Visual Basic
.NET

Primer Plus

Jack Purdum, Ph. D.

SAMS

800 East 96th St., Indianapolis, Indiana, 46240 USA

Visual Basic .NET Primer Plus

Copyright © 2003 by Sams Publishing

International Standard Book Number: 0-672-32485-7

Library of Congress Catalog Card Number: 2002117399

Printed in the United States of America

First Printing: April 2003

06   05   04   03   4   3   2   1

Trademarks

Warning and Disclaimer

ASSOCIATE PUBLISHER
Michael Stephens

ACQUISITIONS EDITOR
Neil Rowe

DEVELOPMENT EDITOR
Kevin Howard

MANAGING EDITOR
Charlotte Clapp

PROJECT EDITOR
George E. Nedeff

COPY EDITORS
Kitty Jarrett
Mike Henry

INDEXER
Rebecca Salerno

PROOFREADER
Carla Lewis

TECHNICAL EDITOR
Jeff Allen

TEAM COORDINATOR
Cindy Teeters

MULTIMEDIA DEVELOPER
Dan Scherf

INTERIOR DESIGNER
Gary Adair

COVER DESIGNER
Alan Clements

PAGE LAYOUT
Michelle Mitchell

CONTENTS AT A GLANCE

TABLE OF CONTENTS

ABOUT THE AUTHOR

Jack Purdum teaches in the department of Computer Technology at Purdue University. He received his B.A. degree from Muskingum College and M.A. and Ph.D. degrees from Ohio State University (and Purdue *still* hired him). He has more than 25 years of teaching experience and has several awards for teaching excellence. He is a best-selling author of more than a dozen programming books and was president of a software firm that specialized in compilers and other programming tools. He also holds a U.S. patent for imaging software he developed and has served as an expert witness for the legal profession for more than 30 years.

DEDICATION

To Joyce, who makes me believe in magic…

ACKNOWLEDGMENTS

First, I'd like to thank a number of people at Sams for their efforts. In particular, I'd like to thank Neil Rowe, Kevin Howard, Kitty Jarrett, George Nedeff, Jeff Allen, and Elizabeth Finney. Their efforts have added immeasurably to the final product.

Others who have helped along the way are Katie Purdum, John Purdum, Kuber Maharjan, Nancy Head, and my students who have endured far too many teaching experiments. I'd also like to mention Jay Crannell, Don Dudine, Phil Engle, Doug Felkins, Jim Hallett, Bill Jones, Mark Keenan, Jim McAllister, Bob McFarling, John Marsh, Jeff Neely, Jeff Nelson, Steve Plopper, Larry Powers, Jim Rheude, Bill Shaw, Mike Shore, Jim Spuller, and John Strack who, in thinly veiled attempts to make me miss a putt, constantly asked, "Is that book done yet?" Particularly effective was John Wilson, whose swing defies every known law of physics.

And, in saving the best for last, a special note of thanks and appreciation to Joyce Scarfo, who has been involved in this work from the start and provided loving support every step of the way. From endless readings and corrections of the manuscript to warm encouragement, you and your efforts are sincerely appreciated. I couldn't have done it without you.

Jack Purdum, Ph.D.

Department of Computer Technology, Purdue University

December 22, 2002

WE WANT TO HEAR FROM YOU!

As the reader of this book, *you* are our most important critic and commentator. We value your opinion and want to know what we're doing right, what we could do better, what areas you'd like to see us publish in, and any other words of wisdom you're willing to pass our way.

As an associate publisher for Sams Publishing, I welcome your comments. You can email or write me directly to let me know what you did or didn't like about this book—as well as what we can do to make our books better.

Please note that I cannot help you with technical problems related to the *topic* of this book. We do have a User Services group, however, where I will forward specific technical questions related to the book.

When you write, please be sure to include this book's title and author as well as your name, email address, and phone number. I will carefully review your comments and share them with the author and editors who worked on the book.

Email: feedback@samspublishing.com

Mail: Michael Stephens
            Associate Publisher
            Sams Publishing
            800 East 96th Street
            Indianapolis, IN 46240 USA

For more information about this book or another Sams title, visit our Web site at www.samspublishing.com. Type the ISBN (excluding hyphens) or the title of a book in the Search field to find the page you're looking for.

INTRODUCTION

Welcome to *Visual Basic .NET Primer Plus*. I appreciate the confidence you've expressed in me by purchasing this book. Obviously, I think you made a good choice, but you'll be the final judge. In any event, I think you'll find the study of Visual Basic .NET to be both exciting and rewarding.

Who Should Read This Book

Obviously, I think you should read this book. Whether you are a seasoned programmer or just beginning to explore computer programming, this book will be helpful to you. Embodied in this text are decades of teaching experience that have helped me to understand the learning process. I understand some of the major stumbling blocks students face while learning computer programming and how to get around them.

If you're just getting started, this book can help you become a good computer programmer. If you're an experienced programmer, this book can help you become a better programmer. Clearly, you'll be the final judge as to whether the book is successful in these endeavors.

Assumptions About the Reader

In a way, it would be nice if you had no programming experience. If that were the case, you would have no preconceived notions about how to program. Your mind would be unfettered by any bad programming habits.

Alas, you probably do have some programming experience. Even so, this book proceeds as though you've never seen a computer program. The book makes no heavy assumptions about your math background other than knowledge of some elementary algebra, at most. Although the assumption of no prior programming experience might make some topics seem pretty simple to you, I encourage you to read this book from cover to cover. Little nuggets of information are scattered throughout this text, and you never know where they're hiding until you read them.

Coverage

To make the learning process easier for you, I've made a very conscious effort to limit the scope of each chapter to one major topic. Some texts swamp you with 100-page chapters, but I've tried to keep the chapters of this book as short as possible while still covering the topic thoroughly. Presenting a single topic in each chapter makes the learning process more manageable.

I encourage you to answer each of the review questions at the end of each chapter. Answering the questions at the end of each chapter is a great way to find out what you *don't* understand. Discovering these shortcomings in understanding early in the process is important because you need to master each new topic before you move on to the next one. This is another reason I've limited the scope of each chapter. Small, bite-sized chunks of information are easiest to assimilate and learn. I want you to gain confidence as you progress through the book, and successful completion of the review questions will help you attain that goal.

Also, I *expect* you to make mistakes along the way. Programs rarely execute as expected the first time you run them. Discovering and correcting program errors, or *bugs*, is an integral part of the learning process. The best way to gain this experience is to write programs. Many chapters offer suggestions for improving the coding examples in the book. Making the suggested modifications is a great way to test your understanding of the topics at hand.

Some program bugs, once uncovered, make you say to yourself, "I never saw that one coming!" Other bugs result in the flat forehead effect: That's when you slam the heel of your hand to your forehead and say: "D'oh! How could I be so stupid?" The good news is that both types of bugs provide learning experiences, and you should view them in that light. We've all made mistakes, and you shouldn't expect otherwise. The bad news is that you'll move on to bigger and better bugs as you gain experience. Still, it's all part of the process of becoming a programmer, and each bug you dispatch is another stripe on your sleeve.

Objectives of This Book

At my institution, students who want to major in computer technology are required to take a two-semester introductory programming course. The language used in those two courses is Microsoft's Visual Basic. On the first day of class, I dutifully ask the students what they think the purpose of the course is. Invariably, most of the students say that the purpose of the course is to learn Visual Basic. Although learning Visual Basic is one objective of the course, it is *not* the primary objective.

The primary goal of the course is to teach the student to think like a programmer. As we journey through those two semesters, I strive to impart to the students the mental discipline, critical thinking, and creative processes that are all components in computer programming. The fact that we use Visual Basic as the vehicle for the learning processes is almost incidental. After all, there have been some pretty sharp programmers emerge during the past five decades who did not use Visual Basic as their first programming language.

The primary goal of this book is the same: to teach you to think like a computer programmer. To do this, I discuss things that are going on "under the hood" moreso than other introductory texts. Most programming texts do not discuss compiler symbol tables and `lvalue` and `rvalue` values. This one does. Armed with these and similar details, you'll be better prepared for the future as a computer programmer.

In the field of computer technology, one thing is certain: Things change. Among those things are programming languages themselves. Mastering one language is fine...until a better language comes along. If this book can teach you to think like a programmer, you'll be able to master *any* language the future might throw at you. To paraphrase an old saying: "Give people a fish, and they eat for a day. Teach them to fish, and they feed themselves forever." My goal in this book is to give you the tools today to survive the future. If I can help you do that, I've done my job.

The secondary goal of this book is to teach you how to use Visual Basic .NET. As you already know, Visual Basic .NET is but one component of a suite of programming tools embodied in Visual Studio .NET.

Finally, Visual Basic .NET is *substantially* different from earlier versions of Visual Basic. If you're new to Visual Basic and have no previous experience, great! If you have prior experience with Visual Basic, you're going to have to unlearn some things that you are accustomed to. Not only is the language itself different, so is the environment in which it runs. Change is afoot, and it's wearing big shoes!

For Instructors

This book was written as a self-teaching instrument. However, much of the material has been pre-tested in my courses at Purdue University. We're on a semester system, with 15 weeks in each semester. Because the introductory programming course is a two-semester sequence, I've written this book to fit those constraints.

Of the 15 weeks available each semester, about 13 weeks are available for instruction. (Exams, breaks, and vacations eat up the other two weeks.) Therefore, the text is comprised of 26 chapters. This means that an average of one chapter is to be covered each week. This is a very manageable reading load on the students. Because we use a lecture and lab approach in teaching this course, this sequencing works nicely for a two-semester course that meets for three hours per week.

If you're in a teaching environment that involves four or five hours of instruction per week, it would be possible to cover the entire book in one semester.

For beginning programming students, the chapters should be read in sequence. Coding examples in one chapter likely draw on programming constructs discussed in earlier chapters. This is why I encourage you to read the entire text from start to finish.

Conventions

To help you differentiate between different types of information presented in this book, we've used different text styles and layout:

- Important words and new terminology appear as *italic words*.

- Text written onscreen by the computer looks as follows:

```
I'm your trusted computer
```

- Text written onscreen and typed by you looks as follows:

```
Hello computer, are you there?
```

- While writing text onscreen, special keys pressed by you, such as the Enter key, are symbolized by **\<enter\>**.

- Code shown as part of code examples has the following appearance:

```
Private Sub MySub()
```

- The line continuation symbol in Visual Basic .NET is the underscore character. In those cases where a program line is too long, you'll see an underscore at the end of the line. The remainder of the line will be indented further than normal code conventions use, thus making it easier to spot these longer lines.

When you must navigate a menu sequence, you'll see the sequence of selections you should make. For example, to start Visual Studio .NET, you would select Start, Programs, Microsoft Visual Studio .NET, Microsoft Visual Studio .NET.

Finally, interspersed throughout the text are programming tips that provide additional details about a topic related to the text under discussion. These programming tips are displayed using the following style:

Programmer's Tip

A programmer's tip provides additional details about the topic at hand. It might discuss common programming mistakes, performance tips, or other useful techniques.

Contacting the Author

I'm always grateful for feedback on almost anything you care to address about the book. If you have a better way to explain a certain topic and would like to share it, great. If you think a topic in this book is unclear, I would like to know about it. It's always helpful if you can pinpoint the problems, and suggested cures are always welcomed. If you like the way a topic was handled, it's always nice to read good comments, too.

If you find an error or typo in the book, please let me know as soon as possible, including the page number and line number.

My email address is `jjpurdum@yahoo.com`

CHAPTER 1

GETTING STARTED WITH VISUAL STUDIO .NET

You will learn about the following in this chapter:

- Installing Visual Studio .NET
- Checking the Visual Basic .NET installation
- Running your first program
- Ending a programming session with Visual Basic .NET

*I*n this chapter, you will learn how to install Visual Studio .NET and how to write a simple Visual Basic .NET program. It is important that you follow the installation instructions carefully. Visual Studio .NET is huge, and it will likely take you about an hour to install it. Following the instructions in this chapter should help minimize the possibility of something going wrong during the process.

The short program you will write at the end of this chapter serves two purposes. First, it introduces you to Visual Basic .NET and its environment. Second, if the program runs, you can be fairly certain that the installation was successful. So with all that in mind, let's get started.

This chapter is devoted to installing Visual Studio .NET and its various components. At the chapter end, you will write a short program in Visual Basic .NET. The purpose of this trivial program is more of a check that Visual Basic .NET was installed properly than a real educational experience. Still, you should type in and complete the program because it does illustrate some fundamental aspects of programming in Visual Basic .NET.

When you are ready to begin the installation of Visual Basic .NET, make sure you have closed all other applications before you begin the installation process. Also, you should allow at least an hour to complete the installation. You will be asked questions along the way, and you will have to swap CD-ROMs, too. Take your time…it's a lot easier to get it right the first time than to redo the installation. Let's get started!

Installing Visual Studio .NET

Visual Studio .NET is available in Professional, Enterprise Developer, and Enterprise Architect Editions. This book uses the Visual Studio .NET Professional Edition for all its program examples. I made this choice because the Professional Edition is the least expensive version, yet it embodies most of the feature set you need to understand and use Visual Basic .NET. However, all the programs in this book function identically, regardless of edition of Visual Studio .NET you install.

Visual Studio .NET Professional Edition comes on five CDs or one DVD. The installation discussed here assumes an installation using five CDs.

This section provides a series of steps you need to follow to ensure that Visual Studio .NET is installed properly. If you have already installed Visual Studio .NET and everything is working properly, you can skip this section and go directly to the section titled "Running Your First Program," later in this chapter. If you have not installed Visual Studio .NET or are experiencing some problems, you might want to read this section.

I have written the installation process as compactly as possible, as it is my experience that most readers will already have the software installed. In all other sections of the book, I make every effort possible to explain what I am doing and why. In this section, I simply want you to be able to install the software and move on to the good stuff: learning Visual Basic .NET. Sometimes there is beauty in terseness, and I think this is one of those times. With that caveat in mind, let's press on.

To install Visual Studio .NET, follow these steps:

1. Close down all currently open applications. Insert into your CD-ROM drive the Visual Studio .NET CD labeled Disk 1 of 5. The setup routine should start automatically. If it does not, you can use the Run option from the Windows menu and simply double-click `setup.exe` on Disk 1 to start the setup procedure. You should see something similar to what is shown in Figure 1.1.

FIGURE 1.1
The Visual Studio .NET
Setup screen.

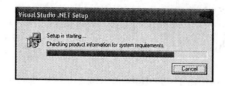

2. The setup program determines whether your machine requires any Windows components to be updated (see Figure 1.2). If it does, you must install different versions of those Windows components by clicking Windows Component Update.

3. Because you will host Web projects, you should select the Install Components option in the screen shown in Figure 1.3.

FIGURE 1.2
The component update
screen.

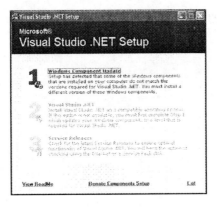

FIGURE 1.3
The Web Project
Requirements screen.

4. Replace Disk 1 with the CD that is labeled Disk 5 of 5 (see Figure 1.4). This is the
    Windows Component Update CD.

FIGURE 1.4
The Insert Disk screen.

5. If you insert the wrong CD, you get the message shown in Figure 1.5. To correct this
    error, simply replace the current CD with Disk 5 and then click OK.

FIGURE 1.5
The incorrect disk error
message.

6. When the correct CD is inserted, the setup program continues. Your screen should display a progress meter similar to that shown in Figure 1.6.

FIGURE 1.6
The installation progress meter.

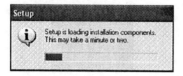

7. Read the End User License Agreement, and then select the I Accept the Agreement radio button and click Continue (see Figure 1.7).

FIGURE 1.7
The End User License Agreement screen.

8. The next screen displays all the Windows components that are required for Visual Studio .NET. Click Install Now to install the required components. Your screen should look similar to the one shown in Figure 1.8.

FIGURE 1.8
Installing Windows components.

9. It might take several minutes to complete the component update process. You should see the update progress on the installation progress bar for each component, as shown in Figure 1.9.

FIGURE 1.9
The component Install
Progress bar.

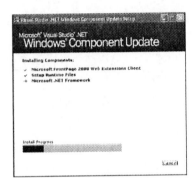

10. After all the Windows components are installed, you see a Congratulations dialog box
    (see Figure 1.10). At this point, click Done to complete the component update process.

FIGURE 1.10
The completed compo-
nent installation.

11. Now you are ready to install Visual Studio .NET. The screen shown in Figure 1.11
    appears. Click Visual Studio .NET to install Visual Studio .NET.

FIGURE 1.11
Installing Visual Studio
.NET.

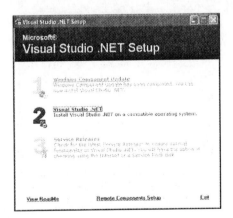

12. You are prompted for a disk change. Replace Disk 5 with Disk 1, and then click OK. The screen that appears should look similar to Figure 1.4.

13. The setup program continues loading installation components. Once again, you should see the progress bar, similar to the one shown in Figure 1.6.

14. Read the End User License Agreement, and then select the I Accept the Agreement radio button. (Of course, I am assuming that you do accept the terms stated in the agreement. If you do not, you should terminate the installation process.) Type your name in the Your Name text box. Enter the product key, which is printed on your CD case, in the Product Key boxes. Click the Continue button to proceed to the next section. See Figure 1.12.

FIGURE 1.12

Entering license agreement information.

15. On the Options page, select the components you want to install (see Figure 1.13). If you are unsure which components to install, simply click Restore Defaults. Then click the Install Now button.

FIGURE 1.13

Selecting Visual Studio .NET Professional Edition items to install.

16. It might take several minutes to complete this part of the installation process. The progress bar should give you an estimate of how long it is going to take to complete the installation. This might be a good time to take a walk and grab a cup of coffee. Figure 1.14 shows the starting screen for the installation.

FIGURE 1.14

The Visual Studio .NET installation screen.

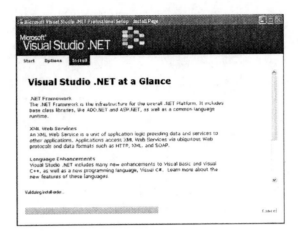

If you have any applications open, you get the message shown in Figure 1.15. You should not get that message if all applications are closed. If you need to close any Windows applications, do so now and then click Retry.

FIGURE 1.15

An error message about an open application.

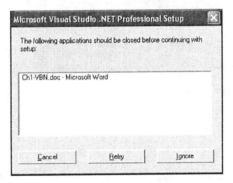

17. Near the bottom of the setup screen, the program displays the estimated time remaining for completion of the installation of Visual Studio .NET (see Figure 1.16).

    This part of the installation process should take about an hour to complete. The exact time it takes depends on your hardware configuration. In all cases, it takes a while, but don't run off.

18. The setup program prompts you to change CD-ROMs along the way, as shown in Figure 1.17. When you are prompted to do so, insert Disks 2, 3, and 4, clicking OK when needed.

19. When the installation is complete, click the Done button (see Figure 1.18).

FIGURE 1.16
The time remaining for the installation.

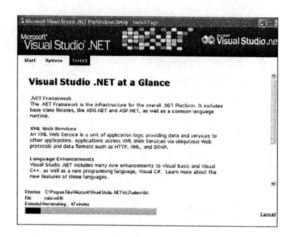

FIGURE 1.17
A screen that prompts for a disk change.

FIGURE 1.18
The Setup Is Complete screen.

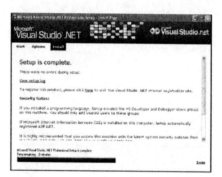

20. At this point you need to check for the services releases. Click Service Releases, as shown in Figure 1.19.

21. Microsoft strongly recommends that you update your machine with the latest system security patches from the Windows Update Web site, www.windowsupdate.com. Make sure that your computer is connected to the Internet, and then click Check for Service Releases on the Internet (see Figure 1.20). This Web site will then check for new service releases and update your computer if necessary.

22. At the time this book is being written, there are no service releases available, as shown in Figure 1.21. Click OK if there are no service releases available when you install Visual Studio .NET. If there are service releases available, install them by following the onscreen instructions.

FIGURE 1.19

Installing service releases.

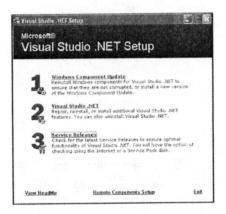

FIGURE 1.20

The Service Releases screen.

FIGURE 1.21

The No Service Releases Available screen.

23. Check whether any service packs are available for the .NET Framework from `http://msdn.microsoft.com/netframework/downloads/sp1/default.asp`. Click Download Now to download and install any service pack that is available. Create an appropriate directory to which to download the file. I recommend that you create a download directory such as `C:\Downloads\Microsoft` to download any files from Microsoft. Figure 1.22 shows the starting dialog box for the service pack download.

FIGURE 1.22

The Microsoft .NET Framework Service Pack screen.

24. Select the appropriate language from Download Now, and then choose Save This Program to Disk (Save) and save the file to the `C:\Downloads\Microsoft` directory as `MSNFrameWorkSP1.exe` (renaming the file if necessary). After the download is complete, double-click the `MSNFrameWorkSP1.exe` file to launch the Service Pack 1 setup. Follow the onscreen instructions to complete the installation of the service pack. The Service Pack Download screen is shown in Figure 1.23.

FIGURE 1.23

The Microsoft .NET Framework Service Pack 1 Download screen.

25. If you have chosen to install the SQL Server Desktop Engine setup files, exit the service pack setup and launch `Setup.exe` from the `..\Setup\MSDE\` subfolder under the main Visual Studio .NET installation folder on your local hard drive. The installation option for installing the Microsoft Development Environment (MSDE) is shown in Figure 1.24.

The configuration takes approximately two minutes to complete, as shown in Figure 1.25.

FIGURE 1.24
The setup screen for the
MSDE.

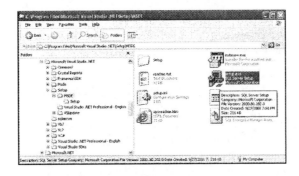

FIGURE 1.25
The progress bar for
installing MSDE.

You are done installing Visual Studio .NET and all its components!

Checking the Visual Basic .NET Installation

Now that the Visual Studio .NET Professional installation is complete, you should check to see that everything in the installation works properly. A good way to do that is to write a simple Visual Basic .NET program.

Starting Visual Studio .NET

Before you can write your first Visual Basic .NET program, you need to get Visual Basic .NET up and running. The easiest way to do that is to click the Windows Start button. Then select Programs, Microsoft Visual Studio .NET, and Microsoft Visual Basic .NET. The Visual Basic .NET development environment launches.

When you see the opening screen, select File, New, Blank Solution (see Figure 1.26). If you've done this correctly, your screen should look similar to that shown in Figure 1.26.

FIGURE 1.26
Creating a new solution
from the Visual Basic
.NET startup screen.

Chapter 2, "The Basics of Object-Oriented Programming," discusses solutions, projects, and files, and other programming details. For now, you can just follow the directions in this chapter and know that you'll learn the details later.

Using Figure 1.27 as a guide, select Windows Application from the Templates box and type **HelloWorld** in the Name box. The Location box asks you where you want to store the program you are about to write. This is entirely up to you. However, I urge you to have some method to your madness. In the example in this chapter, I have selected the directory named **C:\VBN\Ch1**. As you might guess, this means that I have a **VBN** directory on disk drive **C:** with a subfolder for each chapter in this book. Using this type of method makes it easy to find the programs you write as you progress through the chapters in the book. You should enter whatever directory you want to use in the Location box. If the directory does not already exist, you can check the Create Directory for Solution box, as shown in Figure 1.27. You can click More to view the project path. When you're done making all the needed changes to this screen, click OK to continue.

FIGURE 1.27
The New Project screen.

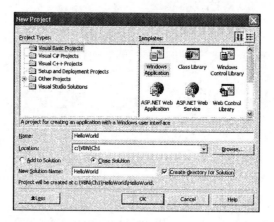

You are now prompted to save the changes you have made thus far (see Figure 1.28). Click Yes to save the changes you have made.

FIGURE 1.28
Saving the changes for a project.

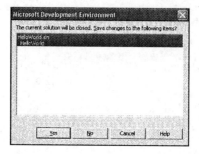

The Visual Basic .NET Integrated Development Environment

At this point, your display screen should look similar to Figure 1.29. This is the Visual Basic .NET Integrated Development Environment (IDE). Virtually all your program-writing activity takes place in the IDE. The IDE is a single program in which you write programs, run and test programs, correct program errors, and make subsequent program modifications. Virtually all phases of program development are done within the IDE.

FIGURE 1.29

The Visual Basic .NET IDE.

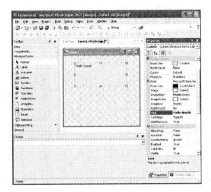

The Toolbox

Approximately the left third of the Visual Basic .NET IDE is a toolbox that holds the basic objects you will use to create programs. The objects in the toolbox are often called *components*, or *controls*, and each of them is designed to perform some specific programming task.

Programmer's Tip

Programmers who have experience using earlier versions of Visual Basic often prefer the term *controls* over *components* to describe the objects presented in the toolbox. This preference goes back to the days when Visual Basic first introduced ActiveX controls. It's not important whether you call them components or controls: Simply keep in mind that they are actually objects that you can use in programs. This book refers to them as controls.

The Forms Window

The middle third of the Visual Basic .NET IDE is the Forms window, with a form shown in that window. You can think of a form as an object on which you place components from the toolbox. By arranging the desired toolbox objects on a form, you can create the visual appearance of what you want a program to look like. You can also click on the tab near the top of the middle window to examine any code that might be associated with the form or any of its components.

The Properties Window

On the right third of the Visual Basic .NET IDE is the Properties window. In the Properties window in Figure 1.29, you can see a label control outlined with a shaded box and the words Hello World in it. The eight small white squares on the outline of the label show that Visual Basic .NET is currently working with that label component. There could be dozens of other components on the form, but the one with the little white squares has Visual Basic .NET's attention at the moment. Because Visual Basic .NET is concentrating on the label control in the Forms window, the Properties window shows all the properties associated with that label control.

The *properties* of a component describe the current *state* of the component. What is meant by the term *current state* of a component? Suppose, for example, that someone asked you to describe yourself. What would you tell that person? You might describe your height, your weight, the color of your eyes and hair, what you are wearing, your age, and so on. Each of those things is a property, or an attribute, and collectively those properties describe your current state. Next month, you might have lost weight, dyed your hair, put in colored contact lenses, had a face lift, and changed your clothes; this would lead to an entirely different description of yourself—an entirely different *state*. In other words, you can change your state by changing the values of the properties, or attributes, that describe you.

In similar fashion, you can also change the properties of a `Label` control. For example, if you look closely at Figure 1.29, you see a property labeled `Text` that is currently set to `"Hello World"`. (You can also see this in the Forms window.) If you change the `Text` property of the label, you also change the state of the label object. You can scroll through the list of properties to see all the attributes that collectively define the current state of the `label` object.

If there were another object on the form in the center of Figure 1.29, you could click it, and the small white squares would outline the object. This would mean that Visual Basic .NET would then be focused on the object you just clicked. You would also notice that the Properties window would change to display the properties associated with the object you just clicked on in the Forms window. Therefore, clicking an object in the Forms window causes the Properties window to be updated with the properties for that object.

Moving an Object from the Toolbox to a Form

To select a component from the toolbox, you click on the Windows Forms bar just below the toolbox bar. (You can see this in Figure 1.29.) A menu of components that you can add to a form then appears. Suppose you want to select a label component and place it on the form. There are two ways to add a component to a form. One way is to click the A Label component and then move the cursor over to the form and click the form to deposit the label on the form. A second way is to double-click the A Label object, which automatically places a label near the middle of the form. It really doesn't matter which method you use. When the label object is on the form, you can drag it to the place where you want it to reside on the form. Notice the little white squares that outline the form and tell you that Visual Basic .NET is watching everything you are doing with the label.

Changing a Property Value

As mentioned previously, Visual Basic .NET is watching what you are doing with the label object, and the Properties window presents a list of all the properties associated with a label object. As an example of changing a property value, move to the **Text** property in the Properties window, place the cursor in the text box to the right of the Text field, type **Hello World**, and press the Enter key.

Right below the **Text** property in the Properties window is the **TextAlign** property. (By default, the properties are listed in alphabetical order in the Properties window.) If you click on **TextAlign** property's text box, you are presented with a drop-down arrow that, when clicked, presents a graphical representation of where you can align the text within the label object. In Figure 1.29, the **TextAlign** property is set to its default value of **top-left**. By clicking the graphical box representation, you can position the text almost anywhere you want within the **label** control. After you've selected a position via the graphical selection process, Visual Basic .NET translates your selection into English and writes it in the **TextAlign** property's text box. You can try playing around with the **TextAlign** property to see this in action. Make sure you understand how the **TextAlign** property works and the effect the different choices have on the placement of the text within the label.

Just for grins, try selecting the **Font** property, and then click the **Bold** option; notice the effect this has on the text in the label on the form. Now move up to the **BorderStyle** property and select the **Fixed3D** option and observe its effect. Personally, I almost always have the **Font** property for labels and text boxes set to **Bold** and the **BorderStyle** property for labels set to **Fixed3D**. These are my personal preferences, and you are free to use whatever looks best to you.

Running Your First Program

In order to execute the simple but complete Visual Basic .NET program you have created, you need to compile it. When you *compile* a program, you are changing the visual and textual state of the program that you see onscreen to a set of instructions that your computer can understand and execute. To compile a program, you select Build, Build Solution. You could also press Ctrl+Shift+B to cause the program to compile the program. Either method builds the program.

Building Versus Compiling

So why do we say *compile* the program, but Visual Basic .NET says it's going to *build* the program? Compiling a program only translates the part of the program that you wrote into executable instructions. To form a complete program, Visual Basic .NET splices a bunch of prewritten mini-programs and routines into the program that it needs in order to make everything work. (You will learn more details about all this in later chapters.) Although Visual Basic .NET does in fact compile a program during the build process, it also links in many other components and objects to create a fully functioning program. Therefore, Visual Basic .NET does compile the part of the program that you wrote, but your code is only a subpart of the build process that is necessary to make a complete Visual Basic .NET program.

Other Ways to Run a Program

Note that you can also compile, build, and run a program by selecting Debug, Start. Or you can simply press the F5 key. In either case, Visual Basic .NET automatically activates the Visual Basic .NET Debugger. The Visual Basic .NET *debugger* is a tool that is used to track down program errors (called *bugs*) as the program executes. The debugger and the process of debugging a program are discussed in great detail in Chapter 19, "Error Processing and Debugging."

You can also run a program with a simple mouse click. Look closely just below the Help menu in Figure 1.29, and you should see the word *Debug* in a text box. Just to the left of that text box is a small, right-pointing blue triangle. If you click that triangle, the program immediately begins execution.

Regardless of the method you use to run a program (you should try all of them), the output of the program should look similar to that shown in Figure 1.30. To end program execution, click the X that you see near the upper-right side of the form. The program terminates, and you are returned to the IDE. Congratulations! You have successfully created, compiled, and run your first Visual Basic .NET program!

FIGURE 1.30
A sample program run.

Ending a Programming Session with Visual Basic .NET

To close Visual Basic .NET, you select File, Exit, and Visual Basic .NET shuts itself down. You can also use the Alt+Q key combination or click the X near the upper-right side of the screen to terminate Visual Basic .NET. If you have not yet saved the program you're closing, Visual Basic .NET asks if you'd like to save your work before it closes down.

I encourage you to save the simple program you created in this chapter so you can return to it a little while from now and play around with it some more. I especially encourage you to place a `TextBox` control on the form and play around with its properties. You might also want to tinker around with the label properties that we have not discussed in this chapter to get a feel for them.

Experimenting with a program like this is a great way to learn about Visual Basic .NET. Don't worry about messing something up. If you see smoke coming out of the computer cabinet…just kidding! There's nothing you can change in the Properties window that's going to hurt anything.

Experiment and have fun!

Summary

In this chapter, you've installed all the necessary Windows components for Visual Studio .NET, installed Visual Studio .NET Professional Edition, checked for Visual Studio .NET service releases, installed needed service packs for Visual Studio .NET, and created your first Visual Studio .NET program. Not bad—but the fun has just begun!

Review Questions

1. What is the primary purpose of the toolbox?

A. The toolbox holds a selection of objects that you can use in your programs. Throughout most of this book, you will use the Windows Forms tab of the toolbox. The Windows Forms tab contains the most-frequently used objects that you will use when you write your own programs.

2. What is the Forms window?

A. The Forms window is located in the center of the Integrated Development Environment screen and serves two purposes. First, it can display the form object upon which you place various control objects that you wish to use in your program. Second, when you double-click on the form or one of its objects, the Forms window converts to the Code Window. The Code window shows you the program statements associated with the current form.

3. What is the Properties window and how is it used?

A. The Properties window shows you the properties, or attributes, of the currently active object in the Forms Window. You can invoke the Properties window for a form object by pressing the F4 key.

4. What does a programmer mean when he refers to the *state* of an object?

A. In the world of object oriented programming (OOP), everything is viewed as an object. You, for example, can be viewed as an object. If you were meeting a stranger at the airport, how would you describe yourself so he would recognize you? You might say: "I'm 6' tall, weigh 200 pounds, have blonde hair, and I'll be wearing a blue suit with a yellow tie." Notice how you use properties to describe yourself. In other words, you hair color and clothing help define your current state. Several months from now you could be 20 pounds lighter, have red hair, and wear different clothes, thus changing your state. Your state, therefore, is defined by the current values of the properties that define you as an object.

5. How can you run a Visual Basic .NET program?

A. There are three basic ways. First, you can use the Debug-Start menu sequence. Second, you can press the F5 key. Third, you can click the Start icon on the toolbar.

CHAPTER 2

THE BASICS OF OBJECT-ORIENTED PROGRAMMING

In this chapter, you will learn the following:

- A brief history of computer programming
- Why object-oriented programming has developed
- The three cornerstones of OOP
- How a small OOP program written in Visual Basic .NET works
- The part that classes play in Visual Basic .NET

This chapter begins exploring the world of object-oriented programming (OOP). It starts that journey with a brief history of programming, which will help you understand the development path that languages have taken in the past 50 years. After all, there's a reason OOP is gaining such wide acceptance. You will also learn how the problems that have arisen in the past 50 years are best addressed by the OOP paradigm. This chapter then discusses the major elements of OOP and concludes with a sample OOP program written with Visual Basic .NET.

All this is pretty neat stuff, so let's start the journey that leads you to becoming an OOP programmer.

A Brief History of Computer Programming

Computer programming has a history that is less than a blink in time's eye. As recently as the 1960s, computers were actually programmed by plugging wires into jacks on boards that would then be plugged into slots in the computer. These boards determined the sequence of instructions that would operate on the data stored in the computer's memory. It's not surprising that the early programmers were often the same engineers who built the computers in the first place.

A significant breakthrough came when John von Neumann suggested that the instructions the engineers were "wiring" into the computer might be stored in the computer's memory, just like the data. Eventually, the sequence of instructions, called *stored programs*, did become stored in the computer's memory—and the art of computer programming was born.

Programming Languages

There are a multitude of programming languages, but they all must ultimately be reduced to the native language of the computer. That language is called *machine language*. Therefore, we will begin our historical journey of programming languages with a peek at machine language programming.

Machine Language

The first computer programs were written in *machine language*, a language that is specific to the particular computer being used. A machine language instruction is nothing more than a precise sequence of 1s and 0s that causes a specific action to take place in the computer. Because computers only understood these two states—1s and 0s—they were called *binary computers*. Even today's computers use the same 1s and 0s as those early computers. (Today's computers are called *digital computers* because the old tube-based analog circuits have been replaced with all digital circuitry.)

Programming a computer consisted of flipping a set of toggle switches off (a binary 0) or on (a binary 1) to create a certain machine-language instruction. Each toggle switch represented a bit in the computer's memory. When the proper bit pattern for the instruction was represented by the toggle switches, pressing yet another button "deposited" the instruction in the computer's memory. By depositing enough instructions in exactly the correct order, a computer program was created and stored in the computer's memory.

As you might imagine, there was a lot of switch-flipping going on for even the simplest of programs. Indeed, you could often identify programmers by the "binary blisters" they had on their index fingers from flipping the switches. (I used to build PCs from kits in the mid-1970s, and I did enough programming to develop "binary calluses"—a clear sign of extensive programming experience back then.)

The sequence of 1s and 0s can be viewed as a number in a variety of ways. Most people are accustomed to using a base-10 (or *decimal*) numbering system, where numbers "roll over" on every tenth digit. In other words, you might start counting at 0 and count up to 9. Then you roll over a 1 to the left of the digit and start over at 0 again. This process forms the number 10 in a base-10 counting system. You then count up 10 more digits (0 through 9), which then gives you the numbers 10 through 19, and you roll over another digit and reset the first digit to 0. You then have 20. This numbering system has served humans well for more than 1,000 years. Computers, however, don't like a base-10 numbering system.

Computers prefer a base-2 (or *binary*) numbering system because it uses only two numbers: 0 and 1. As mentioned earlier, each bit in a computer's memory is either on (a 1) or off (a 0). (We won't get into too much detail about it here; you will learn the details of binary numbers in Chapter 4, "Data Types and Numeric Variables.") It's possible to view a sequence of such computer memory bits by using different numbering bases, depending on how you want to group the bits. In the early days of computers, most computer memory instructions were designed to use 8- or 16-bit instructions. As a result, most machine language instructions used a base-8 (or *octal*) or a base-16 (or *hexadecimal*, often called simply *hex*) numbering system. Octal-based systems grouped the binary bits into groups of 3 bits, and hex-based systems grouped them into groups of 4 bits. A group of 8 bits taken together is called a *byte*, and 4 bits is called a *nibble*. (I'm not making this stuff up.)

Of the two predominant numbering systems, hex is used more often than octal in PCs. Using the hex numbering system, a computer instruction to jump to memory location 3,000 for a certain computer processor might be written like this:

```
C3 68 06
```

The programmer has to remember that the computer instruction for jumping to a certain memory location is an operation code (or *op code*) of C3, followed by a two-byte memory address. This is hardly a user-friendly programming language. As you will learn later, the number 3,000 in base-10 numbers becomes 668 in hexadecimal. The early PC chips stored numbers in the computer's memory with the least significant byte first, followed by the most significant byte. That's why 668 appears as 68 06 in our example. Again, some details are presented in Chapter 4.

Assembly Language

Eventually, programmers got a little tired of machine language programming and looked for easier, and more productive, ways to program computers. One of the earliest attempts was to create a more easily recognized set of abbreviations for the machine language op codes. For example, the op code sequence C3 86 06 could be replaced with this:

```
JUMP 3000
```

JUMP was a form of shorthand, or *mnemonic*, for C3—and it was a lot easier to remember. Other mnemonics were created for each op code in the computer's machine language instruction set. Collectively, the resulting set of mnemonics was called *assembly language*. An actual computer program would be a sequence of these assembly language mnemonics, arranged in such a way as to perform a specific task. Collectively, these mnemonic instructions for the program are called the *source code* of the program.

Even though assembly language was a huge step in the right direction, it still had several shortcomings. First, even something as simple as adding a few numbers together might require dozens of assembly language instructions. Although it was better than machine language, assembly language was still tedious, at best. Second, assembly language was specific to the central processing unit (CPU) of a particular computer. Each CPU had its own unique set of machine language instructions and, hence, its own assembly language. Therefore, if you wrote a program in assembly language for the Motorola 6800 CPU, that same program would have to be rewritten if you wanted it to run on the Intel 8080 CPU. In a nutshell, assembly language is not portable from one computer system to another.

Assembly language is still used today. Indeed, Chapter 4 shows how to look at a Visual Basic
.NET program and see the assembly language that the Visual Basic .NET compiler creates for
the program. Although you may never need to understand or use assembly language, it's com-
forting to know that Visual Basic .NET makes it available to you if ever you do need it.

Virtual Machine Language and Interpreters

In the 1950s, computer programmers created virtual machine languages. The idea was to produce a unified set of mnemonics that were the same for all computers. Then, as a program was
running, the computer would translate those virtual instructions into the actual machine code
for a particular computer. For example, to process the instruction JUMP 3000, the computer
would compare the JUMP mnemonic with a table of instructions, called the *instruction table*,
that was stored in another part of the computer's memory. That table would then say that the
mnemonic JUMP should be interpreted as the machine language op code C3. The table would
also say something like "JUMP must be followed by a memory address. Take the number that
follows the JUMP instruction and form it into a two-byte memory address." Seeing this, the
program would then read the number 3,000 and form it into a 2-byte memory address (that is,
86 06 in hex, stored with the low byte of the memory address first, followed by the high byte
of the 2-byte memory second). The program then had a machine language instruction it could
execute.

The benefit of this approach is that if you changed the instruction table stored in the computer's memory, the JUMP 3000 instruction in the program could be coded for any CPU. For
example, if you wrote a program to do a company's payroll in assembly language on an 8080
CPU, the instruction table for that CPU would be loaded into memory and you could run your
program. If you took the same payroll program to a computer using a 6800 CPU and loaded in
the instruction table for the 6800, you could run the program on a totally different CPU. This
was the benefit of a virtual machine: You could run the same program on different types of
computers! That was the good news.

The bad news was that the program ran slower using this approach than using assembly language. As you might guess, reading a line of the program's virtual machine language source
code, looking up what it should be translated to in machine language in the instruction table,
and then executing those instructions took a lot of time. Such languages that must interpret
what each instruction means in terms of machine code are called *interpreted languages*. The
program that reads the program's source code and performs the interpretation is called an
interpreter.

It's important to note that the interpreter must be sitting someplace in memory before a program can be run. Also, the interpreter needs the source code for the program to be loaded into
memory before it can begin its interpretation tasks.

Because interpreted language programs were easier to write and understand than their
machine code equivalents, programmer productivity increased dramatically. After all, the programmer no longer had to cope with an endless sequence of 1s and 0s. In their stead was a
more easily remembered set of mnemonics that could be used to write programs. Another real
plus was the fact that the programmer didn't have to learn a new machine language each time

a new CPU was developed. The only significant downside was that the interpreted languages spent so much time looking up each instruction that they ran slowly—perhaps as much as 30 times slower than a machine language program. This seemed like a true dilemma—there were two choices, and both were bad.

Compiled Languages

One day, a programmer (often said to be Grace Hopper) suggested that perhaps it would be possible to let the interpreter perform all its table lookup translations and then run the program after all the interpretations had been performed. This is the idea behind a *compiler*. A compiler translates the program's source code into machine code and then stores the resulting machine language program (often called *binary code*) for later use. When you want to run the program, you just load in the already translated machine language program and run it at full speed. Using a compiler provides the ease-of-use of the interpreted languages but generates a program that can run at the speed of machine language.

So which is better: a compiled language or an interpreted language? It depends. If you're typing in your name on the computer as part of a program, does it really matter that a compiled program can process your typing at the rate of 2 billion characters per second, but an interpreted program can only do it at a rate of 500 million characters per second? Both programs are going to be sitting there twiddling their thumbs, waiting for you to hit the next key. On the other hand, if the program is not waiting for user input and is just crunching the numbers or doing some other more complex processing, the compiled program is going to finish faster than the interpreted program. So how much faster is it?

Several years ago a fashionable pastime was cracking the security encryption used on the Web. Someone was able to crack one such encrypted message in "just" two weeks on a huge supercomputer. My guess is that the program was compiled. If the program had been an interpreted one, the same result may have taken several months to accomplish. I am fairly confident that most of the users of the program would have favored the compiled version. This, however, is a pretty extreme example.

Most programs process a program's data fairly quickly—a time that is often measured in milliseconds or less. If the compiled version takes 35 milliseconds and the interpreter takes 125 milliseconds, is a human's perception of time granular enough to notice the difference? Often it is not. Also, as you will see in later chapters, interpreters have certain advantages that make writing programs for them easier than writing programs when using a compiler.

Visual Basic .NET is an interpreted language. I say this because the output of the Visual Basic .NET compiler is not machine code. Instead, the Visual Basic .NET compiler produces an intermediate code called Microsoft Intermediate Language (MSIL) that ultimately becomes translated into machine language. (Again, these are fussy details that you need not worry about yet.) Therefore, programs written with Visual Basic .NET run a little slower than compiled versions of the same programs might run. Still, in the age of 3GHz processors, Visual Basic .NET is usually more than fast enough for the vast majority of applications.

High-Level Languages

During the 1950s and 1960s, there was a move away from assembly language toward high-level languages. The trend was to move the programming language away from the machine code the computer understood toward a more English-like language the programmer understood. Several languages emerged during the 1950s and gained a large following, including ALGOL, COBOL, FORTRAN, and LISP. These languages are still in use today.

One benefit of such high-level languages is that because they are not written in machine code, program source code can be moved from one computer to another and run, even if the two computers have totally different machine code instructions. A compiler or an interpreter must simply be written for the CPU of each machine for the language of choice. The programmer is then freed from having to cope with the underlying machine architecture and can concentrate on solving the programming problem at hand.

Sequential Processing

While computers and their languages were improving over time, so were the programmers. The earliest programs were executed in a sequential fashion. That is, the computer started with the first line in the program's source code, executed it, proceeded to line 2, executed that line, proceeded to line 3, and so on, until there were no more program lines to execute. The execution sequence of the program's instructions, called the *program flow*, was from the start of the program to its end, with no detours in between. This *sequential processing* worked, but it wasn't necessarily the most efficient way to write a program (see Figure 2.1).

FIGURE 2.1

Sequential processing in an early BASIC program.

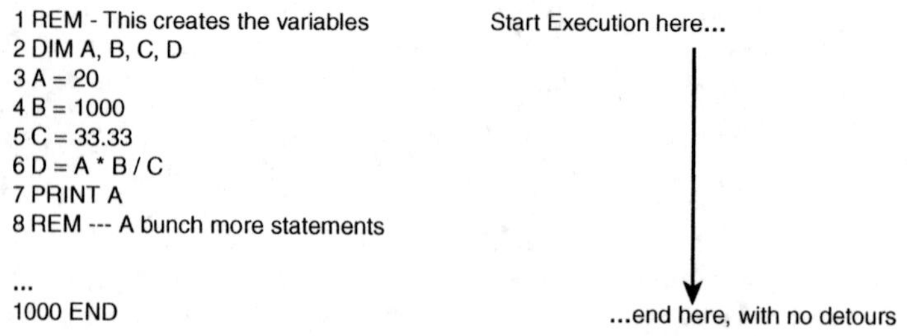

```
1 REM - This creates the variables       Start Execution here...
2 DIM A, B, C, D
3 A = 20
4 B = 1000
5 C = 33.33
6 D = A * B / C
7 PRINT A
8 REM --- A bunch more statements

...
1000 END                                 ...end here, with no detours
```

Programs that used sequential processing had certain drawbacks. For example, as the program was executing, the user might be asked to type some information into the program at 10 different points in the program. With sequential processing, the code necessary to collect the keystrokes from the user would appear at each of the 10 points in the program's source code. This process is shown in Figure 2.2. (Only three instances are shown in the figure, but the others would be similar, just having different program line numbers.)

Notice that the code is essentially the same in each of the three instances in Figure 2.2.

FIGURE 2.2

Duplicate code used in
early programs.

```
1 REM - Start Program
...
120 S = Kinput
121 IF S <> "" THEN
122    V = V + S
123    GOTO 120
124 END IF
...
270 S = Kinput
217 IF S <> "" THEN
272    V = V + S
273    GOTO 270
274 END IF
...
550 S = Kinput
551 IF S <> "" THEN
552    V = V + S
553    GOTO 550
554 END IF
...
```

Subroutines

Programmers quickly observed that certain processes in a program were repeated over and over (refer to Figure 2.2). They reasoned, "Why not write the code that accepts keystrokes from the keyboard and place it at a certain line number (for example, line 900) in the program and simply branch to that line number whenever the program needs some data to be entered by the user? Just so we don't get lost in the process, we'll remember the line number where we make the branch (for example, line 125) and resume executing at the next line (for example, line 126) when the user has finished typing the new information into the program." Thus was born the concept of the subroutine.

A *subroutine* is simply a small piece of program code that is designed to perform a specific task more than once. The phrase *calling a subroutine* is simply a programmer's way of saying that the program flow is temporarily redirected to the subroutine. Using a subroutine in a program is depicted in Figure 2.3. Note how the subroutine is called each time the user is expected to enter some data from the keyboard, and then program control returns to the line following the one where the subroutine was called. It's also clear from Figure 2.3 that at this stage, programs were no longer forced to use sequential processing. Programs could now branch to whatever subroutine was needed, have the subroutine complete its task, and resume program execution back where it left off before the branch to the subroutine.

With a subroutine, the GOSUB keyword caused the program to jump to the subroutine at the stated line number (for example, 900 in Figure 2.3). The code in the subroutine was then executed. The RETURN statement in the subroutine caused the program to branch back to the line number following the subroutine call (for example, 121 in Figure 2.3).

Think about what this simple idea means. Suppose a subroutine consists of 30 lines of code. A sequential program, with its 10 requests for user input, would have 300 lines of (mostly) duplicate code, whereas a program that used a subroutine would have only 30 lines of code to perform the same 10 tasks. This creates two significant advantages: the program requires less memory than it does with sequential processing and the programmer has 270 fewer lines of code to write, test, correct, and maintain. Memory savings was very important during the early stages of computing, and it was not uncommon for even large mainframe computers to run everything in as little as 32KB (that is, 32,000 bytes) of memory. (32KB of memory is actually 32,768 bytes of memory. Programmers love to simplify things!)

FIGURE 2.3

Using a subroutine to avoid code duplication.

```
1 REM - Start Program
...
120 GOSUB 900
...
270 GOSUB 900
...
550 GOSUB 900
...
900 S = Kinput
901 IF S <> "" THEN
902    V = V + S
903    GOTO 550
904 END IF
905 RETURN
...
```

Today, it's not uncommon for a PC to have 256MB or more of memory. (256MB of memory is actually 268,435,456 *million* bytes of memory!) Clearly, memory restrictions are a lot less imposing today than they were 40 years ago, although memory and other resource use should always be a concern to programmers. However, when it comes to the actual cost of writing and running a computer program, it is the cost of writing, testing, correcting, and maintaining the program that is highest. Memory is cheap; programmers are not.

The advent of subroutines also significantly simplified the process of writing, testing, and debugging a program. It looked like subroutines were going to save the day by lowering the costs of writing new programs significantly. But, as you'll learn in the next section, that didn't happen.

Structured Programming

All the jumping around to process subroutines led to the creation of programs that lacked logical structure. Programs were getting larger and more complex, as were computers. With that growth came even higher expectations from the computer user of what the next generation of computers would do. As the hardware technology experienced explosive growth during the 1960s and 1970s, the programmers' bag of tricks just didn't seem to keep pace. Programmers knew that without some kind of structure and discipline in their programs, things were going to get worse before they got better. And, over time, that's exactly what happened. Program development costs continued to spiral, even though the actual computational costs were starting to decline.

A lot of very bright people began work on developing a formal methodology for writing computer programs. One of these pioneers was Nicklaus Wirth, who was a strong proponent of a new way to write programs using structured programming techniques. The Pascal programming language was Wirth's brainchild; Wirth developed it with structured programming in mind from its inception. The structured programming methodology did result in programs that had more structure and, because of that structure, the programs were easier to test, debug, and maintain than earlier programs. Structured programming techniques ushered in other innovations, too, as described in the next section.

Functions

One major contribution to structured programming was the concept of functions. A program *function* is much like a subroutine, except you can pass data to the function, have the function operate on that data, and then have the function return a data value when it is done processing the data. Although we're not fully ready to discuss the implications of this yet, functions in structured programming were an early attempt at *data hiding*. By hiding certain pieces of data from other parts of the program, data was less likely to become contaminated as the program executed.

Another major player in the language arena was C. Developed in the early 1970s by Dennis Ritchie and Ken Thompson, the language grew from modest beginnings to become the most dominant language of the 1980s and early 1990s. C suited the philosophy of structured programming nicely. Its capability to use functions provided a way to divide a program problem into small, often reusable, parts. It also provided improved ways to hide the program's data from other effects in the program as it executed. C was a nice, powerful language. Alas, software costs continued to rise, despite falling hardware prices. Clearly, there had to be a better way to write programs.

OOP

OOP represents a unique way of thinking about the entire programming process. Although OOP may appear to be a relatively new programming process, its basic concepts can be traced back to early simulation problems of the 1960s. One particular simulation involved trying to simulate people arriving at a hospital elevator and waiting to get on. Programmers were frustrated because each time they wanted to simulate another person arriving at the elevator, they had to write new code to simulate that new person's arrival at the elevator doors. They realized that the simulation would be relatively simple if they could just tell the new arrival, "Create yourself and quit bothering me!"

Lightning struck, thunder boomed, and programmers had an epiphany. Up until that time, every programming problem had been viewed from two separate perspectives: the data necessary to represent the problem and the code necessary to operate on that data to yield a solution to the problem. In that system, computer programs were reduced to defining the data and writing the subroutines and functions to manipulate the data in such a way that the solution to the problem became known. An OOP methodology works differently. OOP *combines* the data and the code that manipulates that data into a single concept called an *object*.

Let's return to the hospital elevator simulation mentioned earlier. Say there's a `Doctor` object, a `Nurse` object, a `Patient` object, and a `Visitor` object. Buried inside each of these objects is a piece of code that can react to the message "Draw yourself." The `Doctor` object might draw itself with a stethoscope around its neck. The `Nurse` object might be very similar but exclude the stethoscope and instead carry a clipboard. Likewise, the **Patient** object would forego the clipboard and stethoscope and have a head bandage and wear one of those fetching gowns we all hate. The **Visitor** object might draw itself in a jacket, carrying a bouquet of flowers. What's really interesting here is that a single message to each object—DrawYourself—produces similar, yet distinct, behavior from each object. That is, sending a **DrawYourself** message to the **Doctor** object produces a result that is visibly different from the same message sent to a **Visitor** object. How is this possible? Although the answer is not simple, it can be explained in terms of three basic OOP concepts: encapsulation, inheritance, and polymorphism.

Encapsulation

Encapsulation means that the data for an object and the instructions that operate on that data are part of the object itself. Figure 2.4 shows how you might view a **Doctor** object as a series of three layers in the shape of a ball. Collectively, the outer layer is the shell that is labeled the **Doctor** object.

FIGURE 2.4

The **Doctor** object.

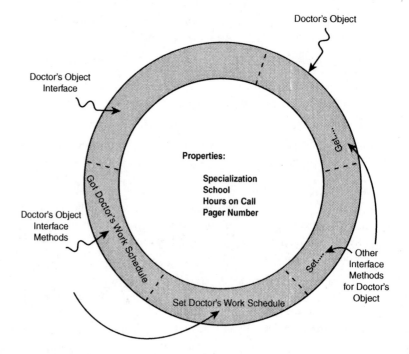

The Properties of an Object

In the center layer, or core, of the **Doctor** object is the data that describes the object. The exact nature of this data depends on how you describe the object. For the **Doctor** object, the data might include the doctor's area of specialization (for example, cardiology, urology), where the doctor went to school, days or hours on call (that is, the work schedule), plus any other information you might think necessary to describe an object called `Doctor` and make that object useful. Often you hear the data of an object referred to as the *properties*, or *attributes*, of the object.

The properties of an object are the data that describes not only the object itself but its state as well. Properties help answer the "so-tell-me-about-yourself" kinds of questions. For example, you might have a `Person` object, and one data item might be named `Occupation`. If you are a student and the object is being used to describe you, I can examine that property and learn something about you. Using the `Doctor` object discussed earlier, you might have a property named `OnCall` that has a value of `1` when a certain doctor is on call and `0` when the doctor is not on call. In this case, you can examine the state of the doctor: Is the doctor on call or not? These are the types of questions that the properties of an object often address.

Clearly, the properties of any object can change, and objects of the same type can assume different values. For example, one `Doctor` object may have a specialization in cardiology, but a different `Doctor` object might specialize in pediatrics. One `Doctor` object might be on call on Saturdays, and another might be on call on Mondays. Although each `Doctor` object may have the same list of properties, the value of each of those properties can vary from one `Doctor` object to the next. Therefore, the values that the properties assume for the object define the *state* of the object. This also means that by inspecting the properties of an object, you can distinguish among individual objects even though they may all be the same type of object (for example, `Doctor`).

The Interface of an Object

Note in Figure 2.4 that the properties of the `Doctor` object are at the core of the object: They are not directly exposed to the outside world. This type of hiding is done by design in the OOP world. As much as possible, the OOP methodology wants to hide the data of an object (that is, its properties) from the outside world. The only way to access the data of an object, therefore, is through a set of methods that clearly define how people can access the properties of the object. In Figure 2.4, the methods for accessing the object's properties form the second layer of the object.

It is this second layer that dictates how the outside world interacts with the properties of the object. Because this second layer describes and defines how the outside world communicates with the object, the second layer defines the *interface* for the object. The object's interface is defined by the *methods* by which all communication is done with the object's data. In other words, you use the methods of the object to examine the properties of the object. Therefore, the interface gives you access to the state of the object.

Note that methods are not simply limited to fetching and changing property values. Methods often address the "so-what-do-you-do?" types of questions. A `Doctor` object might have a `PerformHeartSurgery` method. A `Nurse` object might have a `GiveInjection` or `ThisMightStingABit` method. Methods, therefore, may imply some form of action on the part of the object. For example, one method might be called `GetDoctorsWorkSchedule`. If your program needs to know the work schedule for a given `Doctor` object, you request the `GetDoctorsWorkSchedule` method to get that information for you. The code associated with the GetDoctorsWorkSchedule method then looks up the Doctor object's work schedule as it is stored in the object's list of properties.

Similarly, there will likely be another method called SetDoctorsWorkSchedule that enables you to change the work schedule for each Doctor object. Indeed, it's common to find these Set and Get methods in pairs for many of the attributes of an object. The purpose of a Set method is to change the object's property, and the Get method is used to read the current value of the property. It should also be clear that the object's Set methods are used to change the state of the object.

Methods usually affect one or more property values, but they are not required to do so. You, the programmer, must make these decisions. All this might seem a bit overwhelming at the moment, but it actually gets easier as you dig deeper into the art of OOP programming. You'll see.

It is important to note that the outside world is forced to use an object's interface in order to know anything about the state of the object. That is, the programmer must use the methods found in the second layer of the object to gain access to the properties found at the core of the object. This is the whole idea behind encapsulation: Keep the data and everything that can affect that data in one place—as part of the object itself.

Inheritance

The idea behind inheritance is that after you've defined an object, you can extend the object to create new objects. For example, you might create an object called Drink. For now we'll assume that the only property for an object called Drink is the size of the glass that holds the fluid (as measured in ounces).

Conceptually, you can then create a new object called WaterDrink that is extended from Drink but has a new property called Water. You might create yet another Drink object, called BeerDrink, with a property called BeerType. And you might create another object derived from Beer called Ale, which has a slightly different set of attributes than does Beer. Other possible objects that might be created from the basic Drink object are SoftDrink, LiquorDrink, FruitDrink, AdeDrink, WineDrink, and so on. This hierarchy is shown in Figure 2.5.

FIGURE 2.5
The Drink object hierarchy.

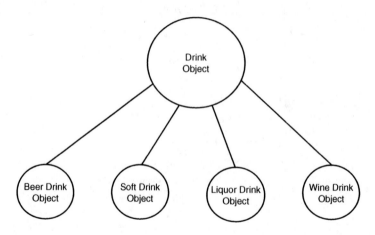

By adding new properties and methods to a previously defined object, it is possible to create new (and slightly different) objects. Because these new objects inherit attributes and methods from existing objects, your job, as a programmer, is simplified because you can build on objects that already exist and reuse the code from the existing object. We will return to this concept of inheritance many times in the course of our study of Visual Basic .NET.

Polymorphism

The third ingredient in the OOP mix is polymorphism. The word *polymorphism* comes from the Greek for "many shapes," but it takes on a slightly different meaning when applied to OOP. What it means in the context of OOP is that you can send a single message to a group of different objects, and each object knows how to process the message in its own distinct way.

Using the hospital elevator example, you could send a `DrawYourself` message to each object, and the `Doctor` object would draw itself with a stethoscope, the `Nurse` object would draw itself with a clipboard, and so on. You don't have to tell the object how to draw itself; it already knows how because each object has a method that responds to the `DrawYourself` message in its own unique way. As a result, the same message sent to different objects produces slightly different results in that the shapes are drawn differently. A single message produces many shapes; hence, this is polymorphism.

Using the hospital example again, you could send a `DoSomething` message to the interface of each of the objects. As a result of receiving this message, the `Doctor` object would perform an operation, the `Nurse` object would give the `Patient` object an injection, the `Patient` object would say "Ouch" and complain, and the `Visitor` object would say, "I bet that hurt." Again, the important thing to notice is that the same message sent to different objects causes different behavior to occur for those objects.

For a language to be considered an OOP language, it must support encapsulation, inheritance, and polymorphism. Some languages come close but do not support all three elements of OOP. Up through release 6.0, Visual Basic had encapsulation and polymorphism, but it lacked inheritance capabilities. Visual Basic .NET removes this shortcoming, and it is a full-featured and robust OOP language. Other languages, such as C++, have all the elements but don't require you to use OOP techniques. Visual Basic .NET, on the other hand, has all three elements of OOP *and* forces you to use OOP techniques. This is why you need to have a basic understanding of OOP fundamentals early in this book.

A Program Example Using OOP

Now that you know something about OOP, you can write a simple program with Visual Basic .NET and examine it with your new understanding of OOP. Assume that you have properly installed Visual Basic .NET according to the instructions in Chapter 1. Also assume that you are ready to start a new program and that your computer screen looks similar to Figure 1.29 from Chapter 1.

If you click the New Project button, you quickly see a screen similar to that shown in Figure 2.6. In that figure, notice that Visual Basic .NET has selected Visual Basic Projects by default as the project type. Also notice that Visual Basic .NET has selected Windows Application for the template type by default. Both of these default selections are fine for your application. (The environment used to write Visual Basic .NET programs in this book is capable of writing programs using other languages, too. However, we will stick to Visual Basic .NET for the time being.)

FIGURE 2.6

The New Project dialog box.

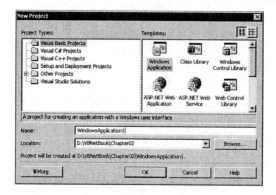

Near the middle of Figure 2.6, you should see the Name text box filled in with the default name for the new project. In the figure, Visual Basic .NET has automatically supplied the name `WindowsApplication1`. This default project name follows a naming convention that is used consistently throughout this book: The first letter of each word in a project name is capitalized. (Notice the *W* and *A* in the default project name in Figure 2.6.) In fact, the same naming convention is used for other elements in a program. You'll learn more about naming objects in Visual Basic .NET in subsequent chapters, especially Chapter 4.

The project name `WindowsApplication1` isn't very informative. You can't tell much about the project from that name. Therefore, replace the name `WindowsApplication1` with the name `FirstProgram`, which gives at least some idea of what the program is.

Below the project name in the New Project dialog box is a text box where you can specify where you wish to store the project on your computer. In Figure 2.6, Visual Basic .NET knows that I have been saving my recent programs in a disk directory named `VBNetBook\Chapter02` on my `D:` disk drive. You should type in the name of the disk directory where you would like to have this project saved, as you will be using this project again later in the book.

Now click the OK button in the New Project dialog box. In a few moments, you should see a screen similar to that shown in Figure 2.7. This screen should look familiar to you because you saw it while you were testing the installation of Visual Basic .NET in Chapter 1. You need to spend some time with the Integrated Development Environment (IDE) now so you can become familiar with the many features that are available to you.

At first blush, Figure 2.7 looks like a good candidate for information overload: There are a lot of things being presented to you all at once. But if you're going to eat an elephant, you need to do the task one bite at a time, until the job is done. And that's exactly what you're going to do here. Rather than flood your brain with an explanation of each and every button and icon on the screen, you will ease into the features of the IDE, learning about each one as you use it.

FIGURE 2.7
The Design window for Visual Basic .NET.

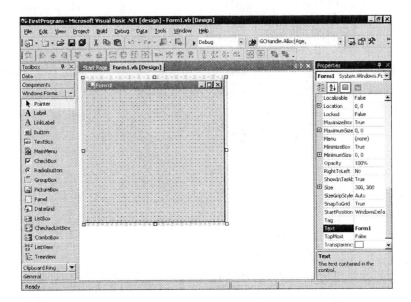

The Design Window

The Design window appears at the center of Figure 2.7. At the top of the Design window are two tabs that are labeled Start Page and Form1.vb [Design]. Because the Form1.vb [Design] tab is highlighted, you know that the IDE shown in Figure 2.7 is in Design mode for something called `Form1.vb`.

If you look below the two tabs, you should see a form displayed in the Design window with `Form1` written on its title bar. You should also notice that eight small boxes surround the form, connected by a light-gray line. As you learned in Chapter 1, this means `Form1` has the focus of the IDE.

The Properties Window

Near the right side of Figure 2.7 is a window labeled Properties. (If you do not see the Properties window, press F4.) Remember from earlier in this chapter that OOP is all about objects and that the state of each of those objects is determined by its properties. The form you see in the Design window is an object of type `Form`. At the present time, Visual Basic .NET has given this `Form` object the default name `Form1`. In fact, Visual Basic .NET has supplied numerous default values to all the properties that describe the form, and that's the purpose of the Properties window: The Properties window allows you to see the current values of the form's properties and also allows you to change them.

Look closely at the Properties window in Figure 2.7. Notice that the **Text** property of **Form1** is highlighted and that the box next to it shows the word **Form1**. If you move your mouse cursor onto the word **Form1** and double-click the mouse, you cause the word **Form1** to be highlighted. Now you can simply type the words **My First Program** and press the Enter key. Your screen should now look similar to the one shown in Figure 2.8.

FIGURE 2.8
The Design window after you change the **Text** property.

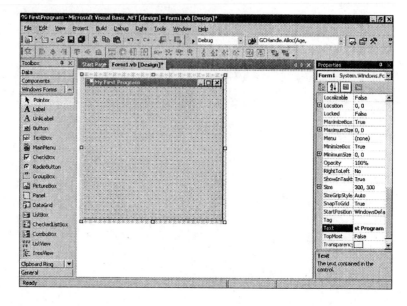

Notice that the title bar now shows the words you just typed. You have just changed the **Text** property of your first **Form** object! You're on a roll, so try changing another property of the form. Scroll the Properties window so that the top of the window is visible. You can do this by placing your mouse cursor on the scrollbar and, while holding the left mouse button down, dragging the scroll box to the top position. When you are done, your screen should look similar to Figure 2.9.

Notice in Figure 2.9 that the **Name** property is changed from **Form1** to **frmFirstProgram**. You can see this new name spelled out just below the title bar for the Properties window. This change illustrates several things. First, it shows that every form has a **Name** property that you can change to just about any name you want. Second, even though you have the freedom to select any name for the form that you want, you should prefix the name with **frm**. This is a convention that is followed by almost every Visual Basic .NET programmer. Prefixing the form name with **frm** makes it easier to identify which object is being referred to if you need to reference the form in the program's code. Now any time you see **frmFirstProgram** in the program code, you know the code is referring to a form object named **FirstProgram**.

FIGURE 2.9

Changing the Name property.

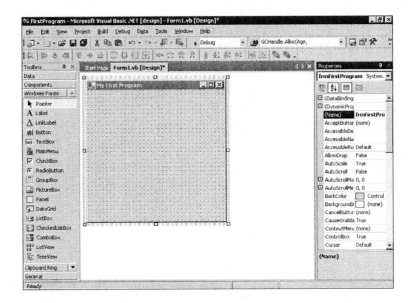

Programmer's Tip

If you were eavesdropping on several programmers who were working on the `frmFirstProgram` program, you would probably hear them refer to the form as `FirstProgram` rather than `frmFirstProgram`. Experienced Visual Basic .NET programmers recognize that the `frm` element of the form's name is a naming convention, but the `FirstProgram` part of the form's name is what actually identifies the form.

You can scroll through the Properties window and examine the many properties that define the `Form` object. If you'd like a little additional information about the property you're examining, look at the gray area at the bottom of the Properties window, which gives additional information. For example, Figure 2.8 illustrates how the explanation window sheds a little more light on what the `Text` field is all about.

Expanding Properties

You might have noticed that in the Properties window, some properties have little boxes with plus signs in them at the left margin. This is Visual Basic .NET's way of telling you there is additional information associated with a property. For example, if you scroll down to the `Location` property, you see a box with a plus sign in it. If you click the plus sign, you see two new rows appear below the `Location` property row. These new rows are labeled `X` and `Y`, and they correspond to the x,y-coordinates of where the form is positioned on the screen. Also notice that what was the plus sign now appears as a minus sign inside the box. This is Visual Basic .NET's way of telling you that you are viewing the expanded definition of the `Location` property. If you click the minus sign, the `X` and `Y` property rows disappear and only the `Location` row is now visible. Also, the plus sign is now inside the box again.

Visual Basic .NET uses this plus box notation at several points in the IDE. We will explore the other plus boxes at the proper time. For the moment, remember that you can click the plus box to reveal additional information associated with the row where the plus box appears. Clicking the box a second time collapses that additional information back to its original, pre-expanded, state.

Adding Objects to a Form

On the left side of the Design window shown in Figure 2.9 is another window, named Toolbox. The toolbox presents a scrollable list of predefined objects, or components, that you can add to a form. As you can see from the list, the toolbox provides a fairly large selection of labels, boxes, and other components that you can add to forms.

To add a label object to your form, you simply place the mouse cursor over the `Label` object in the toolbox and click. Then move the cursor over the form and click the mouse again. Your form should look like the one in Figure 2.10.

FIGURE 2.10

Adding a `Label` object to `frmFirstProgram`.

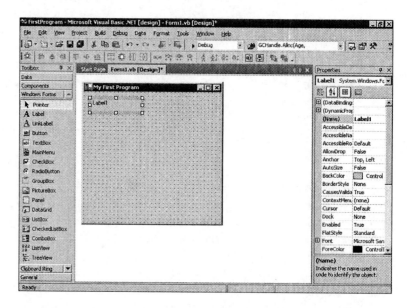

Notice that the `Label` object has the focus of Visual Basic .NET. This means that the Properties window is displaying the properties that are available for the `Label` object.

Let's change a few of the `Label` control's properties. First, scroll down to the `Text` property and change the text to `My name is Joyce`. Next, right below the `Text` property is the `TextAlign` property, which simply determines where the text appears within the `Label` object. If you click this property, you are presented with nine boxes, which represent the positions where you can set the text. By default, the upper-left box is depressed, indicating that the text in the `Label` object will be positioned in the upper-left portion of the object. Clicking the box in the center causes the text to be centered in the `Label` object. If you press the Enter key (or click another part of the display screen), you see the `TextAlign` property filled in with the word `MiddleCenter`. You should also see that the `Text` property you just filled in is now centered within the `Label` object.

Now scroll the Properties window up to the top and change the `Label` object's `Name` property to `lblName`. Notice that the Visual Basic .NET naming convention of `lbl` is used to prefix the `Name` label for the `Label` object. While you're there, also change the `BorderStyle` property to `Fixed3D`. If you've made all these changes correctly, your display should look similar to that shown in Figure 2.11.

FIGURE 2.11

Setting the properties for the `lblName` object.

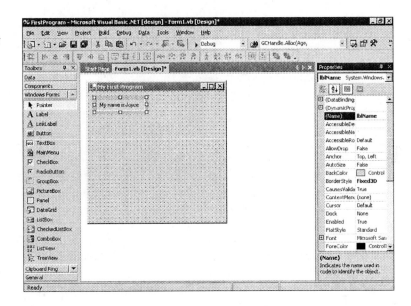

Now, add two more objects to the form. To do so, you click the `Button` object in the toolbox list and then double-click the `Form` object to deposit the button on the form. Notice that double-clicking an object in the toolbox automatically places that object on the form. Now click the `Button` object on the form and, while holding down the left mouse button, drag the button toward the bottom-left side of the screen. Scroll the Properties window toward the bottom of the list and set the button's `Text` property to `&Change`. (You'll learn why the ampersand is there in a moment.) Now scroll the Properties window to the top of the list and change the `Name` property to `btnChange`. The Visual Basic .NET naming convention is to prefix all `Button` objects with `btn`.

Now that you're a pro at adding objects to a form, add a second `Button` object to the form and give it the name `btnExit`. You should also change its `Text` property to `E&xit`. If you've done this correctly, your form should look similar to the one shown in Figure 2.12.

FIGURE 2.12
The Form object with three component objects on it.

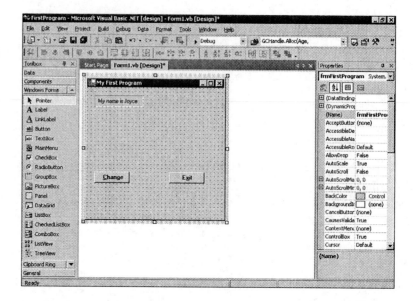

Note the appearance of the text on each button. The letter C is underlined on the btnChange button object and the x is underlined on the btnExit button object. This happens because you placed an ampersand before these two letters on the buttons. These letters then become hotkeys for these buttons. That is, you could activate the btnChange object by clicking it with the mouse, or you could press the Alt+C key combination to activate it. Likewise, the btnExit object could be activated by using the Alt+X key combination. This is a standard Windows convention whereby the user can either use the mouse to click an object to activate it or use the object's hotkey—the key with the underline—to activate the object.

Compiling Your First Program

If you tried to compile your program now, you would get an error message stating that Sub Main is not found. This error message means that Visual Basic .NET doesn't know where to start executing the program. The reason Visual Basic .NET needs this information is because you can write programs that have more than just one form in them. Therefore, even though your simple program has only one form, Visual Basic .NET still wants you to specify which form should be used to begin program execution.

To supply the missing information, select View, Solution Explorer. (Note that Ctrl+R also activates the Solution Explorer menu option.) If you have done this correctly, your screen should look like Figure 2.13.

FIGURE 2.13

The Solution Explorer
window.

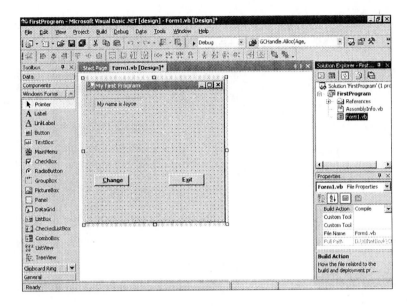

Notice that the Properties window has been pushed down, and the Solution Explorer window
appears near the top-right portion of the screen. Because you need to tell Visual Basic .NET
where to start your program, you need to click the second line, FirstProgram1. When you do
this, the five icons you see directly below the Solution Explorer title bar collapses to three
icons, as shown in Figure 2.14.

FIGURE 2.14

The Properties ToolTip
for FirstProgram1.

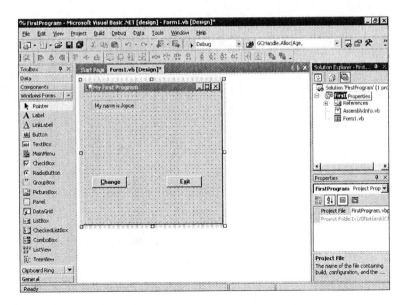

If you click the rightmost icon, which is the Properties icon for FirstProgram1, the display changes to that shown in Figure 2.15.

FIGURE 2.15
Setting the
FirstProgram1 startup
object.

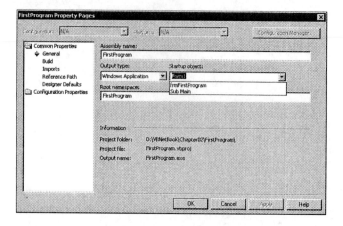

Near the middle of the form is a field labeled Startup Object. If you click the down-arrow at the right edge of the field, your display should look like that shown in Figure 2.15. Visual Basic .NET is asking you to select the object that should be used to start your program. Because you have only one form, you should select frmFirstProgram as the startup object and then click the OK button. The screen should revert to the one shown in Figure 2.14.

Now select Build, Build Solution. Visual Basic .NET compiles your program, and you should see a display similar to the one shown in Figure 2.16.

FIGURE 2.16
The display after a suc-
cessful compilation.

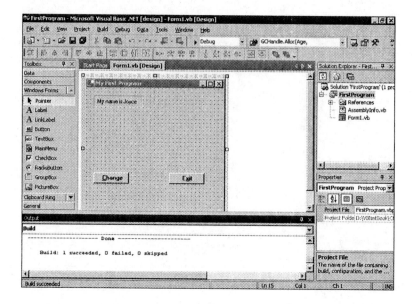

As you can see in the Build window, near the bottom of the display screen, the build of your program is successful. You can now run the program.

Running a Visual Basic .NET Program

There are two ways to run a Visual Basic .NET program while you are in the IDE. The first way is to click the Start button (the right-pointing triangle to the right of the Debug text box).

If you click the Start button, there is a delay as Visual Basic .NET does some behind-the-scenes work, but eventually you should see a display screen similar to that shown in Figure 2.17.

FIGURE 2.17

The My First Program program.

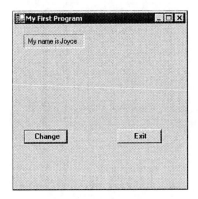

Your program is now running, even though you haven't really written any code! All the code that was needed to actually run the program was written behind the scenes by Visual Basic .NET.

The first thing you should notice is that all those dots that you saw while you were designing your program are gone. Actually, those dots were never part of the program in the first place. Visual Basic .NET simply puts them on the form to make aligning the various objects on the form a little bit easier.

The second thing you should notice is that nothing happens if you click either of the `Button` objects on the form. Indeed, you have to click the close box to terminate the program. This seems a bit crude, and you will learn how to fix this problem in the next section.

Recall that there are two ways to run a program in the IDE. The second way is to simply press the F5 key. This method executes the program in Debug mode, which is a little bit different from simply clicking the Start button as you did before. You will learn a lot more about Debug mode in later chapters. For now, you can just use the Start button to run your programs.

Adding Code to Your Program

After you've run the program, the display screen should look something like Figure 2.18, which shows a Debug window near the bottom of the display.

FIGURE 2.18

The display screen after program execution.

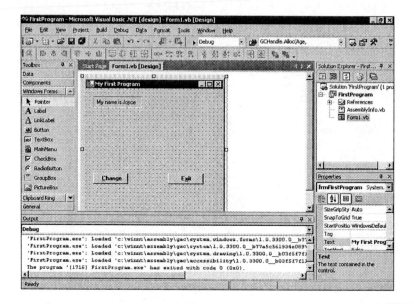

Right above the Debug window is the title bar for the Output window. To the extreme right of that title bar you should see an icon that looks like a push-pin and then the close box. Click the close box to dismiss the Output window. Your display should once again look like Figure 2.14. Now you are ready to write some code for your program.

First, you need to move your mouse cursor over the Change button and double-click it. The display changes to reveal the Code window, as shown in Figure 2.19. First, notice that there are two tabs at the top of the Code window. The highlighted tab reads Form1.vb* and represents the Code window. The other tab reads Form1.vb [Design]* and represents the Design window. If you click that tab, the display changes to look like the Design window shown in Figure 2.14. For now, select the Code window, as shown in Figure 2.19.

Notice that the cursor is sitting right below the word `Private`, waiting for you to type some code into the program for the `btnChange` object. Specifically, Visual Basic .NET is waiting for you to write some code for the `btnChange` object's `Click()` event. You know this from the information on the line above the cursor, which starts out like this:

```
Private Sub btnChange_Click(...
```

(The three periods after the opening parenthesis are called an *ellipsis* and indicate that additional details are present but not being shown. We will explain those missing details in Chapter 4.) Simply stated, these words say: "This marks the beginning of the code the program wants to execute each time the user clicks the btnChange button object." If you look directly below the cursor in Figure 2.19, you should see the words End Sub. This line marks the end of the code you want to execute each time the btnChange object is clicked.

FIGURE 2.19

The Code window for the btnChange object's Click event.

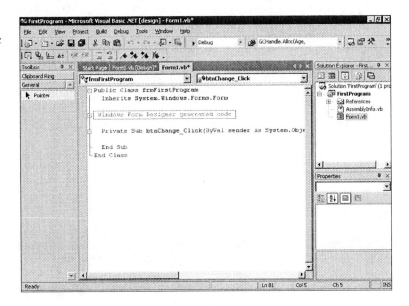

At the point where the cursor is located, type in the following code:

```
lblName.Text = "My name is your-name"
```

You should substitute your name for *your-name* in this code. For example, if your name is Nicholas Hartman, you type this:

```
lblName.Text = "My name is Nicholas Hartman"
```

Without getting bogged down in too many details, the following sections consider what this line does.

The Dot Operator

Look at Figure 2.14 and recall that you added a Label object, named lblName, to your program. At that time, you set the Text property to My name is Joyce. The new code line you have added simply changes the Text property to display your name instead of Joyce's name. Notice the syntax you need to observe in order for this to work correctly:

ObjectName.PropertyName

Anytime you want to examine or alter the property of an object, you must first supply the name of the object (for example, lblName), followed by a dot (that is, the dot operator), followed by the name of the property (for example, Text) you want to examine or change. The dot operator is simply a period that is placed between the object you are working with and the property you want to examine or change.

Don't underestimate the power of the dot operator! Think of the dot operator as the magic key that lets you gain access to the (encapsulated) object. Without the dot operator, all you can do is stand around outside the object and stare at it. Although such activity may be interesting, it's not terribly productive. The dot operator lets you get inside the object, and that's where the action is.

The line you just typed into the program, therefore, is designed to change the `Text` property from `My name is Joyce` to `My name is Your Name` when the user clicks on `btnChange` object. In other words, what you are really saying to Visual Basic .NET with the line:

```
lblName.Text = "My name is your-name"
```

is "Find the object I named `lblName`, locate its `Text` property, and change whatever might currently be there to `My name is your-name`."

Now you can try a similar change to the `btnExit` object. First, click the Design window tab at the top of the Code window to change the display back to what is shown in Figure 2.14. Double-click the `btnExit` object. The Code window again appears, but it looks as shown in Figure 2.20.

FIGURE 2.20
The Code window for the `btnExit` object's `Click()` event.

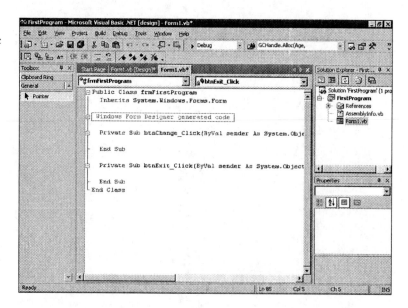

As before, the cursor is waiting for you to type in some code for the `btnExit` object's `Click()` event. This time, instead of changing an object's property, you should invoke a method associated with a particular object, as described in the following section.

Invoking an Object's Method

To invoke a method associated with a particular object, you can begin by adding to the `btnExit` object some code that will cause the program to end when the user clicks the Exit button. This is pretty standard stuff for a Windows program. To end a program, you need to tell Visual Basic .NET to close down the currently active form that is being displayed. Because you have only one form, you can type the name of the form, followed by the dot operator. After you do this, your screen should look as shown in Figure 2.21. This is called an *automatic property list*, which lists the available properties for the object you've typed.

FIGURE 2.21

Automatic property lists.

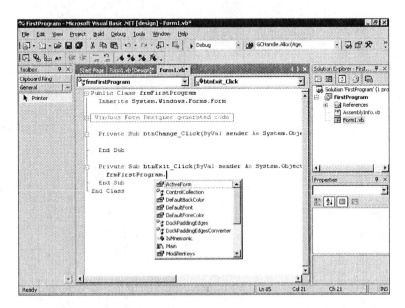

Visual Basic .NET is smart enough to know that you want to perform some type of operation on your form, and it presents you with a list of properties from which to choose. You are interested in the `ActiveForm` attribute, so press the A key and press the spacebar. Visual Basic .NET automatically fills in the line with `ActiveForm`. Now, push the Backspace key to remove the blank space you just added. (This is a pain-in-the-butt step that Microsoft needs to address soon.) Now, press the period key to add another dot operator. Your screen should look like the one shown in Figure 2.22.

Scroll the list down until you see the `Dispose` method, as shown in Figure 2.22. Double-click the `Dispose` method, and Visual Basic .NET fills it in on your program line automatically. The `Dispose` method for a form is used to dispose of the current form. Because you have only one form in your program, the `Dispose` method has the effect of ending your program.

You have now added code to handle what the program should do when the user clicks the `btnChange` and `btnExit` objects. To compile the new version of your program, you can either select Build, Build Solution or simply press Ctrl+Shift+B. At the bottom left of the display screen you should quickly see a "Build succeeded" message, stating that everything went okay.

Now you can click the Start button to run the program. When you click the Change button, you should see the display change to look like Figure 2.23.

FIGURE 2.22
Automatic method lists.

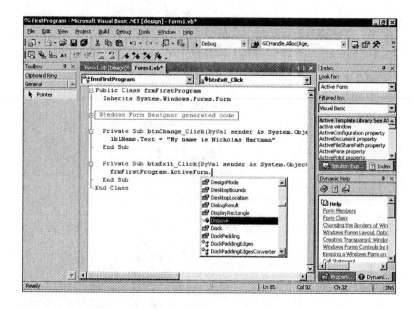

FIGURE 2.23
The new version of
`FirstProgram` after a button's `Click()` event.

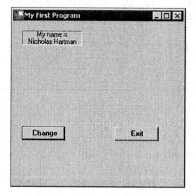

In Figure 2.23, because the new name is longer than the label is wide, Visual Basic .NET folds the text to fit in the label. If you click the Exit button, the program ends.

The `Me` Keyword

The following program line is quite a mouthful, but it accurately describes the currently active form in a program:

```
frmFirstProgram.ActiveForm.Dispose()
```

However, when you write Visual Basic .NET programs, referencing the currently active form is such a common task that Visual Basic .NET provides a shorthand form for it. If you change the preceding line to this:

```
Me.Dispose()
```

the program operates exactly as it did before. Therefore, you can use Me as a shorthand notation for the currently active form.

Me is an example of a keyword in Visual Basic .NET. A *keyword* is any word that has special meaning to Visual Basic .NET. Other keywords you have seen (but that we haven't actually discussed yet) include Private, Sub, and End. Because keywords have special meaning to Visual Basic .NET, they can be used only within certain contexts. For example, you cannot use any Visual Basic .NET keyword as the name of an object, such as a form or a button. Therefore, using a Visual Basic .NET keyword as an object name is an inappropriate context within which to use a keyword. (We will continue the discussion about keywords in Chapter 4.)

Experimenting with the Sample Program

As an experiment, try expanding the width of the lblName object. You can do this several ways. First, while in the Design window, you can move the mouse cursor over the middle box on the right side of the object. When you have the cursor positioned correctly, the cursor changes shape and becomes a double-pointed arrow. You can then click the mouse button and, while holding the button down, drag the cursor to the right to increase the width of the Button object.

A second way to change the width of the lblName object is to do it through code when the program runs. In that case, you add the following line to the btnChange object's Click() event code:

```
lblName.Width = 200
```

The Code window should look like Figure 2.24.

FIGURE 2.24

Modifying the btnChange object's Click() event code.

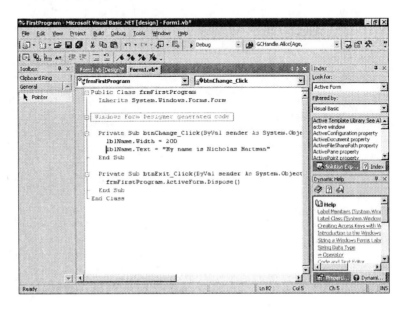

As you've probably guessed, this line expands the width of the `Label` object. It changes the `Width` property to `200`. (The original value was `100`.) You can see that this change causes the new line of text to be displayed without being folded as before, but what does this line actually do? It changes the width of the `lblName` object from `100` to `200`. But what units of measurement are being used?

In earlier versions of Visual Basic the unit of measure defaulted to *twips*, which is a standard measure used in the printing business. (One inch is about 1,440 twips.) However, most programmers are more comfortable using pixels than twips when talking about display screens, so Visual Basic .NET uses pixels as its measure. A pixel is one dot on a display screen. Your code change simply tells Visual Basic .NET to expand the width of the `lblName` object from 100 pixels to 200 pixels when the user clicks the `btnChange` object.

Notice that this change in the width of the `lblName` object, via the new line of code, causes the width to be changed as the program executes. This is called a *runtime* change in the property of an object. When you increase the width of the `lblName` object by using the mouse cursor to widen the `lblName` object before the program was run, this is called a *design-time* change. It's important to realize that you can change most properties of an object either at design time or at runtime. Which method is better depends on the task at hand. You'll learn more about these tradeoffs in later chapters.

Summary

You bit off quite a chunk of the elephant in this chapter. You should pat yourself on the back because you now have a pretty good understanding of what OOP is about and how Visual Basic .NET uses objects in a simple program. I encourage you to experiment with the `FirstProgram` code and try changing different properties to see what effect they have on the program when it runs. Keep in mind that you can change the properties by using the Design and Properties windows (design-time changes), or you can do it by actually adding new lines of code to the program (runtime changes), as shown in Figure 2.24.

Believe me when I tell you that you will learn more if you use runtime changes. Using runtime changes forces you to think about what you're doing more than using design-time changes does—and that's what learning is all about. Sometimes, the long way is the better way. Furthermore, if one of your changes *doesn't* work as expected, you shouldn't get discouraged. It's great experience to try to figure out on your own what has gone went wrong and why. Ferreting things out on your own is a terrific way to learn. Doing this now will prevent a lot of problems later on. We've all had the kind of problems that make us say, "How could I make such a stupid mistake?!" Trust me, we've all been there and, alas, most of us still visit there from time to time.

You should experiment and have some fun making changes to the program before you move on to the next chapter. If any program change doesn't work, so much the better. If you learn to be a good detective, you'll enjoy programming that much more.

Review Questions

1. What is a major disadvantage of machine language?

A. A major disadvantage of machine language is that it is specific to the CPU for which it is written. The instruction set for one CPU is almost never the same as the instruction set of another CPU. Programs written in machine language cannot be run on a computer that is different from the one on which it was developed. Therefore, machine language programs are not portable.

2. What is a mnemonic?

A. A mnemonic is a shorthand notation, or abbreviation, for a machine language instruction. For example, if the machine language instruction for a jump to a memory location is C3 (hex), the mnemonic might be JMP. The mnemonic is simply easier to remember than its numeric equivalent.

3. What is source code?

A. Source code is the human-readable form of a program. For today's computers, any program ultimately resolves to binary digits. This means the program is a long sequence of 1s and 0s. It is the program source code that was translated into the binary code. The source code could be written in machine language or Visual Basic .NET, or anything in between.

4. What is the difference between an interpreter and a compiler?

A. A compiler takes the source code of a program and converts it into binary code which is then saved as a program file. Therefore, when a compiled program is loaded into memory, it is ready to run because it is already in memory as binary instructions. An interpreted program is loaded into memory, but each program instruction must be converted into binary code by an interpreter. This means that both the program source code and the interpreter must be in memory at the same time. Because the interpreter must decode each instruction before the computer can execute it, interpreted programs run more slowly than compiled programs.

5. What is a subroutine and why is it useful?

A. A subroutine is a piece of program code that is designed to perform a specific task. The advantage of a subroutine is that is can be used many times in a program and may be used in different programs. For example, if you write a subroutine that checks for valid phone numbers (that is, is there an area code and the proper number of digits), you can reuse that subroutine to check any phone number, be it a home, work, or cell phone. Without a subroutine, you would have to duplicate the code three times in the program to check the three types of phone numbers. Therefore, subroutines reduce the amount of code that must be written, tested, debugged, and maintained.

6. What are the three cornerstones of OOP?

A. The three cornerstones of OOP are encapsulation, polymorphism, and inheritance.

7. How would you fully qualify the `Text` property of a button control object named `btnExit` in a program that is placed on a form named `frmTest`?

A. `frmTest.btnExit.Text`.

CHAPTER 3

THINKING ABOUT PROGRAMS

In this chapter, you will learn the following:

- Algorithms
- Five programming steps
- Sideways refinement
- UML
- UML class diagrams

The purpose of this chapter is to introduce you to program design. Over the years, many formal program design methodologies have been developed. Some of these design methodologies are relatively complex, whereas others are fairly simple. In all cases, however, the goal was the same: to help the programmer write programs that were easy to write, debug, and maintain.

In this chapter, we'll begin our program design discussion with a very simple design methodology. Although this simple methodology is fairly basic, it serves the purpose of starting you to think about the design of a program. After you've studied this simple methodology, I'll present a more formal methodology called UML. UML is a popular design methodology especially suited for object-oriented programming.

Why Bother?

Each semester, I see the same thing happen. I assign a lab problem to the class. Within seconds, there's a clickety-clack of keystrokes as the students start typing in the code to solve the problem at hand. Invariably, however, there's one student who takes out a piece of paper and starts writing "stuff" on the paper. Minutes pass, but eventually the student starts typing program code into the computer. Almost without exception and despite the late start, that student finishes the assignment faster and with a better solution than does the rest of the class. Why?

If you look at the "stuff" the student wrote on the paper, you would find it's a program design for the problem. Some students have fairly elaborate designs filling up several pieces of paper, whereas other designs are fairly terse. The important thing, however, is that these students *have* a program design.

Algorithms

Every program should have a design, or plan, for the programmer to follow. In the parlance of the programmer, every program needs an algorithm. Simply stated, an *algorithm* is a statement of a systematic means for solving a specific problem. To programmers, an algorithm is the blueprint, or recipe, that we follow to produce a program.

Macro Versus Micro Algorithms

Algorithms come in different flavors. We can talk about the algorithm used to write a given program. At this level, we're talking about algorithms at the macro level. The algorithm tries to capture the general aspects of the program as an overview rather than grapple with the nitty-gritty details of each aspect of the program.

We can also discuss an algorithm at the micro level. At this level, we get down to the nuts, bolts, and glue that hold one particular aspect of the program together. For example, if you have data that must be sorted before it can be used, there are dozens of sorting algorithms from which to choose. Selecting one sorting algorithm addresses one aspect of the program. Once you've sorted the data, you need another micro algorithm to display the data.

As you might guess, we can collect all the micro algorithms to create a macro algorithm. If we start with the micro algorithms and work up to the macro view of the program, we're doing what's called *bottom-up* program design. If we start with a macro algorithm and work down toward the micro algorithms, we're doing *top-down* program design.

So, which method is best? If you take all the articles that have been written on which design approach is better and laid them end-to-end, you would never reach a conclusion. Each approach has its good points and bad points.

Regardless of which design approach you use, you must have some design for the program. At the very least, you need a statement of the programming problem at hand and a plan for addressing the problem. Once you understand the problem, you can start figuring out how to solve it. You'd be amazed how many false starts I've seen because the users and the programmers did not communicate the problem to be solved.

Because I believe a solid understanding of the problem to be solved is an essential first step in programming, I might favor the top-down program design approach. With that in mind, let's use a macro approach to viewing virtually every programming problem.

Five Programming Steps

Every program, no matter how complex, can be reduced to five fundamental steps. These steps are

1. Initialization

2. Input

3. Processing

4. Output

5. Cleanup

Let's examine each of these steps in greater detail.

Initialization Step

The initialization step is the first step you should think about when you design a program. The initialization step includes everything the program should do *before* the program begins interacting with the user. At first, the concept of doing things before interacting with the user might seem strange, but you've probably seen many programs that do exactly the same thing.

For example, we've all used Microsoft's Word, Excel, or similar programs. With such programs, you know that you can click on the File menu option and see a list of the files you worked with recently near the bottom of the menu. They didn't get there by magic. The program probably read the list of recently used files from a disk data file and appended that list to the File menu. Because this list is read before the program displays anything to the user, it falls under our Initialization step.

Anther common task that's often relegated to the Initialization step includes reading setup files. Such setup files might include information about the path names where certain database or other disk files can be found. Depending on the type of program being run, setup files might also contain information about display fonts, printer names and locations, foreground and background colors, screen resolution, and similar information. Other programs might read information about network connections, Internet access and security privileges, passwords, and other sensitive information.

In your own programs, you need to think about what type of information your program must have before it can do its job. If your design requires any type of setup or pre-program information, the Initialization step is probably where you should handle it.

Input Step

The Input step is exactly what you expect it to be. It's the step that collects whatever inputs the program needs to accomplish its task. In most cases, if you think about what the program is supposed to accomplish, defining the list of inputs is fairly simple. For example, if you're writing a loan interest program, you know you'll need to ask the user for the amount of the loan, the interest rate, and the length of the loan.

In other cases, however, you really need to think about what inputs should be requested of the user. For example, if you're writing an address book program, do you really want to ask the user to type in the name of the disk file that holds the address book and the location of that file each time you run the program? In other words, some of the Input step can, and properly should, be pushed into the Initialization step. The exact nature of amount of information that can be read in the Initialization step depends on the nature of the program. However, as a general rule of thumb, most users would like repetitive information stored in a setup or initialization file rather than re-entering it each time they run the program.

Where the inputs come from is a design decision. Setup files are great and should be used whenever possible. Obviously, other input information cannot be known until the user types it in, as in our loan interest example. In such situations, you'll likely use text boxes to collect the information from the user for use in the program. Because the user must interact with these text boxes to supply program information, the way you lay out the text box, labels, menus, and other program elements defines an important element of the *user interface* for the program.

Entire books have been written on how to design an effective user interface. There's no way that I can do the topic justice right now. However, it never hurts to keep in mind that a lot of people in the world read from left to right, top to bottom. If you expect the user to skip around all over the screen filing in a bunch of randomly placed text boxes, chances are that the user's going to be a little miffed. I'll have a lot more to say about the design of a user interface as we progress through the text.

Processing Step

The Processing step involves acting on the inputs to produce the result desired from the program. In our loan example, the program would accept the inputs (that is, the loan amount, interest rate, and term of the loan), plug them into a financial equation, and solve the equation to yield the desired result (that is, a monthly payment amount). Stated differently, the Processing step accepts the inputs, "crunches" them, and produces an answer to the problem.

Note that the Processing step usually does *not* display anything on the screen. Its sole purpose is to act on the data to generate a result. There's one notable exception to this rule, however. If you know beforehand that the Processing step is going to take a long time, it's usually a good idea to provide some feedback to the user that the program is still running. We've all run programs where a progress bar shows us what percentage of the task at hand has been completed. Another common example is programs that provide an estimate of the time remaining before completion. A lot of Web-based program use this approach. These situations need some form of feedback so that the user knows the program is still working. However, in situations in which the Processing step is fairly quick, displaying information to the user normally isn't done.

Output Step

In a sense, this is the whole purpose of the program in the first place: to give the users an answer to whatever problem it was they wanted solved. Many of our sample programs display an answer in a single text box. If, for example, you wrote a program to calculate a monthly loan payment, just displaying the payment in a text box is all that the Output step needs to do.

Other programs, however, are much more complex. Perhaps you've run programs that read your name, address, phone number, and perhaps a half-dozen other pieces of information from a database and then display them on the screen. Such complex programs might need several dozens of text boxes to display the necessary output information. In some situations, displaying the results cannot be done efficiently in text boxes. For example, displaying a table filled with customer data might better be done with a grid control or a list box that the program fills in as needed.

The important thing to note in the Output step is that because you're displaying results to the user, it's also part of the user interface. You saw earlier that the Input step was an element in the user interface because it collected data from the user. In the Output step, the user interface interacts with the user in a more passive manner, but still needs to consider the needs of the user in the design. Presenting information in an informative manner is almost an art form. I'll have more to say about Output step considerations as we get into more complex programs in later chapters.

Cleanup Step

The Cleanup step is used to gracefully shut down a program after it has completed its task. You can think of this step as the counterpart to the Initialization step. Although many simple programs can simply end without any further work by the programmer, more complex programs might need some help. For example, if your program reads a setup file to initialize some variables during the Initialization step, the Cleanup step probably should update those variables in the setup file with the user's latest information.

The Cleanup step is often associated with closing disk data files, including setup and database files. Some programs track how long a user ran a program and writes that information to what's called a *log file*. It isn't uncommon for log files to track the name of the people who were running the program, the dates and times they started running the program, and when they stopped using the program.

Another type of log file is called an *error log file*. The purpose of an error log file is to record information about any errors that were encountered as the program ran. Programmers can use the content of the error log file to help them debug the program should the need arise.

The actual tasks that are performed in the Cleanup step depend on the needs of the program itself. However, chances are that if something needs to be done in the Initialization step, some form of matching tasks is likely needed in the Cleanup step. Opening and closing different types of disk files is a common task for these two steps.

Five Steps for Every Program?

Does every program require all five programming steps? No. As you'll see in the next few chapters, we have a number of sample programs that don't need the Initialization or Cleanup steps. The sample programs are so simple that there's no need for these two steps. Normally, the Initialization and Cleanup steps appear in the design as the complexity of the program increases.

As you gain experience in writing programs, you'll develop a knack for knowing which programs need all five programming steps and which don't. However, you should always approach a programming design problem under the assumption that all five steps are needed. It's always easier to throw away steps later in the design than it is to squeeze them in once the design is well underway.

Sideways Refinement

I stated earlier that I tend to favor a top-down, macro algorithm as a starting point in the program design process. After all, you have to understand the problem before you can solve it. Still, the time will come when we have to look at the micro issues that must be addressed to solve the problem. As we proceed from the general overview of the program to its specifics, we're increasing the details, or *granularity*, of our view. Stated another way, we're moving from the general to the specific.

We can use the five programming steps as the starting point for our macro view of the design process. Next, we can take each of these steps and provide more detail about what each step involves. This process is called *sideways refinement*. An example will help you to understand the process.

Suppose that you have a user that has a database file that holds all the user's appointments in it. These appointments are stored in the database in chronological order by the date of the appointment. The user, however, wants to be able to view the appointments in alphabetical order, based on the last name of the person the user is meeting. Let's see how we might use a sideways refinement approach to designing a solution.

Sideways Refinement of the Initialization Step

We already know that the user has a database of the appointments. We also know the user wants a list of the appointments in alphabetical order by last name. This is our macro view of the algorithm.

So, what should the Initialization step do? Well, it seems clear that we need to open the appointments database. We also need a Visual Basic .NET form to display the results after the appointments have been sorted. We'll assume that our task is a little easier because we know where the database is located on the network, and we can also determine the user's name and password from the same database as soon as the user starts the program. With this information in mind, our first sideways refinement might look like the one shown in Figure 3.1.

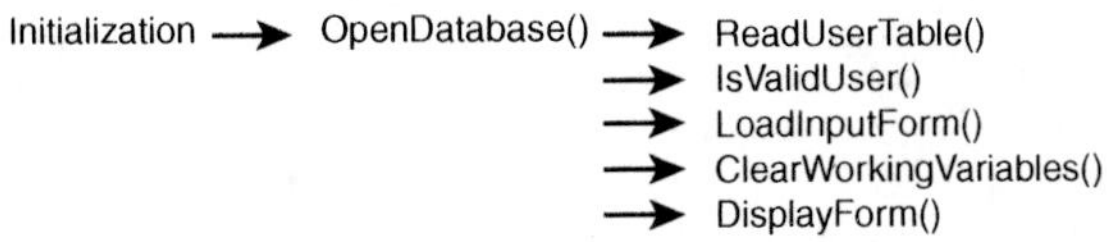

FIGURE 3.1

A sideways refinement of
the Initialization step.

Initialization ——▶ OpenDatabase() ——▶ ReadUserTable()
  ——▶ IsValidUser()
  ——▶ LoadInputForm()
  ——▶ ClearWorkingVariables()
  ——▶ DisplayForm()

Notice how the detail increases as we move sideways from left to right in Figure 3.1. In the fig-ure, the sideways refinement presents a list of subroutines or functions that the step needs to accomplish its task. These subroutines and functions will be similar to those we discussed in Chapter 2, "The Basics of Object-Oriented Programming." Each small routine has a specific task to accomplish.

Pseudo Code

We can continue to further refine each step by the use of pseudo code. *Pseudo code* is an algo-rithm for the routine stated using an English-like syntax. For example, we might take the IsValidUser() routine and write its pseudo code as follows:

```
IsValidUser() → If CurrentUserName Not in ValidUserList
    Display Invalid User Error Message
    Terminate Program
    Else
    Return ValidUserIDNumber
     End
```

Notice how the pseudo code describes what the routine is supposed to do, but without the formal syntax of the programming language being used. Pseudo code is *not* a language-based syntax. Pseudo code is an algorithmic statement of what the routine is supposed to do.

The real advantage of pseudo code is that, because it's very English-like, you can share it with the (non-programming) user in the design stage to see whether you're addressing the problem correctly. This review process with the user at an early stage of the design is a huge benefit to both of you. Catching design errors and program changes early in the process prevents a lot of nasty problems down the road. Involving the user at the outset usually results in a better pro-gram produced in less time with fewer changes later on. It's a win-win approach to program design.

Once you have an understanding of the purpose of the routine stated in pseudo code, translat-ing the pseudo code into actual program code is pretty simple. Good design promotes easier program development.

I encourage you to stop reading at this point and take a moment to do a sideways refinement of the remaining four program steps for our appointment program. You might also take a crack at trying to write the pseudo code for each refinement you create in the list. Even though I realize that most of you won't take the time to do this, there are a few of you die-hards who will. Trust me…it's well worth the effort.

What Is UML?

To this point, we've taken a fairly informal approach to program design. The five programming steps are a good starting point for thinking about program design. The sideways refinement of the five programming steps is the second phase in designing a program. Using pseudo code to expand the detail of the refinement is extremely helpful in program design. Although the five-programming-step approach to program design is useful, some prefer a more rigorous approach. The Unified Modeling Language, or UML, is such an approach.

> The **Unified Modeling Language (UML)** is a standard language for specifying, visualizing, constructing, and documenting the artifacts of software systems, as well as for business modeling and other non-software systems. The UML represents a collection of best engineering practices that have proven successful in the modeling of large and complex systems.[1]

Simply stated, UML is a formalized methodology for software development.

A Brief History of UML

As mentioned in Chapter 2, object-oriented programming (OOP) has been around since the 1960s. Although OOP was relatively young, several objected-oriented modeling languages were developed between the mid-1970s and late 1980s. By the mid-1990s, more than 50 modeling languages had been developed. Clearly, so many attempts without producing a language that was embraced by the programming community suggests that there was more work to be done.

Part of the problem was competing methodologies. The leading contenders at the time were Jim Rumbaugh (General Electric), Grady Booch (Rational Software), and Ivar Jacobson (Objectory). These three leaders beat each other up for years in a fascinating zero-sum game in the modeling language arena.

In 1994, Rumbaugh left General Electric and joined Booch at Rational Software, thus ganging up on Jacobson. A year later, Rational Software bought Objectory and the three major players (sometimes called the Three Amigos) were under one roof. In June of 1996, UML 0.9 was released.

In the years since then, the Object Management Group (OMG) has served as a focal point for refinements to UML. In mid-2001, OMG members began their work on a major upgrade to UML 2.0. Currently, UML includes visual modeling, simulation, and development environments. A number of UML modeling tools are commercially available. Some of these tools include Rational Rose 2002 from Rational Software Corporation, Describe Enterprise from Embarcadero Technologies, and Visio 2002 from Microsoft. (We'll use Visio 2002 for our UML design efforts, primarily because of university agreements with Microsoft.)

---

1 http://cgi.omg.org/news/pr97/umlprimer.html

UML Diagrams

UML is a visual tool and employs many types of diagrams. Each UML diagram is designed to let developers and customers view a software system from a different perspective in varying degrees of abstraction. Table 3.1 presents a list of the UML diagrams commonly created by these visual modeling tools.

TABLE 3.1   Some Common UML Diagrams

Use Case Diagram	Displays the relationship among actors and use cases.
Class Diagram	Models class structure and contents using design elements such as classes, packages, and objects. It also displays relationships such as containment, inheritance, associations, and others.
State Diagram	Displays the sequences of states that an object of an interaction goes through during its life in response to received stimuli, together with its responses and actions.
Sequence Diagram	Displays the time sequence of the objects participating in the interaction. This consists of the vertical dimension (time) and horizontal dimension (different objects).
Collaboration Diagram	Displays an interaction organized around the objects and their links to one another. Numbers are used to show the sequence of messages.
Activity Diagram	Displays a special state diagram in which most of the states are action states and most of the transitions are triggered by completion of the actions in the source states. This diagram focuses on flows driven by internal processing.
Component Diagram	Displays the high-level packaged structure of the code itself. Dependencies among components are shown, including source code components, binary code components, and executable components. Some components exist at compile time, at link time, at runtime, or combinations of each.
Deployment Diagram	Displays the configuration of runtime processing elements and the software components, processes, and objects that live on them. Software component instances represent runtime manifestations of code units.

Each of the diagrams presented in Table 3.1 deserves a chapter (perhaps more) of its own. However, we are primarily concerned with how UML can be used with class diagrams and how they can help us to develop programs that embrace the philosophy of OOP.

OOA, OOD, and OOP

Just what you need...more abbreviations and terms to contend with. Actually, it's not all that bad and we can dispatch these fairly quickly.

Object-Oriented Analysis

Object-oriented analysis, or OOA, is a methodology for the analysis of the software development process. When using OOA, we need to think of everything in the software development process in terms of classes. We talked about classes in Chapter 2 as they related to the hospital elevator example. In that example, each hospital individual (that is, doctor, nurse, patient, and visitor) was a class. You'll also remember that each new individual that we created from a class was called an *instance* of that class. The OOA process is primarily concerned with how we derived the classes that are needed by the system.

The core issue in OOA is concerned with answering the "What" types of questions that arise in the software development process. Typical OOA questions and concerns are "What are the classes in my program?", "What will my program do?", "What does each class object do to help solve the problem?", and "What are the responsibilities of this class in my program?". At the OOA stage, the emphasis is on the analysis of the objects, tasks, and responsibilities of the actual software system.

Object-Oriented Design

The focal point of object-oriented design phase is concerned with the "How" issues of the software system. Typical issues that are addressed in the design phase include "How will this class gather the data?", "How will this class calculate a tax return?", and "How will this class print the report?". In terms of our discussion from Chapter 2, this level is concerned with all the attributes, properties, and methods of a class.

Therefore, the OOA component seeks to identify the classes that are necessary to accomplish the software objectives. Having done that, OOD focuses on the implementation of those classes and the attributes, properties, and methods that are at the core of each class. Coupling the two activities and developing the links that connect the classes are all part of the complete OOP process.

UML Class Diagrams

The standard UML diagram, or notation, for a class is a rectangle that's divided into three compartments. Starting at the top of the class diagram, the first compartment contains name of the class. The second compartment contains attributes of the class. (You'll also hear the attributes of a class referred to as the *properties* or *variables* of the class.) The third compartment contains class methods. The methods of the class tell us what the class can do.

Figure 3.2 shows a class diagram with the class name `Vehicle` in the first compartment. The standard naming convention for class names is to begin the class name with an uppercase letter. If the class name contains more than one word, each word in the class name is in uppercase. For example, class names that follow this naming convention would include `Vehicle`, `PassengerCar`, and `IncomeStatement`. There are no spaces between the words in a class name.

FIGURE 3.2

A sample UML class diagram for a class named `Vehicle`.

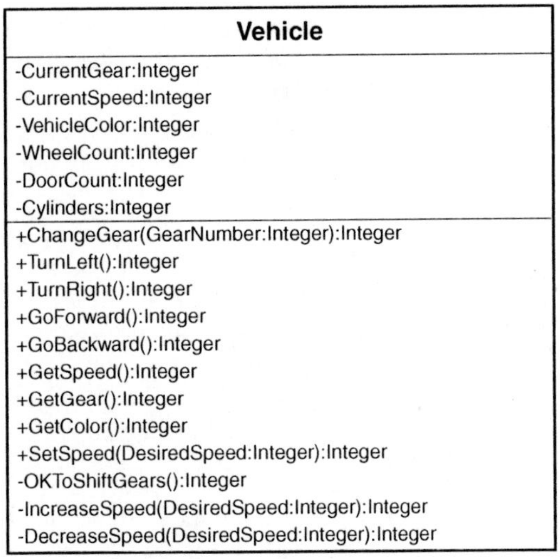

Vehicle
-CurrentGear:Integer
-CurrentSpeed:Integer
-VehicleColor:Integer
-WheelCount:Integer
-DoorCount:Integer
-Cylinders:Integer
+ChangeGear(GearNumber:Integer):Integer
+TurnLeft():Integer
+TurnRight():Integer
+GoForward():Integer
+GoBackward():Integer
+GetSpeed():Integer
+GetGear():Integer
+GetColor():Integer
+SetSpeed(DesiredSpeed:Integer):Integer
-OKToShiftGears():Integer
-IncreaseSpeed(DesiredSpeed:Integer):Integer
-DecreaseSpeed(DesiredSpeed:Integer):Integer

Class Properties (Attributes)

In our example, compartment two has six `Integer` attributes. In a more complete example, there could be dozens of attributes for a class. Visual Basic .NET tends to refer to these attributes as the *properties* of the class. Each property can assume different values. Collectively, the current values of the properties describe the state of a class object. For example, if the `CurrentGear` value is `4` and `CurrentSpeed` is `55`, it seems reasonable to assume that the `Vehicle` object is going forward at 55 miles per hour. Therefore, the state of the object is such that it is moving forward at 55 mph. If we can draw an English analogy, the properties of an object are like the nouns of a sentence.

Plus Signs and Minus Signs

You'll notice that each entry in the second compartment has a minus sign in front of it. In the third compartment, some entries have plus signs, whereas others have minus signs. The plus sign (+) signifies that the item on that line is available outside the class. Stated in a different way, the plus signs means that we can use these items to affect the state of the class object. The plus signs, therefore, denote `Public` elements of the class.

If an entry is prefixed with a minus sign (-), it means that the item is available for use only within the class itself. The item is not visible or accessible outside of the class. The minus signs, therefore, mark the `Private` elements of a class.

As a general rule, making an item `Private` is a good thing and is consistent with our goal of hiding data whenever possible. This is an integral part of the idea of encapsulation that we discussed in Chapter 2. By encapsulating the data, we minimize the chance of inadvertently changing the data in some part of the program outside of the class. This makes finding program errors much easier.

The plus and minus signs, therefore, denote the access specifiers for each element in a class. (There is a third access specifier named `Protected` that's denoted by the sharp symbol, `#`. We won't discuss this access specifier until Chapter 16, "Class Properties.") You can think of the plus signs as defining the way you interact with class objects, whereas the minus signs tells you what's available only to the class itself. (We'll delve into these program elements in Chapter 15, "Encapsulation.")

Class Methods (Operations)

Compartment three lists the operations that are available in the class. Although UML notation calls the items in compartment three *operations*, when using Visual Basic .NET, the tendency is to refer to these operations as *methods*. Methods tell the programmer how they must interact with the class. If you look at the names of the items in compartment three, each seems to imply an action of some sort. If properties are the nouns of a sentence, methods are the verbs.

You'll often hear other programmers refer to the methods as the *procedures* of a class. Even though there's nothing seriously wrong with this term, you should remember that procedures can exist outside of a class. However, methods are almost always tied to a particular class object.

Class Methods with Arguments

Sometimes a method needs outside information to perform its task. For example, in Figure 3.1, we see the following line:

```
+SetSpeed(DesiredSpeed:Integer):Integer
```

The plus sign says that `SetSpeed()` is a `Public` method, so it can be used in conjunction with a class object. Between the parentheses, we see that a data value is passed to the `SetSpeed()` method of the `Vehicle` class. This data value is given the name `DesiredSpeed` and it is an `Integer` data type. (You'll learn more about data types in the next chapter. For now, just think of `DesiredSpeed` as a number.)

After the closing parentheses, we see a colon (`:`) followed by the word `Integer`. This means that `SetSpeed()` will return an integer value to the part of the program that wanted to use the `SetSpeed()` method. Although we can't be sure at this point, the return value is probably used to indicate whether or not we were able to set the speed. After all, things can go wrong. For example, `SetSpeed()` probably doesn't work too well if the `Vehicle` object isn't running. Likewise, setting the speed to `150` is probably not wise if the current gear is `Reverse`.

Now look at the two lines:

```
-IncreaseSpeed(DesiredSpeed:Integer):Integer
-DecreaseSpeed(DesiredSpeed:Integer):Integer
```

These look very similar in terms of their purpose and use. In fact, such similarities should tip you off that it might be possible to simplify things. Could we replace these two methods with the following method

```
-ChangeSpeed(DesiredSpeed:Integer):Integer
```

with the understanding that if `DesiredSpeed` is positive, it represents the amount we want to raise the speed whereas a negative number is the amount we want to decrease the speed? For example, consider what the following code might do:

```
Dim MyVehicle as New Vehicle
Dim ObjectSpeed as integer

' Some code that does something...

ObjectSpeed = MyVehicle.GetSpeed()
ObjectSpeed = MyVehicle.ChangeSpeed(-ObjectSpeed)
```

First we create a `Vehicle` object named `MyVehicle`. Then we call the `GetSpeed()` method for the `MyVehicle` object. Notice how a dot (called the dot operator) separates the object name from the method name. All Visual Basic .NET objects use this syntax format.

Let's assume that the vehicle is presently traveling at 55 mph. The value of `ObjectSpeed` is assigned the value of **55**. If we then pass the negative value of the current speed (that is, **-55**) to the `ChangeSpeed()` method, we can cause the car to stop.

I realize that there are a lot of syntax details that you don't understand about this example right now. Not to worry. We'll cover all of those details in subsequent chapters. For now, however, I just want you to get an idea of what a UML class diagram is and the type of information it conveys.

Why are some of the methods marked with minus signs? Obviously this means they are `Private` methods and not available outside of the class. Such methods are helper methods that are used internally by the class itself to accomplish its tasks. For example, the method `OkToShiftGears()` might check the `CurrentGear` and `CurrentSpeed` values to see if it's safe to shift gears. If the `CurrentSpeed` is 55, it might not be a good idea to shift into Reverse right now. Therefore, the `ChangeGear()` method might call `OkToShiftGears()` to help it decide whether it's safe to change gears.

The idea behind a UML class diagram is that is gives you a quick, concise overview of what the class does and how you as a programmer are expected to interact with it. If you think of a class as a black box, the minus signs indicate things inside the black box you shouldn't mess around with as a user of the class. The plus signs indicate the means you *must* use to interact with the properties and methods of the class. In other words, the `Public` items of a class define the interface for the class object and how you must interact with it.

Programmer's Tip

Always keep in mind that it's the `Public` methods that dictate how programmers must use your class. As long as you don't change how these methods are used, your interface with those programmers doesn't change. This lends consistency to your class.

On the other hand, you can change the `Private` methods to your heart's content and never need to worry about getting the programmers ticked off at you because you've changed the way they work. After all, they never see or use the `Private` methods anyway. This usually means keeping the `Public` methods as simple as possible and using the `Private` methods to manage the details of the task at hand.

We'll revisit UML class diagrams again in later chapters. For now, just review the material in this section to become comfortable with the nature of information UML class diagrams provide.

Summary

In this chapter, you've learned how virtually any programming problem can be summarized with five simple steps. You've also seen how you can use these five steps as a starting point for designing your own programs. You saw how a sideways refinement of each step could be used to add detail to a program design. Finally, we used a UML class diagram as a more conventional methodology to think about program design.

Take a few moments to think about classes and objects. If you can, think of a class you'd like to have and use the five program steps to outline its design. Having done that, convert that design into a UML class diagram. Think about the interface you've created with the design and ask yourself whether it's complete enough to perform the task of the class, but simple enough to be used easily. These are the types of questions you should always ask yourself over and over during the design process.

Class and program design gets easier as you gain experience doing it. Although this may seem like alchemy right now, you'll probably grow to enjoy it over time!

Review Questions

1. What is an algorithm?

A. An algorithm is an organized statement of a how a specific problem or questions will be solved. A well-designed algorithm presents a step-by-step process that leads to the solution to the problem.

2. What are the five programming steps?

A. The five programming steps are Initialization, Input, Processing, Output, and Cleanup.

3. What does *sideways refinement* mean?

A. Each of the five programming steps represents a macro view of a program. For example, the Input step might require getting data from the keyboard, and then reading a setup table from a database, and finally reading more information from a different database. A sideways refinement is the process in which you take a programming step, such as the Input step, and add more and more detail as you move from the macro view of the step to the micro details that get the job done. For example:

Input Step→ReadKeyboard()

ReadSetupTable()→ReadTable1()→(Code)

ReadTable2()

ReadTable3()

Each movement toward the right adds more and more detail to the task at hand. Ultimately, the sideways refinement stops when the actual code for a function is written for the task at hand.

4.   What is UML and why is it beneficial?

A.   UML stands for *Unified Modeling Language*. The benefit of UML is that it forces you to think about programming problems in an organize fashion using OOP techniques. The basic building blocks of UML are the class, its attributes, and its methods. UML class diagrams bring all three of these OOP elements into one convenient diagram.

5.   In terms of OOP, what does it mean when we say that some object's attribute is either `Public` or `Private`?

A.   The terms `Public` and `Private` in OOP refer to the access that is afforded to the object's attribute. If an attribute is `Private`, it can be changed only using the means provided by the class to which it belongs. If the attribute is `Public`, any other object has full access to the attribute, including the capability to change its value. The idea behind encapsulation is to make all data as private as possible to prevent contamination by outside agents.

CHAPTER 4

DATA TYPES AND NUMERIC VARIABLES

*I*n this chapter you will learn about the different types of data that are inherently part of Visual Basic .NET. You will also learn how to think like the Visual Basic .NET compiler. This process will not only make you a better programmer but also make you more adept at correcting program errors (that is, debugging). Understanding what Visual Basic .NET does behind the scenes will help give you a more comprehensive understanding of how programs work and, hence, make you a better programmer.

Visual Basic .NET Data Types

What is data? Simply stated, data is information. From a programmer's perspective, however, the information contained in a piece of data can be stored in a computer many different ways. Given that you have choices about how to store data in a computer, how do you select the "correct" way to store a given piece of data in the computer? It depends.

As a starting point in making a decision about which data type to use for a specific task, you first need to know what the data type choices are. Table 4.1 presents a list of the common data types that are supported by Visual Basic .NET. The table also presents additional information about each data type to help you better understand the use for which each data type is best suited.

TABLE 4.1 Visual Basic .NET Basic Data Types

Type	Storage (Bytes)	Value Range
Boolean	2	True or False
Byte	1	0 through 255 (unsigned)
Char	2	0 through 65535
Date	8	0:00:00 January 1, 0001, through 11:59:59 December 31, 9999
Decimal	16	0 through ±79,228,162,514,264,337,593,543,950,335 with no decimal point; 0 through ±7.9228162514264337593543950335, with 28 places to the right of the decimal; the smallest nonzero number is ±0.0000000000000000000000000001 (±1E-28)
Double	8	−1.79769313486231570E+308 through −4.94065645841246544E-324 for negative values; 4.94065645841246544E-324 through 1.79769313486231570E+308 for positive values
Integer	4	−2,147,483,648 through 2,147,483,647
Long	8	−9,223,372,036,854,775,808 through 9,223,372,036,854,775,807
Object	4	A value of any Object type
Short	2	−32,768 through 32,767
Single	4	−3.4028235E+38 through −1.401298E-45 for negative values; 1.401298E-45 through 3.4028235E+38 for positive values
String	*	0 to approximately 2 billion Unicode characters
User Defined	*	A range determined by the structure member's data type that is independent of the ranges of the other members

*The amount of storage depends on the implementing platform.

A quick look at Table 4.1 shows that there is a considerable range of values among the various data types. Sometimes the data type you need to use is obvious. For example, if you need to store the data value 1000 in a program, the Boolean and Byte data types will not work because they are not capable of storing the value 1000. However, Char, Decimal, Double, and several other data types are quite capable of storing the value `1000`. How do you decide which of them to use?

Which Data Type to Use?

In all facets of life, decisions often involve tradeoffs. In terms of computer programming, the tradeoff often involves trading memory usage for speed or vice versa. In other cases, you have to trade memory usage for range. For example, if you use a `Single` data type, you use less memory for each number (4 bytes) than if you use a `Double` data type (8 bytes), but you are forced to accept a smaller range of values.

As a general rule, programmers are less concerned today about memory limitations than they are about the speed at which data is processed. Because the speed at which data is processed is very important, it seems to make sense that the smaller the number of bytes the program needs to manipulate while processing the data, the faster the program will run.

Well…not really.

Data Type Selection and CPU Registers

When chipmakers design central processing unit (CPU) chips, they design them in such a way that certain parts of the chip, called *registers*, are most comfortable with data of a certain size. For example, most of the CPU chips that run the Windows operating system have registers that handle 4-byte data very efficiently. As a result, `Integer` data is a good choice in many situations, provided that the data falls within the range of an integer variable. In fact, in some instances, `Integer` data is processed faster than some of the data that uses fewer bytes simply because the smaller data types don't fit the "natural" size of the CPU's registers.

Let's reconsider our earlier decision about whether to use a `Single` or `Double` data type for very large numbers. The `Single` data type has fewer bytes, and if we don't need the extra range that a `Double` offers, it would seem that the `Single` data type should be a good choice. After all, it's only 4 bytes, just like an integer, and should fit naturally within the CPU registers, right?

Well, there's a little glitch in this thinking. The `Single` and `Double` data types are designed to represent floating-point numbers. *Floating-point numbers* are numeric values that may have fractional values, resulting in numbers that have decimal points in them. Because of this, floating-point numbers are not processed in the same way that integer numbers are. (Integer numbers are whole numbers and cannot have fractional values.)

Processing floating-point numbers is inherently slower than processing integer numbers. In fact, the processing is so much slower that chip manufacturers have recently begun to build small floating-point processors (FPPs) into CPU chips. (Prior to being part of the CPU itself, the FPP was a separate chip, like the 8087 by Intel.) The registers inside the FPPs are designed for 8-byte data values. Because of this, even though the `Single` data type uses fewer bytes than the `Double` type, it actually runs more slowly in most applications because it doesn't naturally fit the register size of the FPP. (This is because code must be executed to add an extra 4 bytes of empty data to the `Single` data type, and this operation takes time.) As a result, the `Double` data type is often the best choice for programs that crunch a lot of floating-point numbers.

Oh my…you want to know the time, and I'm telling you how to build a watch. Still, the devil is in the details, and the more details you know, the better programmer you will be. Sometimes you can make better programming choices if you have a complete understanding about the hardware you're working with. As a friend of mine once said: "If you don't like these details, you should consider another line of work." There's a large chunk of truth there, so let's plow on.

Details About the Visual Basic .NET Data Types

The following sections briefly describe the data types presented in Table 4.1.

The `Boolean` Data Type

A `Boolean` data item can hold only one of two values in Visual Basic .NET: `True` or `False`. No other values are allowed for `Boolean` data items. `True` and `False` are keywords in Visual Basic .NET and equate to the values -1 for `True` and `0` for `False`. (A complete list of Visual Basic .NET keywords is presented later in this chapter, in the section "Keywords.") This means that a `Boolean` data item can accept the values `True`, `False`, -1, or `0`, and that's it; nothing else is allowed.

So, should you use `True` or -1 if you want a `Boolean` data item to have a `True` value? Just what you need…more decisions to make. Well, actually, this one's pretty easy. You should use `True` instead of -1. This is the correct decision for two reasons. First, suppose you want to use a `Boolean` variable named `Sick` to describe how you feel. Which line is easier for you to understand?

```
Sick = True
```

or

```
Sick = -1
```

Clearly, using the Visual Basic .NET keyword `True` imparts more information about how the variable `Sick` is being used than does -1. Using the keyword `True` gives the person reading the code at least some idea of how the variable `Sick` is being used. In other words, the use of the keyword `True` or `False` provides better documentation of how the variable is being used in the program. Don't forget that there may be other people who will have to understand your code, too.

A second reason for using `True` and `False` instead of their numeric equivalents concerns changes that might occur to Visual Basic .NET in the future. Suppose Microsoft decides that using the value of -1 for a true state of a `Boolean` variable was a bad idea, so it changes the `True` value to 1. If all the `Boolean` variables in a program were assigned a -1 value instead of

`True`, you would have to go through all those programs and change every occurrence of the -1 value to `1`. This could involve a lot of search-and-replace effort as you searched through all your programs' source code, looking at each -1; this process would be prone to errors.

However, if Microsoft changes the numeric value of the `True` state and you have used the keyword `True` throughout your code, everything still works correctly, and you don't have to make any changes to your programs' source code. All you then have to do is recompile your programs. This is the case because the new Visual Basic .NET compiler would know that everywhere it finds the keyword `True`, it must use the value `1` instead of -1, as it did before. Why should you make all the conversions when the Visual Basic .NET compiler can do it all for you?

You will see other examples of where it makes sense to use words to represent numeric values in later chapters.

The `Byte` Data Type

A `Byte` data item uses a single byte of memory. Remember from Chapter 2, "The Basics of Object-Oriented Programming," that each byte in memory has 8 bits. Each of these 8 bits can assume only one of two possible values: `1` or `0`. If you take the number 2 (that is, the number of possible values for a bit) and raise it to the 8th power (that is, the number of bits available in a byte), you find the following:

$2^8 = 256$

This means that a byte of memory is capable of representing 256 unique values. Because 0 is a valid value for a byte, the range of values for a `Byte` data type is 0 through 255.

`Byte` data items are not used very often in Visual Basic .NET programs. However, they are used to store values that represent the American Standard Code for Information Interchange (ASCII) character set. Each time you press a key on the keyboard, a byte of information is sent from the keyboard to the computer as an ASCII character. For example, if you press the lowercase letter *a* on your keyboard, the ASCII value sent to the computer is the numeric value 97. If you hold the Shift key down and press *a* again, a capital *A*, with an ASCII value of 65, is sent to the computer. A complete list of the ASCII codes is presented in Appendix A, "The ASCII Character Set."

If your program needs to manipulate ASCII data as it is received from the keyboard, the `Byte` data type might be a good choice. In situations in which you need to manipulate character data, the `Char` data type might be more appropriate, as discussed in the following section.

The `Char` Data Type

The `Char` data type is used to store character data. That might seem strange because I just told you that the `Byte` data type is often used to store character data. Well, the World Wide Web is changing everything. If you write a program for the Web, it might be run in countries other than the United States. We're pretty fortunate in the United States because we can present each of the characters in our character set in 1 byte. If you count the number of keys on your keyboard, you'll see that there just aren't that many to worry about. This is not so for many Asian countries. A Chinese typewriter might have several thousand character keys on it. Clearly, a `Byte` data type doesn't have the range to store such a large character set.

The information age is drawing the world into a closer community, and Visual Basic .NET embodies the concept of a locale. *Locale* simply reflects the environment in which Visual Basic .NET is being used. For example, in the United States, people would use the notation 5/24/02 to represent the date May 24, 2002, whereas Europeans would use the notation 24/5/2002. If you set the Visual Basic .NET locale to the proper location, information is displayed in a format that is common to the locale selected. If you are writing programs in the United States, your locale uses the ASCII character set. However, if you are programming in China, your locale might be using the Katakana character set.

To accommodate the more extensive character sets found in some locales, programmers around the world have accepted the *Unicode* character set. Unlike the ASCII character set, the Unicode character set uses 2 bytes (16 bits) to represent each character in the character set of the locale being used. Note that Visual Basic .NET uses the Unicode character set in the United States, even though the ASCII character set would be sufficient. Keep in mind that the "double-wide" Unicode character set is the default mechanism for working with characters in Visual Basic .NET.

Given that Unicode uses 2 bytes for each character, how many characters could it represent? Let's do the math. There are 16 bits, with two possible states for each bit:

$2^{16} = 65,535$

With more than 65,000 possible characters, Unicode can handle just about any character set that a locale might ever need.

The `Decimal` Data Type

The `Decimal` data type is a fixed-point numeric data type that uses 16 bytes (128 bits) for storage. Of the 128 bits, 96 are used to represent the number itself, and 1 bit is used for the sign bit. (A *sign bit* is used to determine whether the number is positive or negative. If the sign bit is `0`, the number is positive. If the sign bit is `1`, the value is negative.) The remaining bits in the number are used as a base-10 scaling factor. If you do the math, you get the following large number:

$2^{96} = 79,228,162,514,264,337,593,543,950,335$

As you can see in Table 4.1, the smallest nonzero number that can be represented with the `Decimal` data type is approximately $\pm 1\text{E}^{-28}$. (You can get additional details about the mechanics of the `Decimal` data type by using the Visual Basic .NET help system; search for the phrase "decimal data type.")

Programmer's Tip

The smallest value for the `Decimal` data type is ±0.0000000000000000000000000001. This value is known as the *Epsilon* value and can be important in certain situations. The reason it becomes important is because if you test a value that is less than the Epsilon value against the value 0, the value is so small that Visual Basic .NET cannot detect the difference between that value and 0. That is, a value smaller than ±0.0000000000000000000000000001 is so small that Visual Basic .NET interprets it as 0.0. Although this is usually not a problem, it does point out a potential danger of comparing floating-point numbers to 0.

Because the `Decimal` data value is a fixed-point number, `Decimal` is often used for financial calculations that require large numbers of significant integral and fractional digits with no round-off errors.

The `Double` and `Single` Data Types

This section discusses the `Double` and `Single` data types together because they are similar in nature. As you can see in Table 4.1, the `Double` data type uses 8 bytes for storage, and the `Single` data type uses only 4 bytes for storage. Because of their different storage requirements, the range of values for a `Single` data type is less than that for a `Double` data type. It is also true that the `Single` data type has fewer digits of *precision*. That is, if you use a `Single` data type, you can rely on the number having only 7 significant digits of precision. The `Double` data type has up to 15 significant digits of precision.

Given that both data types are used to store floating-point numbers (that is, values that can have decimal points in them), which type should you use? As mentioned earlier in this chapter, the CPU chips used for the Windows operating system have FPPs that are most efficient when processing 8-byte data values. For that reason, the `Double` data type is often the best choice because the values are processed faster than `Single` values. Keep in mind, however, that if memory restrictions are critical, you might want to use the `Single` data type because it requires less memory for storage.

The `Integer`, `Long`, and `Short` Data Types

This section discusses the three data types `Integer`, `Long`, and `Short` together because they are all integral data types (that is, no decimal point is allowed), differing only in their storage requirements and, hence, their range of values.

The `Integer` data type takes 4 bytes (32 bits), of which 1 bit is used as the sign bit, leaving 31 bits for the number itself. Therefore, the possible range of values for an `Integer` data type is

-2^{31} through 2^{31} = $-2,147,483,648$ through $2,147,483,647$.

An `Integer` data type has a positive value when the sign bit is positive and a negative value when the sign bit is negative.

The `Long` data type is similar to the `Integer` data type, but it takes 8 bytes (64 bits) for storage, again using 1 bit for the sign bit. Therefore, the `Long` data type has a range of

$$-2^{63} \text{ though } 2^{63} = -9,223,372,036,854,775,808 \text{ through } -9,223,372,036,854,775,807$$

A `Long` data type has a positive value when the sign bit is positive and a negative value when the sign bit is negative.

Finally, the `Short` data type uses only 2 bytes (16 bits) for storage, including the sign bit. As a result, its range of value is

$$-2^{15} \text{ through } 2^{15} = -32,768 \text{ through } 32,767$$

A `Short` data type has a positive value when the sign bit is positive and a negative value when the sign bit is negative.

Note that these three data types support only integral data values. That is, no decimal point is allowed with these three data types. Obviously, you should not use these values if you are working with data such as money or interest rates that may have fractional values. As you will learn, integral data types are perfect for counting things, and you will use them extensively in later chapters.

Of the three integral data types, the `Integer` data type is usually the most efficient to use, provided that it has the range of values you need in your program.

The `Object` Data Type

As mentioned in Chapter 2, Visual Basic .NET is an object-oriented language. Therefore, the programs you write with it often manipulate objects in various ways as the programs execute. Although we are not ready to dig in to this topic fully at this time, I can tell you that the 4 bytes mentioned in Table 4.1 as the storage value for the `Object` data type is actually the number of bytes required to store the *memory address* of an object, not the object itself. This might seem a bit strange at first, but as you will see later in this chapter, it makes a lot of sense when it comes to processing your objects in a program.

For the time being, you can simply think of the 4 bytes associated with an `Object` data type as a means by which Visual Basic .NET knows where to look in your computer's memory for an object. You'll learn more details later in this chapter.

The `String` Data Type

The `String` data type is one of the few data types that does not have a fixed storage requirement. The reason for this has to do with the nature of `String` data. The `String` data type is used to store character data. For example, suppose you have a `String` variable named `MyName`. You might have a program statement like this:

```
MyName = "Joyce"
```

In this case, `MyName` would use 10 bytes of memory (plus a few more overhead bytes). Why doesn't it use just 5 bytes plus a few overhead bytes? Remember that Visual Basic .NET is a global language that uses the Unicode character set, so each character requires 2 bytes of memory.

If you changed the program statement to this:

```
MyName = "Clive Cussler"
```

the storage requirement would increases to 26 bytes plus the overhead bytes. Note that the blank space between the first and last name counts as a character, so there are 13 letters in the name, requiring 26 bytes of memory.

Programmer's Tip

The *overhead bytes* I keep mentioning with respect to the `String` data type are used by Visual Basic .NET to process certain `String` operations efficiently. The number of overhead bytes is fixed and does not change with respect to the number of characters present in the `String` variable. As a general rule, you do not need to concern yourself with these overhead bytes, and they are not mentioned again in any subsequent discussions about the `String` data type.

It should be obvious that most of the times that you want to represent information that is not numeric in nature, you use the `String` data type. You can safely assume that a `String` data type can store up to about 2 billion Unicode characters, which is usually enough characters for the problem at hand.

The `User Defined` Data Type

The `User Defined` data type requires a variable amount of memory for storage. There are circumstances in which a program might be more efficient with a blend of data types than with just one of the types presented in Table 4.1. In such cases, Visual Basic .NET allows you to define your own data type. Because you have the freedom to define `User Defined` data types as you see fit, there is no way to know how many bytes you need for one until after you have defined it.

I like to think of `User Defined` data as "data for adults." `User Defined` data types are an advanced topic that is covered in Chapter 12, "Program Loops."

Variables

Now that you have an idea of the types of data that Visual Basic .NET makes available to you, let's explore how you can actually use these data types in a program to get something productive done.

When you think about it, a computer program is usually designed with one thing in mind: manipulating data. When you write an email message to a friend, the program accepts the keystrokes you make, formats the text into an email message, and then passes along the message to your friend. If you run a program to figure out how much a bank loan will cost you per month, you type in the amount of the loan, the interest rate, and the number of months, and then you press the Enter key; the monthly payment is then calculated. In each of these cases, the program accepts data from you via the keyboard, processes that data, and presents new data based on what you typed in to the program.

Regardless of the exact purpose of the program, the basic sequence is the same: Get some data from the user, process that data, and then display the result to the user. The sequence can be simplified to three basic steps (as described in Chapter 3, "Thinking About Programs"):

1. Input the data.

2. Process the data.

3. Output the results.

Clearly, the program needs some place to hold the data after you type it in to the program. The place where the program holds the data is called a *variable*.

Variable Name

You define a *variable* to hold a data item. You create a variable's name yourself, and there are certain rules that you must follow when you create a valid variable name:

1. The variable name must start with a letter or an underscore character.

2. The variable name cannot have punctuation marks or special characters in it.

3. The variable name cannot be a Visual Basic .NET keyword. (You'll learn more about keywords in the following section.)

Consider the variable names presented in Table 4.2.

TABLE 4.2   Valid and Invalid Variable Names

Variable Name	Valid or Invalid	Comment
MyName	Valid	Meets all rules
Hatsize	Valid	Meets all rules
34Waist	Invalid	Violates Rule 1; starts with a number
My.Phone.Number	Invalid	Violates Rule 2; has period characters
Date	Invalid	Violates Rule 3; Date is a Visual Basic .NET keyword
Negative-Number	Invalid	Violates Rule 2; has hyphen sign character
_As	Valid	Meets all rules; note leading underscore character
As	Invalid	Violates Rule 3; As is a Visual Basic .NET keyword

Visual Basic .NET programmers follow some naming conventions for variables, and you'll learn when you start writing your own programs in later chapters. For now, you should know that you need to follow the three naming rules for variables.

Keywords

Rule 3 for variable naming states that you cannot use a Visual Basic .NET keyword as a variable name. A *keyword* is a word that has special meaning to Visual Basic .NET. A keyword causes Visual Basic .NET to perform a certain action or process associated with the keyword. You will learn what each of the Visual Basic .NET keywords mean as you progress through this book. The following are the keywords for Visual Basic .NET:

AddHandler	AddressOf	Alias	And
AndAlso	Ansi	As	Assembly
Auto	Boolean	ByRef	Byte
ByVal	Call	Case	Catch
CBool	CByte	CChar	CDate
CDec	CDbl	Char	CInt
Class	CLng	CObj	Const
CShort	CSng	CStr	CType
Date	Decimal	Declare	Default
Delegate	Dim	DirectCast	Do
Double	Each	Else	ElseIf
End	Enum	Erase	Error
Event	Exit	#ExternalSource	False
Finally	For	Friend	Function
Get	GetType	GoTo	Handles
If	Implements	Imports	In
Inherits	Integer	Interface	Is
Let	Lib	Like	Long
Loop	Me	Mod	Module
MustInherit	MustOverride	MyBase	MyClass
Namespace	New	Next	Not
Nothing	NotInheritable	NotOverridable	Object

On	Option	Optional	Or
OrElse	Overloads	Overridable	Overrides
ParamArray	Preserve	Private	Property
Protected	Public	RaiseEvent	ReadOnly
ReDim	#Region	REM	RemoveHandler
Resume	Return	Select	Set
Shadows	Shared	Short	Single
Static	Step	Stop	String
Structure	Sub	SyncLock	Then
Throw	To	True	Try
TypeOf	Unicode	Until	Variant
When	While	With	WithEvents
WriteOnly	Xor	#Const	#ExternalSource
#If...Then...#Else	#Region		

Remember that you cannot use keywords as variable names. If you try to create a variable name by using a keyword, you get an error message from Visual Basic .NET.

The Dim Statement: Defining Variables

Before you can use a variable in a program, you need to define it. For example, suppose you want to create a variable named Age for use in a program. Further assume that you are only interested in using a person's age as an integer value. That is, you only care if a person is 37, not 37.5. To define the Age variable, you would type the following line into your program:

```
Dim Age As Integer
```

When you type this line and press the Enter key, Visual Basic .NET examines it. In other words, Visual Basic .NET scans, or *parses*, the line you typed to see if the line conforms to the rules of valid Visual Basic .NET statements. A *statement* is nothing more than a sequence of expressions, or words, that obey the rules of the Visual Basic .NET language. These language rules are called the *syntax rules* of the language. If you type something into a program that Visual Basic .NET determines does not obey the syntax rules, Visual Basic .NET issues a syntax error. Visual Basic .NET is smart enough to write a squiggly line under the word (or words) that cause a syntax error. (The squiggly line is the result of Visual Basic .NET's IntelliSense feature.) Because you do not get a syntax error when you type in the program code line

```
Dim Age As Integer
```

you know you have entered a statement that conforms to the Visual Basic .NET syntax rules.

The `Dim` keyword at the start of this statement tells Visual Basic .NET that you want to create a variable for use in the program. The word immediately following the `Dim` keyword is the name you want to use for the variable (`Age` in this example). The last two keywords, `As Integer`, tell Visual Basic .NET the data type, also called the *type specifier*, to use for the variable named `Age`. Because you have obeyed all the syntax rules of Visual Basic .NET in this statement, you now have a variable named `Age` that you can use in your program to store integer-type data.

Behind the Scenes: The Visual Basic .NET Symbol Table

Although it seemed in the previous chapter that Visual Basic .NET instantaneously created the new variable `Age` for use in your program, a lot of things were going on between the time you pressed the Enter key and when the cursor moved to the next line. Let's look under the hood to see what Visual Basic .NET did in that brief moment of time.

First, Visual Basic .NET parsed the line you typed to see if it obeyed all the syntax rules. If you had misspelled `Dim` as `Dem`, or misspelled `Integer` as `Intger`, or made some other spelling mistake in a keyword, Visual Basic .NET would have told you so by sending a syntax error message. If you had violated one of the naming rules for `Age`, Visual Basic .NET would have issued a syntax error message to you. Because you spelled everything correctly, placed each keyword in the proper place, and followed the proper naming rules for the variable, Visual Basic .NET was happy.

The Symbol Table

Thus far, Visual Basic .NET knows that the `Dim` statement is properly written. The next thing Visual Basic .NET does is make sure it can create a variable name `Age` with the `Integer` properties you gave it. To do this, it first examines something called a symbol table. A *symbol table* is a table that Visual Basic .NET creates automatically in the background to keep track of each and every data item used in a program. Visual Basic .NET uses the symbol table to track dozens of attributes about each data item, and two of the primary attributes kept in the symbol table are the name of the variable and its data type.

After Visual Basic .NET is happy that you obeyed its syntax rules, it scans its symbol table to see if you have already dimensioned (that is, defined) a variable with the name `Age`. If you have already created a variable named `Age` in the program, Visual Basic .NET displays a squiggly line under the word `Age` in the `Dim` statement. If you then try to compile the program, Visual Basic .NET would issue an error message like this:

```
Local variable Age is already declared in the current block.
```

This message tells you that you tried to create a variable that has the same name as a variable that already exists. If you created two variables with the same name, Visual Basic .NET wouldn't know which one to use; therefore, it issues an error message to prevent such confusion.

If there is not another **Age** variable already defined in the program, Visual Basic .NET attempts to find a place in memory to store the **Age** variable.

Actually, Visual Basic .NET cannot store something by itself; it needs the permission of the operating system. For Visual Basic .NET, the operating system is Microsoft Windows. Therefore, Visual Basic .NET sends a message to Windows saying, "Hey, Windows! My programmer is trying to create an **Integer** variable. Can you give me a memory address that currently is not being used where I can store 4 bytes of data?" (Table 4.1 tells you that an **Integer** data type needs 4 bytes of memory, remember?)

The Windows memory manager then looks through its available memory blocks for 4 bytes of unused memory that it can release for use by Visual Basic .NET. If the memory manager finds 4 bytes of free memory (which it usually can), it sends a return message that says: "Hey, Visual Basic .NET! You can use the 4 bytes of memory starting at memory address 123456." (Obviously, the actual memory address will vary. Also, the memory address is expressed using the hexadecimal numbering system described in Chapter 2. I use the decimal numbering system here just to keep things simple.) Visual Basic .NET then stores that memory address (123456) in its symbol table, along with the variable's name (**Age**) and its data type (**Integer**). If the memory manager cannot not find 4 bytes of free memory, it tells Visual Basic .NET it is out of memory, and Visual Basic .NET passes the bad news along to you in the form of an error message. If all goes well, Visual Basic .NET creates a variable named **Age** for use in your program.

Note
It is pretty rare for an "out of memory" error message to occur at the time you are writing a program (that is, design time). You are more likely to see such a message after the program starts running. You'll learn more about "out of memory" error messages and how to fix them in later chapters.

lvalue **and** rvalue

Figure 4.1 shows what is associated with the **Age** variable in the symbol table.

FIGURE 4.1
The **lvalue** and **rvalue** for **Age**.

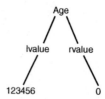

As you can see in Figure 4.1, the left value in the diagram, called the **lvalue**, represents the memory address where the variable named **Age** is stored. The right value in the diagram, **rvalue**, is what is stored at that memory address. You can think of the **lvalue** as the "where" and the **rvalue** as the "what."

Because Visual Basic .NET initializes all newly created variables with the value **0**, the `rvalue` for **Age** is **0**. In other words, the `lvalue` is *where* **Age** is located in the computer's memory, and the `rvalue` is *what* is actually stored at that memory location. Think of a variable as a bucket that can hold a data item; the `lvalue` is where the bucket is located, and the `rvalue` is what's inside the bucket. The variable's type specifier tells how big the bucket is. Visual Basic .NET uses the `lvalue` to locate the variable named **Age** any time you need to use it in your program.

The Visual Basic .NET symbol table for your program might look as shown in Table 4.3.

TABLE 4.3 A Visual Basic .NET Symbol Table

Variable Name	Data Type	Bytes	Lvalue	Other Attributes...
Age	Integer	4	123456	...
...	...	...	...	...

The column names in Table 4.3 should be familiar to you now. The last column, Other Attributes, indicates that the symbol table is considerably more complex than the one we are showing here. It would not be unusual to have several dozen attributes maintained in a symbol table for each data item. Table 4.3 just shows the attributes that we are currently interested in.

Operands and Operators

Now that you have a variable named **Age** available for use in your program, you should do something with it. Consider the following Visual Basic .NET program statement:

```
Age = 34
```

This is a valid Visual Basic .NET program statement that assigns the numeric value **34** to the **Age** variable. This program statement uses the assignment operator, the equal sign (=), to change the value of **Age** from its current value of **0** to **34**. To Visual Basic .NET, a valid assignment statement is expressed as follows:

Operand1	*AssignmentOperator*	*Operand2*
Age	=	34

In Visual Basic .NET, a properly constructed assignment statement has these three parts:

- **Operand1**—Often a variable name
- **AssignmentOperator**—The equal sign
- **Operand2**—The value to be assigned into *Operand1*

Because the assignment operator requires two operands, it is called a *binary operator*. If either operand is missing, or if the operator is missing, Visual Basic .NET issues an error message.

How Visual Basic .NET Processes an Assignment Statement

When Visual Basic .NET sees this program statement:

```
Age = 34
```

it breaks the statement into three parts: *Operand1*, *AssignmentOperator*, and *Operand2*. When Visual Basic .NET reads the equal sign, it knows there must be two operands. Because this program statement does have two operands, Visual Basic .NET proceeds with the next phase of the program statement.

In the next phase, Visual Basic .NET goes to the symbol table to see if *Operand1* has been defined. Visual Basic .NET scans through the symbol table, looking for *Operand1* (that is, **Age**). If you have properly defined the variable named **Age**, Visual Basic .NET finds an entry for *Operand1*, much like the entry shown in Figure 4.2. Visual Basic .NET then looks at the other attributes in the symbol table for *Operand1* and does the following sequence of operations:

1. It looks up the `lvalue` of *Operand1* (that is, **123456** in Figure 4.2).

2. It formats the value in *Operand2* (that is, **34**) into an **Integer** data type, using the required number of bytes for the data type (that is, 4 bytes for an **Integer** variable).

3. It moves those 4 bytes of data into memory, starting at the memory address specified by the variable's `lvalue`.

When Visual Basic .NET finishes these three steps, the information previously shown in Figure 4.1 looks like the information shown in Figure 4.2.

FIGURE 4.2
The `lvalue` and `rvalue` for **Age** after the assignment statement is processed.

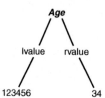

As you can see, Visual Basic .NET does a lot simply to change the value of **Age** from **0** to **34**.

The Inspector Program

The Inspector program allows you to see the actual `lvalue` and `rvalue` of a variable. Figure 4.3 shows a sample run of the program.

FIGURE 4.3

The Inspector program.

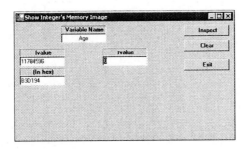

As you can see, the program has a defined variable named `Age`, and it has asked the Windows operating system for enough memory (that is, 4 bytes) to store the `Integer` variable named `Age`. Evidently, the request is successful, as you can see from the `lvalue` of `11784596`. (The program displays the memory address in hexadecimal notation as well as in decimal because that is the numbering system that Windows uses for memory addresses.) You can also see from Figure 4.3 that the `Age` variable has been initialized with the value of `0`, which is the current (default) rvalue for `Age`.

Now, type the number `34` into the `rvalue` text box and then click the Inspect button. Doing this produces the information shown in Figure 4.4.

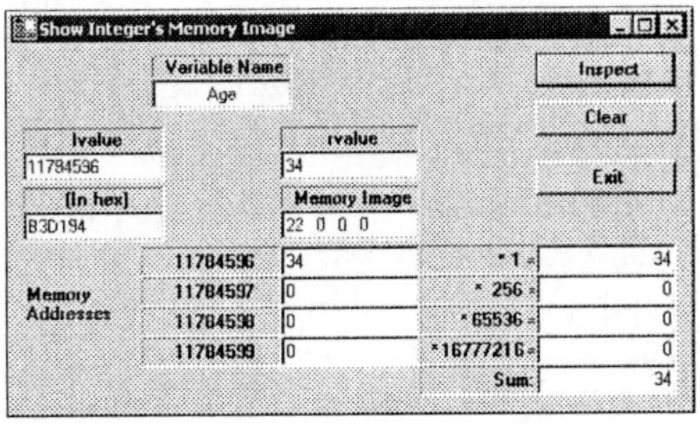

FIGURE 4.4

Output of the Inspector program after the assignment statement is processed.

Note the changes in the display. First, look at the text box below the Memory Image label. It shows these values:

`22 0 0 0`

This is the value `34` expressed in hexadecimal. (Because hexadecimal is a base-16 numbering system, you take the first 2, multiply it by 16 to get 32, and then add the second 2 to get 34.) Therefore, the first memory byte used by `Age`—memory address `11784596`—has the numeric value `34` stored in it. The other three memory addresses used by `Age` are all `0` because the value `34` can be stored in a single byte. Therefore, any value stored in the first byte is scaled by the value 1. If you had a value stored in the second byte, it would be scaled by 256 because the first byte can only store a value between 0 and 255. Remember that

$2^8 = 256$

Because the first byte in an Integer data type uses 8 bits, anything stored in the second byte must be scaled by 256 to determine its actual (decimal) numeric value.

In similar fashion, anything stored in the third byte is scaled by this:

$2^{16} = 65536$

and the fourth byte is scaled by this:

$2^{24} = 16777216$

Adding all the values together determines the final Integer value that is stored in the 4 bytes associated with the variable named Age.

Try using a value for Age that is larger than will fit in a single byte: Use an rvalue of 1000. The result is shown in Figure 4.5.

FIGURE 4.5

The Inspector program, using the rvalue 1000.

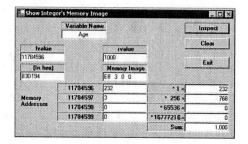

When you do the conversion, the hex value E8, as stored in the first byte, is 232 in decimal. When multiplied by its scalar value of 1, its value is 232. The second byte of the Integer variable Age has the value 3. After it is multiplied by its scalar value of 256, its value becomes 768 (that is, 256 × 3 = 768). The remaining bytes for Age are 0, yielding scaled values of 0. Adding the numbers produces a decimal value of 1,000, which is exactly what the rvalue of Age should be.

Figure 4.6 shows one more run of the Inspector program, using the one million for the rvalue.

FIGURE 4.6

The Inspector program, using the value of 1,000,000.

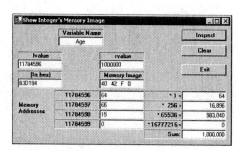

You should be able to convince yourself that the proper `rvalue` has been assigned to `Age`.

There is one more thing to notice in Figures 4.3 through 4.6. In each run of the program, the `lvalue` of `Age` does not change. Although this has no real impact on how the program runs, it does illustrate an important point: It is the operating system, not Visual Basic .NET, that determines the `lvalue` for a variable. For this reason, a Visual Basic .NET program you write should *never* attempt to change the `lvalue` of a variable. If you tried to change an `lvalue`, you might assign a value into a piece of memory that Windows is using for some other purpose, and that is almost never a good thing!

One more thing you can prove by using the Inspector program is that Windows stores memory addresses in a rather weird way. If you type in the `lvalue` (that is, `11784596`) as the `rvalue`, you should see the `lvalue` expressed in hex in the Memory Image text box. This is shown in Figure 4.7.

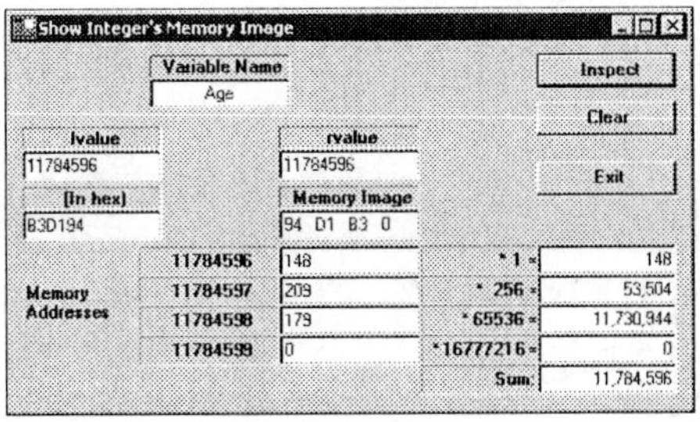

FIGURE 4.7

The Inspector program, using the `lvalue` of `Age` as the `rvalue`.

Notice that the `lvalue` in hex is `B3D194`, but the `rvalue` is stored as `94 D1 B3`. Yet when you look at the scaled number, everything works out correctly. The reason it works this way is because the CPU stores memory addresses with the least significant memory byte first, progressing to the most significant memory bytes. There are some technical reasons the chipmakers use this format for memory addresses, but you need not concern yourself about that at this point. Still, you might want to keep this tidbit of information in mind because you never know when this topic will come up at a cocktail party.

Visual Basic .NET Program Errors

As you saw in this chapter, Visual Basic .NET requires you to play by certain rules when writing programs. Some rules concern the way in which you create names for variables. Other rules must be followed when creating program statements. Collectively, the rules that you must follow are called the *syntax rules* for Visual Basic .NET. You know that in this assignment statement:

```
Age = 34
```

the equal sign (=) is the assignment operator and that it requires two operands. When operands and operators are combined together correctly, they form an *expression*. One or more expressions form a program *statement*. By arranging program statements in a very specific way, you can create a program that you can run to solve a specific problem. You can see this relationship is Figure 4.8.

FIGURE 4.8
Progressing from operands and operators to a Visual Basic .NET program.

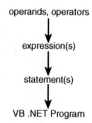

operands, operators

↓

expression(s)

↓

statement(s)

↓

VB .NET Program

Semantic Errors

You can write a program that abides by the syntax rules but still doesn't work properly. You can do the same thing in English. For example, an English sentence usually has a noun and a verb. This sentence:

The dog meowed.

has a noun and a verb, and it abides by the syntax rules of English, but it doesn't make sense because dogs don't meow. This type of error is called a *semantic* error. In such errors, the syntax rules are followed properly, but the words (or operands, in the case of programming languages) are used out of context. You can write programs in Visual Basic .NET that have semantic errors. The bad news is that Visual Basic .NET may not be equipped to catch such errors.

You can also write programs that don't have either syntax or semantic errors but still produce incorrect results. Such errors are most often caused by problems with the design of the program, or its logic.

Any error in a program is called a *bug,* and the process of correcting and removing program errors is called *debugging* the program.

Note

The term was coined back in the early days of computers, when a moth flew into a computer and shorted out several wires. The engineers had to dismantle part of the computer to remove the body of the moth, hence the term *debugging.* Believe it or not, this little piece of trivia actually *has* come up at a cocktail party! This was also the answer to a million-dollar question on a popular game show. (The contestant answered it correctly.)

As you write programs throughout this book, I actually ask you to introduce bugs into them. I do this because it gives you some familiarity with how Visual Basic .NET handles program bugs. It also helps you become a better detective in isolating and correcting other bugs that might creep into your programs. Seeing Visual Basic .NET error messages under controlled circumstances is a valuable learning tool.

A Simple Math Program

In this section you'll write a simple program, the Math program, that exercises some numeric data. Although the program is quite simple, it illustrates some common tasks that you must consider when working with numeric data.

Start a new project and add three labels and three text boxes, as shown in Figure 4.9. Name the top text box `txtNumber`, name the second text box `txtSquare`, and name the last text box `txtSquareRoot`. You should name the Calculate button `btnCalc` and the Exit button `btnExit`. Notice that these names follow the naming conventions mentioned in Chapter 2.

You can leave the label names unchanged because you will not reference them in the program. However, the labels will look best if you set their properties as follows:

Property	Setting
BorderStyle	Fixed3D
Font	Microsoft Sans Serif
Font Style	Bold
TextAlign	MiddleRight

You should also modify the `Text` property for each label to correspond to the text shown in Figure 4.9.

FIGURE 4.9

The Math program form.

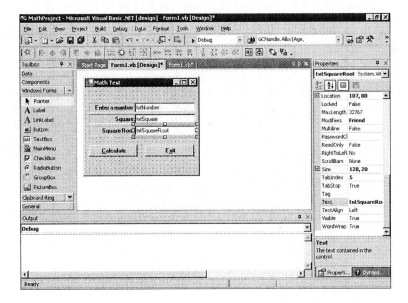

Notice that the **Text** property for each of the buttons has an ampersand (**&**) embedded in it. For example, the **Text** property for the **btnCalc** button is **&Calculate**, and the **btnExit** button has the **Text** property set to **E&xit**. Using the ampersand like this means the program's user can use the Alt+C and Alt+X key combinations to activate the buttons instead of clicking the buttons with a mouse.

The only code you need to add to the program is that for the Calculate button. Add the following code to the **btnCalc** object's **Click()** event:

```
Dim Square As Double, SquareRoot As Double

Square = CDbl(txtNumber.Text)
txtSquare.Text = CStr(Square * Square)
txtSquareRoot.Text = CStr(Sqrt(Square))
```

The first line simply creates two variables named **Square** and **SquareRoot**, using the **Dim** statement discussed earlier in this chapter.

Data Type Conversions

Visual Basic .NET does not like to fit square pegs into round holes. That is, Visual Basic .NET does not like to assign a text variable into a numeric variable. Therefore, you need to use a conversion routine when you try to perform assignments between different data types.

The second line:

```
Square = CDbl(txtNumber.Text)
```

converts the number that the user types into the **txtNumber** text box into a **Double** data type by using the built-in Visual Basic .NET **CDbl** keyword. (If you look at the table of keywords earlier in this chapter, in the section "Keywords," you should notice that **CDbl** is a Visual Basic .NET keyword.)

Why do you have to use the **CDbl** function? You use this function because the data in the **txtNumber.Text** text box is **String** data, not numeric data. The purpose of the **CDbl** function is to convert the **String** data to **Double** data. The value returned from the **CDbl** function is a numeric value of the **Double** data type. For example, suppose you pressed the 2 and the 5 keys, resulting in the character string **"25"** being placed in the **txtNumber** text box. These two ASCII characters correspond to the decimal values **50** (the 2 character) and **53** (the 5 character), as you can see in Appendix A. The two values **50** and **53** are stored in memory as **String** data types. Because you cannot perform mathematical operations directly on **String** data, you use the **CDbl** function to convert the string **"25"** to a **Double** data type with the numeric value **25**.

Therefore, this line:

```
Square = CDbl(txtNumber.Text)
```

becomes this:

```
Square = CDbl("25")
```

which then becomes this:

```
Square = 25.0
```

This line assigns the numeric value **25.0** to the variable named **Square**.

The next line in the **btnCalc** object's **Click()** event is this:

```
txtSquare.Text = CStr(Square * Square)
```

This line does almost the opposite action of the previous line. In this case, **Square** holds a numeric value, but you want to assign the product of **Square** multiplied by itself to a text box. The problem is that **Square** is a numeric **Double** data type, but **txtSquare.Text** demands a **String** data type. As you might have already guessed, **CStr** is a Visual Basic .NET built-in function that converts numeric data into **String** data. Therefore, this line:

```
txtSquare.Text = CStr(Square * Square)
```

first multiplies **Square** by itself (the **Square * Square** expression) and then converts the result of that operation into a **String** data type. The **String** data returned by **CStr** can then be assigned directly to **txtSquare.Text**.

Now let's look at the last line:

```
txtSquareRoot.Text = CStr(Sqrt(Square))
```

This line looks a little confusing, but it's actually pretty simple. Remember that expressions inside parentheses are resolved before anything else in the expression. Therefore, it appears that a function named **Sqrt** is called using the numeric value of **Square** as an argument. However, if you look at the list of keywords in the section "Keywords," earlier in this chapter, you can't find **Sqrt**. So what is **Sqrt**? The answer is found in something called a *library*.

Visual Basic .NET Libraries

Sqrt is actually a math function that returns the square root of a number. However, the **Sqrt** function is not an inherent part of Visual Basic .NET. Instead, the **Sqrt** function is a routine found in the math library that comes with Visual Basic .NET. The math library is not automatically included in every program simply because not every program needs the functionality provided by the math library.

However, when you need some functionality from the math library, as you do here, you can tell Visual Basic .NET to include the math library in the program. You do this by adding the following line to the very top of your program:

```
Imports System.Math
```

This line tells Visual Basic .NET to include the math routines in the program. Doing this gives you access to the **Sqrt** function and other functions. In your program, if **Square * Square** is 25, the **Sqrt** function returns the **Double** numeric value 5. However, because this is a **Double** data type, you must again use the **CStr** function to convert the **Double** data type into a **String** data type so you can assign the result into **txtSquareRoot.Text**.

The only other code you need to add is the line:

```
Me.Dispose()
```

You add this line to the `btnExit` object's `Click()` event. Remember that `Me` is shorthand notation that always refers to the currently active form. The `Dispose()` method simply ends the program if the user clicks the `btnExit` button.

Figure 4.10 shows what the program output should look like if the user enters `25` in the `txtNumber` text box.

FIGURE 4.10
A sample run of the Math program.

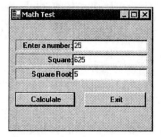

The Math program shows you how to convert from numeric to string data and string to numeric. Indeed, if you look at the keywords that begin with *c*, you can see that a number of built-in functions are provided for converting from one data type to another. You can use Visual Basic .NET's help system to get additional details on how to use these conversion routines.

Binary Numbers

Before you leave this chapter, you need to examine the binary numbering system in some detail. As mentioned in Chapter 2, a computer understands only two things: on and off. Because a computer understands only these two states, it interprets all values by using base-2, or binary, arithmetic. Figure 4.11 shows how a byte is interpreted using binary arithmetic.

FIGURE 4.11
The binary numbering system.

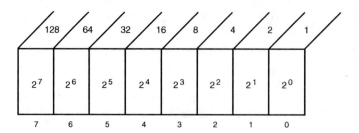

In Figure 4.121 the numbers along the bottom correspond to the bit positions in an 8-bit byte of memory. When viewed this way, the rightmost bit is called the *least significant bit* and the leftmost bit is called the *most significant* bit. The numbers along the bottom simply number the bits, from most significant (that is, bit number 7) to least significant (that is, bit number 0), reading from left to right.

Each bit position has a numeric value that is equal to its bit position as a power of 2. For example, if the bit in bit position 0 is turned on, it has a value equal to 2^0, which equals 1. If the bit in bit position 1 is turned on, its value is 2^1, which equals 2. The upper row of numbers in Figure 4.11 shows the value for each bit position if that particular bit is turned on, expressed as a decimal number. Summing across all bit positions gives you the binary value for the memory byte. How does this work?

Suppose a byte in memory has the following bit pattern:

00001010

You can see that bits 1 and 3 are turned on; all the other bits are turned off. You can depict this bit pattern as shown in Figure 4.12.

FIGURE 4.12

Determining the value of bit pattern 00001010.

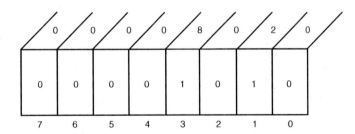

If you look at the bits that are turned on and raise 2 to the bit position's power, you get the row of numbers seen near the top of Figure 4.12. In other words, you have

$(2^7 \times 0) + (2^6 \times 0) + (2^5 \times 0) + (2^4 \times 0) + (2^3 \times 1) + (2^2 \times 0) + (2^1 \times 1) + (2^0 \times 0)$

$= 0 + 0 + 0 + 0 + 8 + 0 + 2 + 0$

$= 8 + 2$

$= 10$

This shows that the bit pattern 00001010 is the binary representation for the decimal number 10. You should see that if all bits are turned on, 11111111 has a decimal value of 255. What would the value be if a "nibble" were turned on? That is, what is 00001111 in decimal arithmetic?

What if you need a number larger than 255? No problem. You add another 8 bits on the left side of Figure 4.12 and label its rightmost bit position 2^8 and continue leftward. The last bit position would be 2^{15}, which equates to a value of 32,768. Now look at the range of values for a **Short** data type in Table 4.1. Do you see any relationship? (The value appears to be off by 1, but that's because of the way the sign bit is used in binary arithmetic.)

What happens if you slide the bits to the right one position so the bit pattern in Figure 4.13 becomes this:

00000101

You should find that the decimal value is 5. This is an old assembly language trick: Shifting the bits to the right one position divides the number by 2, and shifting the bits to the left one position multiplies by 2. Try it. This shouldn't be too surprising because we're using base-2 arithmetic. In decimal arithmetic, if you take a 1 and shift it one position to the left, it becomes 10. The left-shift by one position multiplies by the base being used. Take 100 and right-shift it one position, and it becomes 10, which is the same as dividing the number by 10. Just think how you will be able to amaze your friends with all this stuff at your next dinner party! Because the CPU instruction sets include bit shifting, which is a much faster operation than multiplying or dividing, bit shifting is a common compiler optimization trick.

Although you might not use binary arithmetic directly in your programming endeavors, it is important that you understand the basics of it. If nothing else, it should help you understand why the values presented in Table 4.1 have the values they do.

Summary

This chapter introduces the basic data types that are available in Visual Basic .NET and discusses the basic characteristics of these data types. You should now have a better idea of what data types are suitable for different tasks. In this chapter you have also learned how to create a valid variable name and how Visual Basic .NET processes statements that create variables. This chapter also goes into considerable detail about what Visual Basic .NET does behind the scenes with something as simple as an assignment statement. Knowing such details will make you a better programmer and help you detect and correct program bugs.

You will learn a lot more about the topics introduced in this chapter as you progress through the book. You should spend whatever time is necessary to become familiar with the concepts of operands, operators, expressions, statement, `lvalue`, and `rvalue`. A little time invested now will yield large dividends later on.

Review Questions

1. What does Visual Basic .NET have so many data types?

A. Many years ago, some dialects of BASIC only had one data type. However, one size fits all just does work very well where data is concerned. Some data is numeric, other data is text, plus many other types. By having data types that fit the data you find in real life, your programs are more efficient at processing that data.

2. Why does Visual Basic .NET require you to define the type of a variable?

A. One important reason is that Visual Basic .NET needs to know how much storage is required to store the variable. Data definitions provide Visual Basic .NET with the information it needs to store and track the data as the program executes.

3. Why is it that some data types that use less memory are not processed as efficiently as other data types that require more memory?

A. Every CPU has a set of registers that are used to process data. Most Windows PCs use CPUs that are best suited for 4-byte integer data and 8-byte floating point data. Data that doesn't fit these natural CPU register sizes often has to be padded or trimmed to fit the CPU registers; a process that takes time.

4. What is a symbol table and what does it do?

A. A symbol table is a table of information that Visual Basic .NET maintains in memory about a program. Some of the more important responsibilities of the symbol table are to keep track of the names of the variables being used in the program and where each variable is located in memory.

5. What is an **lvalue**?

A. An **lvalue** (location value) is the memory location of where a data item is stored in memory. The lvalue for each variable in a program is maintained in the symbol table. Visual Basic .NET uses the **lvalue** to locate where any specific variable is stored in memory.

6. What is an **rvalue**?

A. An **rvalue** (read value, or sometimes called a register value) is the data that a variable contains. The **lvalue** is used to find the variable in memory, and the **rvalue** is what is stored at the memory location.

7. Why does Visual Basic .NET have to know the data type of a variable?

A. Visual Basic .NET not only keeps the name of the variable and its **lvalue** in the symbol table, it also keeps that variable's data type. Because each data type requires a known amount of memory, Visual Basic .NET can use the **lvalue** to go to the memory address of the variable and the data type determines how many bytes Visual Basic .NET must fetch to get the data (**rvalue**) of the variable. Without the data type, Visual Basic .NET would not know how many bytes to fetch from memory to get the data associated with the variable.

CHAPTER 5

SUBROUTINES AND FUNCTIONS

You will learn the following in this chapter:

- What subroutines and functions are available in Visual Basic .NET

- Why subroutines and functions are different from each other and when you should use one instead of the other

- How to pass subroutine and function arguments

Recall from Chapter 2, "The Basics of Object-Oriented Programming," that one of the breakthroughs in the early development of languages was the advent of the subroutine. In Chapter 2 you learned how subroutines simplify program structure by avoiding duplicate code for repetitive processes. Subroutines reduce program complexity and program size. This chapter examines both subroutines and functions in considerable detail. It also uses your understanding of `lvalue` and `rvalue` from Chapter 4, "Data Types and Numeric Variables," to demystify how information is passed to subroutines and functions.

Subroutines

Simply stated, a *subroutine* is a set of instructions designed to accomplish one specific task. For example, you might write a subroutine named `CheckRange()` that checks certain numeric values to make sure they fall within a certain range. You might write another subroutine named `CalcSalesTax()` that calculates the sales tax for an order. In each case, the purpose of the subroutine is to accomplish one narrowly defined task.

Why Use Subroutines?

One of the primary reasons to use subroutines is to eliminate duplicate code. For example, if a program asks the user to enter a dozen numeric values into the program, you could write a

`CheckRange()` subroutine once and then use it to check all 12 numbers. Which is better: writing a dozen almost identical sections of code to check each number or writing a subroutine once and being done with it? Using subroutines eliminates the need for duplicate code in many programs.

A second reason for using subroutines results from the first: Subroutines simplify programs. Because subroutines reduce the amount of code in a program, there is less code to read and understand. This also means there is less code to debug and maintain. These are good things.

A third reason for using subroutines is that doing so promotes modularity. That is, when you write a subroutine, you compartmentalize the code. When you write a subroutine, you give it some kind of descriptive name, such as `CalcSalesTax()`. Next year, when your state is going broke and decides to raise the sales tax rate, you know *exactly* where to go in your code to make the necessary change. You don't have to go searching through all your code, looking for all the places where the sales taxes are figured. With a subroutine, you need to make one program change and—bingo!—you're done.

A fourth reason for using subroutines derives from the third reason. Because subroutines promote modular code, they help you more easily reuse code. For example, if you write a new program that deals with sales taxes, you can steal the `CalcSalesTax()` code from your existing program and use it in the new one. One reason stealing something is so popular is because it's much easier than working for it. The same is true in programming. Reusing fully functional and debugged code is easier than writing new code.

Writing a Simple Subroutine

Suppose you have a program that saves a person's name and phone number to a disk data file. Further assume that there is a Save button that saves the data to the file. Also assume that the Save button is also responsible for clearing out the text boxes after the data is saved. This simple program might use a form that looks like the one shown in Figure 5.1.

What you want to do is write a simple subroutine that clears out the `txtName` and `txtPhone` text boxes when the user clicks the `btnSave` button. The following is the general syntax structure for a subroutine:

```
Private Sub SubName()

 ` Code statements that are the body of this subroutine

End Sub
```

The first line of a subroutine begins with the word `Private`. The word `Private` is an access specifier. We don't discuss access specifiers until Chapter 7, "Arrays," so for now you can think of `Private` as meaning that this subroutine can be used only by code in the currently active form. In other words, if the program had multiple forms, this subroutine would only pertain to, or be private to, the form shown in Figure 5.1.

FIGURE 5.1

A program form for saving a name and phone number.

The second word in the first line is **Sub**. As you have probably guessed, this is an abbreviation for the word *subroutine*. **Sub** tells Visual Basic .NET that you are in the process of defining a subroutine.

The third word in the first line, *SubName()*, is the name of the subroutine that you are defining. In naming subroutines, you must follow the same rules that you follow for naming variables. You should make the name of the subroutine descriptive so that it gives you (and anyone else who might read the code) a good idea of what the subroutine does. In your simple program, you might choose to name the subroutine **ClearTextboxes()** because it describes what you want the subroutine to do.

The last program statement is **End Sub**. This marks the end of the subroutine. Everything between the first and last lines forms the code that is called the *body* of the subroutine. The body of the subroutine contains all the program statements that are necessary for the subroutine to accomplish its task.

In the simple program you're writing, you simply want the subroutine to clear out the text boxes after the information is saved to disk. The actual code for the subroutine is very simple, as shown in Listing 5.1.

LISTING 5.1   Code for the **ClearTextboxes()** Subroutine

```
Private Sub ClearTextboxes()
  txtName.Text = ""
  txtPhone.Text = ""
End Sub
```

All the subroutine does is set the **txtName** and **txtPhone** text boxes to contain empty strings.

Calling a Subroutine

Now that you have written a subroutine, how do you use it? When you want to execute the code associated with a subroutine, you *call* the subroutine. To call a subroutine, all you have to do is write the name of the subroutine as a program statement at that point in the program where you want the subroutine to be executed. In your sample program, you would probably place the call to the subroutine in the btnSave object's Click() event, as shown in Listing 5.2.

LISTING 5.2   Code for the btnSave_Click() Event Subroutine

```
Private Sub btnSave_Click(ByVal sender As System.Object, ByVal e As _
            System.EventArgs) Handles btnSave.Click
 SaveNameAndPhoneNumber()
 ClearTextboxes()
End Sub
```

In the code in Listing 5.2, it appears that there are two subroutines. The first subroutine that is called is named SaveNameAndPhoneNumber(). As you might guess, the purpose of calling this subroutine would be to save the name and phone number that was just entered by the user to a disk data file. After that subroutine finishes its task, the ClearTextboxes() subroutine is called.

There are several things to notice in this simple piece of code. First, the btnSave object's Click() event is itself a subroutine. Indeed, all button Click() events (plus many others that are examined in later chapters) are subroutines that have their skeleton code written automatically by Visual Basic .NET whenever they are added to forms.

What's skeleton code? Perhaps you've noticed that whenever you add a button object to a form, Visual Basic .NET automatically writes this subroutine "header code":

```
Private Sub btnSave_Click(ByVal sender As System.Object, ByVal e As _
            System.EventArgs) Handles btnSave.Click
```

Visual Basic .NET also automatically supplies this subroutine "tail code":

```
End Sub
```

All you, as the programmer, have to write is the body of the subroutine. In the subroutine example in Listing 5.2, the body code is simply the two subroutine calls.

Subroutine Parameters

You should notice that in Listing 5.1, the ClearTextboxes() subroutine is immediately followed by a set of empty parentheses. However, in the btnSave_Click() subroutine in Listing 5.2, the parentheses are not empty.

Sometimes, subroutines need additional data in order to perform their specific task. This needed information can be passed to the subroutine as a *subroutine parameter*. If a subroutine parameter is needed, the name of the subroutine parameter appears between the two parentheses.

If a subroutine needs a subroutine parameter, you must supply the name of the parameter, along with its data type. For example, in Listing 5.2, you can see that the `btnSave_Click()` subroutine has two subroutine parameters, named `sender` and `e`. At this point you don't need to completely understand the details of everything you see between the parentheses; the important thing to notice is that two subroutine parameters are being passed to the subroutine, and they are separated by a comma.

Programmer's Tip

We have been referring to the data that is passed to the subroutine as *parameters*, but it is not uncommon to call the data being passed as subroutine *arguments*. Programmers use the two terms interchangeably.

How do you know whether to use subroutine parameters? Alas, there is no hard-and-fast rule. If the subroutine needs to know about some information that is hidden away in some other part of the program, you probably need to pass that data to the subroutine as a parameter. You are free to use zero or as many parameters as you need. All you need do is separate the parameters with commas.

A Sample Program with Subroutine Parameters

To put your knowledge of subroutines to use, you can now write a simple program that calculates the sales tax due on a sale of an item. To begin, create a new project named `SalesTax` and supply it with the objects shown in Figure 5.2. The two text boxes are called `txtCost` and `txtTax`, and the two buttons are the names we normally use: `btnCalc` and `btnExit`.

FIGURE 5.2
The objects for the
`SalesTax` project.

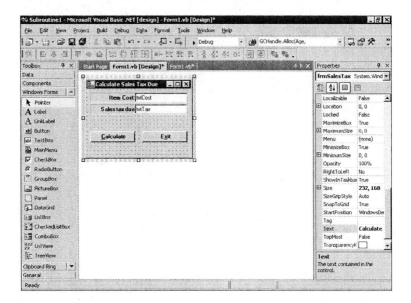

Your job is to write a subroutine that calculates the sales tax due on the sale of a particular item. You can use the subroutine name presented earlier in the chapter: `CalcSalesTax()`.

The Parameters to Use

You now need to think about the design of the `CalcSalesTax()` subroutine. A reasonable starting place is to determine what information the subroutine needs to perform its task. In order to calculate the amount of sales tax to collect, the subroutine needs to know the cost of the item being purchased. Also, the subroutine needs to know the sales tax rate. Finally, the subroutine needs to return to the caller a numeric value that is the amount of the sales tax to be collected. (The *caller* is the name of the routine that called the subroutine. You'll learn more on this in a moment.)

You can summarize the data needs for the `CalcSalesTax()` subroutine as follows:

- Cost of item

- Sales tax rate

- Sales tax due

Now that you know what information the subroutine needs, you need to consider the form this information should take.

In the `SalesTax` program, the cost of the item could vary substantially each time the program is run. The sales tax due will also vary because it is dependent on the item's cost. In the short run, however, the sales tax rate will probably *not* vary. Data that will likely not vary in the short run are usually not candidates for subroutine parameters. Still, the subroutine needs to have the sales tax rate in order to perform its calculation. So how should we handle this design issue?

You could make the sales tax rate a symbolic constant. A *symbolic constant* is a data item that is assigned a constant value. You could use the following line of code to define a symbolic constant for use in the `SalesTax` program:

```
Const SalesTaxRate As Double = 0.05
```

This line of code defines a symbolic constant named `SalesTaxRate` as a `Double` data type. The `Const` keyword tells Visual Basic .NET that this data item is a constant and its value will not change during the life of the program. The name of the symbolic constant (`SalesTaxRate`) follows the `Const` keyword, which is then followed by the data type being defined (that is, `As Double`). The last part of the definition simply assigns the numeric value for the symbolic constant. Note that you must perform this assignment as part of the definition. (This makes sense. After all, what's the purpose of a constant if you can reassign it later in the program?) When the value is assigned to the symbolic constant, its value is etched in stone, and any attempt to change it generates an error message.

This definition should be placed after the `Inherits` statement in the program. You can see the `Const` statement near the top of the Form window in Figure 5.3.

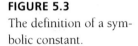

FIGURE 5.3

The definition of a symbolic constant.

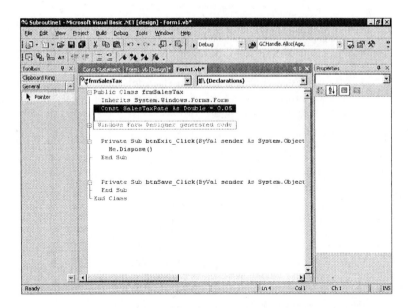

Why use a symbolic constant? Why not just use a variable and assign it a value? Well, you could do that, and the program would work just fine…in this particular program. However, using a symbolic constant offers certain advantages.

First, if you make `SalesTaxRate` a constant, there is no way that its value is going to be changed unintentionally by any other part of the program. This is simply a defensive method of coding to make sure that something that could never happen (for example, somebody being stupid enough to intentionally change the sales tax rate) doesn't. This is especially a good idea when a team of programmers develops a program.

Second, because `SalesTaxRate` is a constant, its definition is made at a known place in the program. Convention places such definitions near the top of the program code, after the `Inherits` keyword. Several years from now, when the tax rate changes, the `SalesTaxRate` constant will make it easy to locate the data item.

A third reason to use a symbolic constant relates to the second reason. Suppose your best friend wants you to write a program, but your friend is colorblind. Therefore, you decide that your program is going to manage the foreground and background color of every piece of text your friend is ever going to read in the program. Your friend can see white text on a blue background.

If the program is fairly complex, there could be hundreds of places where you need to change the foreground and background colors of the text box. This means there could be hundreds of lines of code, in dozens of forms, that look similar to this:

```
txtFirstName.ForeColor = &H00FFFFFF& ' This is white
txtFirstName.BackColor = &H00FF0000  ' This is blue
```

The notation used for the values shown here is for hexadecimal constants; this is a common way to state color values. For the moment you need not concern yourself with how these values are derived.

Finally, you finish the program, and your friend loves it. As he is leaving your office, you open the door a little too quickly and bang his head pretty hard with the door. After he quits seeing stars, he looks at the computer and notices that he can no longer read white text on a blue background. After a little experimentation, you discover that he can now read green letters on a red background.

So you begin the process of performing hundreds of search-and-replace changes throughout every aspect of the program code. This is a very error-prone process. Surely there is a better way.

If you had defined the following two symbolic constants:

```
Const ForegroundText as Long = &H0000FF00& ' This is green
Const BackgroundText as Long = &H000000FF&RGB(0, 0, 255)  ' This is red
```

and used them throughout the program as follows:

```
txtFirstName.ForeColor = ForegroundText
txtFirstName.BackColor = BackgroundText
```

All you'd have to do to accommodate your friend's new color scheme is change the color values in the definitions of the two symbolic constants and recompile the program. In a matter of seconds, Visual Basic .NET could change the hundreds of assignment statements for the foreground and background colors to use the new color values.

Symbolic constants are perfect for values that will not change in the short run but might change at some future date. Also, symbolic constants can often make code more understandable. For example, which of the following statements gives you a better idea of what the program is doing at this point—this:

```
due = p * .05
```

or this:

```
due = p * SalesTaxRate
```

Selecting meaningful names for symbolic constants (or any variable, for that matter) helps document what the code is doing.

Now you know that there is no reason to make the sales tax rate an argument to the subroutine. You can simply define the sales tax rate as a symbolic constant named `SalesTaxRate`, as shown in Figure 5.3. Now you can press on to writing the subroutine.

The `CalcSalesTax()` Subroutine

You now know that you need two parameters passed to the subroutine: the price of the item and the sales tax to be collected. Therefore, you might write your code as shown in Listing 5.3.

LISTING 5.3 Code for the `CalcSalesTax()` Subroutine

```
Private Sub CalcSalesTax(ByVal Price As Double, ByVal SalesTax As Double)
 ' Purpose: This subroutine calculates the sales tax
 '     that is to be collected for a given item.
 '
 ' Arguments:
 '  Price   the purchase price of the item
 '  SalesTax the sales tax amount to collect
 '
 ' Caution: the calculation uses the symbolic constant
 '     SalesTaxRate, which holds the current sales
 '     tax rate.

 SalesTax = Price * SalesTaxRate
End Sub
```

Notice in Listing 5.3 that program comments are used to state the purpose of the subroutine and the parameters it uses. A cautionary statement appears at the end of the comments to tell the reader what the **SalesTaxRate** is. After the comment is the actual body of code for the subroutine. This subroutine is very simple and only needs a single line of code.

Programmer's Tip

It is always a good idea to document what a subroutine does. The format shown in Listing 5.3 is simply a guideline. You can use whatever format works for you. However, when you select a format, you should use it consistently, to make it easier to read the code months from now, especially if there are others on the project.

Also, you should place your subroutine code in the same place in programs, as much as possible. For example, I prefer to place my subroutines at the bottom of the program code, sorted alphabetically by subroutine name. Then, if I ever need to check the code, I just drag the thumb control to the bottom of the code listing to find the needed code. (You can also click the drop-down box shown near the top of the Form window in Figure 5.3 and then click the subroutine name. However, I find it easier to just scroll the code window. Either way works.)

Calling a Subroutine

When the code for your subroutine is finished, you need to add the following lines to the `btnSave` object's `Click()` event:

```
Dim ItemPrice As Double, SalesTaxDue As Double

ItemPrice = CDbl(txtCost.Text)
CalcSalesTax(ItemPrice, SalesTaxDue)      ' Call the subroutine
txtTax.Text = CStr(SalesTaxDue)
```

The first line defines two **Double** data types for use in the program. The second line simply converts the cost the user types into the program into a **Double** and assigns it to the **ItemPrice** variable. The third line is the actual call to the subroutine. Notice that the first parameter in the parentheses is **ItemPrice** and the second parameter is the **SalesTaxDue** variable. This sequence is important, and it must match the parameter sequence for the

`CalcSalesTax()` subroutine. Imagine how things would get messed up if you reversed their order.

Now compile and run the program. A sample run is shown in Figure 5.4.

FIGURE 5.4

A sample run of the `SalesTax` program.

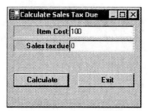

Wait a minute. If the item price is $100 and the sales tax rate is .05, the `txtTax` text box should be displaying 5, not 0. Something's not right. The following sections explain the problem and how you fix it.

The `ByVal` and `ByRef` Keywords

If you type the following statement line into the `SalesTax` program:

```
Private Sub CalcSalesTax(Price As Double, SalesTax As Double)
```

and press the Enter key, Visual Basic .NET immediately changes the program line to this:

```
Private Sub CalcSalesTax(ByVal Price As Double, ByVal SalesTax As Double)
```

Notice that Visual Basic .NET immediately prefixes both parameter names with the keyword `ByVal`. The `ByVal` keyword is the default method for passing a parameter to a subroutine. The impact that `ByVal` has on parameters is extremely important for you to understand.

Simply stated, `ByVal` means that a *copy* of the parameter's current value is passed to the subroutine. In terms of the discussion in Chapter 4, it is the `rvalue` of the parameter that is passed to the subroutine. In Figure 5.4, you can see that the user typed in the value `100`, so that this statement in the `btnSave` object's `Click()` event:

```
ItemPrice = CDbl(txtCost.Text)
```

finds the variable `ItemPrice` equal to `100`. Now, let's see what the next statement does:

```
CalcSalesTax(ItemPrice, SalesTaxDue)     ' Call the subroutine
```

Because Visual Basic .NET says that the parameters in the `CalcSalesTax()` subroutine are `ByVal`, when Visual Basic .NET sees the call to `CalcSalesTax()`, it creates copies of the current values for `ItemPrice` and `SalesTaxDue` and sends those copies to `CalcSalesTax()`. How does Visual Basic .NET send the copies of `ItemPrice` and `SalesTaxDue` to the subroutine? It does it via a mechanism called the stack, described in the following section.

The Stack

The *stack* is a chunk of memory that is used to hold temporary values while a program executes. What's interesting about the stack is that it works like a last-in, first-out (LIFO) buffer.

To envision how a stack works, think of the stack of salad plates at a buffet line. The busboy comes out and starts putting plates on the stack. Each new plate pushes the previous plate deeper into the stack. When the busboy is finished, the last plate he put on the stack is the first one a customer uses. That is, the last plate in the stack is the first plate off the stack.

A computer stack works much the same way as the stack of salad plates. When the `CalcSalesTax()` subroutine is called, the first thing Visual Basic .NET does is push the memory address of the *next* program instruction on the stack. For example, if the call to `CalcSalesTax()` is located at memory address 50,000, Visual Basic .NET pushes the next memory address, 50,001, on the stack. Why does it do this? When it does this, the last thing to come off the stack when the subroutine is done doing its job is the memory address of where the program should resume execution. This memory address takes 4 bytes of stack memory.

In the `btnSave` object's `Click()` event, the two variables of interest are `ItemPrice` and `SalesTaxDue`. Assume that `ItemPrice` is stored at memory address 80,000 and `SalesTaxDue` is stored at 80,100. Figure 5.5 shows how their `lvalue` and `rvalue` values look just before you call `CalcSalesTax()`.

FIGURE 5.5

lvalue and rvalue values for `ItemPrice` and `SalesTaxDue`.

The next thing Visual Basic .NET does is copy the current value of `Price` onto the stack. Because `Price` is a `Double`, Visual Basic .NET makes a copy of `Price`'s rvalue (`100`), forms it into a `Double`, and shoves that 8-byte copy onto the stack. Finally, it takes the current **rvalue** of `SalesTaxDue`, which is `0` by default, makes it into an 8-byte `Double`, and shoves it onto the stack. Figure 5.6 shows what the stack looks like the instant before program control is sent to `CalcSalesTax()`.

FIGURE 5.6

A picture of the stack when `CalcSalesTax()` is called.

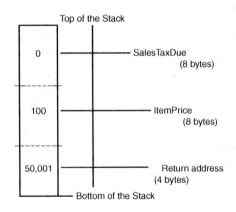

Now let's look at the code for `CalcSalesTax()` and see what Visual Basic .NET does there. Because Visual Basic .NET has made the parameters `ByVal` variables by default, Visual Basic .NET knows that the stack has copies of data on the stack. Therefore, Visual Basic .NET creates two temporary variables named `SalesTax` and `Price`, each of type `Double`. How does Visual Basic .NET know that these two variables are on the stack? It knows because the first line of the subroutine says there are two `Double` data types being passed to the `CalcSalesTax()` subroutine.

Assume that Visual Basic .NET places the two temporary variables at the `lvalue` values shown in Figure 5.7.

FIGURE 5.7
Temporary stack variables created for `CalcSalesTax()`'s parameters.

Figure 5.7 shows the `rvalue values`, with question marks because Visual Basic .NET knows that the "real" values for these temporary variables are on the stack, so there's no reason to initialize their `rvalue values` to `0`. That would be a waste of time. Therefore, the actual `rvalue` values for `Price` and `SalesTax` at the moment they are created are whatever random bit patterns happen to exist at memory locations 5,000 and 6,000.

As mentioned earlier, Visual Basic .NET knows that there are two `Double` values on the stack. It also knows that the last parameter in the parameter list will be the first one to be popped off the stack because the stack is a LIFO buffer. Therefore, the first thing Visual Basic .NET does is pop off the top value (all 8 bytes of it) from the stack and shove it into `SalesTax`. The stack now looks as shown in Figure 5.8.

FIGURE 5.8
The stack after `SalesTaxDue`'s rvalue is popped off.

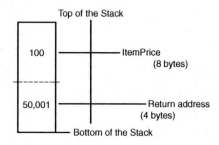

Because the value of `SalesTax` has been popped off the stack, there are only two data items left on the stack, as shown in Figure 5.8. Likewise, Figure 5.7 has now changed because you've taken off the second parameter and made it the `rvalue` of `SalesTax`. This is shown in Figure 5.9.

FIGURE 5.9

lvalue and rvalue values for Price and SalesTax after the first parameter is popped off the stack.

Notice that the only difference between Figures 5.7 and 5.9 is the zero value that was popped off the stack and into the **rvalue** for **SalesTax**.

The next thing Visual Basic .NET does is pop the **rvalue** for **Price** off the stack. The stack picture now looks as shown in Figure 5.10.

FIGURE 5.10

The stack after Price's rvalue is popped off.

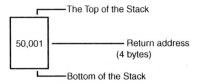

Now the only data left on the stack is the memory address where program execution resumes when **CalcSalesTax()** is finished. Visual Basic .NET has popped the first parameter value off the stack and assigned it to **Price**. The final values for the temporary variables are shown in Figure 5.11.

FIGURE 5.11

lvalue and rvalue values for Price and SalesTax after both parameters are popped off the stack.

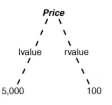

Visual Basic .NET now has the parameter values set up properly, and you can execute the next program statement in the subroutine. This is the program line:

```
SalesTax = Price * SalesTaxRate
```

Using the **rvalue** values in Figure 5.10, that line becomes this:

```
SalesTax = 100 * .05
SalesTax = 5.0
```

As a result, the **rvalue** for **SalesTax** becomes **5.0**, as shown in Figure 5.12.

FIGURE 5.12

lvalue and rvalue values for Price and SalesTax after Price is multiplied by SalesTaxRate.

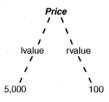

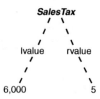

Here is where you went wrong: The instant Visual Basic .NET sees the End Sub statement in Listing 5.3, it discards the temporary variables Price and SalesTax—and all the data associated with them. Good grief! You do all that work and then just toss the results away when the End Sub is executed. In fact, when Visual Basic .NET sees the End Sub, it releases the memory for Price and SalesTax, and then it pops off the last value on the stack. Visual Basic .NET knows that this last value is the memory address where it should resume program execution, so Visual Basic .NET jumps to memory address 50,001 and starts executing the instructions stored at that address. Price and SalesTax are gone completely, as are their lvalue and rvalue values.

Back in the btnSave object's Click() event, ItemPrice and SalesTaxDue are the same as they were before. After all, their lvalue values were unknown to the CalcSalesTax() subroutine. How can you expect CalcSalesTax() to change SalesTaxDue if the subroutine doesn't know the lvalue where SalesTaxDue is in memory? There is no way anything can change SalesTaxDue if it doesn't know the lvalue. Think about it. Given that CalcSalesTax() doesn't know the lvalue of SalesTaxDue, how can you fix the problem?

Fixing the Problem

If the CalcSalesTax() subroutine had the lvalue of SalesTaxDue, it could change its rvalue. The fix is simple. You take the first program line for the CalcSalesTax() subroutine and change it so it looks like this:

```
Private Sub CalcSalesTax(ByVal Price As Double, ByRef SalesTax As Double)
```

The only change to this line is that you change the ByVal keyword for SalesTax to ByRef. The ByRef keyword means that the parameter is being passed "by reference" to the subroutine. In our words, instead of sending a ByVal copy of SalesTaxDue to the subroutine, you are sending its ByRef lvalue instead. Because an lvalue is being sent, Visual Basic .NET does *not* create a temporary variable for SalesTax. Instead, CalcSalesTax() uses the lvalue passed to it for anything that might involve SalesTax. In other words, CalcSalesTax() is really using the SalesTaxDue variable that was defined in the btnSave object's Click() event.

This one-word change makes a huge difference in the way things work in the subroutine. First of all, the stack picture in Figure 5.6 now becomes that shown in Figure 5.13.

Note that you are now sending the lvalue of SaleTaxDue— not the rvalue—to the subroutine. Obviously, this means that CalcSalesTax() now knows where to find the SaleTaxDue variable in memory.

FIGURE 5.13

A new picture of the stack when `CalcSalesTax()` is called.

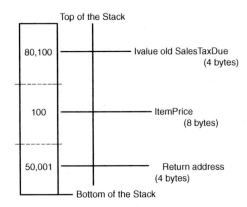

Because of the change to the first line of `CalcSalesTax()`, Visual Basic .NET also knows that the first parameter off the stack is not an **rvalue**, but rather an **lvalue**. Therefore, Figure 5.10 now changes to Figure 5.14.

FIGURE 5.14

lvalue and **rvalue** values for `Price` and `SalesTax` after you make `SalesTax` a `ByRef` parameter.

Notice that the **lvalue** for `SalesTax` in `CalcSalesTax()` is the same as `SalesTaxDue` in the `btnSave` object's `Click()` event. Now, when the subroutine multiplies `Price` by `SalesTaxRate` in the program line:

```
SalesTax = Price * SalesTaxRate
```

Visual Basic .NET takes the result, **5.0**, and places that value as a `Double` into memory address 80,100, as shown in Figure 5.14. It then sees the `End Sub`, cleans up the temporary variable named `Price` that it created, and resumes execution at memory address 50,001. There is no cleanup for `SalesTax`. Visual Basic .NET knows not to create a temporary variable because an **lvalue**, not an **rvalue**, was sent for `SalesTax`.

You should now change the first line in the `CalcSalesTax()` subroutine to use the `ByRef` keyword and recompile the program. As you can see in Figure 5.15, all is now right with the world.

FIGURE 5.15

A sample program run after you use the `ByRef` keyword for the `SalesTax` parameter.

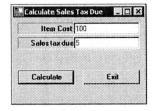

Define Versus Declare

Throughout this book I have been very precise in my use of the term *define*. When I have said something like "The `Dim` statement defines a variable named `ItemPrice`," I have had a very precise meaning. Specifically, the term *define* means that storage for the object is returned by Windows, and a new `lvalue` is now available for that object in the symbol table.

Programmers often use the terms *define* and *declare* as if they are interchangeable. They are not. When you define an object, storage is allocated for the object, and an `lvalue` is determined and written into the symbol table. When you declare an object, you are simply filling in attributes about the object (for example, the data type, the name), but no storage is requested and no `lvalue` is returned.

In the previous section, the second parameter in the `CalcSalesTax()` subroutine is named `SalesTax`. However, because it is a `ByRef` parameter, its storage and, hence, its `lvalue`, are determined *before* program control ever reaches the `CalcSalesTax()` subroutine. Therefore, any `ByRef` parameter references are data declarations, *not* data definitions. Visual Basic .NET uses data declarations so that it knows how to process the object, not where to create it. However, `ByRef` objects already exist and have `lvalue` values because they must have been previously defined elsewhere in the program.

I admit that this is some pretty hairy stuff. However, it is critical that you understand the difference between `ByVal` and `ByRef` because they are used in parameter lists. Understanding these keywords will help you understand how to use a subroutine to change the value of a variable that is defined in some other section of the program. Please, I *beg* you, reread this material until you are sure you understand it. It will make life *a lot* easier later on if you take the time to understand it now!

Functions

A program function is slightly different from a subroutine in one important way: A function can return a value to the caller. Let's use the previous subroutine program from earlier in this chapter as a starting point to show the difference.

First, you need to change the `btnSave` object's `Click()` event code to the following:

```
Dim ItemPrice As Double, SalesTaxDue As Double

ItemPrice = CDbl(txtCost.Text)
SalesTaxDue = CalcSalesTax(ItemPrice)      ' Call the function
txtTax.Text = CStr(SalesTaxDue)
```

Note that the only change appears in the third line. You have removed `SalesTaxDue` from the parameter list and, instead, used it in an assignment statement after the call to `CalcSalesTax()`.

Now you need to change the code line for the `CalcSalesTax()` subroutine to the code shown in Listing 5.4.

LISTING 5.4   Using `CalcSalesTax()` as a Function

```
Private Function CalcSalesTax(ByVal Price As Double) As Double
  ' Purpose: This subroutine calculates the sales tax
  '     that is to be collected for a given item.
  '
  ' Arguments:
  '  Price   the purchase price of the item
  '  SalesTax the sales tax amount to collect
  '
  ' Return Value:
  '  double  the sales tax due for this sale
  '
  ' Caution: the calculation uses the symbolic constant
  '     SalesTaxRate, which holds the current sales
  '     tax rate.

  CalcSalesTax = Price * SalesTaxRate
End Function
```

First, notice that the second word in the first line of Listing 5.4 is `Function`, not `Sub`, as before. This tells Visual Basic .NET that you are about to define a function rather than a subroutine.

Second, at the end of the first line, after the closing parenthesis, are the words `As Double`. This tells Visual Basic .NET that this function is designed to return a `Double` data type to the caller. This is what makes the function different: It returns a value to the caller. Listing 5.4 defines the function to return a `Double` data type. You can, of course, write functions that return any type of data you want. However, you must append `As ???` to the end of each new function definition so Visual Basic .NET knows what the function is to return to the caller.

Third, notice that in the documentation for the function, several new lines that begin with `Return Value:` have been added. This provides the reader additional details about the `Double` data type that is being returned by this function. You should get in the habit of providing such documentation notes.

Fourth, a single statement forms the body of the function:

```
CalcSalesTax = Price * SalesTaxRate
```

This statement does two things. First, it calculates the sales tax that is due for this sale, as the product of `Price` multiplied by the `SalesTaxRate`. Using the values suggested in Figure 5.5, `Price` is 100 and `SalesTaxRate` is .05, yielding a tax due of 5. This product is then assigned into `CalcSalesTax` as though it were a variable, when it is actually the name of the function. All functions must use the following syntax in order to return a value to the caller:

```
FunctionName = ValueToBeReturned
```

This is the proper way to tell Visual Basic .NET what value is to be returned.

Fifth, notice that the last line of the function in Listing 5.4 is changed to read `End Function` rather than `End Sub`.

How does Visual Basic .NET actually get the value (that is, **5**) back to the caller? It pushes the value **5** on the stack as a **Double** data type. After the last line in the **CalcSalesTax()** function executes, the stack looks as shown in Figure 5.16.

FIGURE 5.16
The new picture of the stack when **CalcSalesTax()** is called.

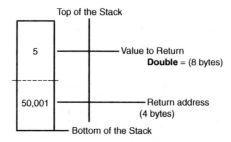

In fact, the last line in the program does calculate the sales tax due, and then it fakes an assignment into **CalcSalesTax**. The "assignment" really tells Visual Basic .NET to place the return value on the stack and return to the caller.

Now look at the program statement in the calling routine that set everything in motion in the first place:

```
SalesTaxDue = CalcSalesTax(ItemPrice)      ' Call the subroutine
```

Because Visual Basic .NET knows that **CalcSalesTax()** returns a **Double** data type, it knows it must pop 8 bytes off the stack and shove those bytes into the memory address (that is, the **lvalue**) for **SalesTaxDue**. If you use Figure 5.11 as a reference, you can see that Visual Basic .NET pops 8 bytes off the stack and puts them into the memory locations starting at address 6,000. This has the effect of changing the **rvalue** of **SalesTaxDue** to **5**. Think about it. It then pops the memory address for the next program instruction from the stack (50,001) and resumes program execution at that address. Pretty neat, huh?

Summary

In this chapter you have learned what subroutines and functions are. More importantly, you should now understand why they are different from one another. The primary difference is that functions can return values to the caller using the stack, but subroutines cannot.

In this chapter you have also learned the difference between **ByVal** and **ByRef** parameters. It is imperative that you understand the difference between these two parameter types. You have also learned that a variable definition is not the same thing as a variable "declaration." Understanding these concepts will help you to better understand the topics in Chapter 8, "Scope and Lifetime of Variables."

You should spend enough time on this chapter so that you know the topics well enough to teach them to someone else. If you can argue convincingly that definitions and declarations are different and the person agrees with you, you're ready for the next chapter. You should work the exercises at the end of this chapter, too.

Review Questions

1. What is a subroutine and why are they used in programs?

A. A subroutine is a series of program statements designed to accomplish a specific task. The advantage of a subroutine is that it can be called from any point in a program, thus reducing the need for duplicate code. This also reduces the amount of code that needs to be written, tested, debugged, and maintained.

2. What does the phrase "calling a subroutine" mean?

A. Calling a subroutine means that the program flow is about to be transferred to the code that comprises the subroutine. After all the statements in the subroutine body are executed, program flow is returned to the point following the subroutine call. The point at which the subroutine is called is often referred to as *the caller*. The caller is not a person per se. Rather, the caller refers to a point in the program where the subroutine is called.

3. What is a subroutine parameter?

A. Often, a subroutine needs some form of data to perform its task. This data is passed to the subroutine in the form of a parameter. For example, if a subroutine is supposed to calculate the amount of sales tax that is due from a sale, the subroutine might be called with parameters for the purchase price of the item, the sales tax rate, and the amount of sales tax. The last parameter would be empty when the parameter is passed to the subroutine and then filled in with the proper value when the subroutine has finished its task.

4. What is a symbolic constant?

A. A symbolic constant is simply a program value to which you have assigned a name. For example, you might use the statement:

```
Const SalesTaxRate as Double = .06
```

You can then use the constant in an expression like:

```
SalesTaxDue = PurchasePrice * SalesTaxRate
```

Using symbolic constants helps to document how a statement is using the constant.

5. What is a stack?

A. A stack is a section of memory that can be used for a variety of programming tasks. With respect to subroutines, the stack is used to pass parameters and the return address to a subroutine. The stack behaves like a LIFO buffer. Data is pushed on the stack just before the subroutine is called, and then the data is popped off the stack in the subroutine. The subroutine uses the data that was popped off the stack for whatever purposes that data serves in the subroutine. The stack also contains the return address of where program execution is to resume once the subroutine finishes its task.

6. Why is a function different from a subroutine?

A. Functions and subroutines are very similar with one major exception: a function can return a value to the caller. The stack is used to return the value to the caller.

7. Write a function that converts a Fahrenheit temperature to Celsius. The formula is

$$C = 5/9 \ (F - 32)$$

A. The code for the program is

```
Public Class frmTemperature
 Inherits System.Windows.Forms.Form

' Windows Form Designer generated code


 Private Sub btnCalc_Click(ByVal sender As System.Object, _
     ByVal e As System.EventArgs) Handles btnCalc.Click
  txtCelsius.Text = Format(ConvertTemp(CDbl(txtFahrenheit.Text)),_
          "###.00")
 End Sub

 Private Function ConvertTemp(ByVal Fahrenheit As Double) As Double
  Return ((5 / 9) * (Fahrenheit - 32))
 End Function


 Private Sub btnExit_Click(ByVal sender As System.Object, _
     ByVal e As System.EventArgs) Handles btnExit.Click
  Me.Dispose()
 End Sub
End Class
```

CHAPTER 6

STRING VARIABLES

In this chapter, you will learn the following:

- Strings
- Working with the String class in Visual Basic .NET
- Other string methods

*I*n this chapter, you'll learn the various ways that you can use and manipulate string data in your programs. You'll discover that there are several different levels at which strings can be used in Visual Basic .NET programs.

Strings

String data is a cornerstone of almost any program. Names, addresses, almost any piece of information that isn't purely numeric is represented as a string. If you recall from our discussion of data types in Chapter 4, "Data Types and Numeric Variables," string data is simply one or more characters treated as a single data item. As we'll see in this chapter, however, using the String data type is a bit different from the numeric data types inherent in Visual Basic .NET.

The String data type is implemented in Visual Basic .NET as a string class rather than as an inherent structure like the numeric data types. Because string variables are class objects, you can work with string data on two different levels. First, you can manipulate the string data using functions that are built into Visual Basic .NET (we'll study these functions first in this chapter). Second, because strings are implemented as class objects in the .NET framework, you can also use the methods that are inherent in the string class to manipulate the data.

Text Boxes and Strings

You've seen in earlier programs that you can type characters into a text box as the program runs. The sequence of characters you type into the text box is treated as a string. Consider the following program lines:

```
Dim MyString as String

MyString = txtString1.Text
```

The first statement creates a `String` variable named `MyString` and finds a place for it in memory. The next program statement takes the characters you typed into the `txtString1` text box and assigns them as a `String` into `MyString`. In this example, the `Text` property of the `txtString1` text box holds the string data that you typed in from the keyboard as the program executed. Because the `Text` property of the `txtString1` text box can change according to whatever the user wants to type into the text box, the `Text` property behaves like a `String` variable.

Now consider a slight modification to these two program lines:

```
Dim MyString as String

MyString = "Lunch time"
```

In this situation, the content of `MyString` is assigned a fixed sequence of characters. Unless something later in the program modifies `MyString`, its contents always remain `"Lunch time"` throughout the life of the program. Anytime you see a sequence of characters surrounded by double quotation marks as shown in the preceding code, the double-quoted sequence of characters is referred to as a *string literal*. In this case, we're assigning a string literal into a string variable named `MyString`.

Manipulating Visual Basic .NET String Data

Perhaps the best way for you to learn how to work with strings is to write a simple program in Visual Basic .NET that manipulates a string for you. To write the program, start a new project and call it MyStringProgram. Add four label controls, six text box controls, and two button controls as shown in Figure 6.1. The names for the various text boxes are as shown in the figure. The Calculate button is called `btnCalc` and the Exit button is named `btnExit`. The names you give to the label controls aren't important because they aren't actually referenced by any expressions in the program.

Add the following line to the `btnExit Click` event:

```
Me.Dispose()
```

You'll recall from previous programs that this line releases all the resources used in the program when we're finished with them and terminates the program. The keyword `Me` is simply a shorthand notation for the currently active form. Because our program has only one form, releasing the form ends the program in a graceful manner.

FIGURE 6.1
Control layout for
MyStringProgram.

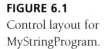

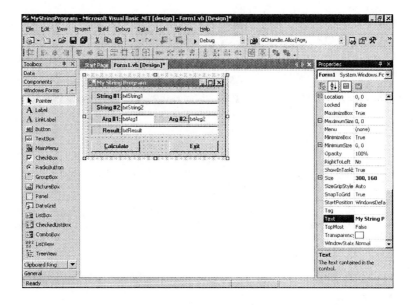

FIGURE 6.1
Control layout for
MyStringProgram.

After you've added the necessary controls and code to the form, save the project. We'll make minor changes to the program throughout this chapter to show you how you can manipulate string data in Visual Basic .NET.

String Concatenation

Perhaps one of the simplest operations on string data is to add two strings together to form a new (longer) string. The process of adding two strings is called *string concatenation*. You can concatenate strings by adding one line of code to the `btnCalc Click` event:

```
txtResult.Text = txtString1.Text + txtString2.Text
```

This statement simply takes the string held in the `txtString1` text box and adds it to the string held in the `txtString2` text box. The statement then assigns the new string into the `txtResult` text box.

Programmer's Tip

The plus sign (addition) operator is used to indicate that the two string expressions, `txtString1` and `txtString2`, are concatenated together. Note, however, that you can also use the ampersand operator, `&`, in place of the plus sign to indicate a string concatenation operation. Many Visual Basic .NET programmers prefer the ampersand operator because it reinforces the idea that it is string data that is being added, not numeric data. We'll use the ampersand operator from now on.

Now compile and run the program. A sample run is shown in Figure 6.2.

FIGURE 6.2

Sample run of MyStringProgram using string concatenation.

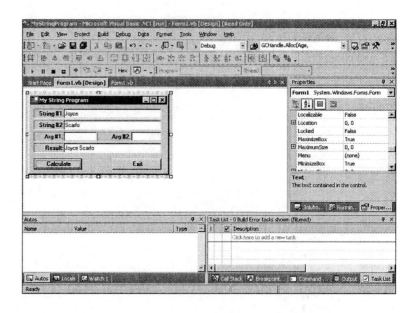

What isn't obvious from the sample run is that there is a blank space in the **txtString1** text box after the word **Joyce**. If we had not added this blank space, the result would look like a single word **JoyceScarfo** rather than **Joyce Scarfo**.

Because string concatenation is a fairly simple string process, we didn't need to use the other text boxes on the form. We'll make use of them in later sections.

Shorthand Operator for String Concatenation

String concatenation is commonly used to build a single longer string from a series of smaller strings. In fact, string building is such a common thing, Visual Basic .NET provides a shorthand operator for it. You could build the string with the statement:

```
txtResult.Text = txtResult.Text & txtString2.Text
```

But that's sort of like sliding down a staircase…on the stairs. Verbally, the statement says, "Take the string in **txtResult** and add to that string a second string named **txtString2** and take the result of the string concatenation of the two strings and reassign it into **txtResult**." Makes me tired just saying it.

Instead, you can simply use

```
txtResult.Text &= txtString2.Text
```

Notice the **&=** operator in the middle of the statement. If we verbalize this statement, it says, "Take the string in **txtResult** and add **txtString2** to it." This shorthand operator for string concatenation saves you from typing the **txtResult.Text** operand in the expression a second time. This shorthand operator simplifies the statement and it uses the preferred string concatenation operator (**&**).

String Length

In some programs, you'll need to know how many characters the user typed into a text box or a string. The number of characters held in a string variable is known as the *length* of the string. To show you how to calculate the length of a string, remove the old program statement in the `btnCalc` Click event and replace it with the following new statement:

```
txtResult.Text = CStr(Len(txtString1.Text))
```

This program statement says to use the `Len()` function that's built into Visual Basic .NET to calculate the length of the string held in the `txtString1` text box. The `Len()` function returns the number of characters in the text box.

However, there is a problem. Because the data type returned from `Len()` is a numeric data type, we must use the `CStr()` function to convert the numeric value returned by `Len()` to a `String` data type before assigning the result into `txtResult.Text`. Doing so forces the data type on the right side of the assignment operator (that is, the equal sign) to match the data type on the left side of the assignment operator (or string-into-string assignment, in this expression).

Programmer's Tip

Recall from Chapter 2 that the assignment operator is a binary operator. This means that it requires two operands to work properly. In Chapter 2, we expressed this relationship as

operand1 = *operand2*

The `CStr()` function forces *operand2* to be the same data type as *operand1* before the assignment takes place, and that is always a good thing!

Although the data type conversion using the `CStr()` function isn't required in this example, it's always a good idea to have the data types match when using the assignment operator. There are instances in which Visual Basic .NET does not automatically convert from one data type to another. In those cases where the types do not match, Visual Basic .NET might get a little cranky and tell you there is a type mismatch in the program expression. Whenever you see such an error message, you'll probably need to use one of the conversion functions to make the data types used in the expression match. (You can find a list of these conversion functions in Table 4.3 in Chapter 4. The conversion functions start with the letter `C` followed by the type they convert to, such as `CBool`, `CByte`, `CChar`, and so on. You can also use the generic CType function, too.) We'll use many of these conversion functions in later chapters.

Figure 6.3 shows a sample run using the `Len()`function. In this sample run, the `txtResult` text box shows the number of characters present in the `txtString1` text box. Because `Len()` can return the length of only one string at a time, the other text boxes in the program aren't used.

FIGURE 6.3

Sample run using the
Len() function.

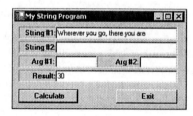

One more thing about the Len() function. It does *not* return the number of bytes of storage used for the string. Remember that strings are stored using Unicode, which is a double-byte character set. Also, some overhead bytes are associated with strings that exist independently of the string content. Therefore, you should not equate string length with string storage requirements. They are not the same.

Substring Operations

There are times when you'll want to extract part of one string and make it a new string. For example, suppose that the user types in Mr. Jim Hallet, but you don't want the Mr. part of the string. Instead, you want just Jim Hallet. Stated another way, you want a substring of Mr. Jim Hallet that is simply Jim Hallet. Visual Basic .NET provides you with several built-in functions that can be used to extract a substring from a string.

The Left() Function

The Left() function has the following syntax requirements:

Substring = Microsoft.VisualBasic.Left(*Str, LenOfSubstr*)

First of all, what's this Microsoft.VisualBasic. stuff that comes before the Left() function all about? Well, it's there to avoid confusing Visual Basic .NET. The problem is that Left() isn't only a string manipulation function; it's also the name of a property in a Windows form. For example, if you want to place a form named frmMyForm 200 pixels from the left edge of the screen, you could use the program statement:

frmMyForm.Left = 200

In this statement, Left is a property of frmMyForm. By fully qualifying Left with Microsoft.VisualBasic.Left, Visual Basic .NET knows that you want to use the built-in Left() string function, not a Visual Basic .NET property named Left.

Note that there are two arguments to the Left() function. The first is the string we want to use. The second argument is an integer value that tells Visual Basic .NET how many characters from the start of the string to use when forming the new substring. For example, if the expression is

SubStr = Microsoft.VisualBasic.Left("Aunt Nancy", 4)

the variable SubStr would be assigned the string value Aunt.

With that information in mind, remove the old program statement from the btnCalc Click event and change it to

```
txtResult.Text = Microsoft.VisualBasic.Left(txtString1.Text, _
    CInt(txtArg1.Text))
```

Note that we use the CInt() conversion function to convert the text in the txtArg1 text box into an integer variable, as required for the second argument used in the Left() function.

Programmer's Tip

In the program line, notice how the line ends with the underscore character, _. This is the *line continuation character* in Visual Basic .NET. Recall that a complete Visual Basic .NET program statement must be contained on a single line. However, some program statements, such as the one shown, are fairly long, hiding parts of the statement when viewed within the program editor. If you want to make such long lines visible, break up the line using the underscore character. Note that you must place the underscore after an operator or an operand. You cannot, for example, place the underscore in the middle of a Visual Basic .NET keyword or variable name. If you do use the line continuation character, it's usually good practice to indent the rest of the line as shown here. This helps tip off the reader that the indented expression is part of a single (longer) program statement.

Figure 6.4 shows a sample run of the program.

FIGURE 6.4
Sample run of Left()
function.

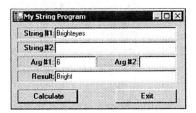

The sample run shows what happens when we extract the leftmost six characters from Brighteyes and treat the result as a substring, as shown in the txtResult text box.

The Mid() Function

The Mid() function is used when you want to extract a substring from a position other than at the beginning of the string. The syntax for the Mid() function is

```
Mid(String, Start, [length])
```

Notice that we've placed the third argument (that is, *length*) in square brackets. Square brackets around an argument mean that it's an optional argument to the function. The first argument (that is, *String*) is the string from which we want to extract the substring. The second argument (*Start*) is the starting position for the substring. If you supply the optional *length* argument, that many characters are returned in the substring. If you do not supply a *length* argument, everything to the right of *Start* is returned as the substring.

For example,

```
SubStr = Mid("James Earl Jones", 7, 4)
```

would assign `Earl` into `SubStr` because we want to start our substring with the seventh character (that is, the `E`), but only return four characters. On the other hand,

```
SubStr = Mid("James Earl Jones", 7)
```

would assign `Earl Jones` in `SubStr` because no *length* argument is given. In this example, everything to the right of character position seven is returned as the substring. Note that we do not need to supply the `Microsoft.VisualBasic.` in front of the `Mid()` function because there is no form property named `Mid`.

To test the `Mid()` function, remove the current line from the `btnCalc Click` event and replace it with the following lines:

```
If txtArg2.text = "" Then
 txtResult.Text = Mid(txtString1.Text, CInt(txtArg1.Text))
Else
 txtResult.Text = Mid(txtString1.Text, CInt(txtArg1.Text), _
 CInt(txtArg2.Text) )
End If
```

Unfortunately, we're forced to use a Visual Basic .NET language construct that we haven't studied yet: the `If-Then-Else` statement. Simply stated, the `If` statement tests to see whether the user typed in something into the `txtArg2` text box. If the `txtArg2` text box does not contain any characters (that is, an empty string or `""`), the user wants to return everything from the starting character to the end of the string. If the user does type something into the `txtArg2` text box, we assume that he is supplying a *length* argument to the `Mid()` function.

Figure 6.5 shows a sample run in which the user has supplied a length argument; Figure 6.6 shows the same run, but without a length argument. Notice how the substring is affected.

FIGURE 6.5
`Mid()` function with a length argument.

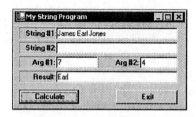

FIGURE 6.6
`Mid()` function without a length argument.

Figure 6.6 shows that the remainder of the string is returned when the optional third argument is not supplied.

The `Right()` Function

It should come as no surprise that if there is a `Left()` function, there's probably a `Right()` function, too. The syntax for the `Right()` function is

```
Right(String, Length)
```

The `Right()` function does not need a starting position because the starting position is calculated from the *Length* argument. For example, suppose that the *Length* argument equals 5. What the `Right()` function really says is, "Give me the rightmost five characters of the string." In other words, the starting position is counted backward from the end of the string for *Length* characters. Therefore, the program statement

```
SubStr = Right ("James Earl Jones", 5)
```

would find `SubStr` equal to `Jones` because that is the last five characters in the string.

Remove all the current program statements from the `btnCalc Click` event and replace them with

```
txtResult.Text = Microsoft.VisualBasic.Right(txtString1.Text, _
        CInt(txtArg1.Text))
```

Again, because Windows forms have a `Right` property, we need to fully qualify the `Right()` function so Visual Basic .NET doesn't get confused. As usual, we need to use the `CInt()` conversion function to convert the length argument held in `txtArg1.Text` as a string into an `Integer` data type. Figure 6.7 shows a sample run for the `Right()` function.

FIGURE 6.7

Sample run of the `Right()` function.

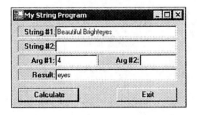

Notice that the rightmost four characters from the string are returned as a substring.

The `InStr()` Function

There will be times when you need to determine the starting position of a substring within a larger string. For example, you might want to extract the last name from a string that holds the first name followed by the last name. In this case, the string might be `James Bond` and you want to create a substring using only the last name, `Bond`. That's exactly what the `InStr()` function is designed to do.

The syntax for the `InStr()` function is

```
StartPosition = InStr(StringToUse, SubstringToFind)
```

The first argument to the `InStr()` function is the string we want to search, and the second argument is the substring we want to find. Note that the substring we want to find can hold one or more characters. The value returned by `InStr()` is the starting position of the first instance of the substring being searched. In our example, we would use

```
StartPosition = InStr("James Bond", " ")
```

which says we want to locate the blank space substring between the first and last names.

If `InStr()` can find a match on the search substring, it returns the starting position for the substring. In the preceding example, `InStr()` would return **6**. If `InStr()` cannot find a match on the substring, it returns **0** to indicate that no match was found in the string. (As a test of your understanding, how would you use the value in `StartPosition` to return the last name in the string? Hint: Think about the `Mid()` function and keep in mind that most last names don't start with a blank space.)

To test the `InStr()` function, remove all the current program statements from the `btnCalc` `Click` event and replace them with

```
txtResult.Text = InStr(txtString1.Text, txtArg1.Text)
```

and compile and run the program. Figure 6.8 shows the results of a sample run. Unfortunately, you can't see that I typed in a blank space for `txtArg1`, but that's the substring we're searching for.

FIGURE 6.8
Sample run using the
`InStr()` function.

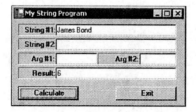

You might also rerun this program, but change the search string from a blank space to `"on"` and study the results. Also, try entering a substring that does not exist in the string and observing the results.

Working Directly on the `String` Data Type

All the string functions that we've discussed thus far work directly on the String data using functions that are built into Visual Basic .NET. The string manipulations we've examined all require that you specify the string as an argument to the function. Stated in terms of what we discussed in Chapter 2, each of these string manipulation functions needs the `lvalue` of the string passed to the function as a function argument. In other words, these string functions are sitting out there in memory somewhere waiting to help you. All you have to do is pass them some information about the string and what you want to do with it.

In the next section of this chapter, we discuss string operations as they exist within the `String` *class*. The string operations performed on the `String` class work a little differently, even though they can provide the same functionality as the `String` functions discussed earlier in this chapter. The `String` class methods provide more ways to manipulate `String` data and are often easier to use.

Working with the `String` Class in Visual Basic .NET

When you manipulate string objects, you'll use the methods that are part of the `String` class. There are two flavors of `String` class methods. They are

- **Shared methods**—These are inherent in the `String` class itself. As such, they don't require an instance of the `String` class to function.

- **Instance methods**—These methods are derived from the specific instance of a `String` object. This means that an instance method is always qualified with the name of the `String` object.

The distinction between these two method types will become clearer when we start using them. To begin our discussion of using the `String` class, let's explore how several of our earlier `String` functions can be duplicated with methods of the `String` class.

The `Length` Method

You already saw how we can calculate the length of a string using the `Len()` function. You can accomplish the same thing using the **Length** method of the `String` class. To test this method, remove all the lines from the `btnCalc Click` event and add the following new lines:

```
Dim buff As String

buff = txtString1.Text
txtResult.Text = CStr(buff.Length)
```

First, we define a variable named `buff` of type `String`. Next, we move the string data from the `txtString1` text box into `buff` using the assignment operator. Now look at the right side of the assignment statement in the third line. The expression

```
buff.Length
```

in essence is telling Visual Basic .NET: "Use the `Length` method of the `String` class to find how many characters are currently stored in the variable named `buff`." Note that the dot operator is used to separate the instance name of the string variable from its method name.

Because the Length method requires us to specify the name of the variable being used, Length is an instance method. Recall that *instance* is an OOP term that refers to a variable that has been properly defined, often with a Dim statement. In our example, *instance* means that we have a variable named buff that exists in memory (that is, it has an lvalue) that we can use in our program.

Figure 6.9 shows a sample run. As you would expect, it yields the same results as does the Len() function.

FIGURE 6.9

Sample run using the Length method of the String class.

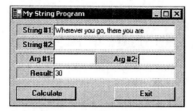

Notice that the output in Figure 6.9 is identical to that shown in Figure 6.3. So far, so good.

The Concat Method

String concatenation is very simple. Remove the current lines from the btnCalc Click event and add the following line:

```
txtResult.Text = String.Concat(txtString1.Text, txtString2.Text)
```

String concatenation using the String class Concat method simply uses a comma-separated list of the strings you want to concatenate together. A sample run is shown in Figure 6.10, using the same data we used for Figure 6.2. It should come as no surprise that the results are identical. (Don't forget to add the trailing blank space after Joyce.)

FIGURE 6.10

Sample run using the Concat method.

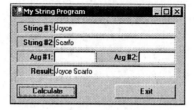

Note that the Concat method is *not* prefaced with the name of a variable. Instead of a string variable name, it's prefaced with the keyword String. After the String keyword comes the dot operator, the Concat method name, and finally the parenthesized list of strings to be concatenated. Because the method is prefaced with the String class name, the Concat method is an example of a *shared* String method.

Programmer's Tip

The `Concat` method is not limited to concatenating two strings at a time. You can concatenate as many strings as you want. Simply place them in order, going from left to right, and separate each one with a comma. For example

```
SubStr = String.Concat(Str1, Str2, Str3, Str4, Str5)
```

would concatenate five strings together and assign the result into `SubStr`.

Optimizing String Concatenation

String data is sometimes used to store data in rather strange ways. For example, I was involved with a project that had to track each unique word as it appeared in a database of medical terms. This required reading the database and appending each new term to a string, followed by a comma. On completion of reading the database, the (rather large!) string contained a comma-separated list of all the unique (17,000+) medical terms in the database.

When the program was written, the string concatenation statement looked like

```
MedicalTerms = MedicalTerms & NewTerm & ","
```

The program execution was extremely slow. A little digging around showed that a surprising amount of the execution time was being spent on the concatenation statement. We scratched our heads for a few minutes and then had a flat-forehead epiphany: Strings in Visual Basic .NET are immutable, which means you can't change them after you create them. This also means that, as the program executed, Visual Basic .NET was passing 17,000+ messages back and forth to Windows asking for storage for a new (longer) string.

We changed the code with the following modifications:

```
Dim TempStr As New System.Text.StringBuilder(255000)
Dim MedicalTerms As String, Term as string

            ' Some details left out...

   TempStr.Append(Term)
   TempStr.Append(",")
            ' More details left out...
MedicalTerms = TempStr.ToString
```

The key change is the definition of the `TempStr` object, which is an instance of a `StringBuilder()` object. We defined the object to be capable of holding 255,000 characters, or about 15 characters per term. The code uses the `Append()` method of the `StringBuilder()` object to build the string. (The `Append()` method statements are actually inside a program loop; a topic we'll discuss in Chapter 12, "The `For` Loop.") The final statement of `TempStr` into `MedicalTerms` is necessary because the `StringBuilder()` object is different from a `String` data type.

What did we gain from the program changes? The actual execution speed was approximately three times faster than before. However, the execution speed of the loop that built the string of terms was almost 30 times faster than before. Clearly, the `StringBuilder()` object is optimized by Visual Basic .NET to perform string concatenation and minimizes message passing between Visual Basic .NET and Windows.

The `SubString` Method

The `SubString` method has functionality that's similar to the `Mid()` function we studied earlier in this chapter. To experiment with this method, remove the current lines from the `btnCalc` `Click` event and add the following lines:

```
Dim buff As String

buff = txtString1.Text
txtResult.Text = buff.SubString(CInt(txtArg1.Text), CInt(txtArg2.Text))
```

Note that the `SubString` method is prefaced with the name of the variable we want to use. Therefore, `SubString` must be an instance method. The first argument of the method (that is, `txtArg1.Text`) is the starting position for the substring. The second argument of the method (`txtArg2.Text`) is the number of characters, or length, we want to extract. Because these two arguments are stored in text boxes, we use the `CInt()` conversion routines to change them from `String` data to numeric data, which is the data type the `SubString` method expects for both arguments.

Figure 6.11 shows a sample run of the `SubString` method. The sample run uses the same data that we used for the sample run shown in Figure 6.6. Oh-oh…the results aren't the same. What's the problem?

FIGURE 6.11
Sample run using the
`SubString` method.

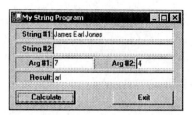

Character Counting with the `String` Class

Well, it's really not a problem. It's just the old off-by-one syndrome. The reason that the results aren't the same is because all `String` class methods treat the first character in the string as character number 0. On the other hand, built-in Visual Basic .NET functions such as `Mid()`, treat the first character in the string as character 1. In the string `James Earl Jones`, if you treat the first `J` as character 1, `E` becomes the seventh character. However, if the first `J` is character 0, the `a` becomes the seventh character.

The lesson is simple: If you use the built-in Visual Basic .NET string manipulation functions, characters are counted from left to right, starting with 1 for the first character. You'll often hear these referred to as *one-based* calculations. If you're using the `String` class methods for string manipulation, characters are counted from left to right, starting with 0 for the first character. The `String` class methods are often referred to as *zero-based* calculations.

So, how do we modify our sample program run to produce the same results? Well, because `String` class methods are zero-based operations, we need to subtract one from our starting position. This is shown in Figure 6.12. (Don't forget the **4** for the second argument.)

FIGURE 6.12

Sample run of the `Substring` method, accounting for zero-based calculations.

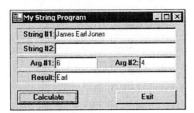

Now the results in Figure 6.12 agree with those shown in Figure 6.6.

Emulating `Left()` and `Right()` Using the `SubString` Method

There are no `String` class methods that match the `Left()` and `Right()` functions directly. However, it's easy enough to emulate them using the `SubString` method. For example, suppose that we want to emulate the `Left()` string function. Remove the current lines from the `btnCalc Click` event and add the following line:

```
Dim buff As String

buff = txtString1.Text
txtResult.Text = buff.SubString(0, CInt(txtArg1.Text))
```

So, what does this program statement do? It says that we want to extract a substring that starts at position 0 with a length that equals the number held in the **txtArg1** text box. This is the same thing that the `Left()` function does. A sample run of the new code is shown in Figure 6.13, using the same string used in Figure 6.4. As expected, the results are the same.

FIGURE 6.13

Emulating the `Left()` function with the `SubString` method.

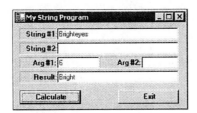

Emulating the `Right()` function is similar, but takes a little more code to accomplish. Add the following code to the `btnCalc Click` event:

```
Dim buff As String
Dim SubLength As Integer, SubStart As Integer

buff = txtString1.Text
SubLength = CInt(txtArg1.Text)        ' Get substring length
SubStart = buff.Length - SubLength    ' Where to start
txtResult.Text = buff.Substring(SubStart, SubLength)
```

First, notice that we've defined two new variables in the `btnCalc Click` event. As you can see from the preceding code, `SubLength` is an integer variable that we use to hold the number of characters we want for the new substring. We get this number by converting the content of the `txtArg1` text box into an integer using our old friend `CInt()`.

The next line determines the starting position in the string from which the substring is to be extracted. For example, if the string is `Bluebird` and we want to extract `bird` as the substring, the calculation becomes

```
SubStart = buff.Length - SubLength
SubStart = 8 - 4
SubStart = 4
```

Plugging this information into the final expression finds

```
txtResult.Text = buff.Substring(SubStart, SubLength)
txtResult.Text = buff.Substring(4, 4)
```

Because `String` class operations are zero-based, character position 4 is the `b` in the string `Bluebird`, so the substring becomes the rightmost four characters, yielding `txtResult.Text` being assigned the substring `bird`.

Searching for Substrings

The `String` class provides the `IndexOf` method for finding the starting position of a substring in a way that is similar to the `InStr()` function we examined earlier. The syntax for the `IndexOf` method is

```
StartPosition = TheStringToSearch.IndexOf(SubStringToFind)
```

To implement this method, remove the existing code from the `btnCalc Click` event and add

```
Dim buff As String
Dim SubStart As Integer

buff = txtString1.Text
SubStart = buff.IndexOf(txtArg1.Text)
txtResult.Text = CStr(SubStart)
```

The real work is done by the program statement in the fourth line. The `IndexOf` method searches the string named `buff` for the substring held in the `txtArg1` text box. If a match is found, the `IndexOf` method returns an integer that corresponds to the character position where the match occurred. If no match is found, a value of 0 is returned by the `IndexOf` method.

Note that we don't have to convert the value returned by the `IndexOf` method to an integer using the `CInt()` conversion routine. The reason is because Visual Basic .NET already knows that the `IndexOf` method returns an integer value, so a conversion is unnecessary.

Figure 6.14 shows a sample run using the same inputs as shown in Figure 6.8. Recall that we were trying to find the blank space between the first and last name. (There's a blank space in the `txtArg1` text box used for the search string even though we can't see it.) Once again, the results in Figure 6.14 differ from those shown in Figure 6.8. The reason for the difference is because the current program uses a zero-based count, whereas Figure 6.8 uses a one-based count for the character positions.

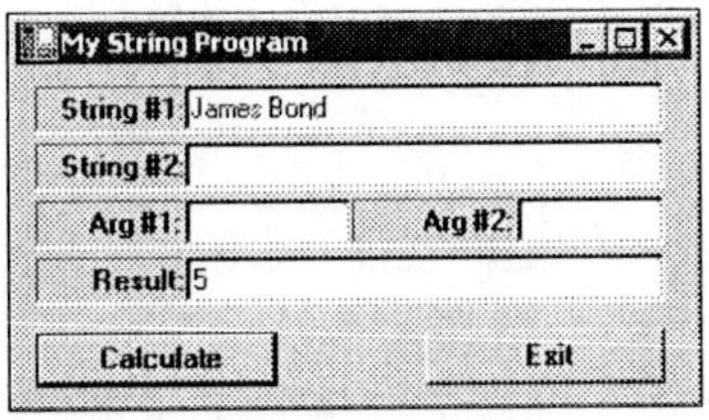

FIGURE 6.14

Sample run using the `IndexOf` method.

The `LastIndexOf` Method

The `LastIndexOf` method is a useful variation of the `IndexOf` method. To illustrate, suppose that you have some information in a string that contains the city, state, and ZIP Code all packed into a single string:

```
"Mt. Holly, NJ 08060"
```

Let's further suppose that you want to extract the ZIP Code as a substring. There are several ways to do it. One way would be to use the `Right()` function and extract the five rightmost characters. Good plan, until someone slips in one of those nine-digit ZIP Codes we're supposed to be using.

Another way would be to search for a blank space between the state and the ZIP Code. The problem here is that there are two spaces in the string (that is, between the period and the H and between the comma and the N) before we get to the space we need. Hmmm…

Not a problem. Simply use the `LastIndexOf` method. This method works much the same way as the `IndexOf` method, but the search starts at the end of the string and works backward toward the start of the string looking for a match. In other words, if you had the following code

```
buff = "Mt. Holly, NJ 08060"
SubStart = buff.LastIndexOf(" ")
```

`SubStart` would equal **13**, which is the zero-based character position of the last blank space in the string.

Finding Out What Is Stored at a Given String Position—The `Chars` Method

Sometimes you'll find that it's more efficient to use string data to encode information. For example, suppose that you want to store the information about a college student. Let's further assume that class standing is encoded as 1 for a freshman, 2 for a sophomore, 3 for a junior, 4 for a senior, 5 for a master's student, and 6 for a Ph.D. student. Now let's assume that 0 is used to represent a female student and 1 is a male student. Let's also assume that computer science majors are encoded as a 7, and college of business majors are an 8. Finally, we'll assume that the student's class standing is stored in position 0 of a string, the student's sex is in position 1, and their major is stored in position 2. Therefore, the string

```
"407"
```

tells us that this student is a female student in her senior year majoring in computer science. That's quite a bit of information about the student stored in only three bytes of data.

Note that we could have created three separate variables to store this information. In this case, we've decided to trade off clarity for compactness. That is, it isn't intuitively obvious that the string `407` contains all the information that we've encoded into it. Because the data is encoded, we need to unpack the information from the string if we want to use the information contained in it. We can use the `Chars` method to help us extract the information.

The syntax for the `Chars` method is

```
CharacterStoredThere = MyString.Chars(PositionToExamine)
```

The `Chars` method has a single argument, which is an integer value that corresponds to the character position in `MyString` we want to examine. The `Chars` method then returns the character stored in that position as a character data type. (In the strictest sense, the `Chars` method does return a `Char` data type, but Visual Basic .NET is smart enough to promote it automatically to a `String` data type if you assign its return value into a string.)

Remove the program statements from the `btnCalc Click` event and add the following program statements:

```
Dim buff As String

buff = txtString1.Text
txtResult.Text = buff.Chars(CInt(txtArg1.Text))
```

The argument to the `Chars` method is the character position in the string you want to examine. Figure 6.15 shows a sample run.

In Figure 6.15, the value held in text box `txtArg1` is the character position we want to examine; position 2, in this example. The result is shown in the `txtResult` text box, which is `7`. Again, while it looks as if the `7` is in position 3, the `String` class performs all of its operations using zero-based indexing. With that in mind, you can see that the `Chars` method returns the character stored at the position indicated.

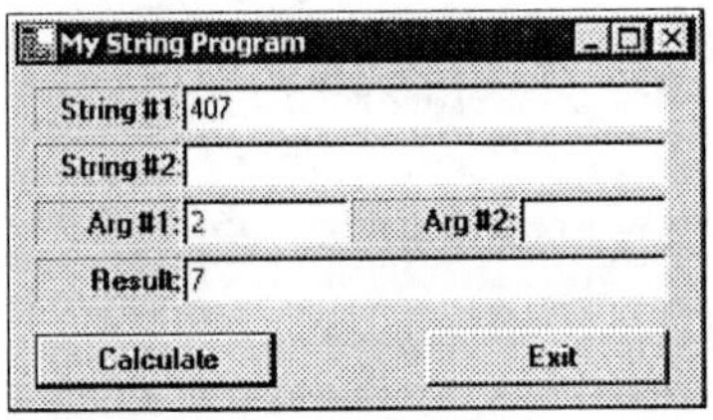

FIGURE 6.15

Sample run using the Chars method.

Comparing Strings—The Compare Method

A common task in a computer program is to compare one string against another string. For example, the user might type in the last name of a customer and then have the program search through a list of all customers trying to find a match to see whether the customer is a new or existing customer.

The Compare method enables you to compare two string values. The syntax for the Compare method is

```
Result = String.Compare(MyString, YourString)
```

The Compare method compares *MyString* to *YourString* and returns an integer value to indicate the outcome of the comparison. If the value returned by Compare is 0, the two strings are identical. A non-zero value means the two strings are different. In most cases, that's all you need to know about using the Compare method. If you're into details, a positive return value means that *MyString* is greater than *YourString*. Think of this value as being determined by a subtraction of the Unicode values in the two strings. For more details, search the Visual Basic .NET online Help for "string comparison" for the index of the search. I'll provide additional details in a minute.

To use this method in our test program, remove the current program statements from the btnCalc Click event and add

```
txtResult.Text = String.Compare(txtString1.Text, txtString2.Text)
```

There are two things to notice in this program statement. First, this is a shared method of the String class. This is why the Compare method is prefixed with String. rather than the name of a string variable. The second thing to notice is that even though Compare returns a numeric value, Visual Basic .NET is smart enough to convert the numeric value to a string and then assign the result into the txtResult text box. (It wouldn't hurt anything, of course, if you enclosed everything on the right side of the equal sign in the parentheses of CStr(), thus converting the integer result to a string.)

Now let's examine some sample runs using the Compare method, as shown in Figure 6.16.

In Figure 6.16, the two strings are different and the result is nonzero as expected. Why is the value a positive 1? If you look at the ASCII codes in Appendix A, you'll find that the value for a capital J is 74. Because both strings begin with a J, 74 minus 74 yields zero. So far, the strings match. Visual Basic .NET then examines the second character in each string and compares them. The o in Joyce is compared to the a in Jack. A lowercase o has an ASCII value of

111, whereas the letter a has an ASCII value of 97. Therefore, because 111 minus 97 produces a result that's greater than 0, the value 1 is returned from the Compare method.

FIGURE 6.16
Sample run using the Compare method; unequal strings.

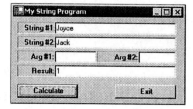

Hmmm. If that's the case, the same logic should produce -1 if we reverse the two strings. This result is shown in Figure 6.17.

FIGURE 6.17
Sample comparison run, reversing the strings.

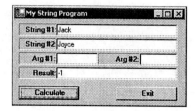

Now try comparing JOYCE with joyce. This test is shown in Figure 6.18.

FIGURE 6.18
Sample comparison run, using uppercase versus lowercase letters in the strings.

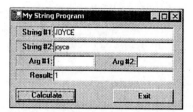

If you look in Appendix A, you'll find that the uppercase J is 74, whereas the lowercase j is 106. If we do the math, 74 minus 106 is −32, which should yield a return value of −1, not a positive 1. Well, Visual Basic .NET throws us a curve here. When comparing strings with the Compare method, Visual Basic .NET scales uppercase letters so that they're numerically greater than lowercase letters. This explains why our other two sample runs performed as expected, but this example does not.

Programmer's Tip

Remember that uppercase letters are scaled to have values that are greater than their lowercase equivalents when used with the Compare method. This might save you some head-scratching later on.

The `Insert` String Method

There are times when you'll need to alter the content of a string variable. Although there are many alternative ways to accomplish such tasks, the `Insert` and `Replace` methods are perhaps the easiest to use. Let's look at the `Insert` method first.

Remove the current program statements from the `btnCalc Click` event and add

```
Dim buff As String
Dim InsertPosition As Integer

buff = txtString1.Text
InsertPosition = CInt(txtArg1.Text)
txtResult.Text = buff.Insert(InsertPosition, txtArg2.Text)
```

In this example, the integer variable is used to tell Visual Basic .NET where to insert the new text into the string. The text to be inserted is held in the `txtArg2` text box, while `txtArg1` holds the character position for the insertion. Figure 6.19 shows a sample run.

FIGURE 6.19

Sample run using the `Insert` method.

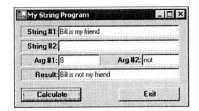

For this sample run to work properly, the word **not** in `txtArg2` does have a blank space after it to give the proper spacing in the result string shown in the `txtResult` text box. Convince yourself that the value of **8** for the first argument produces the proper results.

The `Replace` String Method

The `Replace` method enables you to replace one substring with another. Again, you could write code on your own to accomplish the same thing, but using `Replace` is a lot easier than writing the code yourself. (Who needs to reinvent the wheel?)

Remove the current program statements from the `btnCalc Click` event and add

```
Dim buff As String

buff = txtString1.Text
txtResult.Text = buff.Replace(txtArg1.Text, txtArg2.Text)
```

In this example, the substring held in `txtArg1` is replaced with the text held in `txtArg2`. A sample run is shown in Figure 6.20.

FIGURE 6.20

Sample run using the `Replace` method.

The `txtString1` text box shows the initial string, whereas `txtResult` shows the result after the substring has been replaced. In essence, the `Replace` method locates the first substring, marks its position within the string, deletes the substring characters from the string, and then inserts the replacement string at the position of the original substring. Simple.

As you can see from Figure 6.20, the lengths of the original and replacement substrings do not have to be of equal length. The `Replace` method is smart enough to take care of the details for us.

Other `String` Methods

There are a number other `String` methods available to you, but we're not quite ready to fully understand what they do and how they're used. We'll use some of the other methods in programs that we'll write in later chapters. To whet your appetite for the moment, you can experiment with a program named StringProgram. A sample run using the StringProgram is shown in Figure 6.21.

FIGURE 6.21

Sample run of StringProgram.

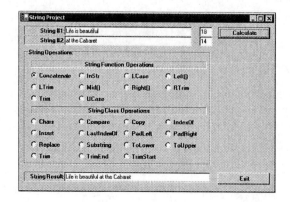

In general, you can get additional information by using the online Help facility with Visual Basic .NET. For now, simply try running StringProgram and figure out what each of the options does and how to use it. By the way, making mistakes running the program won't hurt anything. As I've said before, making mistakes is a great way to learn, especially in a controlled environment! Have fun and experiment.

Summary

In this chapter, I've shown you some of the many ways in which you can manipulate string data in your program. In some cases, we used string functions to manipulate the data. In other cases, we used the methods of the `String` class to manipulate the data.

I also showed you that in some cases, the `String` method and functions provide the same functionality. In those instances where you can use either approach, which is better? Perhaps the correct answer is, "Use either one." However, my choice is to use the `String` class methods whenever possible. It's an OOP world out there, and you might as well get used to it.

Review Questions

When you answer the questions that involve writing code, you can place the statements in the form `Load` event and place a breakpoint at the `End Sub` statement at the end of the form `Load` event. You can then place the cursor over each variable you use and it will show you the value.

1. What is a string variable?

A. A *string variable* is used to store text data in memory.

2. What is the difference between a string variable and a string literal?

A. A string variable can hold any sequence of character data that might be assigned to it. A string literal is a sequence of characters that are surrounded by quotation marks. In the statement

```
buff = "This is a string literal"
```

the variable `buff` is a string variable and the phrase surrounded by quotes is a string literal.

3. Suppose you want to extract the first name from a string. How would you do it? For example, if the name is `Jennifer Hartman`, how would you extract `Jennifer` from the string?

A. First, think about what you want to do. You need to separate the first and last names into two parts and retrieve the first part. You know they are separated by a blank space. Therefore, this problem can be solved using a two-step process: 1) Find where the blank space is, and 2) return everything to the left of the blank space. The code would be

```
Dim Blank As Integer, buff As String, First As String

buff = "Jennifer Hartman"
Blank = InStr(buff, " ")
First = Microsoft.VisualBasic.Left$(buff, Blank - 1)
```

The `InStr()` function returns the character position of where the blank space is. The `Left$()` function returns the leftmost characters from the string named `buff` starting at position 0 and going to position `Blank`−1. If we didn't subtract the 1, we would also have the blank space as part of the first name.

4. With `Option Strict` turned on, Visual Basic .NET does not allow blind casts. (A *blind cast* is when you try to assign one data type into a different data type.) With that in mind, fix the following statement:

```
txtResult.Text = 10
```

A. You need to avoid a blind cast by using a type converter:

```
TxtResult.Text = CStr(10)
```

5. What's the difference with respect to string between a shared method and an instance method?

A. A shared method is one that is inherent to the string class. For example, the statement

```
buff = String.Concat(s1, s2, s3)
```

is a shared method that is inherent for all string class variables. On the other hand, an instance method exists only for an instance of the string object. An example would be

```
length = buff.Length
```

where `Length` is an instance method that is associated with the `buff` string.

6. It's not uncommon to pack data into a string. Suppose that you want to keep information about club members. Let's further assume that the first two bytes are the number of years the person has been a member, the next byte is the member's classification (that is, a Junior, Regular, or Senior member), and the next four characters is the person's club number. Extract the information for the string:

```
"15R0501"
```

A. You can use the substring instance method to derive the results:

```
Dim Years As Integer, Type As String, Num As Integer

buff = "15R0501"
Years = CInt(buff.Substring(0, 2))
Type = buff.Substring(2, 1)
Num = CInt(buff.Substring(3))
```

The `Substring()` method is overloaded. This means you can use it in more than one way. In the first two uses, the first argument is the starting position within the string, and the second argument is the number of characters you want to examine. In the last use, you simply pass in the starting position. In that instance, `Substring` uses everything from that position to the end of the string.

7. What is the difference between and ASCII and Unicode character sets?

A. An ASCII character only uses 7 bits to represent a character. As a result, ASCII defines 128 characters in the ASCII character set. If you look at your keyboard, you'll see that there are fewer than 128 characters shown, so ASCII works fine for the characters we use in the English character set. Unicode characters are 16-bit characters, which means that there can be more than 65,000 different characters in a Unicode character set. Some character sets, such as Chinese or Japanese, may use thousands of characters in their character sets. The Unicode character set accommodates their needs. By default, Visual Basic .NET uses the Unicode character set.

8. Suppose that you have a large block of text stored in a variable named `buff`. You want to search the text for the substring `Vanessa` to find its position in the text. How would you do this?

A. You would use the `IndexOf()` instance method:

```
Position = buff.IndexOf("Vanessa")
```

If the string is found, `Position` will hold the index value of where the substring starts. If `Position` is `-1`, the substring was not found.

CHAPTER 7

ARRAYS

You will learn about the following in this chapter:

- Single-dimensioned arrays and data lists

- User interface design

- Dynamic arrays

- Multidimensional arrays and data tables

- How to determine array boundaries

*I*n this chapter you will learn about a basic data structure called an array. Arrays are used in many computer programs because they afford a convenient way of organizing data. As you will see, arrays are usually an extension of the basic data types provided by Visual Basic .NET. This chapter shows you how you can use arrays in your own programs.

Organizing Data with Arrays

Simply stated, an *array* is a group of one or more data items that share a common name. In previous chapters, we have used a data definition similar to the following statements:

```
Dim DayOfWeek as String
DayOfWeek = "Monday"
```

As you know from earlier chapters, after processing the `Dim` statement, Visual Basic .NET creates an entry in its symbol table and allocates space in memory for a `String` variable named `DayOfWeek`. The second program statement assigns the string literal `"Monday"` into the variable named `DayOfWeek`. This works fine as it is, but what if you want to have variables for each day of the week?

In that case, you could do something like the following:

```
Dim Day0 As String, Day1 As String, Day2 As String, Day3 As String
Dim Day4 As String, Day5 As String, Day6 As String

Day0 = "Monday"
Day1 = "Tuesday"
Day2 = "Wednesday"
        ' We'll skip the obvious statements that follow...
```

You get the idea. This code works fine, but it is not very convenient to use in a program. Obviously, what you want in this case is a list of the days of the week. The code here forces you to reference the seven days of the week as seven different variables. Clearly, the days of the week are conceptually related to each other, and that's the way you would like to reference them: as a related list. That is exactly what arrays allow you to do.

You can simplify the day-of-the-week code as follows:

```
Dim DaysOfTheWeek(6) As String

DaysOfTheWeek (0) = "Monday"
DaysOfTheWeek (1) = "Tuesday"
DaysOfTheWeek (2) = "Wednesday"
        ' ...and so on...
```

The first thing to notice is that you've decreased the number of data definitions from seven to one. Now you have a single data definition of a string array named `DaysOfTheWeek(6)`. What distinguishes this data definition from the previous `String` definitions is the `(6)` after the variable name. The purpose of `(6)` is to set the number of elements in the `DaysOfTheWeek` string array.

Array Elements

Elements? What is an array element? When you define any type of array, you are actually defining a set of variables of the same data type that can be referenced by a single name. Each one of those variables is called an *element* of the array.

So how many elements have you defined for the `DaysOfTheWeek()` array? By default, all arrays in Visual Basic .NET begin with element 0, not element 1. Therefore, this statement:

```
Dim DaysOfTheWeek(6) As String
```

defines array elements `DaysOfTheWeek(0)` through `DaysOfTheWeek(6)`. This means that you have actually defined *seven* elements for the string array named `DaysOfTheWeek()`.

When Visual Basic .NET sees this statement, it pretty much does the same thing it does with any other `Dim` statement. First, it checks to see whether you already have a variable named `DaysOfTheWeek` defined anywhere in the program. If you don't, Visual Basic .NET asks the Windows operating system for enough memory to hold a string array with seven array elements in it. If there is enough free memory for a string array with seven elements, Windows sends a message to Visual Basic .NET, saying everything's okay, and returns an `lvalue` (that is, a memory address) of where to put the array in memory.

Now let's review the next three statements:

```
DaysOfTheWeek (0) = "Monday"
DaysOfTheWeek (1) = "Tuesday"
DaysOfTheWeek (2) = "Wednesday"
```

You already know that the equal sign in such a program statement performs an assignment of the expression on the right of the equal sign into the variable on the left side of the expression.

So what is the purpose of the values in parentheses in each of these expressions? The next section explains.

Array Indexes

To distinguish one element of an array from the others, each element of an array is associated with an *index number*. That index number is used to reference each distinct element of the array. Therefore, the first program line assigns "Monday" into the first element of the DaysOfTheWeek() array, the second line assigns "Tuesday" to the second element of the array, and so on.

Programmer's Tip

Many programmers use the word *subscript* to refer to the index number of an array. The two terms may be used interchangeably.

If you think about the Dim statement for the array, you should now understand the purpose of the 6 in the statement: The value in the parentheses in the Dim statement sets the upper limit of a valid index number for any element in that array. If you tried to access element DaysOfTheWeek(7) of the array, Visual Basic .NET would get upset because it only got enough memory from Windows to access up through element DaysOfTheWeek(6) of the array. If you attempted to access an element larger than the upper limit that was defined for the array, you would get an "Index was outside the bounds of the array" error message. You would also get that error message if you used a negative index number for an array element.

A Simple Program Example Using a String Array

To test your new knowledge of arrays, start a new Visual Basic .NET project and name it StringArray01. Place the controls shown in Figure 7.1 on the form, using the names indicated for the text boxes. The button used to show the day of the week should be named btnShowDay and the Exit button should be named btnExit.

Add the following code to the btnExit object's Click() event:

```
Me.Dispose()
```

This code line for the btnExit button should be fairly familiar to you by now. For this reason, this line is not mentioned in subsequent programs unless you need to add some additional code to the btnExit object's Click() event.

Now add the following code to the btnShowDay object's Click() event:

```
Dim DaysOfTheWeek(6) As String

DaysOfTheWeek(0) = "Monday"
DaysOfTheWeek(1) = "Tuesday"
DaysOfTheWeek(2) = "Wednesday"
DaysOfTheWeek(3) = "Thursday"
```

```
DaysOfTheWeek(4) = "Friday"
DaysOfTheWeek(5) = "Saturday"
DaysOfTheWeek(6) = "Sunday"

txtDay.Text = DaysOfTheWeek(CInt(txtIndex.Text))
```

FIGURE 7.1
Components used in the
`StringArray01` project.

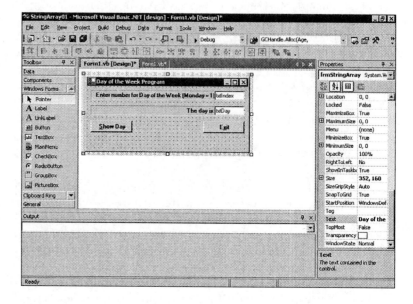

This code should look familiar and probably doesn't need much explanation. The `Dim` statement defines a string array named `DaysOfTheWeek()` that has seven elements. The next seven
lines simply initialize each element of the array with the appropriate string literal for the day,
as determined by the index number for each array element.

The last program line converts the number entered by the user in the `txtIndex` text box into
an integer by using the `CInt()` conversion routine, and it assigns that element of the
`DaysOfTheWeek()` array into the `txtDay` text box. For example, if the user enters the number `3`
into the `txtIndex` text box, the assignment statement is processed as follows:

```
txtDay.Text = DaysOfTheWeek(CInt(txtIndex.Text))
txtDay.Text = DaysOfTheWeek(CInt("3"))  ' "3" is still a string
txtDay.Text = DaysOfTheWeek(3)      ' Now it's a numeric index
txtDay.Text = "Thursday"
```

The user would then see `Thursday` displayed in the `txtDay` text box.

Program Refinements

The `StringArray01` program works fine as it is, but it has a confusing user interface. (The
term *user interface* refers to the screen the user is expected to use to interact with the program.) The user interface is a little confusing because it shows two text boxes on the form as

the program executes, but it expects the user to fill in only the first one. The second text box is used to display the output of the program.

The problem is that users are accustomed to filling in a text box when they see one on a program form. You really don't want the user to type anything into the **txtDay** text box. To fix this problem, make the following changes to the program:

1. Click the label that contains the caption **The Day is:**. (This is probably called **Label2** in your program.)

2. Go to the Properties window. Click the **Visible** property and set its value to **False**. You can see the **Visible** property in the lower-right part of Figure 7.2. You can also see the drop-down list box that shows the value **False** highlighted.

FIGURE 7.2

Setting the **Visible** property for **Label2** to **False**.

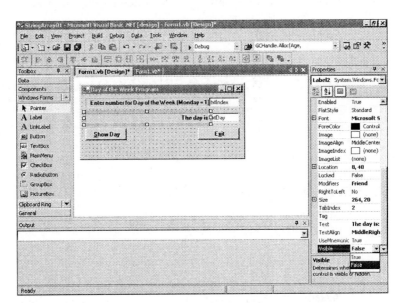

3. Click the **txtDay** text box and set its **Visible** property to **False**. You have now made the **Label2** label and the **txtDay** text box invisible when the program begins execution.

4. Make the following new lines the last two lines in the **btnShowDay** object's **Click()** event:

```
Label2.Visible = True
txtDay.Visible = True
```

5. Compile and run the program. When the program begins execution, it should look as shown in Figure 7.3.

Now the user can only type into the **txtIndex** text box, which is exactly what you want the user to do. After the user types a value into the **txtIndex** text box and clicks the **btnShowDay** button, the last two lines of the program make the second label and the **txtDay** text box visible by changing their `Visible` properties to `True`. The program output would then look like that shown in Figure 7.1, but with the proper day of the week shown in the `txtDay` text box.

FIGURE 7.3
`StringArray01` program execution after you modify the `Visible` property.

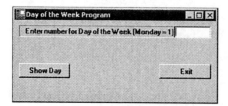

Although the program is now a little more complex than it was before, the user can now more easily interact with the program. It is almost always a good idea to make things as simple as possible for the user, even if it means you must add new code to a program.

Changing the Base Index of an Array

At times, starting an array with an index value of 0 seems counter-intuitive. For example, do users really think of Monday as the zeroth day of the week, or do they think of Monday as the first day of the week? I vote for the second option. Indeed, when a user runs the program shown in Figure 7.1 for the first time, he or she probably wouldn't even think of entering a zero for the index value, even though the label for the text box tells the user that Monday equates to 0. This points out a programming truism: *Users don't read program labels.*

Whether the users read the labels or not, it would be nice to define the array in a way that is consistent with the way you expect to use the array. In the day-of-the-week program, it would make more sense to have Monday have an index value of 1 than an index value of `0`. There are several ways to accomplish this. First, you could change the code to make it look like the following:

```
Dim DaysOfTheWeek(7) As String

DaysOfTheWeek(0) = ""
DaysOfTheWeek(1) = "Monday"
DaysOfTheWeek(2) = "Tuesday"
DaysOfTheWeek(3) = "Wednesday"
        ' ...and so on for the other days...
```

In this solution, you dimension the array for one additional element and assign an empty string to element `0`. The good news is that Monday now has an index value of `1`. The bad news is that you've wasted the memory associated with element `0`. The other bad thing about this approach is that, even though you never intend to use element `0`, because it is there, you could inadvertently use it in a program. As you gain more programming experience, you will find that program bugs often hide in good intentions such as these.

I refer to code like this as RDC (that is, really dumb code) because it wastes memory and it's a potential breeding ground for bugs. Nope, it is not a good solution to the problem. You are better off sticking with your original code, with a minor modification.

First, you need to change the text in the label for the `txtIndex` text box to this:

```
Enter number for Day of the Week (Monday = 1)
```

Next, you need to change the program line that indexes into the `DaysOfTheWeek()` array to the following:

```
txtDay.Text = DaysOfTheWeek(CInt(txtIndex.Text) - 1)
```

Note that the only change here is that you subtract 1 from the array index value typed in by the user. Now, when the user enters 1 for the first day of the week, the statement processes the information as follows:

```
txtDay.Text = DaysOfTheWeek(CInt(txtIndex.Text) - 1)
txtDay.Text = DaysOfTheWeek(CInt("1") - 1)
txtDay.Text = DaysOfTheWeek(1 - 1)
txtDay.Text = DaysOfTheWeek(0)
txtDay.Text = "Monday"
```

This minor program change leads to a much more intuitive interface for the user. The days of the week now run from 1 through 7, which makes more sense than a range of 0 through 6. Two relatively minor program changes have made the program a little bit easier for the user to understand.

Programmer's Tip

Some programming languages allow you to set the lower bound index value of an array to a value other than 0. Indeed, earlier versions of Visual Basic had this feature. Such is no longer the case: All arrays in Visual Basic .NET have a lower bound value of 0.

Dynamic Arrays

In some situations you cannot anticipate how large to make an array. For example, you might have a program that asks the user to enter the names of his or her friends. One user might want to enter four or five names, and another user might want to enter several dozen names. How can you, as the programmer, set the size of the array to accommodate the variation expected in the array size?

One approach is to simply estimate the maximum size that you might reasonably expect the array to have. For example, you might reason that no one is going to enter more than 100 names of friends into the program. This is an RDC approach to the problem, for several reasons.

First, Murphy's Law states that the minute you set the array size to 100, some user is going to try to enter 101 names. This would cause an error, and the program would die an ungraceful death right before the user's eyes. Not good.

Second, some users might have a very limited list of names to enter. If a user enters a list of five names and you've fixed the array size at 100, you've wasted the memory associated with the remaining 95 empty array elements. Although the program would run properly in this case, you should get a nagging feeling in the back of your mind, telling you that you're being wasteful.

The solution to this dilemma is to define a dynamic array. A *dynamic array* is an array that can have its element size set after the array is defined in a program. We can use our previous program to see how to use a dynamic array.

First, you remove the old `Dim` statement from the `btnShowDay` object's `Click()` event and replace it with the following line:

```
Dim DaysOfTheWeek() As String
```

Notice that the new line is almost the same, but you have removed the size (that is, the element count) of the array from the definition. How does Visual Basic .NET handle an array definition with no element size given? Actually, Visual Basic .NET does pretty much the same thing as when the element size is given: It creates an entry in the symbol table for the `DaysOfTheWeek()` string array, but instead of asking Windows for memory, Visual Basic .NET says to Windows: "Hey, Windows! I'm creating an entry for a string array named `DaysOfTheWeek()`, but I don't know exactly how big it is right now. I'll get back to you later." Visual Basic .NET then fills in the symbol table with what it does know about the array (that is, it's a string array and its name is `DaysOfTheWeek`) and postpones the remaining details until later.

Now add the following line to the program's `btnShowDay` object's `Click()` event, immediately following the `Dim` statement you just entered:

```
ReDim DaysOfTheWeek(6)
```

This program statement is used to dimension the `DaysOfTheWeek()` array with elements `0` through `6`. In other words, this statement redimensions the array that you defined earlier (hence the `ReDim` keyword). When Visual Basic .NET sees this program statement, it sends the following message to Windows: "Hey, Windows! Me again. Remember that string array we didn't know the size of? Well, the programmer finally got around to telling me about it, and I need enough memory for a string array with seven elements." The Windows memory manager then looks for enough memory for seven string elements and passes an `lvalue` back to Visual Basic .NET, to specify where the array will reside in memory. If there isn't enough free memory, Visual Basic .NET issues an error message.

The code in the `btnShowDay` object's `Click()` event should now look like this:

```
Dim DaysOfTheWeek() As String

ReDim DaysOfTheWeek(6)

DaysOfTheWeek(0) = "Monday"
DaysOfTheWeek(1) = "Tuesday"
DaysOfTheWeek(2) = "Wednesday"
DaysOfTheWeek(3) = "Thursday"
DaysOfTheWeek(4) = "Friday"
DaysOfTheWeek(5) = "Saturday"
DaysOfTheWeek(6) = "Sunday"

txtDay.Text = DaysOfTheWeek(CInt(txtIndex.Text) - 1)
Label2.Visible = True
txtDay.Visible = True
```

Only the first two lines are different from the earlier version of the program, but the `DaysOfTheWeek()` array in this example uses a dynamic array.

A Subtle Feature of Runtime Use of `ReDim`

In the dynamic array example discussed here, you hard-code the `ReDim` statement to give seven elements in the `DaysOfTheWeek()` array. Obviously, if you know we want seven elements, as you do in this situation, you can just use the old `Dim` statement to define the `DaysOfTheWeek()` array. You really don't need to use a dynamic array.

Suppose, however, that you are working with a "list-your-friends" type of program. Further suppose that a text box, called **txtSize**, prompts the user to enter a number that tells the program how many names of friends he or she wants to enter. Now you could do something like this:

```
Dim MyFriends() As String

ReDim MyFriends(CInt(txtSize.Text) - 1)
```

For example, if the user typed **12** in the **txtSize** text box, the code would be processed like this:

```
ReDim MyFriends(CInt(txtSize.Text) - 1)
ReDim MyFriends(CInt(12) - 1)
ReDim MyFriends(12 - 1)
ReDim MyFriends(11)
```

This would define elements **0** through 11—a total of 12 elements. You should be able to convince yourself that, no matter what number the user would type into the **txtSize** text box, the program would create enough elements in the **MyFriends()** array to hold the list of friends. Note that this method means you can get exactly the storage requirements you need, at runtime, for the **MyFriends()** array. There's no muss, no fuss, no wasted storage by trying to guess what the user *might* need.

The purpose, therefore, of the **ReDim** statement is to dynamically allocate array space when you do not know how much storage is needed at design time. Usually, you have a program determine how much storage is needed at runtime and then use the **ReDim** statement to set the array size. You will see additional examples of the proper use of the **ReDim** statement in later chapters.

Forcing an Error

Obviously, you can generate program errors if you do not use **ReDim** properly. Try changing the **6** for the element size in this **ReDim**:

```
ReDim DaysOfTheWeek(6)
```

statement to **5**, and then recompile the program. The program compiles without error. Now run the program. When the program gets to this line, it dies:

```
DaysOfTheWeek(6) = "Sunday"
```

The program dies because you are trying to index into an element of the array that does not exist.

Note that this error manifests itself while the program is running. Errors that go undetected before the program is run but show up while the program is running are called *runtime errors*. Visual Basic .NET does a good job of catching syntax errors before you even try to run the program. However, there are errors that Visual Basic .NET cannot detect until the program starts running. These runtime errors are usually evidence of semantic or logic errors in the program.

What would happen if you changed the **6** in the **ReDim** statement to **12**? In that case, the program would run without error because you have defined enough elements for every element referenced in the program. The bad news is that you would waste some memory with elements you really don't need.

The Preserve Keyword

Suppose that you have written a program that asks the user to enter a list of friends. Further assume that you have done it correctly and used the **ReDim** statement to resize the array to the size actually needed by the user. For the sake of argument, assume that the user has five friends. Finally, assume that before the program ends, you write the list of five friends to a disk data file so you can retrieve it at a later time.

Now suppose that the user has met a new friend and wants to update the list stored in the disk data file. Through some programming magic that is covered in Chapter 23, "Disk Data Files," the program starts, discovers there are five names stored in the disk data file, and redimensions the name array to hold the five names. Uh-oh. The array can hold only five names, but you want to add a sixth to the list.

This shouldn't be a problem. All you need to do is use another `ReDim` but increase the `ReDim` size by 1 to include the new friend. Changing the `ReDim` from this:

```
ReDim MyFriends(4)
```

to this:

```
ReDim MyFriends(5)
```

provides another element for the user's new friend. However, like any other `Dim` statement, `ReDim` initializes the elements in the array. In the case of the `String` data type, Visual Basic .NET initializes each element in the array to be an empty string. This means that you will have lost the names of the original five friends. Not good.

Fortunately, the problem is easily solved with the `Preserve` keyword. Changing the `ReDim` statement to this:

```
ReDim Preserve MyFriends(5)
```

tells Visual Basic .NET to preserve whatever is currently stored in the array and add any new element(s) to the end of the array. Any new element(s) is initialized to an empty string, but the original five names remain intact.

You do not have to redimension an array one element at a time. That is, if the array currently holds 5 names and you think you might need 10 elements, a single `ReDim` for 10 elements does the job. This is true for `ReDim` statements with or without the `Preserve` keyword.

Programmer's Tip

The `ReDim` statement causes some message passing to occur between Visual Basic .NET and Windows when the statement is executed. This message passing takes time, although the user might not notice it. However, if a program is such that you expect the user to add several new items to an array, it is probably most time-efficient to bump the size up by several elements at a time rather than keep bothering Windows over and over by increasing the array size by one element at a time. Most programmers are willing to waste a few memory resources to make their programs run faster.

You can use the `ReDim` statement to decrease the size of an array. This requires two `ReDim` statements. The first `ReDim` statement is used to set the array's initial size, and the second `ReDim` is used to shrink its size. Although using the `ReDim` statement to shrink an array is a bit unusual, you might find a situation in which it makes sense to do so, perhaps if memory is at a premium.

Multidimensional Arrays

As you have seen, an array is great for holding a list of data. The list of data might be the names of friends or things needed from the grocery store. Other situations, however, require that you have a table of data. A data table is multidimensional. That is, tables of data have two dimensions: rows and columns. For example, suppose you wanted to have a table of squares for the integer values **0** through **5**. You might write that table on a piece of paper like this:

Number	Square
0	0
1	1
2	4
3	9
4	16
5	25

In this example, the table has six rows and two columns. You can reconstruct this table with a simple program.

You should start a new project and call it **TableProgram**. Then, you need to place two labels, two text boxes, and two buttons on the form, as shown in Figure 7.4. As shown in Figure 7.4, you should name the Calculate button **btnCalc** and the Exit button **btnExit**. As in the days-of-the-week program, you need to set the **Visible** property of the **txtResult** text box and its associated label (**lblResult**) to **False** so that they are invisible until after the Calculate button is clicked.

Now you need to add the following code to the **btnCalc** object's **Click()** event:

```
Dim SquaresTable(5, 1) As Integer

SquaresTable(0, 0) = 0
SquaresTable(0, 1) = 0
SquaresTable(1, 0) = 1
SquaresTable(1, 1) = 1
SquaresTable(2, 0) = 2
SquaresTable(2, 1) = 4
SquaresTable(3, 0) = 3
SquaresTable(3, 1) = 9
SquaresTable(4, 0) = 4
SquaresTable(4, 1) = 16
SquaresTable(5, 0) = 5
SquaresTable(5, 1) = 25

txtResult.Text = CStr(SquaresTable(CInt(txtNumber.Text), 1))

lblResult.Visible = True
txtResult.Visible = True
```

FIGURE 7.4
Component placement for the `TableProgram` program.

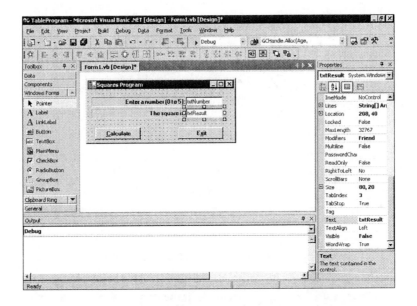

You should look at the dimension statement for the `SquareTable()` array. The `Dim` statement tells Visual Basic .NET to define an array that has **0** through **5** rows and **0** through **1** columns. This array layout is shown in Table 7.1.

TABLE 7.1   Indexes for the `SquaresTable()` Array

N	Square of N
0, 0	0, 1
1, 0	1, 1
2, 0	2, 1
3, 0	3, 1
4, 0	4, 1
5, 0	5, 1

The next 12 program statements fill in the actual values for the array. These 12 program statements result in a table that looks like Table 7.2.

TABLE 7.2 Values in the `SquaresTable()` Array

N	Square of N
0	0
1	1
2	4
3	9
4	16
5	25

This statement:

```
txtResult.Text = CStr(SquaresTable(CInt(txtNumber.Text), 1))
```

simply converts the value typed in by the user into an integer value that is to be used as the index into the array. For example, if the user types **4** into the `txtNumber` text box, the statement is processed as follows:

```
txtResult.Text = CStr(SquaresTable(CInt(txtNumber.Text), 1))
txtResult.Text = CStr(SquaresTable(CInt("4"), 1))
txtResult.Text = CStr(SquaresTable(4, 1))
txtResult.Text = CStr(16)     ' Position 4,1 in Table 7.2 is 16
txtResult.Text = "16"     ' Made into a string for text box
```

The string `"16"` is placed in the `txtResult` text box. The remaining two lines simply make the `lblResult` and `txtResult` controls visible. A sample run of this program is shown in Figure 7.5.

FIGURE 7.5
A sample run of the `TableProgram` program.

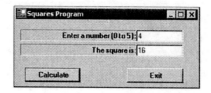

You should walk through each line of code shown in Listing 7.1 and confirm that the program displays the proper result:

LISTING 7.1 Complete Code for the `TableProgram` Program

```
Public Class frmTable

 Inherits System.Windows.Forms.Form

 Private Sub btnCalc_Click(ByVal sender As System.Object, ByVal e As
 System.EventArgs) Handles btnCalc.Click
```

LISTING 7.1   Continued

```
Dim SquaresTable(5, 1) As Integer
Dim MyArray(,) As Integer

'  ReDim MyArray(10, 10)

ReDim MyArray(3, 5)

SquaresTable(0, 0) = 0
SquaresTable(0, 1) = 0
SquaresTable(1, 0) = 1
SquaresTable(1, 1) = 1
SquaresTable(2, 0) = 2
SquaresTable(2, 1) = 4
SquaresTable(3, 0) = 3
SquaresTable(3, 1) = 9
SquaresTable(4, 0) = 4
SquaresTable(4, 1) = 16
SquaresTable(5, 0) = 5
SquaresTable(5, 1) = 25

txtResult.Text = CStr(SqaresTable(CInt(txtNumber.Text), 1))

lblResult.Visible = True
txtResult.Visible = True

End Sub

Private Sub btnExit_Click(ByVal sender As System.Object, ByVal e As
System.EventArgs) Handles btnExit.Click
  Me.Dispose()
End Sub
End Class
```

Multidimensional Arrays with More Than Two Dimensions

You can create a multidimensional array that has more than two dimensions. For example, this statement:

```
Dim MyCube(10, 5, 3) As Integer
```

defines an array named **MyCube()** with 11 rows, 6 columns, and a depth of 4 integers. This array could be visualized as a cube.

So, how many dimensions can an array have? Visual Basic .NET gives you the ability to define an array with 32 dimensions. However, I'm not as smart as Stephen Hawking and have never used anything with more than 3 dimensions. Indeed, I have tried to think of an example using 4 or more dimensions, and all I have to show for my efforts is a headache.

Dynamic Multidimensional Arrays

Earlier in the chapter you learned how to define a dynamic array and use the `ReDim` statement to redimension an array to a new size. Can you also redimension multidimensional arrays? Suppose you try the following:

```
Dim MyArray() As Integer

ReDim MyArray(5, 5)
```

If you try to compile a program with these two lines in it, Visual Basic .NET gets upset and tells you `ReDim cannot change the number of dimensions of an array`. In other words, Visual Basic .NET thinks that the `Dim` statement is for a one-dimensional array—information that Visual Basic .NET recorded in its symbol table when it processed the `Dim` statement. Therefore, the `Dim` statement must not be conveying the proper information to Visual Basic .NET. How can you tell it to create a multidimensional array in the `Dim` statement without supplying any index values in the `Dim` statement?

Remember that when you wanted a one-dimensional dynamic array, you simply left out any value for the index in the `Dim` statement. Would the same concept apply in a multidimensional dynamic array? Suppose you left out the actual numbers but left in the comma between the two numbers:

```
Dim MyArray( , ) As Integer

ReDim MyArray(5, 5)
```

These two statements compile without error. Make sure you notice the lonely comma between the parentheses in the `Dim` statement. The comma tips Visual Basic .NET off to the fact that you want to create a two-dimensional dynamic array.

What if you need a three-dimensional dynamic array? In that case, this allows you to define a three-dimensional dynamic array:

```
Dim MyArray( , , ) As Integer

ReDim MyArray(10, 5, 4)
```

The rule is simple:

> To create an N-dimensional dynamic array, place N–1 commas inside the parentheses in the array's `Dim` statement.

As you just saw, a two-dimensional dynamic array (that is, N=2) requires one comma inside the parentheses (2–1=1 comma). A three-dimensional array requires two commas (that is, 3–1=2). A four-dimensional array requires three commas (that is, 4–1=3) plus a lot more math skills that I possess.

Determining the Size of an Array

As shown in this chapter, you can increase or decrease the size of a dynamic array according to the needs of the program. Although this offers you great flexibility, there are times when you need to know how many elements are currently defined for the array. After all, if you try to access an element that is larger than the array is dimensioned for, you get a runtime error message from Visual Basic .NET.

In such situations, it would be nice to know exactly how large the array is. Being armed with information about the size of an array allows you to write code that can trap values that could cause errors in the program. Such defensive coding is called *error trapping*. You will learn a lot more about error trapping in Chapter 19, "Error Processing and Debugging."

To determine the size of the dynamic array you created earlier, you can add the following new lines to the `btnShowDay` object's `Click()` event:

```
Dim MyArray( , ) As Integer
Dim lo As Integer, hi As Integer

ReDim MyArray(5, 3)

hi = UBound(MyArray)
lo = LBound(MyArray)
```

The first line simply defines a two-dimensional dynamic array of integers named `MyArray()`. The second line defines two new integer variables that you can use in the program. The third line redimensions the dynamic array to have six rows and four columns. (Remember that the numbers in the `Dim` and `ReDim` statements are the upper limits of valid index values. And because arrays begin with element 0, you always get one more element than it appears you have defined.)

The `UBound()` function returns the largest valid row index number of the `MyArray()` array. In our example, the variable `hi` would be assigned the value `5`. The `UBound()` value is always equal to the first dimension of the array. That is, if you reversed the dimensions so that the `ReDim` statement is read as follows:

```
ReDim MyArray(3, 5)
```

the variable `hi` would equal `3`, not `5`. This would be true regardless of the number of dimensions in the array.

The next program statement uses the `LBound()` function to return the index value of the lowest valid index number for the `DaysOfTheWeek()` array. Actually, `LBound()` is a lot less useful in Visual Basic .NET than it is in earlier releases of Visual Basic because the lower boundary for all arrays in Visual Basic .NET is now always `0`. Remember that earlier releases of Visual Basic allow you to set the lower boundary value for the array to something other than `0`.

Armed with information about the lower and upper bounds of the array (as stored in the values for `lo` and `hi`), you can check the value entered by the user *before* you use it to index into the array. You will see exactly how to write such error trapping code in Chapter 19. For now, you just need to know that there is a way to determine the size of an array while the program is running.

Summary

In this chapter you have studied a data structure called an array. You have learned that one-dimensional arrays are useful for storing lists of data and two-dimensional arrays are often used for data tables. You have also seen how you can change the size of an array during program execution by using dynamic arrays.

Keep in mind that even though this chapter uses only string and integer arrays, you can define arrays for any data type supported by Visual Basic .NET. You should try typing in the programs presented in this chapter and experimenting with them. In particular, you should try to access array elements that are not defined to see how Visual Basic .NET handles such errors. You might also modify the `TableProgram` program to process the `Double` data type so that fractional values can be entered into the program. Once again, experimentation is a great way to learn, and I encourage you to experiment as much as possible.

Review Questions

1. What is an array?

A. An array is a data structure that allows you to reference multiple values of a data type by using a single name.

2. What's wrong with the following data declaration?

```
Dim MyArray as Integer
```

A. First, the statement is attempting to define a data item, not to declare it. The problem is that Visual Basic .NET does not see the definition as an array definition. Instead, it defines a single integer variable named `MyArray`. To make an array of 10 integers, you would define it like this:

```
Dim MyArray(9) as Integer
```

3. In the following statement, how much storage is required for the array?

```
Dim MyArray(10) as Double
```

A. Visual Basic .NET uses the number 10 in this statement to determine how much storage to request from the operating system. Each `Double` data type takes 8 bytes. Remember that arrays start with element 0 by default, and the number `10` in the statement is the highest subscript allowed for the array. Therefore, elements 0 through 10 are valid, which means 11 numbers have 8 bytes each—88 bytes total. Therefore, Windows returns 88 bytes of storage.

4. What role does the type specifier play in fetching an array value?

A. Suppose you have an array named **MyArray** that contains 10 integers that are stored starting at memory location **1000**. Because the type specifier tells you the type for the data item being stored, and because each integer takes 4 bytes of storage, the array looks like this in memory:

	1004		1012		1020		1028		1036
0	1	2	3	4	5	6	7	8	9
1000		1008		1016		1024		1032	

To read element 5 (which is actually subscript 4), Visual Basic .NET takes the **lvalue** of **1000**, and adds the product of the subscript (**4**) multiplied by the storage required for each element of the array (**2** bytes), and adds that product to the **lvalue**. This gives Visual Basic .NET the proper memory address to fetch the value. Using the information provided:

MemoryAddress = lvalue + (Subscript × BytesPerItem)

MemoryAddress = 1000 + (4 × 4)

MemoryAddress = 1016

Therefore, **MyArray(4)** is located at memory address **1016**, which agrees with the array diagram. It also follows that Visual Basic .NET uses the type specifier to figure out the proper offset from the **lvalue** to fetch the proper element of the array.

5. How do you define a dynamic array?

A. Defining a dynamic array is a two-step process. First, you define a reference to the array with this statement:

```
Dim MyArray() as String
```

This places a reference variable in the symbol table, but no actual array storage is yet defined. At some later point in the program, you need this statement:

```
ReDim MyArray(9)
```

which defines an array of 10 strings (that is, 0–9). If you later want to increase the array so that it has more than 10 elements, you would use this:

```
ReDim Preserve MyArray(19)
```

This causes 10 new (empty) strings to be added to the array, but it preserves the string content for the first 10 elements.

6. Suppose you want to define an array whose first element is 1 instead of 0. How would you define the array?

A. You don't. All arrays in Visual Basic .NET start with 0.

7. How do you define a multidimensional array that will be used to store a table of values? The first dimension should be used to hold the number, and the second dimension should hold the square of that number. You should make the array large enough to hold the values 0 through 100.

A. This is the statement to define this multidimensional array:

```
Dim MyArray(100,1) as Integer
```

Too often, students define this array as `MyArray(100,100)`, which is wasteful. The proper assignment for the number 5, for example, would be this:

```
MyArray(5,0) = 5
MyArray(5,1) = 25
```

8. Suppose you have a text box named `txtNumber` into which the user types a number. Further assume that an array named `MyArray()` is capable of storing 1,000 numbers. The value typed into `txtNumber` is to be copied into the element that matches the number that was typed in. For example, if the text box holds the value 100, `MyArray(100)` should equal `100`.

A. The following statements should do the trick:

```
Dim MyArray(1000) As Integer, Index As integer

Index = cint(txtNumber.Text)
MyArray(Index) = Index
```

CHAPTER 8

SCOPE AND LIFETIME OF VARIABLES

> **You will learn about the following in this chapter:**
>
> - Scope
> - Local scope, block scope, and module scope
> - Namespaces
>
> - Variable lifetime
> - Storage classes

O ne of the central themes of object-oriented programming (OOP) is encapsulation. As discussed in Chapter 2, "The Basics of Object-Oriented Programming," the idea behind encapsulation is to hide the data and methods associated with an object so they can't be contaminated by outside forces. In some non-OOP languages, making a program change in one section of code has side effects in other, seemingly unrelated, sections of the program. It's like trying to pull on one thread in a spider web and expecting all the other threads to remain unmoved: It just doesn't happen that way.

As an OOP language, Visual Basic .NET provides ways to minimize the impact of these side effects rippling through your code. In this chapter, you will learn how to isolate code and keep it from being contaminated by outside forces. Clearly, this is a good thing and will help you to write better, more bug-proof, code.

What Is Scope?

Scope refers to the visibility and life of a data item or object. Perhaps an example will help you to understand the concept of scope. Chapter 6, "String Variables," discusses a number of string functions that Visual Basic .NET provides. Some examples of these are the `Len()`, `Left()`, `Right()`, and `Mid()` functions.

In a sense, these string functions are like black boxes. You shove some data through the front door of the black box, and some desired result emerges from the back door. You can't see what's inside the black box. You have no idea what variables, objects, or other data items might be used inside the box. Although you can be relatively sure that some data items are being used inside the black box, it's an exclusive club to which you don't belong. In other words, the data that is defined inside the black box is not visible to you. Because you know nothing about the black box's data, the *scope* of the data being used inside the black box is visible (and usable) only inside the black box.

The concept of scope, therefore, relates to the accessibility of a data item or object. In most cases, you want to limit the scope of an object. That is, you want to keep the scope of a data item confined to only those objects and methods that need to have access to it. The more data that you can hide in little black boxes, the less chance there is of someone or something else messing it up. You want to define your data in such a way that the data exists only on a "need-to-know" basis. In OOP terms, you want to *encapsulate* your data as much as possible.

In the following sections you'll write a short program that will expand your understanding of what scope is and how you can use it to your advantage.

Local (Procedural) Scope

To examine the concept of scope in greater detail, you should create a new project and name it `LocalScope`. Add two buttons to the form and name them `btnCalc` and `btnExit`. The form should look something like the form shown in Figure 8.1.

FIGURE 8.1
The form for the
`LocalScope` project.

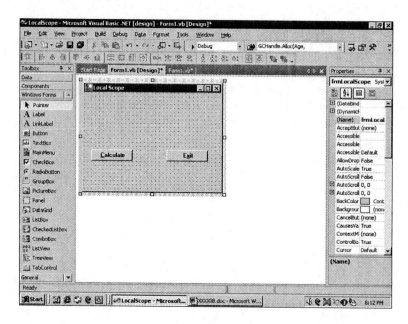

Add the code shown in Listing 8.1 to the `btnCalc` object's `Click()` event.

LISTING 8.1   Code for the `btnCalc` Object's `Click()` Event

```
Private Sub btnCalc_Click(ByVal sender As System.Object, ByVal e As _
              System.EventArgs) Handles btnCalc.Click
  Dim MyVariable As Integer

  MyVariable = 10

End Sub
```

All you've done is define a variable named **MyVariable** and assigned the value **10** to it. Now you need to copy the assignment statement to the **btnExit** object's **Click()** event so that its code reads as follows:

```
Private Sub btnExit_Click(ByVal sender As System.Object, ByVal e As _
              System.EventArgs) Handles btnExit.Click

  MyVariable = 10
  Me.Dispose()

End Sub
```

If you compile the program, what happens? You get the following error message:

```
'MyVariable' is not declared.
```

That's strange. You defined the variable named **MyVariable** in the **btnCalc** object's **Click()** event, but Visual Basic .NET is telling you it has no clue what **MyVariable** is.

The reason Visual Basic .NET doesn't know about **MyVariable** in the **btnExit** object's **Click()** event is that you defined **MyVariable** in the **btnCalc** object's **Click()** event. Whenever you define a variable within a subroutine, as you did with **MyVariable**, the scope of that variable extends from its definition statement (that is, its **Dim** statement) to the end of the subroutine in which it is defined. Therefore, **MyVariable**'s scope extends only from the **Dim** statement to the **End Sub** for the **btnCalc** object's **Click()** event. This is an example of *local scope*. A variable with local scope exists only within the subroutine or function in which it is defined.

Programmer's Tip

Local scope is sometimes referred to as *procedural scope* because subroutines and functions are also called *procedures* in Visual Basic .NET. You can use the terms interchangeably, although I prefer the term *local scope*. Also, rather than write *subroutines and procedures* each time some concept applies to both, I simply refer to them collectively as *procedures*.

Because you tried to use **MyVariable** inside **btnExit**, Visual Basic .NET does not know about **MyVariable** because it is out of scope. The scope for **MyVariable** does not extend to the **btnExit** subroutine; therefore, there is no way for Visual Basic .NET to know about **MyVariable** outside **btnCalc**. Listing 8.2 shows the scope for **MyVariable**.

LISTING 8.2   The Local Scope for `MyVariable`

```
Private Sub btnCalc_Click(ByVal sender As System.Object, ByVal e As _
          System.EventArgs) Handles btnCalc.Click
 Dim MyVariable As Integer  ' MyVariable scope starts here....
        ' ...still in scope...
 MyVariable = 10    ' ...still in scope...
        ' ...still in scope...
 End Sub          ' MyVariable scope ends here...out of scope
```

The important thing to keep in mind about local scope is that variables that have local scope only live within the function or subroutine in which they are defined.

How does Visual Basic .NET keep track of a variable's scope? You don't really need to know the details of how Visual Basic .NET tracks a variable's scope; basically, it uses a coding scheme to index each variable's scope and maintains that information in the symbol table.

Scope and Duplicate Definition Errors

Another way to prove the idea of local scope is to place a second definition for `MyVariable` at the same local scope level as the first. This is shown in Listing 8.3.

LISTING 8.3   Two Variables with the Same Name and the Same Scope

```
Private Sub btnCalc_Click(ByVal sender As System.Object, ByVal e As _
          System.EventArgs) Handles btnCalc.Click
 Dim MyVariable As Integer

 MyVariable = 10
 Dim MyVariable As Integer

 End Sub
```

You should make the code changes shown in Listing 8.3. (It's the same as Listing 8.1, except for the second `Dim` statement.) Then if you compile the program, you get this error message:

```
Local variable 'MyVariable' is already declared in the current block.
```

Visual Basic .NET is trying to tell you, "I'm confused. You have already defined a variable named `MyVariable` at this scope level, and now you're trying to do it again. Don't do that!" In other words, Visual Basic .NET has looked in the symbol table and found that a variable called `MyVariable` already exists at that scope level. Because two variables cannot have the same name at the same scope level, Visual Basic .NET has no choice but to issue an error message.

The Same Variable Name, Different Scope Levels

What would happen if you used the same variable name as before but defined it in a different procedure? To see what happens in this case, place a duplicate definition statement for `MyVariable` in the `btnExit` object's `Click()` event. The code for both events appears in Listing 8.4.

LISTING 8.4   Variable Definitions with the Same Name but Different Levels of Local Scope

```
Private Sub btnCalc_Click(ByVal sender As System.Object, ByVal e As _
            System.EventArgs) Handles btnCalc.Click
  Dim MyVariable As Integer

  MyVariable = 10

End Sub

Private Sub btnExit_Click(ByVal sender As System.Object, ByVal e As _
            System.EventArgs) Handles btnExit.Click
  Dim MyVariable As Integer

  MyVariable = 20
  Me.Dispose()

End Sub
```

Now if you try to compile the program, you don't have any problem, do you? Why doesn't Visual Basic .NET complain about the variable named `MyVariable` being defined twice in the program? The reason Visual Basic .NET doesn't complain is because they are *not* the same variable. The variable named `MyVariable` that is defined in the `btnCalc` object's `Click()` event has a level of scope that extends only to the `End Sub` statement for the `btnCalc` object's `Click()` event; that is, `MyVariable` only lives inside the `btnCalc` object's `Click()` event. `MyVariable` is invisible outside the `btnCalc` object's `Click()` event. The two `MyVariable` variables are different variables with different `lvalue` values. The same applies to the `MyVariable` variable defined in the `btnExit` object's `Click()` event. It lives only within the body of the `btnExit` object's `Click()` event subroutine. Outside that subroutine, `MyVariable` does not exist.

Because each instance of `MyVariable` has a scope that is limited to the subroutine in which it is defined, there is no name conflict between subroutines. Local scope means the life and visibility of a variable with local scope are limited to the procedure body in which it is defined.

Clearly, local scope is a good thing for variables because it has a black-box effect. In essence, the black box is the statement body for the procedure in which the variable is defined. There is no way for anything outside the statement body to access a variable with local scope. This also means there is no way for any outside agent to alter the value of a data item that has local scope. In almost all situations, this data privacy is a good thing.

Programmer's Tip

As you have seen in this section, variables that are defined within a procedure have local scope. Programmers often refer to such variables as *local variables*. This simply means that the variables have local scope and are not accessible outside the procedure in which they are defined.

Block Scope

Although it is not used all that often in Visual Basic .NET programs, an even more restrictive scope level than local scope is available within a subroutine or function. *Block scope* applies to all data items that are defined with a statement block. (Although we haven't covered the keywords fully, this is the proper time and place to discuss block scope.) The statements that can be used in conjunction with block scope are `If-Then-Else`, `For-Next`, and `Do-Loop`.

An example will help you understand how block scope works. To begin, remove the present code from the `btnCalc` object's `Click()` event and then add to it the code presented in Listing 8.5.

LISTING 8.5   An Example of Block Scope

```
Dim i As Integer      ' Local scope

If i = 0 Then
 Dim j As Integer     ' Start of block scope for j
 j = 10       ' Block scope for j
End If        ' End of block scope for j

Debug.WriteLine(j)
```

Now if you try to compile the program, you get the following error message:

```
Name 'j' is not declared.
```

The line that causes the error message is the `Debug.WriteLine(j)` statement. This happens because you have defined the variable name j within the `If-Then` statement block. The statement block extends from the opening `If` statement to the closing `End If` statement. Any code between these keyword statements is considered part of the `If` statement block. The variable j, therefore, is in scope only from its `Dim` statement to the `End If` statement. Because `Debug.WriteLine(j)` attempts to use j outside its statement block, Visual Basic .NET issues an error message.

Programmer's Tip

The `Debug.WriteLine()` statement in Listing 8.5 is a debug method that is provided by Visual Basic .NET. It allows you to print variables and other data contained within the parentheses in the Debug window while the program runs.

The Same Variable Name at Different Scope Levels

If you changed the references to j in Listing 8.5 to i, would you get a duplicate variable error message? The code fragment that changes the reference follows:

```
Dim i As Integer      ' Local scope

If i = 0 Then
 Dim i As Integer     ' Start of block scope for i
 i = 10        ' Block scope for i
End If       ' End of block scope for i
```

```
Debug.WriteLine(i)
```

In this case, you get an error message that states Variable 'i' hides a variable in an enclosing block. This happens because i is used in the If statement and, therefore, becomes part of the If statement block. Now you should move the definition of i outside the Click() event, toward the top of the program, after this statement:

```
Inherits System.Windows.Forms.Form
Dim i as integer
```

When you compile the program now, does Visual Basic .NET issue the same error message?

The answer is no: If you move the definition of i outside the button's Click() event, you do not get a duplicate variable error message. The reason is because the second definition for variable i occurs at a different scope level. The first i is at the module scope level, and the second definition of i is at the block scope level. Variables defined at different scope levels can have the same name.

Another interesting issue to determine is which i is used in this statement from the preceding code block:

```
i = 10       ' Block scope for i
```

As the comment suggests, the assignment applies to the i defined at the block level. As a general rule, if two variables with the same name are both in scope, the most-recently defined variable is the variable that is being accessed. Note that the first i defined in the code fragment has a different scope level, called *module scope*, so it is in scope from its definition to the end of the module. (Module scope is explained in the next section. For the moment, just recognize that module scope is different from local scope.) This also means that its scope wraps around the scope for the variable i that is defined within the If statement block. However, the i that is defined within the If statement block takes precedence in the If statement block because it is the variable that was defined last.

Now determine which variable i is used in this statement:

```
Debug.WriteLine(i)
```

It must be the i with module scope because the i with block scope no longer exists. It died when you left the If statement block.

As you can see, block scope is limited to whatever keyword pairs (If-End If, For-Next, and so on) form the statement block. Any data item that is defined within a statement block has its scope limited to that statement block. This is similar to local scope in that local scope extends from the Dim within the subroutine or function to its End Sub or End Function statement.

Block scope extends from its `Dim` to the end of the statement block. However, because statement blocks usually appear within a procedure block, block scope is usually more restrictive.

Variables that employ block scope are a bit unusual. I could present a rather contrived example, but it's not really necessary to do so. You should remember that block scope exists because there may come a time when it proves useful to you.

Module Scope

Earlier in this chapter you saw how local scope keeps you from having a variable that is defined in one subroutine changed by being used in some other subroutine. This means that you can use local scope to hide data. That data privacy helps keep the data from being contaminated by other segments of the program.

However, hiding is not always a good thing (in courtship, for example). Even in programs, there are times when you want multiple procedures to have access to a single piece of data. In terms of this chapter's earlier example, you might want both `btnCalc` and `btnExit` to have access to `MyVariable`. You can make this happen by defining a data item so that it has module scope.

Module scope means that every procedure within that module has full access to the data item. For the moment, you can think of the program form as being the module that grants module scope. Look carefully at Listing 8.6. It presents all the code currently associated with the form named `frmLocalScope`.

LISTING 8.6   All the Program Code for the Module `frmLocalScope`

```
Public Class frmLocalScope
 Inherits System.Windows.Forms.Form
 Dim MyVariable As Integer

 Private Sub Form1_Load(ByVal sender As System.Object, ByVal e As _
          System.EventArgs) Handles MyBase.Load
 End Sub

 Private Sub btnCalc_Click(ByVal sender As System.Object, ByVal e As _
          System.EventArgs) Handles btnCalc.Click
  MyVariable = 20
 End Sub

 Private Sub btnExit_Click(ByVal sender As System.Object, ByVal e As _
          System.EventArgs) Handles btnExit.Click
  MyVariable = 20
  Me.Dispose()
 End Sub
End Class
```

Notice that the definition of `MyVariable` has been moved from the `btnCalc` object's `Click()` event to the third line from the top of the program in Listing 8.6. In Listing 8.2, the definition of `MyVariable` is within the `btnCalc` object's `Click()` event. Because the definition occurs within the `btnCalc` subroutine, it has local scope in Listing 8.2.

Class Definition

In Listing 8.6, notice the first line:

```
Public Class frmLocalScope
```

and the last line:

```
End Class
```

As you might guess, everything between these two lines defines the statement body for the class named `frmLocalScope`. With the exception of four lines in Listing 8.6, Visual Basic .NET automatically wrote the class definition for `frmLocalScope`. Collectively, you can call all the code in Listing 8.6 the `frmLocalScope` `Class` module; `frmLocalScope` is the module to which module scope applies.

The third line in Listing 8.6 is the definition of `MyVariable`. Note that the definition of `MyVariable` is outside any procedure but is contained within the `frmLocalScope` module. Because the class definition for `frmLocalScope` is the module for the program, `MyVariable` has module scope.

The code in Listing 8.6 compiles without error, even though you have accessed `MyVariable` in both the `btnCalc` and `btnExit` objects' `Click()` events. Your earlier attempts to use `MyVariable` in `btnExit` objects' `Click()` event drew error messages because `MyVariable` was out of scope.

In Listing 8.6, because the definition of `MyVariable` occurs outside any procedure, `MyVariable` has module scope. Because it has module scope, you can use the variable at any point in the module after it has been defined (that is, after the `Dim` statement in line 3). Therefore, the good news is that `MyVariable` is accessible everywhere in the `frmLocalScope` class definition. The bad news is also that `MyVariable` is accessible everywhere in the `frmLocalScope` class definition. Data items that have module scope cannot hide from anything within the module. By giving `MyVariable` module scope, you give up data privacy for `MyVariable` in the `frmLocalScope` class definition.

When should you sacrifice the benefits of data privacy and use module scope? Alas, I cannot fully answer that question now because there are additional details about Visual Basic .NET that you need to understand first. However, you will learn more about this in later chapters.

Dim, Private, and Module Scope

The placement of the definition of `MyVariable` in Listing 8.6 gives it module scope. As discussed in the preceding section, module scope means that everything within the module has access to `MyVariable` and can change the value of `MyVariable` if it wants to. `MyVariable` has module scope with respect to the `frmLocalScope` class definition. Stated another way, everything within the `frmLocalScope` class knows the `lvalue` of `MyVariable`.

What about access to `MyVariable` outside the `frmLocalScope` class definition? By default, the definition of `MyVariable`, as shown in this statement, is private to the `frmLocalScope` class:

```
Dim MyVariable As Integer
```

This means that if the program had multiple forms and modules, none of those other forms or modules would be able to access the variable named `MyVariable`.

The scope of `MyVariable` is confined to the `frmLocalScope` module, and it is a common convention in Visual Basic .NET to replace the module scope definition shown in Listing 8.6:

```
Dim MyVariable As Integer
```

with this definition:

```
Private MyVariable As Integer
```

Most Visual Basic .NET programmers prefer this notation because it reaffirms that the variable is private to this module and is not available for use in any other form or module in the program.

Namespaces

Chapter 2 points out that the .NET Framework is a huge collection of thousands of classes that are made available to you. The granddaddy of all these classes is the `System` class. Virtually everything in the .NET Framework is derived from this one class.

However, in an attempt to make this massive collection of classes more manageable, Visual Basic .NET divides the `System` class into smaller groups of classes, each with its own namespace. The *namespace*, therefore, is the way you reference classes in Visual Basic .NET to avoid ambiguity. You have already seen examples of this when you have used forms in your sample programs. The components you have used in this chapter are part of the `System.Windows.Forms` namespace. If you look near the top of Listing 8.6, you see this line:

```
Inherits System.Windows.Forms.Form
```

This line is necessary because you want to use the functionality provided by the Visual Basic .NET forms and the objects you can use with forms. Therefore, in Listing 8.6, you are making the classes that are part of the `System.Windows.Forms` namespace available to you.

It might not be obvious that Visual Basic .NET automatically creates a namespace for every executable program file you create. The namespace has the same name as your project. For example, suppose you create a new project named `MyNewProject`. Further assume that your program is somewhat large, and you have three forms in the program. To keep this example simple, assume that these forms are named `InputForm`, `DisplayForm`, and `PrintReportForm`.

Now assume that you have a variable named `MyPrinter` that is defined with module scope in the `PrintReportForm` module. You can use this variable anywhere in the `PrintReportForm` module by simply using the name `MyPrinter`. But to the other two forms, the variable is not even visible because it is out of scope. Remember that module scope for a variable extends from its point of definition to the end of the class definition.

The Purpose of Namespaces

Suppose you were presenting a paper on a program you wrote, and you wanted to say something about the `MyPrinter` variable. To do this properly and without ambiguity, the reference would have to be: `MyNewProject.PrintReportForm.MyPrinter`. Notice that this reference format clearly identifies where the `MyPrinter` variable exists. As you can see, the purpose of namespaces is to reduce ambiguity and prevent name collisions.

A *name collision* occurs when you attempt to define a second variable with the same name and at the same scope level as another variable. (A name collision produces a duplicate definition error, as you saw earlier in this chapter, in the section "Scope and Duplicate Definition Errors.") The proper use of a namespace, however, helps prevent name collisions. For example, how many forms have you created that have `btnExit` buttons on them? A bunch, and that's just an estimate. Why isn't there a name collision for `btnExit`? Even though you have in many different programs a button object that uses the same name, it's not a problem because the full namespace for the `btnExit` object is prefixed with the namespaces for both the form that holds the button and the project that holds the form.

In the hypothetical program mentioned in the preceding section, even if the `InputForm`, `DisplayForm`, and `PrintReportForm` modules all have `btnExit` buttons, there is no name collision. The reason is that the namespace for each button is unique (for example, `MyNewProject.InputForm.btnExit` versus `MyNewProject.DisplayForm.btnExit`). Even though the `btnExit` buttons share the same name, Visual Basic .NET uses the full namespace to reference each one, so there is no collision.

Namespace Scope

You saw earlier in this chapter that if you move the definition of `MyVariable` outside any procedure, it has module scope. You also saw that, by default, the scope of `MyVariable` is limited to the module in which it is defined. But what if you want other elements of the program outside the module in which `MyVariable` is defined to have access to `MyVariable`? You can make that happen by changing the definition of `MyVariable` and giving it namespace scope.

To illustrate namespace scope, you can add a second form to the `LocalScope` project. To add a second form, select Project, Add Windows Form. When Visual Basic .NET prompts you for the form name, type **frmForm2**. Then add a label with the text `MyVariable:` and a text box named `txtValue`. If you do this correctly, your screen should look similar to Figure 8.2.

Now you can double-click the form to activate the Code window for `frmForm2`. Add the following code to the form's `Load()` event for `frmForm2`:

```
Private Sub frmForm2_Load(ByVal sender As System.Object, ByVal e As _
            System.EventArgs) Handles MyBase.Load
 MyVariable = 10
End Sub
```

FIGURE 8.2

The IDE screen for the second form in the LocalScope project.

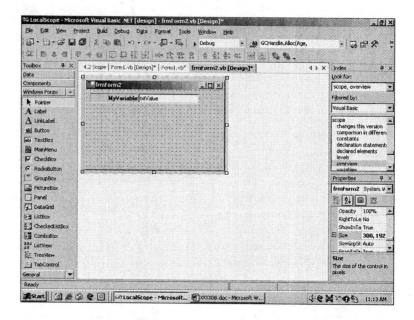

You need a way to invoke the second form shown in Figure 8.2. Therefore, you should add the following lines of code to the btnCalc object's Click() event of the frmLocalScope form:

```
Dim F2 As New frmForm2()

MyVariable = 20
F2.ShowDialog()
```

The Dim statement defines an instance of the second form. This means that F2 is an instance of the frmForm2 class. The second line simply assigns the value 20 to MyVariable. The third line calls the ShowDialog() method for the F2 object. The impact of this statement is that it shows frmForm2 onscreen. Now if you compile the program, you get this error message:

```
Name 'MyVariable' is not declared.
```

This error message is telling you that Visual Basic .NET has no clue what the variable named MyVariable that is referenced in the frmForm2 form's Load() event is. It is undefined. Hmmm. What if you try using the namespace for the first form? Modify the line in the frmForm2 form's Load() event so it looks like this:

```
frmLocalScope.MyVariable = 10
```

Then try to compile the program. Now you get a different (and more promising) error message:

```
'LocalScope.frmLocalScope.MyVariable' is not accessible in this context _
because it is 'Private'
```

Visual Basic .NET is telling you that it found the variable named MyVariable in frmLocalScope, but the variable is defined with module scope that is private. This is exactly as it should be, remember? Only data items in the module in which the definition occurs have access to the variables with `Private` module scope.

What if you changed the `Private` access specifier in Listing 8.6 to `Public`? You can change the third line in Listing 8.6 to this and then recompile the program:

```
Public MyVariable As Integer
```

The compile still didn't work, but what's the problem? You get this error message:

```
Reference to a non-shared member requires an object reference.
```

The error message is saying that `MyVariable` is defined in such a way that it is not accessible to the code in the second form. You have to remember that Visual Basic .NET has the creative thinking ability of a box of rocks. You and I know that `MyVariable` is defined in the `frmLocalScope` form, but Visual Basic .NET can't make the logical connection between the two forms by itself. Could it be that because we had to create an instance of the `frmForm2` form in the first form, you need to do the same thing in the second form?

Listing 8.7 shows the code for `frmForm2`.

LISTING 8.7   The Code for `frmForm2`

```
Public Class frmForm2
 Inherits System.Windows.Forms.Form
 Dim OtherObject As New frmLocalScope()

 Private Sub frmForm2_Load(ByVal sender As System.Object, ByVal e As _
            System.EventArgs) Handles MyBase.Load

  txtValue.Text = CStr(OtherObject.MyVariable)

 End Sub
End Class
```

Notice the definition of `OtherObject` near the bottom of Listing 8.7:

```
txtValue.Text = CStr(OtherObject.MyVariable)
```

This creates an instance of the `frmLocalScope` object that you can reference in `frmForm2`. The line simply uses the instance of the `frmLocalScope` object named `OtherObject` to access the `MyVariable` member. Now if you compile the program, it works without error. The program compiles now because you have created an instance of the `frmLocalScope` object that contains `MyVariable` in `frmForm2`.

Figure 8.3 shows a sample run of the program.

As you can see, the program executes and does load and show the second form.

But there's a problem. When you modified the `btnCalc` object's `Click()` event code, you assigned `MyVariable` the value 20 and then called the second form with the `F2.ShowDialog()` statement. Given that you did all that, why does Figure 8.3 show the value for `MyVariable` to be 0 and not 20? You need to go back to the drawing board.

FIGURE 8.3
A sample run of the modified `LocalScope` project.

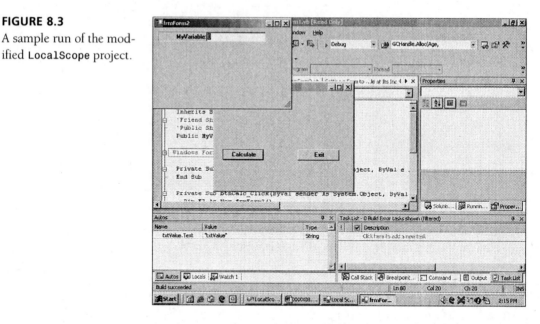

Sharing Variables Between Forms

Whenever you create an instance of an object, you also create new instances of all the data items that are part of that object. In the preceding section, you created a new instance of the `frmLocalScope` object, which means you got your own brand-new version of the `MyVariable` variable, too. In other words, the `lvalue` of `OtherObject.MyVariable` is not the same as the `lvalue` for `frmLocalScope.MyVariable`. Even though they share the common name `MyVariable`, they are in different namespaces. Therefore, they are different variables with different `lvalue` values and cannot be expected to have the same `rvalue` values.

But what if you want them to be the same variable? What if you want the variable `MyVariable` in the `frmLocalScope` object to be the same `MyVariable` in the `frmForm2` object? In other words, what if you want the forms to share a single `lvalue` for `MyVariable`? Well, if that's what you want, you need to tell Visual Basic .NET about it. (More rocks, remember?) To do that, you change the third line in Listing 8.6 from its present form:

```
Public MyVariable As Integer
```

to this:

```
Public Shared MyVariable As Integer
```

This change tells Visual Basic .NET that you want the variable named `MyVariable` to be available to other objects in the program (via the `Public` keyword), and you also want only a single `lvalue` for `MyVariable` defined for all instances of the `frmLocalScope` object. Stated in different terms, you want the scope of `MyVariable` to extend to all objects in the project.

Programmer's Tip

Some programs have dozens of classes in the project. It is fairly common to refer to the all the classes associated with a single project as the *assemblies* for the project. Therefore, saying something like "Variable MyVariable has namespace scope for the assemblies" simply means that all objects in the project have access to MyVariable.

If you now recompile and run the program, you find that MyVariable in the second form now has the value 20.

Lifetimes

As you saw earlier in this chapter, the scope of a data item determines what parts of a program can have access to that item. You can think of scope in terms of its restrictiveness. Block scope limits the accessibility of a data item to the block in which it is defined. Local scope limits access to the statement body of the procedure in which it is defined. Module scope limits access to the module in which the definition occurs. Namespace scope expands module scope to include all classes within the assembly, provided that you've used the proper access specifiers (for example, Public and Shared).

The concept of the lifetime of a data item or object is slightly different from the concept of scope. Suppose you have the following code fragment in a program:

```
Private Sub btnCalc_Click(ByVal sender As System.Object, ByVal e As _
          System.EventArgs) Handles btnCalc.Click
 Dim Counter As integer

 Counter = Counter + 1

End Sub
```

In this example, the variable Counter is defined with local scope. Each time the btnCalc object's Click() event is executed, Counter is defined and incremented. Because Counter has local scope, its lifetime is limited to the time it takes to execute the btnCalc object's Click() event. Counter's life ends when the End Sub is reached.

However, suppose you want to keep track of how many times the user clicks the btnCalc button. Clearly, because the lifetime of Counter extends only to the end of the Click() event, the largest count you will ever have is 1. Because Counter is "reborn" each time the user clicks the Calculate button, it is initialized to 0 each time you enter the procedure.

What you really want to do is extend Counter's lifetime beyond that associated with a normal variable with local scope. You would like Counter not to be reborn each time you enter the btnCalc object's Click() event, but extend its lifetime to that of the program. That is, as long as the program is running, the same definition of Counter exists in the program.

The `Static` Storage Class

What you need is a way to prevent a variable from dying when it goes out of scope. To extend `Counter`'s lifetime, you can change its definition as follows:

```
Static Counter As Integer
```

The `Static` keyword changes the way the `Counter` variable is defined in the program. The `Static` keyword causes Visual Basic .NET to make a special notation in the symbol table that says: "Even when this variable goes out of scope, do not destroy it. Keep its `lvalue` in the symbol table, and never re-create it, even if we enter this procedure another time." In other words, after a static variable is defined, it doesn't go away until the program ends. Therefore, its lifetime is the same as the program's lifetime. As long as the program is running, `Counter` exists.

This means that `Counter` can now hold its current value, even after you leave the scope in which it is defined. Big deal, you say. Why not just give `Counter` namespace scope by moving its definition outside `btnCalc` and give it shared public access? Well, that would work, but you would lose one important advantage: With the `Static` keyword, the scope of `Counter` is still local to `btnCalc`. Because `Counter`'s scope is still local, nothing else in the program can inadvertently change its value! Data hiding is almost always good.

Keep in mind that the `Static` keyword extends the lifetime of a data item but does not change its scope. Using the `Static` keyword is perfect for data items that must track a running total of something but that you don't want to expose to other sections of the program.

Summary

This chapter discusses the concept of scope and the impact it has on the visibility of data in different sections of a program. It describes how `Public` and `Private` keywords can be used to alter a variable's scope. Finally, it discusses what the lifetime of a variable is and how the `Static` keyword can be used to extend the lifetime of a variable.

Some issues related to both scope and lifetime are not discussed in this chapter. You will learn about them later in the book, when they are in contexts that makes more sense.

Review Questions

1. What is meant by the scope of a variable?

A. The scope of a data item refers to the accessibility of the data item. For example, if you define a variable within a procedure, such as a subroutine, you can only access that variable within the subroutine in which it is defined. Therefore, the scope of the variable is the subroutine in which it is defined.

2. What is meant by the lifetime of a variable?

A. Normally, the lifetime of a variable is the same as its scope. That is, the lifetime of a variable starts with its definition and ends when the variable goes out of scope. Therefore, for normal variables defined within procedures, the lifetime starts when the program control enters the subroutine and ends when program control exits the subroutine. A Static variable is an exception: Its lifetime is equal to that of the program.

3. What does the Static keyword do to the attributes of a variable?

A. When a variable is defined with the Static keyword, Visual Basic .NET tags the variable with a special attribute that says that the lifetime of the variable starts when the program begins execution and ends when the program terminates. This is true even if the scope of the variable is limited to a subroutine.

4. What are the different scope levels?

A. The different scope levels are local (or procedure) scope, block scope, module scope, and namespace scope.

5. Which scope level is best to use in a program?

A. Each scope level has a purpose, and one size does not fit all. However, as you move up the scope scale and expose a data item to larger and larger sections of the program, the chance of contaminating the data increases. This risk increases as you increase the exposure of the data item to other sections of the program. Therefore, all things being equal, the more restrictive the scope level, the better, because you are hiding the data and more effectively protecting the data from outside contamination.

6. Say you want to display the number of times a certain procedure named CountHits() is entered. The name of the form that needs this feature is frmMain. How would you write the code to display the number of times CountHits() is entered on the title bar of the form?

A. The following might be one solution:

```
Private Sub CountHits()
 Static MyCounter as Long

 MyCounter += 1
 frmMain.Text = "Hits: " & CStr(MyCounter)

 ' Whatever other code might be in the procedure

End Sub
```

This code defines MyCounter as a Static data type, so its lifetime equals that of the program. Therefore, its value is initialized only once, at program startup. After that, the definition statement is never executed again, and its value persists until the program ends.

7. If a data item is defined with local scope and it is entered 12 times while the program is running, what is displayed on the title bar of the form when you use the following code?

```
Private Sub ThisProc()
 Dim i as Integer

 i += 1
 Me.Text = CStr(i)

 ' Other statements
End Sub
```

A. The number displayed will always be 1. Because the variable has local scope, it is initialized to 0 each time the procedure is entered. Because it is then incremented by 1, the value 1 is always displayed.

CHAPTER 9

ARITHMETIC AND ASSIGNMENT OPERATORS

You will learn the following in this chapter:

- What arithmetic operators are
- What an assignment operator is
- What a unary operator is
- What a binary operator is
- What operator precedence is
- How to change operator precedence

This chapter explores the various assignment operators that are available in Visual Basic .NET. First, it discusses the operators that are used in arithmetic expressions. After that, it explains the assignment operators. You have used the assignment operator in numerous programs already, but as you'll learn in this chapter, there are some very useful variations that you need to know about.

Arithmetic Operators

Simply stated, arithmetic operators are special symbols that cause Visual Basic .NET to process program expressions in a very specific manner. Table 9.1 presents the arithmetic operators that are available in Visual Basic .NET.

TABLE 9.1 Arithmetic Operators

Operator	Type	Description
*	Binary	Multiplication
/	Binary	Regular division
\	Binary	Integer division
^	Binary	Exponentiation
Mod	Binary	Modulus division
+	Binary	Addition
-	Binary	Subtraction
+	Unary	Unary plus
-	Unary	Unary minus

There may be a few surprises for you in Table 9.1. First, notice that there are two division operators. The forward-slash division operator (/) is the division operator that you are likely to use most often. The backward-slash division operator (\) is limited to integer division and is used less often because any remainder from the division is dropped. However, integer division is very fast and may be useful to you in some limited applications.

The exponentiation operator (^) is one you've used before, at least indirectly, in the discussion of binary arithmetic in Chapter 4, "Data Types and Numeric Variables." Remember when I said 2^8 equals 256? You could produce this result in Visual Basic .NET by using the exponentiation operator with this statement:

```
Result = 2 ^ 8
```

After you process this statement, `Result` equals `256`.

The `Mod` operator returns the remainder after integer division. For example, in integer division, 5 divided by 2 equals 2, with a remainder of 1. Therefore, this statement:

```
Result = 5 Mod 2
```

would find `Result` equal to `1`, not `2`. Again, the reason is because the `Mod` operator returns the remainder of the division, not the quotient. A common use for the `Mod` operator is to determine whether a number is odd or even. In this expression:

```
Result = Number Mod 2
```

`Result` equals `1` any time `Number` is an odd number, and it equals `0` any time `Number` is an even number.

Unary Plus and Unary Minus

The unary plus (+) and unary minus (-) operators are a little strange because they are unary operators rather than binary operators. Recall from Chapter 4 that a binary operator takes two operands.

The binary arithmetic operators listed in Table 9.1 have this general form:

```
ArithmeticResult = Operand1 Operator Operand2
```

The unary operators, however, have this form:

```
ArithmeticResult = Operator Operand1
```

Notice that only a single operand is used in this expression. An example should help explain how this works. Consider the following code fragment:

```
Num = 10
Result = -Num
```

In this example, we are using the unary minus operator to change `Num` from `10` to `-10`. Note that the unary minus operator works by subtracting the operand (in this case, `Num`) from `0`.

What does the following code fragment assign to `Result`?

```
Num = -10
Result = +Num
```

If you said `Result` equals `10`, you are wrong! The reason is that unary plus simply returns the operand; it does not change the sign of the operand. If you need the absolute value of the number, you use the `Abs()` function, found in the `Math` library. (If you forgot about the `Math` library, check out how the `Sqrt()` function is used in Chapter 4.)

A Sample Program Using the Arithmetic Operators

A good way to explore the arithmetic operators is to write a simple program that lets you enter values for the operands and operators and see what the result is.

To create this program, you need to start a new project and call it `MathOperators`. Then, add controls to the form as shown in Figure 9.1.

The layout of the objects on the form is similar to that of a Visual Basic .NET assignment statement. As you learned earlier, a simple assignment statement in Visual Basic .NET has this form:

```
ArithmeticResult = Operand1 Operator Operand2
```

In Figure 9.1, the objects are arranged such that the statement looks like this:

```
txtResult = txtOperand1 Operator txtOperand2
```

FIGURE 9.1

Placement of controls for the arithmetic operators program.

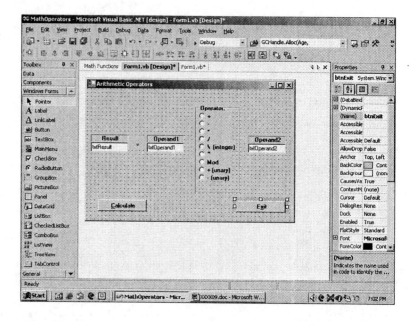

The user supplies the two operands by typing them into the appropriate text boxes and clicking the operator he or she wants to use. The user then clicks the Calculate button, and the operation is performed.

The complete code for this program is presented in Listing 9.1.

LISTING 9.1   The Arithmetic Operators Program

```
Public Class frmArithmeticOperators
 Inherits System.Windows.Forms.Form
 Dim WhichOne As Integer
 Windows Form Designer generated code

 Private Sub Form1_Load(ByVal sender As System.Object, ByVal e As _
    System.EventArgs) Handles MyBase.Load
  RadioButton1.Checked = True
 End Sub

 Private Sub RadioButton1_CheckedChanged(ByVal sender As System.Object, _
    ByVal e As System.EventArgs) Handles RadioButton1.CheckedChanged
  WhichOne = 1
 End Sub

 Private Sub RadioButton2_CheckedChanged(ByVal sender As System.Object, _
    ByVal e As System.EventArgs) Handles RadioButton2.CheckedChanged
  WhichOne = 2

 End Sub
```

LISTING 9.1   *Continued*

```
Private Sub RadioButton3_CheckedChanged(ByVal sender As System.Object, _
    ByVal e As System.EventArgs) Handles RadioButton3.CheckedChanged
 WhichOne = 3

End Sub

Private Sub RadioButton4_CheckedChanged(ByVal sender As System.Object, _
    ByVal e As System.EventArgs) Handles RadioButton4.CheckedChanged
 WhichOne = 4

End Sub

Private Sub RadioButton5_CheckedChanged(ByVal sender As System.Object, _
    ByVal e As System.EventArgs) Handles RadioButton5.CheckedChanged
 WhichOne = 5

End Sub

Private Sub RadioButton6_CheckedChanged(ByVal sender As System.Object, _
    ByVal e As System.EventArgs) Handles RadioButton6.CheckedChanged
 WhichOne = 6

End Sub

Private Sub RadioButton7_CheckedChanged(ByVal sender As System.Object, _
    ByVal e As System.EventArgs) Handles RadioButton7.CheckedChanged
 WhichOne = 7

End Sub

Private Sub RadioButton8_CheckedChanged(ByVal sender As System.Object, _
    ByVal e As System.EventArgs) Handles RadioButton8.CheckedChanged
 txtOperand2.Text = ""
 WhichOne = 8

End Sub

Private Sub RadioButton9_CheckedChanged(ByVal sender As System.Object, _
    ByVal e As System.EventArgs) Handles RadioButton9.CheckedChanged
 txtOperand2.Text = ""
 WhichOne = 9

End Sub
Private Sub btnCalc_Click(ByVal sender As System.Object, ByVal e As _
            System.EventArgs) Handles btnCalc.Click
 Select Case WhichOne
  Case 1
   txtResult.Text = CStr(CDbl(txtOperand1.Text) + _
            CDbl(txtOperand2.Text))
  Case 2
   txtResult.Text = CStr(CDbl(txtOperand1.Text) - _
            CDbl(txtOperand2.Text))
```

LISTING 9.1 Continued

```
      Case 3
       txtResult.Text = CStr(CDbl(txtOperand1.Text) * _
                  CDbl(txtOperand2.Text))
      Case 4
       txtResult.Text = CStr(CDbl(txtOperand1.Text) / _
                  CDbl(txtOperand2.Text))
      Case 5
       txtResult.Text = CStr(CInt(txtOperand1.Text) \ _
                  CInt(txtOperand2.Text))
      Case 6
       txtResult.Text = CStr(CDbl(txtOperand1.Text) ^ _
                  CDbl(txtOperand2.Text))
      Case 7
       txtResult.Text = CStr(CInt(txtOperand1.Text) Mod _
                  CInt(txtOperand2.Text))
      Case 8
       txtResult.Text = CStr(+(CDbl(txtOperand1.Text)))
      Case 9
       txtResult.Text = CStr(-(CDbl(txtOperand1.Text)))
     End Select
     WhichOne = 1
    End Sub

    Private Sub btnExit_Click(ByVal sender As System.Object, ByVal e As _
           System.EventArgs) Handles btnExit.Click
     Me.Dispose()
    End Sub
End Class
```

There appears to be a lot of code in Listing 9.1, but much of it is duplicate code. Note at the top of the program the integer variable WhichOne. Because it is defined outside any procedure, WhichOne has module scope and is available to every procedure.

Each of the operators is associated with a radio button. Because all the operator radio buttons are grouped within a group box, clicking on one radio button automatically deselects whatever button was previously clicked. There are nine radio buttons, and their code is contextually identical. Consider the code for the first radio button:

```
Private Sub RadioButton1_CheckedChanged(ByVal sender As System.Object, _
    ByVal e As System.EventArgs) Handles RadioButton1.CheckedChanged
  WhichOne = 1
End Sub
```

In this code, you can see that when RadioButton1 is clicked, WhichOne is assigned the value 1. If you look at the code for all the other eight buttons, you see that the only change in most of them is the value that is assigned to WhichOne.

Note that radio buttons 8 and 9 set the text box for the second operand to be empty. You have them do this because these two operators are unary operators and do not require a second operand.

All the work is done in the `Select Case` statement in the `btnCalc` object's `Click()` event. You will not learn about the `Select Case` statement until Chapter 11, "Making Decisions," but you should get an idea of what it does from the code in Listing 9.1. Given a value for `WhichOne`, the `Select Case` statement executes the code for the case that corresponds to `WhichOne`.

You can also see in Listing 9.1 that the first radio button is selected by default when the program starts. If there is code that you want to have executed the moment the program begins execution, you can place it in the `Form1_Load()` event. This statement:

```
RadioButton1.Checked = True
```

simply sets the first radio button in the operator list (that is, the addition operator) to `True`.

That's all there is to it. A sample run of the program is shown in Figure 9.2.

FIGURE 9.2

A sample run of the arithmetic operators program, showing the result of a modulus operation.

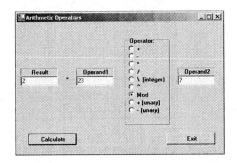

The sample run shows that `23 Mod 7` is `2`. Recall that the modulus operator returns the remainder of division; you can see the result is correct. You should experiment with the program, especially the modulus and integer division operators, to make sure you understand how they work.

Shorthand Operators

Certain types of arithmetic operations are performed a lot in most computer programs. These common arithmetic operations perform some arithmetic operation on the original value of a variable and then reassign the new value back to the original variable. A common example is the statement that increments a variable by 1, which is written as follows:

```
Num = 10
' Do some other stuff...
Num = Num + 1     ' This increments Num by 1
```

In the last statement, you take the original value of `Num` (that is, `10`), add 1 to it, and then assign the new value back to `Num`. In short, the last statement simply increments `Num` by 1.

The increment statement, `Num = Num + 1`, has this general form:

```
Operand1 = Operand1 ArithmeticOperator Operand2
```

Because such operations are so common, Visual Basic .NET supplies shorthand operators to simplify these statements. With a shorthand operator, the increment statement can be rewritten as this:

```
Num += 1
```

The effect on Num is identical; its value is incremented by 1.

As you can see, the shorthand operator replaces this syntax:

```
Operand1 = Operand1 ArithmeticOperator Operand2
```

with this:

```
Operand1 ArithmeticOperator= Operand2
```

The only catch is that the arithmetic shorthand operators must do the assignment into themselves. Whereas Operand2 can be a variable, a numeric constant, or another expression, Operand1 must be a variable. The shorthand operators are listed in Table 9.2.

TABLE 9.2   Shorthand Arithmetic Operators

Shorthand Operator	Operation	Full Expression	Shorthand Expression
+=	Addition	X = X + 1	X += 1
-=	Subtraction	X = X + Y	X -= Y
*=	Multiplication	X = X * 8	X *= 8
/=	Division	X = X / 2	X /= 2
\=	Integer Division	X = X \ 3	X \= 3
^=	Exponentiation	X = X ^ 2	X ^= 2

The shorthand operators don't give you anything you didn't have before. They simply give you a shorter way to write the statements. (By the way, don't forget the shorthand operator for string concatenation, &=, for building strings.)

Operator Precedence

Suppose you saw the following statement in a program:

```
Num = 2 + 3 * 5
```

What does Num equal? Does Num equal 25 or 17? In other words, is the expression resolved as this:

```
Num = 2 + 3 * 5
Num = 5 * 5
Num = 25
```

or is the expression resolved as this:

```
Num = 2 + 3 * 5
Num = 2 + 15
Num = 17
```

As it turns out, `Num` is equal to `17`. The reason is because of the concept of *operator precedence*, which determines the order in which complex expressions are resolved. This statement:

```
Num = 2 + 3 * 5
```

has two binary arithmetic operators (that is, + and *) and one assignment operator. Clearly, the arithmetic operations must be resolved before the assignment can occur. Operator precedence determines the order in which the arithmetic operations are performed. Table 9.3 presents the precedence order for the arithmetic operators, starting with the highest operator precedence (exponentiation) and proceeding to the lowest operator precedence (addition and subtraction).

TABLE 9.3   Arithmetic Operator Precedence

Type of Operator	Operators
Exponentiation	^
Unary plus, unary minus	+, -
Multiplication, division	*, /
Integer division	\
Modulus arithmetic	Mod
Addition, subtraction	+, -

Using Table 9.3, you can see that in this statement:

```
Num = 2 + 3 * 5
```

the multiplication operator (*) and its operands (3 and 5) are resolved first (15 = 3 * 5) because multiplication has higher precedence that does addition. Therefore, the operands for the addition operator are 2 and 15, causing a result of 17 to be assigned into `Num`.

Associativity

As you can see in Table 9.3, several arithmetic operators have equal precedence. The unary operators share the same precedence level, as do multiplication and division and addition and subtraction. When these operators are used in a single statement, how does Visual Basic .NET decide which expression to resolve first?

The rules of *associativity* determine the order of resolution for expressions that have operators of equal precedence. All binary operators are left associative. This means the operators are resolved in a left-to-right order. For example, in this statement:

```
Num = 5 * 4 / 2
```

the expressions are resolved in the following manner:

```
Num = 5 * 4 / 2
Num = 20 / 2
Num = 10
```

Notice that the expression for multiplication is done first, followed by division. Visual Basic .NET simply starts with the leftmost expression; it resolves that expression, and the result becomes the operand for the remaining binary expression.

It is important that you recognize that this statement:

```
Num = 5 * 4 / 2
```

contains three subexpressions. The three binary expressions are resolved according to the rules of associativity. The associativity rules cause the resolution to be multiplication, then division, then assignment. You could rewrite the statement to illustrate this order of resolution:

```
Num = 5 * 4 / 2
```

which you can reduce to this:

```
Num = operand1 * operand2 / operand3
Num = ResultantOperand1 / operand3
Num = Result
```

Notice how this:

```
operand1 * operand2
```

forms a binary expression for the multiplication operation. If you plug in these numbers:

```
operand1 * operand2
5 * 4
```

You see that the value `20` becomes *ResultantOperand1* in the second expression:

```
Num = ResultantOperand1 / operand3
Num = 20 / 2
```

After this binary expression is resolved, the assignment expression becomes this:

```
Num = 10
```

This causes the `rvalue` of `Num` to assume the value `10`.

You might be saying, "Wait a minute. If the operators group left to right, why isn't the assignment expression resolved first?" It's because the binary assignment operator has the second-lowest precedence of all operators. (The comma is last.) Therefore, the arithmetic expressions are resolved before the assignment expression is processed.

Altering Precedence Order

At times you might need to have an expression execute in a specific order, even if it disagrees with the precedence rules. For example, suppose you have a business that sells items after a

20% markup. Further assume that the sales tax rate for your state is 5%. Therefore, the cost to the customer is the cost of the item plus the 20% markup plus the 5% sales tax on the marked-up item price. Therefore, the sales equation is this:

```
CustomerPrice = Cost + Markup * SalesTax
```

You might write this equation in Visual Basic .NET as follows:

```
CustomerPrice = Cost + .2 * Cost * 1.05
```

You need to multiply by 1.05 because the final price to the customer is 105%, after tax is added. If you resolve this equation, assuming that the item costs $100, you get this:

```
CustomerPrice = Cost + .2 * Cost * 1.05
CustomerPrice = 100 + .2 * 100 * 1.05     ' Do first multiplication
CustomerPrice = 100 + 20 * 1.05     ' Do second multiplication
CustomerPrice = 100 + 21      ' Now do addition
CustomerPrice = 121       ' Now do assignment
```

Therefore, you collect $121 from the customer, and he literally bolts out of the store amid the sounds of muffled laughter. Hmmm. Clearly, the item was sold too inexpensively because you let the natural precedence order resolve the equation.

The error arose because you need to figure the sales tax on the combination of the base price plus the markup. To save your equation, you need a way to alter the order of precedence you are using. You can do that with parentheses.

If arithmetic operators eat operands, parentheses are at the top of the food chain. In any complex expression that involves subexpressions, expressions that are surrounded by parentheses are resolved first, regardless of the operators in the subexpression they surround. For example, you can rewrite your pricing statement as follows:

```
CustomerPrice = (Cost + .2 * Cost) * 1.05
```

Because subexpressions in parentheses are processed first, you can see the impact that the parentheses have on the final assignment:

```
CustomerPrice = (Cost + .2 * Cost) * 1.05
CustomerPrice = (100 + .2 * 100) * 1.05
CustomerPrice = (100 + 20) * 1.05
CustomerPrice = (120) * 1.05
CustomerPrice = 126
```

Now the purchase price plus the tax has been calculated correctly.

Expressions contained within parentheses are resolved before expressions that are not in parentheses. In cases where there are two or more subexpressions in parentheses, the subexpressions are resolved according to the left-to-right rules of associativity. Consider the following complex statement:

```
X = (A + B) + (C / D) * (E - F)
```

In this statement, all the values within the subexpressions in parentheses are resolved first. Supplying some numeric values helps you understand this process:

```
X = (10 + 5) + (100 / 2) * (50 - 48)  ' Resolve parenthesized sub expressions
X = 15 + 50 * 2      ' normal rules of precedence resume; multiplication
X = 15 + 100         ' Now add
X = 115              ' Now assign
```

Notice that after the expressions in parentheses are resolved, the normal precedence order takes over.

Summary

This chapter examined the arithmetic operators provided by Visual Basic .NET. It also showed how some of the arithmetic operators have shorthand versions that you can use. It then explained what operator precedence is and how precedence can affect program statements. Next, the chapter explained that some operators have equal precedence levels and that the rules of associativity come into play to resolve such expressions. Finally, the chapter showed how you can use parentheses to alter the order of precedence and associativity.

It takes a little experience to become comfortable with the rules of precedence and associativity, but they play a crucial part in programming.

Exercise

Write a program to convert temperatures from Celsius to Fahrenheit and vice versa. The formula looks like this: F = (9/5)C + 32, where F = Fahrenheit and C = Celsius.

Review Questions

1. What is an operand?

A. An operand is a subexpression that resolves to some value. For example, if you are adding two numbers, the addition operator requires two operands—in this case, the two numbers to be added together.

2. What is meant by the term *binary operator*?

A. If an operator is a binary operator, it requires two operands to perform its function. This is the general format for a binary operator:

```
Operand1 Operator Operand2
```

For example, the addition operator is a binary operator and hence needs two operands. Therefore, to add the numbers 10 and 20, *Operand1* becomes **10**, and *Operand2* becomes **20**:

```
10 + 20
```

The result of this addition expression evaluates to 30.

3. Suppose you want to have a variable named `Odd` equal 1 if a number is odd and 0 if the number is even. Assume that a variable named `Number` holds the value to test. Write the code that sets `Odd` correctly.

A. You need to write a single statement

```
Odd = Number Mod 2
```

The `Mod` operator returns the remainder of division. Therefore, an odd number `Mod 2` will yield 1 whenever `Number` is odd.

4. What is a shorthand operator?

A. Some operations are performed so often that Visual Basic .NET provides a shortened version of the operator. For example, incrementing a variable is normally done like this:

```
number = number + 1
```

This is the shorthand operator for the same operation is:

```
number += 1
```

Each of the arithmetic operators has a shorthand version. The base operator precedes the assignment operator:

```
Operand1 Operator= Operand2
```

You simply replace *Operator* with the operator you want to use. For example, to subtract 5 from a variable named `Result`, you use this:

```
Result -= 5
```

5. What is operator precedence?

A. Operator precedence refers to the way in which complex expressions are resolved. For example, in the expression:

```
Result = 5 * 10 + 50 /2
```

what does `Result` equal? If you didn't know anything about operator precedence, the answer would be ambiguous. However, because certain arithmetic operators are performed before others, you can determine that the answer should be 75.

CHAPTER 10

RELATIONAL AND LOGICAL OPERATORS

You will learn the following in this chapter:

- What relational operators are and how to use them

- What logical operators are and how to use them

- How to use bitwise operators

- What operator precedence is for relational and logical operators

This chapter explores the relational and logical operators in Visual Basic .NET. You use these operators to make decisions in programs by comparing one value against another. Indeed, a fundamental task of almost any computer program is the capability to make decisions based on data that is present in the program. The relational and logical operators, therefore, are a cornerstone in the decision-making capability of a computer program.

Relational Operators

The *relational operators* are used to compare values. These operators are presented in Table 10.1.

TABLE 10.1 Visual Basic .NET's Relational Operators

Relational Operator	Meaning
=	Equal
<>	Not equal
<	Less than
>	Greater than
<=	Less than or equal to
>=	Greater than or equal to

All the relational operators are binary operators. Recall from earlier chapters that a binary operator requires two operands. Therefore, the general syntax for the group of relational operators is as follows:

```
Operand1 RelationalOperator Operand2
```

When a statement uses a relational operator, the statement is said to be performing a *relational test* between two values (that is, operands). There are only two possible outcomes from a relational test: logic `True` or logic `False`.

A Simple `If-Then-Else` Statement

Relational tests are often performed by using `If-Then-Else` statements. Although you have used this statement in programs in earlier chapters, you have not learned its syntax. This is the syntax for the `If-Then-Else` statement:

```
If Expression1 Then
   Execute if Expression1 is True
Else
   Execute if Expression1 is False
End If
```

The `If` statement block extends from the `If` keyword to the `End If` keywords. *Expression1* is usually a relational test that either evaluates to logic `True` or logic `False`. If the relational test of *Expression1* is logic `True`, the second line of the `If` statement is executed. If the relational test of *Expression1* is logic `False`, the line following the `Else` keyword is executed.

Programmer's Tip

By convention, the logic `True` and logic `False` statements of an `If-Then-Else` statement block are indented one tab stop. You will learn more about the `If-Then-Else` statement in Chapter 11, "Making Decisions."

Next, you can write a simple program that allows you to exercise both the If statement and the relational operators. Start a new project and call it **RelationalOperators**. Add the text boxes and buttons shown in Figure 10.1. (You could reuse the program you wrote for testing the arithmetic operators in Chapter 9, "Arithmetic and Assignment Operators," if you like.)

FIGURE 10.1

The form for the relational test program.

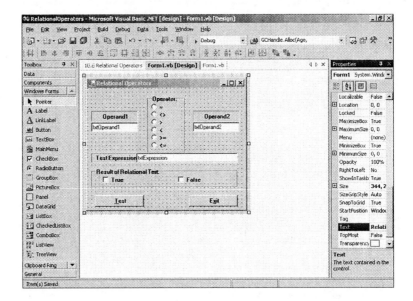

Figure 10.1 shows a text box for each operand named **txtOperand1** and **txtOperand2**, and a third text box for the expression that is being tested. In other words, the text box named **txtExpression** presents the operands and operator that is called *Expression1* in the syntax format for the If-Then-Else statement presented earlier. Near the bottom of the form in Figure 10.1 is a group box that holds two check boxes, which will show whether the relational test being performed is logic **True** or logic **False**.

The code for the program is simple. The operator group box contains six radio buttons, one for each of the relational operators. The code for the first radio button is presented in the following code fragment:

```
Private Sub RadioButton1_CheckedChanged(ByVal sender As System.Object, _
    ByVal e As System.EventArgs) Handles RadioButton1.CheckedChanged
 WhichOne = 1
End Sub
```

Whenever a radio button is clicked, the value of **WhichOne** is set to the selected radio button. **WhichOne** is an integer variable that is defined with module scope.

After the user types the two operands into his or her text boxes and selects the relational operator to test, he or she clicks the Test button. Listing 10.1 shows the complete code for the **btnTest** object's **Click()** event.

LISTING 10.1 Code for the **btnTest** Object's **Click** Event

```
Private Sub btnTest_Click(ByVal sender As System.Object, _
            ByVal e As System.EventArgs) _
          Handles btnTest.Click
 ckbTrue.Checked = False    ' Set to false to begin with
 ckbFalse.Checked = False
 Select Case WhichOne
  Case 1
   txtExpression.Text = txtOperand1.Text & " = " & txtOperand2.Text
   If txtOperand1.Text = txtOperand2.Text Then
    ckbTrue.Checked = True
   Else
    ckbFalse.Checked = True
   End If
  Case 2
   txtExpression.Text = txtOperand1.Text & " <> " & txtOperand2.Text
   If txtOperand1.Text <> txtOperand2.Text Then
    ckbTrue.Checked = True
   Else
    ckbFalse.Checked = True
   End If
  Case 3
   txtExpression.Text = txtOperand1.Text & " > " & txtOperand2.Text
   If txtOperand1.Text > txtOperand2.Text Then
    ckbTrue.Checked = True
   Else
    ckbFalse.Checked = True
   End If
  Case 4
   txtExpression.Text = txtOperand1.Text & " < " & txtOperand2.Text
   If txtOperand1.Text < txtOperand2.Text Then
    ckbTrue.Checked = True
   Else
    ckbFalse.Checked = True
   End If
  Case 5
   txtExpression.Text = txtOperand1.Text & " >= " & txtOperand2.Text
   If txtOperand1.Text >= txtOperand2.Text Then
    ckbTrue.Checked = True
   Else
    ckbFalse.Checked = True
   End If
  Case 6
   txtExpression.Text = txtOperand1.Text & " <= " & txtOperand2.Text
   If txtOperand1.Text <= txtOperand2.Text Then
    ckbTrue.Checked = True
   Else
    ckbFalse.Checked = True
   End If
 End Select
End Sub
```

The code in the procedure begins by setting the values of both of the check boxes to `False`. Then a `Select Case` statement is used to select the proper case to execute based on the value of `WhichOne`. In each `Case` of the `Select` statement, the `txtExpression` string is built by concatenating the operands in the `txtOperand1` and `txtOperand2` text boxes. The two operands are separated with a string literal that represents the relational operator being tested. A simple `If` test then determines whether to check the `True` check box or the `False` check box. All the `Case` statement blocks work in the same manner.

That's all there is to it. A sample run of the program is shown in Figure 10.2.

FIGURE 10.2

A sample run of the `RelationalOperators` program.

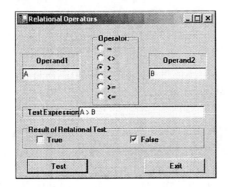

The sample run in Figure 10.2 shows that you can also test string data with the relational operators. The example shows the test expression `A > B` is logic `False`. Why is the expression `False`? Recall that string comparisons are made by using the numeric codes for the letters `A` and `B`. Because `A` equates to `65` and `B` is `66`, the expression `A > B` is `False`. Of course, you can test numeric values for the two operands, too.

You should experiment with the program so you become comfortable with how the relational operators work. You should use both numeric and string data for your experiments. Each string variable may contain more than a single character. For example, what happens if you test `JOYCE` against `Joyce` and why?

Logical Operators

A *logical operator* compares Boolean operands and returns either `True` or `False` (a Boolean result). Table 10.2 presents a list of the logical operators that Visual Basic .NET makes available.

TABLE 10.2   The Visual Basic .NET Logical Operators

Logical Operator	Type	Meaning
And	Binary	Logical And
Or	Binary	Logical Or
Xor	Binary	Logical exclusive Or
Not	Unary	Logical negation
AndAlso	Binary	Short-circuit And
OrElse	Binary	Short-circuit Or

As you can see in Table 10.2, all but logical Not are binary operators. The following sections explore each of these logical operators in detail.

The Logical And Operator

The logical And operator compares two operands and returns logic True if, and only if, both operands are logic True. You can see this relationship by looking at the truth table for the logic And operator. A *truth table* is a table that shows a list of all possible combinations for the two operands and their logical And result. Table 10.3 presents the truth table for logical And.

TABLE 10.3   The Truth Table for the Logical And Operator

Operand1	Operand2	Result
True	True	True
True	False	False
False	True	False
False	False	False

Notice in Table 10.3 that the only way to get a True result with a logical And operator is when both operands are True. Any other combination produces a False result. Consider the following expression:

```
Result = 10 > 5 And 100 > 60
```

If you evaluate each relational test in this expression, you get this:

```
Result = 10 > 5 And 100 > 60
Result = True And True   ' Cols 1 and 2 in Row 1,Table 10.3
Result = True       ' Row 1, Column 3 in Table 10.3
```

Because **10** is greater than **5**, the first relational test is **True**. Also, **100** is greater than **60**, so the second relational test is also **True**. Therefore, the second line of this example shows that the logical test that is actually being performed is **True And True**. From Table 10.3, because both operands are **True**, the expression is **True**.

Let's try a variation on the same expression but change the relational operator for the second operand:

```
Result = 10 > 5 And 100 < 60
Result = True And False   ' Cols 1 and 2 in Row 3,Table 10.3
Result = False      ' Row 2, Column 3 in Table 10.3
```

Here are some additional examples, with the results shown in the comments at the ends of the statements:

```
Result = 10 = 5 And 100 > 60          ' False
Result = 10 >= 5 And 100 <> 60        ' True
Result = 10 <> 5 And 100 <> 60        ' True
Result = 10 > 5 And 100 <= 60          ' False
Result = 10 > 5 And 100 > 60 And 20 < 80  ' True
Result = 10 > 5 And 100 < 60 And 20 < 80  ' False
```

Work through each example and convince yourself that the result is as it indicated. The last two statements show that you can have more than just one logical **And** operator in a single statement.

The Logical Or Operator

The logical **Or** operator compares two operands and returns a logic **True** if either of the operands is logic **True**. The truth table for the logical **Or** operator is shown in Table 10.4.

TABLE 10.4   The Truth Table for the Logical **Or** Operator

Operand1	Operand2	Result
True	True	True
True	False	True
False	True	True
False	False	False

A logical **Or** test produces a **True** result any time either of the operands is **True**. Only when both operands are **False** does the logical **Or** test produce a **False** result. Let's use the same examples as before, but test them using the logical **Or** operator:

```
Result = 10 = 5 Or 100 > 60          ' True
Result = 10 >= 5 Or 100 <> 60         ' True
Result = 10 <> 5 Or 100 <> 60         ' True
Result = 10 > 5 Or 100 <= 60          ' True
```

```
Result = 10 > 5 Or 100 > 60 Or 20 < 80     ' True
Result = 10 > 5 Or 100 < 60 Or 20 < 80     ' True
```

Because at least one expression using the relational operators here is `True`, `Result` is `True` for all the expressions. You might want to compare the results of using `And` and `Or` to make sure you understand why they are different.

The Logical Xor Operator

The `Xor` operator is the exclusive `Or` operator. The `Xor` operator returns `True` if one, and only one, of the operands evaluates to `True`. If both operands are `True` or both operands are `False`, the result is `False`. The truth table for the `Xor` operator is presented in Table 10.5.

TABLE 10.5   The Truth Table for the Logical `Xor` Operator

Operand1	Operand2	Result
True	True	False
True	False	True
False	True	True
False	False	False

Let's again use the same examples as before, but test them using the logical `Xor` operator:

```
Result = 10 = 5 Xor 100 > 60            ' True
Result = 10 >= 5 Xor 100 <> 60          ' False
Result = 10 <> 5 Xor 100 <> 60          ' False
Result = 10 > 5 Xor 100 <= 60           ' True
Result = 10 > 5 Xor 100 > 60 Xor 20 < 80     ' True
Result = 10 > 5 Xor 100 < 60 Xor 20 < 80     ' False
```

The first four statements are fairly easy to understand, but the last two might benefit from a little explanation. Let's work through the first of these two statements:

```
Result = 10 > 5 Xor 100 > 60 Xor 20 < 80
Result = True Xor True Xor True
Result = False Xor True
Result = True                  ' True
```

The tricky part comes in step 2. Because you are evaluating an expression that has two `Xor` operators, the precedence levels are the same for the two operations. Therefore, step 2 actually behaves as though it were written like this:

```
Result = (True Xor True) Xor True        ' True
```

As you can see from Table 10.5, when both operands are `True`, `Xor` yields a `False` result. In the final step, `False Xor True` yields a `True` value for `Result`.

For the other complex statement, the resolution is as follows:

```
Result = 10 > 5 Xor 100 < 60 Xor 20 < 80
Result = (True Xor False) Xor True
Result = True Xor True
Result = False                  ' False
```

This resolves to **False** because the final expression must resolve two **True** expressions.

Quite honestly, you probably won't use the **Xor** operator that much. However, it can be very useful in manipulating images in graphics programming.

Bitwise Operations Using Logical Operators

There are times when you need to get down to the bit level of a piece of data. Common examples of this need can be found in decoding of data that has been encoded, communications software, and some graphics programming. To explore the bitwise operations, we can use the code from the program shown in Figure 10.1. You need to add lines to the **btnTest** object's **Click()** event so that the procedure is written as shown in Listing 10.2. Only the top few lines are shown because the rest of the listing remains unchanged from the code shown in Listing 10.1.

LISTING 10.2   A Partial Listing for the **btnTest** Object's **Click()** Event

```
Private Sub btnTest_Click(ByVal sender As System.Object, ByVal e As _
          System.EventArgs) Handles btnTest.Click
 ckbTrue.Checked = False   ' Set to false to begin with
 ckbFalse.Checked = False
 Dim Result As Boolean     ' New code line here!

 Result = Cbool(5 And 4)       ' The last new line here!

 Select Case WhichOne
  Case 1
      ' The rest of the code for the procedure
```

Notice the two new lines in Listing 10.2 that define a variable named **Result** as a **Boolean** data type. The next line simply has an **And** test on the values **5** and **4**. You should compile the program with the two new lines, but you shouldn't run it yet.

Setting a Debugger Breakpoint

With the code for the **btnTest** object's **Click()** event showing in the Form window, you need to click in the left margin of the line that has the **Select Case** statement. A brownish-red colored line that is similar to the one shown in Figure 10.3 should appear. This brownish-red colored line is called a *breakpoint line*, and it indicates that you have set a breakpoint in the program on this line.

FIGURE 10.3

Setting a breakpoint in the **btnTest** object's **Click()** event.

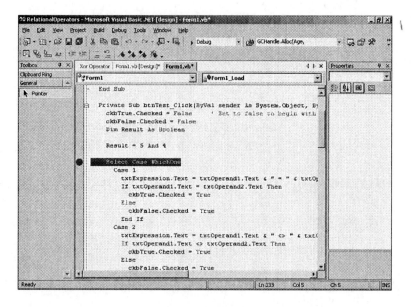

A *breakpoint* is a feature of the Visual Basic .NET program debugger that allows you to stop program execution at the breakpoint line. When the breakpoint line is reached, Visual Basic .NET suspends program execution at the selected line. You can use a breakpoint to inspect the values of variables as they exist at any present moment during program execution.

After you have set the breakpoint and compiled the program, you should press the F5 key. (Remember that pressing the F5 key is another way of starting the program to run.) You should then click the Test button. Figure 10.4 shows the program when the breakpoint is reached.

FIGURE 10.4

Reaching a breakpoint in the **btnTest** object's **Click()** event.

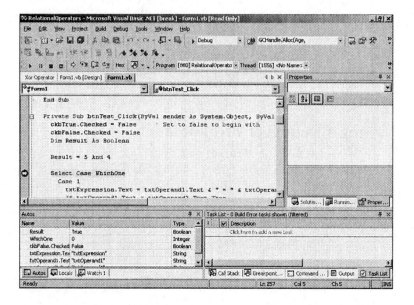

Notice that the program suspends execution at the breakpoint. The brownish-red line has changed color to yellow, to indicate that the program is currently suspended at the yellow-colored line. Near the lower-left side of Figure 10.4, you see tabs that are labeled Autos, Locals, and Watch 1. Click the Locals tab. The display should look similar to Figure 10.5. (You can stop the debugger by selecting Debug, Stop Debugging or by pressing the blue square on the toolbar.)

FIGURE 10.5

Viewing the Locals window for the `btnTest` object's `Click()` event.

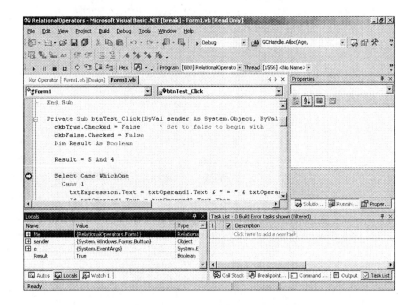

As you can see in Figure 10.5, the Locals window is displaying the variables that have local scope. Among these is the `Result` variable, which has the value `True`. In other words, the logical `And` of `5` and `4` yields Boolean `True`. Why is the test `True`? Because the values of `5` and `4` are nonzero, they are viewed as logic `True` operands, hence the `True` assignment to `Result`.

Next, you should change the definition of `Result` from a `Boolean` data type to `Integer`:

```
Dim Result As Integer
```

After you make the change, recompile and run the program. The output should look similar to that shown in Figure 10.6.

`Result` now has the value `4` rather than `True`. This happens because you have defined `Result` as an `Integer` instead of a `Boolean`. When `Result` was defined as a `Boolean`, it could only assume the values `True` and `False`. `Result` is now free to hold the answer to the bitwise `And` of `5` and `4`. What's going on?

A bitwise `And` operation does a bit-by-bit comparison of the two values, logically `And`ing each bit in the two numbers. These are the binary representations for the two numbers:

```
5 = 00000101
4 = 00000100
```

FIGURE 10.6

Result as the outcome of a bitwise And operation.

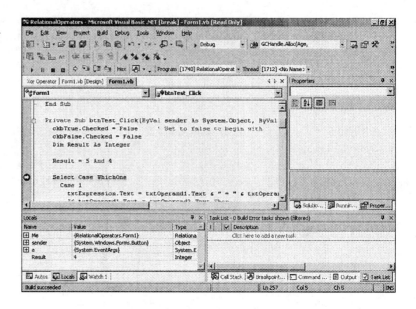

Remember that the first bit in a number is actually the rightmost bit. For **5**, the first bit is **1**. For **4**, the first bit is **0**. Remember from Chapter 4 that you can view a 1 as logic **True** for the bit and **0** as logic **False**. Therefore, the first bit for **5** is **True**, and the first bit for **4** is **False**. Now look at Table 10.3. For a logical **And** operator, **True And False** yields a logic **False** result, or **0**.

If you repeat this logical **And** for each bit of the two numbers, you get the following result:

```
5 = 00000101
4 = 00000100
------------
   00000100 = bitwise And of 5 and 4
```

Notice that only bit position 3 yields **1** from the **And**ing of each of the bits. This is because both bits are logic **True** in bit position 3. If you convert the binary result to a decimal number, the value is **4**. This is exactly what **Result** equals in the Locals window in Figure 10.6.

Try some different values and see what happens. Try changing the values to **16** and **4**, recompile the program, and observe the results. Here's the outcome with these values:

```
16 = 00010000
 4 = 00000100
------------
    00000000 = bitwise And of 16 and 4
```

In this case, because none of the bits have matching 1s in both numbers, the result is **0**.

Bitwise `Or` and `Xor`

You can use the `Or` and `Xor` functions in bitwise operations. To see this in action, change the `And` statement from Listing 10.2 to this:

```
Result = 5 Or 4
```

Then recompile and run the program to see the result. Using Table 10.4 to generate the bitwise results, you find this:

```
5 = 00000101
4 = 00000100
- - - - - - - - - - - -
    00000101 = bitwise Or of 5 and 4
```

The value is **5**. This is because logical `Or` is `True` if *either* operand is `True`. What about `16 Or 4`?

```
16 = 00010000
 4 = 00000100
- - - - - - - - - - - -
    00010100 = bitwise And of 16 and 4
```

If you convert the binary value, you find that the value is **20**.

Now try `Xor` on the two numbers **5** and **4**, using Table 10.5:

```
5 = 00000101
4 = 00000100
- - - - - - - - - - - -
    00000001 = bitwise Xor of 5 and 4
```

Because `Xor` returns logic `True` only when the bits are different, only the first bit is `True`. The value is **1**. What about **16** and **4**?

```
16 = 00010000
 4 = 00000100
- - - - - - - - - - - -
    00010100 = bitwise Xor of 16 and 4
```

In this case, the result is again **20**.

Most programs you write will probably not use the bitwise operators. However, there are instances in communications work (for example, working with modems), image processing, and encoding–decoding algorithms in which the bitwise operations may prove useful.

Operator Precedence

Until this point, we have covered the arithmetic, relational, and logical operators that Visual Basic .NET makes available. In complex expressions, you might use all three operators in a single program statement. How does Visual Basic .NET decide how to process each expression in such complex statements? Once again, operator precedence determines the sequence that Visual Basic .NET will follow.

Table 10.6 presents the order for all of Visual Basic .NET's operators, starting with the highest precedence and working down to the lowest precedence. (Note that Table 10.6 includes a few operators that are covered in later chapters.)

TABLE 10.6 Visual Basic .NET Operator Precedence

Operator	Name	Type
^	Exponentiation	Arithmetic
-	Negation	Arithmetic
*, /	Multiplication, division	Arithmetic
\	Integer division	Arithmetic
Mod	Modulus arithmetic	Arithmetic
+, -	Addition, subtraction	Arithmetic
&	String concatenation	String concatenation
=	Equality	Relational
<>	Inequality	Relational
<, >	Less than, greater than	Relational
>=	Greater than or equal to	Relational
<=	Less than or equal to	Relational
Like	String comparison	String comparison
Is	Object comparison	Object comparison
TypeOf...Is	Type comparison	Type comparison
Not	Negation	Logical
And, AndAlso	And, AndAlso	Logical
Or, Xor, OrElse	Or, Exclusive Or, OrElse	Logical
=	Assignment	Assignment

As a general rule, the arithmetic operators have highest precedence, followed by the relational operators, followed by the logical operators. You might want to dog-ear this page because you will probably need to refer to this table later on, when the program examples become a little more complex. You should keep in mind that you can override the operator precedence by using parentheses to force the order in which expressions are evaluated (refer to Chapter 9).

Summary

In this chapter you have learned how relational and logical operators can be used in programs. You have also learned how truth tables can be used to verify logical operations on different operands. We also discussed how precedence affects both types of operators. Finally, you have learned how the logical operators can be used to determine bitwise values on the operands. Although you might not need some of these techniques in your programs right now, you should tuck this information in the back of your head because the day may come when they provide an elegant solution to a vexing problem.

Review Questions

Programmer's Tip

As you try the short programs presented in this section, you can type the code into the form's `Load()` event. You do not need to add text boxes or other controls to the programs. To test the programs, you simply set a breakpoint on the `End Sub` statement at the end of the form's `Load()` event. You can, of course, move the cursor over any variable you want to examine while the program is running.

1. What is the purpose of relational operators?

A. Relational operators are used to compare values. Because relational operators are used to compare two values, they are binary operators that require two operands to do their job. Relational operators are the starting point for making decisions in a program based on the values of data.

2. Suppose a variable named `Gender` assumes the value `0` for females and `1` for males. How would you write the code that tests the value of `Gender` and uses a message box to display `Male` or `Female`, based on the outcome of the test?

A. The code might look like:

```
Dim Gender As Integer

Gender = 0

If Gender = 0 Then
 MessageBox.Show("Female")
Else
 MessageBox.Show("Male")
End If
```

In this example, you use an `If` test, by using the relational equality operator, to determine which sex to display, via a call to `MessageBox()`.

3. What is the value of `Result` after the following statement is executed?

```
Result = 10 > 5
```

A. You can answer this question by executing the following code:

```
Dim Result As Integer

Result = 10 > 5

MessageBox.Show(CStr(Result))
```

Before you try running the program, what do you think the value of `Result` will be, and why? Now run the program and, if the outcome is not what you expected, try to resolve why the answer was different than you expected. (Hint: Visual Basic .NET translates logic `True` to -1 and logic `False` to `0`.)

4. What is the value of `Result` in the following statement?

```
Result = (10 > 5) And (5 > 7)
```

A. You can test the answer by using the following code:

```
Dim Result As Integer

Result = (10 > 5) And (5 > 7)

MessageBox.Show(CStr(Result))
```

Is the answer what you expected and, if not, why was your answer wrong?

5. What is the value of `Result` in the following statement?

```
Result = (10 > 5) Or (5 > 7)
```

A. You can test the answer by using the following code:

```
Dim Result As Integer

Result = (10 > 5) Or (5 > 7)

MessageBox.Show(CStr(Result))
```

You should be able to explain the value that is calculated for `Result`. It is important that you know the difference between this answer and the answer to Review Question 4.

6. What is the value of `Result` in the following expression?

```
Result = Not 3
```

A. You can test the answer by using the following code:

```
Dim Result As Integer

i = 3
Result = Not 3

MessageBox.Show(CStr(Result))
```

The outcome of a unary **Not** operation is the bitwise complement of the expression—in this case, the value **3**. This is the binary representation of the value **3**:

`00000011`

When you determine the bitwise complement of a number, the value of each bit in the expression is flipped, so the binary representation after the **Not** expression is this:

`11111100`

Note that all the 1s become 0s and all the 0s become 1s. However, because the sign bit is now set, the outcome of the expression is viewed as a negative number. Because of the way negative numbers are processed, the answer is –4.

7. Suppose a function named **IsItOdd()** returns a nonzero result if the number passed to it is odd, and it returns **0** if the number is even. What is displayed in the message box when this program runs?

```
Private Sub Form1_Load(ByVal sender As System.Object, ByVal e As _
          System.EventArgs) Handles MyBase.Load
  Dim Result As Integer, TestValue As Integer

  TestValue = 55 < 100

  If IsItOdd(TestValue) Then
   MessageBox.Show("Hello")
  Else
   MessageBox.Show("Good-Bye")
  End If
End Sub
Private Function IsItOdd(ByVal num As Integer) As Integer
 num = num Mod 2
 Return num
End Function
```

A. The interesting section of code is in the **If** test. First, the logical test that 55 is less than 100 is logic **True**, which assigns -1 into **TestValue**. The call to **IsItOdd()** passes the -1 to the function, which is an odd (negative) number. The return value, therefore, is -1. Upon return from the function, the **If** test examines the return value of -1 and, because any nonzero value is deemed to be logic **True**, the program displays "**Hello**" in the message box.

8. The present value of an income stream can be determined by the following equation:

`PV = Income / (1.0 + InterestRate) ^ Years`

For example, if **Income** is $100 and the interest rate is 5% and the number of years is 2, the present value is $90.70. This means that if you put $90.70 in an asset that yields 5% for 2 years, you would have $100 in two years. Write the code necessary to calculate the present value of $200 for 3 years at 5%.

A. Here's the code:

```
Dim Value As Double

alue = 200 / (1.05) ^ 3
```

The answer is $172.77. Are the parentheses needed? Why? You might try to generalize this program to use text boxes for the interest rate, the amount, and the number of years, and then display the result in another text box.

CHAPTER 11

MAKING DECISIONS

You will learn the following in this chapter:

- How decision making is accomplished in programs

- How to use If-Then-Else statements

- How to make multiple decisions by using ElseIf

- How to use the Select Case statement

- How to make your code more readable by using enumerations

- How to use the short-circuit operators

*I*t is the computer's capability to make decisions that makes it useful. A computer program can measure data and make comparisons, and from those comparisons, the program can make decisions based on the data that is available to it. It's not that the computer can do something you and I can't do. However, the computer can do things much faster than we can. You and I can go through 100,000 files one-by-one and say, "Nope, that's not the one," and keep right on looking. Days later, we might find the name we are looking for and then proceed to the next step. What would take us days to accomplish the computer can accomplish in seconds. Like humans, the computer can say, "Nope, that's not the one," but it can do it thousands of times a second. Better still, it doesn't get bored, it doesn't get eye strain or headaches, and if the computer is properly programmed, it doesn't make mistakes. Even if the decision is a simple yes or no, being able to do it thousands of times a second is pretty powerful stuff.

This chapter explores some of the ways in which a program can make decisions. You have learned about the If statement in earlier chapters. You have not, however, seen the complete picture. In this chapter we dig into the details of how you can harness that the computer's power.

Simple If Statements

The most elementary decision-making statement is the If statement, which has the following general syntax:

```
If Expression1 Then
  ' If statement block
End If
```

The key to the `If` statement is the logical result of *Expression1*. If *Expression1* evaluates to logic `True`, the statements in the `If` statement block are executed. If the outcome of the test of *Expression1* is logic `False`, the `If` statement block is bypassed. In that case, program execution resumes with the next program statement following `End If`.

An example will help you see how the `If` statement works. Consider the following code fragment:

```
If Burglary = True Then
 ActivateAlarms()
 CallPolice()
End If
```

The `If` statement performs a relational test between `Burglary` and logic `True`. (You can assume that some earlier code is responsible for setting the `Burglary` variable to `True` if someone breaks in to the house.) If the relational test determines that `Burglary` is logic `True`, the `ActivateAlarms()` procedure is called, followed by a call to the `CallPolice()` procedure. On the other hand, if `Burglary` is logic `False`, program execution skips the two procedure calls and proceeds to execute the next program statement following the `End If` statement.

Figure 11.1 shows how the program flow is executed, depending on the outcome of the relational test on *Expression1*.

FIGURE 11.1
Program execution
sequence for an `If`
statement.

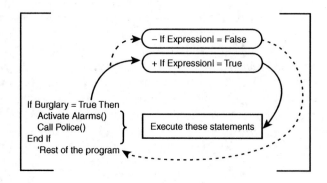

In Figure 11.1, when the relational test is `False`, program flow is diverted around the program lines that are controlled by the `If` statement block. This means the procedure calls to `ActivateAlarms()` and `CallPolice()` are bypassed.

You can write a simple program to show how the `If` statement works. Start a new project and call it `IfElseProject`. Add two text boxes, two labels, and two command buttons to the program, as shown in Figure 11.2.

Name the Test button `btnTest` and the Exit button `btnExit`. In the `btnExit` object's `Click()` event, add the call to `Me.Dispose()` as you usually do.

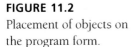

FIGURE 11.2

Placement of objects on the program form.

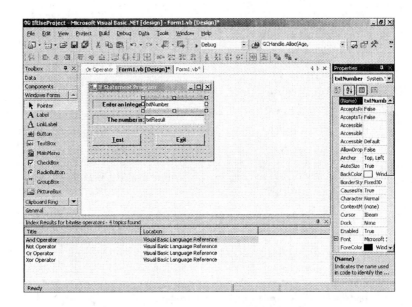

The only additional code needed for this program is shown in Listing 11.1.

LISTING 11.1   Code for the `btnTest` Object's `Click()` Event

```
Private Sub btnTest_Click(ByVal sender As System.Object, ByVal e As _
          System.EventArgs) Handles btnTest.Click
Dim Number As Integer

 Number = CInt(txtNumber.Text)
 txtResult.Text = "Even"
 If Number Mod 2 = 1 Then
  txtResult.Text = "Odd"
 End If

End Sub
```

When the user clicks the Test button, an integer variable named `Number` is defined and assigned the number the user enters in the `txtNumber` text box. Again, you must call `CInt()` to convert the string in the text box into an integer variable. The program then assigns the string literal `"Even"` to the `txtResult` text box.

The `If` statement tests whether `Number` is an odd or even number. It performs the test by using the `Mod` arithmetic operator. Because `Mod` returns the remainder of integer division, any odd number returns `1` as the result of the `Mod` expression. If the number is even, `Mod` returns `0`. The program then performs a relational test to see if the `Mod` expression returns `1`. If the relational test is `True`, the `txtResult` string is changed to `"Odd"`. If the relational test is `False`, the assignment statement of `"Odd"` into the `txtResult` text box is bypassed, and `Even` remains displayed.

Let's examine how the processing of the `If` statement is done if the user enters `10`:

```
If Number Mod 2 = 1 Then
  If 10 Mod 2 = 1 Then
  If 0 = 1 Then
```

How does Visual Basic .NET process the second line of this code? Recall from Chapter 10, "Relational and Logical Operators," that arithmetic operators have higher precedence than relational operators. The second line actually behaves as though it were written like this:

```
If (10 Mod 2) = 1 Then
```

Because 10 divided by 2 is 5, with no remainder, the `Mod` operator returns `0`. The statement then appears as this:

```
If 0 = 1 Then
```

This line uses the equality relational operator to see if 0 equals 1, which it does not. The result of the relational test for equality is `False`, so the statement is reduced to this:

```
If 0 Then
```

Because *Expression1* of the `If` statement is logic `False` (that is, `0`), the `If` statement block code is not executed, and `txtResult` remains unchanged, with the string `"Even"`. It's simple!

Using the Visual Basic .NET Debugger to Watch Program Flow

You can use the Visual Basic .NET debugger to see how different values for `Number` affect the flow of a program. To do this, you need to set a breakpoint on the line where the `If` statement appears in the program. With the program code showing in the Form window, click in the gray area to the left of the `If` statement line. Your display should look similar to Figure 11.3.

FIGURE 11.3
Setting a debugger breakpoint on the `If` statement.

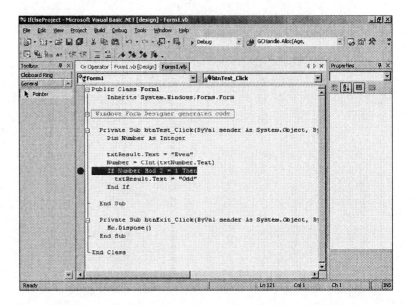

Now run the program, enter the value **10** in the **txtNumber** text box, and click the Test button. Your screen should look similar to the one shown in Figure 11.4.

FIGURE 11.4

Program execution suspended at the breakpoint statement.

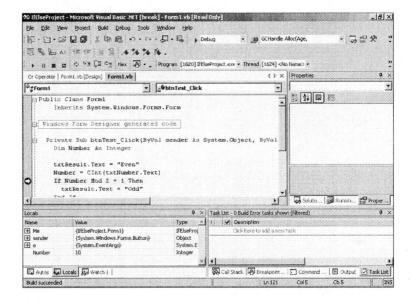

As shown in Figure 11.4, Visual Basic .NET suspends program execution at the statement where the breakpoint is set. Notice that the Locals window shows that **Number** has the value **10**. (If your screen does not show the Locals window, simply click the Locals tab at the bottom of the window.)

You should also notice that the color of the statement line where the breakpoint is changes to yellow. Visual Basic .NET uses this color to show you what line is to be executed next.

Programmer's Tip

When program execution stops at a breakpoint statement, the statement line is shown in yellow. This means that Visual Basic .NET has *not* yet executed the line shown in yellow. In other words, breakpoints suspend program execution *before* the breakpoint statement is executed.

Single-Stepping

When a program reaches a breakpoint, you can cause Visual Basic .NET to execute the next statement to see which statement is executed next. To do this, you can have the debugger execute one line at a time; this is called *single-stepping* the program. To single-step the program, you press the F10 key. The F10 key tells Visual Basic .NET: "Hey, Visual Basic .NET! Wake up from your program suspension and execute the next line in the program!"

If you enter **10** (or any other even number) in the **txtNumber** text box and press the F10 key, you should see the yellow line jump to the **End If** statement. In other words, the **If** test is logic `False`, so the test causes the program to skip the statement in the `If` statement block (that is, the assignment of `"Odd"` to `txtResult`).

Now you should press the F5 key. The F5 key tells Visual Basic .NET to resume program execution at full speed.

If you want to remove a breakpoint from a statement line, you move the cursor to the edge of the screen and click. This action toggles the breakpoint off. If you click again, the breakpoint is reactivated.

You should try running the program several times, entering odd and even numbers to verify that the program behaves as it should. I encourage you to do this with the breakpoint active so you can single-step through the program and see how it behaves.

A Program Simplification

You might have had a nagging feeling in the back of your mind when you saw that the `If` statement was resolved to this when an even number was entered:

```
If 0 Then
```

If you did, good! You remembered that in the general format for the `If` syntax, the value of *Expression1* determines whether the `If` statement block is executed. If that's the case, do you even need the relational test?

What would happen if you replaced this `If` statement:

```
If Number Mod 2 = 1 Then
```

with this:

```
If Cbool(Number Mod 2) Then
```

This second variation of the `If` statement doesn't contain the relational test for equality. If you change the statement to this new variation and compile and run the program, does it behave exactly as it did before? You should single-step the program to find out.

You should discover that the program functions exactly as it did before. This happens because you can treat the value returned by the `Mod` operator as logic `True` or `False`, depending on the value entered for `Number`. If the user enters `13`, for example, the expression becomes this:

```
If Cbool(13 Mod 2) Then
If 1 Then
```

Because 13 divided by 2 is 6, with a remainder of 1, the `Mod` operator returns `1`. The `If` statement interprets this remainder as logic `True` for *Expression1* of the `If` statement, causing the `"Odd"` string literal to be assigned to `txtResult`. Remember that an even number produces a `Mod` value of `0`, and that is viewed as logic `False` for *Expression1*. This causes the `If` test to bypass the assignment of `"Odd"` to `txtResult`.

Programmers love economy of expression (that is, they don't like to type more than they have to). As a result, *Expression1* of an `If` statement is often written without the relational test.

Function Calls and `If` Tests

You can modify your program slightly and write a function that tests for an even or odd number. After all, after you write the function, you can reuse it in other programs if you want. The code for the `OddEven()` function is shown in Listing 11.2.

LISTING 11.2   Code for the `OddEven()` Function

```
Public Function OddEven(ByVal Number As Integer) As Integer
 ' Purpose: This function returns 1 if the number is odd,
 '      and returns 0 otherwise.
 '
 ' Arguments:
 '  Number    The integer number to test
 '
 ' Return Value:
 '  integer   1 if odd, 0 if even
 '
 OddEven = Number Mod 2
End Function
```

In the first line of the function is this statement:

```
Public Function OddEven(ByVal Number As Integer) As Integer
```

This says that `OddEven()` is a function with `Public` scope that has a single `Integer` argument named `Number`. The `As Integer` keywords at the end of the statement line are the type specifier for the function. A *type specifier* tells what data type is returned from the call to the function. Therefore, you know that `OddEven()` returns an `Integer` data type.

The actual code for the function is this single statement:

```
OddEven = Number Mod 2
```

Remember from Chapter 5, "Subroutines and Functions," that a function can return a value. When a function returns a value, it appears that the return value is assigned to a temporary variable that has the same name as the function. (What really happens is that the return value is pushed onto the stack, as explained in Chapter 5.) The result of the `Mod` operation is then returned to the caller.

Now that you have the code for the `OddEven()` function, you should change the code in the `btnTest` object's `Click()` event so that it calls the function. Make the following minor change to the `btnTest` object's `Click()` event code:

```
If OddEven(Number) Then
```

Now when the Test button is clicked and the `If` statement is executed, the program calls the `OddEven()` function. If `Number` is odd, the function returns 1. For example, if `Number` equals 11, the expression is resolved as follows:

```
If OddEven(Number) Then
If OddEven(11) Then
If 1 Then     ' The return value is 1 if Number is odd
```

This resolves the expression to logic `True`, and the `"Odd"` string literal is assigned to `txtResult`. You should think of the `OddEven(11)` call to the function as being replaced with the return value after the function call is completed. (Actually, this abbreviated form of the test expression is slightly faster, too, because the return value from the function call is not assigned into a variable.)

You should try placing a breakpoint on the `If` statement, and then run the program. Enter 11 for the number and click the Test button. The program pauses at the breakpoint. Press the F10 key to single-step into the `OddEven()` function. Keep pressing the F10 key until you return from the function call. You should see the yellow line process the assignment statement of `"Odd"` to the `txtResult` text box.

Programmer's Tip

Pressing the F10 key always single-steps a program. There may be times, however, when you would rather have the program execute the line following a function call than step through each line of code in the function itself. This process of bypassing the code in the function and going directly to the next line after the function call is called *stepping over* the procedure. If you want to step over a procedure (for example, a function or a subroutine), you press Shift+F10. The Shift+F10 key sequence causes Visual Basic .NET to execute the code in the procedure at regular speed and proceed to the next program line after the procedure call.

You should try experimenting with odd and even values for `Number` to confirm that the code actually does behave as it did before you modified the code. You should also single-step through the program to make sure you understand how `If` tests can alter the control flow of a program.

The If-Then-Else Statement

You have seen the `If-Then-Else` statement in several programs in earlier chapters, and in this section, you're going to learn the details. This is the syntax for the `If-Then-Else` statement:

```
If Expression1 Then
  ' Execute this statement block if Expression1 True
Else
  ' Execute this statement block if Expression1 False
End If
```

If *Expression1* evaluates to logic `True`, the statement block following the `Then` keyword is executed. This is exactly the same as in a simple `If` statement. If *Expression1* evaluates to logic `False`, the statement block following the `Else` keyword is executed.

You can make a simple modification to the `IfElseProject` program from earlier in this chapter to illustrate how the `If-Then-Else` statement works. Change the existing code in the `btnTest` object's `Click()` event to this:

```
If OddEven(Number) Then
 txtResult.Text = "Odd"   ' Then statement block
Else
```

```
txtResult.Text = "Even"   ' Else statement block
End If
```

Notice that you have added the `Else` statement to the `If` block. Also, you have moved the assignment of `"Even"` to `txtResult` into the `Else` statement block. If the call to `OddEven()` returns 1, the `Then` component of the `If` block is executed, and `"Odd"` is assigned to `txtResult`. If the call to `OddEven()` returns 0, the `Else` component of the `If` block is executed, and `"Even"` is assigned in `txtResult`.

The `If` Statement Block, the `Then` Statement Block, and the `Else` Statement Block

An `If`-`Then`-`Else` statement actually has three statement blocks. The first is the `If` statement block, which extends from the keyword `If` to the `End If` keywords. Within the `If`-`Then`-`Else` statement block are two more statement blocks: the `Then` and `Else` statement blocks. There can be one or more statements in the `Then` and `Else` statement blocks.

You can think of the `Else` keyword as serving a dual role. First, the `Else` keyword marks the end of the `Then` statement block. Any statements after the `Then` keyword but before the `Else` keyword are part of the `Then` statement block. Second, the `Else` keyword marks the start of the `Else` statement block. Any statements after the `Else` keyword but before the `End If` keywords are part of the `Else` statement block.

Programmer's Tip

By convention, the statements in the `Then` and `Else` statement blocks are indented one tab stop beyond the `If` and `End If` statements that form the complete `If` block. This makes it easy to see where each block starts and ends.

The `If` statement block encompasses both the `Then` and `Else` statement blocks. Sometimes you'll hear a programmer say something like, "The `If` block calls the `OddEven()` function...." In most cases, the programmer is referring to the entire `If` statement block, including the `Then` and `Else` blocks.

Multiple Decisions Using `If`

Life is rarely limited to the either/or type of decisions that the `If`-`Then`-`Else` statement is designed to resolve. Life seems to be filled with lots of gray areas—lots of maybe and perhaps. For example, suppose you are writing a program to price movie tickets. Those under 12 get one price, those over 65 get another price, and those in between these two ages get a third price.

One way to attack this problem is to nest an `If` statement. To *nest* an `If` statement, you place one `If` statement inside another `If` statement. Consider the following code fragment:

```
Dim TicketPrice as Double

' Assume Age is set somewhere else

If Age <= 12 Then
  TicketPrice = 2.5     ' Child price
Else
  If Age >= 65 Then     ' Start of the nested If
   TicketPrice = 6.0  ' Senior price
  Else
   TicketPrice = 8.0  ' Regular price
  End If         ' End nested If
End If
```

You need to assume that Age is determined somewhere else in the program. All you are concerned with in this example is the pricing of the ticket based on Age. The first If expression checks whether Age is less than or equal to 12. If it is, the Then statement block is executed, and TicketPrice is set to 2.5.

If Age is greater than 12, the Else statement block is executed. However, in this example, the Else statement block contains another If statement. That is, a second If block is contained within the first If block. This second If statement block is the nested If statement. The nested If checks whether Age is equal to or greater than 65. If it is, the individual must be a senior citizen, and the (nested) Then statement block is executed. The result is that TicketPrice is set to 6.0.

If the person is not 65 or older and not 12 or younger, he or she must be between 13 and 65 years of age, and TicketPrice is set to 8.0. You know the person's age must fall within these limits because of the first If test that was performed on Age earlier.

The ElseIf Statement

Nested If blocks like the ticket price example in the previous section are so common that Visual Basic .NET provides a semi-condensed expression syntax using the ElseIf keyword. You can rewrite the If statements from the previous section by using the ElseIf keyword as follows:

```
If Age <= 12 Then
  TicketPrice = 2.5     ' Child price
ElseIf Age >= 65 Then     ' Start of the nested If
   TicketPrice = 6.0  ' Senior price
Else
   TicketPrice = 8.0  ' Regular price
End If
```

If you compare this code fragment with the one in the previous section, you should find that the ElseIf version does away with one End If statement and squishes the Else and If keywords into a single ElseIf keyword. Except for some minor indentation changes, everything else is the same for the two versions.

So, which is better: the nested If or the ElseIf? Because the decision has no impact on the underlying code, the choice is more a matter of style than of substance. You should use the one you prefer.

One thing you should avoid is a *cascading If block*. A cascading If block occurs when you have one If block nested within another If block, nested within another If block, nested within another If block, and so on. Cascading If blocks are more difficult to read than they need be.

The need for such nested blocks, however, is more frequent than you might expect. For example, suppose you have a variable named MyDay that assumes the values 1 through 7 to represent each day of the week. Further assume that you want to do something different on each day of the week. You could write this as a series of nested If blocks, but there is a better way: You can use the Select Case statement, as described in the following section.

The Select Case **Statement**

Chapter 9, "Arithmetic and Assignment Operators," provides a brief look at the Select Case statement. This section provides additional details on how to use the Select Case statement. This is the syntax format for the Select Case statement:

```
Select Expression1
  Case 1
    ' Statement block for Case 1
  Case 2
    ' Statement block for Case 2
  Case N
    ' More Case blocks as needed
  Case Else
    ' Catch-all
End Select
```

Expression1 in the Select statement is evaluated. If the expression matches a Case value, that Case's statement block is executed. When all the statements in that Case's statement block are executed, program control is sent to the statement that follows the End Select statement. If *Expression1* does not match any Case value, the Case Else statement block is executed. The Case Else statement is optional, so it is possible for no Case statements to be executed if *Expression1* does not match any Case value.

For example, suppose MyDay can take the values 1 through 7, where 1 is Monday, 2 is Tuesday, and so on. Further assume that certain tasks are to be performed on each day of the week. The Select Case block code to do this might look like that shown in Listing 11.3.

LISTING 11.3   A Select Case Block for Days of the Week

```
Select MyDay
  Case 1     ' Monday
    TakeHeadacheMedicine()
  Case 2     ' Tuesday
    GroceryShop()
  Case 3     ' Wednesday
    PayBills()
  Case 4     ' Thursday
    PayMoreBills()
```

LISTING 11.3 Continued

```
   Case 5    ' Friday
      LeagueNight()
   Case 6    ' Saturday
      Bathe()
   Case 7    ' Sunday
      Rest()
   Case Else ' Catch-all
      MessageBox.Show("Improper value for MyDay")
End Select
```

For any given value of **MyDay**, the associated **Case** statement block is executed. As with other statement blocks, each **Case** statement block can have more than one statement if needed.

Notice how Listing 11.3 uses the **Case Else** statement to trap any unexpected values for **MyDay** that might creep into the program. This is a fairly common practice and is an example of defensive coding. Planning for the unexpected is almost always a good thing.

Select Case Statement Variations

Some very useful variations make the **Select Case** statement especially easy to use. For example, suppose you want to set a variable to the number of days in the month. You could use 12 **Case** statements, but you don't need to. After all, most of the months have either 30 or 31 days. Assuming that 1 equals January, 2 equals February, and so on, consider the following code fragment:

```
Select MyMonth
   Case 2    ' February
      Days = 28 + LeapYear()
   Case 4, 6, 9, 11
      Days = 30
   Case Else
      Days = 31
End Select
```

Notice the middle **Case** statement. You can use a single **Case** statement that resolves to multiple values by simply separating the values with commas. In the code example, if **MyMonth** equals 4, 6, 9, or 11, the statement block that assigns **30** to **Days** is executed. Therefore, **Days** equal **30** for April (4), June (6), September (9), and November (11).

What do you suppose the **Case 2** statement does? It calls a function named **LeapYear()** and adds whatever it returns to 28 and then assigns it to **Days**. Visual Basic .NET does not provide a function named **LeapYear()**, but if it did, the function would probably return **1** for a leap year and **0** otherwise. If that is the way **LeapYear()** worked, **Days** would equal 29 for leap years and 28 otherwise.

Select Case Statements with Ranges of Values

You might have a situation in which you want to test for several values, but there is a range of values that should cause a single statement to be executed. Here's an example to help explain this:

```
Select Number
  Case 1, 2
    Answer = 4
  Case 3 To 6      ' A range of values
    Answer = 6
  Case 11, 13 To 15
    Answer = 8
  Case Else
    Answer = 0
End Select
```

In the second `Case` statement, `Answer` is set to `6` if `Number` equals `3`, `4`, `5`, or `6`. The `To` keyword allows you to specify a range of values for a single `Case` statement. Notice that the range is inclusive. In the next `Case` statement, `Answer` is set to `8` if `Number` is `11`, `13`, `14`, or `15`. In other words, you can have a comma-separated list of numbers and a range that uses the `To` keyword in the same `Case` statement.

Select Case Statements with Limit Ranges

At some point you might want to test several different ranges with a minimum of fuss. Consider the following code fragment:

```
Select Case Number
 Case 1
  txtResult.Text = "1"
 Case 2 To 10
  txtResult.Text = "2"
 Case Is < 20
  txtResult.Text = "3"
 Case Is > 20
  txtResult.Text = "4"
End Select
```

Notice how the first two `Case` statements cover the values between 1 and 10 for `Number`. At first glance, the third `Case` statement seems to overlap the first two `Case` statements, but that is not how the `Is` keyword works in a `Case` statement. The `Is` keyword is followed by a relational operator and then an operand. The relational test is performed with respect to all the previous `Case` values and the operand. In this code fragment, `txtResult` displays `3` for any value of `Number` between 11 and 19. This occurs because the prior `Case` values include the values through 10. The last `Case` statement would be executed for any value of `Number` that is greater than 20. Note that the value `20` is not covered by any of the `Case` statements.

You have to be a little careful when you use the `Is` keyword in a `Case` statement. The next code fragment is the same as the preceding one, except that the first `Case` is moved to the bottom of the `Select Case` block:

```
Select Case Number
 Case 2 To 10
  txtResult.Text = "2"
 Case Is < 20
  txtResult.Text = "3"
 Case Is > 20
  txtResult.Text = "4"
```

```
    Case 1
      txtResult.Text = "1"
End Select
```

If you type this code into your program and enter 1 for `Number`, `txtResult` displays 3, not 1. This happens because `Select` evaluates `Number` (that is, *Expression1*) and then starts looking at each `Case` value for a match. Visual Basic .NET finds a match on `Number` at the `Case Is < 20` statement because `Number` is less than 20 and is not found in the first `Case` using the `To` keyword. Even though the value of `Number` is 1, Visual Basic .NET never gets to the last `Case` when you enter 1.

The `Is` keyword can be useful in a `Select Case` block, but it is a bit tricky to use. You need to be sure you clearly understand the ranges covered and the placement of the `Case` statements when you use the `Is` keyword in a `Select Case` block.

Enumerations: Making `Select Case` Blocks Easier to Understand

Listing 11.3 presents a `Select Case` statement block for the processing of a days-of-the-week type of programming problem. The comments help the reader understand what the code is doing, but you can make it even more understandable by using Visual Basic .NET's enumeration statement. The enumeration statement allows you to define a set of named constants for use in a program. This is the syntax of the `Enum` statement:

```
[AccessSpecifier] Enum EnumName [As Type]
   ' List of Enum members
End Enum
```

If `AccessSpecifier` is not supplied, it is `Public` by default, but it can have other access types as well. (You will learn more about access specifiers in Chapter 15, "Encapsulation.") If you elect to specify the type of data by using the `As` keyword, the data types are limited to `Byte`, `Integer`, `Long`, and `Short`. If you do not specify the type, the enumeration members are `Integer` by default. The scope for enumerations is limited to the module, namespace, and assembly levels. This means that enumerations cannot be defined with local scope.

Consider the following example:

```
Enum ThisDay
   Monday = 1
   Tuesday = 2
   Wednesday = 3
   Thursday = 4
   Friday = 5
   Saturday = 6
   Sunday = 7
End Enum
```

The members of the `ThisDay` enumeration are simply named constants for each day. This definition would appear near the top of the `Class` code, after the `Inherits` statement. Note that you can use the constants in expressions, but you cannot change their values in any way after they are initialized in the `Enum` statement block.

You can now rewrite Listing 11.3 as Listing 11.4.

LISTING 11.4   Using Enumerations in a **Select Case** Statement Block

```
Select ThisDay
  Case ThisDay.Monday
    TakeHeadacheMedicine()
  Case ThisDay.Tuesday
    GroceryShop()
  Case ThisDay.Wednesday
    PayBills()
  Case ThisDay.Thursday
    PayMoreBills()
  Case ThisDay.Friday
    LeagueNight()
  Case ThisDay.Saturday
    Bathe()
  Case ThisDay.Sunday
    Rest()
  Case Else   ' Catch-all
    MessageBox.Show("Improper value for MyDay")
End Select
```

Even though the change from Listing 11.3 to Listing 11.4 has no real impact on the performance of the code, the use of enumerations makes it easier to understand what the code is doing. This is especially true when comments are missing.

Short-Circuiting Operators

Visual Basic .NET provides two new operators: `AndAlso` and `OrElse`. The following sections explain how to use them in your programs.

The `AndAlso` Operator

To appreciate what the new `AndAlso` operator brings to the table, you have to understand what Visual Basic .NET does with complex expressions in an `If` statement. Consider the following `If` statement:

```
If Number > 65 And OddEven(Number) = 1 Then
```

In this statement, Visual Basic .NET must evaluate two relational comparisons. The first comparison tests whether `Number` is greater than 65. The second comparison tests whether the function call to `OddEven(Number)` returns the value 1. Visual Basic .NET evaluates both comparisons, even if the first test is logic `False`.

To observe this processing sequence, you can replace the code from the `btnTest` object's `Click()` event with the following code:

```
Dim Number As Integer

Number = CInt(txtNumber.Text)

If Number > 65 And OddEven(Number) > 0 Then
 MessageBox.Show("Both true")
Else
 MessageBox.Show("At least one is not true")
End If
```

Notice that both comparison expressions use the greater-than relational operator, so their precedence levels are the same. This means the two comparison expressions are evaluated from left to right (that is, `Number` is evaluated first). You should set a breakpoint on the `Mod` statement in the `OddEven()` function. Then compile and run the program, entering the value 1 in the `txtNumber` text box. The program pauses at the breakpoint in the `OddEven()` function.

Because Visual Basic .NET stops at the breakpoint, you know that Visual Basic .NET executed the call to `OddEven()`, even though the first expression evaluated to logic `False`. This is inefficient because if the first expression is logic `False`, the truth table for logic `And` (refer to Table 10.3 in Chapter 10) tells you that regardless of the outcome of the second expression, there is no way the `Then` statement block can be executed. The logical `And` operator requires that both expressions be logic `True` in order for the `Then` statement block to execute. However, after the first comparison on `Number`, a logic `False` condition exists. Why even bother making the call to `OddEven()`? Visual Basic .NET is going to execute the `Else` statement block regardless of what `OddEven()` returns. Indeed, it is wasteful to make the call to `OddEven()`.

Now change the `If` statement to this:

```
If Number > 65 AndAlso OddEven(Number) > 0 Then
```

The only change in the statement is the use of the `AndAlso` operator. Now you should keep the breakpoint in the `OddEven()` function and recompile the program. If you now run the program, using the value 1 for `txtNumber`, what happens?

The program still displays the message for the `Else` statement block, but the breakpoint is never reached. This means that because the first relational test on `Number` returned logic `False`, Visual Basic .NET said, "The heck with the call to `OddEven()`; what's the point?" In other words, the `AndAlso` operator allows Visual Basic .NET to short-circuit the call to `OddEven()` if its relational test cannot alter the outcome of the complex expression. This allows you to avoid an unnecessary call to `OddEven()`.

Programmer's Tip

You can gain efficiency with the `AndAlso` operator only when the first expression evaluates to logic `False`. Therefore, if you plan to use the `AndAlso` operator, you should place the expression that is most likely to be `False` on the left side of the `AndAlso` operator.

The OrElse Operator

As you might expect, there is a short-circuit operator for the logic Or relational operator: the OrElse operator. To understand how it works, you can simply change the AndAlso operator in the If statement of the btnTest object's Click() event to OrElse:

```
If Number > 65 OrElse OddEven(Number) > 0 Then
```

The intention is different now, but a little thought will show what's going on. What you want to do now is execute the Then statement block if Number is greater than 65 or if OddEven() returns a value greater than 1. From the Or truth table in Chapter 10 (that is, Table 10.4), you know that if either relational test is logic True, Visual Basic .NET should execute the Then statement block. Another way of stating this is "If Number is greater than 65, why bother calling the OddEven() function?" When the first relational test is True, OrElse allows you to short-circuit the call to OddEven().

You should now compile the program, but keep the breakpoint in the OddEven() function. Run the program, and enter 66 in the txtNumber text box. The program executes the Then statement block without calling the OddEven() function. (The messages that are displayed are messed up because you changed the logic from a test based on an And comparison to one using an Or, but you should get the idea.) Now try entering a value less than 65 and explain what happens.

Programmer's Tip

You can gain efficiency with the OrElse operator only when the first expression evaluates to logic True. Therefore, if you plan to use the OrElse operator, you should place the expression that is most likely to be True on the left side of the OrElse operator.

Summary

This chapter examined how decisions can be made in a program. It explored the If statement, and its variations, in considerable detail. This chapter also showed how the Select Case statement can simplify code when complex decisions must be made. It also showed how to use enumerations to make code more easily understood. Finally, this chapter discussed the AndAlso and OrElse operators and how they can provide a slight boost in program efficiency.

Decision making is a crucial element in virtually all computer programs. You should experiment with some programs of your own design, using the concepts discussed in this chapter, before moving on to the next chapter. Working the exercises at the end of the chapter should also prove useful.

Review Questions

1. What are the main parts of an If-Then statement?

A. The main parts of an If statement are the If keyword, the test expression (which must evaluate to either logic True or False), and the Then keyword. If the outcome of the test expression is logic True, the If statement block following the Then keyword is executed. Otherwise, the If statement block is skipped.

2. What are the main parts of an If-Then-Else statement?

A. The main parts of an If statement are the If keyword, the test expression (which must evaluate to either logic True or False), the Then keyword, and the Else keyword. In the following statement:

```
If TestExpression Then
  IfStatementBlock()
Else
  ElseStatementBlock()
End if
```

if TestExpression is logic True (that is, nonzero), IfStatementBlock() is executed. If TestExpression is logic False, ElseStatementBlock() is executed.

3. What is a nested If?

A. A nested If occurs when one If statement is part of another If statement. In the following example, the first If tests the age of the person, and the nested If checks the sex of the person:

```
If Age > 21 Then
  If Sex = 0 then
    MessageBox.Show("This is an adult female")
  Else
    MessageBox.Show("This is an adult male")
  End If
Else
  MessageBox.Show("This is a minor")
End If
```

Based on the combined tests, the program displays the appropriate response.

4. When should you use a Select Case statement instead of an If statement?

A. You can use the Select Case statement in place of an If statement any time you want to. However, the Select Case is normally used when there are a number of different actions to be taken, depending on the value of the test expression. An If is normally used when the test expression resolves to a specific value, such as this:

```
If Age > 65 Then
  GiveSeniorDiscount()
End If
```

An `If-Then-Else` statement is often used when there is a specific value and everything else falls into a default category. Here's an example:

```
If Age > 65 Then
  GiveSeniorDiscount()   ' Special
Else
  GiveRegularDiscount()   ' Default
End If
```

In this situation, you want to give one discount to senior citizens (that is, the special case), but everyone else gets the regular discount (that is, the default case).

A `Select Case` statement is best used where the test expression means that different actions are to be taken over a wider range of values. Here's an example:

```
Select Case NaughtySpeed
  Case 60 To 70
    Fine = 60 + ((NaughtySpeed - 60) * 10)
  Case 71 To 80
    Fine = 70 + ((NaughtySpeed - 60) * 20)
  Case 81 To 90
    Fine = 80 + ((NaughtySpeed - 60) * 30)
  Case 91 To 100
    Fine = 500 + TakeTheirCarAwayFromThem()
  Case 101 To 714
    Fine = 2000 + PutThemInJail()
End Select
```

As you can see, the `Select Case` statement is well suited to situations where a variety of actions need to be taken based on the test condition (in this case, `NaughtySpeed`).

5. What are enumerations, and what data types can be used with enumerations?

A. Enumerations are named constants that can be used in a program. A carefully selected list of enumerated constants can help make code more readable. The `Enum` data type is limited to integral data types, and the default starting value in an `Enum` list is zero.

6. Suppose you are writing a program for a university that has freshmen through seniors, plus master's and doctoral students. You know from your preliminary design that there will be a lot of places in the code where knowing the student's class year will be important. How might you classify these students?

A. An `Enum` list would help in this situation. You might try this:

```
Enum StudentYear
  Freshmen = 1
  Sophomore = 2
  Junior = 3
  Senior = 4
  Masters = 10
  Doctoral = 100
End Enum
```

This declaration must appear outside a procedure. Then you could use something like

```
Dim Age, Sex As Integer, ThisStudent As StudentYear
```

```
Select Case ThisStudent
 Case ThisStudent.Freshmen
  ShowThemTheRopes()
 Case ThisStudent.Sophomore
  TimeToSelectAMajor()
 Case ThisStudent.Junior
  TellThemToTowTheRope()
 Case ThisStudent.Senior
  TimeToGetAJob()
 Case Else
  GradSchool()
End Select
```

In your code, the **Case** values determine which tasks to perform based on the **Enum** values. The **Enum** values make it easier to understand what each **Case** means. The code would be more difficult to read if the **Case** statements were simply labeled with numbers.

7. In Exercise 6, why do you make the master's and doctoral students' **Enum** values so much larger than the other students' values?

A. There are two reasons: so you could add up to 90 new master's student classifications without overlapping the doctoral students and so you could do certain tests on the students' numeric values and know something about who they are. Here's an example:

```
Dim StudentValue As Integer, ThisStudent As StudentYear

' Some code that sets the student value to their Enum

If StudentValue / ThisStudent.Masters >= 1 Then
  ThisIsAGradStudent()
Else
  ThisIsAnUnderGrad()
End If
```

Given the way the **Enum** is declared in this example, you could use a **Mod 10** operation on a student's year value to determine whether he or she is an undergraduate or a graduate student. That is, a student year value **Mod 10** would produce a value of **0** for either type of graduate student (master's or doctoral). Again, the **Enum** value makes it easier to understand what the code is doing.

8. What is the basic idea behind the use of a short-circuit operator?

A. The basic idea behind the use of a short-circuit operator is efficiency. If you have a complex test expression that uses a logical **And** or **Or**, the short-circuit operators **AndAlso** and **OrElse** can skip the evaluation of the second test expression. Here's an example:

```
If Class = 4 And Grade = "A" Then
  Graduate()
End If
```

In this case, even if `Class` is not equal to `4`, the code still performs the test on `Grade`. However, this is inefficient because if `Class` is not `4`, there's no reason to even perform the test on `Grade` because the compound expression is already logic `False`, and there is no way to reach the `Graduate()` call.

If you write this code:

```
If Class = 4 AndAlso Grade = "A" Then
  Graduate()
End If
```

if `Class` is not equal to `4`, Visual Basic .NET does not even bother to perform the second test. You short-circuit the second test, and this short-circuit saves time.

`OrElse` works in a similar fashion by saying that if the first test is logic `True`, there's no reason to even perform the second test.

CHAPTER 12

PROGRAM LOOPS

In this chapter, you will learn the following:

- Loop structure

- A simple program loop

- The For-Next loop

- Using a For-Next loop to implement an algorithm

- For loops and arrays

- Exit For—getting out of a For loop early

- Nested For loops

Computers excel at repetitive tasks. Computers don't get bored, they don't get distracted, they (usually) don't take breaks, and they do what they're told. Program loops are often used to automate repetitive tasks. In this chapter, we'll explore how to use program loops to perform certain tasks multiple times. You'll also learn that there are well-behaved loops and there are ill-mannered loops. Obviously, I want you to understand the difference. As you'll discover in this (and the next) chapter, Visual Basic .NET provides you with a variety of loop structures.

Although this chapter concentrates on For-Next loops, you need to have a general understanding of how program loops work. Because you do have a choice as to the type of loop you can use, understanding how each one works enables you to make better choices as to which is best for a given task.

Loop Structure

Program loops are used whenever you want to have one or more program statements executed one or more times. Regardless of the loop structure you use, all loops have three things in common:

- One or more variables must be initialized to some starting value. These variables may be initialized to their starting value before the loop begins execution, or they may be initialized as part of the loop structure itself.

- At least one of the variables must be tested at some point in the loop to decide whether another pass through the loop is to be made. This variable is often referred to as the *loop control variable*.

- The loop control variable is manipulated in some way, usually an increment operation, on each pass through the loop.

If these three conditions are met, the loop at least has a chance of being a well-behaved loop. If the conditions are not met, it's very unlikely that the loop will be well behaved.

What is the likely behavior of a loop if the conditions aren't met? As a broad generalization, if the loop doesn't initialize at least one variable properly, there are two likely possibilities. First, it's possible that the statements within the loop may not be executed at all. This often happens when the first condition mentioned earlier is not met.

A second possibility is that the loop executes forever. Loops of this type are called *infinite* loops and are not usually desirable (exceptions might include fire and burglar alarms that continually loop through a list of sensors). Infinite loops are almost always caused by violating the second condition and third conditions.

A Simple Program Loop

Let's write a simple program that contains a single loop. Create a new project and name it SimpleLoop. Place two text boxes, two labels, and two button objects on the form, as shown in Figure 12.1.

FIGURE 12.1

The form for the simple loop program.

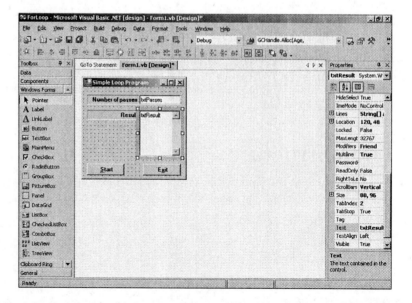

We have named the buttons **btnStart** and, as usual, **btnExit**. The **txtResult** text box is a little different from those we've used before. If you look closely at the Properties window, you'll see that we've set the **Multiline** property to **True**. This allows the text box to show multiple lines of text. We've also set the **ScrollBars** property to **Vertical**. This enables us to scroll the text box contents up and down if we need to.

To implement our loop, we're going to use the Visual Basic .NET equivalent of the old assembly language **JUMP** instruction, similar to the way loops were written 50 years ago! The code is shown in Listing 12.1.

LISTING 12.1   The **btnStart Click** Event Code Creating a Program Loop

```
Private Sub btnStart_Click(ByVal sender As System.Object, ByVal e As _
            System.EventArgs) Handles btnStart.Click
 Dim i As Integer, Sum As Integer, Terminate As Integer
 Dim NewLine As String

 NewLine = Chr(13) & Chr(10)     ' Carriage-Return, Linefeed
 Terminate = CInt(txtPasses.Text) ' Target iterations
 Sum = 0                ' Clear out the running total
 i = 1                  ' This is our loop counter
 txtResult.Text = ""

LoopStart:
  Sum += i              ' Calculate a running total
  txtResult.Text += CStr(Sum) & " (i = " & CStr(i) & ")" & NewLine
  If i < Terminate Then       ' Are we done yet?
   i += 1               ' Nope...increment loop counter
   GoTo LoopStart          ' Do another iteration
  End If

 End Sub
```

The program begins by defining a number of working variables. The **NewLine** variable consists of a carriage return, linefeed pair of characters. When added to a string and displayed, it causes the next sequence of characters to appear on the next line. That is, the carriage return character (that is, the **13**) causes the cursor to move to the beginning of the line. The linefeed character (that is, the **10**) moves the cursor down one line. The effect, therefore, is to display the next part of the string on a new line. This is exactly how we want to display the string that's built in the loop.

The code then sets **txtResult** to an empty string. We do this so that if you run the program a second time, you start with a clean text box.

The **Terminate** variable is set by the user and determines how many passes are made through the loop. **Sum** is used to maintain a running sum of the loop counter. It really doesn't do anything useful as far as the management of the loop is concerned. Notice that we did use the shorthand summation arithmetic operator with **Sum**.

The statement

```
txtResult.Text += CStr(Sum) & " (i = " & CStr(i) & ")" & NewLine
```

simply builds a display string for display in the `txtResult` text box. If you break down the statement, you'll see that it displays the running total of `i` (as stored in `Sum`) and then parenthetically displays the loop counter, `i`. On the first pass through the loop, the `txtResult` text box would display

```
1 (i = 1)
```

Concatenating the `NewLine` variable prepares the next pass of the loop to display the string on the next line in the text box.

The variable `i` is the loop counter. An `If` test checks to see whether `i` is less than `Terminate`. If `i` is less than `Terminate`, we need to perform another pass through the loop. As long as the `If` relational test is `True`, the `Then` statement block is executed. On each pass through the loop, `i` is incremented. (Again, we used the shorthand arithmetic operator for addition.) The `GoTo` statement then sends program control to the label named `LoopStart`.

A `label` statement in Visual Basic .NET is simply a placeholder in a program. (Labels are hangovers from the old days when BASIC programs used line numbers at the start of each program statement.) Label names follow the same rules as do variables, except they must end with a colon character (`:`). If you think about it, what do you suppose Visual Basic .NET puts in the symbol table for a label besides its name? Clearly, it must be a memory address because we're branching back to a previously executed set of instructions in memory. Therefore, an `lvalue` must be one part of the symbol table entry for a label. More specifically, it's the memory address of the program instructions that immediately follow the label. In Listing 12.1, the `lvalue` would be the memory address where the instructions for the

```
Sum += i
```

statement are stored.

Programmer's Tip

Most Visual Basic .NET programmers use the variable names of i, j, and k for Integer loop counters. This naming convention seems to have started about 50 years ago with FORTRAN programmers, but it hangs on today across many languages. We'll continue the tradition.

The program loop is formed by the `LoopStart` label and its corresponding `GoTo` statement. A sample run is shown in Figure 12.2.

You should single-step through this program to watch how **GoTo** sends control back to the `LoopStart` label.

FIGURE 12.2
Sample run of the simple
loop program.

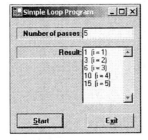

Is This a Well-Behaved Loop?

Yes, it is. Notice that we initialize a loop counter (variable **i**) just before we enter the loop. Also, we have a check to see whether we should terminate the loop or make another pass. Equally important is the increment operation of the loop counter **i** on each pass through the loop so that we know when to stop.

This is a fairly simple loop, but it exhibits all the characteristics of a program loop.

A Short Digression

I have a confession to make. Virtually all programmers hate `Goto` statements in their code. Indeed, when we talked about how early programs got so unwieldy, the greatest single culprit causing the confusion was the `GoTo`. The `GoTo` statement can cause what is called *spaghetti code*; that is, code that's so confusing it's difficult to trace what the program is supposed to do.

Because of these negative aspects of the `GoTo`, you'll hear some people say you should never use it. I think that's a bit too strong. You may find a situation where the `GoTo` provides a clean, easily understood means to solve a particular problem. If that's the case, by all means, use it. Still, they should be used very sparingly.

Well, because I've discouraged you from using the `GoTo` as a loop structure, let's explore a more conventional loop structure.

The `For-Next` Loop

The `For-Next` loop is a good choice for loops where a known number of passes must be made through the loop. For example, if a loop is supposed to total the monthly sales for the year, chances are pretty good that we shouldn't make 13 passes through the loop. If you're doing something with days of the week, it seems reasonable that there will be seven passes through the loop. If you have a good idea of how many passes must be made through the loop, chances are good that the `For-Next` loop will do the job.

The `For-Next` loop has the following basic syntax format:

```
For LoopCounter = StartValue To EndValue [Step BumpIt]
  ' For statement block
Next [LoopCounter]
```

Let's use a For-Next loop in place of our earlier Goto loop. The new code is shown in Listing 12.2.

LISTING 12.2   The Simple Loop Program Modified to Use a **For-Next** Loop Structure

```
Private Sub btnStart_Click(ByVal sender As System.Object, ByVal e As _
            System.EventArgs) Handles btnStart.Click
Dim i As Integer, Sum As Integer, Terminate As Integer
Dim NewLine As String

txtResult.Text = ""
NewLine = Chr(13) & Chr(10)
Terminate = CInt(txtPasses.Text) ' Target iterations
Sum = 0    ' Clear out the running total

For i = 1 To Terminate
 Sum += i
 txtResult.Text += CStr(Sum) & " (i = " & CStr(i) & ")" & NewLine
Next i

End Sub
```

Actually, there aren't too many differences between the two listings. First, we did away with the LoopStart label. We don't need it anymore. Second, because i is initialized at the start of the For statement, we dropped the statement that initialized i equal to 0.

The For statement starts by initializing i to equal its starting value. In our program, we're setting i to equal 1, but it could be any value you want, including negative values. This initialization step is done only once, when we first enter the For loop.

The program then inspects the value for Terminate. In our program, this is the value that's entered by the user. If Terminate is greater than the value of i, the For statement block code is executed. The *For statement block* is the block of statements after the For statement, but before the Next keyword. It's customary to indent the For statement block lines one tab space, as shown in the listing.

Note that if the value of Terminate is less than the initial value of i, the For statement block isn't executed. If the value of Terminate equals the initial value of i, the block statements are executed only once.

Type in the program changes shown in Listing 12.2 and compile the program. Set a breakpoint on the For statement and run the program. Now single-step the program to see how the code is executed. You'll notice that the For statement is never executed a second time. How does the loop know when to stop? That's the purpose of the Next statement.

The Next Statement

When program execution reaches the Next statement, the loop counter variable (i in our example) is incremented and then compared to the number of passes that are to be made through the loop (`Terminate` in our program). As long as the loop counter is less than or equal to the number of passes to be made through the loop, control is sent back to the first statement following the `For` statement. Therefore, control is sent back to the

```
Sum += i
```

statement after `Next` has done its job. We continue this pattern of execution until the termination condition is met. That is, we continue until `i` has been incremented to a value that is greater than `Terminate`.

Programmer's Tip

If you look at the syntax format for the `For-Next` loop, you'll notice that the loop counter name after the `Next` keyword is optional. That means you could write the `Next` statement as

```
Next i
```

as we did earlier, or you can also write it simply as

```
Next
```

omitting the name of the loop counter variable. Although this is a perfect legal way to write the `Next` statement, don't. *Always* place the name of the loop counter variable after the `Next` keyword. It helps document the code and makes it easier to read, especially if you're using nested `For` loops (we'll discuss those later in this chapter).

I strongly urge you to single-step this program to observe how the program control flow is affected. Try values for `Terminate` that are 1, 0, and −1 to see how each value affects the loop. When you can accurately predict how the loop will behave with different values for `Terminate`, you're ready for the next section of the chapter.

Using a For-Next Loop to Implement an Algorithm

Algorithm? An *algorithm* is nothing more than blueprint, or recipe, of how a particular programming problem is going to be resolved. In this section, I'm going to describe to you something I observed, and then let you try to develop an algorithm to solve the problem. After all, this is the way programs are developed in the real world. That is, the potential user describes what he wants and expects you to develop the algorithm(s) necessary to implement it.

Quite by accident, I discovered that for a given number, N, the sum of N odd positive integers is equal to the square of N.

Write a program that demonstrates this mathematical result. Now, read the sentence a few times to let it sink in. Okay, now let's try to make sense of what it says.

First, let's pick a number and see whether the description as given is correct. Let's try N equals 3. Next, it says that if we add up N odd positive integers, the sum of those integers should equal the square of the number. So, we have

```
 N = 3
Sum = 1 + 3 + 5      (Since N equals 3, then 1, 3, and 5
                 are the 3 positive integers.)
Sum = 9
```

Hmmm. It seems to work; N^2 does equal 9. Let's try it for N equal to 5:

```
 N = 5
Sum = 1 + 3 + 5 + 7 + 9
Sum = 25
```

Weird, but it works. Visually, I can explain it. For example, put a single floor tile on the floor and it forms a square. Add three more tiles and you can still form a square. Add another five tiles and you can still create a larger square. I don't have a clue how to state this mathematically, however. Further, because it's never come up at a cocktail party, maybe I don't even care to know!

Now let's design a program that implements the algorithm.

First, we need a text box that accepts the number that we want to square. (This would be our Input step from Chapter 3, "Thinking About Programs.") We'll call it **txtNumber**. We also need some way to display the results (the Output step from Chapter 3). However, rather than just displaying the square of the number, perhaps we should show how the number was derived. After all, we could cheat and just square the number and the user wouldn't know the difference.

Okay, that's good for a start. Create a new project and call it Square. Place the components on the form in a manner similar to that shown in Figure 12.3.

FIGURE 12.3

Component layout for the Square project.

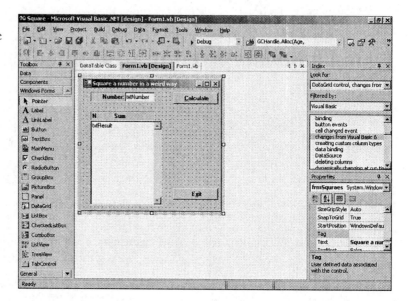

The Calculate button is named `btnCalc` and the exit button is `btnExit`. To be able to "stretch" the `txtResult` text box, you must first set its `Multiline` property to `True`. We've also added vertical scrollbars to the text box.

Now all we have to do is think about how we want to implement the algorithm in code. We definitely need a loop counter and a variable to keep the sum of the odd integers. Because the integer value increases by 2 during each iteration through the loop, we need a variable to track that value, too. Listing 12.3 presents the code.

LISTING 12.3   Code for the `btnCalc Click` Event

```
Private Sub btnCalc_Click(ByVal sender As System.Object, ByVal e As _
            System.EventArgs) Handles btnCalc.Click
  Dim Number, Sum, i, MyInteger As Integer
  Dim Newline As String

  Newline = Chr(13) & Chr(10)
  Sum = 0
  MyInteger = 1
  Number = CInt(txtNumber.Text)
  txtResult.Text = ""

  For i = 1 To Number
   Sum += MyInteger
   txtResult.Text += CStr(i) & "   " & CStr(Sum) & Newline
   MyInteger += 2
  Next

 End Sub
```

An Alternative Syntax to Define Variables

Notice how we've defined the variables in this program. In previous programs, we've defined the variables as

```
Dim Number As Integer, Sum As Integer, i As Integer, MyInteger As Integer
```

specifying the data type for each variable as it is defined. However, Visual Basic .NET enables us to use the format shown in Listing 12.3 with the same result, but using a short syntax notation.

Most of the rest of the code in Listing 12.3 should look familiar to you, so let's concentrate on the `For` loop. Variable `i` serves as our loop counter and `Number` dictates how many iterations through the loop are to be made. `Sum` holds the running total for the loop, and `MyInteger` is used to hold the integer value as the loop executes. Notice how `MyInteger` is initialized to `1` outside the loop.

Code Walk-Through

Now let's do a walk-through of the code. A code *walk-through* is when you take a piece of paper and, without running the program, execute the code in you mind, line by line. You can jot down values of key variables as you mentally run the program. For our walk-through, we'll assume the number to square is 3. This means that the value of `Number` is 3. Use Listing 12.3 as you read this section.

On the first pass through the loop, `Sum` is assigned the value of `MyInteger` in the first statement of the `For` loop statement block. Therefore, *Sum* should equal 1 when `i` equals 1. The next statement displays `i` and `Sum`, which now should both equal 1. The third statement increments `MyInteger` by 2, making its value 3. We now hit the `Next` keyword, which increments `i` by 1. Because `i` is less than `Number`, Visual Basic .NET sends control back to the first statement in the statement block.

`MyInteger` is added to `Sum`. Prior to the addition, `Sum` equaled 1. Because `MyInteger` is now 3, `Sum` equals 4 after the statement is executed. The loop counter `i` is 2 at this point and the values are displayed in the text box. `MyInteger` now has 2 added to its current value of 3, to yield its new total of 5. The `Next` statement bumps `i` by 1. Because `i` is still less than `Number`, control goes back up to the first statement in the block.

Again, `MyInteger` is added to `Sum`. `Sum` currently equals 4 and `MyInteger` equals 5. After the addition, `Sum` equals 9. The loop counter `i` is now 3. The following statement displays the data. `MyInteger` is again incremented by 2, making its value 7.

The `Next` statement increments `i` to 4. However, this time `i` is now greater than `Number`. Therefore, `Next` does not send control back for another pass. Instead, control passes to the statement following `Next` in the program. Because the next program statement is `End Sub`, the program is finished processing the `Click` event.

We've finished our code walk-through, and *Sum* equals 9 and `Number` equals 3. It appears our code does the job. You should compile and run the program to verify that the code works as advertised.

Mental Itching

The code in Listing 12.3 performs as advertised, but an itch in the back of your mind might need to be scratched. `Sum` and `MyInteger` seem to be doing about the same thing in our program. Another thing that bothers us is that we know we can make the `For` loop increment by any value we want by simply adding a `Step` keyword to the statement.

Let's modify the code in the `For` loop to that shown in the following code fragment:

```
For i = 1 To (Number * 2) Step 2
 Sum += i
 txtResult.Text += CStr(MyInteger) & " " & CStr(Sum) & Newline
 MyInteger += 1
Next
```

First of all, notice that we have added a **Step** keyword at the end of the **For** statement. The **Step** keyword tells the **Next** statement how much to increment the loop counter. If **Step** isn't specified, the default increment is 1. In our modified code, we're telling Visual Basic .NET to increment **i** by 2 on each pass through the loop. However, because we're incrementing **i** by 2 on each pass through the loop, we need to double the terminating value of the loop, which is **Number**. If we didn't do this, we wouldn't make the required number of passes through the loop.

The statement

```
Sum += i
```

simply adds **i** to **Sum**. That is, **i** can assume only odd integer values now because we're adding 2 to **i** on each pass. Therefore, if **i** starts at 1, its values become 1, 3, and 5 for the three passes through the loop. Again, this is because we overrode the default **Step** value of 1 used by the **For** loop and made it 2.

The statement to display the output in the **txtResult** text box is the same, except that we're displaying **MyInteger** instead of **i** for the first number displayed. Note that we are incrementing **MyInteger** by 1 now, so we can use it in the display to show which pass we're making through the loop. By the way, the actual assembly language code for incrementing a variable by 1 is usually one of the fastest instructions a CPU can do. Therefore, the increment on **MyInteger** will be extremely fast.

If you make the code changes and compile the program, you'll see that the program does calculate the square correctly.

Which Version Is Better?

Okay, so what do you think of our modifications? Which version of the program do you like better, and why? Think about your decision for a moment.

Personally, I don't like the second version all that much. The required multiplication of **Number** by 2 in the **For** statement confuses the intent of the algorithm. The **Step** instruction is also a distraction. Also, if there is any performance improvement, it's going to be very minor. As a result, I would probably scrap this last effort and stick with our first version of the program.

Some of you are probably a tad miffed at me right now because I made you read a few extra pages and maybe unnecessarily killed an extra tree or two. Well, not really. The process shown here is how things work in the real world. Sometimes your first try at something is the best, but most of the time a little thought will improve it[1]. In this case, it didn't. I apologize. Sometimes the second effort has more warts than the first and, when that happens, you need to admit it and change the code back to the way it was. However, rethinking a solution is almost always a good thing, so even this step backward is a positive learning experience.

---

[2] Jack Purdum, "Pattern Matching in C," *Computer Language*, November 1987. The article shows how minor algorithm changes produced an almost tenfold speed improvement.

Also, one of the primary reasons I think the first effort is better is because the intent of the code is more clearly understood in the first program. Although the second effort may exhibit more cleverly crafted code, clever code isn't necessarily good code. This is especially true when the clever code is difficult to understand. A major component of software development cost is debugging and, *ceteris paribus* (all other things being equal), clever code is harder to debug than simple, straightforward code. Good program managers abide by the KISS principle (Keep It Simple, Stupid) because they know it helps keep development costs down. If you can't resist being clever, make sure that you add enough comments to the code to demystify it.

For Loops and Arrays

A very common use for any loop structure is to process data arrays. Create a new project and call it PhoneNumbers. Add control objects to the form as shown in Figure 12.4.

FIGURE 12.4

Component objects for PhoneNumbers project.

There are two labels, three text boxes, and three buttons. These objects should all be pretty familiar to you now. Note that `txtResult` has the `Multiline` property set to `True` and the `Scrollbars` property is set to `Vertical`. Everything else is old hat by now. Some of the code, however, is not.

Structure **Data Types**

As you can probably tell from the form in Figure 12.4, our program is going to collect a set of names and phone numbers and display them in a text box. Now, we could stuff the names into one array, and then stuff the phone numbers into another array and sort of co-process the two arrays in parallel. It would work, and we'd probably do it that way if we didn't have better alternatives. After all, if the only tool you have is a hammer, pretty soon all your problems look like a nail. Not so with Visual Basic .NET. We have all kinds of tools available to us. Let's look at one that is especially suited to the task at hand. It's called the `Structure`.

Programmer's Tip

Earlier versions of Visual Basic supported something called user-defined data types. Indeed, you may hear programmers refer to user-defined data types as UDTs. UDTs have been replaced in Visual Basic .NET with `Structures`. Although this is a form of abandonment for UDTs, it's a step forward for us because most other OOP languages (C++, C#, and Java) support `Structures`.

The general form for a `Structure` declaration is

```
[AccessSpecifier] Structure StructureTag
    StructureMemberList
End Structure
```

The keyword `Structure` begins the structure declaration. It can be preceded by an access specifier such as `Public`, `Private`, or `Friend`. For the moment, however, we're ignoring the optional access specifier until we're ready to discuss it in Chapter 15, "Encapsulation."

The `Structure` keyword is followed by the *StructureTag*, or name, you want to give to the structure. Next comes the declarations for the members that you want to have in the structure. The `End Structure` keywords mark the end of the list of `Structure` members. The statements between the *StructureTag* and the `End Structure` keywords are the `Structure` statement block.

In our program, we declare a `Structure` named `PhoneList` as shown in the following code fragment:

```
Structure PhoneList
 Dim Name As String
 Dim Phone As String
End Structure
```

Here we have declared a `Structure` with the structure tag name of `PhoneList`. The `Structure` has two members, `Name` and `Phone`, both of which are `String` data types. Notice how the structure members use the `Dim` statement you've seen so many times before. The end of the structure member list and the `Structure` declaration itself are marked by the `End Structure` keywords.

Cool! Now we have a data structure named `PhoneList` that we can shove names and phone numbers into. WRONG!

Structures Are Cookie Cutters, Not Variables

Notice how careful we were to use the word *declaration* in the preceding paragraphs. Remember our discussion from Chapter 4 when we talked about *defining* variables? I stressed that the key element in defining a variable is that the operating system must hand back a valid `lvalue` for the data item to Visual Basic .NET and record it in the symbol table. Use your highlighter pen and highlight the last sentence. It's very important.

In the `Structure` code fragment shown earlier, the `End Structure` keywords tell Visual Basic .NET, "Okay, you now know all the members that belong to the `PhoneList Structure`. Make a cookie cutter that looks like this and keep it in the symbol table, but don't whack out any cookies with it yet."

The purpose of the `Structure-End Structure` keywords is to declare a list of member variables that *can* exist in the program. No storage has been allocated for the `PhoneList` `Structure`. Therefore, there are no `PhoneList` variables yet. Obviously, this also means there are no `lvalues` yet, either.

To get a `PhoneList` variable we can use in our program, we need to define one first. We can define a `PhoneList` variable as follows:

```
Dim MyList() As PhoneList
```

This statement defines a dynamic array of type `PhoneList` named `Mylist()`. Obviously, we'll set the array size later in the program. The key, however, is that we now have a variable named `MyList()` that exists in the symbol table and has an `lvalue`. (Actually, the `lvalue` of a pointer variable is defined at this point. However, the essential point is that an `lvalue` does now exist.)

Structures may not have local scope. Therefore, we need to place our structure declaration outside of any procedure definition. You'll usually give them module or namespace scope.

The concept of a `Structure` enables us to group related data together and treat it as a single data item. Plain old arrays require that the data in the array be homogeneous. That is, all of the data in the array must be of the same data type. No so for structures. The `Structure` members can be whatever data type we want them to be. Yet, the really neat thing is that we can reference this group of related (albeit dissimilar) data by a single variable name. Kim Brand once called structures "arrays for adults" because the array can have complex data members. It's a fitting description.

The btnAdd Click Event

It's pretty obvious that we want the user to type in a name and phone number and then click the Add button to add it to our list. Listing 12.4 shows the code for the `btnAdd Click` event.

LISTING 12.4   Code for the `btnAdd Click` Event

```
Private Sub btnAdd_Click(ByVal sender As System.Object, ByVal e As _
            System.EventArgs) Handles btnAdd.Click
 Static Count As Integer = 0

 If txtname.Text <> "" And txtPhone.Text <> "" Then
  Count += 1
  ReDim Preserve MyList(Count)
  MyList(Count - 1).Name = txtName.Text
  MyList(Count - 1).Phone = txtPhone.Text

  txtName.Text = ""    ' Clear for next entry
  txtPhone.Text = ""
  txtName.Focus()
 Else
  Beep()
  MessageBox.Show("Must enter both a name and a number")
 End If
End Sub
```

First, we define a variable named Count with the Static storage class. Why use the Static storage class? The reason is because Static variables can retain their values after program control leaves the procedure in which they're defined. In other words, Static variables have a lifetime that equals that of the program itself. Non-Static local variables do not. Because we want to maintain a count of the number of names and phone numbers that are entered, Count must be defined as a Static.

Programmer's Tip

True, we could define Count with module scope and it would properly track the count of the number of names and numbers entered. However, giving Count module scope crushes our goal of hiding the data as much as possible. By making it a Static inside of btnAdd, only the code in btnAdd has access to Count. Hiding the data in this way is almost always a good thing.

Although the initialization of Count to 0 is not necessary (Visual Basic .NET does this automatically), I still prefer to initialize it to 0 as a form of *documentation of intent*. That is, it tells everyone that we intend to initialize Count to 0 even if Visual Basic .NET ever decides not to. (Things could change, right?)

Next, the code uses an If statement to make sure that the user entered both a name and a phone number. A logical And operator is used for this check. Notice that if either text box is empty, an error message is displayed.

If all goes well, we enter the Then statement block. First, we increment Count by 1. We then dynamically allocate enough memory for Count elements of the MyList() array. We use the Preserve keyword because the second (and subsequent) time we enter this procedure, we want to preserve all the previously entered names and phone numbers in the array. This is exactly what the Preserve keyword does for us. (If this is fuzzy to you, review Chapter 7, "Arrays.")

The next two statements takes the string data stored in the two text boxes and assigns them into the appropriate members of the PhoneList structure. Why is the array subscripted MyList(Count - 1)?

```
MyList(Count - 1).Name = txtName.Text
```

The reason is because arrays start with element 0, but Count has already been increment to 1. Therefore, even though we might be entering the first person in the list (that is, Count = 1), that first person is actually stored in element 0 in the MyList() array. Think about it.

Once the data is stored in the array, we clear out the text boxes, and move the cursor back to the txtName text box to get ready for another name. The Focus() method of a text box is used to set the focus to the associated text box. Therefore, the Focus() method moves the cursor into the text box.

Programmer's Tip

The astute reader will recall from our discussion in Chapter 7 that ReDim statements are relatively slow. This is because ReDim statements cause messages to be sent to the Windows memory manager. Therefore, isn't it inefficient to call ReDim each time we add a new name and number? Picky, picky, picky. Yes, it is inefficient. However, because Visual Basic .NET can do several thousand ReDims in the time it takes you to hit the next keystroke, we can live with it in this case. Keyboard input and output (I/O) and mouse clicks are so slow relative to a ReDim, it will have no performance impact on our program in this situation.

The btnDone Click Event

When the user has finished entering the names and phone numbers, she clicks the Done button. This causes the list of names and phone numbers to be displayed in the **txtList** text box. The code for the **btnDone Click** event is shown in Listing 12.5.

LISTING 12.5   Code for the **btnDone Click** Event

```
Private Sub btnDone_Click(ByVal sender As System.Object, ByVal e As _
            System.EventArgs) Handles btnDone.Click
Dim i As Integer
Dim NewLine As String

NewLine = Chr(13) & Chr(10)
txtList.Text = ""

For i = 0 To UBound(MyList)
  txtList.Text += MyList(i).Name & "   " & MyList(i).Phone & NewLine
Next
End Sub
```

The code defines several working variables and the **NewLine** string. The **txtList** text box is then cleared and we start executing the **For** loop. Because **UBound()** returns the highest valid index of an array, we can use it to set the terminating value of **i** in the **For** loop.

The loop counter **i** is initialized to **0** because that's the starting element of the **MyList()** array. The statement block is a single statement that displays the name and phone number for each person entered by the user. The **NewLine** string simply causes each entry to start on a new line in the text box.

Notice how we use the loop counter variable **i** to index into the **MyList()** array. **For** loops are perfect for sequential processing of arrays. By the way, could we also use the code shown in the following code fragment?

```
For i = UBound(MyList) To 0 Step -1
 txtList.Text += MyList(i).Name & "   " & MyList(i).Phone & NewLine
Next
```

Yes, it will work, but it also shows a small bug in our program. Because we ReDim for one more index than we actually use, the program never uses the last element in the MyList() array. When you display the list in normal order, this empty array is actually displayed, but we don't notice it because all the MyList() members are unused (empty). However, because the For loop in the preceding code fragment displays the list in reverse order, we can see that the first element displayed (which is the last one in the array) is actually empty. This must also mean that although UBound() is doing its thing correctly, the count of the number of names and phone numbers is actually one less than UBound() tells us. (How would you fix this? Remember: Never use an H-bomb to kill an ant.)

Exit For—Getting Out of a For Loop Early

Our program builds an array of names and phone numbers. In a more useful program, we might want to search this list later for the name and phone number of a particular individual. Indeed, searching lists of data is a common programming problem. At issue here, however, is how to we get out of the loop early? In other words, if we have a list of 200 names and numbers and we find the one we want at index 25, do we really have to plow through 175 additional entries we're not interested in? Clearly, the answer is no.

Consider the following code fragment for our list of 200 names:

```
For i = 0 to 200
 If MyList(i).Name = PersonToFind Then
   Exit For
 End if
Next I
txtList.Text = MyList(i).Name & " " & MyList(i).Phone
```

In this For loop, we use an If statement to see whether we've found the person we're looking for. If so, the Exit For statement is executed. The Exit For statement sends program control outside of the For statement block to the statement immediately following the Next statement. In the code fragment, control would be sent to the assignment statement for txtList.Text (just after the Next statement). Therefore, you can use an Exit For to get out of the For statement block prior to reaching the terminating value of the loop counter.

Nested For Loops

We have seen how a For loop can be used to walk through a list of data. In Chapter 7, I showed how multidimensional arrays can be used to process tables of data. Nested For loops provide an easy way to work with tables of data.

To illustrate a nested For loop, let's create a new project named SquaresTable. Place label, text box, and button objects on the form as shown in Figure 12.5.

FIGURE 12.5

Placement of component objects for SquaresTable program.

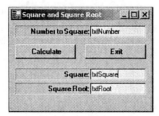

As usual, the Calculate button is named `btnCalc` and the Exit button is `btnExit`. The remaining objects are named as shown in Figure 12.5.

Even though the form would suggest that we calculate the square and square root of the number on the fly, this isn't the case. Instead we calculate all possible values as the program is loading, but before presenting the form to the user. This is a common technique used by Visual Basic .NET programmers.

First, we define an array named `Values()` with module scope. The top several lines of the program are shown in the following code fragment:

```
Imports System.Math
Public Class Form1
 Inherits System.Windows.Forms.Form

 Dim Values(1001, 3) As Double
```

The `Imports` statement for the `Math` library is necessary because we'll be using the square root routine from the library. The `Dim` statement defines a `Double` array with 1001 rows and 3 columns. Listing 12.5 shows how the array elements are processed.

LISTING 12.5 The `Form1_Load` Event

```
Private Sub Form1_Load(ByVal sender As System.Object, ByVal e As _
        System.EventArgs) Handles MyBase.Load
 Dim i, j As Integer

 For i = 0 To 1000
  For j = 0 To 2
   Select Case j
    Case 0              ' The number
     Values(i, j) = i
    Case 1              ' Square root
     Values(i, j) = Math.Sqrt(i)
    Case 2              ' Square
     Values(i, j) = i * i
   End Select
  Next
 Next
End Sub
```

Because we're using two nested loops, we need two loop counter variables, i and j. The outer loop is managed by variable i and the inner loop is managed by j. I've decided to limit the range of numbers from 0 to 1000. The Values() array tracks the value itself, its square, and its square root. (We really don't need the value itself because the array index number is the number being calculated. I just threw the number in to give us an extra number to track.)

We could have used nested If statements to fill in the values, but I decided to use a Select Case statement that uses j to execute the proper statement block. The code in each Case statement is pretty self-explanatory.

All that remains is the btnCalc Click event code, which is shown in Listing 12.6.

LISTING 12.6   The btnCalc Click Event Code

```
Private Sub btnCalc_Click(ByVal sender As System.Object, ByVal e As _
            System.EventArgs) Handles btnCalc.Click
Dim Number As Double

 If Number > 1000 Then
  Beep()
  MessageBox.Show("Only values between 1 and 1000")
  txtNumber.Focus()
 End If
 Number = CDbl(txtNumber.Text)
 txtSquare.Text = CStr(Values(Number, 2))
 txtRoot.Text = Format(Values(Number, 1), "##.#######")
End Sub
```

First, the code checks to make sure that the number entered by the user falls within the proper range. If the user entered a number that is too large, the computer's alarm is sounded via the call to Beep() and an error message is displayed. After the user reads the message and dismisses the dialog box, control is sent back to txtNumber so that the user can enter a new value.

If the number is within range, Number is assigned the user's input after being converted to a Double. The two text boxes are then filled in with the proper values as held in the Values() array. (Notice how we use Number to index into the array. This is why I said Values(i, 0) is unnecessary.)

That's it! Nested loops are most often used when the dimensions of the data table are known. If you try to use a For loop to index into an array and the loop counter exceeds the upper boundary of the array, you'll get an "out of bounds" error message. If you're unsure of the size of the array, use the UBound() function to set the number of possible passes through the loop.

Summary

In this chapter, you learned about program loops and the conditions that must be present to have well-behaved loops. You also learned how to construct a (well-behaved?) program loop using the For-Next statement. We discussed how such loops are perfect for processing problems in which the number of iterations that must be made in the loop is known. I also felt this was a good time to introduce you to Structures because they're often associated with lists of data. Finally, we wrote a simple program to process both single- and multi-dimensioned arrays with For loops.

It's probably safe to say that for any nontrivial program, most of a program's complexity is found in the statement blocks of loops. Spend some time with this chapter's exercises before you move on to the next chapter.

Review Questions

1. What is the purpose of program loops?

A. Program loops are used to repeat a series of program statements multiple times.

2. What are ill-behaved and well-behaved loops?

A. A *well-behaved* loop repeats the series of program instructions in a predictable manner and has a condition that will eventually terminate the loop. An *ill-behaved* manner does not process the loops statements in a predictable manner and often results in an infinite, never-ending loop.

3. What are the conditions that result in a well-behaved loop?

A. There's a minimum of three conditions. First, one or more variables must be initialized to a starting loop value. Second, there must be a test expression that determines whether another pass should be made through the loop body statements. The outcome of the test expression must have the possibility of terminating the loop and is normally determined by a loop control variable. Third, the variable that controls the loop must have the chance to change its state during program execution.

4. Write a program that displays a number, its square, and its cube for the values from 0 to 25 in the debug output window.

A. The program could be written as

```
Dim i As Integer

For i = 0 To 25
  System.Console.Write(CStr(i) & " " & CStr(i * i) & _
        " " & CStr(i ^ 3) & vbCrLf)
Next i
```

The program uses a For loop to generate the data requested. Notice that it possesses the three necessary conditions for a well-behaved loop. Always remember that For loops run inclusively for the terminating value of the loop. In our example, that means the values for 25 are displayed.

5. What is the difference between a pre-test and a post-test loop?

A. A *pre-test loop* has the test expression that determines whether the loop should be executed at the start of the loop structure. A *post-test* loop has the test expression at the bottom of the loop structure. Because the test expression in a pre-test loop is before the statements in the loop body, it's possible that the statements in the loop body will never be executed. However, because the test expression in a post-test loop is at the end of the loop structure, the statements of the loop body are always executed at least one time.

6. What kind of testing (pre-test or post-test) is done with a `For` loop and a `Do-While` loop?

A. The `For` loop is a pre-test loop. A `Do-While` loop can be written as either a pre-test or post-test loop.

7. Assume that you're writing an automated fire alarm system. There are several hundred fire and smoke sensors scattered throughout a building and each sensor is polled every few seconds by your program. The first alarm in the list is assigned the value `StartingAlarmNumber` and the last one is named `EndingAlarmNumber`. The alarm currently being polled is determined by a variable named `CurrentAlarmToTest`. The alarms are numbered sequentially and are integer values. The function responsible for polling the sensors is named `PollAlarms()` and uses `CurrentAlarmToTest` as its argument. If everything is normal, the function returns logic `False` after each sensor is polled and it proceeds to the next alarm. If there's a fire, the function returns the number of the sensor and the program must calls the fire depart using a function named `CallFireDepartment()` with `CurrentAlarmToTest` as its argument. What would the code look like? (You can assume that the code for `PollAlarms()` and `CallFireDepartment()` already exists in the namespace.)

A. Although there are many variations, one solution might be

```
CurrentAlarmToTest = StartingAlarmNumber     ' Initialize to first alarm
Do
 If PollAlarms(CurrentAlarmToTest) Then     ' Start checking them
  Exit Do                    ' If there's a fire, get out
 End If
 CurrentAlarmToTest += 1              ' No fire, look at next alarm
 If CurrentAlarmToTest > EndingAlarmNumber Then ' Start over?
  CurrentAlarmToTest = StartingAlarmNumber ' Yep
 End If
Loop While True
CallFireDepartment(CurrentAlarmToTest)         ' Call for help
```

A `Do-While` loop with a post-test is used. This means we'll always enter the loop at least once. The `If` test calls the `PollAlarms()` function and returns `False` if there is no fire. If there is a fire, the return value from `PollAlarms()` is non-zero and the `Exit Do` statement is executed, which sends control to `CallFireDepartment()`. If there is no fire, `CurrentAlarmToTest` is incremented and tested to see whether we're at the end of the alarm list. If we are at the end, `CurrentAlarmToTest` is reset to its starting value. Because the loop test is set to logic `True`, we've purposely written an infinite loop, so another pass is made through the loop. The program should stay in this loop until there is a fire.

8. Suppose that you have a U.S. stamp collection and you want to track the stamps you have using the Scott number of the stamp (this is a standard classification numbering system used by collector and should be a string), the date you bought the stamp, how much you paid for it, and a brief description. Right now, you're just starting to collect, so you have only 20 stamps. How would you organize the data? (You don't have to set up the text boxes or the like—just show how you would organize the data.)

A. You might use

```
Structure MyStamps
 Dim Scott As String
 Dim PurchaseDate As Date
 Dim Cost As Double
 Dim Description As String
End Structure
```

to organize the data into a **Structure** type. This declaration must appear outside of any procedure call. Because you have 20 stamps, you'll need 20 variables of this structure type. Therefore, elsewhere in the code you would write

```
Dim MyCollection(20) As MyStamps
```

You would now have 20 such structures that you could fill in with the data about each stamp. In Chapter 23, "Disk Data Files," and Chapter 25, "Database Programming with Visual Basic .NET," you'll learn how you can write such data to a data file or a database.

9. How can you exit from a nested **For** loop?

A. The problem is that the **Exit For** statement transfers control out of only the current **For** loop. This still leaves you in the outer **For** loop. For example:

```
Dim i, j, foundit, Goal, ThisOne As Integer

' Some code that sets our Goal
For i = 1 To 100
 For j = 1 To 100
  ' code that sets ThisOne
  If ThisOne = Goal Then
   Exit For
  End If
 Next j
 ' The Exit For puts us here
Next i
```

In the code, if we find what we're looking for, the **Exit For** statement transfers us to the point of the last comment in the code fragment. However, we want to end both loops once we found what we are looking for. In other words, we want to be at the statement following **Next i**, not **Next j**.

To do this, modify the code as follows:

```
foundit = 0
For i = 1 To 100
 For j = 1 To 100
```

```
 ' code that sets ThisOne
 If ThisOne = Goal Then
  foundit = 1          ' Set our success flag
  Exit For
 End If
Next j
 ' The Exit For puts us here
 If foundit = 1 Then     ' Did we have success?
  Exit For             ' Yep, so get outta Dodge
 End If
Next i
```

The code uses what is called a *flag variable* to set a flag when some desired state is reached. In the preceding code, `foundit` is a flag variable that's initialized to `0`. If we find what we're looking for, `foundit` is set to 1 and the `If` test after the `Next j` statement causes the second `Exit For` to be executed and we transfer control out of the nested loops. You should be able to convince yourself that program control will stay in the loops through all passes or until `foundit` is set to `1`.

CHAPTER 13

While **LOOPS**

In this chapter, you will learn the following:

- While End While Loops
- The BinaryConversion Program
- Do While Loops—Flavor One
- Do While Loops—Flavor Two
- Until Loops
- Terminating Do Loops Early
- Sentinels

This chapter continues the discussion of program loops that we began in Chapter 12, "The For Loop." However, the flavor of the loops changes a little from the For loops we studied earlier. You learned how For loops are often used when the number of iterations to be made through the loop is known before the loop begins to execute. In this chapter, we'll study While loops. While loops are often used when the number of loop iterations is *not* known when the loop begins executing.

In this chapter, you'll learn about three different types of While loops and how they differ from each other. You'll also learn what to consider when deciding between the various loop structures during program design.

While End While Loops

The general syntax structure for a While loop is

```
While Expression1
   WhileStatementBlock
End While
```

The While statement is based on the Boolean evaluation of *Expression1*. As long as *Expression1* evaluates to logic True, the program statements in *WhileStatementBlock* are executed. If there are multiple statements in the While statement block, control is sent back to

Expression1 for reevaluation after the last statement is executed. When *Expression1* evaluates to logic **False**, program control is sent to whatever statement follows the **End While** keywords.

While End While Syntax Rules

Let's explore this syntax with the following code fragment:

```
Dim Number as Integer

Number = 10

While Number < 20
  DoThis()
  Number += 1
End While
```

Notice that the **While** loop executes as long as **Number** is less than 20. *Expression1*, therefore, is a relational comparison that must yield a Boolean result of either True or False. The fact that *Expression1* is a Boolean result has two important implications.

First, it's possible for the statements controlled by the **While** loop never to be executed. For example, suppose that we assigned 30, instead of 10, into **Number** in the preceding code fragment. In that case, the Boolean result for *Expression1* (that is, **Number < 20**) would be **False** when it's first evaluated. This means the two statements controlled by the **While** would never be executed.

Second, if *Expression1* evaluates to **True**, the statements controlled by the **While** are executed. Equally important, however, is that some statement in the **While** statement block must be able to falsify the outcome of *Expression1* at some point. If the statements cannot falsify *Expression1*, an infinite loop results. For example, what would happen if we removed the statement

```
Number += 1
```

from the code fragment? In that situation, *Expression1* would always be **True** because no statement in the loop alters the initial value of **Number**. This results in an infinite loop, which would cause the program to hang in the **While** loop. Not good.

It should be clear from this discussion that well behaved **While** loops require the same three conditions we studied in Chapter 12. That is, the variable that's used to control the loop must be initialized, the variable needs to be evaluated by a relational test, and the variable must be able to assume a value that will result in a logic **False** evaluation.

The BinaryConversion Program

Let's write a program named BinaryConversion that uses a **While** loop. The various control objects are shown in Figure 13.1.

FIGURE 13.1

The form and control objects for the BinaryConversion program.

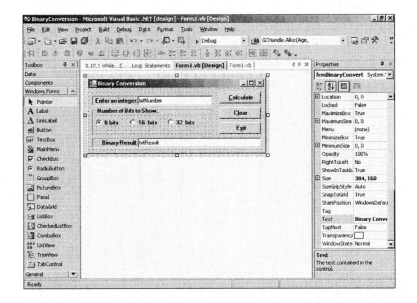

The three buttons are named `btnCalc`, `btnClear`, and `btnExit`. Inside a group box, I've also added three radio buttons named rbBits8, rbBIts16, and rbBits32. These radio buttons are used to select whether the binary number is display with 8, 16, or 32 bits. The Clear button is simply used to clear the `txtNumber` and `txtResult` text boxes.

More Than Meets the Eye

What isn't clear just by looking at Figure 13.1 is that the program is capable of converting either way. That is, if you type a decimal number into `txtNumber` and click the Calculate button, the binary representation of the number is shown in the `txtResult` text box. However, if the `txtNumber` text box is empty and you type a binary representation of a number into the `txtResult` text box and click Calculate, the decimal value for the binary number is shown in the `txtNumber` text box. This means the program can do decimal-to-binary or binary-to-decimal conversions. In other words, this program is actually useful!

First, let's look at the `btnCalc Click` event code. This is shown in Listing 13.1.

LISTING 13.1   Code for the `btnCalc Click` Event

```
Private Sub btnCalc_Click(ByVal sender As System.Object, ByVal e As _
          System.EventArgs) Handles btnCalc.Click
Dim number As Long, BitCount As Integer

 If rbBits8.Checked = True Then        ' 8-bit result?
  BitCount = 8
 Else
  If rbBits16.Checked = True Then      ' Perhaps 16-bit?
```

LISTING 13.1 Continued

```
    BitCount = 16
  Else
    BitCount = 32              ' Must be 32-bit.
  End If
 End If
 If txtNumber.Text <> "" Then        ' Did they enter a decimal number?
  number = CLng(txtNumber.Text)
  txtResult.Text = ConvertToBinary(number, BitCount)
 Else
  If txtResult.Text <> "" Then
   txtNumber.Text = ConvertToDecimal(txtResult.Text)
  End If
 End If

End Sub
```

The code defines two working variables and then does a series of **If** tests to determine whether the user wants the result displayed in a field of 8, 16, or 32 bits. Next, the code checks to see whether the **txtNumber** text box is empty. If the text box isn't empty, we assume the user wants to convert the number in the text box to binary. The code then calls the **ConvertToBinary()** function. The value returned is then displayed in the **txtResult** text box.

If the **txtNumber** text box is empty, the code checks to see whether the user entered a binary number into **txtResult**. If so, the code calls the **ConvertToDecimal()** function. The value returned from the call is displayed in the **txtNumber** text box.

It should be obvious that most of the work is done by the two functions that are called in the **btnCalc Click** event. Let's take a look at these two functions.

The `ConvertToBinary()` Function

The code for the decimal-to-binary converter is shown in Listing 13.2.

LISTING 13.2 The Code for the Decimal-to-Binary Function

```
Public Function ConvertToBinary(ByVal number As Long, ByVal bits As _
                Integer) As String
' Purpose: to convert a number into a string that is the
'      binary representation of the number
'
' Parameters:
'  number the decimal number to convert expressed as a long
'  bits  the number of bits to show
'
' Return value:
'   string the binary representation of the number
'
 Dim Length As Integer
 Dim One As Integer, power As Long
```

LISTING 13.2   Continued

```
Dim bin As String

Length = bits          ' Save bit count

While Length >= 0
 power = 2 ^ Length
 One = CInt(number \ power) ' Divide number by appropriate power
 If One Then
  bin += "1"      ' If big enough
 Else
  bin += "0"
 End If
 number = number Mod power ' Get the remainder
 Length -= 1
End While
         ' This keeps the result within the bit length
ConvertToBinary = Microsoft.VisualBasic.Right(bin, bits)
End Function
```

First, notice that we comment the code so the reader can get an idea of what the function does. We do this because this particular function could be used by other programmers in other programs. After the function's documentation, several working variables are defined. The Length variable is set equal to bits. A While loop begins with a test on the number of bits passed to the function. The number of bits can be 8, 16, or 32, depending on which radio button the user selected.

Notice that the While loop tests Length to see that it is greater than or equal to 0. If the user selects 8 bits, Length equals 8 and we enter the While loop. This code is a little tricky. Because we're going to allow 0 to be a valid condition for another iteration of the While loop, we'll have a total of nine passes through the loop. That's because we allow all positive numbers (that is, the 8 bits) *plus* the pass through the loop when Length is zero. An example will show why we do it this way.

Suppose that the user selects 8 bits, but enters the number 256. The largest number that can be represented in 8 bits is 255. To show the binary value 256 would require 9 bits to display, or

100000000

The program statement near the end of Listing 13.2

ConvertToBinary = Microsoft.VisualBasic.Right(bin, bits)

returns only the rightmost 8 bits of the string, or 00000000. This is exactly what should be returned if the user selects 8 bits. If the user subsequently selects 16 bits, the number can be properly displayed. This also allows the program to work even if the user enters a number that's too large for the number of bits selected (within reasonable limits).

Let's look at the code inside the While loop in Listing 13.2. Suppose the user enters 128 for the number and selects 8 bits. In the first statement, we have

```
power = 2 ^ Length
power = 2 ^ 8
power = 256
```

The next line then becomes

```
One = CInt(128 \ 256)
One = CInt(0)
One = 0
```

Recall that integer division cannot have a fractional value, so 128 divided by 256 is 0. The `If` statement results in a 0 being assigned into `bin`.

The next statement evaluates:

```
number = number Mod power
number = 128 Mod 256
number = 128
```

Because the `Mod` operator returns the remainder of integer division, 256 divides into 128 zero times with a remainder of 128. Therefore, `number` still equals 128. We then decrement `Length` from `8` to `7` and return back to the top of the `While` loop.

Now let's evaluate the next three statements again:

```
power = 2 ^ 7
power = 2 ^ 7
power = 128
```

The next line then becomes

```
One = CInt(128 \ 128)
One = CInt(1)
One = 1
```

The `If` test now adds a `1` to `bin`, which now becomes `01`.

Look what happens in the next statement:

```
number = number Mod power
number = 128 Mod 128
number = 0
```

If we divided 128 by 128, we get 1 with a remainder of 0. Because `number` is now 0, the statement near the top of the loop becomes

```
One = CInt(0 \ power)
```

for the rest of the passes through the `While` loop. You should be able to convince yourself that this will result in seven zeroes being concatenated to `bin`. Because `bin` is already equal to 01, when it finishes the loop, it will equal

```
010000000
```

The final statement at the bottom of the function

```
ConvertToBinary = Microsoft.VisualBasic.Right(bin, bits)
```

means that only the rightmost eight bits are returned, which becomes `10000000`. This is the binary value of 128.

The `ConvertToDecimal()` Function

The `ConvertToDecimal()` function takes a binary number and converts it into a decimal number. The code is presented in Listing 13.3.

LISTING 13.3   The `ConvertToDecimal()` Function Code

```
Public Function ConvertToDecimal(ByVal bits As String) As String
 ' Purpose:  to convert a binary number into a decimal number
 '
 ' Parameters:
 '  bits   the string of bits that is the binary number
 '
 ' Return value:
 '  string  the decimal representation of the binary number
 '
 Dim i, Length As Integer
 Dim result As Long

 Length = bits.Length - 1
 result = 0
 i = 0
 While Length >= 0
  If bits.Substring(i, 1) = "1" Then
  result += 2 ^ Length
  End If
  Length -= 1
  i += 1
 End While
 ConvertToDecimal = CStr(result)
End Function
```

Let's suppose that the user presses the Clear button to remove whatever strings happen to be in the text boxes. Suppose the user types the string `101` into the `txtResult` text box. When the user clicks the Calculate button, the `ConvertToDecimal()` function is called.

`Length` is assigned one less than the length of the string that holds the binary number. In our example, `Length` equals 2. The code then sets `result` and `i` equal to `0` and we enter the `While` loop.

The statement

```
If bits.Substring(i, 1) = "1" Then
```

uses the `Substring()` method to examine a single character in the `bits` string. On the first pass through the loop, the value of `i` is `0`, so we're looking at the first character in `101`, or the first 1 in the `bits` string. (Review Chapter 6, "String Variables," if you don't recall how the

`Substring()` method works.) Therefore, because the `If` test is True, we enter the `Then` statement block.

When we enter the `Then` statement block, the value of `Length` is 2, so the statement

```
result += 2 ^ Length
```

becomes

```
result += 2 ^ 2
result += 4
```

Because `result` was **0** to begin with, `result` now equals 4. Next, `Length` is decremented by 1 and variable `i` is incremented to 1. Program control then goes back up to the `While` statement. Because `Length` is still greater than or equal to 0, the relational test is True and we execute another pass through the loop.

The `Substring()` method now examines the second character in the `bits` string, which is **0**. The `If` test fails, and we again decrement `Length` and increment `i`. Control is again sent back to the top of the `While` loop.

The `Substring()` method now examines the last character in the string, a 1. Because the `If` test is True, we process the result statement. At this point, `result` equals 4, so

```
Result += 2 ^ 0
4 += 1
5
```

which is the value of result after the statement is executed. `Length` is decremented, `i` is incremented, and control goes back to the top of the `While` loop. However, `Length` now equals -1, so *Expression1* is logic False, and the `While` loop is not executed. The final statement in the function is executed and the string value of `result` (that is, 5) is passed back to the caller. Therefore, the binary number 101 is decimal 5. Taa-Daa…it works!

Save your work; these routines may be useful in other programs you write. (Keep in mind that we're experimenting with only positive numbers.) Experiment with different values and single-step through the code to see how the control of the program is affected by the `While` statements.

Do While Loops—Flavor One

Several flavors of `Do-While` loops are available to you. The major difference between them is where the relational test is performed. The first version we will explore has the syntax form:

```
Do While Expression1
  DoWhileStatementBlock
Loop
```

Expression1 is a Boolean expression that evaluates to either logic True or False. If *Expression1* is logic True, the statements in the `Do-While` statement block (that is, *DoWhileStatementBlock*) are executed. When the `Loop` keyword is reached, control is directed back to the Do-While test on *Expression1*. As long as *Expression1* is logic True, the loop statements continue to be executed. When *Expression1* becomes logic False, control is sent to the first statement following Loop.

For example, let's write a program that simulates tossing a coin. Let's further assume that we want to see how many coin tosses it takes before we get a certain number of heads in a row. Start a new project named CoinTosses and add the objects shown in Figure 13.2.

FIGURE 13.2

The placement of objects for the CoinTosses project.

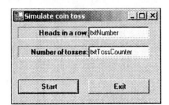

The first text box, named **txtNumber**, is the number of heads we want in a row. Text box **txtTossCounter** shows how many tosses were made before we got the desired number of heads. Consider Listing 13.4 for the **btnStart Click** event.

LISTING 13.4   Code for the **btnStart Click** Event

```
Private Sub btnStart_Click(ByVal sender As System.Object, ByVal e As _
            System.EventArgs) Handles btnStart.Click
Dim Tosses, Heads, ThisToss, Target As Integer

Heads = 0
Tosses = 0

If txtNumber.Text <> "" Then    ' Make sure they entered a number
 Target = CInt(txtNumber.Text)
Else
 MessageBox.Show("You need to enter a number.")
 Exit Sub
End If
Do While Heads <> Target
 ThisToss = TossACoin()  ' Function returns 1 for head
 If ThisToss = 1 Then
  Heads += 1        ' It was a Heads, increment the count
 Else
  Heads = 0         ' Tails...start over
 End If
 Tosses += 1            ' The toss counter
Loop
 txtTossCounter.Text = CStr(Tosses)
End Sub
```

Notice how we check to make sure that the user entered a number into the `txtNumber` text box. If the user didn't enter a number, an error message is displayed and we leave the subroutine.

We've written a function named `TossACoin()` that returns a 1 if a heads was tossed, or `0` if a tails was the result. When we enter the `Do-While` loop, `Heads` is `0`, which means the relational test that `Heads` is not equal to `Target` is logic True. This causes control to enter the `Do-While` statement block. The code for the `TossACoin()` is presented in Listing 13.5.

LISTING 13.5   Function to Simulate Tossing a Coin

```
Private Function TossACoin() As Integer
 ' Purpose: To simulate tossing a coin. The function
 '        return 1 for a Head, and 0 for a tail.
 '
 ' Parameters
 '
 ' Return value
 '   integer    1 for Head, 0 for tails
 '
 TossACoin = Int(2 * Rnd())
End Function
```

A call to the `Randomize()` function seeds the random number generator so that a nonrepeatable series of pseudo-random numbers is produced. The function needs to be called only once before `Rnd()` is used, so we placed the call in the `Form_Load` event. (The `Randomize()` function uses the system timer for this purpose.) The call to `Rnd()` returns a value between 0 and 1 as a `Single` data type. When you want a value to fall between two values, you use the formula:

```
Int((upperlimit - lowerlimit + 1) * Rnd() + lowerlimit)
```

Because we want either a 1 or a 0, our formula becomes

```
Int((1 - 0 + 1) * Rnd() + 0)
Int(2 * Rnd())
```

which is the statement we used in Listing 13.4.

Programmer's Tip

If you call `Rnd()` with a negative number as an argument, such as `Rnd(-1)`, the function returns a repeatable sequence of random numbers. That is, you'll get the same series of random numbers each time. This can be useful when debugging a program. Obviously, if you're seeding `Rnd()` this way, there's no reason to execute a call to `Randomize()`.

I'll assume that by now you're comfortable adding the code for the Exit button. Figure 13.3 shows a sample run.

FIGURE 13.3

Sample run of the
CoinTosses project.

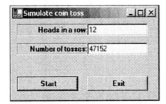

As you can see from Figure 13.3, it took 47,152 tosses before we got 12 heads in a row. If you care to repeat the experiment, I've seen as few as 14 tosses give 12 heads in a row! You might want to put a breakpoint on the **Do-While** statement and single-step the program so that you can see how the loop works.

Do While Loops—Flavor Two

The second type of **Do-While** loop has the following syntax:

```
Do
    DoWhileStatementBlock
Loop While Expression1
```

The only real change is that the test on *Expression1* is moved to the bottom of the loop. The logic, however, is still the same. If *Expression1* is True, another iteration of the loop is made. However, having the test of *Expression1* at the bottom of the loop has one important implication: The loop is always executed at least one time.

When *Expression1* is at the bottom of the loop, the statements in the loop block are executed before the test on *Expression1* is evaluated. For example, suppose that we have a fire alarm system that calls a function that reads all the fire sensors in the building. If there is no fire, the call returns **0**. If there is a fire, the call returns the sensor number where the fire is located. Now consider the following code fragment:

```
Dim Fire As Integer

Fire = CheckSensors()

Do While Fire = 0
    Fire = CheckSensors()
    If Fire Then
      CallSecurity()
    End If
Loop
```

Even though this code is a little simplistic, it does illustrate the point. With the preceding **Do-While** loop, what if the first call to **CheckSensors()** does in fact find a fire? Because **Fire** is nonzero, the loop is never executed and **CallSecurity()** is never called.

So, we change the code to

```
Dim Fire As Integer

Fire = CheckSensors()

Do
  If Fire Then
    CallSecurity()
  End If
  Fire = CheckSensors()
Loop While Fire = 0
```

In this situation, even though `Fire` is already nonzero, we enter the loop and, hence, make the call to `CallSecurity()`. The only difference between the two versions is that the test on whether to execute the loop is made at the bottom of the loop rather than the top.

As an exercise, you could rewrite the coin toss program to use the `Do While` with the test at the bottom. What changes would you have to make in the code?

Until Loops

`Until` loops are very similar to the `While` loops we studied earlier. However, the previous `While` loops had their loop block executed as long as the test condition (*Expression1*) was True. `Until` loops have their statement block executed until the test condition *becomes* True. The `Until` loop kind of reverses the normal loop logic.

Do Until

Like the `While` loop, there are two flavors of the `Until` loop. The first form of the `Until` has the syntax

```
Do Until Expression1
  DoUntilStatementBlock
Loop
```

The statement block for the `Do Until` version executes as long as *Expression1* evaluates to logic False. When *Expression1* becomes logic True, control is sent to the statement following the `Loop` keyword.

For example, in our coin toss program, we could rewrite the loop to use the `Do Until` as shown in the following code fragment:

```
Do Until Heads = Target
 ThisToss = TossACoin() ' Function returns 1 for head
 If ThisToss = 1 Then
  Heads += 1 ' It was a Heads
 Else
  Heads = 0  ' Tails...start over
 End If
 Tosses += 1  ' The toss counter
Loop
```

In this case, we enter the loop with `Heads` not equal to `Target`. As long as `Heads` is not equal to `Target`, the loop statement block continues to execute. When the condition does become logic True, and `Heads` does equal `Target`, the loop block no longer executes. The `Do Until` loop is useful in a "keep-looking-for-something-until-you-find-it" type of situation.

Programmer's Tip

`Until` loops aren't used as often as you might think. Although they're suited to the "keep-looking-for-something-until-you-find-it" type of problem, `Until` loops are predicated on the assumption that whatever you're looking for is actually there to be found. However, in many programming problems, you're searching through a list, unsure that what you're looking for is even in the list. This is like your Mom telling you to keep looking for something in your room when your evil twin sister threw it out two days ago. `Until` loops can become infinite loops if what they're searching for isn't present.

Keep in mind that `Do Until` loops continue to execute as long as the test expression is logic False, not True.

Loop Until

The second type of `Until` loop is the `Loop Until`. It has the syntax form:

```
Do
    LoopUntilStatementBlock
Loop Until Expression1
```

Note that the `Loop Until` evaluates the test expression at the bottom of the loop. Therefore, `Loop Until` always executes the loop's statement block at least once. Just like the `Until` loop, `Loop Until` continues to execute the loop's statement block until *Expression1* becomes logic True.

Could we use `Loop Until` in our coin toss program? Sure. Consider the following code fragment:

```
Do
 ThisToss = TossACoin() ' Function returns 1 for head
 If ThisToss = 1 Then
  Heads += 1 ' It was a Heads
 Else
  Heads = 0  ' Tails...start over
 End If
 Tosses += 1  ' The toss counter
Loop Until Heads = Target
txtTossCounter.Text = CStr(Tosses)
```

This change has no real effect on the program, because we always have to make at least one pass through the loop to simulate a coin toss.

Terminating Do Loops Early

For all the Do loops studied in this chapter, you can use the Exit Do statement to send program control outside the current loop block. For example:

```
Do While 1
   If Names(i) = TargetName Then
     Exit Do
   End If
   i += 1
Loop
```

In this code fragment, we search through a list of names held in the Names() array until we find TargetName. Because the If test is logic True, the Then statement block with the Exit Do statement is executed. This sends program control to the statement following the Loop statement.

What is the meaning of the following line?

```
Do While 1
```

In this case, *Expression1* of the test expression is hard-wired to be logic True. This guarantees that we'll enter the Do While loop. That's the good news. The bad news is that we'll stay in this loop forever unless we find what we're looking for. In other words, what the code is actually saying is

```
Do While True
```

thus creating an infinite loop. This loop is constructed in the belief that we'll eventually find a match and the Exit Do statement will terminate the (otherwise infinite) loop. Loops like this are perfectly acceptable, provided you know an Exit Do statement will eventually be executed.

Nested Do Loops and Exit Do

If you have nested Do loops and use an Exit Do, where does program control go? Does the Exit Do send control out of all the Do loops, or just the one in which the Exit Do appears? Simply stated, an Exit Do sends program control outside of the loop in which the Exit Do statement appears. An example might help you understand what happens:

```
Do While Temperature < Critical
 Do While Ph < Acidic
  If Vat10 = 0 then
   Exit Do
  End if
  Vat10 -= 5
 Loop       ' Ph < Acidic
  Temperature = ReadTemp()
Loop   ' Temperature < Critical
```

In this code fragment, the outer `Do While` is controlled by `Temperature` and `Ph` controls the inner `Do While` loop. If `Vat10` equals `0` (this is, becomes empty), the `Exit Do` statement is executed. This sends program control to the

```
Temperature = ReadTemp()
```

program statement. Any `Exit Do` statement can terminate only the loop in which the `Exit Do` statement appears.

Sentinels

As I mentioned earlier, one of the dangers of using an `Until` loop is that it assumes that the test expression will eventually become logic True. That's not always the case, however. How can you address this problem and still use the `Until` loop?

One way is to know the size of the list you're searching before entering the loop. Often, this isn't a problem. For example, if you're searching a list of names, they might be stored in a `String` array. You can then use the `UBound()` function to find out how large the array is. You might use code like that shown in Listing 13.6.

LISTING 13.6   Using a **Do Until** to Search for a Name

```
Dim i, ListSize as Integer

ListSize = UBound(Names)

Do Until Names(i) = LookingFor
 If i = ListSize then
  Exit Do
 End If
 i += 1
Loop
```

In this code, we march through the list of names looking for a match. However, because we've set `ListSize` to the number of names in the list, the `If` statement with its `Exit Do` guarantees that we won't have an infinite loop. The loop will terminate even if the person's name isn't in the list.

Although the code in Listing 13.6 works, it can be improved. It's not uncommon for today's databases to have several million names in them. Anything we can do to speed up things in loops that might execute millions of times will improve the program. Consider the changes reflected in Listing 13.7.

LISTING 13.7   Using a Sentinel in a `Do Until`

```
Dim i, ListSize as Integer

ListSize = UBound(Names)

ReDim Preserve Names(ListSize + 1)    ' Make room for 1 more
Names(ListSize + 1) = LookingFor

Do Until Names(i) = LookingFor
 i += 1
Loop

If i <= ListSize Then
 MessageBox.Show("Found it!")
Else
 MessageBox.Show("Name not in list.")
End If
```

Let's see what the impact of our changes is. First, we set `LimitSize` to the current size of the list. Let's assume that `LimitSize` is 50,000. We then use `ReDim` to resize the array for one more name. (We use the `Preserve` keyword so the existing list of names remains intact.) The next statement assigns the name we're looking for into this last empty slot in the `Name()` array. This entry is called a *sentinel*. Therefore, element 50,001 in the `Name()` array becomes our sentinel. The sentinel *guarantees* that the `Name()` array now contains the name we're looking for.

Now look at the loop statement block. It no longer contains the `If` statement to check whether we're at the end of the array. Why bother? We know we will at least find a match on the sentinel at element 50,001 and exit the `Do Until` loop. The sentinel guarantees that we'll exit the loop.

Once we're finished executing the loop, all we have to do is decide whether we really did find a match, or if it was the sentinel that terminated the loop. If `i` is less than or equal to `ListSize`, we must have found a real match in the list of names. That is, if `i` is less than 50,001, the `Do Until` loop terminated because it found a match in the list of names. If `i` equals 50,001, we know we found the sentinel, which means the name was not in the list. The `If` statement at the bottom of Listing 13.7 shows how you might handle the decision as to which match was found.

The improvement is that we've added a few new statements *outside* the loop to get rid of an `If` statement inside the loop. If we're searching a list with thousands of names in it, we avoid executing that `If` statement on each pass through the loop. A thousand here, a thousand there, and pretty soon the time savings starts to add up.

In certain situations, sentinels can make a big difference in the performance of a program. One of the most time-consuming aspects of a program's execution time is executing program loops. Loops are frequently a major cause of poor performance, or *bottlenecks*, in a program. If you're unhappy with the time it takes for your program to execute, loops are often a fruitful place to start looking for bottlenecks. In some cases, a sentinel might just be the solution you need to break the bottleneck.

Summary

In this chapter, we studied the various types of **Do** loops that Visual Basic .NET makes available to you. You learned that **Do** loops are often used when the terminating condition is not known when entering the loop. You also learned that **Until** loops are useful when you want to execute a set of instructions until some condition becomes True. Finally, you learned how a sentinel can be used to improve loop performance.

Program loops are very important elements of any program, primarily because they often comprise such a large component of the program's total execution time. Because of this importance, pay close attention to them when you design your programs.

Review Questions

1. When do you use a **While End While** loop?

A. **While End While** loops are normally used when the number of iterations that must be made through the loop is unknown when the loop is entered. This is unlike most **For** loops, where the number of passes to be made is often known before the loop begins execution.

2. Convert the following code to a **While** loop:

```
For i = 20 to 0 Step -1
  Sum += cint(i)
Next i
```

A. One way is

```
Dim i, sum As Integer

sum = 0
i = 20
While i > 0
  sum = sum + i
  i = i - 1
End While
```

Notice that the three conditions for a well-behaved loop are still present.

3. Use a **While** loop to find the factorial of 10. (Recall that a *factorial* is the product of all integer values from 1 to the number being factored. For example, 5 factorial is 5 * 4 * 3 * 2 * 1 = 120.)

A. Again, there are various ways that this could be written, but one simple one is

```
Dim num, factorial As Double

num = 9
factorial = num + 1
```

```
While num > 0
 factorial *= num
 num -= 1
End While
```

4. What is the primary difference between a `Do While` loop and a `Do Until` loop.

A. A `Do While` loop executes as long as the test expression evaluates to logic True. A `Do Until` loop executes as long as the expression is logic False.

5. Assume that a huge text buffer named `buff` holds thousands of words from a text file. You want to count the frequency of each letter of the alphabet found in the text file. Uppercase and lowercase letters are treated the same. At the end of the program, you want to show the counts for each letter. How would you write the code?

A. Try:

```
Dim i As Integer, length As Integer, index As Integer
Dim buff As String, Counts(26) As Integer

buff = "aeeeeeeemmmmmmmg"

For i = 1 To Len(buff)
   index = Asc(UCase(Mid$(buff, i, 1))) - Asc("A")
   Counts(index) = Counts(index) + 1
Next i

For i = 0 To 25
   If Counts(i) <> 0 Then
      Debug.Print Chr$(i + 65); Counts(i)
   End If
Next i
```

6. Suppose that you're a cryptography expert. You're sent a file that you know contains a hidden message. You also know that the letters in the message are *N* letters apart, but you've forgotten what *N* is. Write a program that looks for the correct *N* to decipher the message. You can use the following short piece of text to test your program. When N is correct, a message should appear.

"vBiGl;iowQs fe BhrloZdpiM ylBFwe/']rqadsbaw"

A. One way might be

```
Dim bump, i, length As Integer
Dim buff As String

buff = "vBiGl;iowQs fe BhrloZdpiM ylBFwe/']rqadsbaw"

length = buff.Length
bump = 0

Do While True
   bump += 1
   console.system.write ("bump = "; bump; " ")
```

```
    For i = 1 To length
       If i + bump > length Then
          Exit For
       End If
       console.system.write (Mid$(buff, i + bump, 1))
       i = i + bump
    Next i
    console.system.writeline("")
    If bump > length / 2 Then
       Exit Do
    End If
```

Loop

In the program, **bump** is the factor that sets the spaces between characters. The **For** loop uses **bump** to march along the string. (You could use a **For** loop with a **Step** argument is you chose.) The two **If** statements are used to prevent unnecessary passes through the loop. (How does it do that?)

CHAPTER 14

ADVANCED ARRAY PROCESSING

> **In this chapter, you will learn the following:**
> - Declaring and defining arrays
> - Sorting an array
> - Searching an array
> - Other array properties and methods
> - Arrays as objects
> - Sample program using an array object
> - Collections

*I*n this chapter, you'll learn about some of the more advanced array processing features that Visual Basic .NET makes available to you. In fact, many of these features weren't available in earlier releases of Visual Basic because they're integral parts of Visual Basic .NET's `Array` class.

Before we can tackle these advanced features, it's important that you understand some fundamental differences in the ways that arrays can be defined in Visual Basic .NET. We'll take on that task first.

Declaring and Defining Arrays

In Chapter 7, we discussed how you could define and use arrays in your programs. For example, you learned that the statement

```
Dim Numbers(10) As Integer
```

defines an array of 11 integers. Remember that the number enclosed within the parentheses is the highest index allowed, starting with 0. The number is *not* the number of elements being defined.

I've also been quite emphatic about the distinction between declaring and defining variables in Visual Basic .NET. The `Dim` statement defines the `Numbers()` array because Visual Basic .NET made a call to the Windows memory manager and got enough storage for 11 integer numbers. How much actual storage was given back for the array?

Array Scalars

Actually, that's the real purpose of the word `Integer` in the preceding `Dim` statement. `Integer` serves as a scalar that Visual Basic .NET uses to determine how much storage is needed for the array. Because `Integer` numbers take four bytes each, the scalar for `Numbers()` is 4. Therefore, Visual Basic .NET needs 44 bytes for the 11 integers in the `Numbers()` array. In other words, Visual Basic .NET took the number of integers that were requested for the array (that is, 11) and multiplied it by the scalar size of an integer (that is, 4) to determine it needs 44 bytes of memory. Assuming that Windows could find 44 bytes of free memory hanging around, Windows returned the memory address for those 44 bytes to Visual Basic .NET.

Array Indexing

After you've defined the `Numbers()` array, you may use it in a Visual Basic .NET statement. Suppose that you enter the following assignment statement:

```
Numbers(3) = 20
```

What does Visual Basic .NET do with this statement? Let's assume that the storage for `Numbers()` array is 5000. After the definition of the array, it would look something like that shown in Figure 14.1.

FIGURE 14.1

A memory image for the `Numbers()` array.

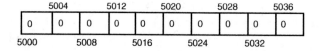

When Visual Basic .NET processes the assignment statement, the first thing it must to is fetch the memory address for `Numbers()`. This is memory address 5000 (that is, its `lvalue`). Next, Visual Basic .NET takes the array index (or subscript) of the element being used; `3`, in our example. It then takes the scalar value for the `Numbers()` array, which is 4 for an `Integer` data type, and multiplies it by the index. The product 12 (that is, 12 = 4 * 3) is then added to the base memory address to get the address where the new `rvalue` is to be placed. We can show this processing as follows:

```
Numbers(3) = 20
lvalue + (index * scalar) = rvalue
5000 + (3 * 4) = 20
5000 + 12 = 20
5012 = 20
```

The assignment statement can be interpreted as the left side of the assignment operator determines *where* in memory to put *what* appears on the right side of the assignment operator. Stated more simply, the left side of the assignment operator is "where" to put the "what" from the right side of the operator. When the processing is finished, the `Numbers()` array looks as shown in Figure 14.2. Notice how the 4 bytes starting at memory address 5012 have changed from Figure 14.1.

FIGURE 14.2

A memory image for the `Numbers()` array after assignment.

	5004		5012		5020		5028		5036
0	0	0	20	0	0	0	0	0	0

5000   5008   5016   5024   5032

It's important for you to understand that indexing into any array is done by calculating an array offset from the base address of the array. The calculation of the array offset is always made using the scalar size of the data item and the index number of the element being used in the expression. Although the math gets a tad more complex, multidimensional arrays use the same array offset method to determine the memory address of a given element.

The good news is that you rarely have to do the indexing math yourself. Visual Basic .NET takes care of all those nasty details for you. However, you should understand how Visual Basic .NET processes array data using array offsets.

Sorting an Array

Let's write a simple program that sorts the data in an integer array. Start a new project and name it RandomNumbers. Figure 14.3 shows the form and objects for the program.

FIGURE 14.3

Form and objects for the RandomNumbers project.

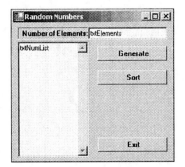

The `txtElements` text box is used to hold the number of elements in the array we're going to use. The `txtNumList` is the text box that will display the contents of the array. For the `txtNumList` text box, you need to set the `Multiline` property to `True` and the `Scrollbars` property to `Vertical`. The three buttons are named `btnGen`, `btnSort`, and `btnExit`. Name the form `frmRandomNumbers`.

First, we need to define the array that will hold the integer values. Place the `Dim` statement so it has module scope, as shown in the following code fragment:

```
Public Class frmRandomNumbers
 Inherits System.Windows.Forms.Form
 Dim Elements, Numbers() As Integer
```

The Dim statement defines two integer variables. The Elements variable is the number of elements the user wants to use in the program. The Numbers() variable is the array of integers.

Listing 14.1 shows how Elements is set in the program.

LISTING 14.1   Setting the Value of Elements

```
Private Sub txtElements_Leave(ByVal sender As Object, ByVal e As_
               System.EventArgs) Handles txtElements.Leave
 Elements = CInt(txtElements.Text)
End Sub
```

Elements is set by using the CInt() conversion function to convert the number typed in by the user and assigning the result into Elements.

The Generate button is used to generate Elements random numbers and store them in the Numbers() array. The btnGen Click event code in Listing 14.2 shows how this is done.

LISTING 14.2   The btnGen Click Event Code

```
Private Sub btnGen_Click(ByVal sender As System.Object, ByVal e As _
              System.EventArgs) Handles btnGen.Click
 Dim i As Integer

 ReDim Numbers(Elements)       ' Set the array size
 txtNumList.Text = ""          ' Clear the output text box

 For i = 0 To Elements
  Numbers(i) = CInt(Rnd() * 100)
  txtNumList.Text &= CStr(Numbers(i)) & vbCrLf
 Next i

End Sub
```

The procedure redimensions the Numbers() array to size Elements. The For loop is used to insert Elements random values into the Numbers() array. Because Rnd() returns values between 0 and 1, we multiply the return value by 100 to get the integer values to fall within the range of 0 to 100.

The second statement in the For statement block simply displays the random numbers in the txtNumList text box. Notice the symbolic constant vbCrLf at the end of the statement. This is the newline character that we built ourselves in several earlier programs.

Programmer's Tip

Move the cursor to the `vbCrLf` constant in the listing and double-click to highlight it. Now press the F1 key. This will present you with a list of the symbolic constants that Visual Basic .NET makes available to you. Any time you want information about a Visual Basic .NET keyword or function, highlighting it and pressing the F1 key will call up Visual Basic .NET's online help for the highlighted item.

If you ran the program at this point, you could get a list of random numbers to be displayed in the `txtNumList` text box. A sample run is shown in Figure 14.4.

FIGURE 14.4

A sample run of the RandomNumbers program.

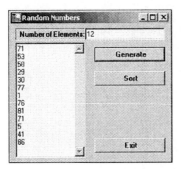

In this example, we've elected to generate 12 random numbers, which we have then displayed in the output window by clicking the Generate button.

To sort those numbers, we need to examine the code associated with the `btnSort Click` event. This code is shown in Listing 14.3.

LISTING 14.3   Code for the `btnSort Click` Event

```
Private Sub btnSort_Click(ByVal sender As System.Object, ByVal e As _
              System.EventArgs) Handles btnSort.Click
 Dim i As Integer

 Array.Sort(Numbers)
 txtNumList.Text = ""
 For i = 0 To Elements
  txtNumList.Text &= CStr(Numbers(i)) & vbCrLf
 Next
End Sub
```

All the work associated with sorting the array is done with a single statement:

```
Array.Sort(Numbers)
```

All arrays in Visual Basic .NET have certain methods that you can use to process the data in the array. The `Sort()` method is one of those methods. As you can tell from Listing 14.3, the `Sort()` method syntax is

```
Array.Sort(ArrayToSort)
```

Notice that the method is prefixed with the `Array` class name, which is integral to Visual Basic .NET. All you have to do is supply the name of the array and the `Sort()` method does all the work for you. What's really nice about the `Sort()` method is that Visual Basic .NET is smart enough to know the type of data that has to be sorted. If you were to write your own routine, you would need to write a separate sort routine for each data type you want to sort, or you would have to write a (more complex) generalized sort routine that could handle all data types.

After the array is sorted, a `For` loop is used to display the sorted list of values in the `txtNumList` text box. A sample run after the list is sorted is shown in Figure 14.5.

FIGURE 14.5
Sample run after the
`Sort()` method is called.

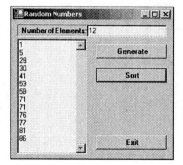

Searching an Array

A common programming task is to search through a list of data for a specific value. The list might be a list of names, phone numbers, part numbers, or any one of a thousand other possibilities. Quite often, the reason for the search is to get a piece of information that can be used to find additional information associated with the list. For example, a list of names might have an account number tied to it, which then opens the door into a database. Therefore, because list searching is often the front end for other aspects of a program, we want it to be as efficient as possible.

Volumes have been written on how to organize and structure data. For the moment, we'll examine only two very simple ways to search data: a sequential search and a binary search.

Sequential Search

The simplest method for search a list of data is to start at the first object in the list and compare it to the object you're looking for. If they match, you're done. If they don't match, you look at the next object for a match. This process of starting at the beginning of the list and proceeding through the list on a one-by-one basis is called a *sequential* search. Clearly, if you get lucky using a sequential search, you could find the object on the first try. If you're unlucky, you might find it after looking at every object in the list.

On average, a sequential search will examine *N*/2 objects in a list of *N* objects before finding a match. Therefore, if you have 100 objects in the list, on average, you'll look at 50 items to find a match. Although this works, it isn't very efficient.

Binary Search

A binary search of a list of data is much more efficient. That's the good news. The bad news is that a binary search requires that the list being searched be in sorted order. To understand how a binary search works, suppose that your friend wants you to guess a number he has in mind that's between 1 and 100. What's the best way to find the number in the fewest guesses? We'll assume that your friend will tell you if your guess is too high, too low, or the correct number.

To illustrate, let's assume that your friend is thinking of the number 77. You should guess 50 on your first try. Your friend responds, "Too low." You now can eliminate half of the numbers in the list because the number must fall between 51 and 100. (We'll assume that your friend doesn't lie.)

With your next guess, you should again try to eliminate half the list, so you would guess 75. Your friend would again respond, "Too low." You now know the number falls between 76 and 100. Again picking the midpoint of the numbers that remain, you guess 88. This time, the response is, "Too high." You now know the number falls between 76 and 87.

Picking the next midpoint yields a guess of 81. The response is, "Too high." The value must fall between 76 and 80. Again selecting the midpoint, you try 78 and the response is, "Too high." Now you know the number is either 76 or 77. You try 77 and get the correct value.

This process of dividing the range in half with each guess is called a *binary search*. Notice how you were able to zero in on the number with only 6 guesses. If you had used a sequential search, you would have had to make 77 guesses to find the number. When the length of the list is in the thousands or millions of items, the performance gain for the binary search is significant.

Let's take a closer look at the binary search process. Given that our program already sorts the data, let's extend the program to perform a binary search.

We need to add a few more objects to our form, as shown in Figure 14.6.

We added a new label named `Label2`, a text box named `txtSearch`, and a button named `btnFind`. The other controls are the same as they were in Figure 14.3.

Visual Basic .NET provides a binary search method that you can use on data arrays. Listing 14.4 shows the code for the program.

LISTING 14.4   Complete Code Using the `BinarySearch()` Method

```
Public Class frmRandomNumbers
  Inherits System.Windows.Forms.Form
  Dim Elements, Numbers() As Integer
```

LISTING 14.4 Continued

```vb
Region " Windows Form Designer generated code "

Private Sub btnGen_Click(ByVal sender As System.Object, ByVal e As _
            System.EventArgs) Handles btnGen.Click
  Dim i As Integer

  ReDim Numbers(Elements)
' Remember if Elements = 10, you actually get 11 (0 - 10)
  txtNumList.Text = ""
  For i = 0 To Elements
   Numbers(i) = CInt(Rnd() * 100)
   txtNumList.Text &= CStr(Numbers(i)) & vbCrLf
  Next i
  txtSearch.Visible = False
  Label2.Visible = False
  btnFind.Visible = False

End Sub

Private Sub btnExit_Click(ByVal sender As System.Object, ByVal e As _
            System.EventArgs) Handles btnExit.Click
  Me.Dispose()
End Sub

Private Sub txtElements_Leave(ByVal sender As Object, ByVal e As _
            System.EventArgs) Handles txtElements.Leave
  Elements = CInt(txtElements.Text)
End Sub

Private Sub btnSort_Click(ByVal sender As System.Object, ByVal e As _
            System.EventArgs) Handles btnSort.Click
  Dim i As Integer

  Array.Sort(Numbers)
  txtNumList.Text = ""
  For i = 0 To Elements
   txtNumList.Text &= Format(i, "00") & " " & CStr(Numbers(i)) & vbCrLf
  Next
  txtSearch.Visible = True
  Label2.Visible = True
  btnFind.Visible = True

End Sub

Private Sub frmRandomNumbers_Load(ByVal sender As System.Object, _
            ByVal e As System.EventArgs) Handles MyBase.Load
  txtSearch.Visible = False
  Label2.Visible = False
  btnFind.Visible = False

End Sub
```

LISTING 14.4   Continued

```
Private Sub btnFind_Click(ByVal sender As System.Object, ByVal e As _
            System.EventArgs) Handles btnFind.Click
    Dim val As Integer

    val = CInt(txtSearch.Text)
    txtSearch.Text &= " = " & CStr(Array.BinarySearch(Numbers, val))
End Sub
End Class
```

FIGURE 14.6

Form and objects for the
binary search program.

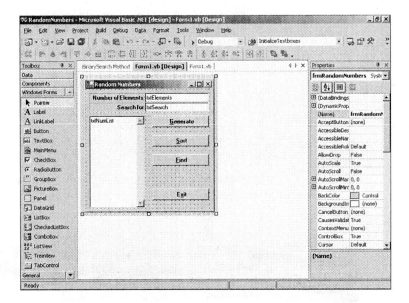

There actually isn't much new in the program. In the **frmRandomNumbers_Load** event, we make
the label and text box for the binary search value invisible. We also set the **Visibility** property for **btnFind** to **False**. These minor details simply prevent the user from trying to find a
value in the list until after the list of sorted values is calculated and displayed.

The real work in the **btnFind Click** event is done with only two statements:

```
val = CInt(txtSearch.Text)
```

```
txtSearch.Text &= " = " & CStr(Array.BinarySearch(Numbers, val))
```

The **txtSearch** text box accepts the user input for the value to find. The second statement
then calls the **BinarySearch()** method of the **Array** class to find the value entered by the user.
The first parameter to the method is the array to search (**Numbers**) and the second parameter is
the value to find (**val**).

If **BinarySearch()** can find a match on **val** in **Numbers()**, it returns the index for the match.
If the value occurs in the array multiple times, the index returned is for the first appearance in

the array. If the value isn't found in the list, a negative value is returned. A sample run is shown in Figure 14.7.

FIGURE 14.7

Sample run for `BinarySearch()` array method.

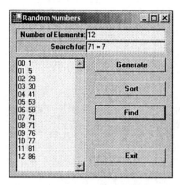

If you look closely at Figure 14.7, you'll notice that there are two values of 71 in the array. In the Search for: text box, you'll see that the `BinarySearch()` method returned the index for the first 71 it found in the list.

Try running the program yourself to confirm the behavior of the `BinarySearch()` method. Also try some values that aren't present in the list. What happens in those cases?

IndexOf

Sometimes the array you want to search isn't in sorted order, and there's no reasonable means by which to sort it. That rules out `BinarySearch()`. Indeed, it may take more time to sort the array than it would just to do a sequential search of it. In such a situation, the `IndexOf()` method provides a viable alternative to the binary search.

The syntax for the `IndexOf()` method is

```
Element = Array.IndexOf(ArrayToSearch, ValueToFind)
```

The first parameter, *ArrayToSearch*, is the array that you want to search. The second parameter, *ValueToFind*, is the value in the array that you want to locate. If the value is in the array, the call returns the index of the element holding the value (*Element*). If the value cannot be found in the array, a negative value for *Element* is returned.

You might try changing the code presented in Listing 14.4 to use the `IndexOf()` method instead of `BinarySearch()`. I leave this as an exercise for the reader.

Other Array Properties and Methods

A number of other properties and methods are available for you to use with arrays. A partial list of some of the more useful array properties and methods are presented in the following sections.

Length

The syntax for this array property is

```
ElementCount = MyArray.Length
```

The property is the *total* number of elements in the array. Note that this is not the same as the upper bound index of an array. For example, if you had an array defined as

```
Dim MyArray(10, 10) As Integer
```

ElementCount would equal 121 for `MyArray()`. That's because each dimension for the array runs from 0 through 10, or 11 elements.

Rank

The syntax for this property is

```
NumDimensions = MyArray.Rank
```

The property is the number of dimensions for the array. The comment tells the `Rank` for each array.

```
Dim MyArray(10,10) As Integer     ' Rank = 2
Dim YourArray(11) As Integer      ' Rank = 1
```

In some circumstances, knowing the `Rank` in conjunction with symmetrical arrays can be useful in loop processing.

Clear

The syntax for this method is

```
Array.Clear(ArrayToClear, StartAtIndex, NumberToClear)
```

The first parameter is the name of the array you want to clear. The second parameter is the starting index to be cleared. Normally, this would be element 0, but this and the third parameter enable you to partially clear an array. The third parameter is the number of elements that you want to clear. For example,

```
Dim X(100) As Integer
```

```
Array.Clear(X, 0, 10)
```

would clear out elements 0 through 9. Please note, however, that the statement

```
Array.Clear(X, 3, 3)
```

clears out elements `X(3)`, `X(4)`, and `X(5)`. Therefore, keep in mind that the middle parameter is an index number, not element position.

Copy

This method makes two forms available to you. The first version is

```
Array.Copy(SourceArray, DestinationArray, NumberToCopy)
```

This version says to copy *NumberToCopy* elements from the *SourceArray* into the *DestinationArray*. Note that the two arrays must have the same Rank.

The second version is

```
Array.Copy(SourceArray, SourceStart, DestinationArray, _
        DestinationStart, NumberToCopy)
```

In this case, you can copy a certain number of elements, starting at a position other than zero. You also can place the source elements in the destination array at a different location. For example,

```
Array.Copy(X, 10, Y, 20, 50)
```

says to copy 50 elements from the X() array starting at index 10 and place them in the Y() array starting at index 20.

GetLength

The syntax for GetLength is

```
NumberOfElements = MyArray.GetLength(WhichDimension)
```

This method yields the number of elements in the array for the dimension specified, as stored in *NumberOfElements*. For example,

```
Dim NumEl, X(10), Y(10,20) As Integer

NumEl = X.GetLength(0)
NumEl = Y.GetLength(1)
```

The first statement would find NumEl equaling 11, whereas the second call would find *NumEl* equal to 21.

This method could be useful with the Rank property of an array. For example, if an array is passed in and you're unsure of its size, Rank could tell you how many dimensions it has and GetLength could tell you the size of each dimension.

Reverse

This method has two flavors. The first is

```
Array.Reverse(ArrayToReverse)
```

This method flips the array so that the last value in the array becomes the first value in the array. In other words, if your array exists in ascending sorted order, after calling this method, the array will be sorted in descending order.

The second version has the syntax:

```
Array.Reverse(ArrayToReverse, StartIndex, Length)
```

In this version, you can reverse just part of the array starting with the *StartIndex* index of the array, reversing *Length* elements. For example,

```
Dim X(10) As Integer
```

```
Array.Reverse(X, 3, 3)
```

would flip positions for elements `X(3)`, `X(4)`, and `X(5)`.

Other array methods and properties are available to you. I've presented some of the more common ones in this section. You can use the Visual Basic .NET online help to explore the others.

All of these array-processing features are made possible because Visual Basic .NET creates arrays as objects of the `Array` class. This makes array processing different from other dialects of Basic you may have used. However, it also makes using arrays in Visual Basic .NET very easy.

Arrays as Objects

Even though all arrays in Visual Basic .NET are actually objects, Visual Basic .NET provides a means for defining array objects that is different from those provided by other dialects of BASIC. We discussed arrays at considerable length in Chapter 7. However, that discussion was based on the standard way to define arrays common to all BASIC dialects. In this section, we explore the more explicit definition of array objects in Visual Basic .NET.

Reference Variables

The following two lines of code define an array object of type `Integer`:

```
Dim Values As Integer()
```

```
Values = New Integer(5){}
```

Notice that the syntax is a little different than we've seen before. The first statement creates a variable named `Values`. In our previous definition of an `Integer` array, `Values` was immediately followed by two parentheses. The parentheses enclosed a number that defined the highest index for the array.

This definition for `Values` is substantially different. The parentheses now follow the `Integer` keyword. Using this syntax causes Visual Basic .NET to place `Values` into the symbol table in a very different way than other BASICs would. Visual Basic .NET performs the usual checks of the symbol table (for example, whether `Values` already exists in the symbol table, and so on) and makes a request to the Windows memory manager for some storage. However, the storage request it makes is *not* for an integer array. Instead, Visual Basic .NET asks for enough storage to hold a reference variable. A *reference variable* is a special variable that is used to hold a memory address as its `rvalue`. Let's see what's really going on with these two statements.

As I mentioned, the first statement defines a variable named `Values` and identifies it as a reference variable. Visual Basic .NET asks Windows for enough memory to store one reference variable. Assuming that there is some free memory, Windows passes back an `lvalue` where `Values` can be stored. It records that `lvalue` in the symbol table and then makes a special note in the symbol table that this variable is a reference variable. It does this because Visual Basic

.NET can do special things with reference variables that it can't do with other (non-reference type) variables.

After the first statement is completed, **Values** can be depicted as shown in Figure 14.8.

FIGURE 14.8

A representation of the **Values** reference variable.

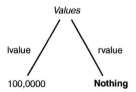

The **rvalue** is initialized by Visual Basic .NET to hold a unique value called **Nothing**. Actually, **Nothing** is a keyword in Visual Basic .NET and it used to indicate an empty **rvalue** for a reference variable. In Figure 14.8, we've assumed that **Values** exists in memory at location 100,000.

Programmer's Tip

Reference variables are similar to pointer variables in other languages, like C++. In those languages, **Nothing** has the same interpretation as a Null pointer.

All Reference Variables Require the Same Storage

What isn't clear from Figure 14.8 is that *all reference variables take the same amount of storage*; 4 bytes for each reference variable. In other words, it wouldn't matter if **Values** were an **Integer** array or an array of **Doubles**, the amount of storage for **Values** would always be the same. The reason is because a reference variable always holds the same thing: a memory address. That is, a valid reference variable will have an **rvalue** that is either a memory address or **Nothing**. That's it…nothing else is allowed! Let's see why.

Let's look at the second statement:

```
Values = New Integer(5){}
```

When Visual Basic .NET sees this statement, it goes to the symbol table and looks for a reference variable named **Values**. If Visual Basic .NET doesn't find **Values** in the symbol table, you'll get an error message stating that **Values** is not declared. (If I were in charge of error messages at Microsoft, the message would say the variable is not *defined*. Given that the person with the most toys wins, I don't think I'm going to get this changed anytime soon.)

Assuming that **Values** is properly defined in the symbol table, Visual Basic .NET then sees the keywords **New** and **Integer**. The **New** keyword tells Visual Basic .NET we want to create a new object. The **Integer** keyword tells Visual Basic .NET what type of object to create. The **5** enclosed in parentheses tells Visual Basic .NET this is an array-of-integers object and that we want enough storage for six integer values. Don't forget, the parenthesized number is the highest index allowed, not the number of elements. In this example, it asks for elements 0 through

5 for a total of six elements. I'll explain what the curly braces (that is, the { and }) mean in a moment.

After reading the entire statement, Visual Basic .NET knows the type of object you want (that is, an array of Integers) and its size (that is, six integers). Visual Basic .NET then sends a message to Windows: "Hey, Windows! Visual Basic .NET here. I need enough storage for six integers. How's it looking?" Assuming that the memory is available, Windows sends a message back saying, "Hey, Visual Basic .NET! It's me, Windows. I found the storage you need. It's located at memory address 80,100." Visual Basic .NET then places that memory address into the symbol table as the rvalue for Values. Our memory image for Values now looks like that shown in Figure 14.9.

FIGURE 14.9

A representation of the Values reference variable after object creation.

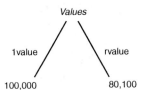

The important thing to notice in Figure 14.9 is that we've replaced the Nothing rvalue for Values with the memory address of where the object is stored in memory.

Note an important difference here between the old-style data definition and the style presented here. With the old style, the statement would have been

```
Dim Number as Integer
```

and Number would be an integer variable, not a reference variable. In this case, if Number had the same lvalue of 100,000, it would occupy memory locations 100,000 through 100,003. Any values held in Number would appear in the memory locations 100,000 through 100,003. (This isn't the case for the Values variable because it's an array.) Therefore, if Visual Basic .NET wants to access Number, it would simply go to the lvalue (that is, 100,000) and return the 4 bytes it finds there.

However, because Values is marked in the symbol table as a reference variable, Visual Basic .NET knows that the rvalue of Values isn't an integer value. Instead, the rvalue of Values is the memory address of where the integer data is found. With a reference variable, to find the value of the first element in the array, Visual Basic .NET reads the rvalue, jumps to that memory address, and fetches the first 4 bytes starting at memory address 80,100. The process of reading a memory address from an rvalue and then jumping to that memory address is called *indirection*. In other words, the memory address in the reference variable Values allows Visual Basic .NET to indirectly fetch the values of the integer array object after jumping to the proper memory address.

Programmer's Tip

Any of you who have taken the time to wade through the assembly language code will recognize that I've taken a few liberties in the precise mechanics of the way things work. However, I feel the simplification is warranted because it makes the explanation that follows a little clearer.

If all this seems like you spent the last 15 minutes talking with Yogi Berra, perhaps Figure 14.10 will help. First of all, let's assume that **Number** is defined as a simple integer number (not an array object). We'll further assume that it's stored in memory starting at address 100,000. For the **Values** reference variable, we'll assume that it's located at memory address 90,000, and Windows has located its object storage at memory address 80,100. We'll further assume that **Number** has the value of 1 and the first 5 elements of **Values** store the integer values 1 through 5.

Given those details, a memory image for both variables appears in Figure 14.10. Note that the figure on the left is for the standard **Integer** definition, whereas the image on the right is for the reference variable.

FIGURE 14.10

The difference between defining an integer and defining an array object.

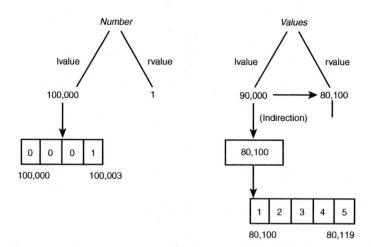

As you can see in Figure 14.10, the standard integer definition has an **lvalue** (100,000) that marks where the integer is stored in memory. Therefore, its **rvalue** actually is the value of the integer (1 in our example).

The reference to an array object is different. Because **Values** is a reference variable, its **rvalue** refers (or points) to the memory location where we find the first element of the array. Therefore, we fetch the **rvalue** (80,100) of **Values**, jump to that memory location via the process called indirection, and then start reading the values in the array from that memory location. Each value in the array is read as a four-byte chunk starting at memory address 80,100.

After the array object is defined, we can use the reference variable in our code just like any other array.

Initializer Lists for Array Objects

When you define an array object, you can also initialize its elements to specified values if you want. For example, the following statement:

```
Dim MyMonths As Integer()
MyMonths = New Integer() {31,28,31,30,31,30,31,31,30,31,30,31}
```

defines the MyMonths Integer array and initializes its 12 elements to the days in each month. You can accomplish the same effect in a single statement:

```
Dim MyMonths As Integer() = New Integer() {31,28,31,30,31,30,31,31,30,31,30,31}
```

If you don't have any values that you want to use to initialize the array, you may use

```
Dim MyMonths As Integer() = New Integer(11) {}
```

Note you must still supply the curly braces at the end of the statement, but the initializer list within the curly braces is empty. Once again, notice that the parameter in the parentheses is the highest index in the array, not the number of elements.

By the way, you can also use an initializer list with the other style of array definition. For example:

```
Dim Numbers() As Integer = {1, 2, 3}
```

would define and initialize an array of three elements. Note that you cannot supply an array size within the parentheses following the array name when you use an initializer list. It should be clear, therefore, that when an initializer list is used, it's the number of values in the list that determines the number of elements in the array.

So, why all the fuss about reference variables? The reason is because reference variables behave differently than normal variables. Because Visual Basic .NET arrays use reference variables, they can be used in ways that might be a little surprising.

Sample Program Using an Array Object

Let's write a short program that uses an array object. The form we want to use is shown in Figure 14.11.

The txtList text box has its Multiline property set to True and its Scrollbars property set to Vertical. The three buttons are named btnCalc, btnShow, and btnExit. btnShow has its Visible property set to False, because we don't want it available to the user when the program first starts running.

The first four lines of the program are shown in the following code fragment:

```
Public Class frmArrayObjects
 Inherits System.Windows.Forms.Form
```

```
Dim MyList As Integer() = New Integer(10) {}
Dim MyCopy As Integer()
```

FIGURE 14.11

Form for the array object program.

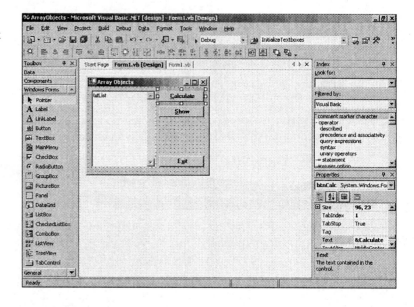

The code starts by defining the **MyList** integer array with module scope. Note that the reference definition and the storage request for the array object are combined into a single statement. This means that **MyList** will have an **rvalue** that points to the storage location in memory after Visual Basic .NET finishes processing this statement.

The next statement defines another reference variable named **MyCopy**, but Visual Basic .NET does *not* create storage for a new array object. Recall that this means that **MyCopy** is created as a reference variable that has an **lvalue**, but its **rvalue** is set to **Nothing**.

Now let's look closely at the **btnCalc Click** event code. This is shown in Listing 14.5.

LISTING 14.5   Code for the **btnCalc Click** Event

```
Private Sub btnCalc_Click(ByVal sender As System.Object, ByVal e As _
          System.EventArgs) Handles btnCalc.Click
Dim i As Integer

txtList.Clear()
For i = 0 To 10
  MyList(i) = i    ' Just fill in some values
Next i

MyCopy = MyList    ' Magic!
```

LISTING 14.5   Continued

```
For i = 0 To 10
  txtList.Text &= MyCopy(i) & vbCrLf
Next
btnShow.Visible = True

End Sub
```

First we clear out the `txtList` text box and then use a `For` loop to fill in some values for the `MyList()` array. Each element simply receives the value of `i` as we progress through the loop.

The next statement assigns `MyList` into `MyCopy`. What does this assignment statement actually do? When you think about it, assignment statements move the `rvalue` of one operand of the assignment operator into the `rvalue` of the other operand. That is, assignment operations are expressions that resolve to `rvalue-into-rvalue` for its operands. (Honestly...think about this before you read further!)

Suppose that `MyList` is stored at memory location 70,000 and the array object is stored at 80,000. Let's further assume that `MyCopy` is stored at memory address 90,000. The image of these two reference variables prior to the assignment statement is shown in Figure 14.12.

FIGURE 14.12
Memory image for
`MyList` and `MyCopy`.

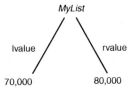

Notice that the `rvalue` of `MyCopy` is `Nothing` because we didn't create a new object for it.

Now consider the assignment statement of `MyList` into `MyCopy`. Because the assignment expression copies the `rvalue` of `MyList` into the `rvalue` of `MyCopy`, the assignment statement:

```
MyCopy = MyList     ' Magic!
```

causes the `rvalue` for `MyCopy` to be changed from `Nothing` to 80,000.

Think about what this assignment means. *Both reference variables now refer to the same object in memory!* Therefore, anything we do to `MyCopy` is actually impacting `MyList`. The rest of the code in the procedure simply displays the `MyList` array values and makes the Show button visible. The state of the program at this point is shown in Figure 14.13.

The purpose of the Show button is to illustrate that `MyCopy` and `MyList` actually reference the same array object in memory. The code for the Show button in Listing 14.6 proves this fact.

FIGURE 14.13
Output of ArrayObjects
program before pressing
the Show button.

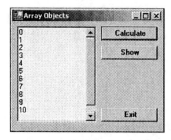

LISTING 14.6   The Code for the **btnShow Click** Event

```
Private Sub btnShow_Click(ByVal sender As System.Object, ByVal e As _
            System.EventArgs) Handles btnShow.Click
Dim i As Integer

MyCopy(5) = 52443   ' Set a new value for copy

txtList.Clear()    ' Clear the old data

For i = 0 To 10    ' Now show ORIGINAL list!
  txtList.Text &= MyList(i) & vbCrLf
Next

End Sub
```

After defining the **For** loop variable **i**, the procedure assigns a number into an element of the
MyCopy array object. Note that we have done nothing with the original **MyList** data. The old
data in the **txtList** text box is cleared out by a call to the **Clear()** method. (The data being
cleared out is the original **MyList** data.)

Now, pay attention! The **For** loop redisplays the **MyList** data. Note we're showing the **MyList**
data; not the **MyCopy** data. Figure 14.14 shows the output of the program after this **For** loop
finishes.

FIGURE 14.14
Program output after
pressing the Show
button.

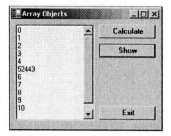

Notice how the output for **MyList(5)** is changed even though the assignment statement for
52443 was performed on **MyCopy(5)**. The reason this works this way is because *both reference
variables point to the same area in memory* for the array object. Therefore, **MyCopy** points to the

`MyList` array object, not a copy of it. While `MyCopy` and `MyList` may have different names, they both reference the same object in memory. This is why the change to `MyCopy` changes the value in `MyList`.

Reference variables are extremely useful things. For example, suppose that we want a function to manipulate the data in an array. Further assume that the array has several hundred thousand elements in it. Which is more efficient: copying several hundred thousand values onto the stack and calling the function, or copying a single 4-byte reference variable onto the stack and calling the function? The choice is a no-brainer.

Collections

This is a good place to introduce you to the concept of a collection. A *collection* is simply a group of related objects. Although you can define your own collections, in this introduction we'll use the predefined `Controls` collection to show how it can be used.

Every form you create has a `Controls` collection. The `Controls` collection object lets you reference all the controls on the form.

Magic Squares

Let's write a program that produces a magic squares matrix. As you may know, a magic squares matrix is one where all the rows, columns, and main diagonals in the matrix add to a single value. The controls for the magic squares form are shown in Figure 14.15.

FIGURE 14.15

The controls for the Magic Squares program.

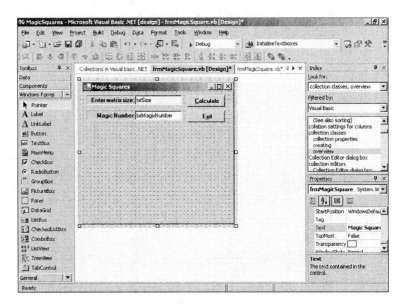

The controls include two text boxes named `txtSize` and `txtMagicNumber` and two buttons, `btnCalc` and `btnExit`. What isn't shown in Figure 14.15 are the text boxes that we add to the form at runtime.

The following code fragment shows the top four lines of the program that defines the array of text box objects:

```
Public Class frmMagicSquare
 Inherits System.Windows.Forms.Form
 Dim txtElement(81) As TextBox
 Dim MatrixSize As Integer
```

The third line says that we have 81 text box objects defined for use in the program. However, because we haven't used the `New` keyword, we haven't actually created an instance of the text boxes at this time. Listing 14.7 shows the code for the `frmMagicSquare_Load` event. As you will recall, the `form_load` event code is the code that executes when the form is first loaded into memory.

LISTING 14.7   The `Form Load` Event for the Magic Squares Program

```
Private Sub frmMagicSquare_Load(ByVal sender As System.Object, _
        ByVal e As System.EventArgs) Handles MyBase.Load
 Dim ctl As Control
 Dim i As Integer

 InitializeTextboxes()

 For Each ctl In Controls
  Console.WriteLine(CStr(i) & " = " & Controls(i).Name)
  i += 1
 Next

End Sub
```

The first thing the procedure does is call a subroutine named `InitializeTextboxes()`. The primary duty of the initialization procedure is to create an instance of the 81 text boxes that we'll use in the program. I'll show that code in a moment. Of greater interest at the moment is the loop that follows the initialization routine.

For Each, Next

The `For Each, Next` loop is used to iterate through a Visual Basic .NET collection. The syntax for the `For Each, Next` loop is

```
For Each ControlVariable In TheCollectionGroup
    ' loop statement block
Next [ControlVariable]
```

`ControlVariable` is a variable that's used to iterate through the elements in the collection. Notice that the name of the control variable (`ControlVariable`) is optional after the `Next` keyword. However, I suggest that you always include it.

The type of the control variable (*ControlVariable*) must match the type in the collection (*TheCollectionGroup*). In Listing 14.7, the *ControlVariable* is named `ctl` and is defined as a type `Control`. The reason it must be of the `Control` type is because we want to inspect the controls on the form. This information is held in the `Controls` collection of the form.

In the statement block, we're simply displaying the name of the controls in the debug window by calling `Console.WriteLine()` to display the control's index number and name. Figure 14.16 shows a sample run, with a breakpoint set and the `End Sub` statement in Listing 14.7.

FIGURE 14.16

The Debug output window showing the text box control names.

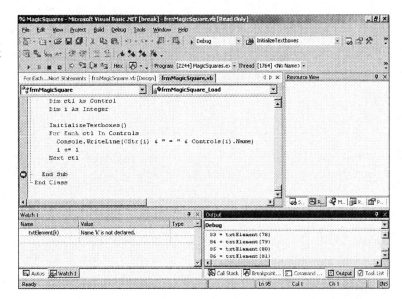

In the lower-right corner of Figure 14.16, you'll see the last few lines that are displayed by the `For Each, Next` loop in Listing 14.7. The information in the Debug window tells us that there are 86 controls on the form. The text box named `txtElement(81)` is the last control in the `Controls` collection for the form. With that in mind, let's now turn to the initialization code that we skipped over a moment ago. This code is presented in Listing 14.8.

LISTING 14.8   Initialization Code for Text Boxes

```
Private Sub InitializeTextboxes()
 ' Purpose: To initialize the array of text boxes.
 Dim i As Integer
 Dim MySize As Size

 MySize.Width = 30
 MySize.Height = 20
 For i = 1 To 81      ' since max size is 9
  txtElement(i) = New TextBox()
  Me.Controls.Add(txtElement(i))
```

LISTING 14.8   Continued

```
     txtElement(i).Size = MySize
     txtElement(i).TextAlign = HorizontalAlignment.Center
     txtElement(i).Visible = False
     txtElement(i).Name = "txtElement(" & CStr(i) & ")"
    Next i
    txtMagicNumber.Visible = False
    lblMagicNumber.Visible = False

  End Sub
```

The `MySize` variable is a type `Size` data type, which is simply an object that holds width and height values, as measured in pixels. We're defining each text box to be 30 pixels wide and 20 pixels high. The program then enters a `For` loop to create an instance of all 81 text boxes. I selected 81 because I chose to limit the maximum size of the (symmetrical) matrix to 9. The first statement in the `For` statement block creates an instance of `txtElement(i)` using the `New` keyword. The next statement places that text box object on the current form using the `Add()` method of the `Controls` collection object.

The next four statements simply set several properties of the text boxes for later use. Notice that we haven't specified a location for the text boxes. Therefore, all 81 text boxes are stacked on top of each other in same default location near the upper-left corner of the form. They aren't visible because we have set the `Visible` property to `False` for each text box.

With, End With

Setting properties of objects in collections is so common that Visual Basic .NET provides a shorthand notation. To illustrate, we can take the lines

```
txtElement(i).Size = MySize
txtElement(i).TextAlign = HorizontalAlignment.Center
txtElement(i).Visible = False
txtElement(i).Name = "txtElement(" & CStr(i) & ")"
```

from Listing 14.8 and replace them with

```
With txtElement(i)
 .Size = MySize
 .TextAlign = HorizontalAlignment.Center
 .Visible = False
 .Name = "txtElement(" & CStr(i) & ")"
End With
```

and the program will function as before. The `With` keyword is followed by the name of the object for which you want to set the properties. Each statement in the `With` statement block begins with the dot operator, followed by the name of the property you want to set. Therefore, the first statement in the `With` statement block:

```
.Size = MySize
```

is syntactically equivalent to

```
txtElement(i).Size = MySize
```

which is the form shown in Listing 14.8. The **End With** keywords mark the end of the **With** statement block. We started with the long form shown in Listing 14.8 so that I could show you how the **With** statement block is used as an alternative. I suggest that you modify Listing 14.8 to use the **With** statement block code.

After the user enters the matrix size she wants to use, that input is checked by **CheckForValidMatrix()** to make sure that it's an odd-sized matrix of size 9 or less. Assuming the matrix size checks out, the **ShowMatrix()** procedure is called. The code for **ShowMatrix()** is shown in Listing 14.9.

LISTING 14.9   Code for the **ShowMatrix()** Routine

```
Private Sub ShowMatrix()
 ' Purpose: This just displays the matrix
 Dim i, j, k, offset, sum As Integer
 Dim Coor As Point

 sum = 0
 k = 1
 offset = 80              ' Pixels from edge
 For i = 0 To MatrixSize - 1    ' rows
  For j = 0 To MatrixSize - 1   ' columns
   Coor.X = 30 * j + 12     ' Position
   Coor.Y = offset
   With txtElement(k)
     .Location = Coor ' Set location
     .Text = CStr(Magic(i + 1, j + 1, MatrixSize))
     .Visible = True
   End With
   k += 1
  Next j
  sum += CInt(txtElement(i + 1).Text)
  offset += 20
 Next i

 txtMagicNumber.Text = CStr(sum)
 txtMagicNumber.Visible = True
 lblMagicNumber.Visible = True

End Sub
```

Basically, all the procedure does is set the location of the text boxes using **Coor** and make the text boxes visible. The call to **Magic()** calculates the numeric value that is to be filled in the text box. The statement

```
Coor.X = 30 * j + 12      ' Position
```

causes each text box to be spaced 12 pixels apart. The expression **30 * j** is necessary because each text box is 30 pixels wide. If you single-step through this expression, you'll see how this results in the spacing of the text boxes. The variable **offset** is used to move the next row below the previous row. That is, **offset** is used to set the Y coordinate.

Notice how a `With` block is used to set the properties of each text box. The last three lines simply display the magic number for the matrix in the `txtMagicNumber` text box.

Figure 14.17 shows a sample run of the program.

FIGURE 14.17

Sample run of the Magic Squares program.

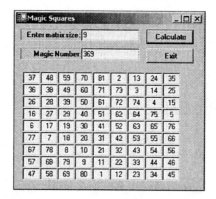

The magic number in Figure 14.17 is 369. Therefore, if you add the numbers in the text boxes for any row, column, or main diagonal, the sum of the values is 369. Although the code is limited to odd matrix sizes of 9 or less, larger odd matrix sizes are possible if you increase the array of text box objects and the size checks. You would also have to enlarge the size of the form. (Algorithms exist for calculating even-sized magic squares, but the code is considerably more complex.)

Summary

In this chapter, we examined some of the array processing features that Visual Basic .NET builds into the `Array` class. We also spent a considerable amount of time discussing how reference variables work. We ended the chapter talking about the `Controls` collection and how the `With` statement can be used to set a series of properties for an object. We'll examine other ways you can use collections of your own design in later chapters.

Review Questions

For testing purposes, simply create a new project without placing any controls on the form. Unless stated otherwise, you can place any code statements in the form `Load()` event for testing purposes.

1. What is an array scalar and why is it important?

A. An array scalar is used to determine how much storage an array needs. Storage requirements are calculated by taking the number of bytes for each element in the array (that is, the size of the type specifier) and multiplying it by the number of elements requested.

For example,

```
Dim MyArray(10) as Double
```

needs 88 bytes of storage. To derive this number, take the number of bytes for the type specifier (8 bytes per **Double**) and multiply the number of elements (11 because the dimension starts with 0) to arrive at the 88 bytes for the array.

2. Will the following statement produce a syntax error? Why or why not?

```
Dim MyArray() as Long
```

A. It will not produce a syntax error. The reason is because the statement defines a dynamic array. At some point in the program before the array is used, however, there needs to be a **ReDim** statement so that the Windows memory manager can allocate storage for the array.

3. What is the syntax form for sorting an array?

A. The syntax is

```
Array.Sort(MyArray)
```

This will sort the array named **MyArray**.

4. What advantage does the **Sort()** method of the array class have over writing your own sort routine?

A. Any time you write your own sort routine, you must write it in such a way that it compares two data items and then decides whether those two items need to be swapped. Because the comparison is for a specific data type (for example, comparing two **Double**s), it's impossible to write a generic sort routine that's capable of sorting all data types. Therefore, if you want to sort an array of **Integer**s and a different array of **Double**s, you would need to write two sort routines. More code, more opportunity for bugs. Using the built-in **Sort()** method of the **Array** class eliminates this problem.

Another advantage is that the **Sort()** method is going to be very efficient. Microsoft is smart enough to know that the **Sort()** method will likely be used heavily and will optimize the routine as much as possible. Indeed, if you write your own sort routine and time it against the **Sort()** method, you'll find a noticeable difference in favor of the **Sort()** method.

5. Although a binary search is an effective search of a data array, what is its major limitation?

A. The disadvantage of a binary search is that the data being searched must be in sorted order.

6. If you have an array that for whatever reason cannot be sorted, and you needed to find a specific value in the array, how would you search the array for that value?

A. One solution is to use the **IndexOf()** method to perform a sequential search of the array. In cases where the array list is short and not sorted, the **IndexOf()** method is faster than sorting the array and then using the **BinarySearch()** method.

7. Suppose a colleague writes some code that uses an array, but you have no idea of the array's dimensions. How could you find out its size?

A. You might use

```
Dim i, TheRank, NumElements As Integer
Dim MyArray(5, 10) As Integer

TheRank = MyArray.Rank
If TheRank > 1 Then
 For i = 1 To TheRank
  NumElements = UBound(MyArray, i)
 Next
Else
 NumElements = UBound(MyArray)
End If
```

In this code, the call to the `Rank()` method tells you how many dimensions the array has. After all, it could be a multidimensional array. The `If` test determines which (overloaded) version of `UBound()` needs to be called. If `Rank()` returns more than one dimension, a `For` loop iterates through the ranks to determine the array boundaries. Otherwise, a single call to `UBound()` is sufficient. You could also use the `GetLength()` method, too.

8. What is a reference variable and why is it different from other variables?

A. A reference variable is used to hold the memory address of another variable or data object. That is, the `rvalue` of a reference variable is designed to hold the memory address of another variable or object. Because of this, the statement

```
Dim Aref as Double()
```

defines a reference variable that is designed to point to a `Double` data type. The `Aref` variable requires 4 bytes of storage because that's how much memory is required to store a memory address. Therefore, even though `Aref` references a `Double` data type (which uses 8 bytes of storage), `Aref` only requires 4 bytes to hold the *address* of where the `Double` is stored.

9. In what ways are collections different from arrays and what advantages do collections offer?

A. Collections are useful for storing related information just like arrays, but they have the advantage of being able to store data of differing types. Whereas arrays are limited to storing one type of data (perhaps an array of type `Double`), collections can contain dissimilar data items. Further, the `Add()` and `Remove()` collection methods make it easier to manage a collection.

CHAPTER 15

ENCAPSULATION

You will learn the following in this chapter:

- How to design and refine a class object
- How to use the Private and Public access specifiers
- How to add a class to a project
- What overloading means

- How to write Public procedures
- What a class interface is
- How to write a program to test a class
- How to add a class to a library file

Until this point, the book has concentrated on teaching the fundamentals of programming in general. You have learned about variables and the various data types they may represent. You have learned about the different types of operators (for example, arithmetic, relational) and how they are used. You have also learned about program structures and loops and how to use them to control what a program does. Along the way, you have also learned about the objects that Visual Basic .NET makes available to you and how to use them. Dozens of other topics have also been discussed. You've come a long way to get to this point.

All the concepts you have learned thus far are applicable to almost any programming language. In this chapter, however, you'll start applying those concepts to object-oriented programming (OOP). This is where we leave the "old" languages behind and move into the 21st century. Although there are still a few hurdles to clear in your quest to master OOP, I think you will find your learning efforts well rewarded.

Creating Your Own Classes

This section concentrates on what you need to know in order to create your own classes. Remember from Chapter 2, "The Basics of Object-Oriented Programming," that classes provide the means by which objects can be created. As you already know, virtually everything in Visual Basic .NET is based on objects. Indeed, there are thousands of objects available to you in Visual Basic .NET. The goal of this section is to show how to add to Visual Basic .NET's list of objects. Being able to create your own classes allows you to extend Visual Basic .NET to meet your own individual needs.

Creating your own classes requires you to think through what you want your new class to accomplish. The following sections present a series of steps that help you design and write the code for a new class.

Step 1: Creating a Rough-Draft Design

For purposes of illustration, this section describes how to create a password class. Most network environments require you to log on with a username and password before you can access the system. Many programs work in a similar manner. In this section, you will learn how to do what I call a *rough-draft design* of a class you want to create.

A rough-draft design is an outline of what you want a class to be able to do. It is a very informal process. In a classroom setting, during the rough-draft design, I state the topic in general terms and then let the students call out a wish list of features the class should have. I write each of these features on the board without any discussion. It's a brainstorming process at this stage, and the goal is to include as many features as possible. This process works well with a programming team, too.

If you're writing code by yourself, you can write your own wish list on a piece of paper. You should write everything that comes to mind. If you have a programmer friend, you can give her a call, tell her the topic, and ask what features she think the class should have. When you cannot think of any more features, stop writing and take a break—preferably a long one of at least several hours. When you return to your work, review the list. Add anything else that might have come to mind while you were away from your work. You should now have a pretty complete laundry list of what you want your class to do.

In this chapter you're going to create the **CPassword** class. You might want to write down your own version of a wish list for the **CPassword** class before you read on. Chances are pretty good that your list will differ from mine. If that's the case and you have a longer list, you should try implementing your version after you've read this chapter. That would be a great way to learn how to program a new class. It would also be a good way to learn whether certain features are worth adding.

The following is a wish list for the **CPassword** class that was taken from a class session of beginning programming students (some really goofy ideas have been deleted):

- Username verification

- Password verification

- Add/edit a user

- Add/edit a password

- Delete an existing user

It's a fairly short list, isn't it? That's exactly the way it should be. If you ever have a really long wish list for a class, chances are pretty good that the functionality needed from the class is not defined clearly. The purpose of a class should be to do one thing well. If you see too many trees, you probably need to create another forest.

The wish list for the **CPassword** class describes the essentials. Can you think of any other items for the list? Some programs need a security clearance level so that different features of a program can be excluded from certain users. For example, viewing the payroll records in an accounting package might require a higher security level than would viewing the inventory records. Therefore, we should add a simple security level to the password program.

At this point we should simplify the wish list a bit, so let's exclude the editing features. We will add a little more realism to this program in Chapter 25, "Database Programming with Visual Basic .NET," when we discuss database programming. For now, however, we will just work on a bare-bones password system.

Step 2: Exploring Your Options for Creating a Class

Now that you have created a wish list for what you want the **CPassword** class to do, you're ready to take the second (often overlooked) step: exploring your options for creating the class. To begin, check the Visual Basic .NET online help feature to make sure an existing class does not fulfill the design needs of the **CPassword** class. To do this, from the Visual Basic .NET main menu, you select Help, Index and type in a word that describes the primary purpose of the class. For example, you might enter **password** and see what comes up.

If the online help shows an entry that seems to fit your needs, you should use it. In most cases, there is no reason to rewrite a class that already exists. (An exception might be when a class has the functionality that you need but you want greater control over the process.) Although an existing class might not be a perfect fit, it might be close enough to serve your needs.

If a class is not a perfect fit, perhaps you can salvage it by grafting some additional functionality onto it. A real advantage of OOP is that you can extend an existing class to fit your specific needs. (The process of extending a class is the subject of Chapter 17, "Inheritance.")

Another alternative is to purchase class libraries from third-party vendors. There are a number of journals and magazines that describe the libraries that are available. You can also check the Web for Visual Basic .NET class libraries. Chances are, someone has already written a library that has the functionality you are looking for. If you value your time at more than a couple bucks an hour, most of these libraries are very cost-effective.

If you can't buy the functionality you need or modify an existing class to suit your needs, then you need to write the class yourself from scratch. Let's assume that this is the case for the **CPassword** class.

Refinement

After you have explored your options and decided to write your own class, you need to refine the class design. Given the design so far, you know you need variables to represent the following data items:

- Username

- Password

- Security level

Each object of the **CPassword** class would be required to have these items. Because these data items are all related to the user, it would make sense to treat them as a single data item. Remember from Chapter 13, "More Loops," that you can use **Structure** to collect these individual data items into a single data structure. Therefore, you can reorganize the data as follows:

```
Private Structure Security      ' Hold relevant info in a structure
 Dim User As String           ' A list of the users for this program
 Dim Password As String        ' The password
 Dim SecurityLevel As Integer  ' Each user has a security level
End Structure
```

It also makes sense that, because each user has this information, you should have an array of these structures to hold the list of authorized users on the system. Therefore, you might have this as part of the class to hold the list of users:

```
Private Shared mUserList() As Security
```

Finally, it would also make sense to track the total number of users on the system. Therefore, you should also add this:

```
Private Shared mUserCount As Integer     ' How many users
```

Programmer's Tip

This chapter follows two naming conventions that are commonly used by Visual Basic .NET programmers. The first is to prefix the data items that are members of a class with a lowercase *m*, as in mUserList() and mUserCount. This makes it easy to see which data items are class members in the code for a class.

The second convention is to use an uppercase *C* to prefix all class names, as in CPassword. This makes it easy to recognize when a variable definition is creating an object that is an instance of a class versus some other type of data.

Notice that all the class members are **Private** and **Shared**. Why?

First of all, the whole concept of encapsulation is to hide the data from the outside world. The outside world is filled with evil things that can contaminate your data. Therefore, you want to limit the scope of the data to the class in which it is defined. That's why the members are **Private**.

If you want the data to be hidden within the class, why do you use the word **Shared** as part of the access specifier? First, remember from Chapter 8, "Scope and Lifetime of Variables," what the word **Shared** means. It does not mean the data is shared with everything else in the program; **Private** assures you of that. What **Shared** does mean is that only one copy of the data item is shared among all instances of the class objects that are created. Therefore, even if you create 1,000 objects of this class, every one of those objects shares the same **mUserList()** and **mUserCount** data items.

This sharing of the two data items makes sense if you think about it. After all, why should every instance of the **CPassword** object have its own copy of the list of users and how many users are in the list? There is no need to duplicate these data items. Declaring them to be **Private** and **Shared** has the dual benefit of hiding (that is, encapsulating) the data and not wasting memory by creating unnecessary copies of the data. Also, if changes are made to the user list, having just one copy makes the change available to all objects. Makes sense, right?

`Private` **Versus** `Public Shared` **Class Data Members**

What would happen if you made the **mUserCount** and **mUserList()** data items **Public Shared** data instead of **Private Shared** data? You would be able to access the **Shared** class data member without even creating an object! That is, you could have the following statement in your program before any **CPassword** object is created:

```
TheUserCount = CPassword.mUserCount
```

Visual Basic .NET would not issue an error message. This works because **Public Shared** class members are created when the class code is first loaded into memory. Because of the **Public** access specifier for the **Shared** member, using the dot operator in conjunction with the class name and the class member makes everything work just fine. You might think this makes **mUserCount** functionally equivalent to a global variable. That's really not true because you must still prefix the variable with the class name and the dot operator.

Now you know that it would be possible to have a **Public Shared** class member. But simply because something works doesn't make it a good idea. Whenever possible, you should try to make all your class members private. That's the whole idea behind encapsulation. If you need to access a **Private Shared** class member before any object is instantiated, you need to write a **Public Shared** method for the member.

A UML Description of `CPassword`

Next you might want to use the Unified Modeling Language (UML) notation discussed in Chapter 3, "Thinking About Programs," to summarize the **CPassword** class. A UML description often helps crystallize the design of a new class. An example of this is shown in Figure 15.1.

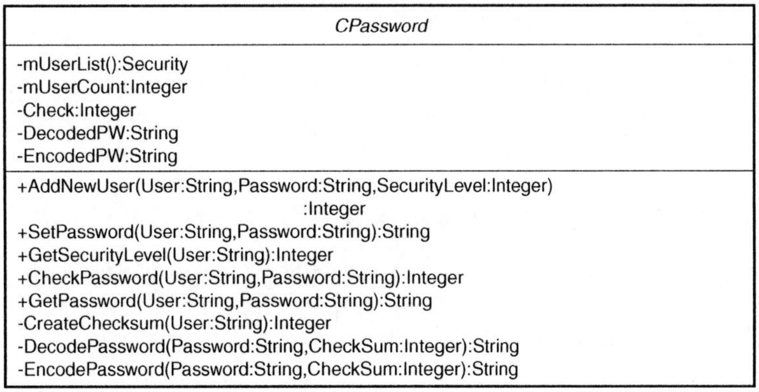

FIGURE 15.1
A UML class diagram for the **CPassword** class.

CPassword
-mUserList():Security -mUserCount:Integer -Check:Integer -DecodedPW:String -EncodedPW:String
+AddNewUser(User:String,Password:String,SecurityLevel:Integer) :Integer +SetPassword(User:String,Password:String):String +GetSecurityLevel(User:String):Integer +CheckPassword(User:String,Password:String):Integer +GetPassword(User:String,Password:String):String -CreateChecksum(User:String):Integer -DecodePassword(Password:String,CheckSum:Integer):String -EncodePassword(Password:String,CheckSum:Integer):String

The top box in Figure 15.1 is labeled `CPassword`, the name of the class. The second box describes the data members, or properties, of the class. (UML notation refers to those data members as *attributes*. This chapter uses the more common Visual Basic .NET term *properties* instead.) Recall that the minus sign before a data item means that the data item is `Private` to the class. The plus sign means that the item is `Public` and, hence, can be accessed from outside the class. All the properties are private to the `CPassword` class.

The final box in Figure 15.1 is a list of the methods that act on the data. (Although the UML notation prefers the term *operations*, this chapter uses the word *methods* instead because it is more common to Visual Basic .NET.) Note that the first five methods are `Public` methods, which means you have access to the class members. The last three methods are `Private` to the class. This means you cannot access these methods outside the class; they are "helper" methods that perform tasks that are required internally by the class.

One nice feature of the UML notation is that it gives a concise summary of all the properties and methods associated with the class. It also provides a summary of how each `Public` method is called by the object and the data type the method returns. A final benefit of the UML notation is that it forces you to think about the design of the class *before* you start writing the code for it.

Programmer's Tip

In the old days, you wrote a program by sitting at a machine that punched holes into 80-column-wide cardboard cards. Each card was one program statement. When the program was finished, you walked the stack of cards to the computer room. This was a locked room shrouded in security, usually with a small window through which you passed your stack of cards. The stack disappeared into the bowels of the earth, and you were given a job number in return. You kept calling a phone number until your job number was called, at which time a printout and your card stack would reappear through the same window. The turnaround time could be as long as several days! That was the bad news.

The good news was that because of the long turnaround time, you spent a lot of time designing and mentally running the program. With today's virtually instantaneous turnaround time, students do not spend nearly enough time in the design phase or thinking about the code they are writing. Good program design has been replaced with trial-and-error programming, and that is *not* a good thing.

You should always think before you write.

At this point, you have a fairly good, albeit rough, idea of what the `CPassword` class should do and the data you need to create the class. Now you can write the code for the class.

Adding a Class to a Project

You can write the code for a class as a single project file. However, writing the code this way is a pain because you still need a test program to exercise, test, and debug the class code. Therefore, the easiest way to start writing a class is to create a new project and make the class code part of the project. (You will see how to put the new class into a library file later in this chapter, in the section "Creating Your Own Class Library.")

First, you need to create a new project called **TestProgram**. Once you have done that, you should select Project, Add Class to add a class to the project. Name the new class **CPassword.vb**, as shown in Figure 15.2.

FIGURE 15.2
Adding the **CPassword** class to a project.

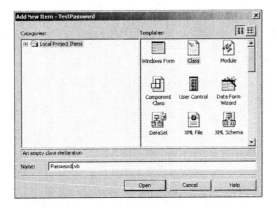

After you click the Open button, Visual Basic .NET automatically adds the class to your project and opens a new Code window, as shown in Figure 15.3.

FIGURE 15.3
The Code window for the **CPassword** class.

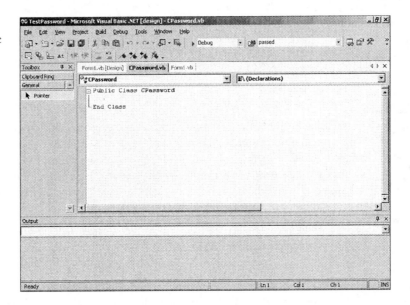

You need to write the new code for the class between the **Public Class CPassword** and **End Class** statements in the file. Later in this chapter, you'll also write code to test the class. You are now ready to start adding code to your new class.

Adding Class Members to a Class

Listing 15.1 shows the first section of code that you need to add to the CPassword class.

LISTING 15.1   The Class Members for the CPassword Class

```
Option Strict On
Public Class CPassword

  '============= Symbolic Constants =====================
  Private Const MINLENGTH As Integer = 4    ' Password must have 4-30 characters
  Private Const MAXLENGTH As Integer = 30

  Private Const MINSECURITY As Integer = 1  ' Ten levels of security clearance
  Private Const MAXSECURITY As Integer = 10
  '=========================================================

  '================= Private Data =======================
  Private Structure Security    ' Hold relevant information in a structure
   Dim User As String         ' A list of the users for this program
   Dim Pass As String         ' The password
   Dim SecurityLevel As Integer  ' Each user has a security level
  End Structure

  Private Shared mUserCount As Integer    ' How many users

  Private Shared mUserList() As Security

  Private Check As Integer
  Private EncodedPW As String
  Private DecodedPW As String
```

Listing 15.1 begins with the definition of several symbolic constants. The first two constants define the minimum and maximum length for a password. Listing 15.1 arbitrarily sets these limits to 4 and 30 characters. The second two constants define the minimum and maximum values for the security levels for the system. You can assume that the lowest security level for the system is 1 and the highest is 10. (In a more sophisticated system, you could have these values stored in the Registry or in an .ini file.)

Next, you declare a Structure that groups the relevant data for a user into one convenient data item, named Security. Note that 15.1 declares it as a Private structure because there is no need for the outside world to have direct access to it.

Notice that each member of the Structure is declared with the Dim keyword. You might think that each of these structure members should also be declared Private, as in this example:

```
Private Structure Security
  Private User As String     ' THIS IS THE WRONG WAY TO DECLARE MEMBERS!!!
  Private Pass As String       ' ALSO WRONG!!!
  Private SecurityLevel As Integer  ' STILL WRONG!!!
End Structure
```

If you try to declare the members by using this syntax, you get the following error message whenever you try to access the members:

```
'TestPassword.CPassword.Security.User' is not accessible in _
this context because it is 'Private'.
```

This error message says that because you have declared the structure members as `Private` to the `Security Structure`, they cannot be accessed outside the `Security Structure`—and that is not a very useful structure. You should use only the `Dim` keyword for declaring the structure members.

The code then declares the `mUserCount` and `mUserList()` variables. These data items are not only `Private` to the class, but they're `Shared` as well, for the reasons discussed earlier in this chapter. The last three statements simply declare three working variables that are used inside the class.

Notice that this chapter is very careful in using the words *declare* and *define*. In a strict sense, nothing in the class exists until an instance of the object for the class is defined, using the `New` keyword. After an instance of the object is defined, all the data items within the class are defined, too.

Adding Class Constructors to a Class

Any class you create automatically has a class constructor associated with it. A *class constructor* is a subroutine that is executed each time a new instance of the class is defined. The default constructor for every class is named `New()`. The code for this constructor is shown in Listing 15.2.

LISTING 15.2   Code for the `New()` Class Constructor

```
Shared Sub New()
  ' If this was being used in a real program, this
  ' code would probably read the user data from a
  ' database file. We just fake it here.

ReDim mUserList(100)

With mUserList(0)
  .User = "Debbie Plesluska"
  .Pass = "Diamonds"
  .SecurityLevel = 8
End With
With mUserList(1)
  .User = "Jay Crannell"
  .Pass = "Whiff"
  .SecurityLevel = 8
End With
With mUserList(2)
  .User = "Jim McAllister"
  .Pass = "Slice"
```

LISTING 15.2 Continued

```
      .SecurityLevel = 6
    End With
    With mUserList(3)
      .User = "Jack"
      .Pass = "Joyce1"
      .SecurityLevel = 10
    End With
    mUserCount = 4

  End Sub
```

The constructor code begins with the keyword `Shared`. This marks the constructor as one that executes only once during the life of the program: It executes when the first `CPassword` object is instantiated. Any subsequent `CPassword` objects that may be defined do not call this `New()` constructor. This is a perfect situation for initializing any `Shared` data that is used in the class, which is exactly the situation with the `CPassword` class.

If this is the first time the constructor is called, a series of `With-With End` statements are executed to fill in several test users for the class. Near the bottom of the constructor, `mUserCount` is set to `4`. If a second object of the `CPassword` class is created, the `Shared` access specifier prevents the `New()` constructor code from being executed a second time; after all, there's no need to execute the code again.

Programmer's Tip

In a real program, the constructor might read the current list of users from a database or another file.

Notice that the constructor serves the same purpose as the `Initialization` step discussed in Chapter 3. The purpose of the constructor is to perform any tasks (often data initialization) that need to be performed before the class object is used. In Listing 15.2, the constructor simply initializes the `mUserList()` and `mUserCount` data items.

Overloaded Constructors

In some programs, the constructor might need to be more complex than the simple constructor you've been working with in this chapter. In fact, you might want an object to be initialized in different ways, depending on the current state of the program. Indeed, if you want subsequent `CPassword` objects to be initialized using code that is different from the code for the first constructor (which in Listing 15.2 is `Shared`), you can overload the `New()` constructor. Because of these varying needs, Visual Basic .NET allows you to have multiple constructors. However, each additional constructor still has the same name—in this case, `New()`.

Wait a minute! If there are multiple constructors, but they all have the same name, how does Visual Basic .NET know which one to use? Easy. Visual Basic .NET looks at the parameter list for each constructor and decides which constructor to execute. Let's look at an example to see how this works.

Suppose you have an array of data that needs to be sorted. However, the data in the array may vary according to the point in the program at which the object is created. You might see something like the following code fragment:

```
Public Sub New(ByVal nums() As Double)
  ' code to sort doubles
End Sub

Public Sub New(ByVal nums() As long)
  ' code to sort longs
End Sub

Public Sub New(ByVal nums() As Integer)
  ' code to sort integers
End Sub

Public Sub New(ByVal str() As String)
  ' code to sort strings
End Sub
```

Assume that the constructors in the code fragment are for the Widget class. Further suppose that you create an instance of the Widget object as follows:

```
Dim MyNums(100) As Double, MyNames(100) As String

' some code that does something

Dim MyWidget as New Widget(MyNums)
Dim AnotherWidget as New Widget(MyNames)
```

Because you are defining the objects with different data types as their parameters, Visual Basic .NET can determine which New() constructor to use when the code executes. Obviously, when MyWidget is defined, the New() constructor that accepts a Double data type as its parameter is executed. Likewise, when AnotherWidget is defined, the New() constructor using the String data type as its parameter is executed.

Do you see what you gain by being able to overload the constructor? You can create a Widget object that uses different data types as the need arises. Even better, the syntax structure to create the object doesn't change, regardless of data type. Although the example here is fairly trivial, being able to overload the constructor makes a class more flexible because it can initialize different data types without changing anything in the Dim statement. In other words, you can move the complexity of handling different data types for the Widget class from outside the class to inside the class, where it belongs.

Another nice thing about constructors is that with a constructor, you, the programmer, don't have to remember to explicitly initialize a data item. If you place the responsibility for initializing the data item in the constructor, the object is automatically initialized properly whenever an object is created.

You can have as many constructors as you need for a class. The only requirement is that the parameters passed to the different constructors must have different parameter lists. That is, each constructor must have a parameter list that uses different data types, a different parameter count, or both. For example, the following code causes no problems for Visual Basic .NET because each constructor has a different parameter list:

```
Public Sub New(ByVal MyInt As Integer)
Public Sub New(ByVal MyStr As String)
Public Sub New(ByVal MyInt As Integer, ByVal Range as Integer)
Public Sub New(ByVal MyInt As Integer, ByVal Range as Double)
Public Sub New(ByVal MyStr As String, ByVal Range as Integer)
```

Adding a New User to a Class

After the CPassword object has been created, all the procedures associated with that class are available through the CPassword object. One of the first things the user of your class might do is add a new user to the existing list of users. The code for doing this is shown in Listing 15.3.

LISTING 15.3 Adding a New User

```
Public Function AddNewUser(ByVal User As String, ByVal Password As String, _
            ByVal SecurityLevel As Integer) As Integer
 ' Purpose  This function is used to add a new user to the system. The
 '      code checks the length of the password and then check to
 '      see if the name entered is already in the list. If either
 '      check fails, logic False is returned.
 '
 ' Argument list:
 '  User      The name of the user
 '  Password      A string that contains the password
 '  SecurityLevel  The clearance for this user
 '
 ' Return Value:
 '  integer      -1 if set OK; 0 otherwise
 '
```

LISTING 15.3   Continued

```
Dim i, length As Integer
Dim buff As String

' See if password length OK
If Password.Length < MINLENGTH OrElse Password.Length > MAXLENGTH Then
 Return 0
End If

' Check security level
If SecurityLevel < MINSECURITY OrElse SecurityLevel > MAXSECURITY Then
 Return 0
End If

' See if the name is already in use.
For i = 0 To mUserCount - 1
 If UCase(mUserList(i).User) = UCase(User) Then
  Return 0
 End If
Next

mUserCount += 1        ' Add one to the list

If mUserCount >= mUserList.GetUpperBound(0) Then  ' See if we need to grow
 ReDim Preserve mUserList(mUserCount + 10)    ' the user list.
End If

' If we get here, it's ok to add them:
With mUserList(mUserCount)
 .User = User
 .Pass = Password
 .SecurityLevel = SecurityLevel
End With

Return -1          ' Everything's fine

End Function
```

In Listing 15.3, all three data items (that is, username, password, and security level) associated with a new user are passed to the **AddNewUser()** function. The code first checks to make sure the password falls between the minimum and maximum password lengths (that is, 4 and 30). Next, the code checks to make sure the security level also falls within the allowable range (that is, 1 to 10). Finally, the code checks to make sure the user's name is not already in the list of current users.

If any of these checks fail, the function returns logic **False** to the caller. The caller can then display an error message and take the appropriate corrective action.

If the checks are passed successfully, the code increments `mUserCount` and then checks whether the `mUserList()` array is large enough to accept another user. If it is not, the array is redimensioned to a larger value. A `With-With End` block then adds the new user to the list. The value logic `True` is returned to the caller to inform the caller that the user has been added to the list successfully.

Public Procedures and the Class Interface

Thus far in the chapter, the procedures (subroutines and functions) have been defined with the `Public` access specifier. You know this means that you can access the procedures from outside the class. Indeed, the `Public` procedures define the interface for the `CPassword` class. The interface of a class dictates how the outside world must interact with the class. Only through the class interface can you gain access to any of the private data contained within the class itself.

One of your goals in creating programs is to make their interfaces as easy to use as possible. Sometimes it's difficult to remember it, but the code you write today might end up being used by someone else tomorrow. You should always attempt to write clear, consistent, and easily understood code, regardless of who might see it in the future. If nothing else, *you* will likely need to review the code sometime, and you'd be amazed at how quickly you forget what you wrote just a few weeks ago.

There are a number of things you can do to make using the class easier: You can document procedures, provide cautionary notes, and be consistent.

Documenting Procedures

You should document every subroutine or function you ever write. You can see an example of my documentation preference in Listing 15.3. You can begin with a section titled `Purpose`, which is a statement of what the procedure should do. In some cases, this is a verbalization of the algorithm used in the procedure. In other cases, the entire procedure may be nothing more than a series of procedure calls to other functions and subroutines. In either case, you should describe the starting state of the data, the transformations made to the data, and the ending state of the data. The user should be able to read this description and understand what the procedure does.

After the procedure description, you should have an `Argument list` section. (You can instead call it a `Parameter list` section, if you like; you can use the terms *argument* and *parameter* interchangeably. My preference is to use argument list, probably because it is a holdover from when I used other programming languages years ago.) This section describes any data that has been passed to the procedure. You should always use descriptive names for the arguments that are passed to a procedure. Listing 15.3 could have used U, P, and S for the arguments that are being passed into the function, and it would make absolutely no difference in the efficiency of the procedure. However, using User, Password, and SecurityLevel sure makes it easier for humans to read and understand the code.

The last section of the comment, titled Return Value:, tells what data type is returned by the procedure call. Obviously, this section would not apply to subroutines because subroutines cannot return values. However, it's a good idea to always have this section present in the description, even in subroutines. First, always having a Return Value: section present adds consistency to the documentation. For a subroutine, you simply use N/A (not applicable) as the return value. Second, you might be surprised at how often you start out with something being a subroutine and then decide later that it needs to return a value, forcing you to change it to a function with a return value anyway. Such changes don't necessarily mean you did a bad job designing the class. When you get into the code, things you might not have foreseen may force you to make changes. Programs continue to evolve over time.

Providing Cautionary Notes

Although a Caution section does not appear in any of the code presented so far in this chapter, you might want to end the comment section with such a section. In some special cases, it might be that a certain program state, or conditions, must be present in order for the function to work properly, even though the code doesn't necessarily show it. For example, say that a procedure writes data to a data file. The code might assume that the file is already open and that the user has access to the file. In such a case, you could add a cautionary note that tells the reader that the code assumes that such-and-such data file is open for writing.

As a general rule, you use cautionary notes to warn yourself and other programmers about things the code cannot check itself. That is, you use cautionary notes when the procedure does something that is based on a state of the program that is dictated by data that is not in scope.

Being Consistent

If you look at the interface for the CPassword class, you'll see that the procedures that have similar arguments are always placed in the same sequence in the argument list. Here's an example:

```
Public Function GetPassword(ByVal User As String, _
        ByVal Password As String) As String
Public Function CheckPassword(ByVal User As String, _
        ByVal Password As String) As Integer
Public Function SetPassword(ByVal User As String, _
        ByVal Password As String) As String
```

All these procedures use User and Password as function arguments. Notice that this example is consistent in placing User first and then Password. Doing this makes it easier to use the CPassword class interface because you know you can expect functions that use these two variables to always place them in the same order. It's a minor thing, but a nice minor thing.

Again, consistency has absolutely no impact on the efficiency of the program. It might, however, increase your efficiency and that of other programmers because it relieves programmers from having to look up the argument order for the functions that use User and Password.

Class Helper Procedures

It is not uncommon to have a number of procedures that simply do subtasks for a class. These are called *helper procedures*. A helper procedure is a subroutine or function that is never part of the class interface. As such, it always uses a Private access specifier and, hence, has its visibility limited to the class itself. A helper procedure cannot be called from outside the class. Listing 15.4 shows a helper function from the CPassword class.

LISTING 15.4   The CreateChecksum() Helper Function

```
Private Function CreateChecksum(ByVal User As String) As Integer
 ' Purpose  This routine is used to create a checksum for a password.
 '        This is done by taking the numeric value of each character
 '        in the user's name and adding it up. The stored value
 '        is the sum modulus 26.
 '
 ' Argument list:
 '   User      The username for this password
 '
 ' Return Value:
 '   integer      The checksum
 '
 Dim i As Integer, sum As Long

 sum = 0
 For i = 0 To Len(User) - 1
  sum += Asc(User.Substring(i, 1))
 Next i
 CreateChecksum = sum Mod 26

End Function
```

The Purpose section of Listing 15.4 tells you that the CreateChecksum() function's only purpose is to create a checksum number from the user's name. Other functions in the class (for example, GetPassword()) use this function for their own purposes. However, by giving it a Private access specifier, you prevent the function from being called outside the CPassword class. By doing this, you are explicitly preventing anyone else from using this function.

The sole purpose of CreateChecksum() is to help the GetPassword() and SetPassword() functions do their jobs. Even so, you still need to follow the documentation and consistency standards for helper procedures. It just makes sense to do so.

Adding the Rest of the CPassword Class Code

Listing 15.5 shows the rest of the code for the CPassword class. The listing includes only procedures that have not already been discussed.

LISTING 15.5   The Remainder of the CPassword Class Code
_____

```
Public Function SetPassword(ByVal User As String, _
        ByVal Password As String) As String
' Purpose  This function is used to encode the password string entered
'      by the user. It does this by adding four numeric characters
'      to the front of the string followed by the password charac-
'      ters themselves. Each character is calculated as the char-
'      acter modulo 26 plus the length of the password.
'
' Argument list:
'   Password    A string that contains the password
'   User        The name of the user
'
' Return Value:
'   string      The encoded password
'
Check = CreateChecksum(User)
EncodedPW = EncodePassword(Password, Check)
SetPassword = EncodedPW

End Function

Public Function GetSecurityLevel(ByVal User As String) As Integer
' Purpose  This routine is used to retrieve the security level of the
'      user.
'
' Argument list:
'   User        The user for this password
'
' Return Value:
'   integer     The security level of the user. It returns 0
'           if the user is not found
'
Dim i As Integer

For i = 0 To mUserCount - 1
  If UCase(mUserList(i).User) = UCase(User) Then
   Return mUserList(i).SecurityLevel
  End If
Next i
Return 0

End Function

Public Function CheckPassword(ByVal User As String, _
        ByVal Password As String) As Integer
' Purpose  This routine is used to check for a password match for a
'      user.
'
' Argument list:
'   User        The user for this password
'   Password    A string that contains the password
'
```

LISTING 15.5   Continued

```
' Return Value:
'   integer    -1 if set if the correct password is given,
'              0 otherwise
'

Dim i As Integer

For i = 0 To mUserCount - 1
  If UCase(mUserList(i).User) = UCase(User) Then
   If UCase(mUserList(i).Pass) = UCase(Password) Then
    Return -1   ' Match
   End If
  End If
Next i
Return 0        ' No match

End Function

Public Function GetPassword(ByVal User As String, _
        ByVal Password As String) As String
' Purpose  This routine is used to check for a password match for a
'       user.

' **********  Right now it is just a way to check the encoding and
' **********  decoding.
'

' Argument list:
'   User      The user for this password
'   Password  A string that contains the password
'

' Return Value:
'   string    the decoded password
'             Empty string otherwise
'

Dim Temp As String, OriginalPW As String

OriginalPW = Password
Check = CreateChecksum(User)
EncodedPW = EncodePassword(Password, Check)

Temp = DecodePassword(EncodedPW, Check)

If UCase(Temp) = UCase(OriginalPW) Then
  Return Temp   ' Match
Else
  Return ""  ' No match
End If

End Function

'================= Helper Functions =====================
Private Function DecodePassword(ByVal password As String, _
        ByVal Check As Integer) As String
```

LISTING 15.5 Continued

```
' Purpose  This routine is used to decode a password. _
       It reverses the encode procedure.
'
' Argument list:
'  password       the password
'  Check     the checksum for the password
'
' Return Value:
'  string   the decoded password
'
Dim i As Integer
Dim length As Integer
Dim s As String, w As String

For i = 0 To 3
  s &= Chr(Asc(password.Substring(i, 1)) - 26)
Next i
length = Val(s.Substring(0, 2))  ' The password length is first 2 chars
Check = Val(s.Substring(2, 2))   ' Next two chars are checksum

For i = 4 To length + 3
  w = w + Chr(Asc(password.Substring(i, 1)) - Check)
Next i
DecodePassword = w

End Function

Private Function EncodePassword(ByVal Password As String, _
        ByVal Check As Integer) As String
  ' Purpose: This routine is used to encode the password string entered
  '       by the user. It does this by adding two numeric characters
  '       to the front of the string followed by the password charac-
  '       ters themselves. Each character is calculated as the char-
  '       acter modulo 26 plus the length of the password.
  '
  ' Parameters:
  '  Password    the password to encode
  '  Check    the checksum for the password
  '
  ' Return value:
  '   string  the encoded password
  '
  Dim s, cs, d, buff As String
  Dim Temp, i, length As Integer

  d = Format$(Len(Password), "00")
  s = Format$(Check, "00")
  buff = d & s

  cs = ""
  For i = 0 To 3        ' Format length and checksum into password
    Temp = Asc(buff.Substring(i, 1)) + 26
```

LISTING 15.5 Continued

```
 cs &= Format$(Chr(Temp))
Next i

d = ""
For i = 0 To Len(Password) - 1 ' Encode the password itself using checksum
 Temp = Asc(Pass.Substring(i, 1)) + Check
 d = d & Chr(Temp)
Next i

s = d
Randomize()
For i = Len(d) To MAXLENGTH - 4 ' Fill in the rest with random chars
 Temp = 0
 Do While Temp < 32 Or Temp > 127
  Temp = Rnd() * 127
 Loop
 s = s & Chr(Temp)
Next i

Password = cs & s        ' Put the pieces together
EncodePassword = Password

End Function
```

It would be worth your time to read through the code in Listing 15.5 so that you understand how the code works. You will also need to refer to this listing a little later in this chapter.

Testing the Code for the CPassword Class

You need a way to test the code in the CPassword class to make sure it works as it should. To do so, you need to create a new project and name it TestPassword. Then, create a form with the controls shown in Figure 15.4.

The button names are btnAdd, btnCheck, and btnExit. The middle two text boxes are named txtPassword and txtConfirm. You cannot see these names in the figure because I have set the PasswordChar property to an asterisk (*). This means that any character typed into these text boxes appears as an asterisk instead of the character typed by the user. This prevents anyone watching the user from seeing the password as it is typed into the program.

The TestPassword Code

The code to test the CPassword class is shown in Listing 15.6. Notice the first line in the listing. This statement tells Visual Basic .NET that the code for any calls to the CPassword class is found in the CPassword library. (You will see how to do this toward the end of this chapter, in the section "Creating Your Own Class Library.") For the moment, you can just think of the CPassword class code as being available via the CPassword library file.

FIGURE 15.4

The form for the
TestPassword project.

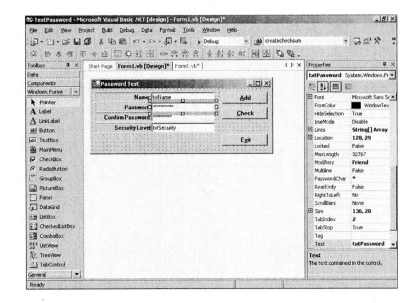

LISTING 15.6   The Code to Test the Password Class

```
Imports CPassword

Public Class frmTestPassword
 Inherits System.Windows.Forms.Form
 Dim MyCheck As New Password()

 Private Sub btnAdd_Click(ByVal sender As System.Object, ByVal e As _
              System.EventArgs) Handles btnAdd.Click
  Dim length, Level, Passed As Integer

  If txtSecurity.Text = "" Then
   MessageBox.Show("Must enter a security level.")
   Exit Sub
  End If
  Level = CInt(txtSecurity.Text)
  Passed = MyCheck.AddNewUser(txtName.Text, txtPassword.Text, Level)
  If Passed = False Then   ' See if this user is OK to add.
   Beep()           ' Guess not...
   length = Len(txtPassword.Text)
   If length < 4 Or length > 30 Then   ' Was the password length OK?
    MessageBox.Show("Error. Password must contain _
             between 4 and 30 characters.")
    txtPassword.Text = ""
    txtConfirm.Text = ""
    txtPassword.Focus()
   ElseIf Level < 1 Or Level > 10 Then   ' How about the security level?
    MessageBox.Show("Error. Security level must be between 1 and 10")
    txtSecurity.Text = ""
    txtSecurity.Focus()
```

LISTING 15.6   Continued

```
    Else                    ' Already in the list.
      MessageBox.Show("Error. User name already in list")
    End If
    Exit Sub
  End If
  ' If we get here, all's OK.
  MessageBox.Show("User added to list successfully")
End Sub
Private Sub btnCheck_Click(ByVal sender As System.Object, ByVal e As _
            System.EventArgs) Handles btncheck.Click
  Dim Password As String, SecurityLevel As Integer

    Password = MyCheck.GetPassword(txtName.Text, txtPassword.Text)
    SecurityLevel = MyCheck.GetSecurityLevel(txtName.Text)

  End Sub

  Private Sub btnExit_Click(ByVal sender As System.Object, ByVal e As _
            System.EventArgs) Handles btnExit.Click

    MyCheck = Nothing        ' This releases the object
    Me.Dispose()
  End Sub


  Private Sub txtConfirm_Leave(ByVal sender As Object, ByVal e As _
            System.EventArgs) Handles txtConfirm.Leave
  If txtConfirm.Text <> txtPassword.Text Then
    MessageBox.Show("The two passwords do not match.")
    txtPassword.Text = ""
    txtConfirm.Text = ""
    txtPassword.Focus()
  End If
End Sub

End Class
```

Near the top of Listing 15.6 is this line, which defines a CPassword object:

```
Dim MyCheck As New Password()
```

The empty parentheses after the CPassword class name simply tell Visual Basic .NET that the CPassword class constructor does not have any parameters passed to it.

When you compile and run the program, a MyCheck object of the CPassword class is created. Given its position in the program, you can see that it has module scope, so you do not need to worry about passing it to other procedures in the program. This scope level is fine for testing purposes, although local scope would be better in a real program.

If you click the Add button, the `btnAdd` object's `Click()` event code is executed. Although the code is somewhat long, it does little more than call the `AddNewUser()` procedure in the `CPassword` class. That is done with this statement:

```
Passed = MyCheck.AddNewUser(txtName.Text, txtPassword.Text, Level)
```

When the call is completed, `Passed` is either -1 or 0. (Again, `Passed` is an `Integer` rather than a `Boolean` because you might want to change the return value later.) If `Passed` is -1, a message is displayed that says the user has been added to the list. All the rest of the code is used to decide what type of error caused `Passed` to be returned as 0. If we coded `AddNewUser()` to return `Integer` values that vary according to the type of error that occurred, you could simplify the code in the test program, perhaps by using a `Select` statement. Implementing such error processing would be a worthwhile exercise for you to try.

Checking a User and Password

You have probably noticed that the `btnCheck` object's `Click()` event really doesn't do anything. However, it appears in the code so you have a convenient place to put a breakpoint so you can observe what is actually taking place in the `CPassword` class.

You should place a breakpoint on the first statement in the `btnCheck` object's `Click()` event. After you have added a few users to the list, try entering a username and password combination that is already in the list. Then click the Check button.

When you reach the breakpoint, single-step the program by pressing the F10 key. When you enter the `GetPassword()` procedure of the `CPassword` class, you see the code from Listing 15.5. The first call is made to `CreateChecksum()`, which returns a value that is assigned to `Check`. The user's password and `Check` are then passed to `EncodePassword()`. The result is passed back and assigned to `EncodedPW`. This string should look very strange. For example, the password `joyce1` comes back as `JPKMw¦tpr>Ayd!Oi6E/EBb3BONUIOho`.

The code then calls `DecodePassword()` with the data you just created. If everything is working right, you should get your original password back in the variable named `Temp`. The code then does a simple test to see if the original and decoded passwords are the same, and it returns `True` or `False` accordingly.

If you make the encoded password accessible through `EncodePassword()`, the procedure could be called and the password written to a database. Then, when anyone viewed the database, he or she would not be able to decipher the user's password. A call to `DecodePassword()` would put the password back into a readable format.

`GetPassword()` is not doing much because it is written simply to test the encoding and decoding of the password. In a real program, this routine would probably be used to encode the user's password before writing it to a database for retrieval at some later time. The constructor code would then be used to read the database table with the password rather than build the dummy list shown in the present constructor code.

Releasing Objects Gracefully

Earlier in this chapter we discussed class constructors and how they are used to initialize an object. It would seem to make sense that if there are class constructors, there would be class destructors, too. This is the case in other languages, such as C++. However, it is not the case in Visual Basic .NET. No class destructor is automatically called when an object goes out of scope. Let's examine the test program a little more closely.

When you end the test program and click the End button, this statement is executed:

```
MyCheck = Nothing
```

In the strictest sense, this statement is not called, but you need to understand its purpose anyway.

Recall from earlier discussions that the New keyword causes an object to be created. (By the term *created*, I mean the object has an lvalue in memory.) Also remember from Table 4.1 in Chapter 4, "Data Types and Numeric Variables," that each object requires 4 bytes of storage. This might have seemed weird at first glance. After all, how can every object use only 4 bytes of memory? What is actually happening is that the variable associated with the New keyword is a reference variable that points to the object being created. In the TestPassword program, MyCheck is a reference variable that points to a memory location where the CPassword object is stored.

It would be nice if, when you are done using the object, you could tell Windows you no longer need the resources associated with the object. You can do that by setting the object to Nothing. The Nothing keyword actually resolves to the default value for the data type of the variable being used. For reference variables, however, Nothing means that the variable is no longer associated with any object. Because the variable is no longer tied to an object, Windows is free to reclaim the resources associated with that object. The process of reclaiming program resources is called *garbage collection*. Note that those resources always involve some amount of memory but could also involve other resources, such as system ports, print resources, database connections, and the like.

Why is garbage collection important? After all, when you end the program, its resources are freed anyway. In complex programs, there is always the risk of running out of system resources. Recall from the discussion of defining variables in Chapter 4 that Visual Basic .NET always has to ask Windows for the necessary memory for the variable. If Windows is getting low on resources, it automatically begins the garbage collection process.

Garbage collection may seem like a very complex process that involves incantations, crushed bat wings, and eye of newt. But stated in simple terms, *garbage collection* is the process by which Windows looks for reference variables that are no longer in use and reclaims the resources associated with those reference variables. Assigning the keyword Nothing to a variable is an explicit way to tell the garbage collection process that the resources associated with the object can be collected and made available for other uses.

Note that the garbage collection process is a background process that Windows does automatically. Because the garbage collection method is part of the System object, however, you *could* directly call the garbage collection method. However, it is not necessary to do so and is probably best left to Windows to decide when to do garbage collection. The only time you need to worry about garbage collection is when a class uses resources other than memory. You will learn more about this topic again in Chapter 26, "Using Visual Basic .NET on the Web," when you begin to use additional (nonmemory) resources. The simple program under investigation here, however, doesn't need to worry about garbage collection.

Creating Your Own Class Library

When you are first developing a new class, it's convenient to tie the new class code to the test program, as you have done in the **TestPassword** project. This allows you to test and debug the class in a fairly straightforward manner. However, the real benefit of classes is to be able to reuse the class objects in other programs. After all, code reuse is one of the primary goals of OOP. Therefore, you need a way to separate the **CPassword** class code from the test program, yet still make the class available for use in other programs. You can do this by creating a class library.

In order to create a class library, the first thing you need to do is copy the code associated with the **CPassword** class. To do this, you simply click the **CPassword** class Code window tab and move the cursor to the beginning of the code. Then you hold the left mouse button down and drag the cursor to the bottom of the Code window, highlighting all the code. Then you press Ctrl+C to copy the highlighted code. At this point, all the **CPassword** code is in the Visual Basic .NET copy buffer. Next, you close the **TestPassword** project.

To create your own class library, you need to select File, New, Project to display the New Project dialog box. Then click the Class Library option in the Templates pane of the window. In the Name field, type **CPassword** as the name for the class library. You should also enter a directory where you would like the library to reside. This is shown in Figure 15.5.

FIGURE 15.5

Naming a new class library by using the New Project dialog box.

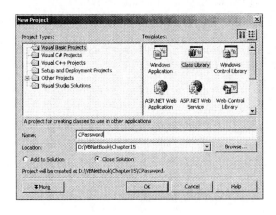

Next, you need to click the OK button to save the information. The screen is then updated to show the default Class Code window (see Figure 15.6).

FIGURE 15.6
The default Class Code window.

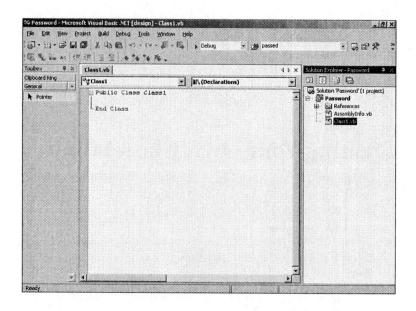

As you can see in Figure 15.6, there is no code for the class yet. Visual Basic .NET has just created an empty Code window named **Class1** that you can use to write the class code. However, because you placed the **CPassword** class code in the Visual Basic .NET copy buffer before you closed the **TestPassword** project, you can copy that code into the empty Code window. To do this, you highlight the two lines in the **Class1** code window and press the Delete key to remove the two lines. Then you press Ctrl+V (or select Edit, Paste) to copy the **CPassword** class code into the Code window. You should then see all the class code in the **Class1** Code window.

If the Solution Explorer window is not already open, you should select View, Solution Explorer (or press Ctrl+R) to open it. Then highlight the **Class1.vb** line and click the right mouse button. This opens a small menu from which you should select the Rename option. This allows you to rename the code from the generic **Class1** name to something more meaningful. Type **CPassword**. The result is shown in Figure 15.7.

You can see the renaming toward the right side of Figure 15.7. After you press Enter, the tab in the Code window changes from **Class1.vb** to **CPassword.vb**.

 Finally, you need to select Build, Build Solution to compile the **CPassword** class code. This causes Visual Basic .NET to generate a dynamic link library (DLL) file named **CPassword.dll**. You now have a library file named **CPassword** that you can use in programs.

Using Library Files

How do you use the library file created in the preceding section? Actually, you already have seen how to use it. If you look at the top of Listing 15.6, you will see this statement:

```
Imports CPassword
```

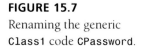

FIGURE 15.7

Renaming the generic
`Class1` code `CPassword`.

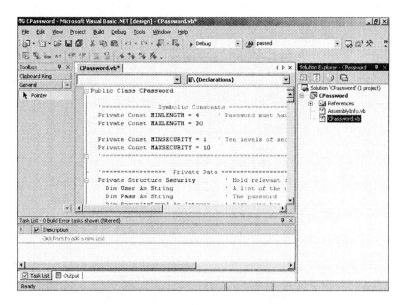

This statement tells Visual Basic .NET to make the code in the **CPassword** file available for use
in the current program. However, because the library file may not be located in the current
working directory, you need to tell Visual Basic .NET where to find the **CPassword** file. To do
this, you simply select Project, Add Reference, click the Browse button, and locate the file.
(Your file should be located in the **bin** directory of the **CPassword** folder.) After you make this
selection, the **Imports** statement knows where to look for the **CPassword** library file. This is all
you have to do to make the **CPassword** class available for use in programs.

Summary

This chapter covers a lot of material. You have seen how to design and write code for your
own classes. You have examined some of the access specifiers you need when you write the
class interface. You have explored class constructors and how you can overload them to meet
special needs when an instance of a class object is created. You have also learned how objects
are destroyed and how their resources are reclaimed by the garbage collection process. Finally,
you have learned how to place the code for an object into a class library so it can be reused in
other programs.

It is probably obvious to you that designing and writing code for class libraries is a very important part of the software development process. Because of this importance, I encourage you to
design, write, and test a new class of your own creation before moving on to the next chapter.
It is very easy to feel confident that you understand a new concept when everything is laid out
in front of you. It is entirely different, however, to start with a blank screen and repeat the
process from scratch with a new class. Please take the time to experiment with the concepts
presented in this chapter before you start the next chapter. Doing so will return great dividends in the long run.

Review Questions

1. In one sentence, what is the major purpose of encapsulation as it relates to OOP?

A. The major purpose of encapsulation is that it hides the data members and the methods that operate on that data within the object itself, thus reducing the possibility of data contamination.

2. What is the difference between a class member and a class method?

A. Class members are like nouns in a sentence. A class member is a property of the class and is normally used to describe the state of the object.

   Class methods are like verbs in a sentence. A class method is a procedure that is used to retrieve or set a class member's data.

3. What does the term *overloaded* mean in OOP?

A. OOP allows a procedure to have multiple class methods that share the same name. If a method does have more than one definition in the current scope, it is called an overloaded method.

4. What is meant by the term *signature* in OOP?

A. The term signature refers to the components of a statement that define the procedure. For example,

```
Public Function MyFunction(arg1 as Integer) as Integer
```

describes the signature for the method named `MyFunction()`. Every procedure and method in a Visual Basic .NET program must have a unique signature. If this condition is violated, a "duplicate definition" error is generated.

5. If a method is overloaded, how does Visual Basic .NET know which method to use?

A. In order to have an overloaded method, each method must share the same name, but have different argument lists and/or return lists. In other words, the signatures for the functions must be different. For example,

```
Public Function MyFunction() as Integer
' The code for the function

Public Function MyFunction(arg1 as Integer) as Integer
' The code for the function
```

illustrates that `MyFunction()` is overloaded because they share the same name, but have different signatures.

6. What is a class Helper procedure?

A. A Helper procedure is a procedure that is designed to accomplish a specific task for the class, but is not to be called from outside the class. Because Helper procedures are to be used only within the class itself, the access specifier for Helper procedures should be `Private`. The `Private` access specifier assures that the procedure is not available outside the class.

7. Suppose you are writing a class named `Golfers` that describe a person who plays golf. You create an `Integer` data member named `mHandicap` that records the player's handicap. Write the property methods necessary to set and retrieve a player's handicap.

A. The methods could be written as follows:

```
Property Handicap() As Integer
 Get
  Return mHandicap
 End Get

 Set(ByVal Value As Integer)
  mHandicap = Value
 End Set
End Property
```

Usually, properties are written in pairs to allow the property to be set or retrieved.

8. Using your answer to question number 7, what would the statement look like to set a player's handicap to 36? To retrieve it?

A. The following is an example:

```
Dim JohnMarsh As New Golfers
Dim Handicap As Integer

Handicap = 36

JohnMarsh.Handicap = Handicap  ' Set it

Handicap = JohnMarsh.Handicap  ' Get it
```

9. Given your answer to question number 8 and that the `Get` and `Set` methods use the same property name, how does Visual Basic .NET know which method to use?

A. This is one case where the context determines which property method is used. If the property method appears on the left-hand side of an assignment operator, Visual Basic .NET knows that a `Set` operation is being performed. If the property method appears on the right side of an assignment operator, Visual Basic .NET knows that a `Get` operation is being performed. Even though the same keywords and variables are used in both statements, their context is very different.

CHAPTER 16

CLASS PROPERTIES

You will learn about the following in this chapter:

- Class properties and their purpose
- The different access specifiers that can be used with properties
- How class properties form part of the user interface

T he **CPassword** class example in Chapter 15, "Encapsulation," uses class members that you never need to read or write directly. That is, in Chapter 15 you never really have a reason to access **mUserList()** or **mUserCount** directly. In many situations, however, you need to write class code where access to the member variables of the class is important. Recall from Chapter 3, "Thinking About Programs," that class member variables represent the properties of the class. Collectively, the values of the properties define the current state of an object of the class.

Unlike the **CPassword** class from Chapter 15, this chapter presents an example in which you want to alter the values of the properties. This chapter shows you how to use property values to affect the state of a class object. As you work through the example presented in this chapter, I hope you feel the same sense of awe I did the first time I used these elements of Visual Basic .NET. There are some pretty bright people in Redmond who have made our lives a whole lot easier. To those people...thanks!

As always, the starting point for any program is to grab a piece of paper and start scratching out a design.

Designing a Program Design

Assume that you are writing a class that models a kitchen oven. You think about it for a while, and you come up with a description, as depicted in the Unified Modeling Language (UML) class diagram shown in Figure 16.1.

FIGURE 16.1

A UML class diagram for the `COven` class.

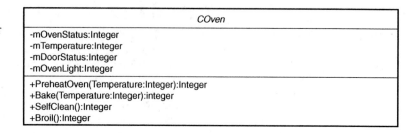

COven
-mOvenStatus:Integer -mTemperature:Integer -mDoorStatus:Integer -mOvenLight:Integer
+PreheatOven(Temperature:Integer):Integer +Bake(Temperature:Integer):integer +SelfClean():Integer +Broil():Integer

The member variables shown in the UML class diagram might be interpreted in the following manner:

- `mOvenStatus`—Is the oven on or off?

- `mTemperature`—What is the temperature in the oven?

- `mDoorStatus`—Is the oven door open or closed?

- `mOvenLight`—Is the oven light on or off?

At this point the oven has four member variables. Although you could add other member variables to the class (for example, an oven might have a sensor you can insert into a roast to read its temperature), this is good enough for a starting point. In the `COven` class, you might want to alter the state of each one of these member variables through the user interface. You can do that with a property procedure. If you write property procedures for member variables, those member variables become properties that are accessible to users of the `COven` class. You have also added four class methods that can be used with the class. Although you might not have thought of everything, this design is a good starting point for the example.

Now you need to create a new project and name it `Oven`. Next, you should create a new class for the project by selecting Project, Add Class, and name the new project `COven` (see Figure 16.2).

FIGURE 16.2

Adding the `COven` class to a project.

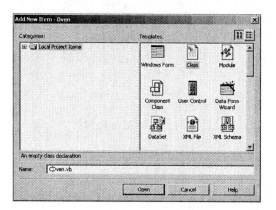

After you press Enter, the screen changes so that the new class is shown in the Code window. (Your screen should look very similar to the screen shown in Figure 15.3 in Chapter 15.) Now you need to enter the following lines of code in the COven Code window:

```
Private mOvenStatus As Integer    ' Is the oven on or off
Private mTemperature As Integer   ' Oven temperature
Private mDoorStatus As Integer    ' Is oven door open or closed
Private mOvenLight As Integer     ' Is oven light on or off

Public Property OvenStatus() As Integer
```

These lines define the properties with the **Private** access specifier. As you know, this means that these class member variables are not directly available outside the **COven** class; that is, their scope is limited to the **COven** class itself.

Property Accessor Methods

When you enter the last line shown in the code fragment in the preceding section and press the Enter key, some pretty neat stuff happens. Immediately, new lines of code are automatically supplied for you by Visual Basic .NET. You should see the following in your Code window:

```
Public Property OvenStatus() As Integer
 Get

 End Get

 Set(ByVal Value As Integer)

 End Set

End Property
```

By default, every property of a class has a property **Get** and a property **Set** method. To distinguish these methods from other class methods, the **Get** and **Set** methods are formally called *accessor methods*. As you have probably guessed, the accessor methods are used to change a property value (the **Set** accessor method) or to read a property value (the **Get** accessor method). Visual Basic .NET automatically supplies a code skeleton for each of these accessor methods. Of course, you must flesh out the details for the accessor methods.

Listing 16.1 shows the code for the **OvenStatus** accessor method.

LISTING 16.1   The Code for the **OvenStatus** Accessor Method

```
Public Property OvenStatus() As Integer
 ' Purpose: To get the current status of the oven.
 '      0 = oven off, non-zero = oven on
 Get
  Return mOvenStatus
 End Get
 ' Purpose: To change the status of the oven. It
 '      is assumed that Value is the desired
```

LISTING 16.1   Continued

```
'        temperature. Value = 0 means the oven
'        is off. Any other value indicates a
'        desired temperature value.
  Set(ByVal Value As Integer) ' Turn oven on or off
    Dim Flag As Integer

    If Value <> OVENOFF Then
      mOvenStatus = OVENON      ' Oven is now on
    Else
      mOvenStatus = OVENOFF   ' Oven is now off
    End If
    Flag = Bake(Value)

  End Set
End Property
```

The `Get` method in Listing 16.1 simply returns the symbolic constant (`OVENON` or `OVENOFF`) for the `mOvenStatus` class member, depending on its current state. (From now on, I drop *accessor* from the term *accessor method*. If you see the terms **Get method** and **Set method**, you should understand that I am talking about accessor methods.) By having a `Get` method for `mOvenStatus` and keeping it `Private`, you are forced to use the interface of the `COven` class to change `mOvenStatus`. Again, using class `Get` and `Set` methods to read or write a class property reinforces the idea of encapsulation for the class.

The `Set` method for `mOvenStatus` is rather involved because you need to change the value of `mOvenStatus`. Note that the `Set` method has a parameter passed to it. The assumption is that a value of **0** for the parameter reflects an oven-off state for the object, whereas a nonzero value says the oven is on. Again, you have defined symbolic constants for these values. (The complete code is presented in the following section, in Listing 16.2.)

Programmer's Tip

A `Set` method can have only one parameter passed to it. Trying to pass more than one parameter causes an error message to appear.

The `COven` Class Code

Listing 16.2 shows the complete code for the `COven` class. Most of the code should look pretty familiar to you by now.

LISTING 16.2   Code for the `COven` Class

```
Option Strict On

Public Class COven
  '========== Constants ==================
  Private Const DOOROPEN = True     ' Oven door open
```

LISTING 16.2   Continued

```
Private Const DOORCLOSED = 0     ' Oven door closed
Private Const OVENON = True      ' Oven on
Private Const OVENOFF = 0        ' Oven off
Private Const LIGHTON = True     ' Oven light on
Private Const LIGHTOFF = 0       ' Oven light off
Private Const BROILTEMP = 550    ' Broiler temperature
Private Const CLEANTEMP = 600    ' Self-clean temperature

'========== class member data ==========
Private mOvenStatus As Integer   ' Is the oven on or off
Private mTemperature As Integer  ' Oven temperature
Private mDoorStatus As Integer   ' Is oven door open or closed
Private mOvenLight As Integer    ' Is oven light on or off


'========== Constructor ===============
Public Sub New()
 ' Purpose: To initialize the variables to their proper values.
 '      Even though some are zero, we set them explicitly.
 mOvenStatus = OVENOFF    ' Oven is off
 mTemperature = 0         ' No temperature
 mDoorStatus = DOORCLOSED  ' Oven door is closed
 mOvenLight = LIGHTOFF    ' Oven light is off

End Sub

'================ Properties ==========
Public Property OvenStatus() As Integer
 ' Purpose: To get the current status of the oven.
 '      0 = oven off, 1 = oven on
 Get
  Return mOvenStatus
 End Get

 ' Purpose: To change the status of the oven. It
 '      is assumed that Value is the desired
 '      temperature. Value = 0 means the oven
 '      is off. Any other value indicates a
 '      desired temperature value.
 Set(ByVal Value As Integer) ' Turn oven on or off
  Dim Flag As Integer

  If Value <> OVENOFF Then
   mOvenStatus = OVENON       ' Oven is now on
  Else
   mOvenStatus = OVENOFF    ' Oven is now off
  End If
  Flag = Bake(Value)

 End Set
End Property
```

LISTING 16.2 Continued

```
Public Property DoorStatus() As Integer
 ' Purpose: This property gets the status of the door
 Get
  Return mDoorStatus
 End Get

 ' Purpose: This property sets the status of the door
 Set(ByVal Value As Integer)
  If Value = 0 Then
   mDoorStatus = DOORCLOSED
  Else
   mDoorStatus = DOOROPEN
  End If
 End Set
End Property

Public Property LightStatus() As Integer
 ' Purpose: This property gets the status of the light
 Get
  Return mOvenLight
 End Get

 ' Purpose: This property sets the status of the light
 Set(ByVal Value As Integer)
  If Value = 0 Then
   mOvenLight = LIGHTOFF
  Else
   mOvenLight = LIGHTON
  End If

 End Set
End Property

Public Property Temperature() As Integer
 ' Purpose: This property gets the oven temperature
 Get
  Return mTemperature
 End Get

 ' Purpose: This property changes the oven temperature
 Set(ByVal Value As Integer)
  Dim Flag As Integer

  If Value < 0 Then
   mTemperature = 0
  End If
  Flag = Bake(Value)    ' Set the oven temperature
 End Set
End Property

'================ Methods ==============
```

LISTING 16.2 Continued

```
Public Function Bake(ByVal Temp As Integer) As Integer
 ' Purpose: This method is used to set the oven temperature
 '     to the temperature passed to this method.
 '
 ' Argument list:
 '  Temp   the desired temperature
 '
 ' Return value:
 '  integer  1 if everything is OK, 0 on error
 '
 If mOvenStatus = OVENOFF Then   ' Oven is now off
  Return 0              ' Error
 End If

 mTemperature = Temp    ' Since oven is on, set temperature
 Return 1          ' Everything's OK

End Function

Public Function Preheat(ByVal Temp As Integer) As Integer
 ' Purpose: This method is used to preheat the oven
 '     temperature to the value passed to this method.
 '
 ' Argument list:
 '  temp   the desired temperature
 '
 ' Return value:
 '  integer  1 if everything is OK, 0 on error
 '
 Return Bake(Temp)

End Function

Public Sub Broil()
 ' Purpose: This method is used to turn on the broiler
 '     in the oven .
 '
 ' Argument list:
 '  N/A
 '
 ' Return value:
 '  N/A
 '
 mTemperature = BROILTEMP

End Sub

Public Sub SelfClean()
 ' Purpose: This method is used to self-clean the oven.
 '
 ' Argument list:
 '  N/A
```

LISTING 16.2   Continued

```
'
' Return value:
'   N/A
'
    mTemperature = CLEANTEMP

  End Sub

End Class
```

The code in Listing 16.2 begins with the definition of a series of symbolic constants. Next, it defines the member variables—that is, the properties—for the class. The access specifier for each of the member variables is `Private`. This forces the user of the class to use the class interface to change the state of the object.

Programmer's Tip

There's nothing etched in stone about the code layout for class code. I prefer to place any symbolic constants first, followed by the member data. I place the constructor code next, followed by the properties, with the methods toward the end of the code. I think it helps to rope off each major section with a comment to make it easy to find the major code sections.

You are free to use whatever sequence you prefer. However, once you adopt a class code layout style, you should stick with it. This is especially true if you are part of a programming team. The coding style you select should also address the style for naming classes and their variables (for example, `mOvenStatus` versus `OvenStatus`), symbolic constants (for example, use all uppercase or lowercase letters), and procedure comments. Adopting a consistent coding practice makes it easier to test and debug code because it gives you at least an approximate idea of where to look for each code section. This is true even if you are writing code by yourself and not as part of a programming team.

Testing the `COven` Class

Now you need to write a shell program that can be used to test your new class. Figure 16.3 shows a form that can be used to test the `COven` class.

There are two buttons on the form. The `btnUpdate` button is used to update the state of the `COven` object, and the `btnExit` button is used to end the program.

The `txtOvenTemp` text box is a little different from other text boxes you have used so far in this book. In this case, you have set the `ReadOnly` property to `True` instead its default value of `False`. Therefore, the user cannot enter anything into the text box.

There are a number of radio button objects on the form. The names of the radio buttons should make it easy for you to decipher their use in the program. For example, the Bake, Broil, Clean, and Off radio buttons are named `rbOvenOn`, `rbBroil`, `rbClean`, and `rbOvenOff`. Equally obvious names are used for the other radio buttons. The names of the buttons, along with the code in the following section, make it clear what the purpose of each button is.

FIGURE 16.3
A form for testing the
COven class.

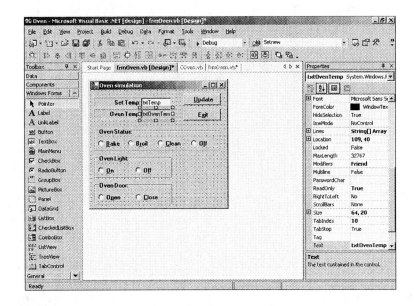

The Code for Testing the COven Class

The code for testing the **COven** class is somewhat long, but it's not too complicated. The code is
presented in Listing 16.3.

LISTING 16.3   Code for Testing the COven Class

```
Option Explicit On
Option Strict On

Public Class frmOvenTest
 Inherits System.Windows.Forms.Form
 Private Const BROILTEMP As Integer = 550    ' Broiler temperature
 Private Const CLEANTEMP As Integer = 600    ' Self-clean temperature

Dim MyOven As New COven()

Private Sub btnUpdate_Click(ByVal sender As System.Object, _
      ByVal e As System.EventArgs) Handles btnUpdate.Click
 ' Purpose: This button acts upon the state of the oven data as set
 '      by the radio buttons and the text boxes.


 If CheckSettings() = 0 Then   ' See if everything in proper state
  Exit Sub
 End If
 If rbOvenOff.Checked = True Then
  txtTemp.Text = "0"
 End If
```

LISTING 16.3   Continued

```
    UpdateOvenTemperature()

    txtTemp.Text = txtOvenTemp.Text

End Sub

Private Sub UpdateOvenTemperature()
  ' Purpose: This routine compares the current oven temperature to
  '          the desired temperature and updates it. To add a little
  '          realism to the process, the change is delayed by using
  '          the VBN DateDiff() function.
  '
  ' Argument list:
  '   None
  '
  ' Return value:
  '   N/A

    Dim Start, Finish As Double
    Dim NewDate As Date
    Dim StartTemp, EndTemp, DiffTemp, Increments, Offset As Integer

    StartTemp = CInt(txtOvenTemp.Text)
    EndTemp = CInt(txtTemp.Text)
    Increments = 5
    Offset = 5
    DiffTemp = EndTemp - StartTemp

    If DiffTemp < 0 Then      ' If we are decreasing the temp
     DiffTemp = 0 - DiffTemp  ' Make it positive
     Increments = -5          ' Count down rather than up
    End If

    While DiffTemp > 0
     NewDate = DateAdd(DateInterval.Second, 1, Now) ' Delay about a second
     While DateDiff(DateInterval.Second, Now, NewDate) > 0
      ' An empty loop
     End While
     StartTemp += Increments
     DiffTemp -= Offset
     txtOvenTemp.Text = CStr(StartTemp)
     Me.Update()                        ' Update the form
    End While

End Sub

Private Function CheckSettings() As Integer
  ' Purpose: This subroutine simply checks to see if all
  '          the radio buttons are consistent with
  '          the action being done
  '
  ' Argument list:
```

LISTING 16.3   Continued

```
'  N/A
'
' Return value:
'  integer  True if OK, False otherwise

' Is the oven on?
If rbOvenOff.Checked = True Then
 txtTemp.Text = "0"
 txtOvenTemp.Text = "0"
 MessageBox.Show("The oven is off")
 Return 0
End If
' Broiling usually has oven door open
If rbDoorClosed.Checked = True And rbBroil.Checked = True Then
 MessageBox.Show("Probably should open the oven door")
 If txtTemp.Text = "0" Then
  txtTemp.Text = CStr(BROILTEMP)
 End If
 Return 0
End If

' If we are baking or self-cleaning, close the door
If rbDoorClosed.Checked = False And rbBroil.Checked <> True Then
 If rbClean.Checked = False Then
  Beep()
  MessageBox.Show("Things bake faster with oven door closed")
  Return 0
 End If
End If

' Show the temperature
If rbDoorClosed.Checked = False And rbBroil.Checked = True Then
 txtTemp.Text = CStr(BROILTEMP)
 Return -1
End If

' If we are cleaning the oven...
If rbDoorClosed.Checked = False And rbClean.Checked = True Then
 Beep()
 MessageBox.Show("Close door during self-cleaning")
 Return 0
End If

' ...set the temperature to the max.
If rbDoorClosed.Checked = True And rbClean.Checked = True Then
 txtTemp.Text = CStr(CLEANTEMP)
 Return -1
End If

Return -1

End Function
```

LISTING 16.3 Continued

```
Private Sub Form1_Load(ByVal sender As System.Object, _
         ByVal e As System.EventArgs) Handles MyBase.Load
 InitializeOven(MyOven)
End Sub

Private Sub InitializeOven(ByVal MyOven As COven)
 ' Purpose: This sets up the starting state of the oven as shown by
 '      the text boxes.
 '
 ' Argument list:
 '   MyOven    a COven object. This does not really need to be
 '             passed in since it has module scope. However,
 '             doing it this way would allow us to change its
 '             scope and still be able to use this procedure
 '             without changing this code.
 '
 ' Return value:
 '   N/A

 If MyOven.OvenStatus = 0 Then    ' Show oven status
  rbOvenOff.Checked = True
 Else
  rbOvenOn.Checked = True
 End If

 If MyOven.DoorStatus = 0 Then    ' Show door status
  rbDoorClosed.Checked = True
 Else
  rbDoorOpen.Checked = True
 End If

 If MyOven.DoorStatus = 0 Then    ' Show door status
  rbDoorClosed.Checked = True
 Else
  rbDoorOpen.Checked = True
 End If

 If MyOven.LightStatus = 0 Then   ' Oven light
  rbLightOff.Checked = True
 Else
  rbLightOn.Checked = True
 End If

 txtTemp.Text = CStr(MyOven.Temperature)    ' Temperature
 txtOvenTemp.Text = CStr(MyOven.Temperature)
End Sub

Private Sub btnExit_Click(ByVal sender As System.Object, _
      ByVal e As System.EventArgs) Handles btnExit.Click
 Me.Dispose()
End Sub
```

LISTING 16.3   Continued

```
' ================= The radio buttons =========================
Private Sub rbOvenOn_Leave(ByVal sender As Object, _
        ByVal e As System.EventArgs) Handles rbOvenOn.Leave
 rbOvenOn.Checked = True
 MyOven.OvenStatus = -1
End Sub

Private Sub rbOvenOff_Leave(ByVal sender As Object, _
        ByVal e As System.EventArgs) Handles rbOvenOff.Leave
 rbOvenOff.Checked = True
 MyOven.OvenStatus = 0
End Sub

Private Sub rbLightOn_Leave(ByVal sender As Object, _
        ByVal e As System.EventArgs) Handles rbLightOn.Leave
 rbLightOn.Checked = True
 MyOven.LightStatus = 0
End Sub

Private Sub rbLightOff_Leave(ByVal sender As Object, _
        ByVal e As System.EventArgs) Handles rbLightOff.Leave
 rbLightOff.Checked = True
 MyOven.LightStatus = 0
End Sub

Private Sub rbDoorOpen_Leave(ByVal sender As Object, _
        ByVal e As System.EventArgs) Handles rbDoorOpen.Leave
 rbDoorOpen.Checked = True
 MyOven.DoorStatus = -1
End Sub

Private Sub rbDoorClosed_Leave(ByVal sender As Object, _
        ByVal e As System.EventArgs) Handles rbDoorClosed.Leave
 rbDoorClosed.Checked = True
 MyOven.DoorStatus = 0

End Sub

Private Sub rbBroil_Leave(ByVal sender As Object, _
        ByVal e As System.EventArgs) Handles rbBroil.Leave
 If rbDoorClosed.Checked = True And rbBroil.Checked = True Then
  MessageBox.Show("Probably should open the oven door")
  Exit Sub
 End If
 MyOven.Broil()
 txtTemp.Text = CStr(BROILTEMP)
End Sub

Private Sub rbClean_Leave(ByVal sender As Object, _
        ByVal e As System.EventArgs) Handles rbClean.Leave
 MyOven.SelfClean()
 txtTemp.Text = CStr(CLEANTEMP)
```

LISTING 16.3 Continued

```
End Sub

' ============= the text boxes =======================

Private Sub txtTemp_Leave(ByVal sender As Object, _
      ByVal e As System.EventArgs) Handles txtTemp.Leave
  If txtTemp.Text = "0" Then
    MyOven.Temperature = 0
    rbOvenOff.Checked = True
  End If
End Sub

End Class
```

The code in Listing 16.3 begins by defining two symbolic constants for the broiling and self-cleaning temperatures. Next it defines a COven class object named MyOven. Because the MyOven definition occurs outside any procedure, it has module scope. If this were a live program, it would be a good idea to place the definition of MyOven inside a procedure to hide it from the rest of the program.

All the action focuses on what happens when the user clicks the Update button. In the btnUpdate object's Click event, the code calls CheckSettings() to see if the radio buttons are in a state that allows the user to operate the oven. For example, if the rbOvenOff button is selected, the oven cannot do anything. If the rbBake button is selected but the oven door is open, an error message is issued. (Trying to bake something with the oven door open slows down the process a bunch.) You can read through the code and see what other states are examined.

The following code fragment is used to inject a small delay each time the txtOvenTemp text box is updated:

```
While DiffTemp > 0
  NewDate = DateAdd(DateInterval.Second, 1, Now) ' Delay about a second
  While DateDiff(DateInterval.Second, Now, NewDate) > 0
    ' An empty loop
  End While
  StartTemp += Increments
  DiffTemp -= Offset
  txtOvenTemp.Text = CStr(StartTemp)
  Me.Update()                    ' Update the form
End While
```

The DateAdd() function sets the date interval to 1 second, and the second parameter to the call creates a 1-second difference between the current date (as held in Now). The return value is assigned to NewDate, which is 1 second in the future. The While loop simply wastes time until the difference between NewDate and Now becomes 0. The remainder of the code updates the displayed oven temperature and updates txtOvenTemp on the form.

The code in Listing 16.3 actually updates things in less than 1 second, probably because of the time lag between the two calls to DateAdd() and DateDiff(). You can experiment with the second parameter in DateAdd() to see the impact it has on the delay.

The `ReadOnly` and `WriteOnly` Properties

There may be times when you would like to have a property that can only be read or that can only be written. For example, you might have a property named `mSerialNumber` that holds the serial number of an oven. (This is not as farfetched as it might seem because many modern ovens are controlled by microprocessors.) There is no reason you would want the user to be able to write a new serial number. You could make the property read-only by using the following code fragment:

```
Public ReadOnly Property GetSerialNumber()
 Get

 End Get
End Property
```

When you press the Enter key after the first line of code, Visual Basic .NET automatically supplies the skeletal code for the `Get` statement block. The `ReadOnly` keyword causes Visual Basic .NET to omit the `Set` statement block because it is not needed with a `ReadOnly` property.

Similarly, if you had a situation in which you wanted to write to a member variable but not make its property part of the class interface, you would use the `WriteOnly` keyword. For example, an oven might track the total elapsed time that it has been in use but not make that information available through the interface. (Such information might be useful in product-life studies, but you wouldn't want the user to have access to the data.) In that case, you might use something like this:

```
Public WriteOnly Property SetHours()
 Set(ByVal Value)

 End Set
End Property
```

Again, Visual Basic .NET automatically supplies the code skeleton after you enter the first line. The `Get` statement block is omitted because the property is write-only. All you need to do is flesh out the details for the `Set` statement block.

Although write-only procedures are less common than read-only procedures, they provide a means for further protecting class data items from outside contamination.

Summary

In this chapter you have learned how to write procedures to provide an interface to the member data of a class. With the material presented in this chapter and in Chapter 15, you should be ready to start designing and writing your own classes. You will learn more about the principles introduced here in later chapters.

Once again, you should take some time to experiment with the code presented in this chapter. You should use the debugger to set breakpoints and walk through the code. It is especially useful to set a breakpoint on the `Dim` statement that creates a class object and walk through its constructor (if any) and its properties and methods. You need to develop an intuitive feel for the flow of a program and its classes, and doing this experimentation can help you develop that feel.

Review Questions

1. What is meant by the term *class properties*?

A. In Chapter 2, "The Basics of Object-Oriented Programming," you learned that encapsulated within an object are member variables that are used to describe the object. These member variables are the properties associated with the object.

2. Why are class properties important?

A. Class properties are important for two reasons. First, the properties are viewed as attributes that can be used to describe or define an object. Second, by knowing the exact values for each property, you know its current state. For example, you might have a class property named `mTerminal` that is a Boolean variable that is used to describe a patient's severity of illness. By examining the value of `mTerminal`, you can learn about one aspect of the state of a patient.

3. Suppose you start using the `COven` class described in this chapter but notice that it doesn't model your oven very well. In particular, your oven has a temperature probe that you can insert into a roast to read the roast's internal temperature directly. What modifications would you have to consider in order to modify the `COven` class?

A. You may have begun your answer by saying that you need to add a new variable, perhaps named `mProbeTemp`, to the `COven` class. That's a good start, but you might want to back up a bit before going any further. The first question you should always ask yourself before adding new properties to an existing class is whether you want to modify the existing class or create a new class. This type of decision is based on an understanding of inheritance, which is the topic of discussion in Chapter 17, "Inheritance." As a general rule, you can make single-property modifications to a class without deriving a new class. However, anytime you want to extend an existing class, you should think about whether to graft the new variable onto the existing class or whether a new derived class should be developed.

The extension you are contemplating in this case is sufficiently easy that you can simply add a new property (for example, `mProbeTemp`) to the class. You will, of course, need to write a new property `Get` procedure for `mProbeTemp`. You can probably omit the property `Set` procedure because it makes no sense to be able to set the probe's temperature; it is a read-only attribute.

4. If you have created a class, is it really necessary to document each property?

A. Yes. You should always document your code. It is amazing how quickly you will forget what you write, even over short periods of time. Although meaningful variable names help, it is always good to document what the class properties are and what they are designed to do. If you cannot read the code for a property accessor method and understand what it is doing, you have not done a good job documenting it.

5. The code for the **COven** class is so simple, why do you bother using symbolic constants for **BROILTEMP** and **CLEANTEMP**?

A. Although the code is very simple and the symbolic constants are not required, when you read the code, do you think the use of the symbolic constants makes it easier to understand what the code is doing? If you answered no, methinks you jest.

6. What is the purpose of the **ReadOnly** and **WriteOnly** keywords?

A. When you use the **ReadOnly** keyword, you are denying users of the class from modifying the property. You use the **ReadOnly** keyword for any property that you do not want changed by users of the class. The **WriteOnly** property allows the user to change the value of the property, but not to read its current value. For example, you might be writing code for a network utility that records the network ID of printer users. Your class would record the activity but not make it available outside the class.

7. What part do properties play in the interface of a class?

A. The property **Get** and **Set** accessor methods define the way in which the user of the class must interact with the properties to change the state of the object modeled by the class.

8. What's wrong with the following class code fragment?

```
Dim mAccountBalance As Double
Dim mAccountStatus As Integer
Dim mDateOpened As Date
Dim mAccountFirstName As String
Dim mAccountLastName As String
Dim mAccountSSN As String

Public Property DateOpened() As Date
  ' Purpose: This property reads and writes the date the account was
  '        opened.

  Get
   Return mDateOpened
  End Get

  Set(ByVal Value As Date)
   MDateOpened = Value
  End Set
End Property

Public Property Balance() As Integer
  ' Purpose: This property reads and writes the account balance

  Get
   Return mAccountBalance
  End Get
```

```
Set(ByVal Value As Integer)
 MAccountBalance = Value
 End Set
End Property
```

A. Several things might need to be fixed in this fragment. First, the `Balance()` property methods should have the `Double` type specifier, not `Integer`. Also, because this property deals with monetary units, the `Decimal` data type might be a better choice. Second, there probably should not be a `Set` property method for `Balance()`. The class should include methods for processing deposits and withdrawals to the account that should set the balance. That would probably be a safer approach than to let the user of the class set the account balance directly.

9. Write an accounting system for General Ledger, Accounts Payable, Accounts Receivable, Payroll, and Inventory by using classes to model all the appropriate objects found in a small business accounting system.

A. Just kidding.

CHAPTER 17

INHERITANCE

You will learn the following in this chapter:

- What inheritance is and how you can use it to simplify programs

- What base classes and derived classes are

- What access specifiers are used with base and derived classes

- How to use a combo box

- What virtual classes are and how they can be used

*I*nheritance is a fundamental element of object-oriented programming (OOP) that promotes code reuse. Any time you can reuse a piece of code that has already been written, tested, and debugged, you enhance programmer productivity.

The basic idea behind inheritance is that although there may be unique properties that precisely define an object, many objects share common properties with other objects. For example, consider a building object. All buildings have certain properties in common. Each has a street address, a property tax rate and amount, a number of square feet, and so forth. However, specific types of buildings have additional properties that distinguish them from one another. Most building codes, for example, require commercial buildings to have a fixed number of parking spots per square foot of lease space. A private home, however, does not have that requirement. Likewise, a private home has properties, such as the number of bedrooms, that don't apply to a commercial building.

This chapter discusses how you can use inheritance to extend the functionality of a class.

Base Classes and Derived Classes

When you design a class, it is often useful to create one class that holds all the common properties and methods of the class and then create other subclasses that hold the unique properties and methods of that class. In OOP, the class that contains all the common properties and methods is called the *base class*. Let's look at an example that helps explain.

Assume that an investor calls you and wants to hire you to create a program to help her manage her real estate investments. The investor tells you that she owns three types of real estate: apartments, commercial office space, and private homes. You agree to take on the job. So, what's the first thing you should do?

Your first thought is probably to create a class for each of the different types of real estate. However, as you dig more deeply into the project, you realize that there are a number of things that all real estate investments have in common. Your preliminary design shows the following list of common properties:

- Purchase price

- Purchase date

- Street address

- Property taxes

- Monthly payment

- Insurance premium

There are probably others, but this serves as a starting point for defining the base class. You decide to name the base class `Building`.

"Is a" Relationships

If you have thought things through correctly thus far, the design should have a base class and one or more derived classes. A *derived class* is a class that inherits the properties and methods of the base class but is uniquely defined by additional properties and methods that are associated with the derived class. You might hear a derived class referred to as a *subclass*.

A properly designed derived class has an "is a" relationship to the base class. For example, you can say that an apartment "is a" building or that a home "is a" building. However, each of the derived classes `Apartment` and `Home` has additional properties and methods that uniquely define it. That is, properties of an apartment make it different from a private home. Likewise, a private home is different from a commercial building, even though both share some properties in common.

Now you ask yourself what properties uniquely identify the three types of real estate investments (apartments, commercial office space, and private homes). After a little thought, you come up with a table of properties, as shown in Table 17.1.

TABLE 17.1 Types of Buildings and Their Properties

Building Type	Properties	Type of Class
All Buildings	Purchase price Purchase date Street address Property taxes Monthly payment Insurance premium	Base
Apartment	Number of units Rent per unit per month Occupancy rate	Derived
Commercial	Square feet of rentable space Rent per square foot per year Parking spaces	Derived
Home	Square feet Rent per month Number of bedrooms Number of bathrooms	Derived

As you can see from Table 17.1, several properties are similar across classes but not exactly the same (for example, rent). Other properties are unique to the specific building type (for example, bedrooms, occupancy rate). The table also shows the properties that all three building types share in common. These properties are the base class properties. You can think of the base class as the common denominator of the derived classes.

Why Have Base and Derived Classes?

Right now you might be thinking, "You're throwing all these new terms at me, and you even dredged up one term from my fifth-grade math class! What's the purpose?" The purpose is to make life easier for you in the long run.

To appreciate what inheritance gives you, let's pretend for a moment there is no inheritance. In that case, you would simply have an `Apartment` class, a `Commercial` class, and a `Home` class. Think about what the investor does to maintain her real estate investments. Each month, she collects the rents and pays the mortgages. Every three months, she pays the quarterly insurance premium for each building. Every six months, she pays the semi-annual property taxes for each building.

Given the activities of the investor, you need to write a `CollectRent()` method, a `PayMortgage()` method, a `PayPropertyTaxes()` method, and a `PayInsurance()` method for each class. Because there are three classes, you have to write 12 methods to cover these activities for all building types.

Then you have an epiphany. If every type of building has these activities in common, why not just write the methods once and let the different classes share these methods? Shazzam! Inheritance!

What are the benefits of using the inheritance approach? First, you have to write only 4 methods instead of 12. Sharing the methods reduces the amount of code you have to write. Second, when there is less code to write, there is also usually less time spent testing and debugging the code. With a smaller volume of code to contend with, it takes you less time to identify, isolate, and correct any bugs that may appear. Third, modifying and maintaining the code over time is also easier with inheritance. All these benefits make you a more productive programmer.

It makes sense to use inheritance when similar classes exhibit common behavior. Once you become used to base and derived classes, you'll wonder how you ever lived without them.

The `Building` Base Class

This section shows the code for the `Building` base class. Based on the discussion to this point in the chapter, the code is presented in Listing 17.1. (Listing 17.1 leaves out a few things from Table 17.1, just to make the code a little more manageable. You might want to add them after you've read the chapter.)

LISTING 17.1   Code for the `Building` Base Class

```
Option Explicit On
Option Strict On

Public Class Building
  ' This is the base class, from which we derive the
  ' apartment, commercial, and home classes.

  ' =============== Symbolic Constants ================
  Private Const APARTMENT As Integer = 0
  Private Const COMMERCIAL As Integer = 1
  Private Const HOME As Integer = 2


  ' ================== Data Members ==================

  Private mAddress As String      ' Street address
  Private mPrice As Double        ' Purchase price
  Private mMonthlyPayment As Double  ' Monthly payment
  Private mTaxes As Double         ' Annual taxes
  Private mType As Integer         ' Building type


  ' ==================== Properties ======================
  Public Property Address()        ' Address Property
   Get
    Return mAddress
   End Get
```

LISTING 17.1   Continued

```
  Set(ByVal Value)
   mAddress = Value
  End Set
 End Property

 Public Property PurchasePrice()    ' Purchase Price Property
  Get
   Return mPrice
  End Get

  Set(ByVal Value)
   mPrice = Value
  End Set
 End Property

 Public Property MonthlyPayment()  ' Monthly Payment Property
  Get
   Return mMonthlyPayment
  End Get

  Set(ByVal Value)
   mMonthlyPayment = Value
  End Set
 End Property

 Public Property Taxes()           ' Property Taxes Property
  Get
   Return mTaxes
  End Get

  Set(ByVal Value)
   mTaxes = Value
  End Set
 End Property

 Public Property BuildingType()    ' Building Type Property
  Get
   Return mType
  End Get

  Set(ByVal Value)
   If Value < APARTMENT OrElse Value > HOME Then
    mType = -1   ' an error
   Else
    mType = Value
   End If
  End Set
 End Property

 ' ========================= Methods =======================
 Protected Sub DisplayBaseInfo()
  Dim BldType As String
```

LISTING 17.1 Continued

```
' Purpose: To display the base member data
Console.WriteLine("Address: " & mAddress)
Console.WriteLine("Purchase Price: " & FormatMoney(mPrice))
Console.WriteLine("Monthly Payment: " & FormatMoney(mMonthlyPayment))
Console.WriteLine("Property Taxes: " & FormatMoney(mTaxes))
Select Case mType
 Case APARTMENT
  BldType = "Apartment"
 Case COMMERCIAL
  BldType = "Commercial"
 Case HOME
  BldType = "Home"
End Select
Console.WriteLine("Building Type: " & BldType)
End Sub

' =========================== Helpers =========================
Protected Function FormatMoney(ByVal num As Double) As String
 ' Purpose: To format a dollar value
 '
 ' Argument list:
 '  num      A double that is the dollar value to format
 '
 ' Return value:
 '  string   A format dollar value string

 Return Format(num, "$##########.00")
 End Function
End Class
```

The code in Listing 17.1 begins by defining several symbolic constants for the three types of investment buildings. Next it defines five `Private` member variables of the base class. Each of these five definitions is followed by a `Public` property access method. This means that the member variables may be changed, but only through the class interface provided by the property access methods.

How could you provide data to a class that is not accessible outside its own class? Simple. You declare the data with the `Private` access specifier, but you do not provide a `Public` property access method for the data members. If you do this, even a derived class cannot have access to the `Private` members of the base class.

This is the first line of the `Address()` property access method:

```
Public Property Address()      ' Address Property
```

Because the property access method is `Public`, the `Address()` property method can be used to change the value of `mAddress`.

What would happen if you changed the `Public` keyword to `Private`? That would limit the property access method to the `Building` class itself. Nothing outside the class could then use it. You would not be able to change the `mAddress` member of the `Building` class from outside the class because `mAddress` and its `Address()` property access method would both be `Private`. Even derived classes would not have access to `mAddress` in such a case.

Listing 17.1 provides `Public` property access methods for all member variables in the `Building` class. It is important to remember that these `Private` data members can be changed, but only after an object of the class has been instantiated. Even after the object has been created, the class member data can be changed only through the class interface you provide via the `Public` property access methods.

The `Protected` Access Specifier

Two methods are provided in the `Building` class. The first, `DisplayBaseInfo()`, is used to display the `Building` class member values for the current object. You use the `Console.WriteLine()` method to display the values in the Debug window. The second method, `FormatMoney()`, is used to display monetary values, each with a dollar sign and two decimal places.

Programmer's Tip

Visual Basic .NET has a function named `FormatCurrency()` that does the same thing as `FormatMoney()`. This section simply uses its own method for illustrative purposes.

Note that the `DisplayBaseInfo()` and `FormatMoney()` methods use the `Protected` keyword. `Protected` is another type of access specifier. However, `Protected` indicates that the programming element (for example, a data item, a method definition) is accessible from within its own class or a derived class.

When you use the `Protected` access specifier, the data and methods are usable within their own class or a derived class. If you used the `Private` access specifier for the `DisplayBaseInfo()` and `FormatMoney()` methods, objects of the derived classes would not have access to those methods. Because you want the derived classes to be able to take advantage of these two methods, you need to use the `Protected` access specifier.

The `Apartment`, `Commercial`, and `Home` Derived Classes

In this chapter you have created three derived classes from the base `Building` class. The code for these derived classes is presented in Listing 17.2. Note that each class is in the same file as the `Building` class. Being able to have multiple classes declared in a single file is something that previous versions of Visual Basic did not allow. This makes it easier to keep the base class and its derived classes collected together in one place.

LISTING 17.2   The Derived Classes from the Building Class: Apartment, Commercial, and Home

```
' +++++++++++++++++++++++++++ Apartment Class +++++++++++++++++++++++++++
Public Class Apartment
 Inherits Building

 Private mUnits As Integer    ' The number of apartments
 Private mRent As Double      ' Rent per unit
 Private mOccupRate As Double ' Occupancy rate for building

 ' ==================== Properties ====================

 Public Property Units()     ' Units
  Get
   Return mUnits
  End Get
  Set(ByVal Value)
   mUnits = Value
  End Set
 End Property

 Public Property Rents()     ' Rents
  Get
   Return mRent
  End Get
  Set(ByVal Value)
   mRent = Value
  End Set
 End Property

 Public Property OccupancyRate() ' Occupancy rate
  Get
   Return mOccupRate
  End Get
  Set(ByVal Value)
   mOccupRate = Value
  End Set
 End Property

 ' =============== Methods ==================
 Public Sub DisplayBuilding()

  DisplayBaseInfo()
  Console.WriteLine("Number of Units: " & mUnits)
  Console.WriteLine("Rent per Unit: " & FormatMoney(mRent))
  Console.WriteLine("Occupancy Rate: " & mOccupRate)
 End Sub
End Class

' +++++++++++++++++++++++++++ Commercial Class +++++++++++++++++++++++++++

Public Class Commercial
 Inherits Building
```

LISTING 17.2   Continued

```
Private mSquareFeet As Integer   ' Rentable square feet
Private mRentPerSF As Double     ' Rent per square foot
Private mParking As Integer      ' Parking spots

' ==================== Properties =====================
Public Property SquareFeet()     ' Square feet
 Get
  Return mSquareFeet
 End Get
 Set(ByVal Value)
  mSquareFeet = Value
 End Set
End Property

Public Property RentPerSF()      ' Rent per square foot
 Get
  Return mRentPerSF
 End Get
 Set(ByVal Value)
  mRentPerSF = Value
 End Set
End Property

Public Property ParkingSpots()   ' Parking spots
 Get
  Return mParking
 End Get
 Set(ByVal Value)
  mParking = Value
 End Set
End Property


' ============== Methods ==================

Public Sub DisplayBuilding()
  DisplayBaseInfo()           ' Call base class
  Console.WriteLine("Square Feet: " & mSquareFeet)
  Console.WriteLine("Rent per SF: " & FormatMoney(mRentPerSF))
  Console.WriteLine("Parking Spots: " & mParking)
 End Sub
End Class

' +++++++++++++++++++++++++++ Home Class +++++++++++++++++++++++++++

Public Class Home
 Inherits Building

 Private mSquareFeet As Integer    ' Home's square feet
 Private mRentPerMonth As Double   ' Rent per month
 Private mBedrooms As Integer      ' Number of bedrooms
 Private mBaths As Integer         ' Number of bathrooms
```

LISTING 17.2   Continued

```
' ===================== Properties ======================
Public Property SquareFeet()     ' Square feet
 Get
  Return mSquareFeet
 End Get
 Set(ByVal Value)
  mSquareFeet = Value
 End Set
End Property

Public Property Rent()        ' Rent
 Get
  Return mRentPerMonth
 End Get
 Set(ByVal Value)
  mRentPerMonth = Value
 End Set
End Property

Public Property Bedrooms()      ' Bedrooms
 Get
  Return mBedrooms
 End Get
 Set(ByVal Value)
  mBedrooms = Value
 End Set
End Property

Public Property Baths()       ' Baths
 Get
  Return mBaths
 End Get
 Set(ByVal Value)
  mBaths = Value
 End Set
End Property

' ============== Methods ==================
Public Sub DisplayBuilding()

 DisplayBaseInfo()         ' Call base class
  ' Console.WriteLine("Building Type: Home")
 Console.WriteLine("Square Feet: " & mSquareFeet)
 Console.WriteLine("Rent per Month: " & FormatMoney(mRentPerMonth))
 Console.WriteLine("Bedrooms: " & mBedrooms)
 Console.WriteLine("Baths: " & mBaths)
 End Sub
End Class
```

The derived classes are very similar to one another, and the mechanics are the same for them all, so this section explains the code for just one of them.

Each derived class begins with the class name and the `Inherits` keyword:

```
Public Class Apartment
 Inherits Building
```

The `Inherits` keyword tells Visual Basic .NET that the `Apartment` class will inherit all the allowable data members and methods of the base class. (Keep in mind that you can use different flavors of access specifiers to limit access of the derived classes to the member data and methods in the base class.)

Member Data and Property Accessors

The next several lines of each derived class list the member data for the class. The member data properties distinguish the derived class from the base class. For the `Apartment` class, these members are the number of apartment units (`mUnits`), the rent per month (`mRent`), and the occupancy rate for the apartment complex (`mOccupRate`). An apartment complex "is a" building, and these additional pieces of information supply details that allow you to identify this building as an apartment building.

After each of these member data items is declared, the property accessor methods are provided for each item. In this simple example, the `Get` method returns the value of each member, and the `Set` method assigns a value to the member. It's interesting to note that Visual Basic .NET is smart enough to make the argument to the `Set` method match the data type of the data member.

Methods of the Derived Classes

The final section of each class is a method named `DisplayBuilding()` that is used to display the member data of the class. Note that this method name is the same for all three derived classes. How is this possible? Isn't there going to be a namespace collision for the method if they appear in all three classes?

No, there is no namespace collision because the `DisplayBuilding()` method is encapsulated into each object. Therefore, if you define three objects, such as `MyApt`, `MyOffice`, and `MyHome`, the method can be accessed only with `MyApt.DisplayBuilding()`, `MyOffice.DisplayBuilding()`, and `MyHome.DisplayBuilding()`. In every case, you must prefix the `Display` method with the object name and dot operator, which prevents any namespace collision in Visual Basic .NET.

Define Versus Declare

Remember that you have to be very careful when using the words *declare* and *define*. The base and derived class code presented thus far in this chapter serve as templates for how Visual Basic .NET will create objects from each of these class declarations.

You cannot do anything with any class until you create an object of the class. At that point, Visual Basic .NET asks Windows for enough memory to create, or instantiate, an object of the class by using the `New` keyword. Only after that definition occurs in the code do you have an object of the class that can use whatever properties and methods may exist for the class.

When you define an object of a class, what does Visual Basic .NET actually give you? For example, after Visual Basic .NET processes this statement:

```
Dim MyApartment As New Apartment()
```

an `Apartment` object named `MyApartment` has been defined, but what is it? In Chapter 4, "Data Types and Numeric Variables," you learned that each object variable requires 4 bytes of memory. Really! How can a class object that has its own properties and methods use just 4 bytes of memory? As you know from Chapter 15, the `Dim` statement actually creates a reference variable named `MyApartment`. Because `MyApartment` is a reference variable, it has an `rvalue` that is the memory address where the actual data for the object is stored. Because a class object's `rvalue` is always a memory address, only 4 bytes of storage are required for any class object.

After you have defined an object in a program, you need to release the resources associated with the object when you are done using it. Therefore, it's good programming practice to set each object variable to `Nothing` when you are finished using it. This allows Visual Basic .NET to gracefully free the resources associated with the object.

How Methods Differ from Functions and Subroutines

Encapsulation makes it possible to differentiate class methods from ordinary Visual Basic .NET functions and subroutines. If you write a Visual Basic .NET function or subroutine, the scope of that function or subroutine is equal to that of the assembly in which it is used. That is, it is global to the project it is in. So what?

There is a huge difference between class methods and general functions and subroutines. Because general functions and subroutines have global scope, their names must be globally unique. If you write a function named `DisplayBuilding()`, you can have only one function with that name in the project namespace. Therefore, if you want that one function to display the class data for different classes, you must increase the complexity of the function so that it can cope with the different display tasks embodied within it. This is not a good thing because the more complexity a routine has, the more chances there are for errors.

Now let's look at class methods. You can have each class use the same method name, and you never need to worry about namespace collision. As shown earlier, encapsulation of the method in the class eliminates this problem because you must prefix the method name with the object name and the dot operator. This removes the namespace problem.

There is another benefit, too. The ability to use the same method name for each class simplifies your programming burden. You can use the same method name in the same manner for all three objects. You don't have a long argument list that has to be memorized because the arguments vary according to the class data to be displayed. Think about all the Visual Basic .NET objects that have `Text` or `Caption` properties. Think how hard it would be for us to remember different method names for the `Text` or `Caption` properties of every object we used in our programs. That's really scary!

If one class needs a different level of processing complexity in its `DisplayBuilding()` method, you can place those differences in that class, where they're needed. The fact that one building type in our example needs a different `DisplayBuilding()` method to display a different class member's list is not a problem. You can tailor each method of the derived class to the unique needs of that class. This means you don't need to bury logic in the method to enable the method to decide which data you are working with, which would be the case for a generalized function or subroutine. Again, this leads to less complex and more easily maintained code. In programming, less is better.

In Listing 17.2, each `DisplayBuilding()` method begins with a call to `DisplayBaseInfo()`. (You can see this method code toward the end of Listing 17.1.) The `DisplayBaseInfo()` method displays the member data of the base `Building` class. After the information of the base class is displayed, the `DisplayBuilding()` method displays the member data that is unique to that class.

You can share the `DisplayBaseInfo()` and `FormatMoney()` methods from the base class because you have defined them with the `Protected` access specifier. This makes each of these methods from the base class available for use in the derived classes. (Some other access specifiers are introduced later in this chapter. Stay tuned.)

The remainder of the code in Listing 17.2, for the `Commercial` and `Home` classes, is very similar to that for the `Apartment` class. The only difference is in the member data for each class. Each of the display methods (that is, `DisplayBuilding()`) for each class calls the `DisplayBaseInfo()` method from the base `Building` class before it displays its own member data. What remains to be shown is the shell that is used to exercise the classes. This is the subject of the next section.

Testing the `Building` Class

Figure 17.1 shows a form that you can use to test the `Building` class and its derived classes. The form includes a series of text boxes that are used to collect the base class member information (for example, street address, purchase price). The following sections discuss various aspects of the test program that need further explanation.

Using Combo Boxes

The last property member of the base class is the property type. Figure 17.1 shows this data being presented to the user in a combo box. You have not used a combo box before, so this section provides a few details on how to use combo boxes. (Additional details about using combo boxes and other Visual Basic .NET control objects are presented in Chapter 21, "Creating Your Own Controls.") The following code fragment shows how you add the list of choices to a combo box:

```
cmbPropertyType.Items.Add("Apartment")
cmbPropertyType.Items.Add("Commercial")
cmbPropertyType.Items.Add("Home")
cmbPropertyType.SelectedIndex = 0
```

FIGURE 17.1

A form for testing the `Building` class.

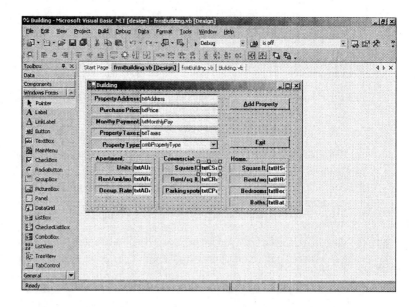

You add the combo box from the toolbar to the form by double-clicking the combo box object in the normal manner and supplying it with the name `cmbPropertyType`.

The first three lines show how you can use the `Add()` method to add an item to the list in the combo box. If the `Sort` property for the combo box is set to logic `False`, the `Add()` method results in a list that appears in the order in which the methods are entered. In this case, you enter them into the combo box in sorted order anyway, so they appear in sorted order, even though you do not have the `Sort` property set to `True`.

The `SelectedIndex` property determines which item in the combo box list is displayed. Because you set the `SelectedIndex` property to `0`, the first item in the list (that is, `Apartment`) is displayed.

Derived Class Member Data

Near the bottom of the form shown in Figure 17.1 are three group boxes, which are used to rope off the member data inputs for each derived class. What is not obvious from Figure 17.1 is that you do not display these group boxes when the program begins execution. Figure 17.2 shows how the program looks just before you select the derived class building type.

Notice that none of the group boxes are displayed at this point in the program. This is because you have set the `Visibility` property for each group box to logic `False`. After the user selects the type of building he or she is entering, the form displays the group box for that building type.

Figure 17.3 shows the form after the `Commercial` building type is selected from the combo box. Notice that only the group box for the `Commercial` building type is displayed. The user interface displays only the group box for the building type that is selected. This user interface design forces the user to consider the base class information before moving on to the specifics of the derived class data. If you compare Figure 17.1 and 17.3, you should see that the user interface is less complex and less confusing if the input text boxes for the other building classes are hidden.

FIGURE 17.2

A form for testing the `Building` class before the building type is selected.

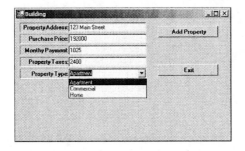

FIGURE 17.3

A form for testing the `Building` class after the `Commercial` building type is selected.

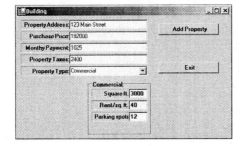

Of course, you could use other designs. The current design has one bad feature. If you never place the cursor in the combo box, you can never fire the `Leave()` event of the combo box. This means the `Apartment` group box would never be displayed because if you are happy with the `Apartment` selection displayed in the combo box, you have no reason to place your cursor in the box, which means the `Leave()` event would never fire. This is not good.

A solution might be to display the group box for the `Apartment` selection when the program starts. If the user selects a building type other than `Apartment`, you could use the combo box's `Leave()` event to hide the `Apartment` group box and then display the group box the user selects. I encourage you to add the code for this improved version to the test program.

Programmer's Tip

As a general rule, with respect to user interface designs, less is better. You should always collect the necessary information with the fewest input fields possible. Although hiding unused input fields may add a little more code to the program, it's a small price to pay for making life easier for the user.

After all the input data has been entered, you can click the Add Property button to show the class data. Figure 17.4 shows the output from the program in the Debug window.

FIGURE 17.4
A form for testing the
Building class after the
Add Property button is
clicked.

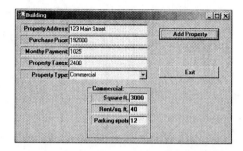

Programmer's Tip

The test program in this chapter simply writes the member data to the Debug window. A more realistic program would use a method to process the data in some way. In this program, for example, you might write this data to a database that the investor can review later.

The code to test the **Building** Class program is presented in Listing 17.3.

LISTING 17.3   Code to Test the **Building** Class Program

```
Public Class frmBuilding
 Inherits System.Windows.Forms.Form
 Dim MyApartment As New Apartment()
 Dim MyBuilding As New Commercial()
 Dim MyHome As New Home()

' " Windows Form Designer generated code "

 Private Sub frmBuilding_Load(ByVal sender As System.Object, ByVal e As _
             System.EventArgs) Handles MyBase.Load

  cmbPropertyType.Items.Add("Apartment")
  cmbPropertyType.Items.Add("Commercial")
  cmbPropertyType.Items.Add("Home")
  cmbPropertyType.SelectedIndex = 0
  grbApt.Visible = False
  grbCom.Visible = False
  grbHome.Visible = False

 End Sub

 Private Sub btnExit_Click(ByVal sender As System.Object, ByVal e As _
             System.EventArgs) Handles btnExit.Click
  MyApartment = Nothing   ' Release the resources
  MyBuilding = Nothing
  MyHome = Nothing
  Me.Dispose()
 End Sub
```

LISTING 17.3   Continued

```
Private Sub cmbPropertyType_Leave(ByVal sender As Object, ByVal e As _
           System.EventArgs) Handles cmbPropertyType.Leave

  Select Case cmbPropertyType.SelectedIndex
   Case 0   ' Apartment
    grbApt.Visible = True
    txtAUnits.Focus()

   Case 1   ' Commercial
    grbCom.Visible = True
    txtCSqFt.Focus()

   Case 2   ' Home
    grbHome.Visible = True
    txtHSqFt.Focus()
  End Select
End Sub

Private Sub cmbPropertyType_Enter(ByVal sender As Object, ByVal e As _
           System.EventArgs) Handles cmbPropertyType.Enter

  grbApt.Visible = False    ' Hide the group boxes
  grbCom.Visible = False
  grbHome.Visible = False

End Sub

Private Sub btnAdd_Click(ByVal sender As System.Object, ByVal e As _
           System.EventArgs) Handles btnAdd.Click


  Select Case cmbPropertyType.SelectedIndex

   Case 0                ' Apartment
    MyApartment.BuildingType = 0
    MyApartment.Address = txtAddress.Text
    MyApartment.PurchasePrice = CDbl(txtPrice.Text)
    MyApartment.MonthlyPayment = CDbl(txtMonthlyPay.Text)
    MyApartment.Taxes = CDbl(txtTaxes.Text)
    MyApartment.DisplayBuilding()

   Case 1                ' Commercial
    MyBuilding.BuildingType = 1
    MyBuilding.Address = txtAddress.Text
    MyBuilding.PurchasePrice = CDbl(txtPrice.Text)
    MyBuilding.MonthlyPayment = CDbl(txtMonthlyPay.Text)
    MyBuilding.Taxes = CDbl(txtTaxes.Text)
    MyBuilding.DisplayBuilding()

   Case 2                ' Home
    MyHome.BuildingType = 2
    MyHome.Address = txtAddress.Text
```

LISTING 17.3 Continued

```vb
        MyHome.PurchasePrice = CDbl(txtPrice.Text)
        MyHome.MonthlyPayment = CDbl(txtMonthlyPay.Text)
        MyHome.Taxes = CDbl(txtTaxes.Text)
        MyHome.DisplayBuilding()

    End Select

End Sub

' ============= Apartment fields ==============
Private Sub txtAUnits_Leave(ByVal sender As Object, ByVal e As _
            System.EventArgs) Handles txtAUnits.Leave
 MyApartment.Units = CInt(txtAUnits.Text)
End Sub

Private Sub txtARent_Leave(ByVal sender As Object, ByVal e As _
            System.EventArgs) Handles txtARent.Leave
 MyApartment.Rents = CDbl(txtARent.Text)
End Sub

Private Sub txtAOccup_Leave(ByVal sender As Object, ByVal e As _
            System.EventArgs) Handles txtAOccup.Leave
 MyApartment.OccupancyRate = CDbl(txtAOccup.Text)
End Sub

' ============ Commercial fields =================
Private Sub txtCSqFt_Leave(ByVal sender As Object, ByVal e As _
            System.EventArgs) Handles txtCSqFt.Leave
 MyBuilding.SquareFeet = CInt(txtCSqFt.Text)
End Sub

Private Sub txtCRent_Leave(ByVal sender As Object, ByVal e As _
            System.EventArgs) Handles txtCRent.Leave
 MyBuilding.RentPerSF = CDbl(txtCRent.Text)
End Sub

Private Sub txtCPark_Leave(ByVal sender As Object, ByVal e As _
            System.EventArgs) Handles txtCPark.Leave
 MyBuilding.ParkingSpots = CInt(txtCPark.Text)
End Sub

' =============== Home Fields =================

Private Sub txtHSqFt_Leave(ByVal sender As Object, ByVal e As _
            System.EventArgs) Handles txtHSqFt.Leave
 MyHome.SquareFeet = CInt(txtHSqFt.Text)
End Sub

Private Sub txtHRent_Leave(ByVal sender As Object, ByVal e As _
            System.EventArgs) Handles txtHRent.Leave
 MyHome.Rent = CDbl(txtHRent.Text)
End Sub
```

LISTING 17.3   Continued

```
Private Sub txtBedrooms_Leave(ByVal sender As Object, ByVal e As _
                System.EventArgs) Handles txtBedrooms.Leave
  MyHome.Bedrooms = CInt(txtBedrooms.Text)
End Sub

Private Sub txtBaths_Leave(ByVal sender As Object, ByVal e As _
                System.EventArgs) Handles txtBaths.Leave
  MyHome.Baths = CInt(txtBaths.Text)
End Sub
End Class
```

There are no surprises in the code in Listing 17.3. The initialization of the combo box is in the `frmBuilding_Load()` event. The `cmbPropertyType.Leave()` event for the combo box is used to display the proper group box after the building type has been selected. For each building type, a `Select Case` structure is used to make the appropriate group box visible and set the focus to the first text box in the group. Because the possibility exists that the `cmbPropertyType.Leave()` event may never fire, you place the assignments for the base class properties in the `btnAdd` object's `Click()` event procedure.

The last statement for each `Case` is a `Focus()` event call to the first text box in the appropriate group box. For example, if the user selected the `Apartment` building type, the last statement for `Case 0` (that is, an `Apartment` type) would call `txtAUnits.Focus()`. This call has the effect of moving the cursor to the `txtAUnits` text box.

The `btnAdd` object's `Click()` event code assigns the member data and then calls the `DisplayBuilding()` method for the selected building type. Notice that the same method is called for each building type. If you used a general subroutine or function instead of a class method, you would have to pass some form of data to the routine so that it could decide which building type to display. Encapsulation and inheritance simplify this considerably. Neat stuff!

Simple Changes to Enhance the `Building` Test Program

If you review the output in Figure 17.4, you might notice that it would be nice if the dollar figures had commas in the appropriate places. Look at the `FormatMoney()` method near the bottom of Listing 17.1. You can modify the statement that begins with `Return` so that it looks like this:

```
Return Format(num, "$#,###,###,###.00")
```

When you rerun the program, the output changes to that shown in Figure 17.5.

Now the dollar figures are formatted with commas in the appropriate places. Notice that because `FormatMoney()` is a `Protected` method in the base class, this change is available to all the derived classes. More importantly, the derived classes don't need to concern themselves about the details of how the change is made: The derived classes get the benefits of the change for free!

FIGURE 17.5
A form for testing the
`Building` class, after the
`FormatMoney()` method
is modified.

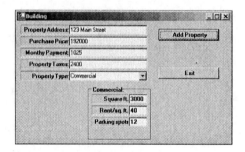

Virtual Classes

At this point, you can sit back and admire your code. Soon, however, your satisfied smile turns
to a frown because you realize you've written some RDC (really dumb code) into the program.
Given the way you've designed the `Building` class, why would anyone ever want to directly
create a `Building` object? The real value of the base `Building` class is that it is a generic collection point for the common data items that are part of a specific type of building. In other
words, the base class probably doesn't have enough specific information to be very useful as a
standalone object.

In situations like this, you might want to prevent users from creating objects from the base
class. You want to use the base class only as a point from which to create derived classes. A
class for which you do not expected to have objects created is called a *virtual class*. (You might
hear programmers refer to virtual classes as *abstract classes*, too. They are the same thing.)
Virtual classes behave like placeholders from which all derived classes are created.

The `MustInherit` Keyword

If you do not want anyone to create an object of class `Building`, you can use the `MustInherit`
keyword. This tells Visual Basic .NET that no object can be created directly from that class. To
implement this feature, you take the top line from Listing 17.1:

```
Public Class Building
```

and change it to this:

```
Public MustInherit Class Building
```

To test this change, you simply add a line that attempts to define an object of the base class. To
do so, look at the top several lines of Listing 17.3, and you should find this:

```
Public Class frmBuilding
 Inherits System.Windows.Forms.Form
 Dim MyApartment As New Apartment()
 Dim MyBuilding As New Commercial()
 Dim MyHome As New Home()
```

Now add the following new line after the preceding code:

```
Dim MyBldg As New Building()
```

The new line is an attempt to create a `Building` object from a virtual class. When you type this line into the program and press the Enter key, Visual Basic .NET gets a tad miffed and flags the statement as containing an error. If you move the cursor over the word `Building` in the statement line, you get this message:

```
'New' cannot be used on a class that is declared 'MustInherit'
```

Visual Basic .NET is smart enough to recognize the error at design time and inform you that you cannot create a `Building` object. (The same error message would be repeated if you tried to compile the program.) The `MustInherit` keyword, therefore, makes the base `Building` class a virtual class from which no objects can be created.

Keywords That Affect Inheritance

Thus far, this chapter has discussed the major structure and keywords that you need to know to create a base class. It has also shown how to extend that base class by deriving new classes from the base class. There are, however, several variations that you can use to alter the basic behavior that exists between base and derived classes. The following sections describe those keywords.

The `Overridable` and `Overrides` Keywords

Oftentimes, a base class contains a property or method that suits the needs of most derived classes but not all. For example, you might have a base class method named `ReadPropertyTaxFile()` that reads property tax data from a data file. However, suppose an investor purchased from the city a piece of property that has special tax incentives if the investor rehabs the building. For such a situation, you might want to create a new derived class named `RehabProperty`. The base class `ReadPropertyTaxFile()` method, however, would not read the proper file for a `RehabProperty` building. In fact, the investor might actually get a credit on his taxes instead of having to pay taxes.

However, because you want to preserve the way the class interface works, you might still want to use the `ReadPropertyTaxFile()` method but change the way it works in the `RehabProperty` class. To do this, you would write the following in the base class:

```
Overridable Sub ReadPropertyTaxFile()
  ' Insert the code to read the normal tax file.
End Sub
```

The `Overridable` keyword tells Visual Basic .NET that derived classes have the capability to replace the `RehabProperty()` procedure in the base class with a different version if they want. If a derived class does not replace the `Overridable` procedure in the base class, the base class procedure is used.

In the `RehabProperty` class, you would write this:

```
Overrides Sub ReadPropertyTaxFile()
  ' Insert the code to read the incentive file.
End Sub
```

The **Overrides** keyword tells Visual Basic .NET that this procedure is overriding a procedure that is defined in the base class. Therefore, any **RehabProperty** object that you define in your program uses the **ReadPropertyTaxFile()** method from the derived class rather than the method with the same name in the base class.

Clearly, the intent of these two keywords is to allow you to accommodate the special cases that arise in the derived classes. Hmmm. Instead of writing all this override stuff, why can't you just write a special method with a different name for the derived class that needs it?

Well, you could do that. However, if you did, you would force yourself to cope with a new method. Worse yet, the method might be used in only one class, and you might totally overlook it. If you can accommodate the necessary special cases for the derived class by using the same method name, you maintain the same interface for each derived class. This simplifies the things for you, the programmer.

Overriding the base class implementation also means that you've hidden away the implementation code for the special cases, which means you can use the same black box for all derived classes, even though what's going on inside that black box might be considerably different for each derived class.

Programmer's Tip

To whatever level possible, you should always try to provide the same methods for all the derived classes in a base class. This makes it easier to use the objects that are created from those classes by standardizing the interface to the class.

The MustOverride Keyword

Suppose you create a base class named **Customer**. From that base class you create derived classes named **WholesaleCustomer**, **RetailCustomer**, and **EducationalCustomer**. The base **Customer** class handles a lot of the expected member data, such as billing address, phone number, sales constants, and other details that customers have in common. However, each derived class has different discounts available. In a situation like this, you know that each derived class needs to calculate its own discount schedule. The base class requires a discount to be applied to each sale, but the details of the discounts must be in the derived classes. The **MustOverride** keyword provides the answer.

In the base class, you might declare a method like this:

```
MustOverride Function GetDiscount() As Double
```

This statement in the base class tells Visual Basic .NET that any class that derives from the **Customer** base class *must* provide a **GetDiscount()** method that returns a **Double** data type. Note that the base class does not provide its own version of the **GetDiscount()** function. This is why I use the term *declare* here, rather than *define*. You are simply telling Visual Basic .NET to make an entry into the symbol table that declares what data type **GetDiscount()** returns and enforce the rule that every derived class must provide an implementation of that method.

In other words, the base class declares the method, but the derived class must define (that is, write the code for) the method.

It follows that you must use the following lines in each of the derived classes:

```
Overrides Function GetDiscount() As Double
 ' Put the discount code here
End Function
```

The `MustOverride` keyword enhances the consistency of the class interface because all classes must supply this method.

The `Friend` Keyword

You learned earlier in this chapter that it's usually a good idea to define the data members in a class by using the `Private` access specifier. In order to have access to those `Private` data members outside the class, it is necessary to provide a property access method for each `Private` data member. This forces the user of the class to go through a consistent interface to gain access to the `Private` data. Again, this is the idea behind encapsulation.

At the other end of the spectrum, you can give the member of the class a `Public` access specifier, which makes the data accessible anywhere there is an object of the class. Because such an access specifier runs counter to the basic idea of encapsulation, I tend to minimize its use with respect to the class data members. The `Protected` access specifier provides an intermediate position from which the base and derived classes gain access to the `Protected` members and methods.

The `Friend` keyword provides a slightly different level of access than `Protected`. Only objects that are defined in the same assembly can access a `Friend` member. Assembly? For the moment, you can think of an *assembly* as being similar to a project. A project that you have compiled is one type of an assembly. Also, if you compile a class into a dynamic link library (DLL) file, as in Chapter 15, "Encapsulation and Creating Your Own Classes," that is also an assembly. `Friend` members are accessible only within the same assembly. In a client/server environment, you might have an assembly that sits on the server with `Friend` members. A different assembly that sits on the client would not have access to the `Friend` members on the server.

If you wanted to add a new member to the base `Building` class called `mBuildingID`, you might use this:

```
Friend mBuildingID as String
```

Now any object of the `Building` class that is in the same assembly has access to the `mBuildingID` member. However, `mBuildingID` is not accessible outside the assembly.

The `MyBase` and `MyClass` Keywords

The section "The `Overridable` and `Overrides` Keywords" explains how the base class might have a method named `ReadPropertyTaxFile()`, but a derived class might override it with its own version. Think again about what this means. There are two `ReadPropertyTaxFile()` methods: one in the base class and another in a derived class.

Now suppose you are in the derived class and suddenly realize that you not only want to use the `ReadPropertyTaxFile()` method in the derived class, but you now need to use the standard `ReadPropertyTaxFile()` method in the base class. (Perhaps you want to compare the two results.) Given the scoping rules that apply, how can you call the base class `ReadPropertyTaxFile()` method from within the derived class?

Simple! All you have to do is prefix the base class method with the `MyBase` keyword, like this:

```
MyBase.ReadPropertyTaxFile()
```

This gives Visual Basic .NET an unambiguous reference to the `ReadPropertyTaxFile()` method in the base class. You can also use the `MyBase` keyword with data members.

You can use the `MyBase` keyword in conjunction with members and methods even if it is not necessary. For example, with the three derived building classes described earlier in this chapter, the first line of the `DisplayBuilding()` method is this, which is defined in the base class and is used to display the base class data members:

```
DisplayBaseInfo()
```

You could change that statement to this, and the program would function exactly as it did before:

```
MyBase.DisplayBaseInfo()
```

The only difference from before is that the line now imparts a little documentation information to reinforce that the `DisplayBaseInfo()` method is found in the base class. Although this change doesn't tell you anything you couldn't find out fairly quickly anyway, it does serve as a memory jogger. For those of us who have drunk from too many aluminum cans over the years, every little bit helps.

The `MyClass` keyword permits similar behavior to `MyBase`, but in a different direction. For example, suppose you have defined an `Overridable` method in a class. This means it is possible for a derived class to override your method definition. By prefixing the method call with `MyClass`, you ensure that the compiler selects your derived class method rather than the base class method.

For example, if you have a `CalculateRents()` method in the base class that can be overridden in any derived classes, this statement in your base class code ensures that Visual Basic .NET uses your method, not one from the derived class:

```
MyClass.CalculateRents()
```

In a way, `MyClass` is similar to `Me`, except that it applies to a class and makes Visual Basic .NET see the method calls as nonoverridable.

The `NotInheritable` Keyword

Visual Basic .NET allows you to build a chain of inheritance classes. For example, you saw earlier in this chapter how the `Home` class is derived from the base class `Building`. However, it is also possible to view `Home` as the base class for new derived classes. These new derived classes from what we might now view as the `Home` base class might be `Ranch` and `Colonial`.

You might decide at some point that this chain of classes has gone far enough and you don't want any further derived classes to be created from the Ranch or Colonial classes. In that case, you would start each class definition with this:

```
Public NotInheritable Class Ranch
.
.
.
End Class

Public NotInheritable Class Colonial
.
.
.
End Class
```

If you do this, Visual Basic .NET does not allow any further classes to be derived from these two classes. The NotInheritable keyword ends the inheritance chain.

Summary

This chapter described how to create derived classes from a base class. It also showed the advantages that you gain from using derived classes when they are appropriate. Finally, this chapter discussed the various access specifiers that you can use to fine-tune how the base and derived classes interact with each other.

Inheritance is a topic that seems a bit intimidating at first. If you feel that way, you should spend a little time reviewing this chapter and writing some sample derived classes of your own. The intimidation will soon dissolve, and you'll throw rocks at any language that doesn't support inheritance.

Review Questions

Programmer's Tip

Students hate questions that begin with "In one sentence…" I believe the reason is because it limits their ability to engage in elocutionary effervescence. Although some topics simply cannot be reduced to a single sentence, those topics are fairly rare. In all other situations, if you cannot define something clearly in a relatively short sentence, you probably don't understand it completely. Also, communicating effectively in relatively few words is an important springboard to corporate advancement. After all, as a manager, would you rather get the same information from a 1-page report or a 14-page report?

1. In one sentence, define what inheritance brings to the programmer's table.

A. Inheritance provides the ability to absorb all the functionality of an existing class as the starting point for the development of a new class.

2. How does a derived class relate to a base class?

A. A base class serves as a collection point for the properties and methods that are expected to be shared in common with a derived class. A derived class adds to the base class properties and methods whatever additional properties and methods are necessary to completely describe the derived class object. In other words, the base class becomes the common denominator for all derived classes.

3. How does the `Protected` access specifier differ from the `Private` access specifier?

A. The `Protected` access specifier indicates that any data item that has this access level is available to any member of the class, including any derived classes. If the `Private` access specifier is used, only the class in which the item is defined has access to the data item.

4. How do you tell Visual Basic .NET that you want the class you are developing to use the functionality of some other class?

A. You use the word `Inherits` in the class that is assuming the existing class's functionality. These statements:

```
Public Class TownHouse
 Inherits Building
```

say that the class being developed (that is, `TownHouse`) inherits all the functionality of the `Building` class.

5. Is it true that a derived class inherits all the functionality of the base class?

A. Not necessarily. By using different access specifiers, you can limit the functionality of derived classes.

6. In one sentence, explain how you can distinguish a function call from a class method call in a program's code.

A. A class method call is prefixed with an object name and a dot operator, whereas a function call is not. (That's the one-sentence answer.) For example, in this statement:

```
ThisPlayersHandicap = Players.Handicap(WhichPlayer)
```

`Handicap()` must be a class method call because it is prefixed with an object name and the dot operator. On the other hand, this statement:

```
ThisPlayersHandicap = Handicap(WhichPlayer)
```

calls a function named `Handicap()`.

7. Suppose an array named `DaysInTheMonths()` holds the number of days in a month, starting with January, and you want to copy those values into a combo box name `cmbDaysInTheMonth`. How would you write the code to do this? (You are only interested in the days in the month as held in the array, not the names of the months. You can also assume that element 1 in the array is January.)

A. The following code provides one way:

```
Dim i As Integer
For i = 1 To 12
 cmbDaysInTheMonth.Items.Add(DaysInTheMonths(i))
Next
```

8. What is a virtual class?

A. A virtual class is a class from which you expect no objects to be created directly. The only purpose of a virtual class is to collect all the common properties and methods that the derived classes will share. The virtual class is the common denominator for the derived classes, but it might not have enough detail in and of itself to be useful.

9. What is the purpose of the `Overridable` keyword?

A. The `Overridable` keyword means that the base class provides a certain method, but the derived classes can implement their own methods by using the same name. If a derived class does write a replacement for the `Overridable` method, it must use the `Overrides` keyword in the definition of the method. Visual Basic .NET always uses the method of the derived class by default in such cases.

10. How is `MustOverride` different from `Overridable`?

A. `MustOverride` means that the derived classes must write code for the `MustOverride` keyword. Whereas `Overridable` gives the programmer the option of writing a replacement, `MustOverride` does not give the programmer a choice; the programmer must write the code for the `MustOverride` keyword. Indeed, the base class does not provide code for the `MustOverride` keyword.

11. How is the `Friend` access specifier used?

A. You use the `Friend` access specifier when you want to make a data item accessible to an entire assembly. `Friend` is one step toward `Public`, and it's a clear step away from `Private` in terms of encapsulation. A common use of `Friend` is when you want to make a data item available to all components compiled on a Web server but hide it from all clients.

12. Give an example of where you might use the `MyBase` keyword.

A. Suppose the base class has an `Overridable` method, and you are writing code for a derived class. However, instead of using the method in the class you are writing, you have one situation where you want to use the base class implementation of the method. If the overridden method is named `CalcTax()`, you could write this statement:

```
ThisTax = MyBase.CalcTax()
```

and your code would call the `CalcTax()` method in the base class rather than the (default) `CalcTax()` method you wrote for the derived class.

13. What is the purpose of the `NotInheritable` keyword?

A. The `NotInheritable` keyword means the current class is the last link in the chain of derived classes. If you write a class using the `NotInheritable` keyword, no further classes can be derived from the class.

CHAPTER 18

POLYMORPHISM

You will learn the following in this chapter:

- What polymorphism is and how it relates to object-oriented programming

- How polymorphism and inheritance work together to simplify programming tasks

- How to use constructors properly

- How to use virtual classes

- How to design an interface

Recall from Chapter 2, "The Basics of Object-Oriented Programming," that the three basic building blocks of object-oriented programming (OOP) are encapsulation, inheritance, and polymorphism. This chapter examines the third component of the OOP trilogy: polymorphism. You will learn what polymorphism is and how to take advantage of it in your programs. By the end of this chapter you will know how to use polymorphism to increase the flexibility of classes, reduce the amount of code required for a given program, and make programs easier to debug and maintain. This chapter ends by showing you how interfaces relate to polymorphism and OOP in general.

What Is Polymorphism?

Simply stated, *polymorphism* is the ability to have different classes implement a common interface in different ways. The *interface* of a class is defined by the properties and methods the class makes available. That is, the interface defines the way we programmers can access the properties and methods of a class (usually through the `Public` elements of the class).

Now that you know something about inheritance, let's add a little flesh to the example discussed in Chapter 2.

Chapter 2 discusses an example in which there is a `Doctor` object, a `Nurse` object, a `Patient` object, and a `Visitor` object—all placed in a hospital setting. (Although Chapter 2 doesn't say so, perhaps each of these objects is derived from a base class object called `HospitalPerson`.)

In the example in Chapter 2, when you issue the message `DoSomething()`, each object reacts to the message in its own way: In response to the `DoSomething()` message, the `Doctor` object performs an operation, the `Nurse` object gives the `Patient` object an injection, the `Patient` object says "Ouch" and complains, and the `Visitor` object says, "I'll bet that hurt." Note that each object reacts differently to the same message. This is polymorphism in action—different objects (`Doctor`, `Nurse`, and so on) reacting differently (for example, an operation by the `Doctor`, an injection by `Nurse`) to the same interface (that is, a `DoSomething()` message).

This is pretty heady stuff. Because a derived class object inherits the capabilities of the base class, any derived class object can be treated as if it were a base class object. This extensibility, however, is a one-way street. Drawing on the `Building` class example from Chapter 17, "Inheritance," you can say that `Home` "is a" `Building` because `Home` is a derived class of `Building`. However, you cannot say a `Building` always "is a" `Home` because a `Building` could also be an apartment or a commercial building (that is, an `Apartment` or a `Commercial` class). Still, inheritance coupled with polymorphism allows you to do some very useful things that would not be possible otherwise.

An Example of Inheritance and Polymorphism

Let's use the `Building` class from Chapter 17 as a basis for the example presented here. The following sections concentrate on the changes you need to make to the code.

A Base Class Constructor

The first change you need to implement is a base class constructor for the `Building` class. The new code for the `Building` class is shown in Listing 18.1.

LISTING 18.1   The Base Class Constructor for the `Building` Class

```
' ================== Constructor ==================
Public Sub New()
 mAddress = "Empty building"   ' The remaining data = 0 anyway
End Sub
```

When you create the `Building` class constructor, you need no arguments. At first blush, the constructor code shown in Listing 18.1 probably seems obvious. Then it hits you: "Wait a minute! The `Building` class is defined as a virtual class, using the `MustInherit` keyword. How can I have a constructor for an object I cannot create?" Good question.

Remember that you can treat a derived class object as if it were a base class object, but not vice versa. Therefore, if you create a derived object of the `Building` class with an empty initializer list, the base class constructor shown in Listing 18.1 is used. Under such circumstances, all the member data values are initialized to `0` (by default), except the `mAddress` member, which is initialized to `"Empty building"`.

If you wanted to initialize the other members of the base class to some nonzero value, you could. However, leaving those members with the value 0 might be a good idea because it reinforces the idea that the object does not yet contain valid data values.

Constructors with Initializer Lists

If you rely on the default constructor for the derived objects of the Building class, you have to use the property methods of the object to fill in the appropriate values. As an alternative, however, you can overload the constructor to initialize the base class members. Listing 18.2 shows the alternative constructor, using an initializer list for the Apartment class; the code is virtually identical for the other derived classes, too.

LISTING 18.2   Constructors for the Derived Building Classes, Using an Initializer List

```
Public Sub New()   ' The Apartment constructor with no arguments

End Sub

' Constructor with initializer list of arguments
Public Sub New(ByVal Addr As String, ByVal Price As Double, ByVal Payment _
        As Double, ByVal Taxes As Double, ByVal Bldg As Integer)
 MyBase.Address = Addr
 MyBase.PurchasePrice = Price
 MyBase.MonthlyPayment = Payment
 MyBase.Taxes = Taxes
 MyBase.BuildingType = Bldg
End Sub
```

The first thing to notice in Listing 18.2 is that each derived class has two constructors. Why? You made the design decision that you will allow the user of the class to create an object with or without an initializer list for the members of the base class. You must therefore provide constructors for both types of object instantiation. This means that the following statements to create an Apartment object are valid:

```
Dim MyApartment As New Apartment("6 North Ben Street", _
         550000, 6000, 12000, APARTMENT)
Dim YourApt as New Apartment()
```

If you did not provide the empty Apartment constructor, the second statement line would force Visual Basic .NET to tell you that you are missing the five arguments required in the constructor's initializer list. If you supplied only the first constructor in Listing 18.2, this statement:

```
Dim MyApartment As New Apartment("6 North Ben Street", _
         550000, 6000, 12000, APARTMENT)
```

would cause Visual Basic .NET to issue a "too many arguments" error message. Therefore, if you want to allow both types of definition statements, you need both constructors in the derived classes.

Note that the code in Listing 18.2 for the second constructor type has an initializer list that only initializes the data members in the base class. You do not require the initializer list to include the members of the derived class. You could do this if you wanted, but I chose not to in this case, in order to keep the code a little bit simpler. If you want to allow a complete initializer list to include those members of the derived class, you should add the class members' parameters to the initializer list in Listing 18.2 for each derived class.

Programmer's Tip

In the strictest sense, it is not necessary to use MyBase in Listing 18.2 because the property accessor methods in the base class are defined by using the Public keyword. However, using the MyBase keyword in the derived classes helps document what the constructor is doing.

Keep in mind that each of the derived classes needs to implement two constructor methods, similar to those shown in Listing 18.2. Only by using two constructors can you allow each derived class to have the option of either an empty or a nonempty initializer list. Given that fact, why don't you just move the constructor with the initializer list into the Building base class and omit it from the derived classes? That would be a good idea, but it won't work because you have declared all the member data in the Building class to be Private. Therefore, you are forced to use the property accessor methods of the base class to affect the values of the members in the base class.

Let's add one more method to your derived classes but force each class to supply the method. In the Building class code, you should add the following line just before the DisplayBaseInfo() method:

```
Public MustOverride Function CallSnowRemoval() As String
```

This statement says that each derived class must provide its own version of the CallSnowRemoval() method. Why would you do this? First, remember that when the base class is an virtual class as the Building class is, its purpose is to serve as a collection point for commonalities shared in the derived classes. Therefore, the properties that distinguish each of the derived classes are properly found in the derived class code.

In other words, MustOverride means you are allowing different actions to be taken for each derived class when snow needs to be removed from the property. For example, the Apartment and Commercial classes can use the CallSnowRemoval() method to call a large commercial snow removal company. The Home class, however, might just call the person renting the home and remind him that his lease requires him to shovel the walk.

Because the base class declares the method, the derived classes must define (that is, implement) the method. Therefore, in each derived class there must be code similar to the following (which uses the Apartment class as an example):

```
Public Overrides Function CallSnowRemoval() As String
 ' Purpose: This routine is called to remove snow for the apartment.
 '
  Return "Apartment snow removal: " & MyBase.SnowRemoval
End Function
```

The use of the keyword `Overrides` in the first statement line tells Visual Basic .NET to override a method that is declared in the base class. Notice that you use the new `SnowRemoval()` property accessor method to read a new member named `mSnowPhone` that you added to the base `Building` class. (The revised code is presented in Listing 18.3.)

The important point to remember is that `MustOverride` requires each derived class to implement its own version of the `CallSnowRemoval()` method. It also follows that the base class does not implement a version of the `CallSnowRemoval()` method. The base class declares the `CallSnowRemoval()` method, and the derived classes define the method.

The complete listing for the `Building` class and the derived classes is presented in Listing 18.3.

LISTING 18.3 Code for the `Building` Class and the Derived Classes

```vb
Option Strict On

Public MustInherit Class Building
 ' This is the base class, from which we derive the
 ' apartment, commercial, and home classes.

 ' =============== Symbolic Constants ===============
 Private Const APARTMENT As Integer = 0
 Private Const COMMERCIAL As Integer = 1
 Private Const HOME As Integer = 2

 ' Default snow removal phone numbers
 Public Const APTPHONE As String = "555-1000"
 Public Const COMPHONE As String = "555-2000"
 Public Const HOMPHONE As String = "555-3000"

 ' ================== Data Members ==================

 Private mAddress As String      ' Street address
 Private mPrice As Double        ' Purchase price
 Private mMonthlyPayment As Double  ' Monthly payment
 Private mTaxes As Double         ' Annual taxes
 Private mType As Integer         ' Building type
 Private mSnowPhone As String      ' Who to call for snow removal

 ' ================== Constructor ==================
 Public Sub New()
  Address = "Empty building"
 End Sub


 ' ==================== Properties =====================
 Public Property Address() As String     ' Address Property
  Get
   Return mAddress
  End Get
```

LISTING 18.3   Continued

```vb
  Set(ByVal Value As String)
   mAddress = Value
  End Set
 End Property

 Public Property PurchasePrice() As Double   ' Purchase Price Property
  Get
   Return mPrice
  End Get

  Set(ByVal Value As Double)
   mPrice = Value
  End Set
 End Property

 Public Property MonthlyPayment() As Double   ' Monthly Payment Property
  Get
   Return mMonthlyPayment
  End Get

  Set(ByVal Value As Double)
   mMonthlyPayment = Value
  End Set
 End Property

 Public Property Taxes() As Double        ' Property Taxes Property
  Get
   Return mTaxes
  End Get

  Set(ByVal Value As Double)
   mTaxes = Value
  End Set
 End Property

 Public Property BuildingType() As Integer   ' Building Type Property
  Get
   Return mType
  End Get

  Set(ByVal Value As Integer)
   If Value < APARTMENT Or Value > HOME Then
    mType = -1  ' an error
   Else
    mType = Value
   End If
  End Set
 End Property

 Public Property SnowRemoval() As String    ' Call for snow removal
  Get
   Return mSnowPhone
```

LISTING 18.3 Continued

```
 End Get
 Set(ByVal Value As String)
  mSnowPhone = Value
 End Set
End Property

' ========================== Methods ========================

' Force the derived classes to figure out who to call.
Public MustOverride Function CallSnowRemoval() As String

Protected Sub DisplayBaseInfo()
 Dim BldType As String

  ' Purpose: To display the base member data
  Select Case mType        ' Which type of building?
   Case APARTMENT
    BldType = "Apartment"
   Case COMMERCIAL
    BldType = "Commercial"
   Case HOME
    BldType = "Home"
  End Select
  Console.WriteLine()
  Console.WriteLine("---------- " & BldType & " ----------")
  Console.WriteLine("Address: " & mAddress)
  Console.WriteLine("Purchase Price: " & FormatMoney(mPrice))
  Console.WriteLine("Monthly Payment: " & FormatMoney(mMonthlyPayment))
  Console.WriteLine("Property Taxes: " & FormatMoney(mTaxes))
  Console.WriteLine("Building Type: " & BldType)
  Console.WriteLine("Snow removal Phone: " & mSnowPhone)
  Console.WriteLine()
End Sub

' ========================== Helpers ========================
Protected Function FormatMoney(ByVal num As Double) As String
  ' Purpose: To format a dollar value
  '
  ' Argument list:
  '  num     A double that is the dollar value to format
  '
  ' Return value:
  '  string   A format dollar value string

  Return Format(num, "$#,###,###,###.00")
 End Function
End Class

' +++++++++++++++++++++++++++ Apartment Class +++++++++++++++++++++++++++
Public Class Apartment
 Inherits Building
```

LISTING 18.3 Continued

```
Private mUnits As Integer    ' The number of apartments
Private mRent As Double      ' Rent per unit
Private mOccupRate As Double ' Occupancy rate for building

Public Sub New()

End Sub

' Constructor with initializer list of arguments
Public Sub New(ByVal Addr As String, ByVal Price As Double, _
        ByVal Payment As Double, ByVal Taxes As Double, _
        ByVal Bldg As Integer, ByVal SnowPhone As String)
 MyBase.Address = Addr
 MyBase.PurchasePrice = Price
 MyBase.MonthlyPayment = Payment
 MyBase.Taxes = Taxes
 MyBase.BuildingType = Bldg
 If SnowPhone = "" Then
  MyBase.SnowRemoval = APTPHONE
 Else
  MyBase.SnowRemoval = SnowPhone
 End If
End Sub

' ===================== Properties =====================

Public Property Units() As Integer    ' Units
 Get
  Return mUnits
 End Get
 Set(ByVal Value As Integer)
  mUnits = Value
 End Set
End Property

Public Property Rents() As Double      ' Rents
 Get
  Return mRent
 End Get
 Set(ByVal Value As Double)
  mRent = Value
 End Set
End Property

Public Property OccupancyRate() As Double ' Occupancy rate
 Get
  Return mOccupRate
 End Get
 Set(ByVal Value As Double)
  mOccupRate = Value
 End Set
End Property
```

LISTING 18.3   Continued

```vbnet
' ============== Methods ==================
Public Overrides Function CallSnowRemoval() As String
  ' Purpose: This routine is called to remove snow for an Apartment.
  '
  Return "Apartment snow removal: " & MyBase.SnowRemoval
End Function

Public Sub DisplayBuilding()

  DisplayBaseInfo()
  Console.WriteLine("      Apartment members:")
  Console.WriteLine("Number of Units: " & mUnits)
  Console.WriteLine("Rent per Unit: " & FormatMoney(mRent))
  Console.WriteLine("Occupancy Rate: " & mOccupRate)
End Sub
End Class

' +++++++++++++++++++++++++++ Commercial Class +++++++++++++++++++++++++++

Public Class Commercial
  Inherits Building

  Private mSquareFeet As Integer   ' Rentable square feet
  Private mRentPerSF As Double     ' Rent per square foot
  Private mParking As Integer      ' Parking spots

  Public Sub New()   ' Constructor with no arguments

  End Sub

  Public Sub New(ByVal Addr As String, ByVal Price As Double, _
        ByVal Payment As Double, ByVal Taxes As Double, _
        ByVal Bldg As Integer, ByVal SnowPhone As String)
    MyBase.Address = Addr
    MyBase.PurchasePrice = Price
    MyBase.MonthlyPayment = Payment
    MyBase.Taxes = Taxes
    MyBase.BuildingType = Bldg
    If SnowPhone = "" Then
      MyBase.SnowRemoval = COMPHONE
    Else
      MyBase.SnowRemoval = SnowPhone
    End If
  End Sub
  ' ===================== Properties =====================
  Public Property SquareFeet() As Integer   ' Square feet
  Get
    Return mSquareFeet
  End Get
  Set(ByVal Value As Integer)
    mSquareFeet = Value
```

LISTING 18.3 Continued

```vb
  End Set
End Property

Public Property RentPerSF() As Double      ' Rent per square foot
 Get
  Return mRentPerSF
 End Get
 Set(ByVal Value As Double)
  mRentPerSF = Value
 End Set
End Property

Public Property ParkingSpots() As Integer  ' Parking spots
 Get
  Return mParking
 End Get
 Set(ByVal Value As Integer)
  mParking = Value
 End Set
End Property

' ============== Methods =================
Public Overrides Function CallSnowRemoval() As String
 ' Purpose: This routine is called to remove snow for a Commercial building.
 '
 Return "Commercial snow removal: " & MyBase.SnowRemoval
End Function

Public Sub DisplayBuilding()
 DisplayBaseInfo()          ' Call base class
 Console.WriteLine("      Commercial members:")
 Console.WriteLine("Square Feet: " & mSquareFeet)
 Console.WriteLine("Rent per SF: " & FormatMoney(mRentPerSF))
 Console.WriteLine("Parking Spots: " & mParking)
 End Sub
End Class

' +++++++++++++++++++++++++++++ Home Class +++++++++++++++++++++++++++++

Public NotInheritable Class Home
 Inherits Building

 Private mSquareFeet As Integer    ' Home's square feet
 Private mRentPerMonth As Double   ' Rent per month
 Private mBedrooms As Integer      ' Number of bedrooms
 Private mBaths As Integer         ' Number of bathrooms

 ' ==================== Properties =====================
 Public Sub New()  ' Constructor with no arguments

 End Sub
```

LISTING 18.3 Continued

```
Public Sub New(ByVal Addr As String, ByVal Price As Double, _
        ByVal Payment As Double, ByVal Taxes As Double, _
        ByVal Bldg As Integer, ByVal SnowPhone As String)
 MyBase.Address = Addr
 MyBase.PurchasePrice = Price
 MyBase.MonthlyPayment = Payment
 MyBase.Taxes = Taxes
 MyBase.BuildingType = Bldg
 If SnowPhone = "" Then
  MyBase.SnowRemoval = HOMPHONE
 Else
  MyBase.SnowRemoval = SnowPhone
 End If

End Sub

Public Property SquareFeet() As Integer      ' Square feet
 Get
  Return mSquareFeet
 End Get
 Set(ByVal Value As Integer)
  mSquareFeet = Value
 End Set
End Property

Public Property Rent() As Double        ' Rent
 Get
  Return mRentPerMonth
 End Get
 Set(ByVal Value As Double)
  mRentPerMonth = Value
 End Set
End Property

Public Property Bedrooms() As Integer      ' Bedrooms
 Get
  Return mBedrooms
 End Get
 Set(ByVal Value As Integer)
  mBedrooms = Value
 End Set
End Property

Public Property Baths() As Integer       ' Baths
 Get
  Return mBaths
 End Get
 Set(ByVal Value As Integer)
  mBaths = Value
 End Set
End Property
```

LISTING 18.3   Continued

```
' =============== Methods ===================
Public Overrides Function CallSnowRemoval() As String
  ' Purpose: This routine is called to remove snow for an apartment.
  '

  Return "Home snow removal: " & MyBase.SnowRemoval
End Function

Public Sub DisplayBuilding()

  MyBase.DisplayBaseInfo()          ' Call base class
  Console.WriteLine("      Home members:")
  Console.WriteLine("Square Feet: " & mSquareFeet)
  Console.WriteLine("Rent per Month: " & FormatMoney(mRentPerMonth))
  Console.WriteLine("Bedrooms: " & mBedrooms)
  Console.WriteLine("Baths: " & mBaths)
  End Sub
End Class
```

The code in Listing 18.3 is very similar to the code in Listing 17.2 from Chapter 17. Listing 18.3 includes added constructors for the base and derived classes. In each derived class constructor, an `If` statement block is used to allow for an "empty" phone number to be passed to the constructor. Consider the following code fragment for the `Apartment` class:

```
If SnowPhone = "" Then
 MyBase.SnowRemoval = APTPHONE ' Use the default snow phone
Else
 MyBase.SnowRemoval = SnowPhone
End If
```

If the argument `SnowPhone` is an empty string, the default snow removal phone number is supplied. (In real life, for example, a newly rented home that is being added to the list of real estate investments might be added before the new tenant has received a new home phone number.)

You should examine the constructors for the derived classes in Listing 18.3 because that code is not present in Listing 17.2. The code itself is fairly straightforward, and you should be comfortable reading it.

Testing Polymorphism

Now that you have finished modifying the derived classes, you need to look at the code used to test your changes. The simple form that is used to test the modified `Building` class and the derived classes is shown in Figure 18.1.

The single text box is named `txtOuput`, and it has the `Multiline` property set to `True`. This text box is used to show the snow removal phone numbers. The two buttons are named `btnProperties` and `btnExit`. The code for the test program is presented in Listing 18.4.

FIGURE 18.1

A form that is used to test the modified `Building` class and the derived classes.

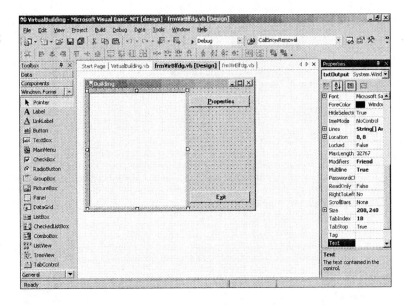

LISTING 18.4   New Code to Test the `Building` Class and the Derived Classes

```
Option Strict On

Public Class frmVirBldg
 Inherits System.Windows.Forms.Form

 Private Const APARTMENT As Integer = 0
 Private Const COMMERCIAL As Integer = 1
 Private Const HOME As Integer = 2

 ' Windows Form Designer generated code


 Private Sub frmBuilding_Load(ByVal sender As System.Object, ByVal e As _
            System.EventArgs) Handles MyBase.Load

 End Sub

 Private Sub btnExit_Click(ByVal sender As System.Object, ByVal e As _
            System.EventArgs) Handles btnExit.Click
  Me.Dispose()
 End Sub

 Private Sub btnProperties_Click(ByVal sender As Object, ByVal e As _
            System.EventArgs) Handles btnProperties.Click
  Dim CurrentBuilding As Building

  Dim MyApartment As New Apartment("6 North Ben Street", 550000, 6000, _
            12000, APARTMENT, "555-1000")
```

LISTING 18.4   Continued

```
Dim MyBuilding As New Commercial("250 Industrial Drive", 320000, 3800, _
                 5800, COMMERCIAL, "")
Dim MyHome As New Home("2 Ghent Court", 140000, 1300, 3300, HOME, "")
Dim delta As New Home()

Dim MyInvestments As Building() = New Building() {MyApartment, _
                 MyBuilding, MyHome, delta}
delta.SnowRemoval = "555-3333"

For Each CurrentBuilding In MyInvestments
 txtOutput.Text &= CurrentBuilding.CallSnowRemoval & vbCrLf
Next
MyApartment.DisplayBuilding()
MyBuilding.DisplayBuilding()
MyHome.DisplayBuilding()
delta.DisplayBuilding()
Console.WriteLine(delta.CallSnowRemoval())

 End Sub
End Class
```

Most of the code in Listing 18.4 is boilerplate code that Visual Basic .NET supplies. The inter-esting stuff takes place in the `btnProperties` object's `Click()` event code, as explained in the next section.

Working with Virtual Classes

The `btnProperties` object's `Click()` event code contains the following line:

```
Dim CurrentBuilding As Building
```

This statement should be a red flag to you. Recall from Chapter 17 that any base class that is implemented by using the `MustInherit` keyword is a virtual (or abstract) class. You cannot instantiate an object of a virtual class. So why doesn't the preceding `Dim` statement cause Visual Basic .NET to generate an error message?

Remember that you can instantiate an object only when you use the `New` keyword. Because the `Dim` statement does not include the `New` keyword, you are not instantiating a `Building` object. Instead, you are defining a *reference variable* that can be used to point to an object of type `Building`. Recall that reference variables have an `rvalue` that is the `lvalue` of where the object is actually stored in memory. Therefore, the statement does not define an object; rather, it defines a pointer to an object. Until the `New` keyword is used, there is no class object created by the statement.

Using a For Each Construct for an Array of Objects

The next four lines in the `btnProperties Click()` event simply instantiate objects of the derived classes. The first three objects are created by using the constructors that have arguments passed to them. The last object (delta) is instantiated without any arguments to show how a base class constructor with no arguments is called.

The following code defines MyInvestments to be an array of Building references:

```
Dim MyInvestments As Building() = New Building() {MyApartment, _
                    MyBuilding, MyHome, delta}
```

You have initialized the references of this array to point to MyApartment, MyBuilding, MyHome, and delta. You can now use the CurrentBuilding reference pointer to walk through each object in the MyInvestments array. A For Each loop is used to iterate through a collection of objects. Because MyInvestments is an array of object references, you can use the For Each construct to iterate through the array. These lines cause the CurrentBuilding reference to point to each object in the MyInvestments array:

```
For Each CurrentBuilding In MyInvestments
 txtOutput.Text &= CurrentBuilding.CallSnowRemoval & vbCrLf
Next
```

For example, on the first pass through the For Each loop, CurrentBuilding is implicitly set as follows:

```
CurrentBuilding = MyInvestment(0)
```

From the initializer list for MyInvestments, you can see that when CurrentBuilding refers to MyInvestment(0), you are actually looking at the MyApartment object. It follows that on the second pass through the For Each loop, CurrentBuilding refers to MyInvestment(1), or the MyBuilding object. The loop continues until all four objects are displayed in the txtOutput text box.

The remaining lines simply show how you might call the DisplayBuilding() method and the CallSnowRemoval() method. A sample run of the program is shown in Figure 18.2.

FIGURE 18.2

A sample run of the test code for the modified Building class and the derived classes.

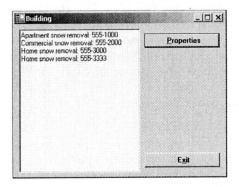

The text box in Figure 18.2 shows the output associated with the passes through the For Each loop, and the Debug window in the background shows the results of the DisplayBuilding() and CallSnowRemoval() calls.

The important thing to note here is that the same message sent to the various building objects produces different results. In each case, the call to the `CallSnowRemoval()` method causes a different string to be displayed. In a more realistic setting, the message might activate an automated dial-up machine that would dial the appropriate snow removal service for the apartments and commercial buildings and then call the tenant of each rental home to remind him or her to shovel the walk.

It would be worth your effort to single-step through the test program to get a feel for how Visual Basic .NET processes the code. Trust me, single-stepping through code is a great way to learn how objects are instantiated and how the base and derived classes interact with each other.

Creating an Interface

In this chapter, you have seen how to use the basic features of inheritance to define an interface based on the interaction between the base class and its derived classes. The `Building` class example shows how you can use a virtual base `Building` class and polymorphic inheritance to provide a `CallSnowRemoval()` method for each derived class. However, there is an alternative way to define an interface.

Recall that the term *interface* refers to the way a class provides access to the properties and methods of that class. You have seen that this statement:

```
Public MustOverride Function CallSnowRemoval() As String
```

in the base class forces each derived class to implement a `CallSnowRemoval()` method. This means that each derived class has to have a method definition that starts with this statement:

```
Public Overrides Function CallSnowRemoval() As String
```

followed by the code that implements the method call. This works fine given the way the classes have been implemented so far. However, suppose a real estate investor decides to purchase some vacation properties. She limits her investments in vacation properties to Florida real estate. She asks you to modify the program to accommodate these new properties. You decide to add a new derived `Building` class named `Vacation`. As you design the code for the new derived class, you see that you must implement a `CallSnowRemoval()` method. But snow removal probably isn't really needed in Florida.

This scenario illustrates a situation you are likely to face in designing classes. In this case, you have several derived classes that have similar needs but one oddball that doesn't fit the mold. Obviously, you could still implement the `Vacation` class as a derived `Building` class and add a `CallSnowRemoval()` method. You'd simply never call the method. That approach would work just fine. However, as you began to write the `CallSnowRemoval()` code for the `Vacation` class, you would probably feel like you were adding a wart to an otherwise unblemished piece of code. You would feel as though there must be a better way to solve this problem. There is.

The solution, as described in the following section, is to write an interface declaration.

Interface Declarations

With interface declarations, any class that wants to use the services of the interface can implement the interface as part of its class definition. Let's stick with the real estate code for this example. You should begin your program modification with the following code:

```
Interface ISnowRemoval
 Function CallSnowRemoval() As String
End Interface
```

An interface declaration begins with the keyword `Interface`, followed by the name of the interface being declared. The default access specifier for an interface declaration is `Public`. Therefore, you could also write the first line of the interface declaration like this:

```
Public Interface ISnowRemoval
```

although most programmers omit the `Public` keyword. In this example, you are calling the interface `ISnowRemoval`.

Programmer's Tip

It is a common Visual Basic .NET programming convention to prefix an interface name with a capital letter *I* (for example, `ISnowRemoval`). Doing this helps document that a class interface is being declared.

Everything between the `Interface` and `End Interface` keywords form the interface statement block. The *interface statement block* lists all the methods and properties that will become part of the interface.

Note that the interface does not contain code to implement the methods or properties. The interface declaration contains just a list of the method and property names that comprise the interface. If any of the methods use arguments, they must be stated as part of the interface declaration. Collectively, the access specifier (for example, `Public`), the method name (`CallSnowRemoval()`), the list of arguments (none in the case of `CallSnowRemoval()`), and the return data type (for example, `String`) form the *signature* of the method or property. Therefore, the interface declaration is little more than a list of signatures for the properties and methods in the interface.

If two methods in this example have the same name, but they have different arguments supplied to them, they have different signatures, and Visual Basic .NET can distinguish between them. (You saw this method overloading when you wrote the two different `New` constructors for the `Building` class earlier in this chapter.) In an interface, you must provide a complete signature for each method or property that is part of the interface. Again, the interface statement block contains only statements that declare the signatures of the methods and properties that make up the interface.

Implementing the Interface

Any class that wants to use an interface must implement it. This is accomplished via a two-step process. First, the class that wants to use the interface must place this statement in its class code:

```
Implements ISnowRemoval
```

Usually, the statement is placed near the top of the code that defines the class. When you place the `Implements` statement in the class code, you are promising Visual Basic .NET that you will implement each and every method and property that is contained in the `Interface` declaration. You might hear that by using the `Implements` keyword in your class code, you are forming a *contract* to write all the code necessary to implement each signature declared in the interface. If you don't uphold your end of the contract, Visual Basic .NET lets you know about it.

The second step in interface implementation requires you to supply the code that is necessary to implement each of the methods and properties contained in the interface statement block. In the example in this chapter, that requires a statement similar to this:

```
Public Function CallSnowRemoval() As String Implements _
               ISnowRemoval.CallSnowRemoval
```

Notice that the `Implements` keyword follows the return data type (`String`) in the statement. This tells Visual Basic .NET that the code that follows is implementing the `ISnowRemoval.CallSnowRemoval` method of the interface.

The complete code for the `Apartment` class is shown in Listing 18.5.

LISTING 18.5   Complete Code for the `Apartment` Class After the `ISnowRemoval` Interface Is Implemented

```
' +++++++++++++++++++++++++++ Apartment Class +++++++++++++++++++++++++++
Public Class Apartment
  Inherits Building
  Implements ISnowRemoval         ' We are making a contract with Visual Basic .NET
here...

  Private mUnits As Integer    ' The number of apartments
  Private mRent As Double      ' Rent per unit
  Private mOccupRate As Double ' Occupancy rate for building

  Public Sub New()

  End Sub


  ' Constructor with initializer list of arguments
  Public Sub New(ByVal Addr As String, ByVal Price As Double, _
          ByVal Payment As Double, ByVal Taxes as Double,
          ByVal Bldg As Integer, ByVal SnowPhone As String)
    MyBase.Address = Addr
    MyBase.PurchasePrice = Price
```

LISTING 18.5   Continued

```
  MyBase.MonthlyPayment = Payment
  MyBase.Taxes = Taxes
  MyBase.BuildingType = Bldg
  If SnowPhone = "" Then
   MyBase.SnowRemoval = APTPHONE
  Else
   MyBase.SnowRemoval = SnowPhone
  End If
End Sub

' ==================== Properties =======================

Public Property Units()      ' Units
 Get
  Return mUnits
 End Get
 Set(ByVal Value)
  mUnits = Value
 End Set
End Property

Public Property Rents()      ' Rents
 Get
  Return mRent
 End Get
 Set(ByVal Value)
  mRent = Value
 End Set
End Property

Public Property OccupancyRate() As Double ' Occupancy rate
 Get
  Return mOccupRate
 End Get
 Set(ByVal Value As Double)
  mOccupRate = Value
 End Set
End Property

' ============== Methods ==================
                ' We fulfill our contract with Visual Basic .NET here...
Public Function CallSnowRemoval() As String Implements _
              ISnowRemoval.CallSnowRemoval
 ' Purpose: This routine is called to remove snow for an Apartment.
 '
 Return "Apartment snow removal: " & MyBase.SnowRemoval
 End Function

Public Sub DisplayBuilding()

 DisplayBaseInfo()
 Console.WriteLine("       Apartment members:")
```

LISTING 18.5 Continued

```
      Console.WriteLine("Number of Units: " & mUnits)
      Console.WriteLine("Rent per Unit: " & FormatMoney(mRent))
      Console.WriteLine("Occupancy Rate: " & mOccupRate)
   End Sub
End Class
```

The fourth line in Listing 18.5 uses the `Implements` keyword to form the contract with Visual Basic .NET to implement the `ISnowRemoval` interface. The first method defined in the class is the `CallSnowRemoval()` method, thus fulfilling the contract between the `Apartment` class and the `ISnowRemoval` interface. Notice how the code for the `CallSnowRemoval()` method matches the signature declared in the interface statement block.

Once again, I am carefully distinguishing the terms *define* and *declare*. The interface statement block is a declaration that tells Visual Basic .NET what is required of any class that wants to use the interface. On the other hand, the actual code that defines how a class wants to implement the methods or properties is placed within the class itself.

The fact that the class is responsible for writing the actual code points to another advantage of using an interface: Each class that uses the interface can implement it any way it sees fit, as long as it conforms to the signature contained in the interface declaration. Different classes requiring different code to implement the specifics of a method or property is not a problem. This makes using interfaces very flexible, yet interfaces provide a consistent means of using a method or property.

So how does an interface benefit the `Vacation` class? You've probably already figured out the answer. Because the `Vacation` class doesn't need to implement a snow removal method, you simply don't add an `Implements` statement to the `Vacation` class. By omitting the `Implements` statement, you are canceling the contract to implement code for the `ISnowRemoval` interface for the `Vacation` class.

To implement the interface for the real estate investment program, all you need do is remove the `MustOverride` statement from the `Building` class and add the `Implements` statement and corresponding code to the classes that want to use the `ISnowRemoval` interface.

To test the new interface, you should substitute the `btnProperties` object's `Click()` event code in Listing 18.6 for the code shown in Listing 18.4.

LISTING 18.6 Code to Test the `ISnowRemoval` Interface

```
Private Sub btnProperties_Click(ByVal sender As Object, ByVal e As _
          System.EventArgs) Handles btnProperties.Click
   Dim CurrentBuilding As Building

   Dim MyApartment As New Apartment("6 North Ben Street", 550000, 6000, _
             12000, APARTMENT, "555-1000")
   Dim MyBuilding As New Commercial("250 Industrial Drive", 320000, 3800, _
             5800, COMMERCIAL, "")
```

LISTING 18.6   Continued

```
Dim MyHome As New Home("2 Ghent Court", 140000, 1300, 3300, HOME, "")
Dim delta As New Home()

Console.WriteLine(MyApartment.CallSnowRemoval())   ' Call it
Console.WriteLine(MyBuilding.CallSnowRemoval())
Console.WriteLine(MyHome.CallSnowRemoval())
Console.WriteLine(delta.CallSnowRemoval())

End Sub
```

If you try to call the `CallSnowRemoval()` method from a class that does not implement the interface, such as the `Vacation` class, Visual Basic .NET issues an error message, telling you that `CallSnowRemoval()` is not a member of the class.

Summary

This chapter showed how you can use polymorphism to cause different objects to respond differently to the same message. This ability to have generic object messages cause objects to respond differently means that you can tailor the behavior of each object to the needs at hand. In this chapter you have seen how you can provide common calling conventions to different types of objects by using the `Implements` keyword to create polymorphic interfaces for class objects. Such interfaces provide an easy way to define common method and property calling across different classes of objects.

Review Questions

1. In one sentence, define polymorphism.

A. Polymorphism is the ability to have different classes implement a common interface in different ways. An important concept behind polymorphism is that each class can respond to a given message in different ways.

2. Why does Visual Basic .NET allow multiple constructors for a class?

A. By allowing multiple constructors, Visual Basic .NET lets you create an object with default values or more specific values. Normally, instantiating an object without passing any arguments to the constructor results in creating the object with a set of default values for the member data. A second contructor must pass at least one argument (so the signatures are different) and allows the programmer to create the object with a different set of values for the member data.

3. What information does the following statement tell you?

```
Public MustOverride Function RentalRooms() As Integer
```

A. This statement tells you a number of things. First, because the `MustOverride` keyword appears in the declaration, the class in which the statement appears is serving as a base class for some other class. Second, the `MustOverride` also tells you that the statement is a signature declaration. This means no lvalue exists for `RentalRooms()` at this point in the code. Third, the `MustOverride` also tells you that all derived classes must write the code for the function named *RentalRooms()*. Finally, the statement tells you exactly how the signature for the function must be written in the derived classes. If you try to write the function using a different name, argument list, or return value, Visual Basic .NET will issue an error message.

4. How would you define a virtual class named `Golfer`?

A. When you begin the class definition, you would use:

```
Public MustInherit Class Golfer
```

The `MustInherit` keyword tells Visual Basic .NET that this class is a virtual class.

5. What do the following statements mean?

```
Interface IKeepScores
Function PostScore() As Integer
End Interface
```

A. The statements mean that an interface is being declared. The `IKeepScores` interface requires that any programmer using the interface must write code for the function named `PostScore()` using the signature shown in the `Interface` statement body. If needed, the interface can have multiple procedures as part of the interface declaration.

6. If an interface is declared in the manner suggested in question 5, what statement is needed to use the interface in your code?

A. The class that wishes to implement the interface must place the following statement in the class:

```
Implements IKeepScores
```

This statement has the effect of creating a contract between you and Visual Basic .NET. You are promising to implement the code for the procedure(s) that are associated with the `IKeepScores` interface. If you fail to implement every procedure in the `IKeepScores` interface, Visual Basic .NET will tell you that you are breaking your contract.

7. Given the answers to questions 5 and 6, write the signature for the `PostScore()` function.

A. The signature must be written:

```
Public Function PostScore() As Integer Implements IKeepScores.PostScore
```

The only difference between writing an interface function and any other function is that you must append the `Implements` keyword, followed by the interface name, the dot operator, and then the function name. You can then write the code for the function as you would write code for any other function.

CHAPTER 19

ERROR PROCESSING AND DEBUGGING

In this chapter, you will learn the following:

- Types of errors
- Sample program for testing the debugger
- Using the Visual Basic .NET debugger

- Unstructured error handling
- Structured error processing
- A program example using exception handling

*I*n this chapter, you'll learn about program debugging and error processing. There are two basic flavors of error processing: unstructured and structured. Although unstructured error processing is losing favor, you should at least know what it is in case you have to maintain code that uses it. Structured error processing provides a more elegant way to process errors, so it becomes the focal point of this chapter.

The second major topic of this chapter is debugging. I've already shown you some of the basics of debugging in other chapters. However, I want to collect the debugging techniques of Visual Basic .NET in this chapter for easier reference in the future. If you're like the rest of us, you'll tend not to repeat the same programming errors…you'll move on to bigger and better ones. The debugger that's integrated into the Visual Basic .NET IDE is an extremely versatile and powerful tool.

Types of Errors

I've stated previously that there are several basic types of errors that can creep into your code. (Aw, let's be honest about it. The errors didn't creep into your code—you put them there.) Before you can expunge an error, you need to understand its type and its exact nature. There are three basic types of errors: syntax errors, semantic errors, and logic errors. Let's look at these a little more closely.

Syntax Errors

Every program statement in Visual Basic .NET is comprised of expressions. These expressions are built up from operators and operands. For example, you know that the statement

x = y

is an assignment expression. It has two operands, x and y, and one (binary) operator, the equal sign. In this case, the program statement is comprised of a single expression.

When you type in any program statement, the instant that you press the Enter key, Visual Basic .NET examines what you typed in to see whether it forms a valid Visual Basic .NET program statement. If the line you typed in doesn't form a valid program statement, Visual Basic .NET places a squiggly line under the offending section of the line containing the error. An example of this is shown in Figure 19.1.

FIGURE 19.1

Example of a syntax error involving an incomplete expression.

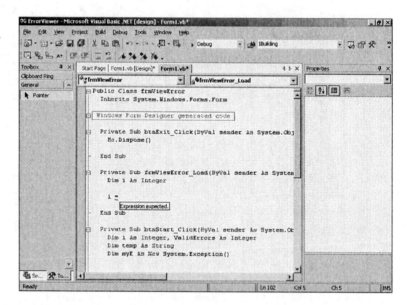

If you look near the middle of the figure, you'll see a squiggly line under the equal sign. What does not show up is the cursor that I placed over the squiggly line. When I did this, Visual Basic .NET displayed the **Expression expected** error message that you see in Figure 19.1. This message tells me that Visual Basic .NET was expecting an expression, but my line did not form a complete expression. (Obviously, I need to add an operand on the right side of the assignment operator.)

When you begin programming with Visual Basic .NET, you should expect to make a lot of syntax errors. After all, this is a new language, and very few people instantly become fluent in any new language. The main point is not to let these syntax errors discourage you. Everyone goes through this phase, and you will, too. To become a Visual Basic .NET programmer, you have to pay your dues, and wading through a swamp of syntax errors is just one of the costs.

The good news is that Visual Basic .NET is extremely good at catching syntax errors. Indeed, it tells you about them the moment you make them. Placing the cursor over the squiggly line causes Visual Basic .NET to issue a message that's usually sufficiently complete for you to figure out what needs to be corrected. After making the correction, the squiggly line should go away if the change results in a syntactically correct program statement.

As you gain experience with Visual Basic .NET, you'll find that the number of syntax errors you make tends to decrease. You'll be able to write dozens and dozens of lines of code and never see the dreaded squiggly line. Yep, the syntax errors virtually disappear after a while. As you gain programming experience and sophistication with Visual Basic .NET, so will your errors. You're ready to move to level 2 errors.

Semantic Errors

We talked about semantic errors before. Just as the English language has rules about how sentences are formed from nouns and verbs, Visual Basic .NET has rules about how program statements are formed from keywords and expressions. If you don't follow the rules, syntax errors like those we discussed in the previous section result.

However, it's possible to obey the rules of the language but construct a sentence that doesn't make sense. Statements that obey the syntax rules, but are taken out of context, are called *semantic errors*. As an example of a semantic error, we used this sentence: "The dog meowed." This obeys the basic rules of English in that the sentence has a noun and a verb, but the sentence doesn't make sense because it does not have the proper context for the noun and verb.

Semantic errors are a little difficult to isolate and change. The reason is because Visual Basic .NET cannot detect semantic errors while you are writing the program the way it can detect syntax errors. For example, suppose that you have the following code fragment in your program:

```
Dim i As Byte
Dim j As Integer

j = 256
i = CByte(j)
```

As you learned in Chapter 4, "Data Types and Numeric Variables," a **Byte** data type has a range of values from 0 through 255. In this code fragment, however, we're trying to assign the value 256 into a **Byte** variable named **i**. If we type this code into our program, Visual Basic .NET doesn't complain. The reason is because each program statement conforms to the syntax rules of Visual Basic .NET.

However, if we try to run the program, Visual Basic .NET issues an error message stating:

```
An unhandled exception of type 'System.OverflowException' occurred in
ErrorViewer.exe
```

```
Additional information: Arithmetic operation resulted in an overflow.
```

This is an example of a semantic error. Visual Basic .NET issued the error message because we attempted to use the variable `i`, which is a `Byte` variable, in the context of an `Integer` variable.

Note the difference between a syntax error and a semantic error. Syntax errors are caught at design time, while you are writing the program. Semantic errors manifest themselves at runtime, while the program is running.

Why can't Visual Basic .NET catch semantic errors at design time as it does for syntax errors? The reason is because syntax errors are checked one line at a time as you enter them. Semantic errors, however, usually involve errors that span multiple lines. In the earlier code fragment, the semantic error is actually caused by a mismatch between the data item being defined (that is, variable `i`) in the first code statement and when it is used in the last assignment statement. Therefore, Visual Basic .NET doesn't detect this type of error until runtime.

Still, Visual Basic .NET is a terrific help because it (eventually) does give you a very clear error message, telling you the nature of the program error. True, it waits until runtime to tell you about the error, but that's still a huge help versus trying to track down this type of error without Visual Basic .NET's help.

Once again, as you gain experience, you'll code fewer and fewer semantic errors. In most cases, semantic errors are called *flat-forehead errors*. Semantic errors earn this name because, on their discovery, you smack the heel of your hand into your forehead while saying, "How could I make such a stupid mistake!" Join the crowd...it's all part of becoming a programmer.

Still, even the semantic errors begin to disappear from the landscape as you gain experience. You have finally graduated to the realm of the level 3 error: the logic error.

Logic Errors

Just about any error that isn't a syntax error or semantic error is a logic error. As a general rule, a *logic error* is simply the manifestation of a difference between what you thought would happen as the program ran and what actually did happen. Your code obeys all the syntax and semantic rules, but the program doesn't produce the results that you expected. The bad news is that, because you have followed all the syntax and semantic rules, Visual Basic .NET can't detect logic errors at either design time or runtime. The good news is that the Visual Basic .NET debugger is a pretty good detective, and you can use it to help track down the culprit.

In terms of the five program steps we discussed in Chapter 3, "Thinking About Programs," the Output step frequently reveals the logic error. However, the actual place where the logic error is hiding could be anywhere in the Initialization step, the Input step, the Processing step, or even the Output step itself. Therefore, the first thing that needs to be done is to isolate the logic error. That is, assuming that the error is repeatable, your first job is to find out which program step is hiding the error. The Visual Basic .NET debugger is the perfect ally for such a task.

Sample Program for Testing the Debugger

Let's write a short program that we can use to exercise the debugger. The form we'll use is shown in Figure 19.2.

FIGURE 19.2
The form used for testing the debugger.

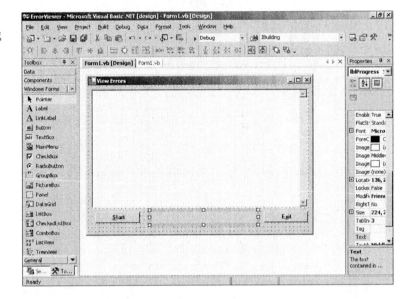

The large text box is named **txtOuput** and it has its **Multiline** property set to **True**. The Start button is named **btnStart**. (I don't really have to tell you about **btnExit** any more, do I?) Note that there's a borderless label named **lblProgress** between the two buttons. The program writes some loop iteration data on the label as the program executes.

The code for the program is presented in Listing 19.1. There really isn't much to the code.

LISTING 19.1   Source Code for the Debugger Test Program

```
Public Class frmViewError
 Inherits System.Windows.Forms.Form
 Private Const UNUSED_ERROR_NUMBER As String = "Application-defined or _
                    object-defined error."

' Windows Form Designer generated code

 Private Sub btnExit_Click(ByVal sender As System.Object, ByVal e As _
            System.EventArgs) Handles btnExit.Click
  Me.Dispose()

 End Sub
```

LISTING 19.1   Continued

```
Private Sub btnStart_Click(ByVal sender As System.Object, ByVal e As _
          System.EventArgs) Handles btnStart.Click
Dim i As Integer, ValidErrors As Integer
Dim temp As String

ValidErrors = 0
For i = 0 To 1000     ' Those below 1000 are reserved
 temp = ErrorToString(i)
 If temp <> UNUSED_ERROR_NUMBER And temp <> "" Then
  txtOutput.Text &= Format(i, "000") & " " & ErrorToString(i) & vbCrLf
  ValidErrors += 1
 End If
 lblProgress.Text = "Processing error number: " & CStr(i)
 Me.Update()

Next
 lblProgress.Text = "Total useable error messages: " & CStr(ValidErrors)
End Sub
End Class
```

Microsoft uses a number of predefined runtime error messages. The program presented in
Listing 19.1 simply displays the runtime error number and its associated error message. It does
this by iterating through a **For-Next** loop while calling the **ErrorToString()** method of the
Err object.

Microsoft documents that it has reserved the first 1,000 error numbers for its own use.
Therefore, the loop tests all possible error numbers from 0 to 1,000. The string constant
UNUSED_ERROR_NUMBER is defined as

```
"Application-defined or object-defined error."
```

Microsoft uses this message to denote error numbers that aren't currently being used, but
might be used at some later time. Rather than clutter the output with these empty errors, the
code skips such empty errors and does not display them in the **txtOutput** text box. Any error
number that does not contain the **UNUSED_ERROR_NUMBER** or an empty string is displayed in the
text box. A sample run is shown in Figure 19.3.

FIGURE 19.3
Sample run of the debug-
ger test program.

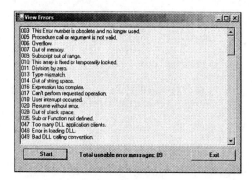

As the program runs, `lblProgress` shows which iteration of the loop is being processed. At completion, the label is used to show the count of runtime error messages that have been displayed in the text box. Figure 19.3 shows that there are (at the time of this writing) 89 runtime error messages. The first column of the output shows the error number (for example, `007`) and its associated error message (for example, `Out of memory`). I wonder if that relationship is by accident?

Using the Visual Basic .NET Debugger

Now let's set up the Visual Basic .NET IDE to exploit the debugger. The first thing you might want to do is activate the debugger toolbar. You do this by selecting the View, Toolbars, Debug menu sequence. This is shown in Figure 19.4.

FIGURE 19.4
Activating the Debug toolbar.

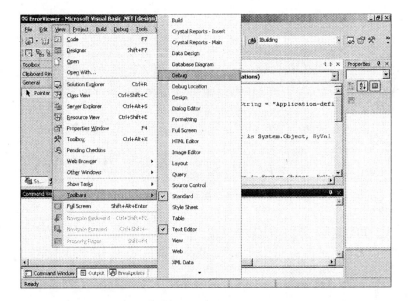

When you do this, the Debug toolbar appears just above the Forms window. The new toolbar is shown in Figure 19.5.

FIGURE 19.5
The Debug toolbar.

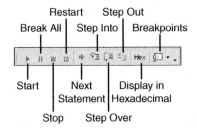

The Debug toolbar provides the following list of options:

- Start—Begins program execution. You can also start a program running by pressing the F5 key.

- Break All—The debugger stops program execution and places your program and the debugger in Break mode.

- Stop—Suspends program execution. It's like a breakpoint and does not end the program.

- Restart—Stops the debugger and restarts the program

- Next Statement—Executes the next program statement. You can also use the F10 key.

- Step Into—If you're on a line that has a procedure call, this option causes the program to step into the procedure and execute the first program line of the procedure.

- Step Over—If you're on a line that has a procedure call, the code of the procedure is executed at normal speed and the program breaks on the first line that is outside of the procedure that was called. Normally, this is the line following the procedure call.

- Step Out—Use this option when you are in a procedure and want to return to the caller. This provides a means of exiting from the procedure without executing all of its code.

- Display in Hexadecimal—Displays numeric values in hex.

- Breakpoints—Shows you a listing of the breakpoints that are set.

Although you might not use all the debugger's features on a regular basis, it's nice to have all of these features in those cases when you do need them.

Setting a Breakpoint

There are two ways to set a breakpoint. The easiest is to move the cursor to the line on which you want to set the breakpoint and press the F9 key. If you press the F9 key a second time while the cursor is on the breakpoint line, the breakpoint is removed. Therefore, the F9 key is a toggle that may be used to turn a breakpoint on or off.

There is a second way to set a breakpoint. Move the cursor into the gray margin to the left of the code window even with the line on which you want to set the breakpoint, and click the mouse. The familiar burnt-red breakpoint line should appear in the Code window. Click on the burnt-red dot in the margin and the breakpoint is removed.

As an experiment, set a breakpoint on the code line

```
ValidErrors += 1
```

as shown in Listing 19.1. Now compile and run the program. Your program should look similar to Figure 19.6.

Program execution is now suspended and we're free to inspect the state of the program.

FIGURE 19.6

The state of the program at a breakpoint.

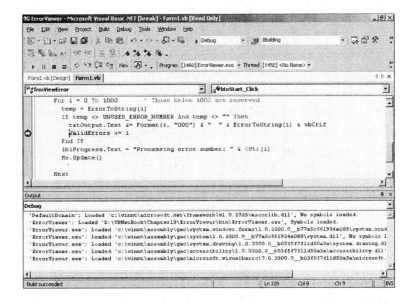

The Locals Window

Suppose you want to examine all the local variables in the program. Recall that local scope applies to all variables that are currently visible in the procedure being executed.

To view the local variables, you need to open the Locals window. To do this, select the Debug, Windows, Locals menu sequence or press the Ctrl+Alt+V keys, and then press the L key. This will open the Locals window near the bottom of the screen, as shown in Figure 19.7.

FIGURE 19.7

The Locals window.

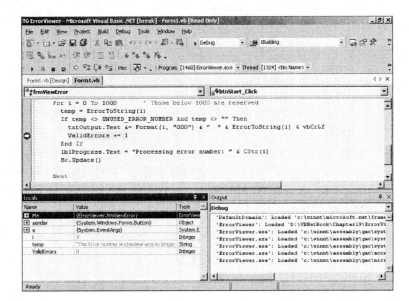

As you can see, variable i has the value 3, temp equals our UNUSED_ERROR_NUMBER symbolic constant, and ValidErrors is 0. The other lines in the window are objects that are also in scope. You might want to click on the small plus sign (+) in the box in front of the variables to expand these entries so that you can see what's being hidden from sight.

The Autos Window

Now let's open the Autos window. To do this, use the Debug, Windows, Autos menu sequence or use the Ctrl+Alt+V keys, and then press the A key. The Autos window will overlay the Locals window. This can be seen in Figure 19.8.

FIGURE 19.8

The Autos window.

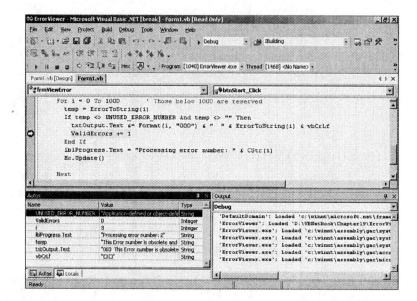

The Autos window shows information that appears to be almost the same as the Locals window, but it is slightly different. The Autos window shows you all the values for the variables that appear in the current (breakpoint) line and the line immediately preceding it. If you single-step to the next line, the Autos window is updated.

Other important things to notice in Figure 19.8 are the two tabs at the bottom-left labeled Autos and Locals. These two tabs enable you to alternate between the Autos and Locals windows by simply clicking the appropriate tab. Note that as we examine other windows, new tabs might appear in this location. This provides a convenient means for activating several debug windows at the same time without cluttering the screen.

The Watch Window

During the debugging process, it is quite often the value of a particular variable that indicates there's a bug. Although the Autos window is helpful for viewing variables on the current and preceding line, those lines might not hold the variable you're tracking. The Watch window provides a better way to observe a variable as the program executes.

The Watch window is selected by using the Debug, Watch, Watch ? menu sequence (where the question mark could be one of four Watch windows), as shown in Figure 19.9.

FIGURE 19.9
The Watch window.

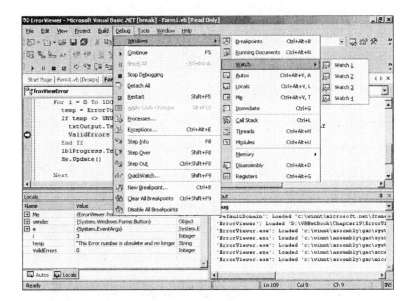

As you can see, you can set multiple Watch windows. If you select the first Watch window, it's added to the list of available Debug windows as can be seen by the new Watch tab at the bottom left of Figure 19.10.

FIGURE 19.10
The Watch tab has been added.

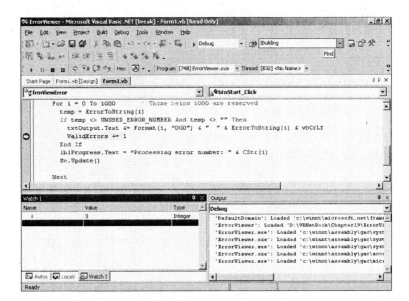

In Figure 19.10, we moved the cursor to the first line of the Watch window and typed in the name of a variable; i in this example. The Watch window then shows the current value of i at this point in the program. You can type in additional variables you want to observe while the program executes.

Why does the debugger provide for up to four different Watch windows? In more complex programs, you might want to track a different set of variables at different points in the program. By having different Watch windows, you can have a less-cluttered window in which to watch the variables you're interested in at different points in the program. You can switch between the different Watch windows by simply clicking on the appropriate tab at the bottom of the window display.

Hit Counter

A new feature has been added to the debugger, and it's one of those "I-wish-I-had-this-five-years-ago" features you've always wished for but never had. This new feature enables you to set a breakpoint and then activate the breakpoint after that line has been hit a specified number of times. In Figure 19.11, I selected the New Breakpoint option from the Debug menu (or use Ctrl+B) and then clicked the Hit Count button to present the screen you see in Figure 19.11. If you select one of the options from the list box, a text box appears to the right of the list box. You can see that I typed in **50** after selecting the Break When the Hit Count Is Equal To option.

FIGURE 19.11

Setting the hit counter.

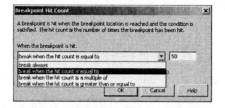

By selecting this option, I'm telling the debugger to run at full speed until the breakpoint line has been executed (that is, hit) 50 times. Only then is the breakpoint executed and the program paused. Although there are other ways to accomplish this type of breakpoint, this approach is very convenient to use. It sure beats banging on the F5 key 49 times to get to the desired iteration in a loop!

The Command Window

The Command window provides a means for you to interact with your code while debugging a program. You activate the Command window using the Debug, Windows, Immediate menu sequence or by pressing Ctrl+G. You'll see the Command window appear near the lower-right side of the screen.

Programmer's Tip

Actually, there are two modes for the Command window. The first is the Immediate mode that we'll discuss in detail here. However, you can also use the Command window in the Command mode, which enables you to issue commands to the Visual Basic .NET environment. Once the Command window is open, you can type in >cmd and press Enter, which switches the Command window to the Command mode. (Yes, you do need to type in the > symbol.) You can now type in a command to Visual Basic .NET. For example, if you type in the letter E, you'll see a drop-down list of the commands that you could enter, such as Exit. If you type in Exit, Visual Basic .NET ends the current programming session.

Once the Command window is activated, you can type in expressions and have Visual Basic .NET use those expressions during program execution. For example, in Figure 19.12, I've typed

```
ValidErrors = 100
```

into the Command window. This expression sets the value of `ValidErrors` to `100`. In other words, the Command window is handy for entering values into the code that you might want to test.

FIGURE 19.12

The Command window.

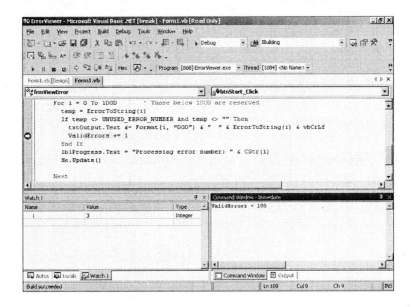

Also note in Figure 19.12 that you can still access the Output window via the tab that appears below the Command window. These tabs enable you to toggle between the Command and Output windows as needed.

Boundary Values

Being able to set the values with the Command windows makes it easy to check certain values that you think might cause problems in the program. A common area of program bugs is in what are called boundary values. A *boundary value* is the first or last value in a set of values that a variable is expected to acquire during program execution. For example, if you have a For loop that's expected to run from 0 to 100, the boundary values for the loop are **0** and **100**. However, perhaps the value **0** doesn't really cause a certain program sequence or value to appear as expected. Likewise, the value **100** might not produce the expected results, either. The Command window makes it easy to type in the boundary values and assess their impact on the program.

Even though boundary values aren't always the culprit for a program error, they're often a good place to start the debugging process. This is especially true in loops that involve array processing.

Other Windows

As you can tell, there are a number of other windows that Visual Basic .NET makes available to you. For example, the Call Stack window shows you the name of each function your program calls and the language it's written in. Likewise, if you want to see what your program would look like if it were written in Assembly language, you could activate the Disassembly and Registers windows. (If nothing else, doing so confirms that using Visual Basic .NET is *a lot* easier to use than Assembly code!)

Although these other windows might be interesting and helpful in certain situations, I won't discuss these here. You can always try experimenting with them, using the Online Help to guide your experimentation. At this point, however, you've been exposed to enough debugging features to track down the vast majority of program bugs.

There is one more thing you might find useful. As I said at the beginning of this chapter, one of your first tasks in debugging a program is to isolate the bug. This often mean setting a lot of breakpoints at different places in the program. You'll eventually narrow your search to one specific section of code. However, in the process of getting there, each time you rerun the program, you have to wade through a dozen or more old (that is, no longer useful) breakpoints to get to the point of interest.

Even though you could toggle each of these old breakpoints off, it's much easier to clear all the breakpoints at once. First, move the cursor to the line where you want to set a breakpoint after you clear all the old breakpoints. Now use the Debug, Clear All Breakpoints menu sequence, or use the Ctrl+Shift+F9 keystrokes to remove all the breakpoints. Finally, press the F9 key to toggle the new breakpoint. The program will now run at normal speed to the line where you set the new breakpoint.

For the remainder of this chapter, I'll show you how to set traps for bugs before they even happen.

Unstructured Error Handling

Earlier versions of Visual Basic did not provide for structured error handling; you were forced to implement unstructured error handling in your programs. Although unstructured error handling is out of favor now, the fact remains that there's a lot of code out there that uses it. For that reason alone, you should at least know how unstructured error handling is implemented.

The On Error Goto Statement

Implementing unstructured error processing is a two-step process. The first step is to activate error handling using the On Error Goto statement. The basic syntax is

```
On Error Goto LabelName
```

where *LabelName* is the Visual Basic .NET program label. Visual Basic .NET program labels follow the same naming rules as variables, but they must end with a colon (:).

To illustrate how we might implement unstructured error handling, we'll modify the btnStart Click event from Listing 19.1 to use the On Error Goto statement. The code change is shown in Listing 19.2.

LISTING 19.2   Using Unstructured Error Handling with On Error Goto

```
Private Sub btnStart_Click(ByVal sender As System.Object, ByVal e As _
            System.EventArgs) Handles btnStart.Click
Dim i As Integer, ValidErrors As Integer

On Error GoTo ShowError    ' Activate the error handler

ValidErrors = 0
txtOutput.Text = ""
For i = 0 To 1000    ' Those below 1000 are reserved
 Err.Raise(i)
 lblProgress.Text = "Processing error number: " & CStr(i)
 Me.Update()
Next i
lblProgress.Text = "Total useable error messages: " & CStr(ValidErrors)
Exit Sub

ShowError:

 If Err.Description <> UNUSED_ERROR_NUMBER Then
  txtOutput.Text &= Format(Err.Number, "000") & " " & Err.Description _
          & vbCrLf
  ValidErrors += 1
 End If
 Resume Next

End Sub
```

The first thing to notice is the statement

```
On Error GoTo ShowError          ' Activate the error handler
```

which enables the error handling. After the statement is executed and if an error is detected, Visual Basic .NET will direct program control to the first line of code *following* the label named ShowError. Toward the end of the btnStart Click event code, you'll see the ShowError label followed by the required colon.

> ### Programmer's Tip
>
> The ShowError label is just that: a label that corresponds to a memory address. There's no code associated with the ShowError label or the colon. In fact, early versions of Visual Basic would not even let you set a breakpoint on a label because there was nothing the debugger could use at the breakpoint. Visual Basic .NET, however, lets you set a breakpoint on a label.

The If statement checks to see whether Err.Description equals our previously defined symbolic constant for an unused error number. So, where did the Err object come from? Err is an object that Visual Basic .NET creates automatically for you when you run a program. As you can see from the code, Err.Description provides a short description of the error, whereas Err.Number holds the error number. The rest of the program behaves as before and the output is virtually identical to that shown in Figure 19.3.

After the On Error Goto statement, we enter a For loop that iterates through the list of predefined error numbers. The statement

```
Err.Raise(i)
```

causes Visual Basic .NET to set the error number to the value of i, thus generating the error condition. The error condition immediately causes Visual Basic .NET to send program control to the code associated with the ShowError label. We then execute the code that follows the ShowError label.

There are a few things about the program and unstructured error handling we need to point out.

Me.Update()

If you look at the two code listings, you'll see that both of them contain the statement

```
Me.Update()
```

In both cases, the statement is contained within the For loop that looks at the error messages. If you've studied the code, you'll have noticed that we want to display the value of the loop counter variable, i, on lblProgress as the program runs. This approach provides feedback to the user that the program is progressing.

As an experiment, try commenting out this line, and then recompiling and running the program. What happens? The program seems to go into never-never land for a few seconds and then it displays the final results shown in Figure 19.3. Without the form's Update() method call, the loop runs to completion before anything is displayed on the form. The purpose of `Update()`, therefore, is to update the screen to reflect the latest changes. In other words, `Update()` forces Windows to *repaint* the screen. Without the call, Windows repaints the screen only after the loop completed its execution.

Why is the call to `Update()` necessary? Why doesn't Windows just update the screen to display the new value written on the label the way the code tells it to? The reason is because it takes a considerable amount of time to repaint a screen. By default, if Visual Basic .NET is in a tight loop where some screen repainting is assumed, Visual Basic .NET postpones the screen updating until after the loop finishes. If you want to override this default behavior, you make the call to `Update()` at those points where you want the screen updated.

Exit Sub

The last statement before the `ShowError` label is an `Exit Sub` statement. This statement is almost always necessary in unstructured error trapping routines. If you did not have an `Exit Sub` statement just before the error trap label (for example, `ShowError`), Visual Basic .NET would fall into the error trapping code even if no error had occurred.

Always remember to place an `Exit Sub` at the point where you want to end the subroutine had no error occurred.

Resume Next

Toward the end of Listing 19.2, you'll see the statement

```
Resume Next
```

The `Resume Next` statement tells Visual Basic .NET to resume program execution at the next line following the line that generated the error condition. Because it was the `Err.Raise()` method that caused the error condition, program control is sent to the line that follows `Err.Raise()`, which is the statement

```
lblProgress.Text = "Processing error number: " & CStr(i)
```

This statement copies the current loop counter value onto the label. The call to `Update()` causes the screen to be repainted so that we can monitor the loop's progress.

Resume

As an alternative to `Resume Next` in Listing 19.2, you could use `Resume`. The `Resume` keyword causes Visual Basic .NET to send program control back to the same line that caused the error to occur in the first place. If we did this in our program, we would produce an infinite loop because we would continue to bounce back and forth between the `Err.Raise()` statement and the error processing code associated with `ShowError`.

In some cases, however, `Resume` provides the proper error handling. For example, if your program is trying to read a file on drive A, but the drive door is open, you could display a message telling the user to close the drive door and click the OK button. The `Resume` statement would then retry the line that sensed the open drive door and then try again to read the file.

On Error Goto 0

The `On Error Goto 0` statement disables the error handler in the current procedure. This means that you can turn off an error handler at any point in a procedure with the `On Error Goto 0` statement. However, any error handler in a procedure is disabled when program control leaves the procedure.

The statement `On Error GoTo -1` also disables error trapping. Because error traps are disabled when program control leaves the procedure in which they are defined, you do not find too many programs that use either of these statements.

The `On Error Goto` statement and its associated statements provide an unstructured means for handling error conditions that might arise as the program executes. However, unstructured error processing is provided by Visual Basic .NET only to allow backward compatibility with earlier versions of Visual Basic. In its place, you're encouraged to use structured error processing.

Structured Error Processing

Perhaps to maintain a respectable distance from unstructured error handling, Visual Basic .NET prefers to refer to structured error processing as *structured exception handling*. *Structured exception handling* is designed to enable the programmer to isolate the code that processes errors. By contrast, it's not uncommon to see code like this:

```
If N <> 0 Then
  Y = X / N
Else
  MessageBox.Show("Divide by 0 error")
End if
```

In this code fragment, the programmer is trying to guard against a divide by zero error. Although this is okay, it tends to mix the error processing code with the non-error code, making the program more difficult to read. Also, if there is a divide by zero error, the preceding code fragment doesn't do anything after the error message is displayed. (You'll often see an `Exit Sub` as the statement line after the message box is displayed.)

Structured exception handling tries to isolate the code that handles the errors from the main program flow. Further, structured exception handling attempts to do this in an organized fashion, using the following syntax structure:

```
Try
    TryStatementBlock
Catch [parameter]
    CatchStatementBlock
[Finally]
    FinallyStatementBlock
End Try
```

I'll discuss each of these keywords in the following sections. After that discussion, I'll present a code example that will help you understand how each statement block may be used.

The `Try` Statement Block

The `Try` statement block contains the code that you think *could* cause an exception to be generated. The statements that appear within the block look like any other Visual Basic .NET program statements. The only difference is that Visual Basic .NET tries to execute those statements within the protective shell created by the `Try-Try End` keywords.

Deciding where you should place the `Try` keyword depends on what you're trying to do. If you're writing code that you know might cause a problem, encapsulate those statements within a `Try` statement block.

The `Catch` Statement Block

There are two flavors of the `Catch` statement. The first flavor is a `Catch` that does not use the optional parameter list. This is often referred to as a *generic* `Catch`. The second flavor does have a parameter list and is referred to as a *parameterized* `Catch` statement. Let's examine each of these in a little more detail.

Generic `Catch` Statement

If you use `Catch` by itself, you're saying that the `Catch` statement block should handle all exceptions that might be generated by the `Try` code. A simple code fragment using this flavor might be

```
Try
  ' Some statements that might generate an error
Catch
  MessageBox.Show("Something bad happened")
End Try
```

As you can see from the code fragment, the `Catch` statement block is a generic exception handler that catches all errors that might occur in the `Try` block.

This code suffers from the dreaded Jack-of-All-Trades syndrome. That is, the exception handler does work and traps all exceptions, but it doesn't do its job very well. Users are not going to find the message `Something bad happened` terribly useful. But that's the nature of the beast. If you catch everything, the error message (or corrective action) by definition must be fairly generic.

Parameterized `Catch` Statement

The second flavor offers more hope. In this case, we add an optional parameter to the `Catch` statement. For example, we might try something like this:

```
Try
  Dim i as Integer
```

```
      i = i / 0          ' Cause a divide by zero error
      ' More statements in the Try statement block

Catch e as DivideByZeroException
  MessageBox.Show("Data produced a divide by zero error")
End Try
```

In this case, the `Catch` statement has an exception parameter that specifically tests for the exception named `DivideByZeroException`. The variable `e` is called the *exception parameter* and holds the value of the exception as determined by Visual Basic .NET.

So, where did the `DivideByZeroException` parameter come from? Visual Basic .NET provides a detailed list of the exceptions that it can detect. To see the broad classifications of exceptions, select the Debug-Exceptions menu sequence or Ctrl+Alt+E. The list is shown in Figure 19.13.

FIGURE 19.13

The Visual Basic .NET exceptions list window.

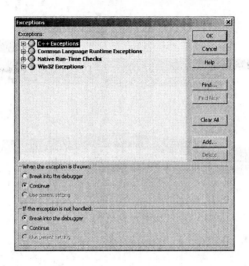

Although you can look at each of these by clicking on its plus box, we're primarily interested in the exceptions found in the common language runtime. If you click on the plus box for the common language runtime, you'll see a list of all the exceptions Visual Basic .NET can recognize in the common language runtime. At the present time, we are interested in the exceptions for the System object, so click on its plus sign. You should see a list similar to that shown in Figure 19.14.

If you look closely, you can see the `DivideByZeroException` defined in the list. You can use any of these exception names in a `Catch` statement to handle that specific exception.

Clearly, a parameterized `Catch` can probably do something more useful from the user's point of view than can a generic `Catch`. The error message can be more specific or perhaps some form of corrective action can be initiated. However, as we'll see in a moment, a generic `Catch` is better than no `Catch` at all.

FIGURE 19.14

A list of the System object's exceptions.

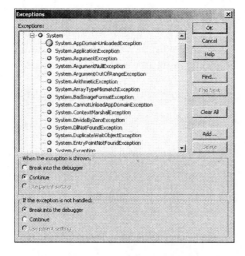

The `Finally` Statement Block

The `Finally` statement block isn't required in structured exception handling. The `Finally` statement block is used to hold code that is always executed, even if no exception is thrown by the `Try` block. However, the `Finally` code is also executed after any `Catch` statement block should an exception occur. Exception or no exception, the code in the `Finally` block is executed.

The `Finally` block enables you to do any cleanup code that must take place before leaving the procedure. This ability obviates the need for a `Resume`-type branch after an exception is encountered.

The `End Try` Statement

The `End Try` statement simply marks the end of an exception-handling statement block. When the `End Try` statement is reached, any exception handling associated with the `Try` statement block is no longer in effect. You may have more than one `Try-End Try` statement block in a procedure and you can nest exception-handling blocks within a procedure.

One last point to notice about structured exception handling: It promotes a top-down program flow. Unstructured error handling often used a `Resume` statement to jump back somewhere in the code, making it more difficult to follow the program flow. Structured exception handling has a smoother flow to it, from top to bottom, and has no need to jump back to some previous section of code. Smooth is better.

Now that we know the basics of structured exception handling, let's try implementing what we've learned.

A Program Example Using Exception Handling

Let's write a program that generates a list of random numbers and then calculates the mean and standard deviation for the list of numbers. The form we'll use is shown in Figure 19.15.

FIGURE 19.15
The form for the exception handler sample program.

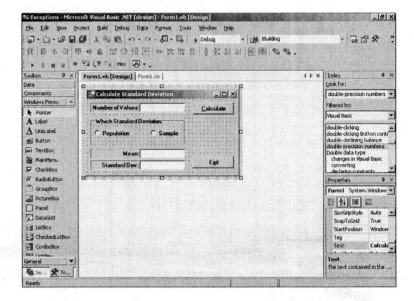

The text box associated with the number of values is named **txtN** and the two text boxes near the bottom of the form are named **txtMean** and **txtSD**. The two radio buttons are named **rbPopulation** and **rbSample**. The command buttons are named **btnCalc** and **btnExit**. I don't really need to get into a statistics lesson here, but the *mean* is simply the average of a list of numbers and the *standard deviation* is a measure of the variability of the numbers. The sample standard deviation has one less degree of freedom than does the population standard deviation; hence the adjustment in the **Term** value in the program code.

The code is presented in Listing 19.3.

LISTING 19.3   Code for the Exception Handling Example

```
Imports System.Math
Imports System.Double

Public Class Form1
 Inherits System.Windows.Forms.Form

' Windows Form Designer generated code
```

LISTING 19.3   Continued

```
Private Sub btnCalc_Click(ByVal sender As System.Object, ByVal e As _
         System.EventArgs) Handles btnCalc.Click
Dim Values() As Double, Mean As Double, SD As Double
Dim N As Long, i As Integer, Which As Integer

txtmean.Enabled = False
txtSD.Enabled = False

N = CLng(txtN.Text)    ' How many values to generate

ReDim Values(N)        ' Set the array size

Randomize()           ' Seed the random number generator

For i = 0 To N - 1
 Values(i) = 101.0 * Rnd()    ' Make up some values
Next

If rbPopulation.Checked = True Then
 Which = 1         ' Do population SD
Else
 Which = 0         ' Do sample SD
End If

SD = StandardDeviation(Values, Mean, N, Which)
If Not IsInfinity(Mean) And Not IsNaN(SD) Then
 txtmean.Enabled = True
 txtSD.Enabled = True
End If
txtSD.Text = Format(SD, "###.#####")
txtmean.Text = Format(Mean, "###.#####")

End Sub

Public Function StandardDeviation(ByVal X() As Double, ByRef Mean As _
     Double, ByVal N As Double, ByVal Which As Double) As Double
 ' Purpose: This function finds the mean and standard deviation
 '      of a series of data.
 '
 ' Argument list:
 '  X()    an array of doubles that holds the data
 '  Mean   the calculated mean, to be filled in by this function
 '  N      the number of observations
 '  Which  calculate pop. SD (Which = 1) or sample SD (Which = 0)
 '
 ' Return value:
 '  Double  the standard deviation for the data set. If an error
 '       is detected, SD is set to NaN and Mean is set to
 '       either positive or negative infinity.
 '
 ' CAUTION: Note that argument Mean is passed by reference
```

LISTING 19.3 Continued

```vb
Dim i As Long, sum As Double, ss As Double, SD As Double
Dim Term As Double

Try
 sum = 0.0    ' Yea, I know...they're set to 0 anyway.
 ss = 0.0
 For i = 0 To N - 1
  sum += X(i)       ' Do the running sum
  ss += X(i) * X(i)  ' Do sums of squares
 Next

 Mean = sum / CDbl(N) ' Calculate the mean

 If Which = 1 Then    ' Population SD
  Term = CDbl(N)
 Else          ' Sample SD, lose one degree of freedom
  Term = CDbl(N - 1.0)
 End If

 If IsPositiveInfinity(Mean) Or IsNaN(Mean) Then ' See if bogus
  Throw New DivideByZeroException()
 End If

Catch e As DivideByZeroException  ' Here if N = 0
 sum = PositiveInfinity

Catch e As OverflowException      ' Here if really big value
 sum = PositiveInfinity

Catch
 sum = NegativeInfinity        ' Here for everything else

Finally
 SD = Sqrt(((N * ss) - (sum * sum)) / (N * Term))
 If IsInfinity(SD) Or IsNaN(SD) Then
  SD = NaN
  Mean = PositiveInfinity
 End If
End Try

 Return SD
End Function

Private Sub btnExit_Click(ByVal sender As System.Object, ByVal e As _
           System.EventArgs) Handles btnExit.Click
 Me.Dispose()
End Sub

Private Sub Form1_Load(ByVal sender As System.Object, ByVal e As _
           System.EventArgs) Handles MyBase.Load
 rbSample.Checked = True
```

LISTING 19.3   Continued

```
      txtmean.Enabled = False
      txtSD.Enabled = False

    End Sub
End Class
```

At the very top of Listing 19.3, you'll see that we have imported two additional namespaces. The `Math` namespace is needed because we use the square root method of the `Math` class. I'll explain the need for the Double namespace in a moment.

The `btnCalc` Click Event

When the user clicks the Calculate button, a number of tasks are initiated. First, we set the `Enabled` property of the two output text boxes to `False`. We do this so that we can better inform the user when an exception has occurred.

Next, we set the number of elements requested by the user to `N`. We then redimension the number of elements in the `Values()` array to permit that number of values. The careful reader will notice that we end up creating one more element than the user requested because arrays start with 0 and `ReDim` sets the highest index value permitted, not the number of elements. Although we could have adjusted the `ReDim` statement accordingly, leaving it as it is doesn't affect what we are trying to accomplish.

After the array is resized, we fill it in with random values that fall between 0 and 100. Next we determine whether the user wants to calculate the sample or population standard deviation. Now that we have things set up properly, we call the `StandardDeviation()` function.

The `StandardDeviation()` Function

The `StandardDeviation()` function is passed in four arguments: the `Values()` array that holds the values; a variable (cleverly) named `Mean` to hold the mean; the number of observations used in the calculations (`N`); and which type standard deviation is to be calculated (`Which`). You can see the call to `StandardDeviation()` in the `btnCalc` `Click` event.

The `StandardDeviation()` Function Argument List

As you'll recall from our discussion in Chapter 5, Visual Basic .NET makes all arguments passed to functions copies of the original data. This means that each argument is automatically given the `ByVal` keyword when you type in the statement for the function. This poses a minor problem for us because functions can return only a single value. We want our function to do double-duty and return both the mean and standard deviation. Hmmm...

Because I want to return the standard deviation and the mean from the function, I elected to have the function return the value for the standard deviation. After all, the name of the function is `StandardDeviation()`, so it seems likely that should be the returned value. So, how do we return the mean?

Simple. In the function's argument list, we change the default pass by value for `Mean` to be pass by reference. This is why `ByRef` is used with the `Mean` argument in the `StandardDeviation()` function definition. This means that we're passing the `lvalue` of `Mean` from the call to the function in the *btnCalc* Click event. Because `StandardDeviation()` is using the `lvalue` for `Mean` from the `btnCalc Click` event, our function has access to the `Mean` defined in `btnCalc`. Therefore, we can change `btnCalc`'s `Mean` while we're executing the `StandardDeviation()`function code.

To prove to yourself that this works, set a breakpoint in the `StandardDeviation()` code on the line just after the *Mean* is calculated. The line is

```
If Which = 1 Then    ' Population SD
```

Now run the program. When you reach the breakpoint, place the cursor over the variable `Mean` in the line above the breakpoint line and note its value. Now scroll to the variable named `Mean` in the `btnCalc Click` event. The values will be the same, even though you've suspended program execution in the code for the `StandardDeviation()` function. This is proof positive that the function is using the `lvalue` of `Mean` in `btnCalc` to affect its value in the `StandardDeviation()` function.

Programmer's Tip

Now you can see why Visual Basic .NET sets procedure arguments to `ByVal` by default. Using `ByRef` in a procedure's argument list exposes that variable to change even though the variable appears not to be in scope. That is, a variable defined with local scope in one procedure can be exposed in a second procedure if the variable is passed to the second procedure by reference. This exposure goes counter to any goals of encapsulation, which is why the default is `ByVal`.

The Exception Handling Code in `StandardDeviation()`

Once we are into the `StandardDeviation()` function code, we set the start of the exception handler using the `Try` keyword. Then we read the data and perform the calculations for the sum (`sum`), sum of squares (`ss`), and the mean (`Mean`). There's an `If` test that sets the denominator for the standard deviation calculation depending on the value of `Which`. Then the mean is calculated.

After the mean is calculated, there's the following `If` statement block:

```
If IsPositiveInfinity(Mean) Or IsNaN(Mean) Then    ' See if the number is bogus
 Throw New DivideByZeroException()
End If
```

We do this just in case the user plays mind games and throws in a value of 0 for `N` in the statement that calculates the mean located immediately above this statement. The `If` test uses the `IsPositiveInfinity()` and `IsNaN()` methods to see whether the calculation of `Mean` threw an exception.

`Double` Data Type and Numeric Overflow

You're probably saying: "Wait a minute! If `N` is zero, why doesn't the code throw a divided by zero exception that's handled in the divide by zero `Catch` block?" Good question.

You've probably seen many examples in other books where that is exactly what happens. However, their code doesn't have our little `If` test. The reason is because they probably used integer variables for the data. If you perform a divide by zero operation using a `Double` data type, however, Visual Basic .NET does *not* throw a divide by zero exception! Instead, it sets the variable to `PositiveInfinity`, `NegativeInfinity`, or NaN (Not a Number), depending on the result of the operation performed. These constants are defined in the `Double` class, which is why we imported its namespace at the top of the program code.

The `If` test uses the `IsPositiveInfinity()` and `IsNaN()` methods to see whether `Mean` has either of these values after the math operation. If either method returns a logic True, we throw a `DivideByZeroException`. We throw…what?

The `Throw` Keyword

We can force Visual Basic .NET to generate an exception by using the `Throw` keyword. In our code, we want to generate a divide by zero exception, so we create a new divide by zero exception with the statement

```
Throw New DivideByZeroException()
```

This causes Visual Basic .NET to generate a divide by zero exception. When this happens, program control is immediately transferred to the `Catch` block that we've written for the divide by zero exception. In this case, the `Catch` block simply sets `sum` to `PositiveInfinity`.

The `Finally` Statement Block

The code found in the `Finally` statement block is always executed, even if there is no exception. In our case, the code calculates the standard deviation (`SD`). However, if any exception was generated along the way, the variable `sum` will have been assigned the value `PositiveInfinity` or `NegativeInfinity`, depending on the exception. (Notice that we also have a generic `Catch` for those exceptions we haven't thought of.)

After `SD` is calculated, we test its value with the `IsInfinity()` and `IsNaN()` methods. If either method is logic True, we reset the values for `SD` and `Mean`. We then return `SD` from the call.

Back in the `btnCalc Click` event, we test the value returned from the `StandardDeviation()` function to see whether it is a Nan. We also test `Mean` to see whether it was set to infinity (notice how we use the unary `Not` operator in the `If` test). If either condition is true, the two output text boxes remain disabled, which causes their background colors to be set to gray. If the tests are passed, the text boxes are enabled and the values displayed on the normal white background.

Can you think of any use for the Command window while using this program to learn about exception handling?

Summary

We covered a lot of ground in this chapter. However, learning how to use the Visual Basic .NET debugger is crucial to be able to track down program bugs. Even though we covered the most important elements of using the debugger, there are still some debug windows and features that we simply did not have time to discuss. For additional details, check the online help categories listed under the general topic `Debug`.

We also discussed both unstructured and structured error handling. I hope that you are now convinced that structured error handling is a better approach to the problem of exception handling. You can even add your own custom error handlers by inheriting from the `Exception` class (that's an advanced topic we're not going to discuss yet.)

I encourage you to experiment with the program presented in Listing 19.3. Set some breakpoints in the code and use the Command window to enter some values that you know will force an exception and see how the exception handlers work. You'll learn a lot from such experimentation.

Review Questions

1. What type of errors is Visual Basic .NET good at catching?

A. Visual Basic .NET is superb at catching syntax errors. Indeed, it catches most of them the instant you press the Enter key to complete a statement.

2. What type of errors is Visual Basic .NET less adept at detecting?

A. Semantic errors are more difficult to detect because they can occur even though the code is syntactically correct. Logic errors are also difficult, if not impossible, for Visual Basic .NET to detect because the rules of the language are being obeyed, but the logic is flawed.

3. What is a breakpoint and how is it used?

A. A *breakpoint* is a debugging tool that lets you pause program execution at a certain line in the program. You create a breakpoint by placing the cursor on the line where you want to set the breakpoint and press the F9 key. This is the breakpoint line.

4. How does a breakpoint help you detect program bugs?

A. Because a breakpoint pauses program execution but does not terminate it, all variables maintain their current values. You can use the various debug windows to inspect these variables to see which variables have values that are different from what you expect at the breakpoint. It is these unexpected values that serve as clues to detecting, isolating, and ultimately correcting the program error.

5. Can you explain what *single-stepping* a program means?

A. *Single-stepping* a program means executing the program one line at a time. You can single-step a program by pressing the F10 key once a breakpoint is reached. Often, you set a breakpoint at a place where you think the program error takes place. Obviously, the best place to place a breakpoint is on the line *before* the statement that causes the error. However, in the early stages of debugging an error, it's difficult to know precisely where the bug is. Therefore, when the program stops at the breakpoint, and you've inspected the values and they still look correct, you can single-step the program and observe what happens to the variables along the way.

6. What does *stepping over a function* mean in terms of debugging a program?

A. While you are single-stepping a program, if a statement calls a function that you wrote for the program, control jumps to the function code and resumes single-stepping in the function. However, in many cases, you don't want to enter the code associated with the function. You want to skip over the call to the function and resume single-stepping the program after the function call. This process of bypassing the single-stepping in the function is called *stepping over a function*. When program execution reaches a statement line with a function call, pressing the Shift+F10 keys causes the program to step over that function call.

7. What does *stepping out of a function* mean?

A. If you're single-stepping the code in a procedure and decide you want to skip the rest of the code, you can step out of the function by pressing the Ctrl+Shift+F10 keys. This causes program control to exit from the procedure and resume on the same statement line that initially called the procedure.

8. What is the difference between the Locals and Autos debug windows?

A. The Locals window shows you all the variables that have local scope. The Autos window shows you all the variables that are being used in the current statement line as well as the statement line before it. Also, the Locals window includes the Me object, which the Autos window does not. The Autos window is a good choice when there are a large number of local variables, but you want to concentrate on those variables being used in the current program statement.

9. What is the hit counter feature of the debugger?

A. The hit counter feature enables you to set a breakpoint that's activated only after the breakpoint statement line has been executed a specified number of times. For example, if you want to inspect the value of a certain variable after 50 iterations through a loop, you can set the hit counter to 49 and single-step from that point to the next iteration. This is much more efficient than pressing the F5 key 49 times. You can set the hit counter using the New Breakpoint dialog box (Ctrl+B).

10. What is a conditional breakpoint?

A. A conditional breakpoint enables you to type in an expression for a breakpoint that is triggered when the conditional expression evaluates to logic True. You can set the hit counter using the New Breakpoint dialog box (Ctrl+B).

11. What purpose does the Command window serve with respect to debugging?

A. You can use the Command window to set values for program variables as the program executes. This enables you to set certain test values at runtime rather than hard coding them into the program at design time.

12. What is unstructured error handling?

A. Unstructured error handling is the way all error processing was performed in all earlier versions of Visual Basic. The error processing was triggered using an `On Error Goto labelname` statement to activate an error trap. The label served as a branch point where program control was sent if an error condition was detected. Unstructured error trapping is less effective than structured error trapping, but is presented because there is a lot of legacy code that uses unstructured error handling.

13. What statements are associated with structured error processing?

A. The core of structured error processing is a `Try-Catch` statement block of the following general form:

```
Try
   TryStatementBlock
Catch [parameter]
   CatchStatementBlock
[Finally]
   FinallyStatementBlock
End Try
```

The *TryStatementBlock* contains the program statements that are processed during normal program execution. The *CatchStatementBlock* are the statements that are to be executed if an error occurs while the *TryStatementBlock* statements are being executed. The optional *FinallyStatementBlock* contains statements that are always to be executed. These are often cleanup statements that must be executed regardless of whether or not an error occurred.

CHAPTER 20

VISUAL BASIC .NET CONTROLS

You will learn about the following in this chapter:

- Visual Basic .NET controls

- The Form control

- The commonly used properties of the Form control

- The commonly used methods of controls

- Combo box controls

One reason Visual Basic .NET is so popular as a Windows programming language has to do with the controls that come with it. The Visual Basic .NET controls are objects that have built-in functionality that you do not have to write yourself. You can write some very useful programs by just combining Visual Basic .NET controls together, without having to write much code. Therefore, new Visual Basic .NET programmers become productive very quickly compared to new programmers working with other Windows programming languages.

Visual Basic .NET has more than three dozen Windows Form controls, and each has dozens of properties and methods associated with it. This chapter discusses the various properties and methods of some of those controls—those that you will most likely use in your programming. Other Visual Basic .NET controls are discussed in the chapters where they are used. For example, the `OpenFileDialog` control is discussed in Chapter 23, "Disk Data Files," and the `DataGrid` tool is discussed in Chapter 25, "Database Programming with Visual Basic .NET."

There are some control properties I have never used in more than 10 years of using Visual Basic. If you think you need to use a property that is not covered in this book, chances are very good that the Visual Basic .NET online help facilities address your questions. Using the online help to answer your own questions is part of the learning process. To paraphrase an old saying, this chapter gives you a fish for today, but the online help teaches you how to fish on your own.

This chapter groups the control properties together to simplify their discussion. That is, rather than discuss the **Text** property of the **TextBox** control and then, later in the chapter, discuss the **Label** control's **Text** property, common properties are discussed together. This chapter discusses the methods of the various controls in the same fashion.

Programmer's Tip

Technically, there is a difference between a Visual Basic .NET component and a Visual Basic .NET control. A Visual Basic .NET component must implement the **Icomponent** interface for the object. A Visual Basic .NET control is a component that is visible at runtime. At this point, however, we can use these terms interchangeably.

The Form Control

You have used the Visual Basic .NET **Form** control in almost every chapter of this book, so you are probably pretty comfortable using it by now. However, there are a few details about the **Form** control that might be useful to you.

First of all, the **Form** control is the canvas on which you paint the user interface for the program. That is, you use a **Form** control to hold the other control objects with which the user interacts while running a program. A form is a container for other controls. To see this in action, let's create a new project called **JustAForm** and consider the **Form** control in its uncluttered state.

The Form Control's Load() Event

So far in this book, each of the program examples has used a single form. When you run such a program, one of the first things that happens is that the form associated with the program is loaded into memory. This is accomplished by the **Form** control's **Load()** event.

The important thing to notice about this event is that it occurs before anything is displayed onscreen for view by the user. To see this for yourself, double-click the form in your project. This switches the Integrated Development Environment (IDE) to the Code window. Your screen should look similar to Figure 20.1. Because you have not given the form a name yet, Visual Basic .NET automatically names the form **Form1**.

Notice the generalized syntax for the **Load()** event:

```
Private Sub ControlName_Event(Args) Handles MyBase.Event
```

Every event that can occur in a Windows program is assigned an event handler. An *event handler* is simply a procedure that is responsible for carrying out the task associated with the event. (You will learn more about event handlers in Chapter 21, "Creating Your Own Controls.") If you look at any of the programs in previous chapters, you'll see that all the event procedures have this general syntax format. (Just turn back to any chapter and look for a button's **Click()** event. All these **Click()** events end with the words **Handles ButtonName.Click**. This is an easy way to locate event handlers in code.)

FIGURE 20.1

The Code window for the Form control's Load() event.

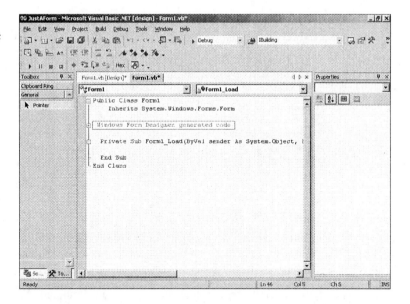

The default access specifier for an event handler is **Private**. This makes sense. For example, if you have a program with multiple forms, each form might have a Close button on it so that the user can close the form when he or she is done with it. Further, each of the Close buttons would probably be named **btnClose**. If you used the **Public** access specifier, there would be name conflicts among the various Close buttons. This is because use of the **Public** access specifier gives namespace scope to the button procedures, leading to the naming conflicts. As a rule, therefore, you should always use the **Private** access specifier for event **Sub** procedures.

For the **Form** control's **Load()** event, the event handler is responsible for loading the form into memory and preparing to display the form to the user. However, the **Form** control's **Load()** event is executed before the form becomes visible to the user. To see this for yourself, you can set a breakpoint on the **End Sub** statement of the **Form** control's **Load()** event and run the program. You should see that the program stops at the breakpoint before the form is displayed.

Recall the five program steps from Chapter 3, "Thinking About Programs." The first step is the initialization step. If your form (or program, if there is only one form) needs some setup or initialization tasks completed before the program actually begins, the **Form** control's **Load()** event is often a good place to put such code. After the code in the **Form** control's **Load()** event is executed, the form becomes visible to the user. The user can then see the form and interact with the user interface that is defined.

Form **Control Properties**

As mentioned earlier in this chapter, there are a lot of properties associated with a form. In fact, there are more than 50 entries in the Properties window for a blank form, and some of those can be expanded to reveal additional properties. This section discusses the properties that you are most likely to use in your programs. The properties are discussed in alphabetical order, so you can easily follow along with the properties shown in the Properties window.

Programmer's Tip

You will get the most out of this section if you start a new project with an empty form. You should click the Design tab in the Form window so you can see the Properties window for the form. As the properties are discussed, you should try changing the default settings to other values and then try compiling and running the program. Even though the program won't do anything, you can still assess the impact of altering the form's properties. Knowing a form's behavior in the absence of interaction with other controls is a useful learning experience.

The `AcceptButton` Property

The `AcceptButton` property tells Visual Basic .NET which button `Click()` event is to be executed if the user presses the Enter key. Therefore, the `AcceptButton` property ties the pressing of the Enter key to a specified button's `Click()` event handler.

To experiment with the `AcceptButton` property, you should add an Exit button to your form. You might want pressing the Enter key to have the same effect as clicking the Exit button. If so, you need to place the cursor in the `AcceptButton` property field; a drop-down list with the names of the form's controls appears. You should select the Exit button from the list. Then, any time a user presses the Enter key, Visual Basic .NET will execute the code you have in the `btnExit` object's `Click` procedure.

The Visual Basic .NET default is not to have an `AcceptButton` property for a form. One reason for this is that new computer users often think that the Enter key is used to terminate text box input. That is, in a form that asks novice Windows users to type in their names, quite frequently they type their names and then press the Enter key. If you have the `AcceptButton` property tied to the Exit button, the moment the user presses the Enter key, the form disappears and the user wonders what went wrong.

To see this effect in action, you should add the following statement to the `btnExit` button's `Click()` event:

```
Me.Dispose()
```

Next, you should add a text box to the form and set the `AcceptButton` field to `btnExit`. Then you should compile and run the program. Finally, you should move the cursor to the text box, type something, and press the Enter key. The form disappears, and the program ends. This could be very confusing to someone who is not familiar with the standard operation of a Windows program.

You can also set the `AcceptButton` property in code. For example, this statement has the same effect as setting the `AcceptButton` property in the Properties window:

```
Me.AcceptButton = btnExit
```

There's nothing wrong with using the **AcceptButton** property. You just need to be careful about what the associated button does when the Enter key is pressed.

The CancelButton **Property**

The **CancelButton** property is similar to the **AcceptButton** property, but it is associated with the action that occurs when the user presses the Esc key. To activate the **CancelButton** property, you place the cursor in its field and select from the drop-down list the button you want to tie to the Esc key. To see how this works, place a button named **btnExit** on the form and set the **CancelButton** property to **btnExit**.

You can also set the **CancelButton** property in code—for example, by using this statement:

```
Me.CancelButton = btnExit
```

This ties the **CancelButton** property to the **btnExit** object's **Click** code. Note that nothing prevents you from using the **btnExit** button for the **CancelButton** control and the **AcceptButton** control if you want to do so.

It is common to be able to terminate the current task in a Windows program by pressing the Esc key. Therefore, the **CancelButton** property is often tied to the code associated with the Exit button.

The ControlBox **Property**

The **ControlBox** property lets you determine whether the control box icon is displayed at the upper-left portion of the form in the title bar. Clicking that icon displays the system control menu, as shown in Figure 20.2.

FIGURE 20.2

The system control menu.

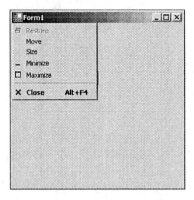

Setting the **ControlBox** property to logic **True** displays the icon. Note that this property also controls the Minimize, Maximize, and Close buttons that appear on the right edge of the form's title bar. However, the user can activate the system menu by pressing Atl+F4. Using the **ControlBox** property is a personal choice, but it doesn't seem to bring much to the party in terms of functionality. (How often have you used the system menu from within a program?)

The Font Property

You can use the Font property to set the print font to be used with a form. Note that virtually every control that has a Text property also has a Font property. To activate the Font dialog box, you can move the cursor to the Font property field and click the ellipsis (…) button. The dialog box that allows you to set the Font property is shown in Figure 20.3.

FIGURE 20.3
The Font dialog box.

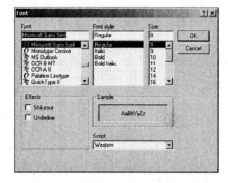

By default, Visual Basic .NET forms use 8-point Microsoft Sans Serif font for regular printing. Whether you elect to change the default is a matter of choice.

Programmer's Tip

My personal choice is to leave the font settings for a form unchanged. However, I do set the Font Style property to Bold for controls that have a Text property that is used as part of an input prompt. Examples of such controls are labels, command buttons, radio buttons, and the like, where the text is used to guide the user's input.

The IsMdiContainer Property

Mdi in the name of the IsMdiContainer property is an abbreviation for multiple-document interface. If you set this property to logic True, you are stating that you want the form to serve as an MDI form. An MDI form is often referred to as the *parent form*. Any form that is subsequently placed within the client area of the parent form is called a *child form*. Usually, the parent form is persistent—that is, it is always visible. The child forms are layered on top of the parent form. Most word processing programs use this approach, and a user's documents are child forms.

We are not going to discuss MDI application programming, so just tuck this information away in the gray matter for later use.

The `Location` Property

The `Location` property determines the upper-left corner of the form, expressed in screen coordinates. As you know, you can click the small plus sign at the left edge of a property field to expand the property and view its details. For the `Location` property, these details are the x- and y-coordinate values. The screen coordinate system is discussed in Chapter 22, "Visual Basic .NET Graphics." For the moment, you can think of these coordinates as being pixel values. To see how these values may be viewed, you can add the following three statements to your form's `Load()` event:

```
Dim x, y As Integer

x = Me.Location.X
y = Me.Location.Y
```

Next, you should set a breakpoint at the statement that follows these statements. You can use the `End Sub` statement of the form's `Load()` event for the breakpoint statement.

Next, you should compile and run the program. If `X` and `Y` are both `0`, your form is at the extreme upper-left corner of the screen.

Next, you should scroll down to the `StartPosition` property (discussed later in this chapter, in the section "The `StartPosition` Property") and select `CenterScreen` from the drop-down list. Then, you should recompile and run the program. Your form should be centered in the screen, and the values for `x` and `y` should be positive values. (The exact values depend on your system settings.)

As you can see, you can set the `Location` property to specific values to position your form wherever you want it. You can also read the `Location` property to find the current location of the form. You might want to use this property in MDI applications to place the child forms at specific locations on the display.

The `Maximize` and `Minimize` Properties

The `Maximize` and `Minimize` properties determine whether the maximize and minimize icons are active for a form. These two icons appear to the left of the Close icon (that is, the icon with the × in it at the right edge of a form's title bar).

If you set the `Maximize` property to logic `False`, the maximize icon is grayed out to show that it is disabled. If you set the `Minimize` property to logic `False`, the minimize icon is likewise grayed out. However, if both the `Maximize` and `Minimize` properties are set to logic `False`, both icons are removed from the title bar. For most programs, you should leave these properties set to their default values of logic `True`.

The `Size` Property

The `Size` property consists of two values: the height of the form and the width of the form. As an experiment, you should add the following lines to a button's `Click()` event code:

```
Dim x, y As Integer
y = CInt(Me.Size.Height * 1.2)
```

```
x = CInt(Me.Size.Width * 1.2)
Dim newpoint As New Size(x, y)
Me.Size = newpoint
```

The first statement defines the working variables x and y. The next two statements set their values to be 20% larger than the current height and width of the form. Because the form's dimensions are expressed in terms of a `Size` object, you can define a `Size` object and pass the values of x and y to the form's `Size` property. The final statement uses the new values to resize the form.

This type of resizing can be useful if you want to hide another control, such as a `DataGrid` control, before it's filled in with a program's output values. When the processing is completed, the user can click a View Output button that expands the form to reveal the hidden `DataGrid` control with the output.

The StartPosition Property

The `StartPosition` property allows you to determine where the form should appear when it is loaded. The `StartPosition` property presents you with a list of alternative starting positions for the form. Note that the `CenterScreen` value is not necessarily the same as `CenterParent`. `CenterScreen` does what it sounds like it does: It centers the form in the display device. `CenterParent` means the form is a child form and centered within the client area of the parent form. If the parent form is skewed to the left, any child form may be centered in the parent's client area but still appear toward the left side of the screen.

I like to use the `CenterScreen` form, but I can't give you a really good technical reason for this preference. I just think it looks good.

The Text Property

The `Text` property of a form controls the text that appears in the title bar of the form. You can use other properties of the form (for example, `Font`) to affect the appearance of this text.

The purpose of the `Text` property is to provide the user with some idea about the purpose of the form. You can use the title bar to display information that changes as the program runs, such as an employee's name. However, you should not rely on the user watching what is displayed in the title bar. My experience is that users tend to ignore what's written in the title bar after they become familiar with the program.

The Window State Property

The `Window State` property lets you determine whether you want the form displayed as normal, maximized, or minimized. When the `Normal` state is set, the window is displayed using the default values for the `Size`, `Location`, and `StartPosition` properties for the form. If you select `Maximized` for the `Window State` property, the form fills the container within which the form is displayed. This is usually the entire display, but it could be the client area of a parent form if the form is a child form. If you select `Minimized`, the form is displayed as a minimized box at the bottom of the screen.

Selecting the `Maximized` state for the form usually looks a little goofy because the default positioning of the controls remains the same. The `Anchor` property (discussed later in this chapter, in the section "The `Anchor` Property") defaults to positioning all controls relative to the top-left corner of the form. So when the `Anchor` property is at its default and the `Maximized` state of the form is selected, the form fills the screen, but it looks like all the controls have been slid toward the upper-left corner of the form. It is not a pretty thing.

As a general rule, you will use the `Normal` (default) state.

`Form` **Control Methods**

Several `Form` control methods may prove useful to you. We have already discussed the `Dispose()` method that is used to close the current form. The following sections describe this and other important methods.

The `Activate` **Method**

The `Activate` method is often used after a form has been loaded but the focus has been given to some other form. You can use this method to activate the form and give it the program focus. For example, it is not uncommon for a program to load several forms when the program first starts but show only one of them. This process fires each form's `Load()` event. At some later time, you might want to show one of the undisplayed forms. The `Activate` method fires when the form is activated but before the form is displayed. Therefore, the `Activate` method gives you a place where you can place code that you want to execute after the form `Load()` event but before the form is actually displayed.

The `Dispose` **Method**

As you learned in Chapter 2, "The Basics of Object-Oriented Programming," you call the `Dispose()` method when you want to release the resources associated with the form and then dispose of the form itself. Note that this is different from hiding a form because the form is removed from memory. If you want to use the form again, you have to reload the form.

The `Hide` and `Show` **Methods**

The `Hide` and `Show` methods are closely related to each other. To see how they work, you can place a new button on your form and place the following statements in the button's `Click()` event procedure:

```
Me.Hide()
MessageBox.Show("Press the button")
Me.Show()
```

The first statement calls the `Hide()` method to remove the form from the display screen. Note that this does not destroy the form or any objects contained on the form. The `Hide()` method has the effect of making the form invisible to the user.

The second statement pauses the program and allows the user to restart it. When the user clicks the OK button of the message box, the `Show()` method causes the form to reappear on the display. Therefore, the `Hide()` and `Show()` methods provide a simple means for temporarily removing a form from the display.

A Sample Program with Controls

In this section you'll learn more about the `TextBox`, `ComboBox`, `ListBox`, `GroupBox`, `RadioButton`, and `Button` controls by building a program that uses them. In the process you'll learn about the common properties and methods that are associated with these controls. The form for this sample program is shown in Figure 20.4.

FIGURE 20.4

The form and the controls for the sample program.

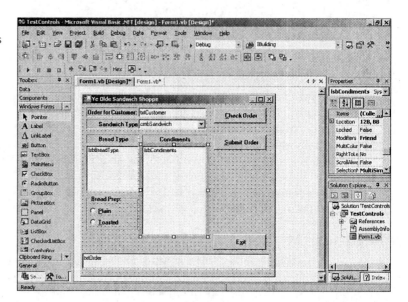

There are two text boxes in this form: `txtCustomer` near the top of the form and `txtOrder` at the bottom of the form. `txtOrder` has its `Multiline` property set to logic `True`.

A number of other controls are placed on the form, and you will learn about how each of them is used in the following sections.

Combo Boxes

The `cmbSandwich` control that is shown in the form in Figure 20.4 is a drop-down combo box. Notice the small downward-pointing arrow at the right end of the combo box. When the user clicks this arrow, the combo box expands to reveal the choices associated with the combo box, as shown in Figure 20.5.

FIGURE 20.5

The options associated
with the `cmbSandwich`
control.

Notice that `Hamburger`, which cannot be seen in the option list in Figure 20.5, is the currently selected item, as displayed in the text box portion of the combo box. If there are more options in the combo box than can be displayed, scrollbars are automatically added to the option list. The text box, however, continues to display the currently selected item from the list.

Programmer's Tip

You can think of a combo box as being built from a `TextBox` control and a `ListBox` control. The text box is used to display the item that has been selected from the list of options that are displayed in the list box portion of the control.

The Anchor Property

Most controls have an `Anchor` property. By default, the `Anchor` property is set to `Top` and `Left`, which means that the position of the control is fixed relative to the top-left edge of the container. The combo box in the program you are creating is contained within a form, and its `Anchor` property is set to `Top` and `Left`, so its location is anchored relative to the form.

Yeah, so what?

Having a control anchored doesn't have any noticeable impact until the user attempts to resize the container (that is, the form). In your form, the upper-left corner of the combo box is 32 pixels down from the top of the form and 130 pixels in from the left edge. If the user attempts to resize the control, your combo box will remain anchored to those coordinates relative to the top-left edge of the form. You can also anchor forms relative to the other edges on the form, but it's fairly standard to reference everything relative to the top-left edge of the form.

The BackColor and ForeColor Properties

You can set the background and foreground colors for many forms. The defaults are often a black foreground and a white background. This is how most text box–like controls are set. However, under certain circumstances, you might want to change the colors, perhaps to draw attention to a combo box. For example, if you wanted to set the background color of the combo box in the sample program, you would move the cursor to the **BackColor** property field in the Properties window and click the drop-down arrow. This would reveal a set of three tabs: Custom, Web, and System. If you click the Custom tab, your screen should look similar to that shown in Figure 20.6.

FIGURE 20.6

The Custom tab of the **BackColor** property.

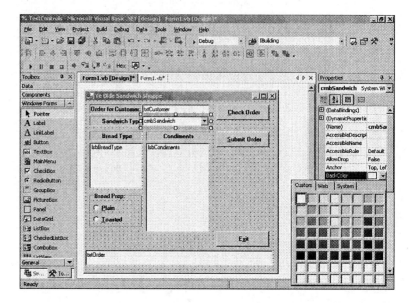

Near the lower-right corner of the Custom tab is a color palette from which you can choose the background color you want to use. (Your palette might look different from that shown in Figure 20.6 due to hardware differences between your system and mine.) When you click the color you want to use, the background color of the combo box changes to that color. Notice that the background color for the drop-down option list also assumes the new color.

Programmer's Tip

Beginning programmers like to use color in their programs. As a general rule, however, you should think twice before changing the normal foreground and background colors of a control. Microsoft has spent more money than you and I will make in a lifetime selecting colors for its controls, even considering the colors' psychological impacts on the user. Color can draw attention to something, and it can also be a distraction. You should carefully think through your user interface before messing around with the default colors of the Visual Basic .NET controls.

The CausesValidation Property

Setting the **CausesValidation** property to logic **True** causes the **Validating()** and **Validated()** events to fire when the focus is leaving the control. In general, *validation* is a process in which you write code to check the input supplied by the user to make sure it is consistent with what you expect the user to enter. You can then add code to these events to check the control's input before the focus is set to the next control in the tab order. If this property is set to logic **False**, the **Validating()** and **Validated()** events are not fired.

Note that the normal sequence of events for a control is **Enter()**, **GotFocus()**, **Leave()**, **Validating()**, **Validated()**, and **LostFocus()**. Although it seems that you might want to use the **LostFocus()** event to do postinput processing, the **Leave()** event is a better choice if the **CausesValidation** property is set to logic **False**. Under certain conditions, it is possible to lock up the program if focus-type code appears in the **LostFocus()** event. (Some additional details are provided in the section "The **TabIndex** Property," later in this chapter.)

The DroppedDown **Property**

You can set the **DroppedDown** property to logic **True** under program control to display the list of items in the combo box. Setting this property to **True** has the same effect as clicking the arrow icon found to the right of the text area: It causes the option list for the combo box to be displayed.

Why would you use this property? In your sample program, the user types in the name of the customer and then selects the type of sandwich he or she wants. If you add the following statement to the **txtCustomer.Leave()** event procedure, the combo box displays the list of sandwich types as soon as the user tabs out of the **txtCustomer** text box:

```
cmbSandwich.DroppedDown = True
```

This eliminates the need for the user to click the arrow icon in the combo box to see the list of choices. That's the good news.

The bad news is that the normal arrow cursor disappears when it is positioned over the combo box. As the user moves the mouse, the user sees the highlighted choice in the combo box change, but there's no arrow cursor. As soon as the user clicks a choice from the list of options in the combo box, the arrow cursor reappears. This is a good idea gone bad. Removing the arrow cursor while selecting a choice seems very unnatural.

To fix this problem (because I like showing the combo box list automatically), you can add the following statement immediately after the **DroppedDown** property is set:

```
Cursor.Current = Cursors.Arrow   ' Set the current cursor type
```

This statement sets the current cursor, which is now invisible because of the **DroppedDown** statement, to the arrow (default) cursor. With the arrow cursor back on the screen, the selection process from the combo box seems normal once again.

Programmer's Tip

You can change the current cursor to a number of different cursor styles (for example, crosshair, I-beam, hourglass) by using the **Cursor.Current** statement. For additional details, see the online help under "Cursors Members."

The `MaxDropDownItems` Property

As you know, when you click on the small arrow icon located at the right end of the combo box text area, the list of items is displayed. The `MaxDropDownItems` property determines how many items are displayed when the user clicks the arrow icon. The default number of items displayed is 8.

If you have enough real estate on the form, you should consider setting the `MaxDropDownItems` property to the total number of items to be displayed. For example, in your sample program, nine items are in the combo box list. Using the default value for the `MaxDropDownItems` property would force the user to scroll the list of items to see all the choices. Simply setting the `MaxDropDownItems` property to `9` removes the need for the user to scroll the list to see all the choices.

Your users will appreciate not having to scroll combo box lists. As a general rule, the fewer keystrokes and mouse clicks the user has to make, the better. Although changing the `MaxDropDownItems` property to reveal the complete list is a small thing, collectively small things like this all add up to help make the interface more user friendly.

The `Sorted` Property

If you set the `Sorted` property to logic `True`, the items in the option list are presented in ascending sorted order. The sort is case-insensitive. The default for this property, however, is logic `False`, which means the items appear in the list in the order in which they are entered. If the `Sorted` property is logic `False`, all new items are added to the end of the list.

Programmer's Tip

Both list boxes and combo boxes provide the `Sorted` property. However, you are not limited to using the `Sorted` property just for the items in the option list. For example, if you have an array of integers named `Vals()` and a list box named `lstTemp` with its `Sorted` property set to logic `True`, you could read the unsorted values from `Vals()` into the list box and then read them back into `Vals()` in sorted order. If you need a sort routine (as in a coding quiz during a job interview), this is a quick-and-dirty way to get the job done.

Adding Data to a `ComboBox` or `ListBox` Control

After you place a `ComboBox` control on a form and set the properties the way you want them, you need to add the items that will appear in the combo box. The following is the general syntax for this:

```
cmbComboBoxObject.Items.Add("Add This Item")
```

This statement adds the quoted string to the `Items` collection of the combo box. If the `Sorted` property is set to logic `True`, the item is entered into the item list in sorted order. If the `Sorted` property is `False`, the item is appended to the end of the list.

After all the items are added to the list, you normally want to have a default selection shown in the combo box. You do that with the following statement:

```
cmbSandwich.SelectedIndex = 0
```

Because the items in the list are zero based, this statement makes the first item in the list the default selection.

The syntax for adding items to a `ListBox` control and setting its default selection is the same for the `ComboBox` control. You will learn how to use some of the other properties for the `ComboBox` and `ListBox` controls later in the chapter, in the section "Multiple Selections in a List Box."

The `TabIndex` Property

With the exception of the `Form` control, any control that can acquire program focus has a `TabIndex` property. This property determines the order in which the controls are selected when the user presses the Tab key. For a Windows program, user input is normally terminated when the user presses the Tab key. Visual Basic .NET detects when the user presses the Tab key and fires the `Leave()` event procedure for the control. Because the user is finished entering data into the current control, Visual Basic .NET needs to move the cursor from the present control to the next control. The `TabIndex` property tells Visual Basic .NET what that next control is.

Programmer's Tip

Earlier versions of Visual Basic use the `LostFocus()` event to override the tab order by using the `SetFocus()` method. You should avoid using `SetFocus()` within `LostFocus()` because it can lead to a state that can cause the program to stop responding.

Suppose, for example, that you have two text boxes named `txtFirst` and `txtLast` for entering a person's name. You want the user to enter the first name first and then enter the last name. You need to set the `TabIndex` property of `txtFirst` to 1 and set the `TabIndex` property for `txtLast` to 2. Then, when the user is finished entering the person's first name and presses the Tab key, Visual Basic .NET fires the `Leave()` event and then examines the tab order of the controls on the form. When Visual Basic .NET sees that `txtLast` has its `TabIndex` property set to 2, it fires the `Enter()` event for the `txtLast` control and places the cursor in the `txtLast` text box.

As you can see, the `TabIndex` property determines the order in which Visual Basic .NET processes the controls on a form.

Programmer's Tip

By default, Visual Basic .NET sets the tab order in the order in which you placed the controls on the form at design time. You can check the tab order by running the program and pressing the Tab key to observe the sequence Visual Basic .NET follows in giving each control program focus. However, an easier way to see the tab order is to select View, Tab Order while in Design mode. This causes Visual Basic .NET to place a small box on each control, with the control's `TabIndex` property written in the box. Selecting View, Tab a second time toggles off the `TabIndex` property values.

Radio Buttons

Two radio buttons are used in your sample program: `rbnPlain` and `rbnToasted`. A radio button control is a binary control because it can assume only one of two states: `True` (that is, checked) or `False` (that is, unchecked). In the form's `Load()` event, this statement sets the `rbnToasted` radio button to its checked status:

```
rbnToasted.Checked = True
```

So what's the status of the `rbnPlain` button?

Normally, radio buttons are grouped together to offer a selection of two or more choices. However, only one choice from the list of available radio button choices can be made. This means that selecting one choice automatically turns off any choice that was previously made. Therefore, if `rbnToasted` is selected in your sample program, `rbnPlain` must be unselected. After all, either the bread is toasted or it isn't. You can't have it both ways, and that's exactly why you use radio buttons.

Does this mean you must write code to manage unchecking one button if another button is checked? Fortunately, the answer is no. If you place two radio buttons within a `GroupBox` control, you tell Visual Basic .NET to treat the radio buttons as a set. Therefore, setting the `Checked` property of one button automatically causes Visual Basic .NET to uncheck the previously checked button. You can use more than two radio buttons in a group box, and the automatic check/uncheck feature works for all buttons.

Running the Sample Program

The remaining control types in this chapter's sample program form are discussed in earlier programs. So let's run the program and then walk through its code. A sample run is shown in Figure 20.7.

The program accepts the customer's name, the type of sandwich the customer wants, the bread type and whether the bread is toasted, and a list of condiments to put on the sandwich. When the user clicks the Check Order button, the program builds an order string that the user could read back to the customer just to make sure everything is correct before sending the order to the kitchen via the Submit Order button.

FIGURE 20.7

A sample run of the controls test program.

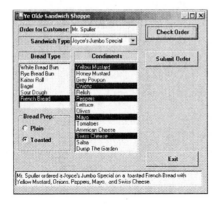

The code for the program is presented in Listing 20.1.

LISTING 20.1   Code for the Test Controls Program

```vb
Public Class frmControlTest
 Inherits System.Windows.Forms.Form

' Windows Form Designer generated code


Private Sub Form1_Load(ByVal sender As System.Object, ByVal e As _
          System.EventArgs) Handles MyBase.Load

  cmbSandwich.Items.Add("Hamburger")        ' Sandwich types
  cmbSandwich.Items.Add("Breaded Tenderloin")
  cmbSandwich.Items.Add("Sub")
  cmbSandwich.Items.Add("Liverwurst")
  cmbSandwich.Items.Add("Ham")
  cmbSandwich.Items.Add("Turkey")
  cmbSandwich.Items.Add("Chicken")
  cmbSandwich.Items.Add("Aunt Nancy's Special")
  cmbSandwich.Items.Add("Joyce's Jumbo Special")
  cmbSandwich.SelectedIndex = 0

  lsbCondiments.Items.Add("Yellow Mustard")    ' Condiments
  lsbCondiments.Items.Add("Honey Mustard")
  lsbCondiments.Items.Add("Grey Poupon")
  lsbCondiments.Items.Add("Onions")
  lsbCondiments.Items.Add("Relish")
  lsbCondiments.Items.Add("Peppers")
  lsbCondiments.Items.Add("Lettuce")
  lsbCondiments.Items.Add("Olives")
  lsbCondiments.Items.Add("Mayo")
  lsbCondiments.Items.Add("Tomatoes")
  lsbCondiments.Items.Add("American Cheese")
```

LISTING 20.1   Continued

```
lsbCondiments.Items.Add("Swiss Cheese")
lsbCondiments.Items.Add("Salsa")
lsbCondiments.Items.Add("Dump The Garden")

lsbBreadType.Items.Add("White Bread Bun")      ' Break types
lsbBreadType.Items.Add("Rye Bread Bun")
lsbBreadType.Items.Add("Kaiser Roll")
lsbBreadType.Items.Add("Bagel")
lsbBreadType.Items.Add("Sour Dough")
lsbBreadType.Items.Add("French Bread")
lsbBreadType.SelectedIndex = 0

rbnToasted.Checked = True
lsbBreadType.Cursor = Cursors.Hand

End Sub

Private Sub btnCheck_Click(ByVal sender As System.Object, ByVal e As _
            System.EventArgs) Handles btnCheck.Click
Dim i As Integer
Dim LastOne As String
Dim buff As String

txtOrder.Clear()  ' Clear out old order
' Build the new order
txtOrder.AppendText(txtCustomer.Text)        ' Customer name
txtOrder.AppendText(" ordered a ")
txtOrder.AppendText(cmbSandwich.SelectedItem)  ' the sandwich
txtOrder.AppendText(" on a ")
If rbnToasted.Checked = True Then          ' toasted?
 LastOne = " toasted "
Else
 LastOne = " plain "
End If
txtOrder.AppendText(LastOne)
txtOrder.AppendText(lsbBreadType.SelectedItem) ' Bread type
txtOrder.AppendText(" with ")

For i = 0 To lsbCondiments.Items.Count - 1    ' Condiments?
 If lsbCondiments.GetSelected(i) = True Then
  LastOne = lsbCondiments.Items(i)
  buff &= LastOne & ", "
 End If
Next
i = InStr(buff, LastOne)       ' Change trailing comma to a period
If (i) Then
 buff = Microsoft.VisualBasic.Left(buff, i - 1) & " and " & LastOne & _
                ". "
End If

txtOrder.AppendText(buff)       ' Display the order
```

LISTING 20.1   Continued

```
End Sub

Private Sub btnExit_Click(ByVal sender As System.Object, ByVal e As _
            System.EventArgs) Handles btnExit.Click
  Me.Dispose()
End Sub

Private Sub txtCustomer_Leave(ByVal sender As Object, ByVal e As _
            System.EventArgs) Handles txtCustomer.Leave
  cmbSandwich.DroppedDown = True   ' Show all the options
  Cursor.Current = Cursors.Arrow   ' Set the current cursor type
End Sub

End Class
```

The following sections describe the important parts of this code.

The Form's Load() Event

The bulk of the code in the form's **Load()** event in Listing 20.1 deals with adding the combo box and list box options. Both the **ComboBox** and **ListBox** controls use the **Add()** method to add the list of options to the **Items** collection. Near the bottom of the procedure, you set the Toasted radio button to be checked because that is to be the default selection.

Just for grins, you set the **Cursor** property for the bread type **ListBox** control to be the hand cursor of the **Cursors** class. When the user places the arrow cursor over the **lstBreadType** list box, the cursor changes to a hand cursor. Moving off the list box automatically restores the arrow cursor. There's no real reason for changing the cursor other than to show you how it can be done.

The btnCheck Object's Click() Event

Visual Basic .NET automatically handles the code to process the selections made by the user. That is, clicking a selection in either the list box or combo box automatically highlights the selection. Therefore, your task is to build a completed order string from the selections made by the user.

The call to the **txtOrder.Clear()** method simply clears out any previous order than might be showing. That call is followed by a series of **txtOrder.AppendText()** method calls. Using the **AppendText()** method is another way of appending text to the contents of a text box. Although the string concatenation operator (**&**) works just fine with text boxes, the **AppendText()** method is considerably faster. In most programs, this speed improvement isn't noticeable. However, if you built a long (multiline) text box string in a tight loop, the efficiency gain might be noticeable.

This statement shows you how to retrieve the string of a selected item from a combo box:

```
txtOrder.AppendText(cmbSandwich.SelectedItem)   ' the sandwich
```

If you look about eight lines further down in Listing 20.1, you can see that selecting an item from a list box uses the same syntax structure.

Multiple Selections in a List Box

The `lsbCondiments` list box code is a little different from the code for processing the `lsbBreadType` list box. The `lsbBreadType` object's `SelectionMode` property is set to `One`, which means that only one item can be selected from the list. If the user changes his or her selection, Visual Basic .NET automatically highlights the new selection and removes the highlight from the old selection. You do not have to write code to manage this feature.

You set the `SelectionMode` property in the Properties window for the `lsbCondiments` list box to `MultiSimple`. This allows the user to select multiple options from the list. Customers might want to add more than one condiment to a sandwich, and setting the `SelectionMode` property to `MultiSimple` allows for multiple condiments.

You use the `GetSelected()` method to determine whether an item in the list box has been selected. If the item is selected, the `GetSelected()` method returns logic `True`; otherwise, it returns logic `False`. This statement is executed if the call to the `GetSelected()` method returns a selected item:

```
LastOne = lsbCondiments.Items(i)
```

This statement then assigns the string associated with the selected item into `LastOne`. (You do this assignment because of some postloop processing you want to perform after all the selections are processed.) The list of items is then built as a comma-separated list and stored in a temporary string named `buff`.

The call to `InStr()` searches `buff` to find the last item added to the list of condiments. The call to the `Left()` function adds the word *and* to the condiment list before the last selected option and replaces the trailing comma with a period. The only purpose of all this postloop processing is to make the resultant order more readable.

After the order string is built, it is copied into the `txtOrder` text box for display.

The `Leave()` event procedure of the `txtCustomer` text box sets the `DroppedDown` property of the `cmbSandwich` combo box to logic `True`. As mentioned earlier in this chapter, this automatically displays the options in the combo box. You set the current cursor to the default arrow cursor to avoid not showing a cursor to the user (which is the default behavior).

You have not implemented any action for the Submit Order button. In a real application, pressing that button would transmit the order to the kitchen so that the sandwich could be made.

You should save this project and then try changing some of the properties for various controls to observe the impact of your changes. You should also add some new items to the menus and use the online help to see if any other properties and methods might prove useful.

Summary

This chapter discusses some of the common controls that you might want to use in your programs. It shows that many of the different controls share common properties, such as `Text`, `Location`, `Size`, and `Visible`. By adding new features to a sample program, you have learned how controls' properties and methods work.

This chapter does not list or discuss all the controls that Visual Basic .NET makes available. Many of the Visual Basic .NET controls are discussed in the chapters where you actually use them. Discussion about database controls, file processing dialog boxes, picture boxes, and similar controls are deferred to the chapters where you can use them in sample programs. This will better help you learn how these controls work than would simply listing them all in this chapter.

As you gain more experience, you might say to yourself, "I wish this control could…." In such cases, the first thing you should do is read the online help for the control to see if there is already some existing property or method that you might be able to use. If the feature you want is not available, you can use inheritance to add the feature because virtually every object in Visual Basic .NET is derived from the `System` object. Using inheritance to enhance existing Visual Basic .NET controls is a real benefit, and it is the subject of Chapter 21, "Creating Your Own Controls."

Review Questions

1. In one sentence, define an event handler.

A. An event handler is simply a procedure that is responsible for carrying out the task associated with a given event.

2. What is the syntax format for an event handler?

A. The statement

```
Private Sub CtrlName_ThisEvent(Args) Handles MyBase.ThisEvent
```

is the signature for the `ThisEvent` event for the `CtrlName` control. This statement form tells Visual Basic .NET that this subroutine processes the `ThisEvent` control event.

3. What is the purpose of the `AcceptButton` property?

A. The `AcceptButton` property links the pressing of the Enter key to a specific button that exists on the form. In other words, if the user presses the Enter key and you want that action to cause the program to behave as though the btnSave button were pressed, you would enter btnSave in the `AcceptButton` property field. After this is done, if the user presses the Enter key, the program will respond as if the user had clicked the `btnSave` button.

4. What is the purpose of the `CancelButton` property?

A. The concept is the same as the `AcceptButton` property, but in this case you are associating the Esc (Escape) key with a button's Click event. Usually, `CancelButton` is tied to the `btnExit` button. Therefore, the `CancelButton` property is normally set to the `btnExit` button. If the user presses the Esc key while the program is running, the form is dismissed.

5. How might the `Show` and `Hide` methods be used in a program?

A. There will be times when you have a sequence of forms that must be filled in by the user. Rather than load these forms as they are needed, the programmer can load them all when the program first starts. After all the forms are loaded, the program can use the `Show()` method to display the first form. After the form is completed by the user, you can use the `Hide()` method to dismiss the current form and use the next form's `Show()` method to display the next form, and so on for all the forms. By using the `Hide()` method rather than the `Dispose()` method, you can redisplay any form as needed with a simple `Show()` method call rather than reloading the form.

6. What is the purpose of the `TabIndex` property?

A. The `TabIndex` property determines one of two things. First, if the form is just now being displayed, the control that has the lowest `TabIndex` value is the control that will receive the program focus when the form is first displayed. Second, the `TabIndex` property determines where program control goes after the user presses the Tab key.

If you are designing a form and double-click on a `TextBox` control on the Windows Form tab of the Toolbox, Visual Basic .NET automatically places a copy of the `TextBox` control on the form. If this is the first control on the form, the `TabIndex` property for the `TextBox` is set to 0. This means that, when the program is run, this text box will receive the program focus when the form is displayed.

If you double-click on the `TextBox` control a second time, the `TabIndex` property is set to 1. In other words, the `TabIndex` property is automatically incremented by 1 for the next control added to the form. It also follows that this second text box would receive the program's focus when the user presses the Tab key while the cursor is in the first text box.

7. Why do you often find radio buttons contained within a `GroupBox` control?

A. Radio buttons are normally used for a mutually exclusive list of program options. That is, if you select the option associated with one radio button, you automatically exclude any and all other radio button options. If the radio buttons are placed on a `GroupBox` control, the radio buttons are treated collectively as a mutually exclusive option list. This simplifies the code necessary to process such option lists.

8. How do you allow for multiple sections from a list box?

A. Set the `SelectionMode` property to `MultiSimple`. You can then use the `GetSelected()` method to determine which items in the list box have been selected.

CHAPTER 21

CREATING YOUR OWN CONTROLS

You will learn about the following in this chapter:

- How to design a control
- How to add properties to a control
- How to add methods to a control
- How to process control events
- How to test a control

A At the time of this writing, more than three dozen Windows Forms controls are being shipped with Visual Basic .NET. If you include other controls that are not used with Windows forms, such as Web controls, the count increases to more than 50 controls. Everything you need is there for you on the toolbar, right? Well, not quite. No matter how many controls are bundled with Visual Basic .NET, each programming task has little nuances of difference that make programmers wish for controls that do this or that. Alas, if the only tool you have is a hammer, pretty soon every problem starts to look like a nail.

You need a variety of tools to do a job right, and Visual Basic .NET gives you a pretty robust selection. If you really do have a problem that one of the Visual Basic .NET tools can't even come close to solving, however, you can check the Visual Basic .NET magazines or the Internet for an appropriate tool. Purchasing off-the-shelf controls is often a cost-effective and smart way to program a solution.

Still, there are a lot of situations in which the Visual Basic .NET tool set comes close to what you need, but it's not quite a perfect fit. The circumstance is not as bad as "round hole, square peg" situation; it's more like a "round hole, oval peg" problem. This chapter shows how to turn oval pegs into round ones; that is, it shows you how to craft your own custom controls.

You can approach the problem of crafting your own custom controls by using any one of three general methods:

- You can add whatever functionality an existing control is lacking via inheritance.

- You can combine several existing controls into a single control to extend their functionality.

- You can build your own control from the ground up.

This chapter shows how to combine the first two methods to build a new control. You'll learn how to build a custom control from three text box controls. Inheritance provides the lion's share of the new control's functionality. When you understand the basics of building a custom control, you will find it pretty straightforward to build new controls from scratch.

The PhoneSSN Control

In this chapter you will build a control called the PhoneSSN control that accepts a phone number or a Social Security number (SSN) from the user. As you know, the format for an SSN is XXX-XX-XXXX, which is essentially a numeric variable stated in terms of three fields. A phone number is similar. It, too, has three fields consisting of the area code, the phone exchange, and the number (XXX-XXX-XXXX). The PhoneSSN control uses three TextBox controls to accept these three field numbers and then formats them into a string that can be treated as the requested data item. A sample run of the control is shown in Figure 21.1.

FIGURE 21.1

A sample run of the PhoneSSN control.

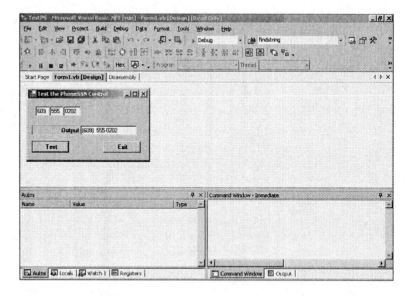

The PhoneSSN control is visible in the upper-left corner of Figure 21.1, and it appears to be nothing more than three text boxes. Indeed, the control is built from three standard text boxes, but it also exposes new properties that simplify the processing of the text boxes. You can resize the width of the control to automatically resize the three text boxes. Also, if you select a different font size, the control automatically resizes the height of the text boxes to accommodate the new font size. This is shown in Figure 21.2.

FIGURE 21.2

A sample run of the PhoneSSN control using a larger font size.

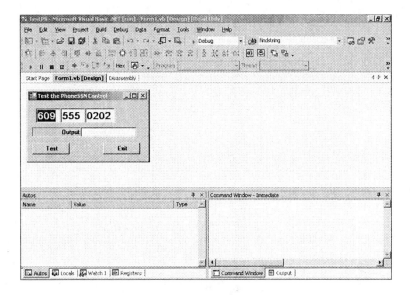

Building a custom control is a little like baking. Unlike cooking, where you can throw things together without a formal recipe and it usually tastes pretty good, baking is a little like chemistry. You need to carefully measure the ingredients and follow instructions precisely. If you don't, you might end up with a cake that's better suited for caulking bath tubs than eating as a dessert. Building your own controls is similar to cake baking, so you should follow the steps in this chapter carefully.

With that caveat in mind, you can start building your custom control.

Setting Up the Project

To begin building your custom control, the first thing you need to do is start a new project. You need to select File, New, Project to open the New Project dialog box. Select the Windows Control Library option from the available options in the New Project dialog box, as shown in Figure 21.3.

FIGURE 21.3

Selecting the Window Control Library option from the New Project dialog box.

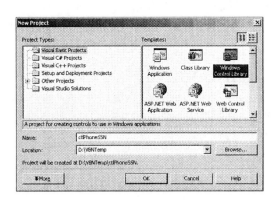

Next you need to type the name `ctlPhoneSSN` for the project and select a location where you want the files to be placed.

> ### Programmer's Tip
> The Standard Edition of Visual Basic .NET does not include the template for the Windows Control Library.

After you fill in the necessary information, you should click the OK button. The display changes to the screen shown in Figure 21.4.

FIGURE 21.4
The Form window for designing a custom control.

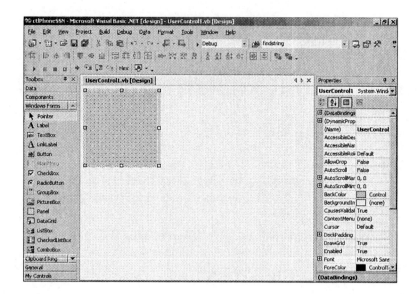

The `UserControl` Form

In the Form window you should see the `UserControl` form. Using the `UserControl` form is very similar to using a normal Visual Basic .NET Windows form. However, the purpose of the `UserControl` form is to act as a container in which you can place the controls you use to build your custom control.

Naming a Custom Control

At this stage of the game, you should supply the name that you want to use for the new control. You named the project `ctlPhoneSSN` so you can tell at a glance what the project contains. However, custom controls are usually not prefixed at this level. For example, Visual Basic .NET refers to the `TextBox` control on the toolbar as `TextBox`. Visual Basic .NET does not use the standard prefix conventions (for example, `txt` for a text box) for controls on the toolbar.

Therefore, a good name for your new control is **PhoneSSN**. Users might want to add a prefix later, but there's no compelling reason for you to do that for them.

To name the control, you go to the Solution Explorer window and click the **UserControl1.vb** entry, as shown in Figure 21.5.

FIGURE 21.5
Naming a custom control.

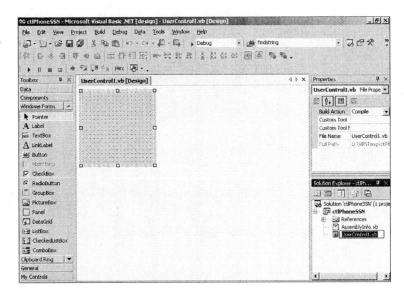

To name the control, you can type **PhoneSSN.vb** in the box and press the Enter key. (You can instead right-click the **UserControl1.vb** entry and select the Rename option from the menu that appears, or you can click the Property icon and enter the filename.) If you've done things correctly, the Solution Explorer should show **PhoneSSN.vb**, and the tab in the Form window should also show the new name.

Placing Text Boxes on a Control

Next you need to place three text boxes on the **PhoneSSN** control, following the guidelines presented in Table 21.1.

TABLE 21.1   Placement and Sizes of the **PhoneSSN** Control's Text Boxes

Control Name	Location Property	Size Property
txtAreaCode	8,8	40,20
txtExchange	48,8	40,20
txtNumber	88,8	48,20

Notice that the first two text boxes have the same size, but the third is slightly larger. After you create the text boxes, you should shrink the **UserControl** control down to about 144×40. If you have followed the directions carefully, your control should look similar to the one shown in Figure 21.6.

FIGURE 21.6
The visual interface for the **PhoneSSN** custom control.

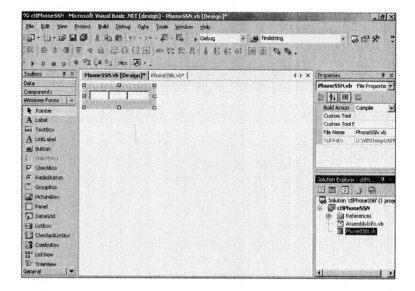

You have now created the visual interface for the **PhoneSSN** control.

Adding Code to the PhoneSSN Custom Control

If you right-click the Form window, you are given an option to view the code, or you can click the Code window icon in the Solution Explorer window. This should be the first line of the Code window:

```
Public Class UserControl1
```

You should change that line to this:

```
Public Class PhoneSSN
```

The second line in the Code window tells you that the **PhoneSSN** class will inherit from the **UserControl** class. This class provides the core functionality for all Visual Basic .NET controls. Therefore, you have already written most of the code needed for your custom control simply by inheriting from the **UserControl** class.

After you make sure that you renamed the project **ctlPhoneSSN**, you should save the project by selecting File, Save All.

Component Attributes

If you look just under the title bar for the Properties window in Figure 21.6, you should see several icons. Perhaps the most familiar icon is the A–Z icon, which presents an alphabetized list of the properties for the control that has the focus. To the left of the A–Z icon are two plus signs. If you click the lower plus sign, the Properties window changes to show you the list of properties arranged by categories, rather than in alphabetic order (see Figure 21.7).

FIGURE 21.7
The Properties window arranged by category rather than by alphabetic order.

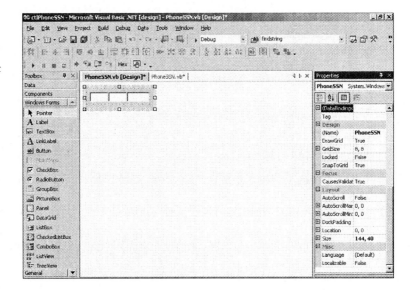

These are the categories for the properties:

- Accessibility
- Appearance
- Behavior
- Configurations
- Data
- Design
- Focus
- Layout
- Misc.

What these categories do should be fairly clear if you look at the way the properties fit into each of these categories.

Sometimes when you're working with a new control, this view of a control's properties may help you understand the organization of the properties. Because you are creating a new control that the user might be unfamiliar with, you should probably take advantage of this feature.

Listing 21.1 shows the beginning of the code for the PhoneSSN control. You will see the complete listing for the control later in this chapter, but for now you need to spend a little time with smaller sections of it.

LISTING 21.1   The First Section of Code for the **PhoneSSN** Control

```
Imports System.ComponentModel
Public Class PhoneSSN

 Inherits System.Windows.Forms.UserControl

 ' Windows Form Designer generated code


 '============ The data members ============

 ' The different formats available
 Enum Selection
  Phone = 0
  SSN
 End Enum

 ' Private members
 Private mBoxType As Selection     ' Do they want a Phone or SSN #?
 Private mAreaCode As String      ' The area code
 Private mExchange As String      ' The exchange
 Private mNumber As String       ' The rest of the number
 Private mComplete As String      ' The complete string

 '============ The property procedures ============

 '            InputType()

 <Description("Will you enter phone numbers or Zip codes?"), _
 Category("Behavior")> _
 Property InputType() As Selection
  Get
   Return mBoxType
  End Get
  Set(ByVal Value As Selection)    mBoxType = Value
  End Set
 End Property
```

The first line of Listing 21.1 imports the ComponentModel object library of the System class. The System class contains the members necessary to work with the Properties window in the manner described earlier.

Using Enum Data Types for Property Choices

The first thing you declare in Listing 21.1 is an Enum data type named Selection that has members that describe the functions of the control. There are only two members: Phone and SSN. Remember that an Enum-End Enum statement block does not define a data object. Rather, it is a declaration that tells what the members of the Enum are. An Enum declaration defines a cookie cutter from which you can create objects of the Enum type.

In the statement line following the Enum declaration is a definition of the class member named mBoxType, which is of type Selection. Why use an Enum for the property choices? You do so because the ComponentModel class knows how to place these choices in a drop-down list for the field of the property. You will see how this works a bit later in the chapter.

The remaining class members are String variables that are used to hold the appropriate string parts of either a phone number or an SSN.

Describing and Categorizing a Property Procedure

Rather than use the property procedure code you've seen before, the property signature in Listing 21.1 is prefaced with this:

```
<Description("Will you enter phone numbers or Zip codes?"), _
Category("Behavior")> _
```

As you have probably guessed, the angle brackets surround category information about the property so that it can be used when the property is displayed in the Properties window. In this case, the Description() method contains a string literal that is displayed at the bottom of the Properties window when the InputType property is selected. The Category() method contains another string literal that tells where the property is to be placed when the Category() option is used to display the properties, as shown in Figure 21.7.

If you do not specify the Category() method, the property defaults to the Misc. property category. You are not limited to the standard categories listed earlier. You can create your own if the need arises. To do so, you simply supply the string literal that you want to use instead of one of the defaults.

If you want to hide a property from being displayed in the Properties window, perhaps because it is a ReadOnly property, you simply change the display information to something like this:

```
<Browsable(False)> _
ReadOnly Property Hush() as Integer
  ' The rest of the property code
```

Obviously, if the property is to be hidden, there is no need for the Description() or Category() methods. The default is for the Browsable() method to be logic True, which is the normal state for most properties. The only time you need to specify the Browsable() method is when you want to prevent the property from appearing in the Properties window.

Programmer's Tip

It is very easy to forget the line-continuation character (that is, the underscore character) when writing the code for the `Description()` and `Category()` methods. Unfortunately, the squiggly line that tells that there's trouble tends to fall on the next method in the list. That is, if you forget the underscore after the `Description()` method, the squiggly line appears under the `Category()` method. However, if you look backward from that point, you see the comma underlined, telling you where Visual Basic .NET expected to find the line-continuation character.

The `InputType` Property Procedure Code

The code for the `InputType` property is similar to the code in Chapter 16, "Class Properties." The only difference is that the return data type from the property `Set()` procedure is the `Selection` data type declared earlier.

You must write property `Get()` and `Set()` procedures for the properties that you wish to expose to the user as part of the control's interface.

Adding a New Tab to the Toolbox

As you gain experience with Visual Basic .NET, you will find yourself writing more and more custom controls. Although you could place your new custom controls on the Windows Forms tab of the toolbox, it is useful to add a new tab to the toolbox and place your controls on it. That way, you can keep your custom controls separate from the standard Visual Basic .NET controls.

To add a new tab to the toolbox, you right-click the toolbox to bring up the menu shown in Figure 21.8.

FIGURE 21.8
Adding a new tab to the toolbox.

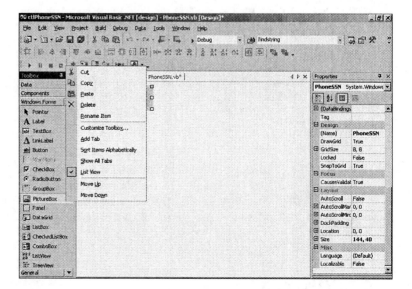

You then select the Add Tab option that appears near the middle of the menu. A text box appears at the bottom of the toolbox. Type **My Controls** (or whatever you would like to name the new tab) in the text box and press the Enter key. The new tab then appears on the toolbox. We will come back to this tab later in this chapter.

The Remaining PhoneSSN Class Code

Listing 21.2 presents the remaining code for your custom control. The code for the properties should look familiar to you by now. However, you need to learn about the new methods for the control. These new methods are discussed in the following sections.

LISTING 21.2   The Remaining Code for the **PhoneSSN** Class

```
'           AreaCode()

<Description("The area code or first three digits of SSN.")> _
 Property AreaCode() As String
 Get
  Return Me.txtAreaCode.Text
 End Get
 Set(ByVal Value As String)
  Me.txtAreaCode.Text = Value
 End Set
End Property

'           Exchange()
<Description("The phone exchange or middle two digits of SSN.")> _
 Property Exchange() As String
 Get
  Return Me.txtExchange.Text
 End Get
 Set(ByVal Value As String)
  Me.txtExchange.Text = Value
 End Set
End Property

'           Number()
<Description("The last four digits of phone number or SSN.")> _
 Property Number() As String
 Get
  Return Me.txtNumber.Text
 End Get
 Set(ByVal Value As String)
  Me.txtNumber.Text = Value
 End Set
End Property

'           Complete()
<Description("A complete phone number or SSN.")> _
 Property Complete() As String
 Get
```

LISTING 21.2 Continued

```
    If mBoxType = Selection.Phone Then
     mComplete = "(" & Me.txtAreaCode.Text & ") " & _
          Me.txtExchange.Text & "-" & _
Me.txtNumber.Text
    Else
     mComplete = Me.txtAreaCode.Text & "-" & Me.txtExchange.Text & "-" & _
Me.txtNumber.Text
    End If
    Return mComplete
   End Get
   Set(ByVal Value As String)
    Me.txtNumber.Text = Value
   End Set
  End Property


  '============ Class methods ============

  ' These constants are derived by taking the ratio of box width to the
  ' control width. This is a little bit of ugliness, but it works.
  Private Const TWODIGITS As Single = 0.19
  Private Const THREEDIGITS As Single = 0.238
  Private Const FOURDIGITS As Single = 0.286

  Protected Overrides Sub OnFontChanged(ByVal e As System.EventArgs)
   MyBase.OnFontChanged(e)
   ResizeFieldBoxes()
  End Sub

  Private Sub PhoneSSNTextBox_Resize(ByVal sender As Object, _
                    ByVal e As System.EventArgs) _
Handles MyBase.Resize
   ResizeFieldBoxes()
  End Sub

  Private Sub ResizeFieldBoxes()
   Dim ControlWidth As Integer = Me.ClientRectangle.Width
   Dim ControlHeight As Integer = Me.ClientRectangle.Height
   Dim TwoBox, ThreeBox, FourBox As Integer

   If ControlHeight < 24 Then     ' Set a minimum control height
    ControlHeight = 32
    Me.Height = 32
   End If

   If ControlWidth < 104 Then     ' Set a minimum control width
    ControlWidth = 104
    Me.Width = ControlWidth
   End If
```

LISTING 21.2   Continued

```
    TwoBox = ControlWidth * TWODIGITS    ' Set relative sizes
    ThreeBox = ControlWidth * THREEDIGITS
    FourBox = ControlWidth * FOURDIGITS

    txtAreaCode.SetBounds(8, 8, ThreeBox, 0)

    If mBoxType = Selection.Phone Then
     txtExchange.SetBounds(ThreeBox + 8, 8, ThreeBox, 0)
     txtNumber.SetBounds(ThreeBox * 2 + 8, 8, FourBox, 0)
    Else
     txtExchange.SetBounds(ThreeBox + 8, 8, TwoBox, 0)
     txtNumber.SetBounds(ThreeBox + TwoBox + 8, 8, FourBox, 0)
    End If

   End Sub

End Class
```

The `Resizing()` Event Code

The methods for the `PhoneSSN` class are primarily concerned with what happens when the user attempts to resize the control. The resizing code for the control is fairly simple because you need to worry about changing only the control's horizontal dimension. This is true because you cannot resize the height of a text box. The only time the height of a text box is changed is in response to a change in the font size or if the text box has the `Multiline` property set to logic `True`.

Font Changes and Resizing

The first method in the `PhoneSSN` class is used to override the `OnFontChanged()` method of the standard `TextBox` control. The `Protected` access specifier is used to limit access to this method for this (and, possibly, any derived) class. Recall from Chapter 18, "Polymorphism," that `Overrides` means that you want this code to be called instead of the code in the base class. The code presented here, however, simply serves as a wrapper around the `OnFontChanged()` call to the base class (via `MyBase.OnFontChanged()`) plus the call to the `ResizeFieldBoxes()` method.

The effect of the `PhoneSSNTextBox()` resizing procedure is to let the base class `OnFontChanged()` method handle most of the work associated with sizing the text boxes in response to a font change. When `OnFontChanged()` finishes its work, you call your own resizing procedure to do the special processing you need for the `PhoneSSN` control.

Resizing the Text Boxes

The `ResizeFieldBoxes()` method is concerned with maintaining the relative sizes of the text boxes if the user changes the size of the `PhoneSSN` control. The method begins by getting the current size of the `PhoneSSN` control and assigning the width and height to `ControlWidth` and `ControlHeight`. You use these two measurements in a couple `If` statements to make sure the user doesn't shrink the control below a size that would obscure the text boxes.

Next, you set three working variables to values that represent the relative width of each text box as a ratio of the control's width. For example, the variable `TwoBox` is the relative control width necessary to hold two-digit characters. `ThreeBox` and `FourBox` are designed to hold three- and four-digit characters, respectively.

The call to the `SetBounds()` method is derived from the `UserControl` class and is used to set the bounds of the control. Therefore, this statement sets the size and location of the `txtAreaCode` text box 8 pixels in from the left side of the control and 8 pixels down from the top of the control:

```
txtAreaCode.SetBounds(8, 8, ThreeBox, 0)
```

The `ThreeBox` variable sets the width of the text box (which is a relative measure of the current width of the control). The last argument in the call is the height of the control, but only a font change can alter the text box height, so you set the height argument to `0`.

Programmer's Tip

As a general rule, any time Visual Basic .NET uses x,y-coordinates in a procedure call, the x-coordinate (horizontal) is presented first, and the y-coordinate (vertical) is presented second.

The `If` statement block checks whether the control is formatting a phone number or an SSN by examining the current state of `mBoxType`. Calls to `SetBounds()` size the remaining two text boxes accordingly.

That's it! All you need to do now is create a test program to see if the control works.

Testing the PhoneSSN Control

At this point, you're all dressed up with no place to go. An inherited user control like `PhoneSSN` cannot exist by itself. Your new control needs a host form in which to exist. Therefore, you need to add a new Windows project before you can proceed.

Adding the TestPS Project

To add a new Windows project, you select File, Add Project, New Project, and then select Windows Application from the New Project dialog box. You should name the project `TestPS` and then name the new form `frmTestPS` and change the `Text` property to `"Test of the PhoneSSN control"`.

At this point, you have two projects showing in the Code window, and you need to tell Visual Basic .NET which one will serve as the startup project. To do so, in the Solution Explorer window, right-click the `TestPS` project and click the Set As Startup Project menu option. Then you can compile the project.

Adding the PhoneSSN Control to the Toolbox

You can now add your custom **PhoneSSN** control to the toolbox. To do this, you click the My Controls tab that you added to the toolbox. This brings that tab to the foreground, although there is nothing on it yet. Next, you right-click the My Controls tab, which brings up a menu selection. Finally, you should click Customize Toolbox and then click the .NET Framework Components tab. You should see a dialog box similar to the one shown in Figure 21.9.

FIGURE 21.9

The Customize Toolbox dialog box.

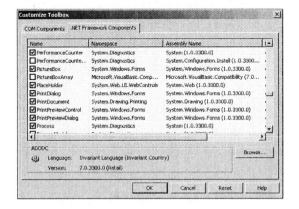

Next you need to click the Browse button in the dialog box and locate the dynamic link library (DLL) file that was generated by the compilation. The file should be located in the **bin** directory of the control project. For example, you created the **ctlPhoneSSN** project in directory **VBTemp** on drive **D**. Therefore, you should find your DLL file in **D:\VBTemp\ctlPhoneSSN\bin**, and the file should be named **ctlPhoneSSN.dll**. If you select the file, the display changes to that shown in Figure 21.10.

FIGURE 21.10

The Customize Toolbox dialog box after the **ctlPhoneSSN.dll** file is selected.

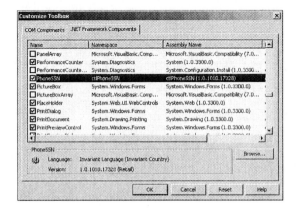

Your DLL file is added to the list of controls, as shown in Figure 21.10. After you click the OK button, the new control should appear on the My Controls tab.

If you double-click the new `PhoneSSN` control, a copy of the control should appear on the test form (that is, `frmTestPS`). Your screen should look like the one shown in Figure 21.11.

FIGURE 21.11
The test form after the
`PhoneSSN` control is
added.

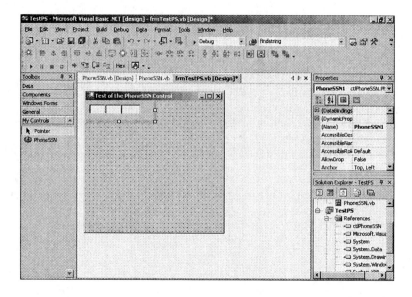

At this point, you should be able to resize the control and see the text boxes change. Note that the height of the text boxes should not change unless you select a new font size. (Try selecting the `Font` property and changing it to a point size of **16**. What happens to the `PhoneSSN` control?)

Now you should add a new text box named `txtOutput`, a label, and two buttons named `btnTest` and `btnExit`, as shown in Figure 21.1. The code in Listing 21.3 shows the complete test code.

LISTING 21.3   Test Code for the `frmTestPS` Project

```
Public Class frmTestPS
 Inherits System.Windows.Forms.Form

' Windows Form Designer generated code


 Private Sub btnTest_Click(ByVal sender As System.Object, ByVal e As _
          System.EventArgs) Handles btnTest.Click
  txtOutput.Text = PhoneSSN1.Complete
 End Sub

 Private Sub btnExit_Click(ByVal sender As System.Object, ByVal e As _
          System.EventArgs) Handles btnExit.Click
  Me.Dispose()
 End Sub
End Class
```

You should click the **PhoneSSN1** control and then move the cursor to the **BoxType** property field. If you click the drop-down icon that appears in the field, you should see the two type members you declared for the **Selection Enum** (see Figure 21.12). The fact that you can see the **Phone** and **SSN** choices in the **InputType** property field tells you that the **UserControl** class is correctly managing our field choices.

FIGURE 21.12
BoxType property
choices.

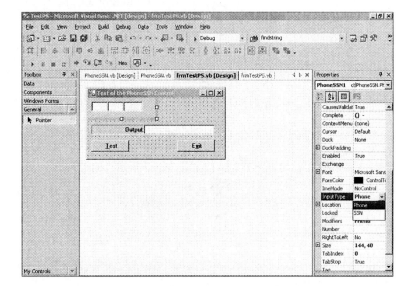

Now you should compile and run the project. You should be able to type in a phone number or an SSN and click the Test button and then see the result of the test. This statement shows how to access the **mComplete** class member through its property **Get()** procedure:

```
txtOutput.Text = PhoneSSN1.Complete
```

Handling Events

Until this point, this chapter has purposely glossed over how event handling works in Visual Basic .NET. But now that you know how to create your own controls, you need to understand what Visual Basic .NET is doing whenever it creates some event-handling code for you. The following sections help you understand this.

Signatures of Event Handlers

In virtually all the program examples in this book so far, there has been an Exit button, the code for which looks like this:

```
Private Sub btnExit_Click(ByVal sender As System.Object, ByVal e As _
        System.EventArgs) Handles btnExit.Click
  Me.Dispose()
End Sub
```

By default, the event `Sub` procedure is created by using the `Private` access specifier. By convention, standard events are named with the control name, followed by an underscore character, followed by the event name:

```
NameOfControl_EventName
```

This is also called the *method name* of the event. For an Exit button, this would be the `Click()` event method name:

```
BtnExit_Click
```

The method name is always followed by an opening parenthesis, a sender object, the arguments for the event, a closing parenthesis, the keyword `Handles`, the control name, the dot operator, and finally the event name. Collectively, these parts of the statement define the *signature* of the event. For example, this is the signature for the `BtnExit_Click()` event:

```
Private Sub btnExit_Click(ByVal sender As System.Object, ByVal e As _
        System.EventArgs) Handles btnExit.Click
```

All the standard controls provided by Visual Basic .NET have predefined event handlers. For example, consider the `btnExit` button as presented in Listing 21.3. While you're in the Code window, you should select the `btnExit` button from the drop-down list of controls and then click in the Declarations section. You should then see a list of predefined event handlers for the `Button` object, as shown in Figure 21.13.

FIGURE 21.13

Predefined event handlers for a Visual Basic .NET `Button` object.

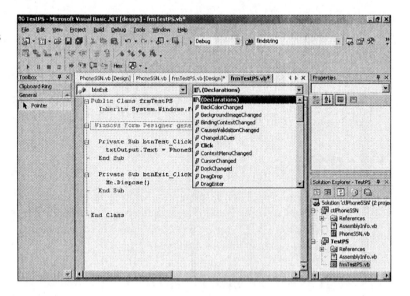

If you click the plus sign for the line in Figure 21.13 that reads `Windows Form Designer generated code` and plow through the code you find there, you should eventually locate this line:

```
Friend WithEvents btnExit As System.Windows.Forms.Button
```

This statement tells Visual Basic .NET that `btnExit` is a `Button` object. The `WithEvents` keyword tells Visual Basic .NET that `btnExit` can generate, or raise, `Button` object–type events. The drop-down list shown in Figure 21.13 is a list of the events that a `Button` object can raise.

If you click one of the events shown in the drop-down list, Visual Basic .NET automatically generates the skeleton code for that event. For example, if you click the `BackColorChanged` option, Visual Basic .NET generates the following statement stub:

```
Private Sub btnExit_BackColorChanged(ByVal sender As Object, ByVal e As _
        System.EventArgs) Handles btnExit.BackColorChanged

End Sub
```

You can add whatever code you want to execute if the `BackColorChanged()` event is fired while the program runs.

Senders, Delegates, and Event Handlers

The button object is often called the *sender* in event processing. In other words, when you click the Exit button, the program sends a `Click()` event message to Visual Basic .NET, saying: "Hey, Visual Basic .NET! The user just clicked on my `btnExit` button." Visual Basic .NET then says to itself: "Oh great. Who is responsible for handling the `btnExit` object's `Click()` event?" Visual Basic .NET then looks through its list of event delegates. A *delegate* is simply another class created by Visual Basic .NET that holds references to the events that it can process. A delegate reference is really a pointer to the procedure that is assigned to handle the event. For example, Visual Basic .NET looks though its list of delegates until it finds the signature that says: `Handles btnExit.Click`. Visual Basic .NET then transfers control to that event handler.

As you have probably already guessed, an *event handler* is simply the code that processes an event. In your program, this procedure is the event that handles the `btnExit` object's `Click()` event:

```
Private Sub btnExit_Click(ByVal sender As System.Object, ByVal e As _
          System.EventArgs) Handles btnExit.Click
 Me.Dispose()
End Sub
```

The `Handles btnExit.Click` at the end of the first statement line is a pretty good clue as to which event is to be processed by this code. When the event handler handles this event, the program simply releases the form and ends the program.

Although this is a pretty slimmed-down explanation, you should be able to decipher what an event handler does and what an event is. For additional information on event handling, you can investigate the online help system.

Summary

In this chapter you have learned how to create your own custom control by extending an existing control. This illustrates the power that inheritance brings to the object-oriented programming table. Just think of all the code you would have to write for your custom control if you were not able to inherit the base functionality of the `TextBox` control!

The `PhoneSSN` control is useful, but it could benefit from some additional work. For example, it should ensure that the data entered in each of the text boxes is numeric only. Also, you might add some formatting options for the phone number. Some people prefer phone numbers in the (123)456-7890 format, and others prefer 123-456-7890 or 123.456.7890. You could use the `Enum` technique presented in this chapter to add a new format property to accommodate these different styles.

Although modifying the code presented in this chapter is a good learning experience, you will learn a lot more if you try to build your own custom control from scratch. I won't even begin to tell you about all the flat-forehead mistakes I made while creating my first custom control. Still, it is an invaluable way to learn how all the pieces discussed in this chapter fit together, so give it a try!

Review Questions

1. What is the first step when designing a new control?

A. The first step is to determine that the control doesn't already exist. Very often the most cost-effective way to implement a new control is to buy it. This is particularly true for commercial software development. If you cannot find exactly what you want in the marketplace, the next step is to determine if you can extend an existing control to suit your needs. More often than not, you can use inheritance to expand the functionality of an existing control. The last resort is to write the control from scratch.

2. If you have the Standard Edition of Visual Basic .NET and wish to develop your own controls, how can you develop your own controls?

A. You can't. Your only alternative is to upgrade your version of Visual Studio.

3. What control considerations should you make part of your control's design?

A. It's very easy to lose sight of the fact that consistency is crucial to programmer productivity. Earlier Visual Basic controls use names like Title, Text, and Caption to write textual information on the control. Even after years of experience, I still had to look up which was which for controls I didn't use that often. Visual Basic .NET does a much better job by consistently using the `Text` property for text that is displayed on a control. As much as possible, follow the lead set by other controls when defining its properties.

4. Looking at the IDE, it appears that developing a control and developing a program are the same. What's the difference?

A. A major difference is that when you are finished developing a control, you have a dynamic link library (DLL) file that you can use in other programs. The result of control development is not an executable program.

5. How do you make the component attributes of a control available to the programmer?

A. You must include the statement:

```
Imports System.ComponentModel
```

in your code to allow the programmer to interact with your control via the Properties window.

6. How do you make a custom control available for inclusion in a program?

A. You need to make Visual Basic .NET aware that the control exists. The easiest way to do this is by placing the new control on the toolbox. To do this, right-click on the toolbox and select the Customize Toolbox option. Now select the .NET Framework Components tab and click the Browse button to locate and select the dynamic link library file that holds the custom control. Visual Basic .NET now adds the custom control to the toolbox. From that point on, you use the control like any other control on the toolbox.

CHAPTER 22

VISUAL BASIC .NET GRAPHICS

You will learn about the following in this chapter:

- The basics of the Visual Basic .NET graphics system

- How to use the Visual Basic .NET coordinate system

- How to use a picture box

- How to use the OpenFileDialog control

- How to use aspect ratio

- How to use graphics line drawing and filling

- How to use graphics pens and brushes

- How to create a graphics control object

This chapter examines how Visual Basic .NET can be used to display various graphics objects on a computer screen (also called a *display*). There are two main topics in this chapter. The first topic discusses how you can use the Visual Basic .NET PictureBox control to display images on your display. The sample program you will develop introduces you to the Visual Basic .NET OpenFileDialog control, too. The second topic shows how to actually draw your own graphics objects. You will write a sample program to develop a simple gauge control, using some of the concepts you learned in Chapter 21, "Creating Your Own Controls."

However, before you jump into the sample programs, you need a little graphics background information.

Your Computer Display

As you probably know, your display consists of thousands of tiny dots called *pixels* (that is, picture elements). Most displays are capable of showing different numbers of pixels. You can access the display settings information by selecting Start, Settings, Control Panel, Display and then selecting the Settings tab. Figure 22.1 demonstrates how to determine your current display setting.

FIGURE 22.1

Determining your display setting by using the Control Panel's Display program.

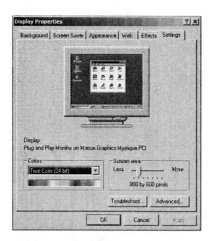

As I am writing this book, I have the display set to 800×600 pixels. You might hear this setting referred to as the *display resolution*. If you do some quick math, you find that my current display resolution uses 480,000 pixels to present information onscreen.

You can change your display resolution by moving the slider control shown in Figure 22.1. If you increase the resolution, everything onscreen gets relatively smaller. This is because you are spreading the same display information over a larger number of pixels. It is important that you understand this because when you start doing graphics programming, what you see in this book might not be what you get. If your display resolution is different from mine, your graphics output might look different.

Display resolution is not the only thing that affects graphics displays. You might see information about a display such as ".26 dot pitch." What's that all about? The dot pitch parameter actually measures the spacing (in millimeters) between the pixels on the screen. As a general rule, the smaller the dot pitch value, the better the quality of any image shown on the display.

Back in the old days, some displays actually had dot pitch values approaching .50. This means that there was a relatively large amount of black space between the pixels. As a result, an all-white screen actually looked gray because the human brain mixes the white pixels with the black background. The higher the dot pitch number, the more black there is between pixels. The result is that colors look subdued and less crisp than on displays that have lower dot pitch numbers. Therefore, an image that looks great on one monitor with a low dot pitch number might look faded or washed out on a monitor with a higher dot pitch.

The Visual Basic .NET Graphics Coordinate System

Windows and Visual Basic .NET use a coordinate system to determine which pixels have which colors. Most modern displays support 24-bit color, which means there are more than 16.7 million possible colors for each pixel. The .NET Framework uses the Graphics Device Interface Plus (GDI+) to manage just about everything that happens on the display.

Every display pixel is uniquely identified by its coordinates. For two-dimensional images, each pixel has an x-coordinate and a y-coordinate. The *x-coordinate* measures the horizontal distance relative to the left edge of the display. The *y-coordinate* measures the vertical distance relative to the top of the display. This system is shown in Figure 22.2.

FIGURE 22.2
The x,y-coordinate system for display pixels.

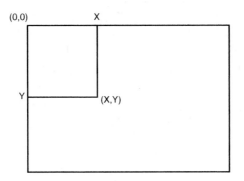

The Visual Basic .NET coordinate system is a little different from what you learned in your high school math class. Most of us are used to thinking of the lower-left corner as the origin (0,0) of a graph, and we extend that expectation to computer graphics. Alas, the Visual Basic .NET graphics coordinate system is different.

The GDI+ system uses the upper-left corner of the display as the origin of the coordinate system. Increasing values of the x-coordinate represent horizontal movement from left to right. You should feel right at home with the x-coordinate and its direction of movement.

It's the y-coordinate movement that throws a curve. You are probably used to thinking of increasing values of y as moving from the bottom of the graph upward. For the GDI+ coordinate system, it's exactly the opposite. Increasing the y-coordinate moves you from the top of the display toward the bottom.

So if my display resolution is 800×600, the lower-right corner of my display has the x,y-coordinates (800,600). A pixel in the center of the display would be found at coordinates (400,300).

Although the display coordinate system might seem a bit weird right now, with a little practice, it will all begin to make sense. This chapter uses the Visual Basic .NET `PictureBox` control to introduce the Visual Basic .NET graphics system.

The `PictureBox` Control

You can use the `PictureBox` control in a variety of ways in the Visual Basic .NET graphics system. At the moment, you should be concerned with its capability to display images. Simply stated, the `PictureBox` control serves as a container within which you can display the types of images shown in Table 22.1.

TABLE 22.1   Image File Formats Supported by the Visual Basic .NET `PictureBox` Control

Image Type	Description
BMP	Bitmap. This is a common Windows image format. BMP files tend to be very large.
GIF	Graphics Image Format. GIF uses a simple, easy-to-program, run-length-encoding scheme to reduce file size. It was very popular in the early 1990s, until a licensing agreement just about killed it.
ICO	Icon. ICO is the standard image format for Windows icons.
JPG	Joint Photographic Experts Group (JPEG). JPG uses a compression algorithm to reduce the storage requirements.
WMF	Windows metafile. WMF is the standard file format for storing Windows metafiles.

Image Storage Size

The earliest PC display devices did not support color. Therefore, an image could store each pixel as a single bit. The pixel was either on or off. Eventually, color displays (for example, Color Graphics Adaptor [CGA] displays) became available, although they were pretty crude by today's standards. As display devices became more technologically advanced, each pixel gained greater capability to display an ever-increasing range of colors. Today's image devices typically use 24 bits to represent the color value for a single pixel. For example, even low-end digital cameras are capable of 1600×1200 image sizes. A little quick arithmetic shows that a color image from a digital camera could require up to 5.5MB of disk storage.

Although disk storage is relatively inexpensive today, the time to load a 5MB image is still noticeable. Smaller image sizes have smaller footprints on the hard drive and quicker load times. Therefore, there has always been a drive to shrink the storage requirements for images while maintaining their quality and fidelity. The GIF and JPEG formats both seek to compress the image storage size while maintaining the image's quality.

In fact, the image shown in Figure 22.6 later in this chapter was stored as both a 1600×1200 BMP image and a JPEG image. That image is a busy image in that it has lots of contrasting textures and colors. Such images do not lend themselves to image compression as well as less busy images do. The BMP version of the image took 5.626M of file storage space. When the image was converted to a JPEG file, the storage requirement dropped to 610KB! This means the converted JPEG image is about 11% of its bitmap size, yet to the human eye there is no noticeable difference in the image quality. There are some very bright people out there!

The `Imageviewer` Project

Your first project in this chapter is a simple image viewer based on the Visual Basic .NET `PictureBox` control. You need to create a new project called `PictureBox` and place a `PictureBox` control and two command buttons on the form, as shown in Figure 22.3.

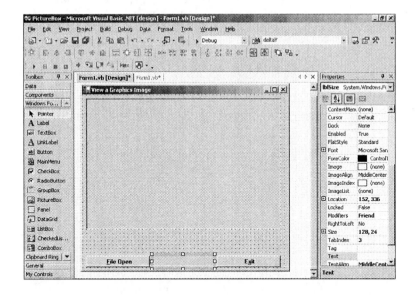

As you can see in Figure 22.3, the PictureBox control is the large panel-looking object on the form. You set the initial size of the PictureBox control to the values 416×272. Because Visual Basic .NET expresses all graphics objects in terms of pixels, the first pixel displayed on the picture box would be at coordinates (0,0), or the upper-left corner of the PictureBox. Similarly, the last pixel shown would be at coordinates (416,272), or the lower-right corner of the PictureBox.

All pixel coordinates for the PictureBox image are expressed in terms of the PictureBox coordinates, not in terms of the form itself. The fact that you placed the PictureBox control on the form at coordinates (8,8) has no bearing on the image displayed in the PictureBox.

The two buttons on the form are named btnOpen and btnExit. Between these two buttons is a label object named lblSize. You will use this label to display the original image size. You set its TextAlign property to MiddleCenter. In addition to these controls, there is a new control in the project—the OpenFileDialog control, which is described in the following section.

The OpenFileDialog Control

To locate the OpenFileDialog control, you need to scroll the toolbox's Windows Forms tab until you see the OpenFileDialog control. Then you should double-click the OpenFileDialog control to move it into your project. Your display should look similar to the one shown in Figure 22.4.

Notice that the OpenFileDialog control does not actually appear on the form itself; rather, it is displayed in its own window below the form. (The OpenFileDialog control is not an object that is visible at runtime, which is one reason it is placed in its own window at design time.)

FIGURE 22.4

The `OpenFileDialog` control.

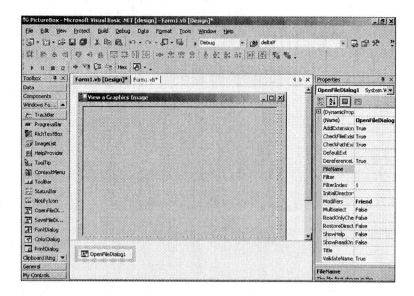

Programmer's Tip

Some programmers refer to the window where the `OpenFileDialog` control is placed as the *component tray*. Visual Basic .NET typically places controls that are not visible at runtime in the component tray. You will see additional examples of the component tray in Chapter 25, "Database Programming with Visual Basic .NET."

The `OpenFileDialog` control has a number of properties that you can set. At the top of the Properties window you can see an expandable entry named `DynamicProperties`. If you expand this entry and click the Advanced button, you see a list of the dynamic `OpenFileDialog` properties that are available. For the sake of this example, you need to use only a few of these properties. (You can use the Visual Basic .NET online help system to get details about the properties that are not used in this chapter.)

Listing 22.1 shows the code that is necessary to use the `OpenFileDialog` control in your project.

LISTING 22.1   The `btnOpen` Code for the `OpenFileDialog` Control

```
Private Sub btnOpen_Click(ByVal sender As System.Object, ByVal e As _
System.EventArgs) Handles btnOpen.Click
Dim path As String
Static InitialSize As Size = PictureBox1.Size ' Save original ctrl size

PictureBox1.Size = InitialSize          ' Reset the control size

With OpenFileDialog1              ' Initialize the file dialog
  .Filter = "Bitmap (*.BMP)¦*.bmp¦Icon (*.ICO)¦*.ICO¦GIF (*.GIF)_
```

LISTING 22.1   Continued

```
          ¦*.GIF¦Metafile (*.WMF)¦*.WMF¦JPEG (*.JPG)¦*.JPG"
 .FilterIndex = 5
 .InitialDirectory = "C:\"
 .Title = "Select Image File"
End With

If OpenFileDialog1.ShowDialog() = DialogResult.OK Then ' File selected?
 path = OpenFileDialog1.FileName
 Me.Text = "View a Graphics Image  " & path
 CalculateControlSize(path)
End If

End Sub
```

The code in Listing 22.1 starts with a definition of InitialSize as Static. Recall from Chapter 8, "Scope and Lifetime of Variables," that a Static data type has the scope of a local variable but a lifetime equal to that of the project. Therefore, InitialSize will retain the original size of the PictureBox for the life of the program. This means that InitialSize is set at program startup and is never reset thereafter. So what?

The reason you need to preserve the original size is that you use the control's size to fit each image within the PictureBox control. If you load in relatively small images, the PictureBox control is resized to fit the smaller picture. The next picture, therefore, would be forced to fit into the now-smaller PictureBox control. If you kept reading smaller images, eventually the PictureBox control would get so small you wouldn't be able to see the image. By resizing the PictureBox control to its original size each time you read another image, you ensure that you won't fall prey to the ever-shrinking-PictureBox-control problem.

The code then uses the With loop structure to move through the OpenFileDialog1 collection. The first property is the Filter property. The Filter property is used to limit the types of files that are shown in the dialog box. Therefore, Visual Basic .NET uses this statement:

```
.Filter = "Bitmap (*.BMP)¦*.bmp¦Icon (*.ICO)¦*.ICO¦GIF (*.GIF)_
     ¦*.GIF¦Metafile (*.WMF)¦*.WMF¦JPEG (*.JPG)¦*.JPG"
```

to place the file choices in the drop-down list box that is part of the OpenFileDialog control. This is shown in Figure 22.5.

Notice that the options presented in the drop-down list box shown in Figure 22.5 match the file choices shown in the code in Listing 22.1.

In the Filter property statement, each drop-down choice has two parts. The first part (for example, Bitmap (*.BMP)) is the string that is shown in the list box when the drop-down arrow is clicked. The second component (for example, *.bmp) is used by Visual Basic .NET as a file search parameter if that particular option is selected. These two parts are separated by the vertical bar character (|). Collectively, these two parts form one file type that might appear in the list box. You can create multiple file types by simply separating each file option with another vertical bar.

FIGURE 22.5

The drop-down list box in the `OpenFileDialog` control.

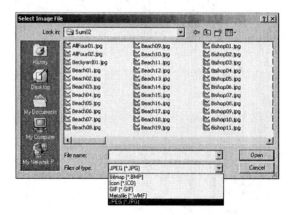

The second property in the collection is `FilterIndex`. This property simply tells Visual Basic .NET which option to place in the list box as the default choice. You need to set this to **5** if you want to show the JPEG image format as the default choice. Note that the index is 1 based, not 0 based, which is why the JPEG choice is **5** instead of **4**.

The third property is `InitialDirectory`. This string causes Visual Basic .NET to use the directory that is specified as the starting point for locating the image files.

The fourth property is `Title`. This string is displayed in the title bar of the `OpenFileDialog` control. The string you select gives the user a hint as to the purpose of the dialog box.

The `ShowDialog()` Method

The `ShowDialog()` method causes Visual Basic .NET to display the `OpenFileDialog` control onscreen, using the properties that you have set. The screen should look similar to the one shown in Figure 22.5. The `ShowDialog()` method returns an `Enum` data type named `DialogResult` that may return the values `Abort`, `Cancel`, `Ignore`, `No`, `None`, `OK`, `Retry`, or `Yes`. You use an `If` statement to test `DialogResult` to make sure valid data is returned from the `OpenFileDialog1` control.

In the `If` statement block, you set a variable named **path** to hold the path and name of the image file. You copy this information to the title bar of the form so that the users know which image file they are viewing. The code then calls the `CalculateControlSize()` procedure to do the rest of the work.

The `CalculateControlSize()` Procedure

The real work for the image viewer is done in the `CalculateControlSize()` procedure. The code for this procedure is shown in Listing 22.2.

LISTING 22.2   The `CalculateControlSize()` Procedure

```vb
Private Sub CalculateControlSize(ByVal path As String)
Dim OriginalX, OriginalY As Integer
Dim NewSize As Size
Dim Aspect As Double
Dim pic As Image = Image.FromFile(path)

OriginalX = PictureBox1.Size.Width    ' Original control size
OriginalY = PictureBox1.Size.Height

lblSize.Text = "(" & CStr(pic.Width) & "x" & CStr(pic.Height) & ")"
Aspect = CDbl(pic.Height) / CDbl(pic.Width)  ' Find the aspect ratio

If Aspect < 1.0 Then          ' If height less than width
 NewSize.Height = CInt(Aspect * OriginalX)
 NewSize.Width = OriginalX
 PictureBox1.Size = NewSize
Else                    ' width less than height
 NewSize.Width = CInt(OriginalY / Aspect)
 NewSize.Height = OriginalY
 PictureBox1.Size = NewSize
End If

' Force image to fit the control
PictureBox1.SizeMode = PictureBoxSizeMode.StretchImage
' Load the picture into the control.
PictureBox1.Image = Image.FromFile(path)

End Sub
```

The code in Listing 22.2 defines some working variables, of which `pic` is the most interesting. The `pic` variable is an instance of an `Image` object that is initialized to the file selected by the user. (You pass the image filename to the procedure by using the `path` argument.) This allows you to determine the height and width of the selected image. You can use these parameters to determine the aspect ratio of the image and to display those parameters on the `lblSize` label. The following section discusses the aspect ratio, which is a critical element in properly displaying images.

The Aspect Ratio

In Listing 22.2, the variables `OriginalX` and `OriginalY` hold the size of the `PictureBox` control. Because you set the size of the `PictureBox` control by using the `Static` variable `InitialSize` in the `btnOpen` object's `Click()` event, `OriginalX` and `OriginalY` are always set to `416` and `272`. These values will rarely equal the exact dimensions of the image you are about to view. Therefore, you need to resize the `PictureBox` control relative to the image size. You do this by calculating the aspect ratio of the image.

The *aspect ratio* is simply the height of the image relative to its width. For example, if you select an image with the pixel dimensions 1600×1200, the aspect ratio is .75 (that is, .75 =

1200 / 1600). The problem is that the `PictureBox` control has an aspect ratio of .6538 (that is, .6538 = 272 / 416). It's the old round-peg-square-hole problem. If you try to shoehorn the image into the `PictureBox` control by using its current size, the image will look distorted. Not good.

You can use the aspect ratio to solve two display problems. First, you want to display the image without having to use scrollbars. Well, there's no way the original 1600×1200 image size is going to fit into a 416×272 `PictureBox` control without scrollbars unless you resize the image or the `PictureBox` control—or both.

The `If` statement block tests the `Aspect` variable, which is the aspect ratio for the current image. If the aspect ratio is less than 1.0, you know the image is wider than it is tall. In that case, you use the aspect ratio to adjust the height of the `PictureBox` control and then set the width to its original value. Some actual numbers will help explain how this works.

Suppose you select an image that is 1600×1200. In that case, `Aspect` would equal .75, which would cause the `If` test to execute this statement:

```
NewSize.Height = CInt(Aspect * OriginalX)
```

which resolves to this:

```
312 = CInt(.75 * 416)
```

This sets the `Height` member of the `NewSize` object to 312. The next statement sets the `Width` member of the `NewSize` object to its original value, `416`:

```
NewSize.Width = OriginalX
```

The next statement uses these new parameters to resize the `PictureBox` control to its new dimensions, 416×312:

```
PictureBox1.Size = NewSize
```

If you divide 312 by 416, you find that it equals .75, which is exactly the aspect ratio of the image you want to display. Because the relative size of the `PictureBox` control matches the aspect ratio of the image, you can display the image without distortion.

If you want to view an image whose height is greater than its width, the aspect ratio is greater than 1.0 and the `Else` statement block is executed. If you work through the math, you find that the `Else` statement block in Listing 22.2 adjusts the width of the `PictureBox` control to maintain the image's aspect ratio.

This statement sets the `SizeMode` property to `StretchImage`:

```
PictureBox1.SizeMode = PictureBoxSizeMode.StretchImage
```

This tells Visual Basic .NET to scale the incoming image to fit within the confines of the (now resized) `PictureBox` control.

Programmer's Tip

You are not limited to forcing an image to fit into a control. You can set the `SizeMode` property to other values. `Normal` places the image in the upper-left corner of the control. If the image is larger than the control, the rest of the image is clipped. `CenterImage` centers the image within the control. If the image is larger than the control, the image's outside edges are clipped. `AutoSize` causes the size of the control to be scaled to match the size of the image.

The final statement loads the image into the picture box and displays it:

```
PictureBox1.Image = Image.FromFile(path)
```

A sample run of the program is shown in Figure 22.6.

FIGURE 22.6

A sample run of the `Imageviewer` project.

The only code not shown for the `Imageviewer` project is the code for the `btnExit` object's `Click()` event, which you already know how to write. As you can see from the sample program, viewing an image with Visual Basic .NET is very easy. In the next section, you will learn how to draw your own graphics objects.

Creating Your Own Graphics Objects

In this section, you'll learn how to use some of the graphics primitives provided by Visual Basic .NET to draw your own graphics objects. Rather than just read about graphics objects, you will build a simple gauge control by using Visual Basic .NET's `Graphics` objects. You will develop the `Gauge` control by using the techniques you learned in Chapter 21. When you are finished, you will have a new control that you can use in other projects.

You should start by creating a new project and then selecting the Add User Control menu option. You should name the new control `Gauge`. The following section shows you how to start adding the code to the `Gauge` control.

The Gauge Control Code

Listing 22.3 shows the members of the Gauge control class.

LISTING 22.3   The Data Members for the Gauge Control

```
Imports System.ComponentModel

Public Class Gauge
 Inherits System.Windows.Forms.UserControl

 ' Windows Form Designer generated code

 '================== Data Members =====================
 Private mMin As Double      'Minimum gauge value
 Private mMax As Double      'Maximum gauge value
 Private mDanger As Double     'Redline danger value
 Private mCaution As Double    'Yellowline cautionary value
 Private mRange As Double     'The range of gauge values
 Private mCurrent As Double    'Current gauge value
 Private mTick As Double      'A tick mark on the scale

 Private mGap As Integer      'The range between tick marks
 Private mTall As Integer     'How tall is the gauge
 Private mWide As Integer     'How wide is the gauge
 Private mLeftSide As Integer  'Where is the left side of the gauge
 Private mTopSide As Integer   'Where is the top of the gauge
```

Listing 22.3 begins by importing System.ComponentModel so you can classify each member and display a help message in the Properties window.

The purpose of each data member of the Gauge control is fairly clear from their names and comments in Listing 22.3. There are, however, two members that may be hard to figure out. The mDanger member allows the user to specify a value at which the color of the gauge changes to red. The mCaution member allows the user to set a value that causes the gauge to display yellow. Together, these two members allow the user to create the effect of redline and yellowline values for the gauge.

The mRange member is the range of values that should be displayed on the gauge. This is set by subtracting mMin from mMax. mTick is set by dividing mRange by 5 and is used for placing the scale values on the gauge. (To simplify things a bit, the number of scale values displayed is limited to five.) The remaining members are used to actually draw the control.

Listing 22.4 shows the property methods for the Gauge control.

LISTING 22.4   The Gauge Control Property Methods

```
'================== The Property Procedures =====================
<Description("The minimum gauge value"), _
Category("Appearance")> _
Property Minimum() As Double  ' Minimum
```

LISTING 22.4   Continued

```
  Get
   Return mMin
  End Get
  Set(ByVal Value As Double)
   mMin = Value
  End Set

End Property

<Description("The maximum gauge value"), _
Category("Appearance")> _
Property Maximum() As Double    ' Maximum
 Get
  Return mMax
 End Get
 Set(ByVal Value As Double)
  mMax = Value
 End Set

End Property

<Description("The gauge danger value where the color changes to red"), _
Category("Appearance")> _
Property Danger() As Double     ' The redline danger value
 Get
  Return mDanger
 End Get
 Set(ByVal Value As Double)
  mDanger = Value
 End Set
End Property

<Description("The gauge caution value where the color changes to yellow"),_
Category("Appearance")> _
Property Caution() As Double    ' The yellowline cautionary value
 Get
  Return mCaution
 End Get
 Set(ByVal Value As Double)
  mCaution = Value
 End Set
End Property

<Description("The gauge height"), _
Category("Appearance")> _
Property Tall() As Integer      ' How tall is the gauge?
 Get
  Return mTall
 End Get
 Set(ByVal Value As Integer)
  mTall = Value
 End Set
```

LISTING 22.4 Continued

```
End Property

<Description("The gauge width"), _
Category("Appearance")> _
Property Wide() As Integer      ' How wide is the gauge?
 Get
  Return mWide
 End Get
 Set(ByVal Value As Integer)
  mWide = Value
 End Set
End Property

<Description("The left edge location of the gauge"), _
Category("Appearance")> _
Property LeftSide() As Integer    ' Where's the left side of the gauge
 Get                ' on the form?
  Return mLeftSide
 End Get
 Set(ByVal Value As Integer)
  mLeftSide = Value
 End Set
End Property

<Description("The top edge location of the gauge"), _
Category("Appearance")> _
Property TopSide() As Integer     ' Where is the top of the gauge on
 Get                ' the form?
  Return mTopSide
 End Get
 Set(ByVal Value As Integer)
  mTopSide = Value
 End Set
End Property

<Description("The present value of the gauge"), _
Category("Data")> _
Property Current() As Double     ' What is current value?
 Get
  Return mCurrent
 End Get
 Set(ByVal Value As Double)
  mCurrent = Value
 End Set
End Property
```

The code in Listing 22.4 is very straightforward. Each property method simply gets or sets the appropriate value for the data member of the control. The real work for the control is done in the remaining methods. The SetGaugeParameters() and Gauge_Resize() methods are shown in Listing 22.5.

LISTING 22.5   The SetGaugeParameters() and Gauge_Resize() Methods

```
'==================== Methods ========================
Private Sub SetGaugeParameters()
  ' Purpose: This subroutine sets some of the parameters that are
  '       used by the gauge.
  '
  ' Argument list:
  '   none
  '
  ' Return value:
  '   n/a
  '
  If mCurrent > mMax Then      ' Value too large?
    mCurrent = mMax
  End If

  If mCurrent < mMin Then      ' Value too small?
    mCurrent = mMin
  End If
  mRange = mMax - mMin         ' Find the gauge range of values
  mTick = mRange / 5.0         ' Find where tick marks should start
  mGap = mTall / 5             ' Find the gaps between tick marks

End Sub

Private Sub Gauge_Resize(ByVal sender As Object, ByVal e As _
      System.EventArgs) Handles MyBase.Resize
  Dim ControlWidth As Integer = Me.ClientRectangle.Width
  Dim ControlHeight As Integer = Me.ClientRectangle.Height

  If ControlHeight < 50 Then    ' Set a minimum control height
    ControlHeight = 50
    Me.Height = 50
  End If

  If ControlWidth < 50 Then     ' Set a minimum control width
    ControlWidth = 50
    Me.Width = ControlWidth
  End If

  mTall = Me.Height * 0.9
  mTopSide = (Me.Height - mTall) / 2 ' location for top edge of gauge
  mLeftSide = Me.Width * 0.05       ' Location for left edge of the gauge
  mWide = Me.Width * 0.2            ' The width of the gauge

  Invalidate()

End Sub
```

The SetGaugeParameters() method is called to check and set some of the member values for
the gauge. For example, if the current value for the gauge (mCurrent) is greater than mMax,
mCurrent is set to mMax. Likewise, if the current value is too small, mCurrent is set to mMin.
After the current value is checked, the mRange, mTick, and mGap values are determined.

Control Resizing

You want the user to be able to resize the control, and the `Gauge_Resize()` method handles the `Resize()` event. Note that resizing is done relative to the control's size, not the size of the gauge. Because you want the gauge to be sized relative to the control's size, all your calculations for the gauge are based on the control size. Therefore, as the user resizes the control, the gauge should increase or decrease in size relative to the changes in the control's size.

This statement is used to determine the current width of the control:

```
Dim ControlWidth As Integer = Me.ClientRectangle.Width
```

`Me`, of course, refers to the `Gauge` control. The `ClientRectangle` method can be used to examine a list of parameters associated with the rectangle formed by the control. This statement returns the current width of the control. Your code examines only the width and height of the control, but the `ClientRectangle` method can be used to return additional information about the rectangle, including `Top`, `Bottom`, `Left`, `Location`, `X`, and `Y` values.

After you have determined the current size of the control, you should check to make sure the user is not trying to make the control too small. In this case, "too small" would be a control size that would not allow the gauge and its values to be displayed. You have hard-coded the minimum width and height to be 50 pixels. This value results in a fairly skinny gauge.

Programmer's Tip

If you need a thinner gauge than shown here, you can change the 50-pixel cutoff to some smaller value. However, doing so clips the scale values that are printed on the control. Therefore, if your version allows the control to assume such small values, you might want to add code to suppress writing the scale values on the control.

These statements set the properties for the new gauge size relative to the new size of the control:

```
mTall = Me.Height * 0.9
mTopSide = (Me.Height - mTall) / 2 ' location for top edge of gauge
mLeftSide = Me.Width * 0.05      ' Location for left edge of the gauge
mWide = Me.Width * 0.2           ' The width of the gauge
```

`mTall` sets the height of the gauge to be 90% of the height of the control. The next calculation sets the top of the gauge (`mTopSide`) so that the gauge is centered within the control's vertical size. The third statement places the left edge of the gauge (`mLeftSide`) so that it is located near the left edge of the control. (Its value is 5% of the control's width.) Finally, the width of the gauge (`mWide`) is set to be 20% of the control's width.

You can change the gauge parameters to suit your own needs. Indeed, you could even make the hard-coded parameters (for example, .90, .05,.20) members of the class and allow the user to set those, too. Although it would take a little more work, you could also orient the gauge to make it horizontal rather than vertical. (Trying to make these changes to the code would be a valuable learning experience!)

After the members have been reset to reflect the control's new size, the code calls the `Invalidate()` method. The `Invalidate()` method call causes Visual Basic .NET to send a message to Windows to redraw the control. Upon return from the call, the control is displayed to the user, using the resized parameters.

The `OnPaint()` Method

The real work for the gauge is done by the `Graphics` object's `OnPaint()` method. This method is designed to paint a Visual Basic .NET `Graphics` object. Each `Graphics` object has numerous methods associated with it, and these methods are responsible for all visual aspects of the object. These responsibilities include changing colors, drawing lines and shapes, filling shapes, drawing fonts, and taking care of other visual elements that appear onscreen. Indeed, every form you've used thus far has an `OnPaint()` method provided by the `System.Windows.Forms.Form` class.

Because it is possible to override the `OnPaint()` method, you can write your own version of the method and use it to draw the gauge. The argument to the `OnPaint()` method is `PaintEventArgs`, which contains a `Graphics` property that you can use for drawing purposes. The code for the `OnPaint()` method is shown in Listing 22.6.

LISTING 22.6   The `OnPaint()` Method for the **Gauge** Control

```
Protected Overrides Sub OnPaint(ByVal e As PaintEventArgs)
 ' Purpose: This subroutine overrides the OnPaint() event to draw
 '       the gauge
 '
 ' Argument list:
 '   e       the paint event arguments
 '
 ' Return value:
 '   n/a
 '
 ' CAUTION: As written, this code assumes there are valid values
 '       for mTop, mLeftSide, mTall, and mWide. No checks are
 '       performed.

 Dim Canvas As Graphics = e.Graphics
 Dim MyPen As Pen = New Pen(Color.Black)
 Dim MyBrush As SolidBrush = New SolidBrush(Color.Green)
 Dim MyStyle As FontStyle = FontStyle.Regular
 Dim MyFont As Font = New Font("Microsoft Sans Serif", 8, MyStyle)
 Dim NumberOffset As Integer, buff As String
 Dim TickOffset As Integer, TopOffset As Integer, TickValues As Double
 Dim i As Integer

 SetGaugeParameters()           ' Calculate some initial values

 If mCaution <> 0 Or mDanger <> 0 Then ' have they set yellow or red lines?
   If mCurrent >= mCaution Then     ' See if value requires a color change
    MyBrush.Color = Color.Yellow
```

LISTING 22.6 Continued

```
   End If
   If mCurrent >= mDanger Then
    MyBrush.Color = Color.Red
   End If
  End If


  ' Draw a rectangle and then fill it with a background color
  Canvas.DrawRectangle(MyPen, mLeftSide, mTopSide, mWide, mTall)
  Canvas.FillRectangle(MyBrush, mLeftSide + 1, mTopSide + 1, mWide - 1, mTall - 1)

  MyBrush.Color = Color.Black       ' Reset brush color for numbers

  TickOffset = mWide + mLeftSide
  TickValues = mMax
  NumberOffset = MyFont.GetHeight(Canvas) / 2

  For i = 0 To 4             ' Draw the tick marks and values
   TopOffset = mTopSide + i * mGap    ' First, draw tick marks
   Canvas.DrawLine(MyPen, TickOffset, TopOffset, TickOffset + 3, TopOffset)
   buff = Format(TickValues - mTick * i, ".00")  ' Now draw scale values
   Canvas.DrawString(buff, MyFont, MyBrush, TickOffset + 5, _
            TopOffset - NumberOffset)
  Next i

  ' Need this because of possible rounding errors for pixel values when drawing
  ' the minimum value tick mark. It draws the minimum tick and value
  Canvas.DrawLine(MyPen, TickOffset, mTopSide + mTall, TickOffset + 3, _
         mTopSide + mTall)
  Canvas.DrawString(CStr(mMin), MyFont, MyBrush, TickOffset + 5, _
         mTopSide + mTall - NumberOffset)

  ' Now draw a filled rectangle for the UNUSED portion of the gauge
  ' using a white brush
  MyBrush.Color = Color.White
  ' This determines how "deep" to draw the new rectangle. The adjustments
  ' by +/- 1 pixel is so we don't overwrite the gauge border
  i = (1.0 - mCurrent / mRange) * mTall + (mMin / mRange) * mTall - 1
  Canvas.FillRectangle(MyBrush, mLeftSide + 1, mTopSide + 1, mWide - 1, i)
End Sub
```

The `OnPaint()` method must use the `Overrides` keyword because you want to override the base class `OnPaint()` method. You use the `PaintEventArgs` parameter e to define a `Graphics` object named `Canvas` that paints the object. (The `Graphics` class has a number of public methods that are associated with it and that are used in this example.) The following statement defines the `Graphics` object:

```
Dim Canvas As Graphics = e.Graphics
```

The variable name `Canvas` reinforces the idea that you are interacting with a drawing object (that is, the surface of the control) when you use an object of the `Graphics` class.

The next two statements define a `Pen` object and a `SolidBrush` object:

```
Dim MyPen As Pen = New Pen(Color.Black)
Dim MyBrush As SolidBrush = New SolidBrush(Color.Green)
```

A `Pen` object is used to draw lines on a `Graphics` object. The `SolidBrush` object is derived from the `Brush` class and is used to draw solid shapes on the `Graphics` object. The `Pen` object draws the gauge, its tick marks, and its text. The `SolidBrush` object fills in the gauge with the different colors.

Visual Basic .NET provides a much larger selection of predefined color names than found in earlier releases of Visual Basic. When you write code to set the color for the `Pen` object or the `SolidBrush` object, Visual Basic .NET presents you with a list of these predefined colors, as shown in Figure 22.7. Visual Basic .NET provides about 150 colors from which to choose.

FIGURE 22.7

The predefined Visual Basic .NET colors.

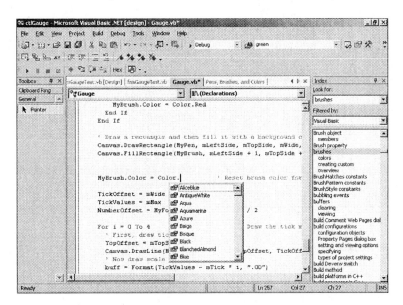

Colors values can now be defined differently than they were in earlier versions of Visual Basic. Previously, a function named `RGB()` allowed you to set the red, green, and blue (RGB) components of a color. Each color had a numeric value that varied between `0` (the absence of the color) and `255` (full intensity of the color). By mixing these color values, you could create different color values.

A fourth color argument, named `Alpha`, has been added in Visual Basic .NET. The `Alpha` component determines the opacity of the color and can assume the values `0` through `255`. If the `Alpha` value is near `0`, the background color bleeds through the RGB components to create a transparency effect. As the `Alpha` value increases, the RGB colors become more "solid," and the transparency effect diminishes. For example, this statement sets the `Alpha` value to `0`, the red component to `255`, and the green and blue values to `0`:

```
MyColor = Color.FromArgb(0, 255, 0, 0)
```

Because the `Alpha` value is `0`, the background color dominates and the red color is totally absent. If you raise the `Alpha` value to `50`, the background color recedes, and the red component increases, yielding a pinkish color. You can achieve some interesting color effects by using the `Alpha` component, especially when overlapping colors are involved.

Setting the Font

These two statements are used to control the font characteristics for the `Gauge` control:

```
Dim MyStyle As FontStyle = FontStyle.Regular
Dim MyFont As Font = New Font("Microsoft Sans Serif", 8, MyStyle)
```

The available font styles are presented in Table 22.2.

TABLE 22.2   The Available Font Styles

Font Style	Description
Bold	Uses boldface on the font
Italic	Italicizes the font
Regular	Uses normal text
Strikeout	Displays each character with a line drawn through the middle
Underline	Underlines each character

Actually, each font characteristic is an `Enum` data type and can be combined together with a logical `Or` to produce combined font effects. For example, if you change the definition of `MyStyle` to this:

```
Dim MyStyle As FontStyle = FontStyle.Regular Or FontStyle.Underline
```

the result is underlined regular text.

The `MyStyle` font style is used to set the font itself. In this statement:

```
Dim MyFont As Font = New Font("Microsoft Sans Serif", 8, MyStyle)
```

the quoted string is the font family name for the font you want to use, followed by the point size and then the font style, as held in `MyStyle`.

You might think that you could select any font from the standard font dialog box, copy the string name into the first argument for the `Font()` method, and be done with it. Well, not exactly. Figure 22.8 shows what happened when I tried to set the font to Monotype Corsiva. The runtime error message makes it clear that all font types may not support all style characteristics.

FIGURE 22.8

An example of an error message for an invalid font style.

If you change the font style for `MyStyle` to `Font.Italics` and use the Monotype Corsiva font in the `Font()` method call, the code works fine.

After the font has been set, several working variables are defined, and a call to `SetGaugeParameters()` is made to initialize some of the values used to draw the gauge, as explained earlier in the chapter.

Using the `Yellowline` and `Redline` Features

The `If` statement block is used to determine the fill color for the gauge:

```
If mCaution <> 0 Or mDanger <> 0 Then ' have they set yellow or red lines?
 If mCurrent >= mCaution Then     ' See if value requires a color change
  MyBrush.Color = Color.Yellow
 End If
 If mCurrent >= mDanger Then
  MyBrush.Color = Color.Red
 End If
End If
```

If either `mCaution` or `mDanger` is nonzero, you can assume that the user wants to activate the yellowline or redline features of the gauge. If the current value (`mCurrent`) is greater than `mCaution`, the brush color is set to yellow. If the current value is greater than `mDanger`, the color is set to red.

Programmer's Tip

Although the `If` statement block is not RDC (really dumb code), it does qualify as DC (doofus code) quality. This is because if `mCurrent` is greater than or equal to `mDanger`, you set the brush color twice. The old adage "If it ain't broke, don't fix it" is sage advice in most cases. However, you can remove the possibility of double-setting the brush color by making a trivial change in the code. You should make this change to the code before you show it to your friends at the next cocktail party. (I've written a lot of code thus far…it's time for you to chip in.)

Figure 22.9 shows a screen shot of the gauge that should give you a better idea of how the rectangles look.

FIGURE 22.9

The **Gauge** control at design time, using the defaults.

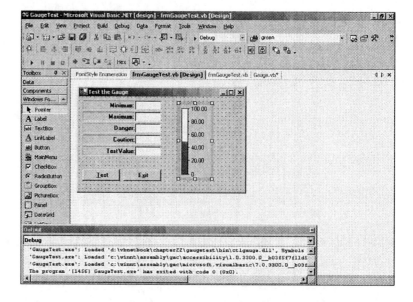

To better understand how the gauge is actually drawn, the most important elements of the gauge are labeled in Figure 22.10. The control size is 62×152 pixels for the gauge shown in Figure 22.9. If you look at the code for the **Gauge_Resize()** event in Listing 22.5 and use the control size of 62×152, you find the following:

```
mTall     = 152 * .9     = 137
mTopSide = (152 – 137) / 2 = 8
mLeftSide = 62 * .05      = 3
mWide     = 62 * .2       = 13
```

FIGURE 22.10

Important measurements on the **Gauge** control.

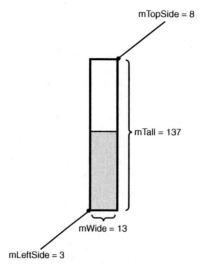

Don't forget that these are pixel (`Integer`) values, so Visual Basic .NET rounds each to the next whole pixel.

Drawing and Filling the Background of a Gauge

When the brush color is set based on the value of `mCurrent` relative to the yellowline and redline colors, you call `DrawRectangle()` to draw the outline of the gauge. This statement:

```
Canvas.DrawRectangle(MyPen, mLeftSide, mTopSide, mWide, mTall)
```

translates to this:

```
Canvas.DrawRectangle(MyPen, 3, 8, 13, 137)
```

using the numbers from Figure 22.10. As you can see from the `DrawRectangle()` statement, the first argument is the pen used to draw the rectangle. The next two arguments are the x,y-coordinates for the upper-left corner of the gauge (3,8). The next argument (`13`) is the width of the rectangle you are drawing, and the final argument (`137`) is its height. When you finish processing the `DrawRectangle()` statement, the outline of the gauge is drawn on the `Gauge` control.

The next statement is used to fill the rectangle:

```
Canvas.FillRectangle(MyBrush, mLeftSide + 1, mTopSide + 1, mWide - 1, mTall - 1)
```

Again, the `FillRectangle()` method uses the same coordinate system as `DrawRectangle()`, with a few minor exceptions. If you have done some graphics programming before, you know that there is a process called *flood fill*. A flood fill method passes in an x,y-coordinates location, a border color (for example, black), and a fill color (for example, green). The method then proceeds to check the pixels around its current location. If the color is the border color, the pixel is not changed. If the color is not the border color, the color is changed to the fill color. The method then changes the coordinates and checks its neighboring pixel colors and repeats the process. When the method is finished, the interior of the object should have been filled in with the fill color.

The problem is that a flood fill spends a lot of time relocating itself and checking pixel values. The advantage of a `FillRectangle()` method is that it doesn't have to perform the border checking tests; it just blasts the color by using the parameters passed to it.

In the call to `FillRectangle()`, you offset each parameter by 1 pixel. The first two parameters (the x,y-coordinates) are each increased by 1 pixel. This has the effect of locating the starting position for the new rectangle just inside the border of the existing gauge. You subtract 1 pixel from the width and height of the gauge. If you think about it, this results in a new rectangle that fits inside the gauge you just drew with the `DrawRectangle()` call. Therefore, this process preserves the black border of the `Gauge` control.

Drawing the Tick Marks and Values

The next four statements calculate some values that are needed to draw the tick marks on the gauge and label them:

```
MyBrush.Color = Color.Black        ' Reset brush color for numbers

TickOffset = mWide + mLeftSide
TickValues = mMax
NumberOffset = MyFont.GetHeight(Canvas) / 2
```

The first statement resets the MyBrush color from the background color of the gauge (that is, green, yellow, or red) to black.

If you look at Figure 22.10 and fill in the appropriate values, you should find that TickOffset results in an x-coordinate value that is just on the right edge of the gauge. TickValues is initialized to mMax. In terms of Figure 22.9, TickValues would be set to 100.

NumberOffset is used to center the numeric values on the tick marks. The GetHeight() method call returns the height (in pixels) for the font you are using. On my system, the value is 12 pixels, so any character that is part of the Microsoft Sans Serif font will fit within a vertical distance of 12 pixels for the font size used. You divide the return value in half and assign it into NumberOffset. By subtracting NumberOffset from the y-coordinate for each character you draw, you locate each string value one-half character higher on the gauge. Using this offset has the effect of centering the numbers on their respective tick marks. You can see the effect in Figure 22.9.

Consider what this For loop from Listing 22.6 does:

```
For i = 0 To 4              ' Draw the tick marks and values
 TopOffset = mTopSide + i * mGap   ' First, draw tick marks
 Canvas.DrawLine(MyPen, TickOffset, TopOffset, TickOffset + 3, TopOffset)
 buff = Format(TickValues - mTick * i, ".00")  ' Now draw scale values
 Canvas.DrawString(buff, MyFont, MyBrush, TickOffset + 5, _
          TopOffset - NumberOffset)
Next i
```

The first statement in this For loop calculates where a tick mark should be drawn. For the dimensions you've been using, you should see that mGap equals 27 pixels. The call to the Drawline() method when i is set to 0 looks like this:

```
8 = 8 + 0 * 27
Canvas.DrawLine(MyPen, 16, 8, 11, 8)
```

The first tick mark (which is a 3-pixel line) is drawn just in front of the value 100.00 in Figure 22.9. On the second pass through the For loop, i should equal 1, so the values change to this:

```
35 = 8 + 1 * 27
Canvas.DrawLine(MyPen, 16, 35, 11, 35)
```

This line becomes the tick mark for the value 80.00 in Figure 22.9. You can check the other values as additional passes are made through the loop.

Now you should look that the calculation of buff:

```
buff = Format(TickValues - mTick * i, ".00")  ' Now draw scale values
```

Recall that `TickValues` was initialized to `mMax`, or `100`. `mTick` is the range of values (range = `mMax` − `mMin` = 100) divided by 5. Therefore, `mTick` is `20`. On the first pass through the loop, `buff` becomes this:

```
"100.00" = Format(100 - 20 * 0, ".00")
```

On the second pass, the calculation becomes this:

```
"80.00" = Format(100 - 20 * 1, ".00")
```

I think you get the idea.

The `DrawString()` method call:

```
Canvas.DrawString(buff, MyFont, MyBrush, TickOffset + 5, TopOffset - NumberOffset)
```

draws the contents of `buff` 5 pixels to the right of the edge of the control (that is, the x-coordinate equals `TickOffset` + 5). The y-coordinate is set by using the calculated value of `TopOffset` minus the font offset (that is, `NumberOffset`).

When the `For` loop finishes, all the numeric string values and their associated tick marks appear on the control. The final calls to `DrawLine()` and `DrawString()` are done outside the loop because you want to align the last tick mark with the bottom of the gauge. Because of rounding errors in calculating the offsets in the loop, the final tick mark might not line up perfectly if you drew it by using the `For` loop calculations. (The technical term for this kind of code is *fudging code*. Not elegant, but necessary.)

Finally, you set the `MyBrush` color to white in preparation for drawing the gauge background color. The calculation of `i` in this statement is used to determine the y-coordinate value for the new rectangle:

```
i = (1.0 - mCurrent / mRange) * mTall + (mMin / mRange) * mTall - 1
```

For example, if the current value, `mCurrent`, is `75` and using the gauge shown in Figure 22.9, the numbers look like this:

```
i = (1.0 - 75 / 100) * 137 + (0 / 100) * 137 - 1
i = (.25) * 137 + (0) * 137 - 1
i = 34.25 + 0 - 1
i = 33.25
```

which means `i` equals `33` because it is an `Integer` data type. This value then becomes the y-coordinate value in this statement:

```
Canvas.FillRectangle(MyBrush, mLeftSide + 1, mTopSide + 1, mWide - 1, i)
```

The call to `FillRectangle()` fills in the gauge with the white color held in `MyBrush`. Because the *entire* Gauge control was previously filled in with appropriate gauge value color (that is, green, yellow, or red, depending on `mCurrent`), the new white rectangle is actually drawing the background color for the gauge based on `mCurrent`. This gives the appearance of setting the gauge color, when in fact you are setting the background color. If you think about this design, the math is actually easier to understand by doing it this way because of the way the graphics system uses the y-coordinate values. The design used here has one other advantage: It works.

You now have everything in place to use the control. All you need is a test shell to exercise the control. The following section describes the testing code.

Testing the Gauge Control

The code to test the Gauge control is very simple. The text boxes shown in Figure 22.9, from top to bottom, are txtMin, txtMax, txtDanger, txtCaution, and txtCurrent. The two buttons are btnTest and btnExit. The testing code is shown in Listing 22.7.

LISTING 22.7   Code for Testing the Gauge Control

```
Public Class frmGaugeTest
 Inherits System.Windows.Forms.Form

' Windows Form Designer generated code

Private Sub btnExit_Click(ByVal sender As System.Object, ByVal e As _
            System.EventArgs) Handles btnExit.Click
  Me.Dispose()
End Sub

Private Sub Form1_Load(ByVal sender As System.Object, ByVal e As _
            System.EventArgs) Handles MyBase.Load
  txtMax.Text = "3000"
  txtMin.Text = "0"
  txtDanger.Text = "2700"
  txtCaution.Text = "2400"
  txtCurrent.Text = "2600"
End Sub

Private Sub btnTest_Click(ByVal sender As System.Object, ByVal e As _
            System.EventArgs) Handles btnTest.Click
  Gauge1.Maximum = CDbl(txtMax.Text)
  Gauge1.Minimum = CDbl(txtMin.Text)
  Gauge1.Danger = CDbl(txtDanger.Text)
  Gauge1.Caution = CDbl(txtCaution.Text)
  Gauge1.Current = CDbl(txtCurrent.Text)
  Gauge1.Invalidate()
 End Sub
End Class
```

When the form is loaded, you initialize some sample test values into the appropriate text boxes. When the user clicks the Test button, these values are passed to the Gauge control to set the member data values for the gauge. The call to the gauge's Invalidate() method causes the gauge to be redrawn using the new values. A sample run is shown in Figure 22.11.

FIGURE 22.11

A sample run of the program to test the **Gauge** control.

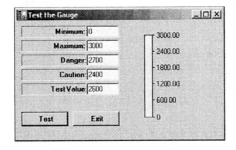

Although you cannot see it, the color in the sample run is yellow because the current test value falls between the Caution and Danger values.

You should type in different test values to see how the gauge responds. You might also try values that do not fall within the current range of the control to see if the control handles them properly. I also encourage you to use the Visual Basic .NET debugger to single-step through the code, looking at the values of the variables in the Locals window. That is a great way to gain a real understanding of how the code works.

Summary

In this chapter you have learned how to use two major features of the Visual Basic .NET graphics system: image processing by using a picture box and shape drawing. This chapter only scratches the surface of what you can do with the **Graphics** object provided by Visual Basic .NET. Indeed, this chapter could be expanded into an entire book by itself. If you dig around in Visual Basic .NET's online help and do some experimenting, you should be able to do just about any graphics programming you might need.

Review Questions

1. What does the term *display resolution* mean?

A. The display resolution refers to the number of picture elements, or pixels, that are present on a display. Most modern displays have display resolutions that are adjustable between 640×480 and 1280×1024.

2. What does the term *dot pitch* mean and how does it impact a display?

A. The dot pitch of a display refers to the distance between pixels. Most modern displays have dot pitch values of approximately .28mm or less. Higher dot pitch values means that there is more black space between pixels. As a result, displays with relatively high dot pitch values produces images that look faded and washed out.

3. What does *image compression* mean?

A. Every image that is displayed on a computer monitor is nothing more than a series of pixels that have specific color values assigned to them. As display device technology improved and increased the range of colors that could be displayed, so did the image's storage requirements. Engineers discovered that it was possible to decrease the storage requirements by encoding, or compressing, the pixel values. While this does decrease the storage requirements, some color detail and fidelity is lost in the process. However, the lost detail is often so small that it is almost undetectable to the human eye even though the image storage requirements may be one-tenth of its orginal value. JPEG is perhaps the most popular image compression currently in use.

4. Suppose you want to use the `OpenFileDialog` control as part of an Access database program. You would like the control to default to Access database files (MDB), but also allow them to view all other file types if they wish. What statements are necessary to meet these design goals?

A. The statements could be written:

```
With OpenFileDialog1   ' Initialize the file dialog
  .Filter = "Access Database (*.MDB)¦*.MDB¦All Files (*.*)¦*.*"
  .FilterIndex = 1
End With
```

The Filter property of the `OpenFileDialog` is used to limit the file types that are displayed. The `FilterIndex` property is used to determine which file type in the `Filter` property's list is used as the default file type. In this example, we have made MDB the default file type by setting the `FilterIndex` property to the first file type specified in the `Filter` list.

5. What is the aspect ratio of an image and why is it important?

A. The aspect ratio is the ratio of an image's width to its height. For example, if an image is 1000 pixels wide and 1000 pixels high, its aspect ratio is 1.0. However, if you try to display that image in an area on the display that is 1000×800, the height of the image is going to be squished so the 1000 pixels of the original image can be shoe-horned into the 800 pixels that are available. As a result, the image will look distorted. To prevent image distortion, the aspect ratio for the image must match the aspect ratio of the display device.

6. Assuming that the original size of an image is too large to be displayed in a `PictureBox` control and you do not want to scroll the image, what steps are necessary to display the control?

A. First, you need to determine the aspect ratio of the image. Next, you resize the `PictureBox` control to have the same aspect ratio as the image. For example, if the image is 1600×1200, the same relative size must be maintained for the `PictureBox` control. A `PictureBox` size of 400×300 would maintain the proper aspect ratio. Finally, you need to make sure that the `SizeMode` property is set to `StretchImage` with a statement similar to:

```
PictureBox1.SizeMode = PictureBoxSizeMode.StretchImage
```

7. What is the difference between a `Pen` object and a `SolidBrush` object?

A. Usually, a `Pen` object is used for drawing shapes, lines, or text. A `Brush` object is used to fill in objects and shapes that have been drawn.

8. Assume a variable named `Where` defines an image name and where to find it. In as few statements as possible, calculate the aspect ratio of the image.

A. The statements might be written as

```
Dim Aspect As Double
Dim Picture As Image = Image.FromFile(Where)
Aspect = CDbl(Picture.Height) / CDbl(Picture.Width)
```

The code defines an `Image` object named `Picture` and initializes it to the image in question. The `Height` and `Width` properties of the `Image` object can then be used to calculate the aspect ratio of the image.

9. What is the difference between the `DrawRectangle()` and `FillRectangle()` methods?

A. The `DrawRectangle()` graphics method uses a `Pen` object to draw an outline of a rectangle using the current properties of the pen (such as the color used to draw the rectangle). The `FillRectangle()` method draws a solid rectangle using whatever properties are currently active for the brush object being used.

10. Suppose you wish to change the default font for a graphics object. What statements would you use?

A. At a minimum, you would need to use a statement similar to

```
Dim MyFont As Font = New Font("Microsoft Sans Serif", 8, FontStyle.Regular)
```

plus whatever statements may be necessary to instantiate a graphics object. You could then use `MyFont` in whatever graphics routine (for example, `DrawString()`) you wished.

CHAPTER 23

DISK DATA FILES

In this chapter, you will learn the following:

- Introduction to Data Files
- Sequential Disk Data Files
- Writing a Text File
- Ramdom Access Data Files
- The frmRandom Class Code

In this chapter, we'll explore how you can save data to files stored on your computer's disk drive. We'll also discuss the various types of data files that you can use and some of the available file options. Further, I'll show you just how easy reading and writing Visual Basic .NET disk data files can be, especially in light of all the ready-to-use tools (for example, `SaveFileDialog`) that Visual Basic .NET makes available to you. Finally, I'll also use this chapter as an opportunity to introduce you to creating menus with Visual Basic .NET. Before we do these things, however, we need to get under the hood and make sure that we understand what disk data files are all about.

Introduction to Data Files

Computers would not be the pervasive tools that they are today if there were no permanent way to save the information contained in the computer. First of all, we would be limited to amount of data that could be stored in memory. That restriction alone would severely limit the computer's usefulness as a business tool. Second, even if we could store all our information needs in memory, shutting the computer down would mean re-entering all that information again each time we wanted to use it. Clearly, there has always been a need for a means of permanent storage of computer data.

When microcomputers first came on the scene in the 1970s, the mass storage device was a cassette tape recorder! I can remember turning on the computer and having the lonely prompt of a bare-bones operating system staring at me. I would then issue a cryptic command telling the computer to load Tom Pittman's Tiny Basic from the cassette tape recorder, press Enter, and go fix lunch. If I made enough sandwiches and the computer was having a good day, when I returned, the 4-*kilobyte* BASIC interpreter would be ready for me to start programming. Although there were ways to save data to the tape recorder, it was so unreliable and slow, I rarely used such data files.

Then Northstar Computers came out with an operating system that supported 90-kilobyte disk drives using 5.25" floppy diskettes. I thought I had died and gone to heaven! The drives were extremely fast (remember the frame of reference) and how could anyone *ever* need more than 90KB of storage? Indeed, I wrote an entire accounting system, including GL, AR, and AP, for my consulting business that fit on one 90KB diskette with room to spare!

I was so excited about the possibilities that I tried to convince one of my clients (a major insurance company) that these small computers would have a major impact on the way their agents would conduct day-to-day business. Alas, they didn't believe it and commented that "...these computers will never do more than play games." Well, in fairness to them, that was back in the late 1970s and there were some serious shortcomings, especially when it came to mass storage devices.

My, oh my, how things have changed. Now you can buy a mega-munch of disk storage for less than a couple of dollars per *gigabyte*. The availability of relatively inexpensive disk storage has played a major role in the acceptance of microcomputers in the business community. With that in mind, let's see how to use some of that storage space.

Sequential Disk Data Files

Data written to a sequential file follows the cassette tape recorder model mentioned earlier. That is, data is usually written starting at the beginning of the file (BOF) and copied byte-by-byte until all the data has been written. At that point, an end of file (EOF) marker is written and the file is closed. The sequential disk data file layout can be seen in Figure 23.1.

FIGURE 23.1
The data layout for a sequential disk data file.

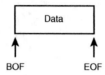

The File Pointer

Try to visualize what happens when you read a disk file. When you open the file, a file pointer is moved to the BOF mark in the file. (Some people find it useful to think of the file pointer as the disk head that actually reads the data.) Each time you read one byte of data from the file, the file pointer moves one byte towards the EOF marker. Eventually, the file pointer reads all the data in the file and reads the EOF marker. The EOF marker tells Visual Basic .NET all the data in the file has been read. As we'll see later, we can move the file pointer anywhere we want in the file.

If you want to add new data to the file, you normally append the new data to the data that's already stored in the file. In other words, when you want to write new data to an existing sequential file, you move the file pointer to the current EOF marker and, starting at that marker, you begin writing the new data. The new data overwrites the old EOF marker and a new EOF marker is written to the end of the file.

Programmer's Tip

Be *really* careful how you open data files. In some cases, if you don't open them correctly, Visual Basic .NET assumes that you want to overwrite any data that already exists in the file. Doing this, of course, destroys whatever data previously existed in the file. Sometimes this is not a good thing.

Figure 23.2 shows the process of appending new data to an existing sequential file.

FIGURE 23.2
Appending data to
sequential disk data file.

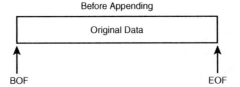

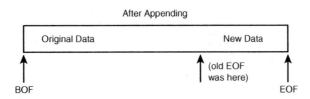

Sequential Files Are Dense

As you can see, adding new data to a sequential file is done by appending that new data to end of the old data. The result is a file that's *dense*. That is, there are no gaps in the data—the bytes are packed one against the other from BOF to EOF and no space is wasted. That's the good news. That's also the bad news.

The problem with sequential files is that they're difficult to update. For example, suppose that you wrote the name of your friend to the file as `Kathy`. Sometime later, after you've added many other names to the file, you discover that Kathy prefers to be called Katherine. Because sequential files are dense, there are no empty spaces in the file that you can reclaim to expand the name. In fact, about the only way to make the change is to copy the old data to a new file up to the point where `Kathy` appears, write the new version, `Katherine`, to the new file, and then continue copying from the old file to the new file.

Given that sequential files are hard to update, why use them? Well, their real advantage is that they are dense data files and result in a very efficient use of disk space. They are perfect for some file types, such as letters and documents that aren't updated all that often. Our first sample program of this chapter is used to read and write a sequential file.

Adding a Program Menu

The first thing we want to do is create a new project named SequentialFile. Now move to the Toolbar and double-click on the `MainMenu` control. Your screen will look similar to that shown in Figure 23.3.

FIGURE 23.3

Adding a `MainMenu` control to a form.

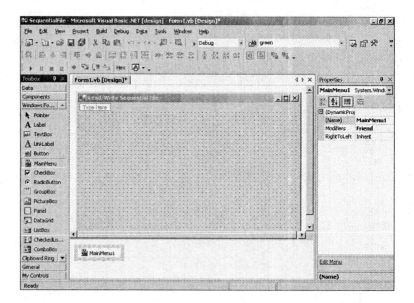

Notice that the `MainMenu` control appears at the bottom of the design window and a small box labeled Type Here appears on the form. (Earlier versions of Visual Basic had a menu editor integrated into the IDE. That editor has been replaced with the `MainMenu` control.)

In the box labeled Type Here, type in the word `&File`, a menu option that's often placed first in a Windows menu list. When you start typing into the box, you'll see two new Type Here boxes. One of these boxes will be located below the File menu, and a second box will appear immediately to the right of File. You've probably already figured out what these choices mean, but we'll go through them anyway.

If you press the Enter or down-arrow key, the cursor moves into the Type Here box that's below the File menu. This enables you to add a new menu option that's a submenu of File. Now type in the word **&New** and press the down-arrow key again. Now type in **&Close** and again press the down-arrow key. Now touch the hyphen (or minus sign) key and then press the down-arrow key. This causes a menu separator to be drawn on the menu. Finally, type in **E&xit**. Your screen should look similar to that shown in Figure 23.4.

FIGURE 23.4

Adding submenu options to the File menu.

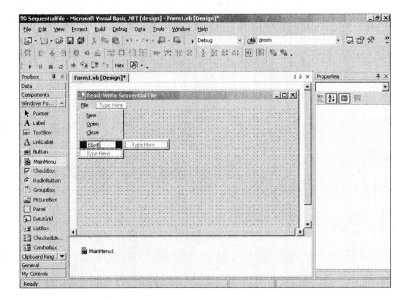

These are the only submenu options for the File menu we need for the moment. Now click on the File menu option you entered earlier and change its name to mnuFile. (If the Properties Window isn't visible, press the F4 key.) Change the names for the submenu options the same way (for example, mnuNew, mnuOpen, mnuClose, and mnuExit).

Now click on the Type Here menu option that's to the right of the File menu option and type in **&View**. Now add &Random and &Sequential submenus to the View menu and set their respective names to mnuView, mnuRandom, and mnuSequential. (We don't actually use these last two menus in this program. However, I want you to see how to move sideways and add new menu options.) We're done with the menus for the program.

Now move to the Toolbar again and add an OpenFileDialog control, a SaveFileDialog control, and finally a rich text box control. If you have done all of these correctly, your display should look similar to that shown in Figure 23.5.

Change the name of the rich text box to rtbOutput. Place rtbOutput so that its upper-left corner is near the upper-left corner of the form. Don't worry about the size of rtbOutput. We'll resize it while the program is running.

FIGURE 23.5

The complete
SequentialFile form.

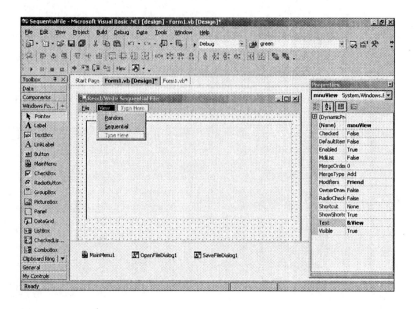

Writing a Text File

First of all, we need to import **System.IO** into our program because it's responsible for all
Visual Basic .NET file processing. Listing 23.1 shows the code necessary for writing a text data
file. Although we could set things up in terms of a reading class or a writing class (did those
just sound like high school electives?), I decided to keep the sequential access code as simple
as possible and place all the code in one place.

First, we import the **System.IO** namespace. The form **Load** event does nothing more than hide
the rich text box.

LISTING 23.1 Code for the **mnuSave** Menu Option

```
Imports System.IO

Public Class frmSequential
 Inherits System.Windows.Forms.Form

' Windows Form Designer generated code


Private Sub frmSequential_Load(ByVal sender As System.Object, ByVal e As _
 '              System.EventArgs) Handles MyBase.Load
 rtbOutput.Visible = False
End Sub


Private Sub mnuNew_Click(ByVal sender As System.Object, ByVal e As _
          System.EventArgs) Handles mnuNew.Click
 rtbOutput.Clear()          ' Clear rtb
```

LISTING 23.1   Continued

```
    SizeRichTextbox()              ' Set up the rtb
    rtbOutput.Visible = True
    rtbOutput.Focus()
End Sub

Private Sub SizeRichTextbox()     ' Resize the rich textbox
  Dim ClientSize, BoxSize As Size

  ClientSize = Me.Size
  BoxSize.Height = ClientSize.Height - 100
  BoxSize.Width = ClientSize.Width - 100
  rtbOutput.Size = BoxSize

End Sub

Private Sub mnuSave_Click(ByVal sender As System.Object, ByVal e As _
             System.EventArgs) Handles mnuSave.Click
  Dim NewFileName As String
  Dim NewFile As SaveFileDialog = New SaveFileDialog()
  Dim MyChoice As DialogResult

  With NewFile
    .Filter = "Text Files (*.txt)¦*.txt¦All Files (*.*)¦*.*"
    .FilterIndex = 1              ' Assume text files
    .DefaultExt = "txt"          ' Ditto
    .InitialDirectory = "C:\Temp\"
    .OverwritePrompt = True        ' Ask before overwriting
    .Title = "Save Text Data File"
  End With

  MyChoice = NewFile.ShowDialog       ' What did they do?

  If MyChoice = DialogResult.Cancel Then ' Bail out?
    Exit Sub
  Else
    NewFileName = NewFile.FileName
  End If

  If NewFileName.Length > 0 Then
    Try
      Dim MyTextData As StreamWriter = New StreamWriter(NewFileName, False)

      MyTextData.Write(rtbOutput.Text)  ' Write the data
      MyTextData.Close()          ' Close the stream
      MyTextData = Nothing          ' Release it
    Catch
      Beep()
      MessageBox.Show("Something went wrong while writing of the data")
    End Try
  End If
End Sub
```

First, notice that we're responding to a menu click event rather than a button click event. Actually, the code is virtually the same whether we respond to a button or menu click.

The mnuNew Click Event

When the user wants to start a new text file, he clicks on the New submenu option of the File menu. To add the code, simply double-click the New menu option in Design mode and Visual Basic .NET switches to the Code window and fills in the subroutine shell for the mnuNew_Click event code.

The code really doesn't do much. First, it uses the rich text box `Clear()` method to erase any text that might be left from a previous run. It then calls `SizeRichTextbox()`, which is a small subroutine we wrote to resize the text box to fill most of the client space for the form. Note that we define two working variables named `ClientSize` and `BoxSize` of type `Size`. The `Size` class enables us to determine the size of the form. We then set the `BoxSize` `Height` and `Width` members to be 100 pixels smaller than the main form's size. This results in a rich text box that fills most of the client area of the form.

After the call to `SizeRichTextbox()`, we set the `Visible` property of the text box to `True` and place the focus in the control. The user can now start typing into the text box. When the user is finished, he can elect to save the contents of the text box to a disk file.

The mnuSave Click Event

When the user clicks on the Save submenu option, the mnuSave Click event code is executed. We define `NewFile` as a `SaveFileDialog()` object. It's very similar to the `OpenFileDialog()` object we used in Chapter 22, "Visual Basic .NET Graphics," and requires similar initialization statements. Because we're interested only in saving text files for the moment, we set the `FilterIndex` property for `NewFile` to default to `*.txt` files and the `DefaultExt` to `txt`. The `DefaultExt` is appended to a filename when the user simply types in a primary filename and does not add the file's extension. Therefore, if the user types in `MyFile` for the filename, the file is actually written to the disk as `MyFile.txt`.

The `OverwritePrompt` property of `NewFile` is important. If the file name entered by the user already exists on the disk, setting this property to logic `True` causes the dialog to ask the user if he wants to overwrite the existing file. If this property is set to logic `False`, the dialog assumes that the writer knows what he's doing (usually *not* a good assumption) and does not ask if he wants to overwrite the file. Because a logic `False` setting for this property could result in losing the existing contents of the file, I think you should always set this property to logic `True`.

`MyChoice` is defined as an object of type `DialogResult` and is used to tell us what the user did with the `SaveFileDialog()` dialog box. If the user elected to cancel the operation, the `If` test on `MyChoice` causes the code to exit the subroutine. Otherwise, we assign the dialog's `FileName` property into `NewFileName`.

If `NewFileName` has a string length greater than 0, we assume that the user wants to save the data to a text file. We define a `StreamWriter()` object named `MyTextData` to write the contents of the rich text box to the data file. In the statement

```
Dim MyTextData As StreamWriter = New StreamWriter(NewFileName, False)
```

the first argument to the `StreamWriter()` constructor is the name of the file that the user entered into the dialog box. The second argument is a `Boolean` that determines whether the data about to be written is appended to the file. If the file already exists and the argument is logic `True`, the data is appended to the file. If the argument is logic `False`, any existing data is overwritten.

We've set the argument to logic `False`, which means that whatever appears in the `rtbOutput` text box overwrites any data that might have previously existed in the file. If you need to preserve the existing data in the file, make sure that you set this argument to logic `True`. For our testing purposes here, overwriting should be fine. The actual writing of the data is a one-line statement

```
MyTextData.Write(rtbOutput.Text)   ' Write the data
```

which writes the text in the `rtbOutput` text box to disk.

The next statement closes the file. It's important that you close the file for two reasons. First, most input/output (I/O) writing operations done in the Windows environment use what is known as *buffered* I/O. Because I/O operations are relatively slow, Windows minimizes the number of physical I/O operations whenever possible. When you use the `Write()` method for a buffered I/O operation, the data is actually moved to a memory buffer, not to disk. In other words, Windows delays the actual I/O activity as long as possible. If the buffer becomes full, Windows flushes the contents of the buffer to disk. If the buffer doesn't become filled, Windows waits until it does become full or you're finished using the file. When you call the `Close()` method, Windows flushes the contents of that memory buffer to disk by performing a physical I/O operation. Therefore, you should call the `Close()` method when you're finished using the file to make sure that the data is written to disk. If you don't make the `Close()` call and something nasty happens (for example, a power loss), the data might be lost.

Programmer's Tip

You can prove that `Write()` operations are buffered by performing the following experiment. First, set a breakpoint on the `MyTextData.Close()` statement. Run the program and type something into `rtbOutput`. Now select the Save menu option, supply a name for the text file, and click the Save button. When the program stops at the breakpoint, end the program. Now try to display the contents of the file you just "wrote" using Notepad. What happens and why?

The second reason for closing the file is so that you can perform the next statement:

```
MyTextData = Nothing        ' Release it
```

This allows Windows to mark the resources associated with the `StreamWriter` object available for garbage collection. By doing this, you don't tie up resources that are no longer needed by the program.

Finally, notice that we embedded the file save code in a `Try-Catch` statement block. After all, things can go wrong, especially with physical I/O devices. We've used a generic `Catch` block, but it would at least give the user a clue that something is amiss. If you want to add a more precise **Catch** block, you can use the exception list (for example, the **System.IO** common language runtime exceptions) found under the **Debug-Exceptions** menu sequence. The details are covered in Chapter 19, "Error Processing and Debugging."

That's it! We've now written code that can move data from a text box to a disk data file. Or, at least we think we did. Let's write the code that enables us to review a text file to see whether we really did things correctly. The **mnuOpen Click** event code is shown in Listing 23.2.

LISTING 23.2   The **mnuOpen** Click Event Code

```
Private Sub mnuOpen_Click(ByVal sender As Object, ByVal e As _
          System.EventArgs) Handles mnuOpen.Click
  Dim FileName As String

  rtbOutput.Clear()
  With OpenFileDialog1
   .Filter = "Random files (*.dat)|*.dat|Text Files (*.txt)|*.txt|All _
          Files (*.*)|*.*"
   .FilterIndex = 2
   .InitialDirectory = "C:\Temp\"
   .Title = "Select File"
  End With

  Try
   If OpenFileDialog1.ShowDialog() = DialogResult.OK Then ' Try to open it
    FileName = OpenFileDialog1.FileName
   Else
    Exit Sub      ' They didn't want to continue...
   End If

   Select Case OpenFileDialog1.FilterIndex
    Case 1      ' Random
    Case 2      ' Text
     Dim MyReadText As StreamReader = New StreamReader(FileName)
     rtbOutput.Visible = True
     SizeRichTextbox()
     rtbOutput.Text = MyReadText.ReadToEnd()
     MyReadText.Close()
     MyReadText = Nothing
    Case Else
   End Select
  Catch
   MessageBox.Show("Something's amiss...", "File Read Error")
  End Try
 End Sub
```

The **mnuOpen Click** event code is used to select and open a text file. The code begins by clearing any previous contents from the **rtbOutput** text box using the **Clear()** method. Next, we initialize the properties of the **OpenFileDialog1** object. These should look familiar to you by now, so we don't need to go over them again here. If you want to review the **OpenFileDialog** properties that we're using, see Chapter 22 or use Visual Basic .NET's Online help.

Again, we nest the code within a **Try-Catch** block in case something goes wrong. The test expression of the **If** statement checks to see whether the user selected a file. If the user cancelled the operation, we exit the subroutine. Otherwise, we assign the filename she selected into **FileName**.

We use a **Select Case** statement block to actually hold the code for reading the text file. (We did this because we'll use this same program to experiment with random access files later in the chapter.) We use the **FilterIndex** property the **OpenFileDialog1** object to determine which **Case** statement block to execute.

In the **Case 2** statement block, we create a **StreamReader** object named **MyReadText**. We create **MyReadText** by passing the **StreamReader** constructor the name of the file that was just selected by the user. We set the **rtbOutput Visible** property to logic **True** and then call **SizeRichTextBox()** to resize the control. All the actual work to read the file is done with the statement

```
rtbOutput.Text = MyReadText.ReadToEnd()
```

which simply reads the selected text file from BOF to EOF (see Figure 23.1) and moves the data to **rtbOutput**. After the data is read, we close the file with the **Close() StreamReader** method and release the resources that we used by setting **MyReadText** to **Nothing**.

A sample run of the program is shown in Figure 23.6. As you can see, reading and writing sequential files is pretty simple. However, there are situations in which the format for sequential files leaves a lot to be desired, especially when we want to selectively retrieve data from a file. It's this selective data retrieval that I want to discuss in the next section.

FIGURE 23.6
A sample run of the SequentialFile program.

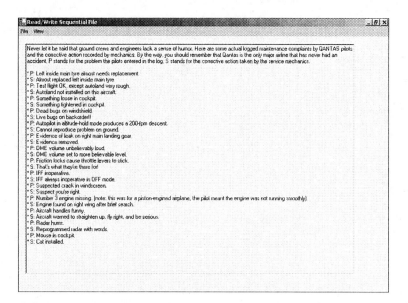

Random Access Data Files

Sequential data files provide an easy way to write data to a disk file. Sequential files are good choice for text files and can even be used for storing comma-separated variables (CSV) in a file. However, a major drawback of sequential files is that there's no convenient way to organize the data for a record-based retrieval system. An example will help explain.

Data Records

Suppose we want to create a data file to store a mailing list. Each person in the list will have a first and last name, an address, and a city, state, and ZIP Code. We'll assume that these pieces of data uniquely describe each person in the list. Collectively, these pieces of data can be grouped together into what is called a *record*. However, one person's record might use only 35 bytes of disk space, whereas the next person's record might use 50 bytes of data. The storage for each record can vary because their names and addresses differ. In other words, if we view the data for each person as a record, each record is a *variable-length* record, the length of which varies according to the actual data in the record.

Although there's nothing to prevent us from writing variable-length records to a data file, getting the data back is a little inefficient. For example, if you need the address for the person you know is the tenth record in the file, you'll have to read through nine (unwanted?) records to get the address you want. Not bad, but not good, either.

Let's try another approach to the problem. Suppose we say that each record will be limited to 100 bytes, no more, no less. We might set these limits as shown in Table 23.1.

TABLE 23.1   Bytes in a Fixed-Length Record

Field Name	Number of Bytes for Field
FirstName	10
LastName	20
Address	30
City	20
State	15
ZIP	5
Total:	100

It's common to refer to each variable in a record as a *field*, and that's how we'll refer to them from now on. Collectively, the fields form a record. If a person's first name is less than 10 bytes, we add enough blank spaces to make that field 10 bytes long. If the last name takes more than 20 spaces, we chop the field off at 20. By padding the fields that are short of the required byte length with blank spaces and truncating any fields that are too long, we can force each record to be exactly 100 bytes in length. So what?

Well, it gives us a very efficient means by which to retrieve records from the file. You saw earlier in this chapter that each file is associated with a file pointer that can be moved around within the file. Now let's return to our friend hanging out in record number 10. Suppose that we place the file pointer at `ByteOffset` and start reading the data:

```
ByteOffset = (DesiredRecord - 1) * FixedRecordLength
           = (10 - 1) * 100
           = 900
```

What would we read? We can figure out the answer by looking at Figure 23.7. If we position the file pointer 900 bytes into the file, we're ready to read the first byte for record number 10. Perfect! The really good news is that we didn't have to read any data we didn't want—we just skipped over the unwanted data by positioning the file pointer to the start of the desired record. Repositioning the file pointer is much faster than reading the data. As a result, we can read a desired record much faster using the approach described here rather than performing a sequential read of the data to the desired record.

FIGURE 23.7

A sample run of the SequentialFile program.

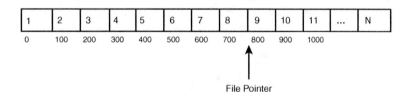

File Pointer

The positioning of the file pointer is similar to the way you fast-forward your VCR recorder. If, for example, you know that Katherine's birthday party starts 90 minutes into the tape, you can fast-forward to the proper place on the tape in a matter of seconds rather than sitting through 90 minutes of Uncle Sonny's mime act.

Programmer's Tip

Most of us are conditioned to count things starting with the number one. If we're listening to an audio CD with 15 songs on it, we think in terms of track 1 through track 15. If we're at an airport, we go to Gate 1, not Gate 0. We just don't think in terms of zero-based counting. Well, computers do. Therefore, record number 1 is really offset zero bytes from BOF. It's because the computer works in zero-based terms that we must subtract 1 from the record number in the equation that calculates the byte offset for positioning the file pointer:

```
ByteOffset = (DesiredRecord - 1) * FixedRecordLength
```

Rather than force the world to realize that record number 10 is *really* record number 9, we just subtract one from the worldly record number and be done with it (look at Figure 23.7 again and think about it).

Using fixed-length records, we can skip to any record in the file that we want without having to read any unwanted data. Files that are based on fixed-length records are called *random access* files. They have that name because we can randomly move around within the file and read a given record. Sequential files don't give us the same flexibility.

Given that we can access records much faster using random access files, what's the downside? The downside is that we'll likely waste disk space because we end up padding a lot of the fields with blank spaces. Still, when you can buy disk storage for a few dollars per gigabyte, most users are more than happy to pay the wasted storage price to gain faster access to the data.

Using Random Access Files

Let's add random access files to our SequentialFile project. We need to make only a few code modifications to frmMain. First, we need to add code that enables us to create a new random access data file. This new code is shown in Listing 23.3.

LISTING 23.3   Code for the mnuNewRandom Click Event

```
Private Sub mnuNewRandom_Click(ByVal sender As System.Object, ByVal e _
        As System.EventArgs) Handles mnuNewRandom.Click
Dim MyRandom As New frmRandom()
Dim FileName As String

rtbOutput.Visible = False

With OpenFileDialog1
  .Filter = "Random files (*.dat)¦*.dat¦All Files (*.*)¦*.*"
  .FilterIndex = 1
  .InitialDirectory = "C:\Temp\"
  .Title = "Select Random File"
End With

Try
  If OpenFileDialog1.ShowDialog() = DialogResult.OK Then
   FileName = OpenFileDialog1.FileName
   Dim MyFile As FileStream = New FileStream(FileName, FileMode.Create,_
                      FileAccess.ReadWrite)
   MyFile.Close()
   MyFile = Nothing
  Else
   Exit Sub      ' They didn't want to continue...
  End If
Catch
  MessageBox.Show("Could not access file")
End Try
MyRandom.FileName = FileName
MyRandom.Show()

End Sub
```

Next, we define some working variables and hide the rich text box that we used to display the sequential files. We then set the `OpenFileDialog1` properties to default to random access data files. I use the filename extension of `.dat`, but you can use any extension you want. A `Try-Catch` statement block is used to catch any I/O errors that might occur. We define a new `FileStream` object, passing it the name that the user typed in for the new file. We don't actually write any data to the file at this time. Instead, we simply create the file by setting the second argument of the `FileStream` constructor to `FileMode.Create`. We then close the file and release its resources.

The statements

```
MyRandom.FileName = FileName
MyRandom.Show()
```

copy the current filename to the `frmRandom` class member named `FileName` and then load the `frmRandom` form. We'll discuss `frmRandom` in a moment, but first I want to discuss the second code change in the `frmMain` form.

The second code change amounts to three new lines to the `mnuOpen Click` event code in Listing 23.2. If you look at the `Select Case` statement block in that listing, you'll see that `Case 1` is empty. Add the following three lines to `Case 1`:

```
Dim MyRandom As New frmRandom()
MyRandom.FileName = FileName
MyRandom.Show()
```

These three lines duplicate the functionality of the last two lines in Listing 23.3. That is, `Case 1` is designed to pass the name of the file the user wants to open to the `frmRandom` class code. Now we can see what `frmRandom` is all about.

The `frmRandom` Class Code

First, `frmRandom` has the form shown in Figure 23.8 associated with it.

The text boxes are named `txtFirst`, `txtLast`, `txtAddr`, `txtCity`, `txtState`, and `txtZip`. The buttons in the middle row of are named `btnAddNew`, `btnRead`, `btnSave`, and `btnExit`. The buttons in the bottom row of are named `btnFirst`, `btnNext`, `btnPrevious`, and `btnLast`. We placed these last four buttons in a group box to reinforce the idea that they're associated with navigating around the random access file.

Adding a Record to the Random Access File

The first time you opt to use a random access file, you select a file name for the random file as part of the `frmMain` code. An empty random file is created and the form shown in Figure 23.8 appears. You then click the New button. (The code for the New button and its associated `ClearForm()` code are shown in Listing 23.4.) The form uses several member variables and defines a `clsList` class object for use by the `frmRandom` class. The name of the random access file that was selected is held in `mFileName`, as shown in Listing 23.3. This shows how easy it is to pass data between class forms without using global data. (We're always mindful of the encapsulation goal of OOP, right?)

FIGURE 23.8

The `frmRandom` form.

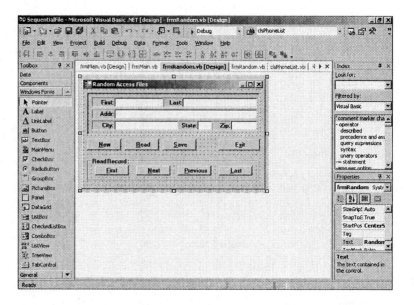

The form `Load` event copies the random access file name into the file name member of the `clsList` class for later use. Next, we get the present record count for the file and assign it into `LastRecord`. We also set the `CurrentRecord` to 1. The `If` test checks to see whether there are any records in the file. If so, a call to `FillARecord()` is made to display the contents of the first record in the file. However, because this is the first time we've run the program, the file is empty and the text boxes remain empty.

LISTING 23.4   The Code for `btnAddNew` and `ClearForm()`

```
Public Class frmRandom
 Inherits System.Windows.Forms.Form

 ' ====================== Members ====================
 Private MyList As New clsList()

 Private mFileName As String
 Private CurrentRecord As Long
 Private LastRecord As Long

 ' Windows Form Designer generated code

 ' ====================== Properties ==================
 Public Property FileName() As String
  Get
   Return mFileName
  End Get

  Set(ByVal NewFileName As String)
```

LISTING 23.4   Continued

```
    mFileName = NewFileName
  End Set

End Property

' ================== Form Load Event ====================
Private Sub frmRandom_Load(ByVal sender As System.Object, ByVal e As _
             System.EventArgs) Handles MyBase.Load
 Dim i As Integer

 MyList.FileName = mFileName         ' Copy open file name to class
 LastRecord = MyList.CurrentRecordCount ' How many records there?
 CurrentRecord = 1
 If LastRecord > 0 Then            ' If there are any records...
  FillARecord(1)                  ' ...show the first one
 End If
End Sub

Private Sub btnAddNew_Click(ByVal sender As System.Object, ByVal e As _
             System.EventArgs) Handles btnAddNew.Click
 Dim NewRecord As Long
 ClearForm()
 txtFirst.Focus()
End Sub

Private Sub ClearForm()     ' Just clear the text boxes
 txtFirst.Text = ""
 txtLast.Text = ""
 txtAddr.Text = ""
 txtCity.Text = ""
 txtState.Text = ""
 txtZip.Text = ""
End Sub

Private Sub txtState_Leave(ByVal sender As Object, ByVal e As _
             System.EventArgs) Handles txtState.Leave
 txtState.Text = UCase(txtState.Text)   ' Convert state to upper case
End Sub
```

At this point, the user starts entering data into the text boxes. There's nothing new going on here. The **Leave** event code for the state text box converts the content to uppercase letters. Other than that, we do nothing with the text boxes.

After all the fields have been filled in, the user clicks the Save button. The code for the **btnSave Click** event is shown in Listing 23.5.

LISTING 23.5   The btnSave Click Event Code

```
Private Sub btnSave_Click(ByVal sender As System.Object, ByVal e As _
            System.EventArgs) Handles btnSave.Click
Dim NewRecord As Integer, ErrorFlag As Integer

MyList.First = txtFirst.Text    ' Copy the data to class members
MyList.Last = txtLast.Text
MyList.Addr = txtAddr.Text
MyList.City = txtCity.Text
MyList.State = txtState.Text
MyList.Zip = txtZip.Text

NewRecord = MyList.CurrentRecordCount + 1 ' Bump the record counter
MyList.WriteRecord(NewRecord)
If ErrorFlag = 0 Then
 MessageBox.Show("Data written to file.")
End If

End Sub
```

The btnSave Click event code copies the data from the text boxes into the clsList members. NewRecord is assigned the current record count of the file as held in the mCurrentRecordCount member of the clsList class. We add 1 to the current value because we're adding a new record to the file. We then call the WriteRecord() method of the clsList class to write the new record data to the random access file. The code for the clsList is shown in Listing 23.6.

Because the clsList class performs file operations, we import the System.IO namespace. The System.IO namespace contains all the file I/O classes we need to work with disk data files.

Using Named Constants

The class begins with a list of named constants that specify the length that we assigned to each field of a random access record. We need to do this because each record in a random access file must be a fixed length.

Why do we use named constants? There are two reasons. First, using named constants avoids magic numbers in the code. Which of the following two statements is easier for you to understand?

```
If Len <= 10 Then
```

or

```
If Len <= FIRST_NAME_LENGTH Then
```

Named constants help document the code and aid in understanding what the code does.

The second advantage of named constants is that if we ever decide to change the size of one of the fields within the record, we need to make the change in only one place and recompile the program. All the places where the named constant are used in the code are automatically updated—we don't have to search through the file looking for magic numbers to change.

In our example, the fixed length of a record is 87 bytes. This means that instead of skipping along in 100-byte chunks as we did in Figure 23.7, we're skipping along in 87-byte chunks. The mechanics used to describe Figure 23.7 still apply; we're just taking smaller steps as we walk through the file. Note that we set mRecordSize to equal the fixed record length.

Why Use Character Arrays Instead of Strings?

Now for the weird part. Notice that we've defined each field member as a character array rather than using a string. The reason for doing this is because there is a better correspondence between the data and the mechanics of writing random access data to the file. Let me explain.

If you write string data to a disk file, Visual Basic .NET prepends some data to the string before actually writing the string data to the file. For example, when writing string data, a FilePut() operation writes 2 bytes of data that describes the data type about to be written to the file, followed by another 2 bytes that tell the length of the string. (In some other languages, these two data items form what is called a *string descriptor block*.) Finally, the actual string data is written to the file.

When Visual Basic .NET reads the file using a FileGet() operation, it uses the string descriptor block information to read the data correctly. The problem is that you might think you wrote only a 10-byte string to the file, but you actually wrote the string plus a 4-byte string descriptor block. Needless to say, this messes up our calculation for the fixed record length.

Note that defining the strings with fixed record lengths, as in

```
<VBFixedString(10)> Public First As String
```

does not solve the problem. The string descriptor block would still be written to the file.

On the other hand, character arrays aren't strings and don't use a string descriptor block. We use the named constants to set the length of each character array. When we actually write the character arrays to the file, we use the binary mode for writing, which avoids writing any descriptor block information to the file. The binary read operations take care of formatting the data into the correct data type when we read the data out from a binary file.

You might ask, "Why not just add the length of the descriptor blocks to the fixed file length and be done with it?" The first reason is because I didn't want to. The second reason is that I don't need the (wasteful) descriptor blocks in the file because the clsList class manages the file data for us. The third reason is because I wanted you to see how to use binary disk files.

LISTING 23.6   The clsList Code

```
Imports System.IO

Public Class clsList

    ' Set the length for each data field
    Private Const FIRST_NAME_LENGTH As Integer = 10
    Private Const LAST_NAME_LENGTH As Integer = 20
    Private Const ADDR_LENGTH As Integer = 30
```

LISTING 23.6   Continued

```vb
        Private Const CITY_LENGTH As Integer = 15
        Private Const STATE_LENGTH As Integer = 2
        Private Const ZIP_LENGTH As Integer = 10


        ' ===================== Data members =======================

        ' Calculate record size, which is currently 87 bytes
        Private mRecordSize As Long = FIRST_NAME_LENGTH + _
                    LAST_NAME_LENGTH + _
                    ADDR_LENGTH + CITY_LENGTH + _
                    STATE_LENGTH + ZIP_LENGTH

        Private mFirst(FIRST_NAME_LENGTH) As Char       ' The actual field data
        Private mLast(LAST_NAME_LENGTH) As Char
        Private mAddr(ADDR_LENGTH) As Char
        Private mCity(CITY_LENGTH) As Char
        Private mState(STATE_LENGTH) As Char
        Private mZip(ZIP_LENGTH) As Char

        Private mFileName As String              ' Name of data file
        Private mCurrentRecord As Long            ' The current record number
        Private mCurrentRecordCount As Long        ' Records in the file

        Private Len As Integer              ' Some working variables
        Private buff As String

        ' =================== Properties ====================
        Public Property First() As String       ' First Name
         Get
          Return mFirst
         End Get
         Set(ByVal Value As String)
          Len = Value.Length
          If Len <= FIRST_NAME_LENGTH Then
           buff = Value & Space(FIRST_NAME_LENGTH - Len)
          Else
           buff = Value.Substring(0, FIRST_NAME_LENGTH)
          End If
          mFirst = buff.ToCharArray()
         End Set
        End Property

        Public Property Last() As String       ' Last name
         Get
          Return mLast
         End Get
         Set(ByVal Value As String)
          Len = Value.Length
          If Len <= LAST_NAME_LENGTH Then
           buff = Value & Space(LAST_NAME_LENGTH - Len)
          Else
           buff = Value.Substring(0, LAST_NAME_LENGTH)
          End If
```

LISTING 23.6   Continued

```
   mLast = buff.ToCharArray()
  End Set
 End Property

 Public Property Addr() As String        ' Street address
  Get
   Return mAddr
  End Get
  Set(ByVal Value As String)
   Len = Value.Length
   If Len <= ADDR_LENGTH Then
    buff = Value & Space(ADDR_LENGTH - Len)
   Else
    buff = Value.Substring(0, ADDR_LENGTH)
   End If
   mAddr = buff.ToCharArray()
  End Set
 End Property

 Public Property City() As String        ' City
  Get
   Return mCity
  End Get
  Set(ByVal Value As String)
   Len = Value.Length
   If Len <= CITY_LENGTH Then
    buff = Value & Space(CITY_LENGTH - Len)
   Else
    buff = Value.Substring(0, CITY_LENGTH)
   End If
   mCity = buff.ToCharArray()
  End Set
 End Property

 Public Property State() As String       ' State
  Get
   Return mState
  End Get
  Set(ByVal Value As String)
   Len = Value.Length
   If Len <= STATE_LENGTH Then
    buff = Value & Space(STATE_LENGTH - Len)
   Else
    buff = Value.Substring(0, STATE_LENGTH)
   End If
   mState = buff.ToCharArray()
  End Set
 End Property

 Public Property Zip() As String         ' Zip Code
  Get
   Return mZip
  End Get
```

LISTING 23.6 Continued

```vb
   Set(ByVal Value As String)
    Len = Value.Length
    If Len <= ZIP_LENGTH Then
     buff = Value & Space(ZIP_LENGTH - Len)
    Else
     buff = Value.Substring(0, ZIP_LENGTH)
    End If
    mZip = buff.ToCharArray()
   End Set
  End Property

  Public Property FileName() As String      ' File name
   Get
    Return mFileName
   End Get
   Set(ByVal Value As String)
    mFileName = Value
   End Set
  End Property

  Public ReadOnly Property RecordSize() As Long       ' record size
   ' ReadOnly because user should never change this
   Get
    Return mRecordSize
   End Get
  End Property

  Public ReadOnly Property CurrentRecordCount() As Long ' record count
   ' ReadOnly because user should never change this
   Get
    If mCurrentRecordCount = 0 Then
     GetRecordCount()
    End If
    Return mCurrentRecordCount
   End Get
  End Property

  ' ===================== Methods ===================
  Public Function WriteRecord(ByVal ThisRecord As Integer) As Integer
   ' Purpose: To write a random record
   '
   ' Argument list:
   '   ThisRecord    the record number to write
   '
   ' Return value:
   '   integer       0 if OK, 1 on error

   Dim ErrorFlag As Integer
   Dim MyFile As FileStream
   Dim MyBinaryObject As BinaryWriter

   Try     ' Set things up to write a record
    MyFile = New FileStream(mFileName, FileMode.Open, FileAccess.Write)
```

LISTING 23.6   Continued

```
  MyBinaryObject = New BinaryWriter(MyFile)
  MyFile.Position = (ThisRecord - 1) * mRecordSize
  MyBinaryObject.Write(mFirst)
  MyBinaryObject.Write(mLast)
  MyBinaryObject.Write(mAddr)
  MyBinaryObject.Write(mCity)
  MyBinaryObject.Write(mState)
  MyBinaryObject.Write(mZip)
  MyFile.Close()
  MyFile = Nothing
  MyBinaryObject = Nothing
  mCurrentRecordCount += 1    ' Up the record counter
 Catch
  MessageBox.Show("Something went wrong in WriteRecord().", "I/O Error")
  ErrorFlag = 1
 End Try
End Function

Public Function ReadRecord(ByVal ThisRecord As Integer) As Integer
 ' Purpose: To read a random record and fill in members
 '
 ' Argument list:
 '  ThisRecord    the record number to read
 '
 ' Return value:
 '  integer       0 if OK, 1 on error

 Dim ErrorFlag As Integer
 Dim MyFile As FileStream
 Dim MyBinaryObject As BinaryReader

 Try
  MyFile = New FileStream(mFileName, FileMode.Open, FileAccess.Read)
  MyBinaryObject = New BinaryReader(MyFile)
  MyFile.Seek((ThisRecord - 1) * mRecordSize, SeekOrigin.Begin)
  mFirst = CStr(MyBinaryObject.ReadChars(FIRST_NAME_LENGTH))
  mLast = CStr(MyBinaryObject.ReadChars(LAST_NAME_LENGTH))
  mAddr = CStr(MyBinaryObject.ReadChars(ADDR_LENGTH))
  mCity = CStr(MyBinaryObject.ReadChars(CITY_LENGTH))
  mState = CStr(MyBinaryObject.ReadChars(STATE_LENGTH))
  mZip = CStr(MyBinaryObject.ReadChars(ZIP_LENGTH))
  MyFile.Close()
  MyFile = Nothing
  MyBinaryObject = Nothing
 Catch
  MessageBox.Show("Read error in ReadRecord()", "I/O Error")
  ErrorFlag = 1
 End Try
 Return ErrorFlag
End Function

 ' ===================== Helpers ====================
```

LISTING 23.6   Continued

```
  Private Sub GetRecordCount()

    Try
     If mFileName.Length <> 0 Then        ' Find out how many records
      mCurrentRecordCount = FileLen(mFileName) / mRecordSize
     End If
    Catch fileexception As FileNotFoundException  ' If a new file
     Dim MyFile As FileStream = New FileStream(mFileName, FileMode.Create,
FileAccess.ReadWrite)
     MyFile.Close()
     MyFile = Nothing
     mCurrentRecordCount = 0
    End Try

  End Sub

End Class
```

Most of the code in the file is used to get and set the properties in the list. The interesting sections of Listing 23.6 are in the methods that read and write the data. Let's walk through the `WriteRecord()` method first.

Writing the Data to the Random Access File

The `btnSave Click` event in `frmRandom` calls the `WriteRecord()` method of the `clsList` class. The argument passed to the `WriteRecord()` method determines which record in the file is about to be written. This record number is assumed to be a one-based record. That is, if the value passed in for `ThisRecord` is 1, this is the first record in the file. As such, it has a 0-byte offset in the file. Notice that when we set the file pointer position with the statement

```
MyFile.Position = (ThisRecord - 1) * mRecordSize
```

we convert the one-based (human) record number to a zero-based (computer) record number.

The actual disk operations are nested in a `Try-Catch` block just in case something goes wrong. First, we open the file using the `FileStream()` method. The statement that opens the file is

```
MyFile = New FileStream(mFileName, FileMode.Open, FileAccess.Write)
```

The first argument is the name of the file we're using. The second argument is the file operation we want to perform. In this case, we want to open the file. (If you look at the `GetRecordCount()` method, you'll see that we used `FileMode.Create` to actually create the new random access file.) The final argument determines how we want to use the file. At this point, we want to write data to the file. The `FileStream()` method returns a `FileStream` object, which we use to create a `BinaryWriter` object:

```
MyBinaryObject = New BinaryWriter(MyFile)
```

After we've defined `MyBinaryObject`, we position the file pointer to the proper offset in the file using the record length as held in `mRecordSize`. Finally, we use the `Write()` method of the `BinaryObject` to actually lay the data on the disk.

Binary disk writes are used because they write raw binary data to the disk. Binary writes do not, for example, write any descriptor blocks to the file. Therefore, when it comes time to read the data back from the disk, we need to use the proper binary **Read()** method. (We'll cover this in the next section of the chapter.) Although we have to give a little more thought to things with random access file data than we did with the sequential file data, the retrieval advantages far outweigh any disadvantages.

We immediately close the file after the data is written and set both file objects to **Nothing.** This allows Windows to perform its magic via garbage collection to free the resources associated with the file objects. If we get this far without an error, the data has been safely written to the disk, so we increment *mCurrentRecordCount* by 1.

Reading a Random Access File

Reading the data back from a random access file parallels the writing of the data. When we define the **FileStream()** object:

```
MyFile = New FileStream(mFileName, FileMode.Open, FileAccess.Read)
```

we simply change the third argument to **FileAccess.Read.** Next, we define a **BinaryRead** object, passing its constructor the name of the **FileStream** object, **MyFile.** The statement

```
MyFile.Seek((ThisRecord - 1) * mRecordSize, SeekOrigin.Begin)
```

uses the **Seek()** method to position the file pointer to the byte position in the file where we want to start reading the data. The first argument calculates the (zero-based) byte offset value, and the second argument is used to determine the frame of reference for the offset. **SeekOrigin.Begin** is an **Enum** that says we want to position the file pointer relative to the beginning of the file (BOF). You can also use **SeekOrigin.Current**, which uses the offset bytes from the current position of the file pointer, or you can use **SeekOrigin.End**, which calculates the offset from EOF.

After the **Seek()** method has done its thing, the file pointer is ready to read the data from the file. The series of read statements that begin with

```
mFirst = CStr(MyBinaryObject.ReadChars(FIRST_NAME_LENGTH))
```

uses the **ReadChars()** method to read the raw character data from the file and assign the data to their respective strings. The **CStr()** conversion is not strictly required because Visual Basic .NET performs a silent cast to convert the data from a character array to a string. However, using **CStr()** helps document exactly what our intensions are. This is a good thing; silent casts are not.

The **BinaryReader** class provides 16 **Read*XXX*** methods for reading binary data from a file (for example, **ReadInt32, ReadString, ReadDouble**, and so on). These different methods enable you to read just about any type of binary data that you want from a binary file. The routines are necessary because, unlike text files that contain formatting data as part of the file (for example, string descriptor blocks), binary data is written to the disk as raw binary data. The various **Read*XXX*** methods provide the means by which Visual Basic .NET can read the raw binary data and format it into the proper data type.

Figure 23.9 shows a sample run of the program. Notice the title bar on the form. It tells us that we're looking at the fourth record in the file.

FIGURE 23.9

A sample run reading a random access data file.

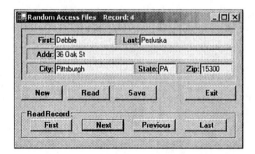

Navigating Through the Records of a Random Access File

Now that we've added a few records to the random access file, we can use the navigation buttons shown near the bottom of the `frmRandom` form shown in Figure 23.9. The code for the buttons is shown in Listing 23.7.

LISTING 23.7   The Code for the Random Access File Navigation Buttons

```
' ===================== Navigation buttons ==========================
Private Sub btnFirst_Click(ByVal sender As System.Object, ByVal e As _
              System.EventArgs) Handles btnFirst.Click
  CurrentRecord = 1
  FillARecord(CurrentRecord)
End Sub

Private Sub btnnext_Click(ByVal sender As System.Object, ByVal e As _
              System.EventArgs) Handles btnnext.Click
  CurrentRecord += 1
  If CurrentRecord > LastRecord Then
    CurrentRecord = LastRecord
  End If
  FillARecord(CurrentRecord)
End Sub

Private Sub btnLast_Click(ByVal sender As System.Object, ByVal e As _
              System.EventArgs) Handles btnLast.Click
  CurrentRecord = LastRecord
  If CurrentRecord < 1 Then
    CurrentRecord = 1
  End If
  FillARecord(CurrentRecord)
End Sub

Private Sub btnPrevious_Click(ByVal sender As System.Object, ByVal e As _
              System.EventArgs) Handles btnPrevious.Click
  CurrentRecord -= 1
```

LISTING 23.7   Continued

```
    If CurrentRecord < 1 Then
     CurrentRecord = 1
    End If
    FillARecord(CurrentRecord)

  End Sub

  Private Sub FillARecord(ByVal rec As Long)
    ' Purpose: This subroutine is used to fill in the form's
    '       text boxes.
    '
    ' Argument list:
    '  rec      a long that is the record number to retrieve
    '
    Dim ErrorFlag As Integer

    ErrorFlag = MyList.ReadRecord(rec) ' Read the class record
    If ErrorFlag = 0 Then
     Me.Text = "Random Access Files  Record: " & CStr(rec) ' Set the title
     txtFirst.Text = MyList.First
     txtLast.Text = MyList.Last
     txtAddr.Text = MyList.Addr
     txtCity.Text = MyList.City
     txtState.Text = MyList.State
     txtZip.Text = MyList.Zip
    Else
     MessageBox.Show("Read failure")
    End If
  End Sub

  Private Sub btnRead_Click(ByVal sender As System.Object, ByVal e As _
              System.EventArgs) Handles btnRead.Click
    Dim response As String

    response = InputBox("Enter the record number:", "Valid Record Numbers 1 _
              through " & CStr(MyList.CurrentRecordCount))
    FillARecord(CLng(response))
End Sub
```

If we click the First button, the `btnFirst` code sets the `CurrentRecord` to 1 and calls
`FillARecord()`, which uses the `clsList` `ReadRecord()` method to read the data. If you look
at the code for the remaining buttons, the same general methodology is used. The
`CurrentRecord` number is adjusted according to the button that was clicked and
`FillARecord()` is called to read and display the data.

One last feature is the Read button. When the user clicks on this button, an `InputBox()` dialog
box pops up and asks the user to enter the record number that he wants to search for. The first
argument is a prompt string, and the second argument is the title for the dialog box. This
sequence is shown in Figure 23.10.

FIGURE 23.10

Using an `InputBox()` dialog box to request a record number.

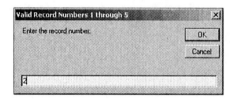

When the user clicks the OK button on the `InputBox()`, the data typed in by the user is returned as a string. We then convert this string data into a `Long` for use as the record number to display using a call to `FillARecord()`.

We didn't add an Edit button to the form, although you could do this easily enough. All you would need to do is call `FillARecord()` to move the edited data into the `clsList` members and then call `WriteRecord()` using the original record number.

Summary

In this chapter, you learned how to read and write sequential and random access data files. We've used only a small fraction of all the file I/O building blocks that Visual Basic .NET makes available to you. If you find that you need to do something different when working with disk files, check the online help first. Chances are pretty good that your question has already been answered.

You should experiment with the SequentialFile project and try to add new features to it. A good starting point would be to add an Edit button to the random access files portion of the program. Again, use the debugger to single-step through the program to follow exactly what the program is doing. Also, try messing things up (for example, opening a file that doesn't exist) and see what happens. Such experiments are the best way to gain a thorough understanding of what the code is doing.

Review Questions

1. When is a sequential data file used?

A. A sequential data file is used when the data can be written to the disk as one long sequential stream of data. A word processing document is a common example. You start at the beginning of the document and write the data letter by letter to the disk data file. The concept of a record is less often used with sequential data files, although random-length records in a sequential data file are possible.

2. What does the term *dense* mean with respect to sequential data files?

A. Sequential data files are usually written as a stream of consecutive bytes with no unused bytes in the file.

3. What is one major advantage and one disadvantage of a sequential data files?

A. The major advantage is that there are no gaps in the data; sequential files are dense. The major disadvantage is that sequential data files are difficult to search. To find a given piece of data, you must start at the beginning of the data file and read through it until you find the data you are looking for.

4. What do BOF and EOF mean?

A. These stand for beginning of file and end of file, respectively. Reading and writing disk data files use the BOF and EOF marks to position the file pointer. This file pointer positioning can be at either mark or as an offset from either mark.

5. What are random access data files and how are they different from sequential files?

A. The major difference between random access and sequential files is that random access files use fixed record lengths. Random access files are organized into records, and each record is allocated a fixed number of bytes. When you perform a read or write operation on a random access file, the operation is done in record-sized chunks of data. Therefore, if a random access record is defined using 100 bytes, the file is always read in 100-byte chunks. This makes searching random access files faster because indexes can be created that can be tied to the fixed position of a random access record. The major disadvantage is that the record size must be fixed to accommodate the largest-sized record, often resulting in a lot of wasted disk space.

6. Explain briefly the purpose of the following two statements:

```
MyFile = New FileStream(mFileName, FileMode.Open, FileAccess.Write)

MyFile.Position = (ThisRecord - 1) * mRecordSize
```

A. The first statement is instantiating a `FileStream` object named `MyFile` and opening the file named `mFileName` for writing. The second statement is determining the byte offset where the new record is to be written. The variable `mRecordSize` is the size (in bytes) of each random access record. The variable `ThisRecord` is the record number to be written. The `-1` is necessary because random access records are zero-based.

7. Why are random access files written in binary mode?

A. When data is written to disk files in a non-binary mode, there can be hidden data associated with each data item written to the disk. For example, writing string to a file writes a descriptor block that stores some overhead information associated with the string (for example, its length). These hidden pieces of information may change the fixed record length needed for random access files to work properly. By writing the data as raw binary data, you can avoid these hidden pieces of information resulting in the true fixed record length needed by random access files.

8. What is the purpose of the following statement?

```
MyFile.Seek((ThisRecord - 1) * mRecordSize, SeekOrigin.Begin)
```

A. The `Seek()` method is used to position the file pointer in a disk data file. The first argument is the product of the record we want to read (`ThisRecord`–1) times the size of each record (`mRecordSize`). This product yields a number that is the byte offset to the record we're seeking. The second argument tells Visual Basic .NET the reference point for the offset. In our example, the reference point is BOF. You can also apply the byte offset to EOF or the current position of the file pointer.

CHAPTER 24

DATABASE FUNDAMENTALS

In this chapter, you will learn the following:

- What is a database?
- ADO.NET
- Using SQL

*I*n this chapter, we'll cover the basic elements of what a database is and how it's organized. As you'll see, you got a good start toward understanding databases in Chapter 23, "Disk Data Files." In fact, many database principles presented in this chapter are simply an extension of the random access files you read about in Chapter 23.

What Is a Database?

A database is simply a collection of related data. For example, your workplace probably has an accounting database that tracks all the income and expenses of the company. If your company is big enough, there's likely another database used in the marketing department that maintains a sales database. Although the marketing department is ultimately interested in the revenues the sales force generates, it also tracks information that wouldn't be directly of interest to the accounting department. Other databases might exist in the maintenance department, another in human resources, and perhaps others are scattered throughout the company.

Regardless of where a database is located, its contents are geared to meet some specific need. Although it would be possible to have one huge monolithic database, it isn't uncommon to find many different databases used by different departments within the company.

What's in a Database?

Obviously, data is what's in the database, but that's not the real issue. What's more important to us is how we interact with a database as programmers. We're less interested in the specific data than in how we can access and present the data. We want to be able to read and write the data and, as such, need to understand how data is organized within the database.

It's the responsibility of the database management system (DBMS) to worry about the details of reading and writing the data to the database. As you probably know, Visual Basic .NET provides the means to use the Access DBMS to read and write database information. However, that doesn't mean that you're limited to using the Access database. Visual Basic .NET can be used to manipulate data of most popular databases, including Microsoft's SQL Server, Oracle, MySQL, and a host of others.

How is it possible for Visual Basic .NET to manipulate the data in such a variety of databases? As you might guess, each company that markets a DBMS is free to design the low-level details of the database in just about any manner it chooses. For example, one manufacturer might elect to represent the `Integer` data type as a 16-bit quantity, whereas another prefers to use 32 bits. Some might decide that floating-point numbers will use 8 bytes, whereas another decides to use 10 bytes. How does Visual Basic .NET get all of these different-shaped pegs to fit into one round hole?

SQL

Fortunately, at an early point in database development history, a group of programmers recognized a need to provide a standardized means by which to access database information. The result was the development of a language written specifically for databases. That languages is called Structured Query Language or SQL. The purpose of SQL (usually pronounced by just saying the letters S-Q-L) is not actually to program the database, but rather to extract information from it. In other words, the initial goal of SQL was to query the database for information; hence the word *query* in the language's name.

Most modern databases vendors implement SQL for use with their database, and Visual Basic .NET is no exception. Visual Basic .NET provides for a robust subset of SQL that may be used directly with an Access database. You can also connect to other databases with Visual Basic .NET by using DLL (dynamic link libraries) and Open Database Connectivity (ODBC) links. Visual Basic .NET provides a means by which to write a user interface (or *front end*) for almost any major DBMS. The actual operations on the database are performed by the ODBC link.

The DLLs take care of the details about how to move the native data found in a database into the Visual Basic .NET environment. Fortunately, we don't need to concern ourselves with how this is done. The details are encapsulated within the libraries, and SQL provides the common denominator through which we can access the data.

I'll have a lot more to say about SQL later in this chapter. However, before we can appreciate what SQL can do for us, we need to understand the basic construction of a modern database system.

The Organizational Structure of a Modern Database

Think of a database as a huge room. Inside the room on the floor are one or more books. One book is titled Customer, another is titled Orders, another is titled Employee, and so on. You pick up the book titled Employee and notice that the first line looks a lot like the guest book at a wedding, with some additional details. The line has an employee's first name, last name, address, Social Security number, the name of the employee's supervisor, plus a bunch of other information about the employee. The next line contains the same information, but for a different employee.

Database Tables

What you discover is that each "book" in the room is actually the equivalent of a database table. A *database table* is a specific subpart of a database and provides detailed information about one subject or topic of interest in the database. The book you examined in the previous paragraph is simply an abstract view of a database table that contains employee information. If you look around at the titles of the other books in the room, you might find names such as Customers, Orders, Products, Payroll, and so on. Each of these books represents a database table.

Figure 24.1 shows you the tables that are found in the `Xtreme.mdb` database that's provided with Visual Studio .NET. This is an Access database (that is, `mdb` = **M**icrosoft **d**atabase) that we'll use for much of our database discussion. (The actual path to the database depends on where you installed .NET. However, you should be able to find it off the main Visual Studio .NET directory in the `Crystal Reports\Samples\Database` directory.)

FIGURE 24.1

The database tables in the `Xtreme.mdb` database.

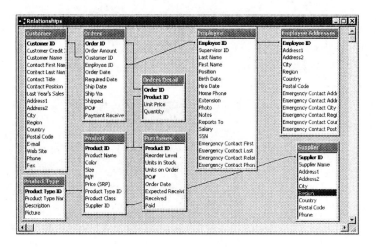

As you can see in Figure 24.1, a number of boxes are displayed. Each of these boxes has a title bar that is the table name in the `Xtreme.mdb` database. Therefore, Customer, Orders, Orders Detail, Employee, Employee Address, and so forth, are all table names that collectively form the `Xtreme.mdb` database.

> ### Programmer's Tip
>
> The database relationships shown in Figure 24.1 were derived from the `Xtreme.mdb` database. I used Access to generate the table shown in the figure. You can replicate this by running Access, selecting the `Xtreme.mdb` database, and then selecting the Tools, Relationships menu sequence.

Fields

In Chapter 23, you learned that each random access record has certain information associated with it. Each piece of information is called a *field*. In Figure 24.1, each line under the table name is a database field. Just as in random access files, each field represents a piece of information that's collected for a table entry. In the Orders table, for example, there is a field for the Order ID, the Order Amount, the Customer ID, and so on for each piece of information in the table.

In the book analogy used earlier, I said that the book had columns labeled in it. These columns correspond to the fields in the table.

Records

If you fill in the fields for a table, that completed row becomes one record in the table. Therefore, where columns represent the fields in a database table, rows represent the records in the table. Figure 24.2 shows an example using the Supplier table from the `Xtreme.mdb` database.

FIGURE 24.2
Sample records from the Supplier table in the `Xtreme.mdb` database.

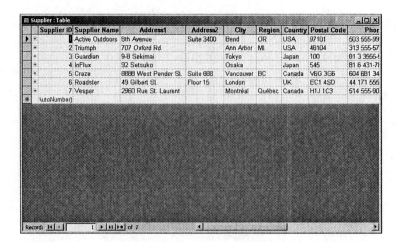

If you look at the field names in Figure 24.1, you'll see those repeated as column headers in Figure 24.2. These columns form the fields for the Supplier table. You can also see that there are seven records in the table. In other words, the information for each of the fields has been filled in to form a total of seven records in the Supplier database table.

Primary Key

If you look closely at Figure 24.1, you'll notice that at least one of the field names in each table is displayed using a boldface font. These fields are the primary key fields for each table. A *primary key* is a field that has an unduplicated value for each record in the table. For example, in the Supplier table, the Supplier ID field is the primary key for the table. This means that no other record in the Supplier table can have the same value for the Supplier ID field. If you look in Figure 24.2, you'll see that no records have the same value for the Supplier ID field.

In some cases, the primary key consists of the combined value of two key fields. If you look at the Orders Detail table in Figure 24.1, you'll notice that the primary key for that table is the combination of the Order ID and Product ID fields. These two table fields, taken together, form a unique combination that isn't duplicated in any other record in the Orders Detail table.

Why do tables even have keys? Because keys represent unique values for records within the table, they can be used to rapidly and efficiently search the records in a table. During the process of creating tables and then adding records to them, the DBMS quietly (and without us knowing about it) constructs indexes to these key fields. When you search a table for a certain record, the DBMS uses these indexes to find the record rapidly.

Relationships

Another reason for having keys in a database table is because they can be used to form relationships with other tables. If you look at Figure 24.1, you'll see a line drawn from the Customer ID field of the Customer table to the Customer ID field of the Orders table. That is, the primary key in the Customer table is used as a field in the Orders table. This means that a relationship exists between the Customer and Orders tables. Because the Customer ID is a primary key, it has a unique value. On the other hand, any one customer can have more than one order. (Indeed, the company hopes that is the case.) The relationship between the Customer and Orders table, therefore, is often described as *One-to-Many*. That is, *one* (unique) customer can have *many* orders.

We can also see that the Employee ID primary key field from the Employee table is also present in the Orders table. Perhaps the employees earn a commission on each sale, so they must include the Employee ID number in each record to ensure that the employee is paid. Because the Employee ID is the primary key of the Employee table, it is unique. This also means that a One-to-Many relationship exists between the Employee and Orders tables. That is, one (unique) employee is associated with many orders.

We can also view the relationships from the Orders table's point of view, too. From this point of view, there's a Many-to-One relationship between both the Customer and Employee tables. Think about it.

Why have relationships exist between various tables? The reason is because it improves the way we can search, or query, the database. For example, it's relatively simple to use SQL to search the Orders table for all orders placed by a certain customer. Likewise, we can use SQL to search the Orders table and find all sales that were closed by a specific employee. It's the relationships between the tables that make these queries faster and more efficient.

Databases that are built with these relationships in mind are called *relational databases*. Virtually all modern databases are relational databases, including the Access database engine included in Visual Basic .NET.

Why All Those Tables?

After seeing Figure 24.1, you might be asking yourself, "Why do we need all those tables?" Actually, we could organize the database in many different ways, and using fewer tables is a possibility. You might, however, want to follow that question with several additional questions: "What's the purpose of the database? What do I want to do with it? What information do I need to maintain to fulfill its purpose?" Given what we see in Figure 24.1, it seems that a primary goal of the database is to track company sales.

If tracking company sales is the goal, we might get by with just one table. For example, we could have an Orders table that stores the customer's name and address, what the customer bought and how many, the name of the employee who made the sale, the name and address of the supplier of the product (so that we can reorder more product when our inventory starts to run low), plus a few other supporting pieces of information. If the Orders table has all this information for each sale, we could do away with almost all the other tables.

This database design would work, but it would be similar to me handing you a shovel and saying, "I want you to build a four-lane highway between New York and Philadelphia...by yourself." You might get the job done, but it's not the most efficient plan for building a highway. Likewise, our single-table database design plan could use some work.

First of all, if our business has repeat customers, our design duplicates their names and addresses in the table for every purchase they make. The same is true for the employee and suppliers names and addresses. It's much more efficient to store a customer's ID number (usually a 4-byte Long) in the Orders table than to use the 50 to 100 bytes it could take to store the customer's name and address. The same idea applies to the employee and supplier IDs, too. An added benefit is that Visual Basic .NET can search a list of numbers faster than it can search a list of strings. This means that if your customer number is 524, we can search through the Orders table and extract all sales with customer ID number 524 much faster than we could by searching the table using your name.

In addition to improving our searching abilities by using ID numbers, we also save a tremendous amount of storage space by avoiding duplicate information. Even though disk storage space is pretty cheap these days, the time it takes to plow through a poorly designed database is not.

What we want to do is create a database design that avoids duplicate data whenever possible, but still have the necessary information to accomplish the task at hand. The use of table indexes and keys in Figure 24.1 shows that whoever designed this database has done a pretty good job.

Programmer's Tip

Volumes have been written on database design and there's no way we can do justice to this important subject. A major goal of such studies, however, is to use a process called *normalization* to avoid redundant data in a database while still providing the requisite information to fulfill the database design goals.

Finding numerous tables in a database is both common and necessary. By creating relationships between the tables, we can provide more efficient ways to search the information in the database and also lessen its storage requirements.

ADO.NET

Visual Basic .NET uses what is called the ADO.NET model for accessing databases. Prior versions of Visual Basic used ADO (ActiveX Data Objects), DAO (Data Access Objects), and RDO (Remote Data Objects) for accessing databases. Each of these database access methodologies had its limitations. Perhaps the most serious limitation was that the technologies were Windows-specific. If the database couldn't be run on a Windows platform, you couldn't talk to it. Further, the underlying format of the data was specific to ADO and exchanging database information was restricted, especially with respect to Internet communications. Also, ADO was not terribly efficient and had the appearance of being an OOP afterthought that was slapped together at the last moment.

ADO.NET removes most of the major drawbacks of earlier versions. Also, it's easy to use XML (discussed in a later chapter) in the ADO.NET model to make data exchanges much simpler.

Using ADO.NET

Before we can obtain any information from a database, we must perform several steps. Those steps are illustrated in Figure 24.3.

FIGURE 24.3
ADO.NET steps for accessing a database.

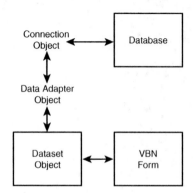

The Connection object serves as a starting point in accessing a database. The purpose of the Connection object is to provide the details about the database that are necessary to make a connection with the database. Although a number of parameters are passed as part of the connection string, the most important are Provider and Data Source parameters. The Provider parameter tells Visual Basic .NET the type of database that we're accessing, and the Data Source parameter provides the full pathname of the database. (I provide examples of these in Chapter 25, "Database Programming with Visual Basic .NET.") As you can see in Figure 24.3, the Connection object becomes our physical connection to the database.

The second step we must perform is to create a Data Adapter object. The Data Adapter object enables us to manage the data associated with the database. The Data Adapter object not only enables us to retrieve data from the table, but also manages any changes we might want to make to the database (for example, adding, deleting, or editing a record).

From the Data Adapter, we can create datasets that are representations of the data we requested from the database. The datasets are held in memory and are therefore temporary. The datasets contain not only the record information we request, they also contain information about the table itself, such as the column names, the type of data stored in a specific field, and other details that might prove useful in manipulating the data. Dataset data is stored in XML documents, which is one reason data exchanges via the Internet are so much easier in Visual Basic .NET than in previous version of Visual Basic. However, we can use the data as though it is stored in native Visual Basic .NET data types.

We don't need to concern ourselves with the XML format at this moment, however, because the objects we'll use to display the information know how to format the XML data for us. Therefore, when we move data between the dataset and a Visual Basic .NET form, Visual Basic .NET takes care of all the data conversion and formatting issues for us.

Using SQL

After we've performed the steps depicted in Figure 24.3, we're all dressed up and ready to go. Ready to go where? So far, all we have in place are the necessary connections between the database and the form upon which we want to display the data. What we need to do now is learn how to pass commands to the database that return the data we're interested in. That's where SQL enters the picture.

This section presents a brief crash course on SQL. We'll cover only the most common SQL commands. A complete review of all the SQL features available is beyond the scope of this book. Indeed, entire books are available that do nothing else but teach you how to use SQL. Still, we can learn enough in a very short period of time to cover most of our needs. With that in mind, let's begin our crash course in SQL.

SELECT

SELECT is the fundamental keyword used in most SQL queries. The SELECT query has the following general form:

```
SELECT ListOfFieldNames FROM TableName
```

The words **SELECT** and **FROM** are SQL keywords and, therefore, have special meaning in SQL. *ListOfFieldNames* is a list of the field names from the table that you want to use. *TableName* is the database table on which you want to use the **SELECT** query.

For example, suppose that you want a list of customer ID numbers and how much each bought for all of your company sales. The **SELECT** query could be written:

```
SELECT [Customer ID],[Order Amount] FROM Orders
```

First, because the designers of the **Xtreme.mdb** database have field names with blank spaces in them, we must surround such field names with square brackets. If the designers had written the field names as **CustomerID** and **OrderAmount**, you could write the same **SELECT** query as

```
SELECT CustomerID,OrderAmount FROM Orders
```

You can add as many field names as you want to the **SELECT** query. Simply separate each field name with a comma. Obviously, it is an error to add a field name to the **SELECT** query if that field does not exist in the table to which you are applying the **SELECT** query. In our example, that means we can use only the field names you see listed in the Orders table in Figure 24.1. Any field names not found in the Orders table will produce an error.

Programmer's Tip

Most programmers use capital letters for the SQL keywords. This helps to make the SQL statement easier to read.

Suppose that you want to examine the values for every field in the Orders table. You could, of course, add all the field names to the comma-delimited list of field names and the **SELECT** query would work just fine. However, SQL provides a shorthand method for such queries. If you write the **SELECT** query as

```
SELECT * FROM Orders
```

all the field values would be returned for each record in the Orders table. Stated another way, this statement returns the entire contents of the Orders database table.

You might be asking, "What do you mean, 'returns the entire contents'?" Refer back to Figure 24.3. Now pretend that you could connect your keyboard to the line drawn between the Data Adapter object and the Dataset object. This might look like Figure 24.4. (I've omitted the Connection object and the Database shown in Figure 24.3 for the sake of brevity.)

FIGURE 24.4

Issuing an SQL **SELECT** query to the database.

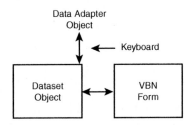

Now suppose that you type in a **SELECT** query in at the keyboard and press the Enter key. Your **SELECT** query travels down the keyboard wire, hangs a right turn and enters the Data Adapter object. The Data Adapter object checks over the **SELECT** query, likes what it sees, and passes it along to the Connection object (refer to Figure 24.3). The Connection object also looks at your **SELECT** query, says "Cool!" and passes it along to the DBMS (probably part of a DLL) that's buried within the code that actually manages the database. (It's the responsibility of the DBMS to process all valid SQL statements for the database.)

When the DBMS finishes gathering the data your **SELECT** query requested, it bundles up the data and sends it back to the Connection object. The Connection object passes the data along to the Data Adapter object. The Data Adapter object then takes the data and shoves it into the Dataset object. At this point, your SQL **SELECT** request has been fulfilled. It's up to the code you write in the Visual Basic .NET form to move the data from the Dataset object and display it on the form (more on that in Chapter 25).

So far, so good. Our **SELECT** query actually returns the entire contents of the Orders table. We would get every record for every sale the company ever had. Although we might actually want this on certain (rare) occasions, more often than not, this would be information overload. There's just too much information to be useful. What we need in most cases is a way to make the **SELECT** query more selective. That is, we need a way to create the **SELECT** query such that it can filter the data to better suit our needs.

We can narrow the focus of the **SELECT** query by using predicates with the **SELECT** query. SQL *predicates* are simply SQL keywords that operate with the **SELECT** keyword in a specific manner. You'll often hear these called *predicate clauses* because they're like a clause in a sentence. Let's see how these predicates might be used.

The WHERE Predicate

The **WHERE** predicate is used in conjunction with a **SELECT** query and has the general form

```
SELECT FieldList FROM TableName WHERE SearchCriteria
```

The **WHERE** predicate specifies a search criteria that we want to apply to the **SELECT** query. The search criterion is normally used to filter, or limit, the number of records that are returned from the database query.

For example, suppose that you're a customer with the company and your Customer ID number is 524. The **SELECT** query

```
SELECT * FROM Orders WHERE [Customer ID] = 524
```

would return a dataset that contains records describing every purchase you ever made with the company.

If your last name is Thomas, you might rewrite the **SELECT** query as

```
SELECT * FROM Orders WHERE [Contact Last Name] = 'Thomas'
```

This seems like it should work, but it won't because the field named `Contact Last Name` doesn't exist in the Orders table. Your last name only appears in the Customer table.

Let's try another query:

```
SELECT * FROM Customer WHERE [Contact Last Name] = 'Thomas'
```

This works fine because we switched from the Orders table to the Customer table. The result would be a dataset that contains a list of all customers who have the last name of Thomas. However, we no longer get the orders information because we aren't searching the Orders table. However, we could use your Customer ID from this query in another query on the Orders table to return your sales records.

Compound WHERE Predicates with AND and OR

We can apply additional data filters by using compound search criteria to augment the WHERE predicate. For example:

```
SELECT * FROM Employee WHERE _
       Salary > 50000 AND _
       Position = 'Sales Representative'
```

Notice the SQL keyword AND in the SELECT query. The AND keyword has the same interpretation that it did when we studied relational operators in Chapter 10, "Relational and Logical Operators." The SELECT query would return all employee records in which the employee's salary exceeds $50,000 and the position is Sales Representative.

Keep in mind that SELECT queries have the potential to return zero records in response to a search. As a general rule, an AND clause returns a smaller number of records from the database than if the AND clause were not used.

You probably guessed that we can also use an OR clause with the WHERE predicate:

```
SELECT * FROM [Orders Detail] WHERE _
    [Unit Price] > 50 OR _
    Quantity > 3
```

This would return more records than if either of the two WHERE predicates were omitted. For example, the statement

```
SELECT * FROM [Orders Detail] WHERE _
    [Unit Price] > 50
```

might return 1000 records, whereas

```
SELECT * FROM [Orders Detail] WHERE _
    Quantity > 3
```

might return 200 records. However, 1,200 records would be returned by using the OR clause. Therefore, OR clauses usually expand the record count when compared to a single WHERE clause.

Compound WHERE Clauses with LIKE

Sometimes you'd like to perform a search using a partial match. For example, perhaps you'd like a list of all employees who live in the Indianapolis metro area. You could use

```
SELECT * FROM [Employee Addresses] WHERE _
    [Postal Code] LIKE '462*'
```

which would return all employee who live in a ZIP Code that starts with 462. This means the records of anyone who lives in a ZIP Code between 46200 and 46299 will be included in the dataset.

Programmer's Tip

You'll notice that some WHERE criteria surround the parameter with single quotation marks (for example, '462*'), whereas others simply present a value (for example, 50). As a general rule, when you're searching for a string literal, you need to surround the parameter with single quotation marks. If the parameter is a numeric data type, you don't need to use the quotation marks.

The ORDER BY Clause

Many databases organize the records within a table according to the primary key for that table. This is usually done to improve the search performance of the database. However, there are times when you want to control the order in which the data are presented. In those cases, you would use the ORDER BY clause. The general syntax is

```
SELECT FieldNameList FROM TableName [WHERE SearchCriteria] _
    ORDER BY FieldNames [ASC ¦ DESC]
```

where the terms in brackets are optional. For example, if you want to present a list of all employees in alphabetical order, you might use

```
SELECT * FROM Employee ORDER BY [Last Name]
```

A variation would be

```
SELECT * FROM Employee ORDER BY [Last Name],[First Name]
```

which would present the same list, but also sort on the first name. In other words, if there are two employees named Smith, the one named John might appear before the one named Fred simply because the primary key causes them to appear that way. If you add First Name to the ORDER BY clause, the dataset would have them in alphabetical order across both the first and last names.

The SELECT query

```
SELECT * FROM Employee ORDER BY [Last Name] DESC
```

would return the records in reverse alphabetical order. The default order is in ascending (ASC) ordering.

You can also use a WHERE predicate, if you want:

```
SELECT * FROM Customer WHERE Country = 'Italy' _
  ORDER BY [Last Name], [First Name]
```

This would produce an alphabetical list of all customers who live in Italy.

There are also SQL commands for inserting new records into a table, deleting records from a table, and for editing existing table records. We'll cover these in Chapter 25. For the moment, however, let's experiment with the basic **SELECT** query to see how it actually behaves.

Using SQL

We can try some of our SQL commands using an SQL test program that we will explore in more depth in Chapter 25. For the moment, however, we'll use it just to see how SQL might be used. Figure 24.5 shows a screen shot of how the program looks after selecting the `Xtreme.mdb` database.

FIGURE 24.5

SQL Tester program after selecting a database.

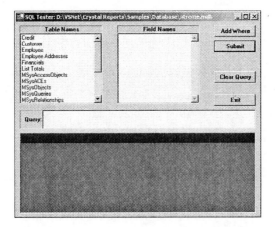

The Table Names list box shows the tables that are contained within the `Xtreme.mdb` database. If you click one of those tables, the program reads the fields from that table and presents them in the Field Names list box. This is shown in Figure 24.6.

Programmer's Tip

Tables that begin with Msys* in Figure 24.5 are internally generated tables that aren't normally used in SQL queries. We could have written the test program to remove these, but we left them in to show you that Access does maintain tables that aren't normally visible to you.

The first entry in the Field Names list box is an asterisk (*) that enables you to select all the fields from the table. Otherwise, you can double-click on the individual fields you want to use in the query. The fields are shown in alphabetical order, but that probably isn't the order in which they're actually stored in the table (more on this issue in Chapter 25).

If you use the wildcard asterisk and don't want to restrict the query with a **WHERE** predicate, you would simply click on the Submit button. A sample run is shown in Figure 24.7.

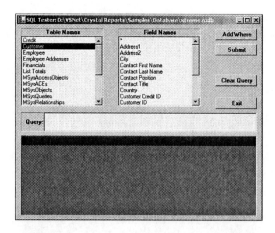

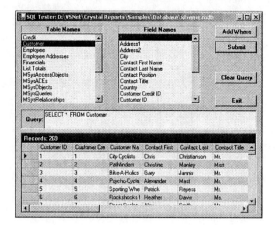

The query that was tested is shown in the Query text box near the center of the display. The
data grid at the bottom displays the results of the query. The title bar for the data grid shows
how many records were returned from the query. Although you might not be able to tell, the
background color for each row alternates between white and a pale green. (This little display
touch should give you a warm fuzzy feeling if you're old enough to remember the mainframe
style of printer paper.)

Adjusting Column Widths

Notice that some of the columns aren't wide enough to show all the data. For example,
although the first column width is okay, the next two column headers are too long to fit within
the default column width. Even though the data for the second column can be seen in full, the
same is not true for column three (Customer Name). However, the data grid control is smart
enough to let the user widen a column at runtime. Figure 24.8 shows the same display after I

expanded the column widths. To widen a column, simply move the cursor to the vertical bar between the two fields. The cursor will change to the double-arrow cursor. Click the left mouse button and drag the bar until the column is the desired width.

FIGURE 24.8
Sample run in Figure 24.7 after increasing column widths.

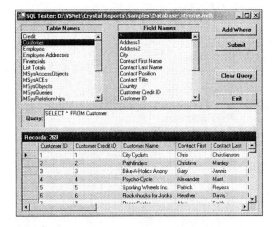

Now you can see the full column header name as well as the data within the columns.

Adding a WHERE Predicate

Figure 24.9 illustrates how to enter a query with a WHERE predicate. After selecting a subset of the available fields, we clicked the Add Where button. The program is now waiting for you to enter the WHERE predicate.

FIGURE 24.9
Adding a WHERE predicate to a query.

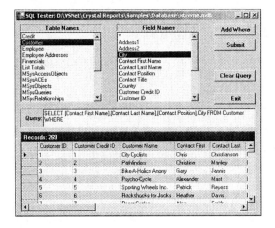

Notice that the query added each field name as I double-clicked it before clicking the Add Where button. If the field name contains a space in it, the program supplies the required brackets around the name (for example, [Contact First Name]). If there is no blank space in the name (for instance, City), no brackets are added.

Programmer's Tip

You can use brackets around a field or table name in a query at any time. However, they aren't required unless the field or table name has a blank space in it.

The program places the WHERE keyword in the query and waits for you to type in the rest of the query. A complete example is shown in Figure 24.10.

FIGURE 24.10
Sample run with a WHERE predicate.

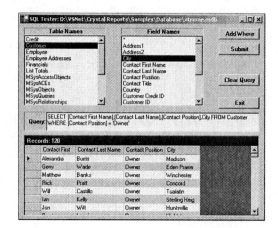

As you can see in Figure 24.10, we filtered the dataset to those instances where the Contact Position in the Customer table was Owner. The query returned 120 records, which is smaller than previous queries. (Compare this with the data grid title bar in Figure 24.9.)

Using an ORDER BY Clause

In Figure 24.10, the records that are returned are in no particular order. We can, of course, add an ORDER BY clause to place the same data set in order. A sample run using an ORDER BY clause is shown in Figure 24.11.

Figure 24.11 shows that the same number of records is returned, but now they're sorted in alphabetical order by last name. You can see the query that was used in the Query text box.

Actually, a simple ORDER BY clause like the one used in Figure 24.11 isn't necessary. The reason for this is because the data grid control is smart enough to sort a single column for us automatically. To place the records in sorted order, simply click on the column head that you want to use for the sort. If you had clicked on the column head titled Contact Last Name in Figure 24.10, you would have produced the same results shown in Figure 24.11.

Does that mean that ORDER BY is unnecessary? No, not at all. Consider the query and results shown in Figure 24.12.

FIGURE 24.11

Sample run using an
ORDER BY clause.

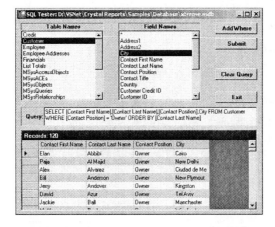

FIGURE 24.12

Sample run using a compound ORDER BY clause.

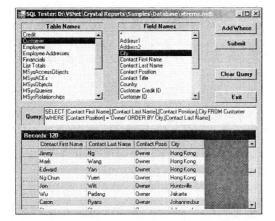

We scrolled the dataset to get to the city of Hong Kong, which has multiple records for that city. Within the records in which the city is Hong Kong, notice how the records are sorted in alphabetical order by last name. We did this by using a compound ORDER BY clause in the query as shown in Figure 24.12. You cannot produce this ordering by simply clicking a column header in the data grid.

Summary

We'll delve into the SQL Tester program in detail in Chapter 25. However, our purpose in this chapter is to simply show you how the SQL language may be used. You should load and compile the same program and experiment with different SQL commands so that you become comfortable with them. Make sure that you try some of the SQL keywords we didn't explicitly use (for example, LIKE).

Review Questions

1. What is a database?

A. A *database* is a collection of related data.

2. What is the general structure of a database?

A. Think of a database as a shell within which are one or more tables. Each table is comprised of columns, called *fields*. Each field represents a data item. Common field names might be `SSN`, `FirstName`, `LastName`, `Address`, `City`, `State`, and `Zip`. If you fill in each field for one row of the table, that row becomes a database record. Usually, the data that comprise each record is unique.

3. What is a primary key and what is its purpose?

A. A *primary key* is a field that has an unduplicated value for each record in the table. In some cases, the primary field is actually two fields. By having a unique primary key in one table, it's possible to use that key in other, related tables for purposes of searching the related tables. A common example of a primary key is a customer ID number in a Customer table, which can then be used to identify all purchases by the customer in the Orders table. In other words, the primary key in the Customer table is used to define a relationship between that table and the Orders table.

4. Explain what the lines are that appear between the tables shown in Figure 24.1.

A. The lines between the tables show how the primary keys are used in other tables. In each case, the primary key is displayed in boldface print. The lines represent how the tables are related to each other. For example, the field named Customer ID is the primary key in the Customer table. However, the Customer ID field is also present in the Orders table, and a line connects the field in the two tables. Therefore, we can search the Orders table and find who placed the order by following the Customer ID number in the Orders table back to the Customer table.

5. Write an SQL statement that selects every customer from the Customers table who lives in the 46220 ZIP Code and presents them in alphabetical order based on their last name. You can assume that the field names are `LastName` and `ZipCode`.

A. The SQL statement would be

```
SQL = "SELECT LastName,ZipCode FROM Customers WHERE "
SQL += "ZipCode = 46220 ORDER BY LastName"
```

6. What is the primary purpose of the Connection object?

A. The purpose of the Connection object is to provide the information necessary to establish a link between Visual Basic .NET and the database. The two most important properties of the Connection object are the Provider and Data Source parameters of the connect string. These two parameters tell the type of database being used and where to find it.

7. What is the purpose of the Data Adapter object?

A. The Data Adapter object enables us to control the data associated with the database. It is from the Data Adapter that we derive the datasets that contain the actual data used in a program.

CHAPTER 25

DATABASE PROGRAMMING WITH VISUAL BASIC .NET

In this chapter, you will learn the following:

- Using Visual Basic .NET wizards to interact with a database
- Adding a DataSet object

- Life without wizards
- Modifying a database

*I*n this chapter, we'll explore how Visual Basic .NET is used to interact with databases. Basically, you have two ways in which to work with databases. First, you can use the wizards that Visual Basic .NET provides to create the skeleton database code. A second way is to forego the wizards and create the code yourself. We'll do both in this chapter. We'll also use the old-style ActiveX Data Object (ADO) along with ADO.NET to interact with a sample database.

Throughout this chapter, we assume that you're working with an Access database. However, the methods used in this chapter apply equally well to Microsoft's SQL Server, Oracle, and other popular databases. (Indeed, some Visual Basic .NET programming elements have been optimized for SQL Server for obvious reasons.) In those instances in which the database flavor makes a difference, I'll point this out to you. When you've finished this chapter, you'll be able to read and write database information using Visual Basic .NET.

Using Visual Basic .NET Wizards to Interact with a Database

Let's begin by creating a new project named DBWizard. We won't concern ourselves just yet with the default form that's created. Instead, locate the Data tab in the Toolbox window and click on it. Your display should look similar to that shown in Figure 25.1.

FIGURE 25.1

The Data tab in the Toolbox window.

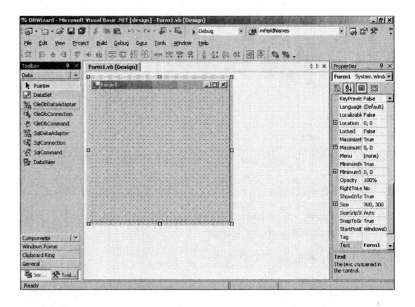

Now double-click on the `OleDbDataAdapter` object to move an instance of the object onto your form. Double-clicking on the `OleDbDataAdapter` object automatically invokes the Data Adapter Configuration Wizard, as shown in Figure 25.2.

FIGURE 25.2

The Data Adapter Configuration Wizard.

The wizard presents an introductory screen to tell you the purpose of this wizard. Click the Next button to proceed to the next screen, as shown in Figure 25.3.

The purpose of this screen is for you to supply the name and path of the database you want to use. Stated another way, Figure 25.3 is asking you to establish the Connection object shown in Figure 24.3 in the previous chapter. The answer you supply here provides the link between the data adapter and the database itself.

FIGURE 25.3

The Data Adapter
Configuration Wizard.

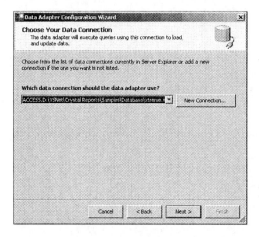

If this is your first time using the wizard, you need to click on the New Connection button to
locate the database file you want to use. We'll assume that no connection exists to the database, so click on the New Connection button. The program loads the Data Link Properties dialog box, changing the display to look like Figure 25.4.

FIGURE 25.4

The Data Adapter
Configuration Wizard
after clicking the New
Connection button.

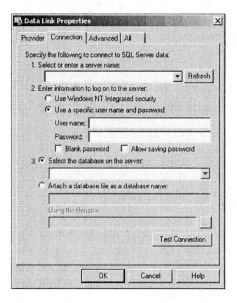

As you can see by the first line on the Connection tab, the wizard assumes you want to connect with Microsoft's SQL Server. (Hmmm…I wonder why?) However, because we want to
work with an Access database, you need to click on the Provider tab first. The display should
now look like Figure 25.5.

FIGURE 25.5
The Provider tab of the
Data Adapter
Configuration Wizard.

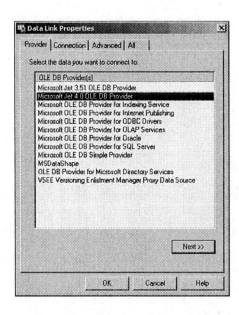

The Provider tab presents a list of currently defined OLE database providers. OLE stands for *Object Linking and Embedding* and is a technology developed by Microsoft to support communication between software objects. The term *Provider* in this instance means that our system has the capability to connect with a specific database.

As you can see from the list in Figure 25.5, a number of providers are listed, including links to Access, Oracle, SQL Server, and ODBC. In our case, we want to select the Microsoft JET 4.0 OLE DB Provider, which is the device driver for Access. Click the Next button.

Your display should now look similar to Figure 25.6. Notice that the Connection tab shown in Figure 25.6 is different from the Connection tab shown in Figure 25.4. The reason is because the content of the Connection tab is context-sensitive to the selection you made on the Provider tab. (You could prove this to yourself by going back to the Provider tab, selecting the SQL Server option, and then clicking the Connection tab. The display would look just like Figure 25.4.)

If you know the pathname to the `Xtreme.mdb` database, you could fill it into the first text box shown in Figure 25.6. Otherwise, click on the ellipsis button (that is, the one with the three dots) and navigate to the proper location and select the `Xtreme.mdb` database. The actual location depends on where you installed Visual Basic .NET. The default is `C:\Program Files\Microsoft Visual Studio .NET\Crystal Reports\Samples\Database`. Your selection then appears in the text box.

We'll accept the rest of the default values for the dialog box. However, as long as we're here, you might want to click on the Test Connection button to make sure that it's functioning properly. If you've filled in the dialog box correctly, you'll see a message box similar to that shown in Figure 25.7. Click on the OK button to dismiss the message box.

FIGURE 25.6

The new Connection tab of the Data Adapter Configuration Wizard.

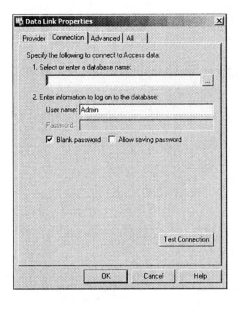

FIGURE 25.7

Testing the database connection.

Now click on the OK button to dismiss the Data Link Properties dialog box. Your screen will look similar to Figure 25.3 and should have the pathname to the `Xtreme.mdb` database shown in the list box. Click on the Next button. The screen should now look similar to Figure 25.8.

FIGURE 25.8

Choosing a query type for the Data Adapter Configuration Wizard.

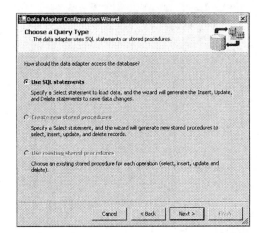

Because we'll be using SQL commands, we'll accept the default choice to use SQL commands. Click the Next button. The screen changes to that shown in Figure 25.9.

FIGURE 25.9

The Data Adapter Configuration Wizard.

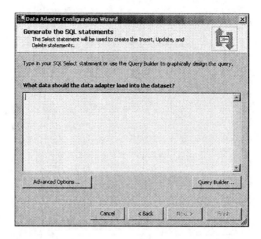

At this point, there are several ways to proceed. Because you already know how to write an SQL **SELECT** statement, you could type in a **SELECT** statement similar to the ones we examined in Chapter 24, "Database Fundamentals," and click the Next button. If you follow this route, your screen should look like Figure 25.10.

FIGURE 25.10

The Data Adapter Configuration Wizard after entering your own **SELECT** query.

As you can see from the first line in Figure 25.10, the data adapter is now configured. You could click on the Finish button to end the Data Adapter Configuration Wizard session.

If you click on the Advanced Options button in Figure 25.9, the display shown in Figure 25.11 appears.

FIGURE 25.11

The Advanced Options display for the Data Adapter Configuration Wizard.

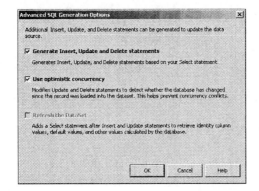

The defaults shown in Figure 25.11 not only enable us to read the database, but also to add new records, edit existing records, and delete records from the database. If you click on the OK button, you're returned to Figure 25.9.

Because we haven't yet provided an SQL query, the Finish button still isn't activated. Therefore, click on the Query Builder button to present the Query Builder. The screen now looks like the one depicted in Figure 25.12.

FIGURE 25.12

The Query Builder dialog of the Data Adapter Configuration Wizard.

This should look somewhat familiar to you because the program we used in Chapter 24 is similar to the Query Builder. For example, select the Customer table from the list of tables shown in Figure 25.12. Click the Add button, and then click the Close button. (Some SQL queries can operate on two tables simultaneously. However, we'll use only the Customer table.) The display will look like Figure 25.13.

Notice the partially constructed SQL query near the middle of the display. In the Customer dialog box, select the City, Contact First Name, Contact Last Name, and Contact Position fields from the Customer table. After each selection is clicked, the SQL query will be updated. When you have finished, the display will look like Figure 25.14.

FIGURE 25.13
The Query Builder after selecting the Customer table.

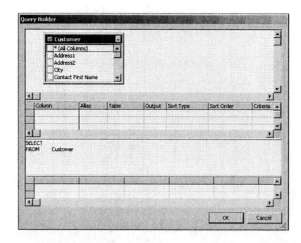

FIGURE 25.14
The Query Builder after selecting the Customer table.

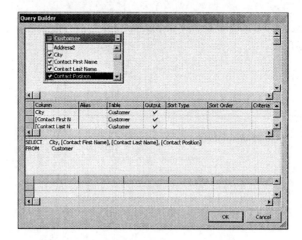

This query is similar to the query we used to generate Figure 24.10 in the previous chapter. Assuming that we're done building our query, click the OK button. Figure 25.15 now appears.

Notice that we're actually back to Figure 25.9, but the query field has been filled in for us. (Because you're such an astute person, you could have just typed in the SQL query in Figure 25.9 and avoided the last six figures. Although I know you didn't need all this extra stuff, we did it just for completeness.) Click the Next button. You'll now see Figure 25.10 displayed. Click the Finish button, which dismisses the Data Adapter Wizard and presents the display shown in Figure 25.16.

FIGURE 25.15

The completed SQL query.

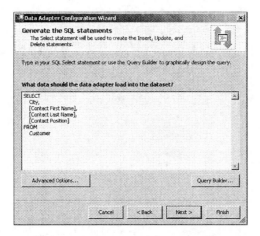

FIGURE 25.16

The addition of the `DataAdapter` object to the project.

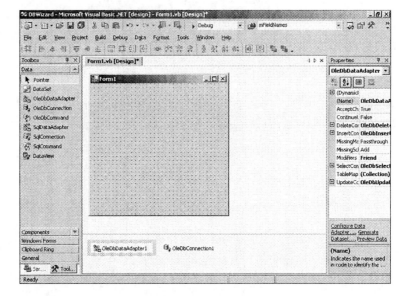

Notice that the `OleDbDataAdapter1` and `OleDbConnection1` objects have been added to our form for us. However, if you recall our discussion from Chapter 24, we still need to have a `DataSet` object for things to work correctly.

Adding a `DataSet` Object

Actually, there are two ways to add the `DataSet` object to our project. We could grab it from the Data tab shown on the Toolbox, but that's the hard way. Instead, select the Data, Generate Dataset menu sequence shown in Figure 25.17.

FIGURE 25.17

The Generate Dataset menu sequence.

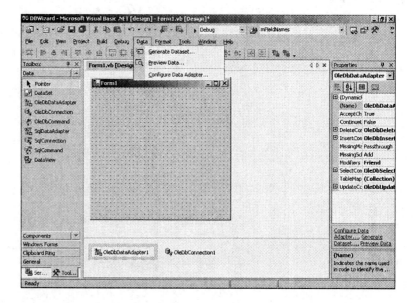

After making the menu selection, the screen shows you the options in Figure 25.18.

FIGURE 25.18

Dialog box for adding the `DataSet` object to the project.

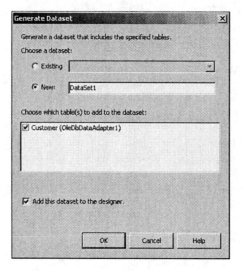

Visual Basic .NET is smart enough to know that we haven't added a `DataSet` object to our project yet. If we had, the Existing drop-down list box would present those `DataSet` objects that have been added to the project. Because that isn't the case, it adds a `DataSet` object named `DataSet1` for us.

The large text box near the middle of the figure presents a list of the tables we want associated with this **DataSet** object. As you can see, Visual Basic .NET got the information from the **OleDbDataAdapter** we built earlier. Because we elected to use only the Customer table when we configured the data adapter, that table is automatically checked for us.

The innocent check box that says Add This Dataset to the Designer determines whether we want the requisite code to use the **DataSet** object added to the project. Life is a lot simpler if you leave it checked. Otherwise, you must add the **DataSet** object code yourself. You can do this, but why bother if Visual Basic .NET will do it for you? Now click OK.

Visual Basic .NET will grind away for a few seconds while it adds the new code to your project. Eventually, your display will look like that shown in Figure 25.19.

FIGURE 25.19
The project after the **DataSet** object has been added.

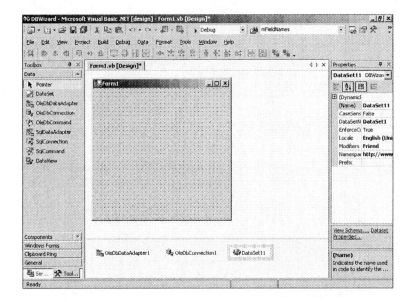

Notice that all three required components we talked about in Chapter 24 (see Figure 24.3) are now present in our project. We have to add only a few more statements to complete the project.

Adding the DataGrid Control

Obviously, we want to use a **DataGrid** control to display the output from our database query. Click on the Toolbox-Windows Forms tab and double-click the **DataGrid** control to place it on our form.

The first thing you need to do is bind the **DataGrid** control to our **DataSet1** object. You do this by setting the **DataSource** property of the **DataGrid** control. When you move to the **DataSource** property in the Properties window, you'll see the **DataSet** object that's associated with the Customer table. Click on **DataSet1.Customer** option. Your screen should now look similar to Figure 25.20.

FIGURE 25.20

The `DataGrid` control after setting the `DataSource` property.

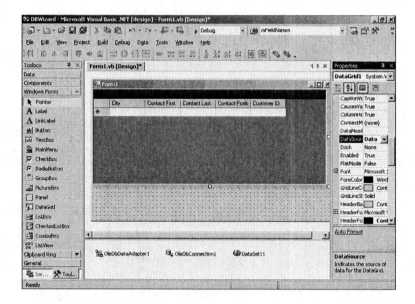

Notice how the column headers are filled in for us by Visual Basic .NET. You'll also see that the last column is Customer ID. We didn't ask for this field, so why is it there? The reason is because Customer ID is the primary key field for the Customer database table. (Refer to Figure 24.1 to see the primary fields for the `Xtreme.mdb` database.) Visual Basic .NET automatically adds the primary key field for us.

As a starting point, we set the `DataGrid`'s size to 500 pixels wide by 200 high. We also set the `AlternatingBackColor-Web` to `GreenYellow` from the predefined list of colors. Suit yourself.

Next, we changed the `Text` property of the form to `"DBWizard Test"`. Finally, we need to link the `DataAdapter` object to the `DataSet` object. You do this by adding one statement to the Form1 Load event. The entire program code is presented in Listing 25.1.

LISTING 25.1   The DBWizard Project Source Code

```
Public Class Form1
 Inherits System.Windows.Forms.Form

 ' Windows Form Designer generated code

 Private Sub Form1_Load(ByVal sender As System.Object, ByVal e As _
            System.EventArgs) Handles MyBase.Load
  OleDbDataAdapter1.Fill(DataSet11)
 End Sub
End Class
```

Now compile and run the project. You should see output similar to that shown in Figure 25.21. (We expanded the columns a bit.)

FIGURE 25.21

Sample run of the DBWizard project.

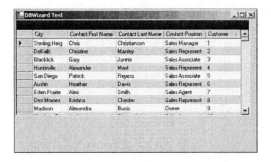

Congratulations! You've just written your own program to read an Access database. Well...actually...you wrote one line of code and Visual Basic .NET wrote the rest of it.

As I said in the first paragraph of this chapter, there are two ways to build a program that can read a database, and we just finished the first way. Using the Visual Basic .NET wizards is the "You-don't-need-to-know-how-to-build-a-car-to-drive-one" approach to database program development. This approach works fine...until your car breaks down in the middle of nowhere. It's my belief that you need to know a little more about what's going on under the hood to appreciate how to really use Visual Basic .NET with databases. That's the topic of the remainder of this chapter. We'll also revisit the wizard again in this chapter.

Life Without Wizards

In this section, we'll examine the code necessary to work with databases, but without using the Visual Basic .NET wizards. We'll also use some old-style ADO along with the new-style ADO.NET. Even though we could do everything with pure ADO.NET, I thought it would be interesting to show you how you can use ADO if needed (there is, after all, a lot of ADO legacy code out there).

Setting Up the Form

The program we're about to write is the SQL test program you saw in Chapter 24. Start a new project and name it SQLTester. You'll need to add the controls shown in Figure 25.22 to the form.

There are two list boxes near the top of the form named `lstTables` and `lstFields`. The buttons are named `btnWhere`, `btnSubmit`, `btnClear`, and `btnExit`. The multiline text box near the center is named `txtQuery`. The `DataGrid` control is named `dtgGrid`. You also need to add an `OpenFileDialog` control named `OpenFileDialog1` (its default name) from the Windows Forms tab of the Toolbox.

Finally, drag copies of the `OleDBConnection` and `OleDbDataAdapter` from the Data tab of the Toolbox onto the form. The default names for each object are fine. When you drag the `OleDbDataAdapter` to the form, Visual Basic .NET automatically starts the Data Adapter Wizard. However, because we want to manage things ourselves now, click the Cancel button to dismiss the dialog box.

FIGURE 25.22
Controls for the
SQLTester project.

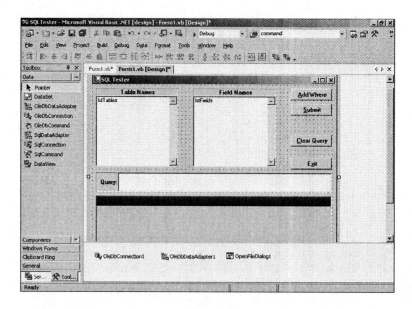

Because we'll be using ADO along with ADO.NET in this project, we need to inform Visual
Basic .NET of that fact. To add the required references, use the Project, Add Reference menu
sequence and click on the COM tab of the Add Reference dialog. Scroll down and click
Microsoft ADO Ext. 2.7 for DDL And Security dynamic link library. Your screen should look
similar to Figure 25.23. Now click the Select button to add the file to our project.

FIGURE 25.23
Controls for the
SQLTester project.

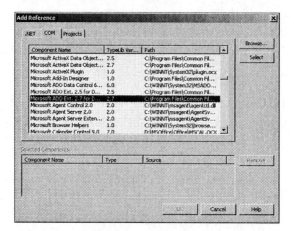

Before you dismiss the Add Reference dialog box, click on the .NET tab. Highlight the **adodb**
component in the list (it should be near the top of the list) and click the Select button. Now
you can click OK to dismiss the Add Reference dialog box. Visual Basic .NET now knows that
we can use the ADO routines in our project.

Adding the Code

Listing 25.2 shows part of the code for the test program. The program begins by importing the necessary namespaces that are required to use ADO.NET. (I'll explain the purpose of the MAX_RECORDS constant later in the chapter.)

The first function in the project is GetFileName(). This function simply asks the user to select the Access database. Because we're working with the sample database that's distributed with Crystal Reports, I've hard coded that directory as the default startup directory (see the InitialDirectory property). Obviously, you should change this directory to reflect your own installation path for Visual Studio .NET. The remainder of the function's code should look familiar to you by now.

LISTING 25.2   The GenFileName() and Form Load Event Code

```
Imports System
Imports System.Data
Imports System.Data.OleDb

Public Class frmMain
 Inherits System.Windows.Forms.Form

 Private Const MAX_RECORDS As Integer = 10000
 Private strConnect As String

' Windows Form Designer generated code

 Private Function GetFileName() As String
  ' Purpose: This function attempts to open an Access database
  '
  ' Argument list:
  '  none
  '
  ' Return value
  '  string   the name of the file selected or an empty
  '         string if cancelled.
  '
  Dim NewFileName As String
  Dim NewFile As OpenFileDialog = New OpenFileDialog()
  Dim MyChoice As DialogResult

  With NewFile
   .Filter = "Access Files (*.mdb)¦*.mdb¦All Files (*.*)¦*.*"
   .FilterIndex = 1          ' Assume text files
   .DefaultExt = "mdb"        ' Ditto
   .InitialDirectory = "D:\VSNET\Crystal Reports\Samples\Database\"
   .CheckFileExists = False
   .ReadOnlyChecked = True
   .Title = "Open Access Data File"
  End With
```

LISTING 25.2   Continued

```
      MyChoice = NewFile.ShowDialog        ' What did they do?

      If MyChoice = DialogResult.Cancel Then ' Bail out?
       NewFileName = ""
      Else
       NewFileName = NewFile.FileName
      End If

      If NewFileName.Length > 0 Then
       Return NewFileName
      End If
    End Function

    Private Sub frmMain_Load(ByVal sender As System.Object, ByVal e As_
               System.EventArgs) Handles MyBase.Load
      ' Purpose: This opens and reads in the table names from the database.
      Dim FileName As String
      Dim AdoConn As New ADODB.Connection()
      Dim MyCat As New ADOX.Catalog()
      Dim tbl As ADOX.Table

      FileName = GetFileName()        ' Get the database file name
      If FileName.Length = 0 Then
       Exit Sub
      End If
      Me.Text = "SQL Tester: " & FileName ' Show the file name

      ' This builds the connect string. It is used later as needed, too.
      strConnect = "Provider=Microsoft.Jet.OLEDB.4.0;Password="""";User _
           ID=Admin;Data Source="
      strConnect &= FileName
      AdoConn.Open(strConnect)
      MyCat.ActiveConnection = AdoConn

      For Each tbl In MyCat.Tables     ' Show the field names
       lstTables.Items.Add(tbl.Name.ToString)
      Next
      AdoConn.Close()

    End Sub
```

The Form Load event code sets things up by a call to GetFileName(). After the database file-name is entered by the user, the code copies the filename and pathname to the form's title bar.

The Connection String

Now the code starts to get interesting. The first thing we need to do is build a connection string that provides the necessary details to Visual Basic .NET to form a connection to the selected database. Because we're connecting to an Access database, we can hard-code the first part of the connection string as

```
strConnect = "Provider=Microsoft.Jet.OLEDB.4.0;Password="""";User _
      ID=Admin;Data Source="
strConnect &= FileName
```

This tells Visual Basic .NET that we'll be using the Provider for Access databases, we aren't using a password, the User ID is **Admin**, and the Data Source is the filename just selected by the user. This connection string comprises the bare-bones essentials needed to form a connection to the database. It's probably obvious that this connection string will vary according to the type of database being used.

Programmer's Tip

If you want to see a more complete list of the parameters that may be used with the connection string, reload the DBWizard project you created at the beginning of this chapter. Expand the Windows-generated code section of the project and look for the `OleDbConnection1.ConnectionString` statement. What you'll find is about eight lines of parameter information that may be used in the connection string. We're using only the essential parameters necessary to form a connection to an Access database (each parameter is delineated by a semicolon).

If you want to connect to a different type of database (for example, SQL Server or Oracle), follow the DBWizard directions, but respond to the wizard questions for the database you want to use. When you're done, examine the connection string in the Windows-generated code section to determine which parameters you need to include in your connection string. In most cases, the first four parameters are sufficient.

Using ADO

Some readers might question my use of the older ADO model in the program. After all, ADO is based upon Microsoft Component Object Model (COM) which, for the most part, is limited to Windows platforms; ADO.NET is not. Still, there are a number of reasons why I chose to include a little ADO code in the program. First, there are things that ADO can do for us that the present incarnation of ADO.NET cannot. For example, ADO.NET does not yet support a data definition language (DDL) for creating your own databases (this is forthcoming, however). Second, sticking your head in the sand doesn't make ADO go away. There is a ton of Visual Basic code out there that uses ADO, and you might learn something useful by studying it. Third, because we're simply using the ADO model to retrieve the table and field information, we aren't taking a significant performance hit. Finally, I wanted you to at least see how easy it is to use an ADO connection if you ever need to. 'nuff said.

After the connect string is formed, we use it to make an ADO connection to the database. The **Catalog** object enables us to retrieve a list of the tables that are associated with the database. We march through the **Tables** collection of the catalog, adding the table names to the **lstTables** list box.

We use the ADO connection in a similar fashion in the **SelectedIndexChanged** event for the **lstTables** list box. This code is presented in Listing 25.3. The same connection string, **strConnect**, is used again to reopen the ADO connection to read the field names for the table that the user selected.

LISTING 25.3   The `SelectedIndexChanged` Event for the `lstTables` List Box

```
Private Sub lstTables_SelectedIndexChanged(ByVal sender As System.Object, _
    ByVal e As System.EventArgs) Handles lstTables.SelectedIndexChanged
  ' Purpose: Construct a list of database fields for the table that was
  '          selected.

  Dim AdoConn As New ADODB.Connection()
  Dim i As Integer, buff As String
  Dim MyCat As New ADOX.Catalog()
  Dim tbl As ADOX.Table, col As ADOX.Column

  txtQuery.Clear()        ' If this changes, clear the query

  AdoConn.Open(strConnect)      ' Open a connection

  MyCat.ActiveConnection = AdoConn
  lstFields.Items.Clear()       ' Clear old field names
  For Each tbl In MyCat.Tables   ' Go through the tables...
    ' for the selected table...
    If tbl.Name.ToString = lstTables.SelectedItem Then
     lstFields.Items.Add("*")
     For Each col In tbl.Columns  ' ...show the fields
      lstFields.Items.Add(col.Name)
     Next
     Exit For
    End If
  Next
  AdoConn.Close()
End Sub
```

The only real difference in the ADO code in Listing 25.3 is that we're also iterating through the **Columns** collection of the database and adding the columns to the **lstFields** list box. We add the wildcard field section (that is, the asterisk) at the top of the list box before adding the field names. As you'll recall from our SQL discussion in Chapter 24, the asterisk means that we want to retrieve all column values from the table for the **SELECT** statement.

As you can see from Listing 25.3, firing the **SelectedIndexChanged** event occurs when the user clicks on one of the database tables listed in the **lstTables** list box. The tables selection then causes the fields for that table to be displayed in the **lstFields** list box.

We're now ready to examine the rest of the program code. The remaining code is presented in Listing 25.4.

Selecting Field Names for the Query

The first subroutine in Listing 25.4 (**lstFields_SelectedIndexChanged**) processes the field choices made by the user. This event is fired any time the user clicks a choice in the **lstFields** list box. The code first checks to see whether the user elected to retrieve all fields by selecting the asterisk. If so, the query text "**SELECT * **" is moved into the **txtQuery** text box and we exit the subroutine.

A little more processing is necessary if the user clicks on a specific field name in the `lstFields` list box. First, we check the length of the `txtQuery` text box. If the length is 0, we're starting a new query and we must add the `SELECT` statement to the text box. If the `txtQuery` length is not 0, it means we're adding another field name to the query. Therefore, we do not need to copy the `SELECT` statement.

The code now must check to see whether the field name selected by the user has one or more words. This check is performed by the `BracketMultiWords()` function. We call `BracketMultiWords()`, passing in the field name that was just selected. If the field name contains two or more words (for example, "Contact First Name" as shown in Figure 25.21), we need to place brackets around the field name. The resulting name is then returned by the function with brackets added, if necessary.

Once that's done, we append the (adjusted) field name to the existing state of the query as held in `txtQuery` and then add a comma at the end of the string. The comma is appended in preparation for adding more field names (more about the comma later on).

Adding a WHERE Predicate

After the field names are added to the query, the user has two choices. First, he can click on the Submit button to submit the query for processing. Second, he can click on the Where button to add a `WHERE` predicate to the query. The code to add a `WHERE` predicate is quite simple.

First, we copy the content of the `txtQuery` text box into a temporary variable named `temp`. We do this so we can use the `LastIndexOf()` string method to see if a `FROM` keyword is already present in the query string. If there is no `FROM` present in the string, we use the `Remove()` string method to remove the trailing comma that was appended while the field names were being added to the query. The code then adds the `FROM` keyword followed by the table name being used in the query. (Once again, we call `BracketMultiWords()` in case the selected table name has two or more words in it.) The resulting string is then copied back into the `txtQuery` text box.

Next, we append the `WHERE` keyword and set the focus to the text box. Finally, we add a trailing blank space to `txtQuery`. Hmmm. Why not just add the space when the `WHERE` keyword is appended? If you use that approach, the `Focus()` method highlights the entire string in the text box. If the user would inadvertently type a keystroke at this point, the entire content of the text box that we have built would be immediately erased. Not good. By setting the focus and *then* adding the blank space, the content of the text box is not highlighted, but the cursor is politely waiting for the user to type in the `WHERE` predicate.

LISTING 25.4   The Remaining Program Code

```
Private Sub lstFields_SelectedIndexChanged(ByVal sender As Object, ByVal e _
        As System.EventArgs) Handles lstFields.SelectedIndexChanged
    ' Purpose: This selects the field names for the query.
```

LISTING 25.4 Continued

```vb
  If lstFields.SelectedItem = "*" Then    ' Did they chose a wildcard?
   txtQuery.Text = "SELECT * "
   Exit Sub                    ' We're done...go home
  End If
  If txtQuery.TextLength = 0 Then
   txtQuery.Text = "SELECT "
  End If
  txtQuery.Text &= BracketMultiWords(lstFields.SelectedItem) & ","
End Sub

Private Sub btnWhere_Click(ByVal sender As System.Object, ByVal e As _
             System.EventArgs) Handles btnWhere.Click
 ' Purpose: Add a WHERE predicate to the query. In preparation, we need
 '      to remove the last comma from the field list.

 Dim FromFound As Integer
 Dim temp As String

 temp = txtQuery.Text
 FromFound = temp.LastIndexOf(" FROM ")    ' See if there is a FROM yet
 If FromFound = -1 Then            ' If not...
  temp = temp.Remove(temp.Length - 1, 1)  ' ...remove trailing comma
  ' and add the FROM and table name
  temp &= " FROM " & BracketMultiWords(lstTables.SelectedItem)
  txtQuery.Text = temp
 End If
 txtQuery.Text &= " WHERE"    ' Now add the WHERE
 txtQuery.Focus()       ' Set the focus so they can add the rest
 txtQuery.AppendText(" ")   ' The order prevents highlighting the query
End Sub

Private Sub FixupTheQuery()
 ' Purpose: This checks for an incomplete SQL query and supplies the
 '      missing parts as needed
 Dim FromFound As Integer
 Dim buff, temp As String

 Try
  temp = txtQuery.Text            ' The current query state
  FromFound = temp.LastIndexOf(" FROM ")   ' Does it have a FROM yet?
  If FromFound = -1 Then           ' Nope, none there...
   temp = temp.Remove(temp.Length - 1, 1)  ' Remove trailing comma
   buff = BracketMultiWords(lstTables.SelectedItem)
   temp &= " FROM " & buff          ' Add in the missing FROM
   txtQuery.Text = temp            ' Copy it back
  End If
 Catch
  MessageBox.Show("Make sure you have selected the table name")
 End Try

End Sub
```

LISTING 25.4   Continued

```vb
Private Sub btnSubmit_Click(ByVal sender As System.Object, ByVal e As _
            System.EventArgs) Handles btnSubmit.Click
  ' Purpose: This sets up the connection and objects and then submits
  '       the query.
  Dim i, j, RecordsRead, WhichField As Integer
  Dim ReConnect As New OleDbConnection(strConnect) 'Reuse connect string...

  ReConnect.Open()            ' ...and reopen the connection
  FixupTheQuery()             ' Complete the query as needed

  Dim MyAdapter As New OleDbDataAdapter(txtQuery.Text, ReConnect)
  Dim MyDataSet As New DataSet()

  Try
    ' How many records were returned?
    RecordsRead = MyAdapter.Fill(MyDataSet, 0, MAX_RECORDS, _
                lstTables.SelectedItem)
    dtgGrid.CaptionText = "Records: " & CStr(RecordsRead) ' Tell how many
    ReConnect.Close()                   ' Close it down

    ' Tie everything to the data grid
    dtgGrid.SetDataBinding(MyDataSet, lstTables.SelectedItem)
    MyAdapter = Nothing        ' Free things up
    MyDataSet = Nothing
    ReConnect = Nothing
  Catch
    MessageBox.Show("Check the SQL query syntax for errors.")
  End Try

End Sub


Private Sub btnExit_Click(ByVal sender As System.Object, ByVal e As _
            System.EventArgs) Handles btnExit.Click
  Me.Dispose()
End Sub


Private Sub btnClear_Click(ByVal sender As System.Object, ByVal e As _
            System.EventArgs) Handles btnClear.Click
  ' Purpose: Just clear out old query, the selected table, and the field
  '       names in case they want to select another table.
  txtQuery.Text = ""
  lstFields.Items.Clear()
  lstTables.ClearSelected()

End Sub

Private Function BracketMultiWords(ByVal Word As String) As String
  ' Purpose: This function checks to see if a table or field name
  '       contains multiple words. If so, it needs to have brackets
  '       around it.
  '
```

LISTING 25.4   Continued

```
' Argument list:
'   Word      a string with the name to check
'
' Return value:
'   string    the string with the brackets added, if needed

Dim SpaceIndicator As Integer
Dim buff As String

SpaceIndicator = InStr(Word, " ")   ' See if field name is multi-word
If SpaceIndicator Then
  buff = "[" & Word & "]"         ' Bracket if it is
Else
  buff = Word
End If
Return buff                   ' Send back the value
End Function

End Class
```

Submitting the Query

After a `WHERE` clause has been added, the user is ready to submit the query for processing. When the user clicks on the Submit button, the first thing we do is reestablish our connection to the database using the `strConnect` string. The call using the `Open()` method reconnects us to the database. However, we need to do a little checking on our query before we attempt to process it.

The call to `FixupTheQuery()` duplicates some of the checking we did with respect to the `WHERE` predicate. The primary check is to see whether the `FROM` keyword is present and add it into the query if it's missing. We surround the code in a `Try-Catch` block just in case the user hasn't selected a table yet. (We don't need to do this in the list boxes because the only way those events can fire is if the table has already been selected. Think about it.)

Next, we create an `OleDbDataAdapter` object named `MyAdapter`, initializing it with the `ReConnect` connection object and the SQL query that's now held in `txtQuery`. We also define a `DataSet` object named `MyDataSet` that will hold the results of the query.

A `Try-Catch` block is used in case something goes amiss. In most cases, an error at this point is caused by an improperly formed SQL statement. The `Fill()` method call

```
RecordsRead = MyAdapter.Fill(MyDataSet, 0, MAX_RECORDS, _
              lstTables.SelectedItem)
```

is overloaded, and we're using the version that takes four parameters. The first parameter, `MyDataSet`, tells the `Fill()` method where to store the results of the query. The second argument specifies the starting record, and the third argument determines the maximum records we want to return. We arbitrarily set this to 10,000 records in the belief that any more than that was probably an error in the SQL statement.

Programmer's Tip

In a real application, you should probably make the maximum number of returned records from a query a member variable of the class that accesses the database. You could then let the user of the class set the maximum number of records returned.

The last argument of the `Fill()` method is the name of the database table being used in the query.

The return value from the `Fill()` method call is the number of records returned by processing the SQL query. We copy this value to the caption text of the data grid so that the user can see how many records were returned by the query.

At this juncture, `MyDataSet` is filled with the results from the SQL query. Therefore, we have what we need, so we immediately close the connection to the database using the `Close()` method of the connection object.

Finally, we bind the results stored in `MyDataSet` to the `DataGrid` control using the `SetDataBinding()` method call and free up the resources associated with the objects. The results of the query are then displayed in the grid control. A sample run is shown in Figure 25.24.

FIGURE 25.24

A sample run of the SQLTester program.

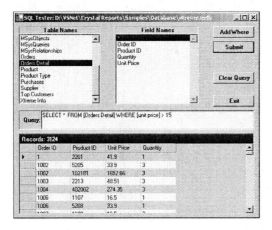

Even though my machine is fairly slow by today's standards (it has a 750MHz clock), response time for the 3,000+ records is about a second using a `WHERE` predicate. Also notice that the field name in a `WHERE` predicate is not case-sensitive.

Finally, if you try a `SELECT` statement in which you need to expand the width of the column, move the cursor to the vertical line that separates the column headers. The cursor will change to a double-arrow cursor. At this point, you could drag the bar to the right to expand the column width, as pointed out in Chapter 24. However, if you double-click when the double-arrow cursor is showing, the column automatically expands to a width that shows the widest entry in the column. Cool stuff.

Navigating a Database

You often need to work with a database in which you're very familiar with its contents. You know all the table names and the field names, and there's really no reason for the user to need knowledge of either. In situations like this, all you might need is a way to navigate through the database and, perhaps, edit or update the content of an individual record. In this section, we'll write a simple program that's designed to navigate through a known database.

Start by creating a new project named DBTextboxes. Place the controls shown in Figure 25.25 on the form.

FIGURE 25.25

The form layout for the DBTextboxes program.

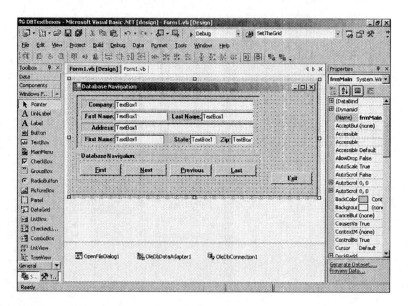

By now, you should be able to look at the code and know what the names of the various controls need to be. Therefore, we won't denude any more of the nation's forests by stating the obvious. The complete code for the program appears in Listing 25.5.

A good portion of the code was copied from the previous project, so we'll concentrate on the new elements of the program.

LISTING 25.5   Source Code for the DBTextboxes Project

```
Imports System
Imports System.Data
Imports System.Data.OleDb

Public Class frmMain
 Inherits System.Windows.Forms.Form
```

LISTING 25.5   *Continued*

```
Private Const MAX_RECORDS As Integer = 10000

Private RecordsRead As Long

Private strConnect As String
Private MyTable As String
Private MyDataSet As New DataSet()

' Windows Form Designer generated code


Private Function GetFileName() As String
 ' Purpose: This function attempts to open an Access database
 '
 ' Argument list:
 '   none
 '
 ' Return value
 '   string   the name of the file selected or an empty
 '            string if cancelled.
 '
 Dim NewFileName As String
 Dim NewFile As OpenFileDialog = New OpenFileDialog()
 Dim MyChoice As DialogResult

 With NewFile
  .Filter = "Access Files (*.mdb)¦*.mdb¦All Files (*.*)¦*.*"
  .FilterIndex = 1              ' Assume text files
  .DefaultExt = "mdb"          ' Ditto
  .InitialDirectory = "D:\VSNET\Crystal Reports\Samples\Database\"
  .CheckFileExists = False
  .ReadOnlyChecked = True
  .Title = "Open Access Data File"
 End With

 MyChoice = NewFile.ShowDialog       ' What did they do?

 If MyChoice = DialogResult.Cancel Then ' Bail out?
  NewFileName = ""
 Else
  NewFileName = NewFile.FileName
 End If

 If NewFileName.Length > 0 Then
  Return NewFileName
 End If
End Function

Private Sub frmMain_Load(ByVal sender As System.Object, ByVal e As _
            System.EventArgs) Handles MyBase.Load
 ' Purpose: This opens and reads in the table names from the database.
 Dim FileName, SQL As String
```

LISTING 25.5 Continued

```
FileName = GetFileName()        ' Get the database file name
If FileName.Length = 0 Then
 Exit Sub
End If
Me.Text = "SQL Tester: " & FileName ' Show the file name

' This builds the connect string. It is used later as needed, too.
strConnect = "Provider=Microsoft.Jet.OLEDB.4.0;Password="""";User _
       ID=Admin;Data Source="
strConnect &= FileName
MyTable = "Customer"
Dim Connect As New OleDbConnection(strConnect) ' Reuse connect string...
Connect.Open()               ' ...and reopen the connection
SQL = "SELECT * FROM Customer"
Dim MyAdapter As New OleDbDataAdapter(SQL, Connect)

Try
 ' How many records were returned?
 RecordsRead = MyAdapter.Fill(MyDataSet, 0, MAX_RECORDS, MyTable)
 Connect.Close()
 SetControlBindings()
 MyAdapter = Nothing       ' Free things up
 Connect = Nothing
Catch
 MessageBox.Show("Something wrong during connecting.")
End Try
WhichRecord()

End Sub


Private Sub btnExit_Click(ByVal sender As System.Object, ByVal e As _
           System.EventArgs) Handles btnExit.Click
 Me.Dispose()
End Sub


Private Sub SetControlBindings()
 txtCompany.DataBindings.Add("Text", MyDataSet, "Customer.Customer Name")
 txtFirstName.DataBindings.Add("Text",MyDataSet, "Customer.Contact First _
               Name")
 txtLastName.DataBindings.Add("Text", MyDataSet, "Customer.Contact Last _
               Name")
 txtAddress.DataBindings.Add("Text", MyDataSet, "Customer.Address1")
 txtCity.DataBindings.Add("Text", MyDataSet, "Customer.City")
 txtState.DataBindings.Add("Text", MyDataSet, "Customer.Region")
 txtZip.DataBindings.Add("Text", MyDataSet, "Customer.Postal Code")
End Sub

Private Sub btnFirst_Click(ByVal sender As System.Object, ByVal e As _
           System.EventArgs) Handles btnFirst.Click
 Me.BindingContext(MyDataSet, MyTable).Position = 0
 WhichRecord()
End Sub
```

LISTING 25.5   Continued

```
Private Sub btnNext_Click(ByVal sender As System.Object, ByVal e As _
            System.EventArgs) Handles btnNext.Click
  Me.BindingContext(MyDataSet, MyTable).Position += 1
  WhichRecord()
End Sub

Private Sub btnPrevious_Click(ByVal sender As System.Object, ByVal e As _
              System.EventArgs) Handles btnPrevious.Click
  Me.BindingContext(MyDataSet, MyTable).Position -= 1
  WhichRecord()
End Sub

Private Sub btnLast_Click(ByVal sender As System.Object, ByVal e As _
              System.EventArgs) Handles btnLast.Click
  Me.BindingContext(MyDataSet, MyTable).Position = RecordsRead _- 1
  WhichRecord()
End Sub

Private Sub WhichRecord()
  ' Purpose: This finds out which record we are looking at and updates
  '       the groupbox text property with the record number.
  Dim where As Long

  where = Me.BindingContext(MyDataSet, MyTable).Position + 1
  gbxDBNavigation.Text = "Navigate Database: Record # " & CStr(where)

End Sub

End Class
```

Because we know the name of the database table we want to use as well as the field names we are interested in, we can push all the real work into the **Form Load** event. We hard-code the query into variable **SQL** and use that string in the **OleDbDataAdapter()** initialization call:

```
SQL = "SELECT * FROM Customer"
Dim MyAdapter As New OleDbDataAdapter(SQL, Connect)
```

The **Fill()** method of the data adapter transfers the data to the **MyDataSet** object. We also fill in **RecordsRead** with the number of records that were returned from the database. We make use of this value later in the program.

The subroutine **SetControlBindings()** does most of the new work in the program. Each text box is tied to a field in the **MyDataSet** object according to the parameters in the call. For example, the statement

```
txtCompany.DataBindings.Add("Text", MyDataSet, "Customer.Customer Name")
```

ties the **txtCompany** text box to the **Customer Name** field of the Customer table. The first parameter (**"Text"**) of the **Add()** method tells which property of the control is being bound. In all cases, we want to bind to the **Text** property of the text boxes. The other calls are similar, changing only the text box name and the field name. (You could also use the Properties window to bind the text boxes, but I wanted to show you how to do it in code.)

If all goes well, you should see the first record of the Customer table displayed in the text boxes. You can navigate through the records by clicking on the buttons in the group box. The code within each button is almost identical, so we just discuss the `btnFirst` button.

The statement

```
Me.BindingContext(MyDataSet, MyTable).Position = 0
```

sets the record pointer for the data set to the first record in the `MyDataSet` object. Because the records are zero-based, the first record is at position 0. Every form has a `BindingContext()` method associated with it when there are bound controls on the form. Because we do bind each text box to the `MyDataSet` object, we can use the `Me` keyword for the base object of the `BindingContext()` method.

With the record pointer set to the desired position, we call `WhichRecord()` to update the record location text for the group box. The remaining buttons work in the same fashion, either incrementing or decrementing the position in the dataset. Note that we use `RecordsRead` to set the position when the Last button is clicked. You could also use the `Count` property, too:

```
Me.BindingContext(MyDataSet, MyTable).Position = _
        Me.BindingContext(MyDataSet, MyTable).Count - 1
```

However, because `RecordsRead` already holds the record count, you might as well use it. A sample run of the program is shown in Figure 25.26.

FIGURE 25.26

Sample run of the DBTextboxes program.

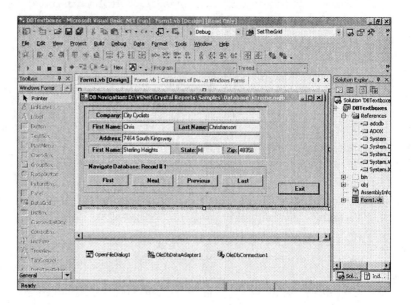

That's all there is to it! The key is to bind the text boxes to a `DataSet` object. Once the dataset is built, the rest is very easy.

You really should experiment with this program. For example, you might try to modify the program so that it would work with other tables. How would you cope with the labels for the text boxes in this situation? Would parts of the SQLTester project be useful? Trying to figure out how to accomplish these tasks is a great way to learn how to manipulate a database.

Modifying a Database

The last topic we need to cover is how you can make changes to an existing database. There are a number of ways that you can modify a database. These are add new records to the database, edit an existing record in the database, and delete a record from the database. We'll explore each of these in a moment. However, before you do anything else, you should make a backup copy of the `Xtreme.mdb` database. Up to this point, we've done nothing that might change what's in the database. However, in this section, we'll be modifying the content of the database. Therefore, you should make a backup copy to preserve the original database content before testing any of the code in this section.

A Delete Digression

I should also mention from the outset that I'm not a big fan of deleting data from a database. Although I'll cover how to delete records from a database, I believe there are better ways to accomplish the same goal. My preference is to create a `Status` field in each table. Early in the design phase, it may seem that a `Boolean` data type is a good choice for a `Status` field because it can mark the absence or presence of some status or condition. For example, either the customer is active or not. The person is either a client or not. The person is either a member of an organization or not. Even though a `Boolean` seems the obvious choice, resist the urge.

Life rarely presents things in pure black or white. Gray is pretty common. For example, members do take a leave of absence. Customers you haven't heard from for years suddenly place an order. By making the `Status` field an `Integer` variable, you can code values that appear later on that you didn't think about during the design phase. For example, `0` might mean the person is not a member, `1` means he's a member, and `2` means he has taken a leave of absence. With a `Boolean`, it's either true or false; there's no room for a design hiccup.

By using a `Status` field, you can alter the status of a table entity without physically removing it from the database. For example, if you're searching a list of active clients, simply use a `WHERE` predicate that ends with `...WHERE Status = 1`. This would exclude all inactive clients. That's not where the real benefit comes in, however.

Just as sure as you're sitting there, right after you delete a client, someone will come in (perhaps an attorney trying to settle a contested will) and ask you to reconstruct all purchases for the client you just deleted from the database. Depending on how you've constructed the database, deleting the client might actually delete all other related records associated with the client (for example, all order information). Reconstructing the information could range from being difficult to impossible.

By using a `Status` field, you aren't physically removing the client from the database. Therefore, reconstructing the data for an inactive client is relatively easy. Indeed, you could create a program that does nothing else but present data for inactive clients.

If you're actually concerned that the dead data is both taking up too much disk space and degrading performance, the `Status` field is still a good idea. You could write a program that copies the dead data to a backup medium and then physically purges the dead data from the database. In this manner, you could still reconstruct the data if necessary, but the dead data is physically removed from the database. The presence of the `Status` field simply makes the task easier.

Okay, I'm stepping off my soapbox and back to level ground. Now let's see how to modify a database. (I'll assume that you've made a backup of the `Xtreme.mdb` database.)

The ModifyDB Project

I would be remiss if I didn't show you the easy way to configure a Visual Basic .NET program for database access. In this section, we'll use the Visual Basic .NET wizards to do almost all the work for us. I can then show you the statements needed to modify the database. Once again, before you start, make sure that you've backed up the `Xtreme.mdb` database because the code and our experimentation in this section will modify the database.

Using the Server Explorer

First, start a new project and name it ModifyDB. Now select the Server Explorer (*not* the Solution Explorer) from the View menu. Figure 25.27 shows what your display should look like.

FIGURE 25.27
Activating the Server Explorer.

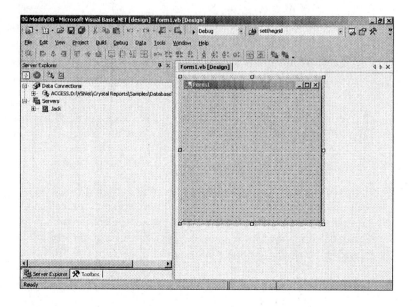

If you look closely, you'll see I already have a data connection to the **Xtreme.mdb** database. However, that's the original database and I don't want to mess with it. Instead, I want to connect with a copy of the database. Therefore, I need to establish a new data connection.

To add a new data connection, right-click the Data Connections icon in the Server Explorer window (it looks like a small drum next to the word Access in Figure 25.27). This opens up a small menu from which you should select the Add Connection option. Your screen should look about the same as Figure 25.4 shown earlier. Click the Provider tab and select the Microsoft JET 4.0 OLE DB Provider and then click Next. Your screen should now look like Figure 25.6. At this point, you should click on the ellipsis button and navigate to the copy of the database that you want to experiment with. After you've done that, it wouldn't hurt to click the Test button to make sure that everything's set up correctly. Now click the OK button. You should now see the new data connection in the Server Explorer window. This can be seen in Figure 25.28.

FIGURE 25.28

The Server Explorer after adding a backup connection to the **Xtreme.mdb** database.

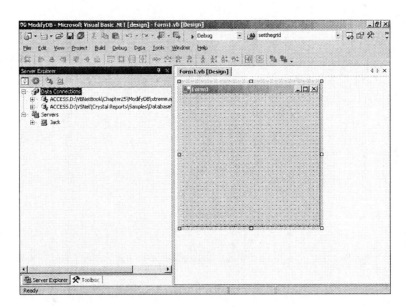

Notice that we've added our new connection to the directory where we're developing the program. So far, so good.

If you click on the expand icon (that is, the plus sign in front of the data connection), you can see the internal structure of the database (tables, views, stored procedures). This can be useful, for example, if you need to know the names of the tables in the database. You can also expand the tables to find the list of fields contained within a table. Useful stuff.

Adding the Data Adapter Object

Now click on the Toolbox tab to bring it to the foreground and then click on the Data tab. Now drag the **OleDBDataAdapter** object onto the form, which will start the Data Adapter

Configuration Wizard (DACW). This time, however, we don't want to dismiss it as we did before. Instead, we want to proceed with the configuration of the data adapter object. Click the Next button to proceed.

The DACW is now asking you to confirm your data connection. You should see the pathname to the **Xtreme.mdb** database. If you need to change the connection, simply select from the drop-down list. (You could also establish a new connection, if you needed to, by using the Add Connection button.) We're good to go, so click the Next button.

If you've done things correctly thus far, your screen should look similar to Figure 25.8 shown earlier. Accept the Use SQL Statements option and click the Next button. The screen will look like Figure 25.9 now. However, this time we want to add the SQL statement that we want to process. To keep things simple, we'll type in

SELECT * FROM Customer

This is shown in Figure 25.29. Now click the Next button.

FIGURE 25.29

Adding a query to the Data Adapter Configuration Wizard.

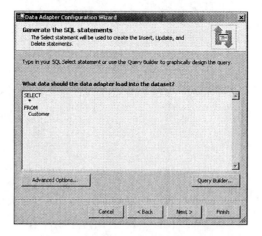

Visual Basic .NET will grind for a few seconds and then display a message saying that it has configured the data adapter. You are told that it has not only set up the **SELECT** statements, but also the table mappings, plus the **INSERT**, **UPDATE**, and **DELETE** statements. It's these last three that we're most interested in here. Click the Finish button and the **OleDbDataAdapter1** object is added to the project.

Creating the DataSet Object

We still need a place to store the data, which is the purpose of our **DataSet** object. From the main menu, click the Data, Generate Dataset menu sequence. Your screen should look the same as Figure 25.18. Click OK to add the **DataSet1** object to the project.

Now all we need is a means by which we can display our data.

Adding the `DataGrid` and Remaining Controls

From the Toolbox on the Windows Forms tab, double-click on the `DataGrid` control to create a grid object on the form. The default name of `DataGrid1` is fine for now. Add four button controls to the form and name them `btnAdd`, `btnEdit`, `btnDelete`, and `btnExit`. Your form should look something like that shown in Figure 25.30.

FIGURE 25.30

Form layout for the ModifyDB project.

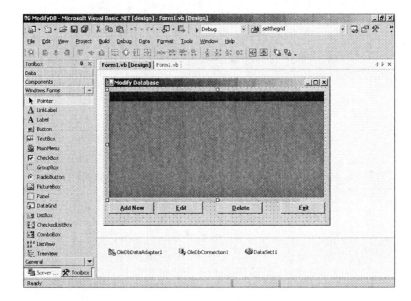

You now need to bind the `DataGrid` control to the database. From the Properties window, move the cursor to the `DataSource` property. Select the `DataSet` object that does not have the database table associated with it. For example, if you named the control `DataSet1`, select it as the `DataSource`, *not* DataSet1.Customers.

Now click in the `DataMember` property and select Customer. Visual Basic .NET knows about the objects you see in the Properties window because of the code that was generated while we were using the wizards.

In the `Form Load` event, add the following lines of code:

```
DataGrid1.CaptionText = "Records Read: " & _
  CStr(OleDbDataAdapter1.Fill(DataSet1))

DataGrid1.AlternatingBackColor = Color.Honeydew
```

The first statement does two things. First, it fills the dataset object with the information from the database via the `Fill()` call. Second, we use the return value from the `Fill()` call to display the number of records that are in the dataset object. The second statement sets the alternating color value to a very pale shade of green. Finally, add the code shown in Listing 25.6 to the program.

LISTING 25.6   The Remaining ModifyDB Code

```
Private Sub btnAdd_Click(ByVal sender As System.Object, ByVal e As _
            System.EventArgs) Handles btnAdd.Click
 ModifyDatabase("Add")
End Sub

Private Sub btnEdit_Click(ByVal sender As System.Object, ByVal e As _
            System.EventArgs) Handles btnEdit.Click
 modifydatabase("Edit")
End Sub

Private Sub btnDelete_Click(ByVal sender As System.Object, ByVal e As _
            System.EventArgs) Handles btnDelete.Click
 ModifyDatabase("Delete")
End Sub

Private Sub ModifyDatabase(ByVal TryingThis As String)
 ' Purpose: This routine does all of the updating for the database.
 Try
  OleDbDataAdapter1.Update(DataSet1)
 Catch ThisEx As Exception
  MessageBox.Show("Error during " & TryingThis & ": " & ThisEx.ToString)
 End Try
End Sub
```

Could the code be any simpler? Each of the buttons calls the same subroutine, named
`ModifyDatabase()`. All that the subroutine does is call the `Update()` method of the data
adapter object using the dataset object as its argument (I'll explain what this does in a
moment).

Using the Program

When you start the program, the data grid is filled in with the Customer table. Figure 25.31
shows a sample run of the program. Now suppose that you want to edit the `Contact Last`
`Name` field for the first record. Because the data grid allows editing, move the cursor to the
desired field. This automatically highlights the current contents of the field. You'll also see a
pencil icon appear in the first (non-writeable) column of the data grid (see Figure 25.31). Now
just start typing in the new value. When you're done, click the Edit button. This calls the
`Update()` method to write the new data back into the database.

FIGURE 25.31
A sample run of the
ModifyDB project.

To delete a row, scroll to the record you want to remove and move the cursor to the extreme-left column and click. This will highlight the entire selected row. Now press the Delete key on your keyboard. The row is removed. If you click on the Delete key, the deletion is made permanent by another call to `Update()`.

Finally, if you want to add a record, scroll to the end of the dataset and place the cursor in the first field and start typing in the new data. When all the fields are filled in, click the Add New button. If you fail to fill in a required field (for example, a primary key field), Visual Basic .NET will let you know.

Obviously, there's a little bit of trickery going on here. All these modifications call the same `Update()` routine to perform the modifications. The reason this works this way is that any changes you make to the data in the grid are really being performed only in memory. Indeed, if you make a multitude of changes and never click one of the buttons, no permanent change is made to the database. (You'll hear programmers refer to this type of update processing as *disconnected* database programming.)

It's also true that you don't have to click on a button after each change. You could make hundreds of changes to the data without clicking any of the buttons. However, after you do click a button, the `Update()` call makes the current state of the dataset object permanent in the database. Likewise, never clicking a button before ending the program leaves the database unchanged.

Summary

We tackled a lot in this chapter. You should feel pretty comfortable now with how Visual Basic .NET works with databases. Still, we've only scratched the surface on some issues. For example, there are many additional features available for use with the `DataGrid` control that we simply don't have space to discuss. However, digging around in the online help and checking in on the Microsoft Web site can also be useful.

You really do need to experiment with the programs presented in this chapter. For example, we hard-coded a lot of variables into the sample programs (for example, some of the SQL statements). You could change these into program variables taken from input text boxes and use them to replace the string literals. Just make sure that you use a copy of a database just in case you modify it in a way that you may not want to make permanent. Don't be afraid of making changes. Nothing's going to go up in flames…or at least I don't think it will.

Review Questions

1. When using the Data Adapter Wizard, what property must be configured first and why?

A. The data provider needs to be set first, even though the wizard shows the Connection tab first. The reason the wizard does this is because it defaults to Microsoft SQL Server as the data provider. You need to make sure that default is acceptable or, if not, click on the

Provider tab and select the correct database provider. This is important because the content of the Connection tab differs according to the database provider selected.

2. When the Data Adapter Wizard finishes its job, where is the code written that is associated with the answers you supplied to the wizard?

A. The code appears in the region named `Windows Form Designer generated code`. The code that appears in that region provides the details necessary for Visual Basic .NET to establish a connection to the database.

3. What is the purpose of the Query Builder?

A. As the name suggests, the Query Builder is used to construct an SQL query of the database. Once again, however, you can use the SQL statements you learned in Chapter 24 to construct your own queries without using the Query Builder.

4. What is the purpose of the `DataSet` object?

A. The `DataSet` object holds the results of any queries that are made on the database. After a query on the database is completed and assuming no errors, the `DataSet` object will contain the records that meet the conditions stated in the query.

5. If you want to write a connect string without using a wizard, how should the string be constructed?

A. The exact nature of the string depends on the database to which you want to connect. If we assume the Microsoft Access database is being used, the connect string might be written

```
strConnect = "Provider=Microsoft.Jet.OLEDB.4.0;Password="""";User _
        ID=Admin;Data Source="
```

Notice that we haven't filled in the `Data Source` parameter yet. This is normally done after the `OpenFileDialog` dialog box has returned the name of the database. After `OpenFileDialog` has finished, and assuming that a variable named `FileName` holds the path and name of the database, the connect string can be completed with

```
strConnect &= FileName
```

You can now use `strConnect` with the `Open()` method.

6. What is a serious limitation of the current implementation of ADO.NET?

A. At the present time, ADO.NET does not implement a data definition language. The DDL is used to create your own databases. As a result, if you want to create a new database on your own, you need to use one of the wizards supplied with Visual Studio or construct the database with the database management (DBM) tools provided with the database. (One of the reasons I elected to use Microsoft's Access database in my examples is because most Windows systems are shipped with Microsoft Office, which contains Access.) Microsoft promises to have the DDL done "real soon now."

7. Assuming that you've built the connect string in **strConnect**, **SQL** holds the query string, and **MyTable** is the table name, what statements are necessary to read the database and retrieve a recordset?

A. You would need to code:

```
Dim MyConnect As New OleDbConnection(strConnect)
MyConnect.Open()            ' ...and reopen the connection
Dim MyAdapter As New OleDbDataAdapter(SQL, MyConnect)
Dim MyDataSet As New DataSet()

Try
 RecordsRead = MyAdapter.Fill(MyDataSet, 0, MAX_RECORDS, MyTable)
Catch
 MessageBox.Show("Check the SQL query syntax for possible errors.")
End Try
```

8. The code you wrote for question number 7 filled in a **DataSet** object with records from the database. Assuming you have a bound **DataGrid** control named **MyGrid**, what statements must be written to display the recordset data?

A. A single statement will suffice:

```
MyGrid.SetDataBinding(MyDataSet, MyTable)
```

9. Suppose that you have a text box named **txtLastName** that you want to bind to the **LastName** field of the Customer table. What statement will accomplish this?

A. The statement is

```
txtLastName.DataBindings.Add("Text", MyDataSet, "Customer.LastName")
```

The first argument states the data type for the field, the second is the data set that holds the data, and the final argument is the table and field name under consideration.

10. What statement would you use to delete a record from a database?

A. This is a trick question. You probably shouldn't delete a record from the database. A better way is to implement a **Status** field for each record. Set the record to **1** when it's created. If you decide at some later time that you can delete it, simply change the **Status** to **0**. If you use a **WHERE** predicate that tests for **Status**, you can return datasets where only the active data are returned. In similar fashion, you could build a query string that would return only the dead data, too!

CHAPTER 26

WEB PROGRAMMING WITH VISUAL BASIC .NET

In this chapter, you'll learn

- What a Web page is and how it works

- The relationship between the client and Web server

- The difference between static and dynamic Web pages

- An overview of how to use ASP.NET to create dynamic Web pages

- How to write a simple Web program using dynamic Web pages

Introduction

In one sense, Web programming is not an integral part of Visual Basic .NET. However, Visual Studio .NET includes provisions for Web programming as part of its IDE. Because you can use Visual Basic .NET code as part of a Web page, I've included this chapter as an extension of Visual Basic .NET programming. However, before we launch into Web programming, you need to understand the basics of how Web pages are written and displayed on a Web browser.

HTML and Static Web Pages

When you visit a Web page on the Internet, you're looking at a display that was built as a Hypertext Markup Language (HTML) script. A *static Web page* is one where the HTML script never changes. Static Web pages always appear the same, regardless of who visits the page, how the viewer arrived at that page, or whether the viewer has visited that page before. There is no interaction between the user and the Web page. The user simply stares at the page.

An example of a static Web page script that uses HTML is shown in Listing 26.1.

LISTING 26.1   A Static Web Page

```
<html>
<title>Sample Static Page</title>
<body>
 <h1>This is a static web page</h1>
 <br>
 Pretty exciting stuff, huh?
</body>
</html>
```

Even though you might never have seen an HTML page before, it will take you about five seconds to figure out how HTML works. An HTML file consists of directives called *tags*. Most HTML tags occur in pairs, using the following syntax:

```
<Tag_Name_start> TagExpressions </Tag_Name_Stop>
```

For example, in Listing 26.1, the line

```
<title>Sample Static Page</title>
```

begins with a `title` tag, followed by the text that is to appear in the title, followed by the ending tag that turns off the `title` tag. Notice how the ending tag is the same as the starting tag, except for the forward slash. This sample HTML line, therefore, causes `Sample Static Page` to appear in the title bar of the browser.

The `body` tag in Listing 26.1 is used to mark the beginning of the HTML body for the Web page. The `h1` tag is used to display text using a relatively large font. The `br`, or break, tag is simply a line break and causes the next line of text to appear on a new line. Notice how all the tags except the break tag appear in pairs. (If you think about it, a break tag doesn't need an ending tag because it doesn't need to be turned off at some subsequent point.) Figure 26.1 shows how our static HTML Web page looks using Internet Explorer 6.0.

You can compare what you see in Figure 26.1 with the HTML script in Listing 26.1 and figure out what each HTML tag does. This all seems pretty simple, but let's dig a little deeper to see how we got from Listing 26.1 to Figure 26.1.

How Web Pages Work

The process of writing a static Web page and having it displayed on a Web browser isn't that difficult. The first step is to write the HTML script for the Web page. As a general rule, static Web pages are pretty simple and can be written with any text editor. In fact, the Web page shown in Figure 26.1 was written with Notepad, a simple text editor that's distributed with Windows. The HTML page is then saved on the Web server.

FIGURE 26.1

A sample static Web page.

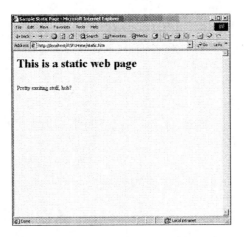

The *Web server* often is a computer that's dedicated to doing nothing else but serving Web pages. What's interesting is that a Web server does not have to be a separate computer. In fact, I'll show you how you can configure your own computer to behave like a Web server later in this chapter. Creating a pseudo Web server on your own computer is a convenient way to test your Web pages without using the Internet.

The second step in displaying a Web page occurs when a user sends a request for the Web page from his Web browser. A *Web browser* is a program that is designed to display Web pages. Microsoft's Internet Explorer and Netscape Navigator are two popular Web browsers, but there are many more. The request for the Web page is sent to the Web server by the browser. If you look closely at Figure 26.1, you can see that I requested a page named `Static.htm` stored at a Web server address of localhost/ASPXHome. The `http` that you see at the start of the address means that we're using the Hypertext Transfer Protocol (HTTP) for exchanging information. Collectively, the line

```
http://localhost/ASPXHome
```

says that we will use the Hypertext Transfer Protocol to communicate with the Web server. The line forms what is known as a *Uniform Resource Locator*, or URL. It is the URL that tells the browser where to find the Web server.

In the third step, the Web server looks for the requested HTML file (for example, `Static.htm`) that was requested by the browser. Assuming that the Web server finds the page, the fourth step sends the HTML page back to the browser. The final step occurs when the browser interprets the HTML sent from the Web server and displays it to the user. This process can be illustrated as shown in Figure 26.2.

FIGURE 26.2

How a Web page is displayed.

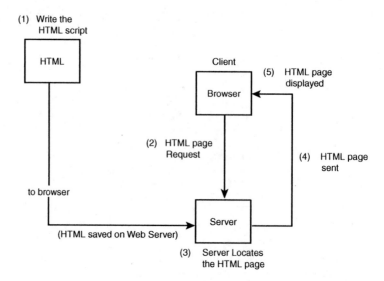

Before you can perform these steps yourself, we must see whether your system has things set up properly to process Web pages. If you have a server in your house, you probably have your system configured to process Web pages. However, most people have just a single computer at home and do not have access to their own server. In the next section, I'll show you how to configure your system to look like a Web server. This will enable you to experiment with Web pages without actually having a separate server. (Of course, you could go out and buy another computer and configure it to be a dedicated Web server if you choose.)

Configuring Your Own Web Server

If you followed the installation instructions in Chapter 1, "Getting Started with Visual Studio .NET," you already have much of the work done for creating your own Web server. The first thing you must do is create a directory where you would like your HTML and other Web files to reside. Use Microsoft's Explorer to create a directory similar to that shown in Figure 26.3. Notice that we've created the new directory off the `inetpub\wwwroot\` directory. The `inetpub\wwwroot\` directory is the default Web directory for our work. You can place your test files in the `MyASPXFiles` (or any other) directory off the root directory.

In the next step, you'll need to use the Internet Information Services (IIS) program that's distributed with Windows. On most systems, you can find IIS using the following Windows directory path:

```
C:\WINNT\system32\inetsrv\iis.msc
```

Although you can use other programs to open IIS, such as the Microsoft Management Console, I just made a shortcut on the desktop to the IIS.MSC program. If you don't want to use a shortcut, type the pathname to IIS into the Open box using the Start, Run menu sequence. After the program begins execution, right-click on the Default Web Site entry in the IIS information tree. Your screen should look similar to the one shown in Figure 26.4. (It's unlikely that your computer is named **jack**. Your screen will tell you the reference name that Windows uses for your computer.)

FIGURE 26.3
Creating a new directory for your Web files.

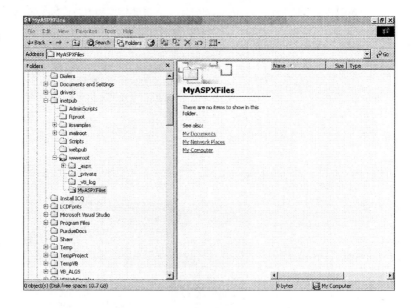

Programmer's Tip

Microsoft's XP version of Home Edition of Windows does not include the IIS program, which would preclude you from running this particular exercise.

For security reasons, it isn't a good idea to use your physical file directory as a Web site location. Instead, you should create a virtual directory name for the physical directory name you created earlier (that is, the directory name you created in Figure 26.3). Figure 26.4 shows how you begin the process of creating a virtual directory once you have IIS running.

After initiating the New, Virtual Directory sequence, you're greeted with the Virtual Directory Creation Wizard dialog box. This is shown in Figure 26.5. Click Next to begin the process of creating a virtual directory.

The program then asks you to enter the name that you want to use as the virtual directory name. The virtual directory name becomes the name that users will use when requesting a Web page from your Web site. I elected to use **ASPXHome** for the virtual directory name in this example. This is shown in Figure 26.6.

FIGURE 26.4
Using Internet
Information Services to
create a virtual directory.

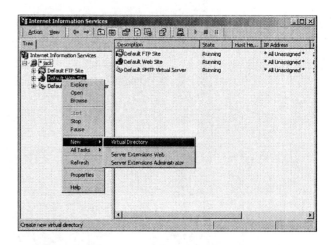

FIGURE 26.5
The Virtual Directory
Creation Wizard dialog
box.

FIGURE 26.6
The Virtual Directory
Creation Wizard dialog
box.

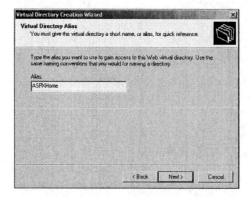

After you've entered the virtual directory name you want to use, click the Next button.

The wizard now asks you to enter the physical directory where the Web site files will reside. This is the pathname that you entered for Figure 26.3. Because we selected C:\inetpub\ wwwroot\MyASPXFiles, that becomes the physical directory entered in Figure 26.7. After you've entered the proper directory name, click the Next button.

FIGURE 26.7
The physical directory name for the Web site.

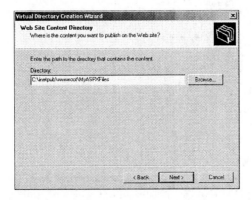

The program now shows you the default access permissions that are to be associated with your virtual directory. For now, just accept the default settings shown in Figure 26.8.

FIGURE 26.8
The Web site access per-missions.

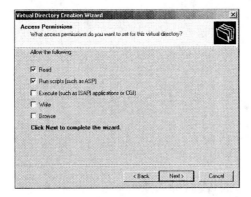

Now click the Next button. The program will display a message telling you that you've com-pleted the creation of your virtual directory. Click the Finish button to dismiss the dialog box. You'll now see your virtual directory listed under the default Web site directory.

If you right-click on your new virtual directory, you can review its properties by selecting the Properties option. The properties for my virtual directory are shown in Figure 26.9.

FIGURE 26.9
The physical directory name for the Web site.

Figure 26.9 shows the physical path (`C:\inetpub\wwwroot\MyASPXFiles`) for my virtual directory (`ASPXHome`) plus the access permissions. Notice that only the Read permission is checked. If you check the Script Source access box, you would allow users to view the source code for your programs. If the Write box were checked, users would be able to not only view the source, but change it as well. Because neither of these options is a very good idea, we leave both of these boxes unchecked (which is the default). Because you went to all the trouble of creating a virtual directory for security reasons, leave the Directory Browsing option unchecked to prevent users from browsing through your physical directories.

Finally, leave the Execute Permissions set to Scripts only. This enables users to execute Web pages that contain scripts as well as static pages. However, it will not allow them to execute any other program files that might be located in the directory. Because we didn't change any of the defaults on this page, just click the Cancel button to dismiss the dialog box.

If you copy the program presented in Listing 26.1 to your physical directory, you should be able to run that program using the virtual directory you just created. For example, I named the file in Listing 26.1 `Static.htm` and copied it to my `C:\inetpub\wwwroot\MyASPXFiles` physical directory. I then started Internet Explorer and typed in my computer and virtual directory names followed by the HTML filename. Therefore, typing in

http://localhost/ASPXHome/static.htm

produces the display you saw earlier in Figure 26.1.

Although our static Web page works, that's about all it does. Watching paint dry and our static Web page are equally entertaining. Clearly, there has to be a more exciting way to interact with the Web. Fortunately, there is.

Dynamic HTML

Let's face it, static Web pages like that shown in Figure 26.1 are pretty boring. Most Web sites you see on the Internet today are built using dynamic Web pages. As you might guess, *dynamic Web pages* have the capability to change their content in response to varying needs, including the interest of the user viewing the Web page. How is it possible to have Web pages on a server that can change?

Actually, the process of creating dynamic Web pages is quite simple. All we need do is insert a special pair of tags in the HTML file that surround non-HTML instructions for the computer processing the HTML. We'll examine the special tags later in the chapter. For now, let's examine the process of creating dynamic Web pages.

Unlike HTML files that end with `.htm` or `.html`, ASP.NET files end with `.aspx`. (The `x` at the end of the filename distinguishes ASP.NET files from the older Active Server Pages files that end with `.asp`.) These ASP.NET files usually contain a blend of pure HTML script and ASP.NET tags. It's what is contained within the ASP.NET tags that enables you to create dynamic HTML files.

On computers that have Visual Basic .NET installed, files that end with `.aspx` are sent to a special dynamic link library (`aspnet_isapi.dll`) for processing. That DLL looks for special tags in the file for subsequent processing. Simply stated, the DLL takes whatever it finds within the special ASP.NET tags, processes those instructions, and generates new HTML script from the instructions. The newly generated HTML is then combined with the original HTML script that was in the file. The newly processed HTML file is then shipped back to the client browser for display.

Server-Side and Client-Side Processing

Notice what has happened in terms of Figure 26.2. When the server determines that an ASP.NET file has been requested by the user, it performs additional processing on that file. In other words, we've added another server step to the process shown in Figure 26.2 because the server now performs additional processing on the file. Because the processing could involve information sent from the client as part of the request, the new HTML file that's sent back to the client can be tailored to the specific needs of the client. This illustrates *server-side* processing because the dynamic Web pages are built on the server.

It's also possible to have *client-side dynamic Web pages*. In that case, the client requests a file from the server, which the server returns to the browser. It becomes the browser's responsibility to process any special instructions that might be embedded in the HTML file. If it finds such special tags, it processes those instructions and generates the new (dynamic) HTML and then displays it.

Client-side processing seems to be losing ground to server-side processing. The primary reason is because not all browsers have the same processing capabilities. Whereas Internet Explorer may process a certain Web file perfectly, Netscape Navigator may not be able to understand the special instructions in the file. Because server-side processing always will have the necessary processing capabilities, they can always generate the new dynamic HTML to be sent back to the browser. Because all browsers can process HTML, there is less chance of a processing failure with server-side processing. That's the good news.

The bad news is that the client's horsepower is going to waste while an ever-increasing burden is being placed on the server. You might be sitting at home with a system that has more computing power than the world did fifty years ago, and all you're doing is displaying HTML. It's the old H-bomb-to-kill-an-ant syndrome. Still, until browser capabilities are standardized, server-side processing is going to be king of the hill. (However, because we're using Visual Basic .NET in conjunction with Internet Explorer, we're fairly safe in assuming that the two pieces of software are compatible.)

Now that you understand the difference between server-side and client-side processing, let's write a simple Web page that uses dynamic HTML and client-side processing. (It's pretty easy to find examples of server-side dynamic Web pages. Client-side examples are a little more difficult to find.)

Home Mortgage Web Page

You've probably seen Web pages that enable you to enter information and, based on what you entered, provide some form of answer after you click a button on the page. In this section, you're going to write a Web page that asks the user for mortgage loan information and then displays the monthly payment.

Create a new project, but this time we want to create a Web-based program. Start a new project and select an ASP.NET Web Application, as shown in Figure 26.10.

FIGURE 26.10
Starting a new Web-based application project.

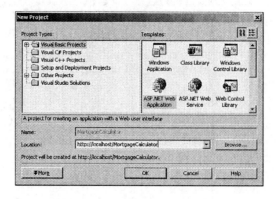

In the Location field shown in Figure 26.10, type in **MortgageCalculator** for the name of the project and click the OK button. Depending on the speed of your computer, Visual Basic .NET will grind away for up to a minute setting things up for Web programming. Eventually, your screen will look similar to Figure 26.11.

FIGURE 26.11

The Visual Basic .NET IDE for Web-based application programming.

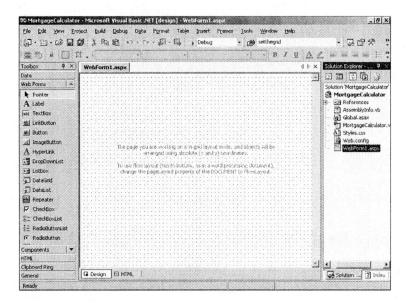

Differences in the Web-Based IDE

There are a number of things to notice when Web programming is being done. First, the design window in the center of the screen looks different. The text in the middle of the design window tells you that you can design a Web page using either a grid layout or a flow layout. Using a *flow layout,* any controls we may place on the form are added without absolute positioning coordinates. Controls are added to the form one after another, flowing from the Toolbox to the form in much the same way as words flow onto a letter. A Web browser, therefore, arranges the controls in whatever order they occur on the page. When a *grid layout* is used, absolute positioning coordinates are used for any controls that may be present on the page.

A second thing to notice is that there are two tabs at the bottom of the design window. In Figure 26.11, the Design tab is highlighted. This is similar to the design mode you've used in earlier chapters. The second tab, named HTML, is new. If you click on the HTML tab, you'll see the skeleton HTML code that Visual Basic .NET has generated for the current (empty) Web page.

A third thing to notice is that the toolbox headings have changed. Rather than seeing a tab named Windows Forms, you now see a tab named Web Forms. Another tab you haven't seen before is the one named HTML, which contains HTML controls. Obviously, neither of these new tabs was needed in our earlier programming efforts.

There are a few other things that are different about the IDE, and we'll discuss those as you write the mortgage calculator program. Let's get started writing our dynamic Web page.

The Mortgage Calculator

The first thing you need to do is put the Design mode window into the Flow layout mode. Click on the Design mode window and press the F4 key to bring up the Properties window. Scroll the window down to the `pageLayout` attribute and select `FlowLayout`. The grid dots will disappear from the form, as can be seen in Figure 26.12.

FIGURE 26.12

Setting the Design mode to Flow Layout.

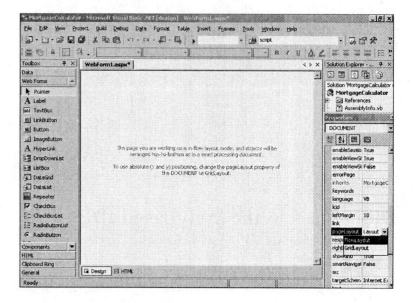

Because we are in the Flow Layout mode, controls are added to the Web page at the point where the cursor is currently located. For that reason, if you place the cursor anywhere on the page and click, the cursor is automatically positioned near the upper-left corner of the display. This confirms what we said earlier about Flow Layout mode: You cannot position a control at a fixed location on the Web page. Instead, the control is positioned at the current cursor location.

We want to place an HTML control on the page, so click on the HTML tab in the Toolbox to reveal the HTML controls. Now double-click on the HTML `Label` control. Your form will look like Figure 26.13.

Move the cursor into the label and backspace over the word Label and type in **Mortgage Calculator**. Because the new text is longer than the label box, select the sizing button and lengthen the label box so that the new text does not fold.

While the label control still has the focus, move to the Properties window, click in the Style attribute field, and then click the ellipsis button. This causes Visual Basic .NET to display the Style Builder dialog box, as shown in Figure 26.14.

FIGURE 26.13
Adding an HTML label
control to the Web page.

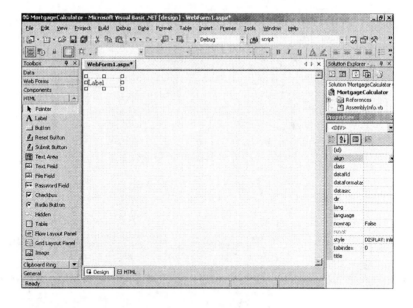

FIGURE 26.14
The Style Builder dialog
box.

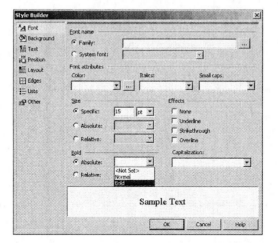

In Figure 26.14, notice that we have set the `Size-Specific` attribute to 15 points and that we have also set the `Bold` attribute. These two changes increase the size of the font and set it to use boldface for display. After you have done this, click the OK button. (Because we've increased the size of the font, you may need to stretch the label a little more to prevent the text from folding.)

You can see that the cursor is still on the same line as the label control you just added. Again, this is because we are in Flow Layout mode. You can try to move the cursor to another position on the page and click, but the cursor remains fixed on the right edge of the label.

However, we want to add a text box now, so press the Enter key to move the cursor to the next line of the page.

Now double-click on the control named Text Field on the HTML control tab. A text box will appear on the Web page. Unlike Windows forms, a Web control does not have a **Name** attribute in the Properties window. Instead, the name of the control is assigned by filling in the **ID** attribute in the Properties window. Type in **txtAmount** in the ID field of the Properties window. Now click back on the Web page. The cursor will be sitting at the right edge of the text box you just named **txtAmount**.

Now double-click on the Label control on the HTML tab. Even though the cursor was at the end of the text box, the new label is placed on a new line. Not a problem. Move the cursor back to the end of the **txtAmount** text box and press the Delete key, and the label will move to the right edge of the text box as shown in Figure 26.15.

FIGURE 26.15
Adding a Label control after a text box control.

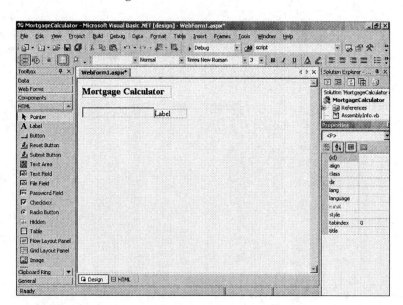

Change the text in the Label control to read Amount. Use the **Style** attribute in the Properties window to change the font to bold using the Style Builder dialog box.

Continue to add text boxes and labels until your Web page looks like that shown in Figure 26.16. Moving from top to bottom, the remaining text boxes are named **txtInterest**, **txtMonths**, and **txtResult**. The button is named **btnCalculate** and its **Value** property is set to **Calculate**. I also used **btnCalculate**'s **Style** property to change the font to bold.

Be careful that you select the correct button control from the HTML tab. You do *not* want to select either the Reset or Submit button styles because they serve different purposes. The Calculate button used in your program should be the plain button style.

FIGURE 26.16
The Web page after all controls have been added.

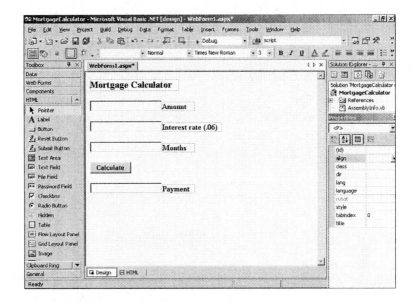

The HTML Script for the Mortgage Calculator

Now select the HTML tab at the bottom of the Design window to see the HTML script that has been generated by Visual Basic .NET. Your display should look similar to that shown in Figure 26.17.

FIGURE 26.17
The HTML script for the mortgage calculator.

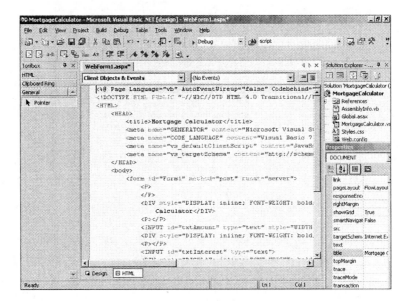

If you look closely at the script between the **HEAD** tags you will see a series of **meta** tags. These are special tags that Visual Basic .NET uses to process the HTML script properly. In particular, the line

```
<meta name="vs_defaultClientScript" content="JavaScript">
```

tells Visual Basic .NET to use the default scripting language as JavaScript. Although the JavaScript scripting language is widely used, it isn't what we want to use in our program.

Programmer's Tip

Virtually all browsers support JavaScript, but fewer support VBScript. However, because we're working in a Visual Basic .NET environment, we'll use VBScript. Although not as ubiquitous as JavaScript, there are still many people using browsers that support VBScript.

We need to change the **meta** line to process VBScript instead of JavaScript. The best way to do this is to highlight and then right-click the line we need to change. This process presents you with a menu of options; select the Properties option. Your screen will now look like that shown in Figure 26.18. Change the Default scripting language for the **Client** to VBScript as shown in Figure 26.18.

FIGURE 26.18
Changing the default scripting language.

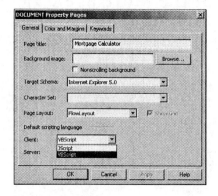

After you click the OK button, you'll see that the **meta** line now reads

```
<meta name="vs_defaultClientScript" content="VBScript">
```

which is exactly what we want.

If you look closely at Figure 26.17, you will see the **</HEAD>** and **<BODY>** tags positioned together. Move the cursor after the **</HEAD>** tag and press the Enter key to create an empty line in the script between the two tags. Now right-click on the line to open a menu selection as shown in Figure 26.19.

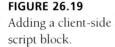

FIGURE 26.19
Adding a client-side
script block.

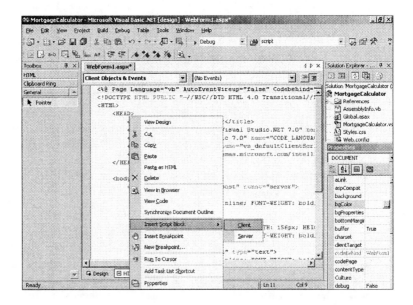

Select the Insert Script Block, Client option. This causes the following empty script block to be
added to the HTML script:

```
<script language=vbscript>
<!--

-->
</script>
```

Notice how the scripting language is now VBScript. What remains to be done, however, is to
add the code necessary to perform the mortgage calculation after the user has supplied the
required information in the text boxes. In other words, we need to add the code associated
with the `btnCalculate click` event.

Place the cursor between the comment markers (that is, the `!--` and the `-->` characters) and
then select the Client Objects and Events drop-down box at the top of the HTML window.
Select the `btnCalculate` object. Now move to the events list box and select the `onclick` event.
Visual Basic .NET automatically supplies the shell stub for the click event. The code for the
subroutine stub should look like the following code fragment:

```
Sub btnCalculate_onclick
  dim result, answer, interest, months, amount, term

  amount = document.all.txtAmount.value
  interest = document.all.txtInterest.value
  months = document.all.txtMonths.value
  interest = interest / 12
  term = (1.0 + interest) ^ months
  answer = interest * amount * (term / (term - 1.0))
  document.all.txtresult.value = FormatCurrency(answer)
End Sub
```

There are several things that need to be explained in the code fragment. First, unlike normal Visual Basic .NET code, no type specifier is associated with a `Dim` statement; in this case, no type fits all. This `Dim` statement appears to use the `Variant` data type from earlier versions of Visual Basic.

Other things that must be explained are the statements that contain the `document.all` specifier. Actually, every Web page is a `document` object. In our case, the `document` object happens to contain a `form` object. Within the `form` object are the HTML controls that you placed on the form. Because we cannot access these form controls directly, we must go through the `document` object first. We do this by using the `All` collection of the `document` object. Therefore, to access any individual control, we must fully qualify the object using the `document.all` specifier to unambiguously define the control we want to use.

The code in the `btnCalculate` click event simply calculates the monthly mortgage payment using the data supplied by the user. The complete HTML script is shown in Listing 26.2. The listing begins with server-side script tags `<%` and `%>`. Like other tag pairs, everything between these two tags is to be processed by the server. The `@_Page` directive supplies information to the server about how the page is to be processed. For example, the `@ Page` directive tells the server that Visual Basic (`vb`) is the language. The `Codebehind` attribute informs the server that the code for the form is found in a file named `WebForm1.aspx.vb`.

The `DOCTYPE` attribute simply defines the version of HTML that's being used by the page. The actual HTML script begins after that attribute. The `meta` attributes are informational and used by Visual Studio to properly process the server- and client-side scripts. These `meta` attributes play an important role in processing the VBScript code contained within the HTML script.

LISTING 26.2   The HTML Script for the Mortgage Calculator

```
<%@ Page Language="vb" AutoEventWireup="false" _
  Codebehind="WebForm1.aspx.vb" _
  Inherits="MortgageCalculator.WebForm1"%>
<!DOCTYPE HTML PUBLIC "-//W3C//DTD HTML 4.0 Transitional//EN">
<HTML>
 <HEAD>
  <title>Mortgage Calculator</title>
   <meta content="Microsoft Visual Studio.NET 7.0" _
       name="GENERATOR">
     <meta content="Visual Basic 7.0" name="CODE_LANGUAGE">
     <meta content="VBScript" name="vs_defaultClientScript">
     <meta content="http://schemas.microsoft.com/ _
      intellisense/ie5" name="vs_targetSchema">
     <script id=clientEventHandlersVBS language=vbscript>
<!--

Sub btnCalculate_onclick
  dim result, answer, interest, months, amount, term

  amount = document.all.txtAmount.value
  interest = document.all.txtInterest.value
```

LISTING 26.2   Continued

```
    months = document.all.txtMonths.value
    interest = interest / 12
    term = (1.0 + interest) ^ months
    answer = interest * amount * (term / (term - 1.0))
    document.all.txtresult.value = FormatCurrency(answer)

End Sub

-->
</script>
</HEAD>

 <body>
    <form id="Form1" method="post" runat="server">
    <P></P>
    <DIV style="DISPLAY: inline; FONT-WEIGHT: bold; _
     FONT-SIZE: 15pt; WIDTH: 191px; HEIGHT: 25px" _
     ms_positioning="FlowLayout">Mortgage Calculator</DIV>
     <P></P>
     <INPUT id="txtAmount" style="WIDTH: 143px; HEIGHT: _
     22px" type="text">
     <DIV style="DISPLAY: inline; FONT-WEIGHT: bold; WIDTH: _
      70px; HEIGHT: 15px" ms_positioning="FlowLayout"> _
      Amount</DIV>
     <P></P>
     <INPUT id="txtInterest" type="text">
     <DIV style="DISPLAY: inline; FONT-WEIGHT: bold; WIDTH: _
      126px; HEIGHT: 19px" ms_positioning="FlowLayout"> _
      Interest rate (.06)</DIV>
     <P></P>
     <INPUT id="txtMonths" type="text">
     <DIV style="DISPLAY: inline; FONT-WEIGHT: bold; WIDTH: _
      70px; HEIGHT: 15px" ms_positioning="FlowLayout"> _
      Months</DIV>
     <P></P>
     <P title="Mortgage Calculator">
    <INPUT id="btnCalculate" style="FONT-WEIGHT: bold; _
      WIDTH: 88px; HEIGHT: 24px" type="button" _
      value="Calculate">
    </P>
     <INPUT id="txtResult" type="text">
     <DIV style="DISPLAY: inline; FONT-WEIGHT: bold; WIDTH: _
      70px; HEIGHT: 15px" ms_positioning="FlowLayout"> _
      Payment</DIV>
    </form>
 </body>
</HTML>
```

The **body** tags surround the HTML that's associated with the text boxes, labels, and the Calculate button. If you examine the attributes contained within the tags, you can figure out what each attribute does for its tag member.

Assuming that you've added the code for the **btnCalculate** click event, you can now compile and run the program in the usual manner (press the F5 key). A sample run is shown in Figure 26.20.

FIGURE 26.20

A sample run of the mortgage calculator.

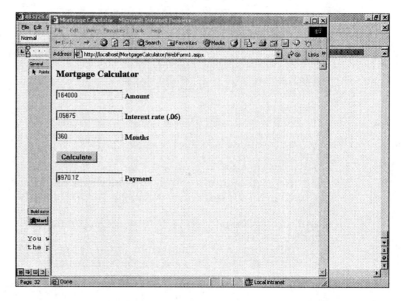

You'll notice that Visual Basic .NET automatically supplied the proper URL to run your Web page. It knows how to find your Web page by using the setup information you supplied at the beginning of the chapter.

Summary

There's no way to cover every aspect of Web programming in this book. Indeed, there are dozens of books available that cover nothing but Web programming using the Visual Basic .NET environment. Most of those books have numerous examples using server-side Web pages using Web controls. As a change of pace, our efforts here have concentrated on using the HTML (client-side) controls. You could, of course, use the Web Form controls instead, using the same general layout as shown in Figure 26.16. (You can distinguish between the two controls by the small box with a green triangle that appears near the upper-left corner of each Web control.) Although the HTML script generated by Visual Basic .NET using Web Form controls is slightly different, you should have no trouble converting between the two types of controls.

In this chapter, you've learned how static and dynamic Web pages work and the difference between client-side and server-side processing of those pages. We also developed a simple client-side program using a dynamic Web page. Once again, you might try your hand at creating your own dynamic Web page application using server-side processing; it would be a worthwhile learning experience.

Review Questions

1. What is the difference between static and dynamic Web pages?

A. Static Web pages are built from HTML scripts that never changes. Dynamic Web pages have HTML scripts that can change in response to the needs of the viewer or other considerations. Dynamic Web pages have this capability because special tags in the HTML can be used to call other scripting languages, such as Visual Basic .NET and JavaScript, to generate new HTML script based on the inputs supplied to the scripting language.

2. What is a *URL*?

A. A URL is a Uniform Resource Locator, which is used to locate the Web server that will provide the HTML for the Web site.

3. With respect to HTML scripts, what is a *tag*?

A. HTML uses tags to determine what action is to be taken by the script. Most of the tags are used in pairs; the first part turns the tag's attribute on and the second part turns the attribute off. For example, the `<title>` tag turns on printing of a page title, whereas the `</title>` tag turns it off.

4. What is meant by *client-side* versus *server-side* scripting?

A. These terms simply describe where the processing of the script is performed. The trend is for less client-side scripting in favor of more server-side scripting.

5. What is a serious limitation of client-side scripting?

A. Client-side scripting relies on the resources that are available on the client side. Because these resources cannot be known with certainty, the client machine might not have all the resources necessary to process your scripts. For example, not all browsers support VBScript, but most do support JavaScript. Server-side scripting eliminates this problem because you can control the server-side resources.

6. What benefits are gained if all clients have the same resource base?

A. If you could assume that every client machine has the resources necessary to process all Web pages, you could push a large part of the processing burden off the (already) overloaded servers onto the (underutilized) clients. It seems terribly wasteful to have a client with a 3GHz machine doing nothing more that displaying HTML scripts at the same time the server is logjammed trying to keep up with the demands that are placed on the server.

7. Suppose that you want the title bar on the Web browser to read `My name's Web Site` (where you supply your own name), and then have the words `I collect 5 dollar bills` in fairly large letters. And in normal-size print display

```
Send your old 5 dollar bills to:
Your Name
123 Your Street
YourCity, YourState, YourZip
```

A. This could be written as a static script:

```
<html>
<title>My Name's Web Site</title>
<body>
 <h1>I collect 5 dollar bills</h1>
 <br><br>
 Send your old 5 dollar bills to:<br>
 Your Name<br>
 123 Your Street<br>
 YourCity, YourState, YourZip<br>
</body>
</html>
```

8. If you want to insert some Visual Basic .NET into an HTML document, what tags are necessary in the HTML document?

A. You might use

```
<script language=vbscript>
<!--
-->
</script>
```

and place whatever code is needed between the comment markers.

9. What are *meta tags*?

A. *Meta tags* are special scripting tags that Visual Basic .NET uses to extend the normal HTML scripting. These tags are not portable to other environments.

10. What tags does Visual Basic .NET use to denote server-side script tags?

A. The tags are `<%` and `%>`. Everything that appears between these two tags is to be processed on the server. These tags are also used by older ASP scripting files.

APPENDIX A

ASCII TABLE

TABLE A.1 ASCII Table

Dec	Hex	Oct	Char
0	00	000	NUL
1	01	001	SOH
2	02	002	STX
3	03	003	ETX
4	04	004	EOT
5	05	005	ENQ
6	06	006	ACK
7	07	007	BEL
8	08	010	BS
9	09	011	HT
10	0A	012	LF
11	0B	013	VT
12	0C	014	FF
13	0D	015	CR
14	0E	016	SO
15	0F	017	SI
16	10	020	DLE
17	11	021	DC1
18	12	022	DC2
19	13	023	DC3
20	14	024	DC4
21	15	025	NAK
22	16	026	SYN
23	17	027	ETB
24	18	030	CAN
25	19	031	EM
26	1A	032	SUB

Dec	Hex	Oct	Char
27	1B	033	ESC
28	1C	034	FS
29	1D	035	GS
30	1E	036	RS
31	1F	037	US
32	20	040	Space
33	21	041	!
34	22	042	"
35	23	043	#
36	24	044	$
37	25	045	%
38	26	046	&
39	27	047	'
40	28	050	(
41	29	051	)
42	2A	052	*
43	2B	053	+
44	2C	054	,
45	2D	055	-
46	2E	056	.
47	2F	057	/
48	30	060	0
49	31	061	1
50	32	062	2
51	33	063	3
52	34	064	4
53	35	065	5
54	36	066	6

TABLE A.1 Continued

Dec	Hex	Oct	Char
55	37	067	7
56	38	070	8
57	39	071	9
58	3A	072	:
59	3B	073	;
60	3C	074	<
61	3D	075	=
62	3E	076	>
63	3F	077	?
64	40	100	@
65	41	101	A
66	42	102	B
67	43	103	C
68	44	104	D
69	45	105	E
70	46	106	F
71	47	107	G
72	48	110	H
73	49	111	I
74	4A	112	J
75	4B	113	K
76	4C	114	L
77	4D	115	M
78	4E	116	N
79	4F	117	O
80	50	120	P
81	51	121	Q

Dec	Hex	Oct	Char
82	52	122	R
83	53	123	S
84	54	124	T
85	55	125	U
86	56	126	V
87	57	127	W
88	58	130	X
89	59	131	Y
90	5A	132	Z
91	5B	133	[
92	5C	134	\
93	5D	135	]
94	5E	136	^
95	5F	137	_
96	60	140	`
97	61	141	a
98	62	142	b
99	63	143	c
100	64	144	d
101	65	145	e
102	66	146	f
103	67	147	g
104	68	150	h
105	69	151	i
106	6A	152	j
107	6B	153	k
108	6C	154	l
109	6D	155	m
110	6E	156	n

TABLE A.1   Continued

Dec	Hex	Oct	Char
111	6F	157	o
112	70	160	p
113	71	161	q
114	72	162	r
115	73	163	s
116	74	164	t
117	75	165	u
118	76	166	v
119	77	167	w
120	78	170	x
121	79	171	y
122	7A	172	z
123	7B	173	{
124	7C	174	I
125	7D	175	}
126	7E	176	~
127	7F	177	DEL

INDEX

Symbols

&= operator, 122
_ (line continuation character), 125

A

abstract classes, 376
AcceptButton property, 440-441
access specifiers, 363
accessing objects, 47-48
accessor methods, 341-342
Activate method, 445
adding
    class members to a class, 316-317
    classes to projects, 314-315
    components, 40-42
    constructors to a class, 317-318
    tabs to the toolbox, 468-469, 473-475
    user to a class, 320-322
AddNewUser() function, 321-322
ADO, 577-589
ADO.NET, 547-548
algorithms, 56, 243-245
Anchor property, 447
And operator, 202-203
AndAlso operator, 229-230
AppendText() method, 455
arguments in subroutines, 103
arithmetic operators, 183-194
arrays
    character arrays, 529-534
    clearing, 291

copying, 291-292
dynamic array, 152-155
dynamic multidimensional arrays, 160
elements, 146-147
example program, 147-150
For loops, 248-253
getting length of, 292
indexes, 147, 150-151
indexing, 282-283
initializer lists, 297
length, 291-292
multidimensional array, 156-160
rank, 291
reference variables, 293-297
reversing, 292-293
sample program, 297-299, 301
scalars, 282
searching, 286-290
size of, 151-152, 161-162
sorting, 283-286
string array, 147-150
subscript, 147
uses, 145-146
ASCII character set, 76
aspect ratio, 489-491
assemblies, 179
assembly language, 25-26
assignment operators, 86, 183-194
assignment statements, 85-86
associativity, 191-192

code
- breakpoint line, 205
- Caution section, 323
- classes, 342-346
- controls, 464
- custom controls, 469-471
- entering, 46-47
- event handlers, 477
- spaghetti code, 241
- testing, 346-352
- walk-throughs, 246

Code window (IDE), 46-47

collections, 301-306

color
- forms, 447-448
- graphics, 484, 501-503

combo boxes, 369-370, 446-451

ComboBox control, 450-451

Compare method, 137-138

comparing strings, 137-138

compiled language, 27

compilers, 27

compiling programs, 19-20, 42-45

components
- adding, 40-42
- current state, 18
- defined, 17
- Icomponent interface, 438
- moving, 18
- properties
    - changing, 18, 38, 40-41
    - current state, 18
    - expanding, 39-40
    - information about, 39-40
    - values, 19
- selecting, 18

computer display screen, 481-482

computer programming
- assembly language, 25-26
- compiled language, 27
- high-level language, 28
- history, 23-35
- interpreted language, 26-27
- machine language, 24-25
- OOP
    - encapsulation, 32-34
    - example program, 35-45
    - inheritance, 34-35

object interface, 33-34
object properties, 32-33
overview, 31-32
polymorphism, 35
- structured programming, 30-35
- virtual machine language, 26

Concat method, 130-131

concatenating strings, 121-122, 130-132

configuring Web servers, 602-603, 605-606

constants
- named constants, 528-529
- symbolic constant, 104-106

constructors
- base class constructor, 386-387, 398-400
- class constructor, 317-318
- initializer lists, 387-396
- overloaded constructor, 318-320

ControlBox property, 441

controls
- ComboBox control, 450-451
- custom controls
    - code, 464, 469-471
    - creating, 459-468
    - fonts, 471, 500-501
    - Gauge control, 492-507
    - naming, 462-463
    - PhoneSSN control, 460-475
    - placing on the toolbox, 468-469, 473-475
    - properties, 465-468
    - resizing, 471-472, 496-497
    - testing, 472, 506-507
    - text boxes, 463-464, 471-472
- defined, 17
- event handlers, 476-477
- Form control
    - Load() event, 438-439, 455
    - methods, 445-446
    - properties, 440-445
    - uses, 438
- ListBox control, 450-451
- methods
    - Activate method, 445
    - AppendText() method, 455
    - Dispose method, 445
    - GetSelected() method, 456
    - Hide method, 445-446
    - InStr() method, 456
    - Show method, 445-446
- number of, 437, 459

forms
        background, 447-448
        child form, 442
        colors, 447-448
        components, 40-42
        drop-down menus, 449-450
        foreground, 447-448
        MDI form, 442
        parent form, 442
        user interface designs, 371
        UserControl form, 462
        validation, 448-449
Forms window (IDE), 17
Friend keyword, 379
functions
        AddNewUser(), 321-322
        CStr(), 123
        data hiding, 31
        defined, 31
        InStr(), 127-128
        Left(), 124-125
        Len(), 123-124
        Mid(), 125-127
        Right(), 127
        type specifier, 221
        uses, 114-116
        versus methods, 368-369

G

garbage collection, 332-333
Gauge control, 492-507
GDI+ (Graphics Device Interface Plus), 482-483
Get method, 341-342
Get property, 341
GetHeight() method, 504
GetSelected() method, 456
GoTo statement, 241
graphics
        aspect ratio, 489-491
        background, 503
        color, 484, 501-503
        coordinate system, 482-483
        display screen, 481-482
        drawing, 503-506
        file formats, 484
        flood fill, 503

        Imageviewer project, 484-491
        painting, 497-500
        PictureBox control, 483-485, 489-491
        storage size, 484
Graphics Device Interface Plus (GDI+), 482-483
greater than operator, 198
greater than or equal to operator, 198
group boxes, 370-371

H

HelloWorld program, 16
help
        debugger, 420
        online help, 437
helper procedures, 324
Hide method, 445-446
high-level languages, 28
HTML
        dynamic HTML, 606-608
        static Web pages, 599-600
        tags, 600

I

IDE (Integrated Development Environment)
        Code window, 46-47
        Debug window, 46
        Design window, 37
        Forms window, 17
        Output window, 46
        Properties window, 18, 37-40
        Solution Explorer window, 42-43
        toolbox, 17-19
        writing programs, 17
If keyword, 198
If statement, 215-218, 220-224
If-Then-Else statement, 198-201, 222-223
images
        aspect ratio, 489-491
        color, 484, 501-503
        displaying
                Imageviewer project, 484-491
                PictureBox control, 483-485, 489-491
        file formats, 484
        storage size, 484

M

P

Pascal programming language, 30
painting graphics, 497-500
parameters of subroutines, 102-108
PhoneSSN control, 460-475
picture elements (pixels), 481
PictureBox control, 483-485, 489-491
pixels, 52, 481
polymorphism, 35, 385-398
precedence of operators, 190-194, 209-210
predefined event handlers for controls, 476-477
preserve keyword, 154-155
primary key (databases), 545
Private access specifier, 363
Private Shared data, 313
Procedures, stepping over, 222
processing
  floating-point numbers, 73
  integer numbers, 73
  sequential processing, 28
  subroutines, 29-30
program errors, 90
program flow, 218-220
program loops
  Do, 274-275
  Do While, 268-273
  Exit For statements, 253
  For, 248-255
  For-Next, 241-248
  infinite, 238
  loop control variable, 238
  loop counter, 240-241
  Loop Until, 273
  naming convention for Integer loop counters, 240
  nesting, 253-255, 274-275
  sample programs, 238-240, 262-268
  sentinels, 275-276
  structure, 237-238
  terminating Do loops early, 274
  Until, 272-273
  While End While, 261-268
programming
  assembly language, 25-26
  compiled language, 27
  high-level language, 28
  history, 23-35
  interpreted language, 26-27
  machine language, 24-25

OOP
  encapsulation, 32-34, 165, 312
  example program, 35-45
  inheritance, 34-35, 357, 377-381, 386-396
  object interface, 33-34
  object properties, 32-33
  overview, 31-32
  polymorphism, 35, 385-398
  structured programming, 30-35
  virtual machine language, 26
programs
  algorithms, 56
  BinaryConversion program, 262-268
  bugs, 90
  building, 19-20
  closing, 20-21
  code, 46-47
  compiling, 19-20, 42-45
  creating, 35-36
  data hiding, 31
  debugging
    breakpoints, 218-219
    defined, 90
    single-stepping, 219-220, 222
  design
    bottom-up design, 56
    cleanup, 59
    importance of, 56
    initialization, 57, 60-61
    input, 57-58
    object-oriented analysis (OOA), 64
    object-oriented design (OOD), 64
    output, 58-59
    processing, 58
    sideways refinement, 60-61
    top-down design, 56
    Unified Modeling Language (UML), 62-68
  display screen, 46
  functions, 31
  HelloWorld program, 16
  Inspector program, 86-89
  Math program, 91-94
  naming, 36
  naming conventions, 36, 38-39
  OOP, 35-45
  processing
    sequential processing, 28
    subroutines, 29-30
  program flow, 28

X